Travels in the Levant

Travels in the Levant:

The Observations of Pierre Belon of Le Mans on Many Singularities and Memorable Things found in Greece, Turkey, Judaea, Egypt, Arabia and Other Foreign Countries (1553)

TEXT ESTABLISHED AND PRESENTED BY ALEXANDRA MERLE

English translation by James Hogarth

HARDINGE SIMPOLE

Published by Hardinge Simpole
an imprint of
Zeticula Ltd,
The Roan,
Kilkerran,
KA19 8LS,
Scotland,
United Kingdom

http://www.hardingesimpole.co.uk
admin@hardingesimpole.co.uk

First published 2012
Translated from the French Edition published by
Editions Chandeigne in 2001.
Copyright © Estate of James Hogarth 2012
Introduction © Alexandre Merle 2001, 2012

ISBN   978 1 84382 196 0 Paperback

Translator's Note

Although Pierre Belon was writing at a time when modern French was enjoying its first great flowering, he was no great stylist. His style can best be described as workmanlike. He wanted above all to record all the information he had gathered during his travels, and he set it down as fully and accurately as possible, on the basis of the notes he had made at the time, adding details as they occurred to him. As a result his sentences are sometimes long and ungainly, often with a string of relative and conjunctive clauses. In translating his text I have got rid of many of the *which*es, the *and*s and the *for*s, which are merely distracting for a modern reader, but apart from this I have not sought to edit Belon's work and have tried to retain something of its original flavour.

The footnotes are based on those in the French edition, though I have sometimes relegated information they gave to the detailed indexes. I have added some additional footnotes for the English edition; they are labelled "T" or "OED".

J. H.
Edinburgh, 2004

Contents

Figure: Portrait of Pierre Belon at the age of 36

Introduction

by Alexandra Merle

When Pierre Belon set out on his journey to the Levant in 1546 he was one of the precursors of the many Frenchmen who travelled about the vast territories of the Ottoman empire in subsequent decades and throughout the 17th century. Before him few westerners had undertaken such a journey and written an account of it, for western interest in the Ottoman possessions was then quite recent.

The capture of Constantinople in 1453 had revealed the existence of the Turks to the western world, but it was some time before they were regarded as a new power to be reckoned with. This came about in 1517, when Sultan Selim I, after defeating the Mamelukes, seized Egypt and the Holy Land, thus adding immense territories to an empire which was already large. Selim also increased his possessions in the Mediterranean, following in the footsteps of his predecessor Beyazit, who had seized many Venetian possessions. By his death in 1521, after a lightning reign which had been a long succession of sensational conquests, Albania and the Morea had been annexed, as well as the greater part of the regions to the south of the Danube, Wallachia, Moldavia and Roumelia.

In the reign of Suleiman, the most glorious of the Ottoman sultans, to whom Europe was soon to give the style of Magnificent, the expansion continued. In the first year of his reign Suleiman took Belgrade. In the following year, 1522, he seized the island of Rhodes, driving out the Knights of St John of Jerusalem. Then he turned on Hungary and won a crushing victory at Mohacs in 1526, thereafter moving on to lay siege to Vienna in 1529. The western powers, particularly the Holy Roman Empire, were now in direct contact with the Turks. Concerned to identify this new enemy and to assess his strength, they set enquiries on foot. Cosmographers sought to establish the origins of the Turks in the writings of the ancients, though without much success, and a great variety of other sources were consulted.

Before 1530 there were very few books about the Ottoman

empire apart from some accounts of pilgrimages to Jerusalem which in any case had little to say about the way of life or the political system of the Turks. In France the few books published in this period were mainly translations of Italian works[1]; two in particular were to become universally quoted sources: a treatise by Spandugino, translated into French in 1519, and above all the monumental work of Paulo Giovio, the Latin version of which, the *Turcicarum rerum commentarius*, was widely read and translated into French in 1538. The following decade saw a proliferation of works on the Turks, in the form of treatises (like that of Antoine Geuffroy, a knight of St John of Jerusalem, which appeared in 1542 under the title *État de la cour du Grand Turc*), accounts of captivity, like that of the Hungarian Bartholomaeus Georgievits, cosmographies (French translations of those of Martin Behaim and Apian) or pamphlets containing exhortations to fight the infidel.

Accounts of travel by French writers which mark the emergence of a new literary genre began to appear during this period. First Guillaume Postel (author of *La République des Turcs*), then Pierre Belon and Nicolas de Nicolay visited much of the Ottoman empire. Thanks to them the French, with the Italians, were the people who had the most direct knowledge of the Turks in the mid 16th century. For this there were economic and particularly political motives. The Italians had good reason to know the Turks, for they had been trading with them for some time. The French also had a special position, for their sovereign, Francis I, had set out to establish friendly relations with this new power which might upset the balance of forces in Europe.

The Ottoman empire in the centre of European policy

The attitude adopted by Francis I to relations with Constantinople was at odds with that of the majority of westerners, and in particular the Spaniards, who saw themselves as defenders of Christendom against the representatives of Islam. Far from wanting to fight the Ottomans, the French king sought to establish trading and also political links with them. Since the beginning of the century French merchants had enjoyed a privileged position in Constantinople, and they were also granted important facilities in Egypt in 1528. The capitulations[2] which followed throughout the century enabled them to make increasing profits in Ottoman territory.

These contacts between Paris and the Sublime Porte were not purely commercial. The French king obtained assurances on the safety of Christian pilgrims and monks in the holy places. More importantly still, he was the first sovereign in Europe to have a permanent embassy to the Grand Signior and to maintain friendly relations with him. Francis I had realised the great weight these relations were to have in European affairs. Suleiman was to become his ally against their common enemy, the Emperor Charles V.

The hostility between the French king and the Emperor was of long standing. Francis could not forget that he had been one of Charles of Habsburg's unsuccessful competitors for the crown of the Holy Roman Empire. Moreover France and Spain had long been rivals in Italy, where there had been perpetual armed conflict. Francis had suffered defeat at Pavia in 1525, fallen into the hands of his enemy and been taken to Madrid, where he was compelled to leave his sons as hostages, sign a treaty which he abhorred and agree to marry Eleanor of Austria. He could not resign himself to seeing the Habsburgs ruling Milan, Naples and Sicily. This rivalry, which the successors of both monarchs inherited, was temporarily laid to rest by the treaty of Cateau-Cambrésis in 1559, under which France renounced its Italian ambitions.

The conflict between Charles V and Suleiman was also in the nature of things. The Emperor for his part had seen it as his duty from the beginning of his reign to continue the work of the Catholic Monarchs, Ferdinand and Isabella of Spain, who had sought to extend their possessions beyond the Mediterranean and considered the Reconquest of Spain from the Muslims of Granada as the first stage in a crusade. North Africa, however, which was the obvious field for Spanish expansion, had linked its fate with the Ottoman empire, since in 1518 Hayrettin Barbarossa, master of Algiers, had sworn allegiance to the Sultan. In addition Charles V was extending his possessions, through the intermediary of his brother Ferdinand, whom he wanted to make king of Hungary, so as to have a common frontier with the Ottoman empire.

The move to establish a diplomatic alliance with the Ottoman empire, which naturally outraged the whole of Europe, probably began after the disaster of Pavia. It is thought that the first contacts were made when the French king was in captivity in Madrid, through the Regent Louise of Savoy, but the embassy which was sent never arrived in Constantinople. Then the king himself sent a Croatian noble, John Frangipani, to Suleiman to ask the Sultan to invade Hungary in order to weaken Charles V, and even to attack Spain directly. Suleiman agreed to the first of these requests, which was in line with his own wishes, and the result was the victory of Mohacs. This aroused the hostility of Europe, which accused Francis of being responsible for the death of the king of Hungary, Louis II, who was the brother-in-law of Charles V and Ferdinand, and recriminations continued throughout the whole of his reign.

These criticisms did not deter Francis from supporting John Zapolya, whom Suleiman had installed on the Hungarian throne. He also tried to justify his alliances by asserting the need to protect Europe against the Habsburgs, and pursued his negotiations to obtain capitulations from Constantinople. He was soon to become the target of further criticism, for soon after the mission of his envoy Antoine Rinçon to the Sultan, in 1529, the Turks marched on Vienna and laid siege to it, without success. The general outcry aroused by this coincidence – which was perhaps not merely a coincidence – obliged Francis to make peace with Charles V in the treaty of Cambrai (1529) and abandon (at any rate in appearance) his scandalous alliance. Under the treaty Charles V gave up his claim to Burgundy, which he had been pursuing for many years (being a grandson of Mary of Burgundy, daughter of Charles the Bold, a relationship which had already brought him Flanders), and Francis recovered the sons who had been hostages in Spain, while at the same time abandoning his Italian ambitions and his erstwhile allies.

This volte-face was merely the first in a long series: Francis, a shrewd strategist, had not ceased to dream of Italy and had not given up the idea of an alliance with the Grand Turk. Thereafter the story of his relations with Charles V and Suleiman was a succession of contradictory treaties and promises, made, given up and then resumed. The French envoys in Constantinople must frequently have had difficulty in explaining to the Sultan the subtleties of their master's policy. First it was Antoine Rinçon who had the difficult task of explaining Francis's intentions to Suleiman. He had also to persuade him to attack Charles V's forces in Italy, but did not succeed in doing so. Francis then signed another treaty, the treaty of Boulogne, which on the face of it was hostile to the Turks, but was merely a scrap of paper designed to restore his brand image in Christendom. Friendly relations therefore continued between Suleiman and France, still through the intermediary of Antoine Rinçon, who carried on new negotiations from Venice in the winter of 1532–1533.

It was then that Francis, with the support of Suleiman's grand vizier Ibrahim, even asked for the help of Barbarossa, the redoubtable corsair in the service of the Ottoman empire. Barbarossa's fleet was to land on the coasts of Naples and in Africa; and the corsair did in fact ravage the coasts of Calabria and Campania and seize Tunis, thus injuring Charles V. Then representatives of Suleiman travelled to France on a highly official mission, landing at Marseilles in October 1534 and spending some time in Paris, to the great displeasure of the rest of Europe. Relations were now excellent between the Sultan and the French king, who then sent to Constantinople his first permanent ambassador, Jean de la Forest.

Thus in 1535 France obtained permission to establish a permanent embassy in Constantinople, well before Venice, although the Venetians had been trading with the Turks for many years and had signed a peace treaty with them in 1502. This was a notable favour; for it was by no means the case that the Sultan considered the king of France, or any other Christian monarch, to be his equal. On the contrary, the Sultan, whether Suleiman or his successors, held himself to be so much their superior that he maintained no ambassador in Europe, deigning only to send envoys extraordinary charged with some particular mission. The capitulations themselves were not treaties between two equal powers but gracious concessions granted by the Grand Signior.

La Forest's mission thus marked a new era in diplomatic relations with Constantinople. It also established a tradition of great importance for the literature of travel, the combination of political negotiations and cultural missions. Thus the ambassador took with him Guillaume Postel, whose mission was to collect manuscripts. Later most French diplomats were accompanied by scholars and men of science who on their journey to Constantinople and their travels in Ottoman territory would have the benefit of the escort which in the conditions of the time was essential, and would make abundant notes destined for publication.

Jean de La Forest, after spending some time in Tunis with Barbarossa, was commissioned once again to ask Suleiman to attack Italian territory. Unfortunately when he landed in Constantinople in June 1535 the Sultan was on campaign in Persia. Charles V took advantage of this respite to seize the Tunisian port of La Goulette and then Tunis itself. In the end the French ambassador managed only to secure a commercial treaty, later extended by capitulations under which France exercised a political and religious protectorate in the Levant and was able to have, in addition to the ambassador in the capital, consuls in the larger towns. Moreover all French people residing in the Ottoman empire were assured of protection and the free movement of their persons and property. Finally the French were granted, in addition to permission to trade throughout the Ottoman empire, the *droit de pavillon*. Henceforth merchants of other nations could sail under the French flag.

The political part of the negotiations was not enshrined in any written document. Suleiman did set out at the head of his fleet in 1537, but it was to direct an operation against the republic of Venice in Corfu, which in the event was unsuccessful. Soon afterwards, however, Barbarossa mounted a victorious expedition against Venetian possessions in the Mediterranean, seizing more than 25 islands: first Syros, Patmos, Ios, Astipalaia, Aegina, Paros, Antiparos and Naxos, then Andros, Serifos, Skiathos, Skyros, etc. There was no longer any question of a joint attack on Italian coastal regions. Suleiman had given priority to his own policies. Francis did not hold it against him, and refused to join the Holy League formed by Charles V, Genoa, Venice and the Pope after Barbarossa's raid on the Mediterranean islands. Later, when the Holy League's enterprises proved unsuccessful and Venice was compelled to negotiate with the Sultan, Francis aided him by informing him of the instructions of the Venetian envoys.

This attitude shows the importance that Francis attached to friendship with the Sultan. Determined to obtain his help, he sent as his envoy Antoine Rinçon, the adroit Spaniard in his service, who replaced La Forest and succeeded in reviving Suleiman's favourable disposition. The Sultan, who was preparing an attack on Charles V in Hungary (after the death of John Zapolya), sent Rinçon back to France to ask Francis to attack the Emperor. Rinçon was received by the king as a hero, but was ill rewarded for his work, for in May 1541, in the course of his return journey to Constantinople, when sailing down the Po, he was captured and killed by the troops of the governor of Milan, perhaps on the orders of Charles V.

Nothing could discourage Francis, who then sent another ambassador, Antoine Escalin des Aimars, called Captain Polin (who became Baron de la Garde in 1543 and later Marquis de Briganson). In Hungary, where Suleiman had just won a victory over Ferdinand's troops, Polin used all his diplomatic skills and soon reached an agreement under which Barbarossa's fleet was put at the disposal of the French king. Accordingly in April 1543 150 ships left Constantinople to spread terror on the Italian coasts, ravaging Calabria, Sardinia, Corsica and Naples and then landing in Marseilles, where joint action was to begin. The great expedition so much looked forward to was about to take place.

Reality, however, did not come up to Francis's or Barbarossa's dreams. The French fleet was not ready to take part in an attack on Admiral Andrea Doria, who was under the orders of Charles V. Operations were therefore restricted to an unsuccessful siege of Nice in August 1543, and Barbarossa then wintered in Toulon at Francis's expense. The allies never managed to reach agreement on an attack on Genoa, while the presence of the corsair's ships in a French port became day by day more ruinous and more scandalous, and there were murmurs throughout Europe that the king of France was about to be excommunicated. Worse still, there were rumours of an agreement between Barbarossa and his supposed enemy Andrea Doria. There was general relief when the corsair's fleet left Toulon with some French galleys, conveying Polin and Jérôme Maurand (an almoner and author of an *Itinéraire d'Antibes à Constantinople*), who thus witnessed the raids on the Italian coasts during the voyage to Constantinople.

A period of coolness followed this abortive expedition. Francis made no effort to improve his relations with Suleiman, signing the treaty of Crépy with Charles V in September 1544 after his victory at Cerisoles. The disadvantages of a mission to Constantinople were then revealed to Monsieur d'Aramont, who had become acting ambassador in the absence of the regular holder of the post, when the Sultan threatened to have him impaled. When Polin returned he succeeded in calming things down. Once again showing his diplomatic skills, he presented the signing of the treaty as a mere demonstration of political skill, and undertook to promote the negotiation of a truce for Ferdinand, Charles V's brother.

The truce, which was to last for a year, was obtained by another French envoy, Jean de Montluc, who arrived in Constantinople in September 1545, for Suleiman also saw some advantage in it. D'Aramont was then able to return to France; but he had no sooner arrived there, at the end of 1546, than Francis sent him back to Constantinople to prepare further joint action against the Habsburgs. This time, to give more *éclat* to the embassy, the king's ministers (particularly Cardinal de Tournon) had the idea of sending with d'Aramont two scholars, Pierre Gilles of Albi and Pierre Belon of Le Mans. The political mission thus became a scientific expedition, on the model of the journey by La Forest and Postel.

The ambassador and his suite left in secret in December 1546. They reached Venice, where they embarked for Constantinople. During a stay in Ragusa (Dubrovnik) they separated: while Belon travelled at leisure round the Greek islands Monsieur d'Aramont continued on his way by land and, arriving in Adrianople, where Suleiman then was, tried, in accordance with his orders, to persuade him to attack Charles V in Hungary and in the Mediterranean at the same time. The Sultan, however, had other plans: for him the enemy of the moment was Persia. He refused, therefore, to march on Vienna, but was prepared to sign another truce, this time for five years, which was concluded on 19th June.

Monsieur d'Aramont's mission thus ended in failure. Francis died before being informed of this, on 31st March 1547. His successor, Henry II, then sent an ambassador extraordinary, Monsieur de Fumel, to inform Suleiman of his father's death. The envoy was able to travel to the East with the Sultan's permission and an escort provided by him. Belon, who arrived in Constantinople in August 1547, accompanied him to Egypt and the Holy Land. When the party got back to Constantinople Monsieur de Fumel returned to France, while d'Aramont, who remained with Suleiman, went with him on his Persian campaign (May 1548 to January 1550). Again Belon travelled with them, at any rate on the first stages of the journey. There were also other observers, like Pierre Gilles and the cosmographer André Thevet, who both wrote accounts of their experiences. Belon soon left them and returned to Constantinople, which he left in the course of 1549 to return to France by way of Venice.

In the end Monsieur d'Aramont's efforts were rewarded. After the Genoese admiral Andrea Doria seized Mahdiya in North Africa for Charles V in September 1550, thus running counter to the interests of the corsair Turgut Reis (or Dragut), who enjoyed the Sultan's protection, the Franco-Ottoman alliance took on a fresh lease of life. Monsieur d'Aramont seems to have managed to persuade Suleiman to break the truce which he had concluded with the Emperor. In January 1551 he returned to France, saying that he had been sent by Suleiman to prepare a joint attack with Henry II against the Spaniards. It is not certain whether he was really acting in accordance with the Sultan's wishes or on his own initiative. However this may be, he overcame Henry II's hesitations; and in May 1551 this indefatigable ambassador left Paris, accompanied by another French traveller, Nicolas de Nicolay, whose name was to become known to posterity.

He now had to persuade Suleiman to send his fleet into the Mediterranean. The first stopping-place on his journey was Algiers, which was governed by Hasan Pasha under Ottoman protection. He failed to persuade him to take part in the French enterprises, and continued on his way to Constantinople. Meanwhile the Ottoman fleet had set sail; but Admiral Sinan Pasha, instead of retaking Mahdiya, preferred to turn on the Knights of Malta and lay siege to Tripoli. After this period of uncertainty and shifting alliances in the Mediterranean joint Franco-Turkish naval operations were launched in the following year. Naples was the objective selected by Suleiman, who was then residing in Adrianople and had been joined there by d'Aramont. The operation ended in an encounter with Andrea Doria's fleet, with equal losses on both sides.

The story of the "scandalous alliance" between Francis I and Suleiman thus boils down to incessant comings and goings between Paris and Constantinople, continuous negotiations, a number of treaties either official or secret, a variety of rumours and much propaganda. Thereafter the Turks were to intervene less and less in the affairs of Europe. The battle of Lepanto in 1571 put a halt to their offensive operations in the western Mediterranean. It is true that the actors changed: Barbarossa died in 1546, Charles V abdicated in 1556 and gave place to a sovereign less interested in universal monarchy, Philip II. In 1559 he signed a peace treaty with France, then involved in civil wars which took up all its energies. Suleiman himself died in Hungary in 1566.

France pursued its intermittent alliance with the Ottoman empire in the reign of Henry IV (1589–1610). Henry wanted to fight Spain, and sought the support of the Sultan in 1595. But the instructions given to his ambassadors François Savary, Seigneur de Brèves, and later Henri de Gontaut-Biron, Baron de Salignac, show that it was less a matter of fighting together against a common enemy than of maintaining good relations. Thus Henry refused to support Persia against the Ottoman empire. Later, under the aegis of Cardinal Richelieu, relations were more commercial than political. The time of conspiracies between Constantinople and the French court was over.

Pierre Belon, naturalist and traveller

Pierre Belon thus travelled in the East towards the end of Francis I's reign, during the final stages of the keenly pursued negotiations between France and Constantinople. He was one of the travellers who accompanied the French ambassadors, one of the scientists who gave additional weight to political missions. Some of them might well have intentions other than the mere desire to learn. This was the case with Nicolas de Nicolay, to whose interest in Ottoman fortresses and ports Stéphane Yérasimos has drawn attention[3]. There is no reason to think, however, that Belon was anything other than a scholar taking advantage of an opportunity to travel in order to extend his knowledge and discover the fauna and flora of a region which was still little known. Not that our traveller was indifferent to the political conditions of the time: he enjoyed the patronage and protection of powerful personages, and the circumstances of his death are still shrouded in mystery.

Pierre Belon was born in a hamlet in the Sarthe region, near Le Mans, in 1517, the year in which Nicolas de Nicolay was also born. Little or nothing is known of his family, which was probably modest, nor of his early years[4]. His interest in scientific matters, however, seems likely to have shown itself at quite an early age, for he became an apprentice apothecary to René des Prez, who was apothecary to the bishop of Clermont. He had the good fortune to enjoy the protection of René du Bellay, bishop of Le Mans, who gave him a taste for botany. With the bishop's support, he set out for Germany and studied at the University of Wittenberg, which was then renowned. He spent a year there (1549–1541) and met the man who was to become his teacher, the great botanist Valerius Cordius, who was also a mineralogist. Belon became one of his favoured companions and travelled with him to the forests and mines of Germany and Bohemia. These expeditions were still present in his memory when, later, he was collecting plants under other skies.

After this instructive stay in Germany Belon returned to France and, seeking to complete his education, went to Paris in 1542 to study medicine. It was at this period that he entered the service of a great personage, Cardinal de Tournon, who was to be the dedicatee of his *Observations* and his most constant patron. François de Tournon, a member of a family of prelates, who was born in 1489, became archbishop of Embrun in 1517, of Bourges in 1525 and of Auch in 1537, and finally cardinal of Ostia, as well as titular abbot of numerous abbeys (including Saint-Germain-des-Prés in Paris); but above all he was a great politician, who was to practise his talents as a statesman continuously for thirty years. In particular he had orchestrated Francis I's marriage with Eleanor of Austria, a match which he had negotiated in person in Madrid. It was this intelligent and cultivated man who was to influence the destiny of Pierre Belon. We do not know what were the young scholar's duties in the cardinal's service. Perhaps he was his apothecary, or possibly a translator; for he spoke several languages, including German. And Cardinal de Tournon was then seeking, on behalf of Francis I, who was in open conflict with Charles V, to establish links with the German Protestants.

Accordingly Belon travelled to Germany and Switzerland in 1542. According to what he himself reveals in the *Chronique* in which he gives an account of his life, and which remained in manuscript, his role on this mission was merely as interpreter. It is known that he was imprisoned in Geneva, but he says that this episode was the result of a lively discussion with Calvinists on religion: a very likely explanation, in view of Belon's later record as an active defender of Catholicism. In any case his stay in prison was brief, and he continued his journey in Cardinal de Tournon's suite to Luxembourg, which had recently been taken by French forces.

Belon then left his patron and joined his teacher Valerius Cordius, who was then travelling in Switzerland and Italy with some of his students. Belon remained with him until his death in Rome in September 1544. On his way back to France he visited a number of famous Italian towns and also found time for botanising. Among other things he saw the gardens of the signoria of Venice in Padua, which he mentions in his *Observations*. He also visited Emilia, the Milanese, Lake Como, Lake Garda and Mont Cenis, taking an interest in fishes, plants and monuments. His knowledge of Roman architecture increased when, in the Dauphiné, he became acquainted with Jean Choul, a keen antiquarian.

When Belon returned to his duties with Cardinal de Tournon, one of Francis I's ministers, he became attached to the court, particularly at the château of Saint-Germain-en-Laye. There he could admire the royal collections, which were justly famed; for the king, who liked "curiosities", had brought together a variety of exotic animals – lions, panthers, camels, ostriches – from distant lands, as well as all kinds of other objects, precious woods from Brazil and rare plants. It was then that Belon, with his great interest in botany, conceived the plan of translating the great works of ancient writers, particularly Dioscorides and Theophrastus, and establishing a concordance of the ancient and modern names of plants.

But he was to have only a brief respite from his travels. In 1546 Cardinal de Tournon sent him to the East in the suite of the French ambassador, Monsieur d'Aramont, who was returning to Constantinople after an earlier stay there. Also in the party was

Pierre Gilles, a protégé of Cardinal d'Armagnac, whose mission was to collect manuscripts and antiquities for the king. In spite of the scientific and cultural character of the journey, Monsieur d'Aramont, as we have seen, had other objectives. His mission could brook no delay, and the party travelled fast. Leaving Paris at the end of December 1546, they went through Switzerland and continued by way of Verona and Padua, to arrive two months later in Venice, where they were received by Jean de Morvillier, an ecclesiastic much involved in politics, later to become bishop of Orleans (in 1552) and minister of justice (in 1568), who had recently come to Venice as representative of the French king.

Monsieur d'Aramont, though in haste to reach Constantinople, was unable to leave Venice until the end of February. He stayed for five days in Ragusa, and then decided that it would be quicker to travel by land. He set out again on 13th March 1547, leaving Belon behind him. Belon then continued on his way by sea, with a much more leisurely timetable which enabled him to pursue his scholarly interests. He travelled by way of Corfu, Zante and Cytherea and on to Crete, then under Venetian rule, and spent some considerable time exploring and observing it. On the way there he had a narrow escape from being captured by pirates, but this event, common enough in the Mediterranean in those days, did not discourage him, and he continued imperturbably with his expeditions. Then he reached Constantinople, visiting on the way Euboea and the Black Sea, where he had another encounter with pirates.

When he arrived in Constantinople Monsieur d'Aramont was already there and Francis I had died. He had plenty of time to explore the city and its surroundings, in the company of Pierre Gilles and probably also of André Thevet, who had come in the suite of Monsieur de Fumel, the ambassador extraordinary of the new king of France, Henry II. After his travels in the surroundings of Constantinople and the towns of Macedonia he returned to the capital, from which he soon set out again, this time with Monsieur de Fumel, for Egypt. The party, with an escort granted by Suleiman, sailed from Constantinople at the end of August 1547. Belon was now to have the opportunity of discovering the great cities of Alexandria and Cairo and the towns of the Holy Land. Leaving

Cairo on 29th October, the travellers arrived in Jerusalem on 18th November. This was not to be Belon's last journey through Ottoman territory, for after returning to Constantinople he set out again in May 1548 to visit Anatolia. Monsieur de Fumel had returned to France, leaving Monsieur d'Aramont master of the situation and the favour of the Sultan. The Sultan was then organising a campaign in Persia, and the French ambassador had been granted permission to go with him. Belon was included in the party, along with Pierre Gilles and the cosmographer André Thevet; but remained with the ambassador only in the early stages of his journey, venturing only as far as Nicomedia. Leaving Monsieur d'Aramont to continue to Palestine and Egypt, which he already knew, he returned to Constantinople, where he found Jacques de Cambray, whom the ambassador had left in charge of the embassy. He stayed there for some time, and then set sail for Venice.

On his return to France after an absence of some years Belon resumed his service with Cardinal de Tournon. But he was no longer at the peak of his political power: the new reign had seen upheavals in the corridors of power, and the cardinal, out of favour, had retired to one of his abbeys. Then the Guise family, now all-powerful, sent him to Rome, where the Pope, Paul III, was dying. Belon accompanied his patron; then, after Paul's death in November 1549 and the election of Julius III in February 1550, he left him in Italy, where he was to remain for many years, and returned to France to occupy the lodging which he had been granted in the abbey of Saint-Germain-des-Prés. There he devoted himself to writing an account of his travels in the East as well as other austerer works. But this indefatigable traveller was not destined to remain sedentary: he travelled to England at least twice, before settling down, from 1551 onwards, to the publication of his works.

The first of these, in 1551, was a *Histoire naturelle des étranges poissons marins,* a treatise illustrated with engravings which, according to Belon himself, were the work of François Périer, a relative of the celebrated 16th century surgeon Ambroise Paré. Then, in 1553, he published in Latin another work devoted to fish, *De aquatilibus,* and two years later a French version, *De la nature & diversité des poissons,* and his copious notes on his travels, brought together under the title *Observations de plusieurs singularités & choses mémorables, trouvées en Grèce, Asie, Judée, Égypte, Arabie, & autres pays étranges,* for which he had obtained a privilege (i.e. in effect copyright) from the king, and which was dedicated to Cardinal de Tournon. In the same year were published two other treatises on different subjects, *De arboribus coniferis* and *De admirabile operum antiquorum.* All this did not prevent Belon from continuing with his travels. In the course of the year 1553 he had a short trip to Lorraine, accompanying a gentleman of the King's Chamber, the Seigneur de Vieilleville, who had been appointed governor of the stronghold of Metz, which had recently been taken from the Spaniards, and took advantage of the journey to study the fauna and flora of the region. He was taken prisoner by the Spaniards, but was promptly freed on payment of a ransom and reappeared at court, probably before the end of 1554[5].

Belon's literary labours were not yet at an end. In 1553, in addition to a slightly reworked edition of the *Observations,* he published his *Histoire de la nature des oiseaux,* illustrated by Pierre Goudet[6]. He was now recognised, and also enjoyed the favour of important personages. Cardinal de Tournon had returned to France in 1552 but was no longer involved in public affairs; but Belon had found a new patron in a great lord who was now all-powerful, a friend of the king's mistress Diane de Poitiers, the Connétable Anne de Montmorency. Montmorency, who shared Belon's interest in botany, had indicated his readiness to finance certain works which he had in preparation. Belon also knew Odet de Coligny, Cardinal de Chatillon, through whose good offices he could also claim the support of the Guise family. He was presented to king Henry II and put forward a proposal to acclimatise exotic species in France. The king granted him a pension, though this was probably merely symbolic.

Pending the realisation of this project, Belon set out again on his travels, visiting various parts of France and then Switzerland and Italy, where he had the privilege of being admitted to the Belvedere gardens. He returned to France by way of Lyons and reminded the king of his promise; but the treasury was empty, and Belon's great projects were put on hold. He did, however, manage to bring in some plants from Italy, and cultivated cypresses, planes and oleanders.

The last period of Belon's life was marked, like that of many of his contemporaries, by the wars of religion between Catholics and Protestants. The accidental death of Henry II in 1559 and the accession of Francis II (briefly the husband of Mary Queen of Scots), followed soon afterwards by that of the boy Charles IX, brought political changes. Cardinal de Tournon reappeared. to end his career as a member of the queen mother's council.

At the same time the French Protestants were now asserting themselves in public. Among them were great personages like Cardinal de Chatillon, who had long shown his sympathies with the Reformation and had now publicly abandoned the Catholic faith. Belon, like Cardinal de Tournon, was fiercely anti-Huguenot, and remained so throughout the confrontations of 1561–1562, which were settled in the peace of Amboise in March 1563. His opinions were well known, and they may well have been the cause of his death. One evening in April 1564[7], when he was returning to the château of Madrid on the outskirts of Paris, recently completed by the architect Philibert Delorme, in which the king had granted him a lodging, he was murdered, apparently by thieves, who then haunted the Bois de Boulogne.

Thus ended the life of Pierre Belon: an adventurous life, nomadic rather than sedentary, wholly devoted to study. From small beginnings he rose to become the habitué of courts. Self-taught, he gained recognition as one of the men of learning of his time, though sometimes becoming involved in jealousies and disputes. This success was due in part to the influence of his patron Cardinal de Tournon: a manifestation of the spirit of patronage of the arts and sciences, then much in vogue in France, to which Belon refers in the dedication of his *Observations*. The cardinal, like the king himself, was known for his culture and his interest in the sciences. Like the king, he liked to surround himself with men of education and learning, to encourage their work by the benefits he was able to offer, and to be accompanied by them on his travels. Belon benefited from these dispositions, which were characteristic of a brilliant reign during which religious conflicts had not yet come to the forefront and overshadowed the cultural flowering. He remained a man of Francis I's reign, as is shown by his frequent praise of the king, whom he constantly refers to as the "restorer of letters".

Some years after Francis's death in 1547, in the preface to his *Observations*, Belon pays homage to him rather than to Henry II. He himself, who continued throughout his life to increase his knowledge in many fields of learning, can justly be regarded as the very model of the humanist in quest of learning, of Renaissance man.

The *Observations*

Belon's account of his travels in the Ottoman empire, written at the end of a period in which the fate of Europe depended on three men – Francis I, Suleiman and Charles V – matches his character as a scholar: it shows less concern with the political preoccupations of the day than with his interest as a naturalist in the flora, fauna and way of life of the regions in which he was travelling. For him observation is predominant, and nothing can distract him from the purpose to which he devoted his whole life. In the course of the many months which he spent in the Ottoman empire, circumstances or his own impulse led him to visit almost the whole of the immense territory ruled by the Turks. From Constantinople, the sole objective of many travellers of the time, a series of long excursions took him not only to Egypt and the Holy Land, regions which were frequently visited, but to Turkey in Asia, then called Anatolia, which attracted fewer westerners. He made quite a long stay there, spending a whole winter and part of the spring in a village called Afyon Karahisar. In his comings and goings he made use of various means of locomotion, travelling by sea, at the risk of falling into the hands of pirates, joining caravans, accompanying great personages, but was not afraid of travelling alone, or almost alone, through regions regarded as dangerous, with the sole object of observing the things that were the objects of his curiosity.

His interests were thus somewhat different from those of the travellers who had preceded him, and particularly those who in the second half of the 16th century and the whole of the 17th were to travel in the same territories. Belon was above all a naturalist, concerned with plants, fish and other animals and extending his observations to people and their customs and way of life. He seems to have practised medicine during his travels[8], taking advantage of his relationship with some powerful personage whom he treated in order to gain access, by an innocent little deceit, to plants and substances which aroused his interest. His *Observations* reflect the life he led in the Levant, a life of free and passionate exploration. They contain, in addition to minute descriptions of the plants and animals which he had come to study, notes on the daily life of the local people, their religion, their amusements, their varied activities. But Belon, with his concern for truth, reported nothing but what he had himself seen, unlike other travellers both before and after him who described the apartments of the "sultanas", to which of course they had never had access. Not that Belon was not interested in the political organisation of the Ottoman empire: from time to time he does let slip some remarks which bear witness to his keen understanding of the system of government of the Turks.

A work to the glory of observation

The title of Belon's book, giving prominence to the key term *observation,* well reflects his approach to his subject during his travels and throughout his whole life. In this he was in the spirit of an age which asserted the value of personal experience and glorified discovery. The extraordinary appetite for knowledge shown by the men of the Renaissance is reflected particularly in the prefaces of the books of travel of the period, in which the writers justify their enterprise. Thus Nicolas de Nicolay says in his *Préface à la louange des pérégrinations & observations étranges déclarant l'intention de l'auteur:* "Reason requires man, and nature seems to command him, to seek, to visit and enquire, to learn to know all the parts and mansions of his universal habitation". Belon would not have disagreed. Both men do honour to the illustrious travellers who have preceded them, headed by Ulysses. Belon, normally inclined to sobriety of language, rises at this point to a lyrical tone: "Neither the terror of shipwreck in the perilous sea, nor the turbulence of the boisterous winds beating on ships and breaking them up amid the waves whipped up by storms, nor the fear of losing their freedom at the hands of inhuman pirates, nor dangerous passages through harsh rocks, nor the intemperance of excessive heat or extreme cold, nor nights darkened by rain clouds with lightning and fearful thunder, nor the danger of crossing uninhabited deserts in fear of wild beasts have been able to repress the ardour of their noble courage, already aflame in their generous heart, and lead them to abandon their enterprise". Nicolay for his part, after referring to the heroes of antiquity, mentions modern travellers, including Postel and Belon, his forerunners, demonstrating the continuity between the ancients and the moderns.

The reference to Greco-Latin antiquity is omnipresent. More precisely, we can observe the development of a theory of knowledge consisting of a compromise between personal observation and information obtained from books. Nicolay gives perfect expression to this in declaring that he proposes to give a description of peoples and territories "extracted in part from the ancient authors, cosmographers, geographers and chorographers, like Ptolemy, Strabo, Pliny, Mela and others, for the most part confirmed and approved by the sure sense of my own eyes". Belon, too, refers in his preface to the authority of the ancients: "After considering ... that anything that we say, having no authority but our own, is not greatly esteemed, it has seemed to me right on occasion to cite passages from good authors to give authority to what I shall say hereafter". In Belon's own words, experience will serve to confirm knowledge previously acquired. This approach applied particularly to fauna and flora. The task that Belon had set himself was an ambitious one: it was to compare the mammals, fish, snakes, birds and plants observed in his travels with the descriptions of the ancients, in order to establish for each of them its Greek or Latin name and to equate these names with the modern names in French, Italian and even in the patois of different parts of France. This plan was followed more systematically and more rigorously in Belon's treatises on each of the fields sketched out in the *Observations*. He might therefore be suspected of desiring to find in nature at any price the animals and plants mentioned by the ancients, an attitude common to many travellers of the time. Belon seems, however, to look more critically at earlier writings and to lay more weight on his own experience.

His references to ancient writers are, on the whole, fairly limited. This was the criticism levelled at him by some of his rivals, who regarded him as a mere amateur. It is true that Belon shows no knowledge of the works of his immediate predecessors, and that even his quotations from the great writers of antiquity are relatively few in number. As Philippe Glardon has recently noted[9], almost all his quotations are from Pliny's *Natural History* and, more rarely, Aristotle's *History of Animals,* which he probably knew in Theodore Gaza's Latin translation, as well as other Latin authors such as Martial, Varro and Columella. Moreover his quotations are sometimes vague, incomplete or slightly inaccurate. It is not surprising, therefore, if his detractors regarded him as but a poor scholar, compared with the celebrated Gesner and Rondelet, his contemporaries.

Such criticisms, however, in no way detract from the qualities as an observer of the self-taught scholar who was Pierre Belon. His minute descriptions, illustrated by numerous engravings, carefully executed and seeking to be true to nature[10], at a time when the public was accustomed to seeing symbolic animals or monsters, have been justly praised. Above all he does not feel himself to be the slave of knowledge inherited from the past, but regards that knowledge as a signpost on the road which leads men to greater knowledge. "Men grow in knowledge on each other's shoulders", he writes in his preface. And so he pours ridicule in advance on those who may criticise his "curiosity" and dismiss his zeal as a waste of time, advising them playfully to return to the rude way of life of the most ancient peoples, who had no need of modern comfort to live.

What is of more importance is that Belon was able to look critically at the writings of the ancients. The respect which he showed them did not prevent him from questioning what they said, with or without the usual precautions, when it was at odds with his observations. Thus in his book on fish he criticises "the great licence and liberty of the ancients in their fables and poetic fictions". Experience can thus show the error of what had been considered certain. For him the ancients are liable to error, and he submits everything, whether in earlier writings or in what he has been told, to the judgment of his reason. Probability and logic were to be his guides. His principal concern, both in the *Observations* and in his other works, was to affirm nothing of which he was not personally certain.

He wrote his *Observations* in accordance with this principle, "resolving in all that I write not to set down anything that I have not first seen for myself", as he declares in his dedicatory epistle to Cardinal de Tournon. Not content with thus affirming the value of actual experience, he focuses in his writings on what he has himself seen and experienced, undistracted by any ulterior motive. Unlike diplomats and merchants, who travel with a precise objective in mind and who, if they write an account of their journeys, can only remark in passing matters which are merely part of the background to their enterprise, Belon's sole aim in his travels was to see and observe. "Those who undertake a distant journey in foreign lands for their private affairs are more curious to look for things necessary for carrying out their purpose than to employ their time in other observations with which they are not concerned, as appears from the business of a merchant, who, despite having made many journeys to India and Newfoundland, nevertheless, having no other aim than to employ his money to advantage in the purchase of goods, is not interested in acquiring the infinite singularities which a curious man might observe".

He presents himself, in short, as the perfect traveller. Or rather, more modestly, he describes himself as a "curious man", a term which depicts him perfectly. Belon is curious about everything, about fauna and flora, about fish, about the mining and use of minerals, but also about the life and customs of people, about human nature. The adverb "curiously" appears very frequently in his writings, implying both a desire for knowledge and a concern with exact detail.

His attitude is always that of a logical observer. His object is to understand and bring order into the world of nature, which for the men of the Middle Ages had been an aggregation of marvels. The collection of "curiosities" or curios was still widely popular in Belon's time, and practised by many of his contemporaries, beginning with Francis I himself, who liked to collect animals and other strange objects brought from distant lands. It is still in evidence in many of the geographical writings of the second half of the 16th century.

Belon, however, is not content with describing singular objects: he shows a constant desire to identify and classify different species, and above all he is ever ready to express his doubts about improbable identifications. If he still uses, and indeed includes in the title of his book, the term "singularities", then much in vogue, his object goes beyond the mere description of them: he seeks always to find connections between them, to establish relationships or differences between them, in short to order them in the scheme of things. In this process of classification he can sometimes fall into error, for example in the case of the hippopotamus. Since his method is based in part on a practical criterion, that of the natural environment, for him the hippopotamus, which lives in water, must, like the crocodile, be of the nature of fish. It was an understandable mistake at a time when the otter was still classed among fish and was eaten during Lent, and need not discredit Belon's work.

In his work of classification, even though it is not perfect nor entirely original, he distances himself sharply from an earlier conception of the world which attached value only to the extraordinary, and which still has its adepts. For example André Thevet, keeper of the king's cabinet of singularities, prides himself on describing in his works only objects which are "singular"[11], that is, rare, and sometimes also fantastic. It was an approach which he erected into a system, as he proclaims in his *Cosmographie universelle:* "Let it suffice, therefore, for the reader that I collect whatever is most remarkable and present to him the rarest objects, and those that will give him most contentment and pleasure". Thevet's prime object is to arouse the reader's wonder, and this leads him to retail without questioning them the most extravagant fables. Belon does not deny *a priori* the existence of all the fabulous animals of which the geographical literature inherited from the Middle Ages is so full, but declares that he has never come across them. He prefers to study what he sees with his own eyes, and does not consider it beneath his dignity to collect specimens of all kinds of plants, even of those also found in Europe, in order to make the most exact comparisons possible. His first reaction on discovering a reptile or a fish is to "anatomise" it, that is, to dissect it immediately, instead of confining himself to its external characteristics, which he already knows.

Unlike Thevet, he did not think he was insulting the Creator by trying to understand His creatures. Thevet believed that God's creatures were meant to be "most frequently incomprehensible and to be wondered at by men. Wherefore it would be impertinent to look for their cause or reason, as many seek daily to do. For that is a true secret of nature, knowledge of which is reserved to the Creator alone" *(Les singularités de la France antarctique)*. The debate about science and discovery in the 16th century was also a theological debate between the heritage of St Thomas Aquinas and that of St Augustine, who condemned curiosity as leading to the sin of pride. For Belon as for many of his contemporaries the increase in knowledge could not but contribute to the glorification of the Creator. Accordingly he never tired of seeking out the secrets of nature and never felt that he had sufficiently succeeded in his quest.

He never hesitated to denounce the false beliefs, the superstitions and misrepresentations that he encountered in the course of his studies. As a rational thinker, he refused to admit that the "sealed earth" which was found on Lemnos and was credited with therapeutic qualities preserved its properties only if it was extracted on a particular day in the year, with particular ceremonies performed by the Greek caloyers on the island. The chapter on this subject has a heading that is sufficiently explicit: "That things which are base and of little esteem are made precious by ceremonies, and that things of little value acquire authority when ennobled by superstition". In Macedonia, observing the "superstitious medicining" practised by a Turk who claimed to be able to cure a man suffering from a disorder of the spleen by drying a piece of bark cut to the size of the affected organ, Belon mocks this poor anatomist who thinks that the spleen is "in the middle of the belly above the navel".

He also derides those who believe that the fish in certain rivers feed on gold and corrects the foolish tales he hears told about the fabulous treasures brought back from the Indies by the Spaniards. With his rational mind, he cannot believe the stories about the miraculous discovery of gold in the Indies ("If you believe what they say, anyone arriving in India has only to dig ... to find gold, which he has only to pack up for loading on a ship"). He demonstrates that the great quantities of gold brought back by the Spaniards in their early days in America came from the pillaging of treasures accumulated over many years, and that this gold could only have come from a mine, extracted at the cost of great labour.

His work of demystification is not confined to the manners of foreign peoples. He vigorously denounces a practice which to a modern reader seems totally repugnant but was common in European courts, and even in the court of France. This was the use made of "mummy" from Egypt, a term which applied both to the embalmed body and the embalming substance. It was credited with valuable properties, particularly that of liquefying congealed blood, and therefore was administered to those who had injured themselves in a fall. What they were given, in fact, was usually a kind of pap made from the body of some unknown Egyptian which had been dried in the sun or in an oven and contained not a trace of any aromatic substance.

An account without artifice

This designedly scientific approach sets the tone of Belon's narrative, which in many places reflects the austerity of its author. He disdained to seek the easy effects which were all too common in the writings of most of his contemporaries. Not only did he not feel obliged to describe sumptuous ceremonies (at which in any case he could not have been present), or to paint the picture of Constantinople which was becoming classic and was repeated endlessly in later accounts, but he refused to over-dramatise his own anecdotes. Thus he relates in a very matter-of-fact way how he went to the baths on the wrong day and found himself among an assembly of women, at the peril of his life. Another writer would undoubtedly have made a scene of comedy out of this misadventure, but Belon merely recounts his experience in a few lines, without any salacious suggestions.

Belon explains the reason for choosing this style in his dedication to Cardinal de Tournon: he declares that he has written his book "in our ordinary French tongue" in order to be understood by as many people as possible, and has deliberately adopted a plain style, "using no artifice or elegance of speech, but in simple terms, telling of things truly as I found them in foreign lands".

This absolute refusal to seek effect marks the whole of his account. Admittedly it leads on occasion to a certain dryness of tone; but this deliberate austerity is the counterpart of a scrupulous respect for truth and a rigorous quest for authenticity. We can be sure that none of Belon's assertions are made lightly. What he writes, he has seen. He is never tempted to recount rumours in order to give his work a character of originality.

Men and manners

In the course of his travels Belon had the opportunity of observing many of the "nations" which co-existed in the Ottoman empire: Turks, of course, but also Greeks, Arabs, Egyptians and Jews, to mention only the largest groups. In his dealings with them all he showed an admirable openness of mind and curiosity. His approach was at the opposite extreme to that of Thevet, who describes his feelings on setting out on his travels in the Levant in these words: "I was much dismayed at the thought of leaving France, where I was born, to acquaint myself with an unknown land and infidel peoples, where I could look forward to no friendship or trust and where I should have to become accustomed to different garments, customs and language". Belon, on the other hand, was determined to observe before making any judgment.

He also employed this scientific method, developed in his study of fauna and flora, in his observation of people and their way of life. Throughout his book he attaches great importance to the details of everyday life in the countries in which he is travelling, for example to their food and drink, and makes it a point of honour to try them himself before expressing his opinion of them. Of course, there is no such thing as a purely objective observer, since he inevitably looks on everything in relation to what for him is the norm; but Belon is well aware of this and frequently refers to it, arriving at the conclusion that everything is relative. He also follows another principle which had guided his study of fauna and flora: comparison. Observing the manner of drinking of the Greeks, he distinguishes it from that of the Turks, and finds it more like that of the Germans. He will even venture to compare the rhythms of the chanting of Arabs in their mosques with the chanting of Latin psalms.

Conditions under Turkish rule

Belon frequently remarks on the situation of towns and ports and their systems of defence, with systematic descriptions of fortresses, castles and town walls which he comes across in the course of his travels. Thus he notes that "this island of Crete is difficult for a hostile force to attack. Since it can be reached only by sea and has few harbours, it is thus sufficiently well fortified", that on the island of Lemnos "there is no large fortress that could resist an attack by force of arms", and that towns in Turkey are not usually walled, while of the many monasteries on Mount Athos "there are none that are not strong and securely enclosed by walls, both to withstand the violence of enemies if they were to be attacked and to resist sea corsairs if the need should arise".

Is Belon discussing such matters of deliberate intent, or is he merely following a tradition of travel writing which gives a preponderant place to the walls and other defensive structures as features no less worthy of attention than the fertility of the surrounding country? The latter hypothesis seems to the present editor more probable. Similarly Belon's concern in his description of the Grand Signior's gold and silver mines[12] is not merely with the quantity produced but above all with the techniques of extracting the gold and minting it into coins.

Nevertheless, if Belon does not think it necessary to describe the ceremonies of the Sultan's court and does not discuss the political conflicts of the day, this does not mean that he is not interested in questions of government: in fact, he is particularly concerned with their effects on the life of the various peoples. Like other western travellers, he observes the decadence of the Greeks, who, after giving the world so many illustrious thinkers, have fallen "into such a marvellous state of ignorance that there is not a town in all their country that has a university; and also they take no pleasure in learning letters and sciences". Visiting Mount Athos, he writes: "Formerly there were good books, written by hand, to be found on the mountain, for the Greeks in the monasteries were in past times much more learned than they are at the present time. Now there are none who know anything, and it would be impossible to find on the whole of Mount Athos more than a single caloyer with some learning in any of the monasteries". It is not so much the economic manifestations of decadence as the cultural decline that shocks him; but, contrary to the general tendency of his time, he does not attribute it to the Turks, who were then universally regarded as responsible for the ruin of the nations that they had conquered. "We must attribute this ruin of Greek books," he says, "to the carelessness and ignorance of the peoples living in Greek lands, who are totally bastardised. And not only within our memory, but also in times long past, there has been no one of learning in the whole of Greece".

Belon's great merit is that he understands the limits and the methods of Turkish rule: it was political and economic, but not cultural. The Turks did not radically change the way of life of the conquered nations. Although the Greeks under Turkish rule adopted Turkish dress, and those subject to the Venetians dressed like them, the inhabitants of country areas retained all their customs and their language. It is an illustration of Belon's great principle that "each nation retains something of the nature of its country", as he says in speaking of the Egyptians.

Everywhere he goes he is concerned to identify the different peoples and to note the languages spoken by the inhabitants of all the regions through which he travels. He thus offers direct evidence of the medley of races in the Ottoman empire, frequently a result of the Turkish policy of moving certain populations according to the needs of the moment. "When the Turk conquers a province he carries off the peasants from the villages and sends them to found colonies and cultivate land round Constantinople or elsewhere which was previously unpopulated". Thus the gold mines of Macedonia wee worked by workers of diverse origin ("The metals are refined here by the labour of Albanians, Greeks, Jews, Wallachians, Circassians and Servians as well as Turks"), and the Jews of Kavala and neighbouring towns had been brought from Hungary to repopulate the region.

Belon also brings out the religious liberty enjoyed by all the subjects of the Ottomans. "I found that the inhabitants of the islands live in accordance with their religion almost as they did before, and even those who live on Cyprus, Rhodes, Lemnos, Chios, Imbros, Thasos, Patmos, Cos, Metelin, Corfu, Zante, Naxos, Crete and other islands have remained in the Christian faith, even though they are ruled by the Turk, as do also others on the mainland of Europe and Asia", he writes. He says the same thing in more general form: "The Turks compel no one to live in the Turkish fashion, but each man is permitted to live in accordance with his faith", and reaches a conclusion of political significance: "This is what has always maintained the Turk in his greatness; for when he conquers a country it is sufficient for him to be obeyed, and provided he receives tribute he does not concern himself with men's souls". He seems, therefore, to regard this method of government as effective, an opinion which is of some interest in an age when the principle of *cuius regio, eius religio,* under which the subjects of a ruler must adopt his religion, was the subject of passionate debate.

The tolerance of the Turks (subject to the payment of tribute) is thus well established. Moreover the Ottoman empire is seen as an ordered world. For Belon the masters of Constantinople and immense territories conquered by force of arms are not blood-stained barbarians. In his view they are more like the Romans, whose place, in some sense, they have taken. In the course of his travels he takes care to mention the monuments inherited from these glorious predecessors, without indulging in lamentations on the decadence of nations and the changes wrought by time.

Belon, however, does not overdo his praise of the Turks, and he cannot be suspected of magnifying the Turks in order to criticise Christians. The *Observations* are not a polemical tract. The organisation of the Ottoman empire was far from being perfect. Thus Belon does not gloss over the avarice of the Turkish officials who, having purchased their offices, recover the cost of their investment by holding travellers to ransom. He himself, having suffered in this way at the hands of the voivode of Lemnos, bitterly remarks on "what robberies the Turks will resort to when you are at their mercy". He observes that these practices are the result of the system for the appointment of officials: "They do that because a man may be governor of a province for a longer or shorter period, perhaps only for a month or a year, and will then have to leave it and take up another post a thousand leagues away; and so if they have any occasion for plunder they will not let it pass them by". The mobility of Turkish officials never ceases to surprise him, and he goes more deeply into the matter when he is in Jerusalem, interrogating a sanjak and describing his career.

The portrait of the Turks that emerges from Belon's account is thus a picture of contrasts. Among their most notable qualities he ranks the charity of those who build hospitals, their concern for hygiene (the Turks, he says, are "the cleanest people in the world"), the continence and physical toughness of their soldiers, which he was able to observe in the members of the escort given to the French ambassador, Monsieur de Fumel: "The Turkish soldiers attached to Monsieur de Fumel throughout the journey carried enough biscuit to eat on the way from Cairo to Mount Sinai and back, and still brought some back, which seemed to us very great continence in their manner of living, which men of another nation would be unable to achieve". This praise is no cause for surprise, for the warlike character and the sobriety of the Turks were among the prime qualities generally attributed to them. Their valour was accompanied by no hint of braggadocio, but rather by good sense and modesty: "The Turks in time of peace are of modest demeanour, leave their weapons at home and live peaceably, ... And if a man were found to have fought with his companion he would not on that account be deemed valiant."

Belon does not shrink from comparing this behaviour with that of those Europeans who play the braggart well away from any field of battle. Finally he pays the Sultan's soldiers on campaign the supreme compliment of comparing them with Romans. On the other hand he contradicts the reputation for bravery of the janissaries, who were not Turks by birth. Those who accompanied Monsieur de Fumel on an excursion to Jerusalem, for example, showed only cowardice, abandoning the travellers when they feared attack by a band of Arabs.

More unusual and more courageous is Belon's attitude when he seeks to correct certain generally held prejudices about the Turks. They were commonly accused of ruthless pillage and rapine in conquered territory; but on several occasions Belon bears witness to the contrary.

On his visit to the island of Rhodes, which had been conquered from the Knights of St John of Jerusalem by Suleiman in 1522, he writes: "All the buildings of the knights of Rhodes, both French and of other nations, still stand entire everywhere, for the Turks have not removed any of the coats of arms, paintings, sculptures or carvings and signs that they found there ... I must say also that the Turks have always had this custom, that any castle or fortress that they have ever taken has been left in the state in which they found it, for they never demolish any buildings or carvings." Continuing this process of rehabilitation, he adds: "The walls of Rhodes are in the same state as they were when [the Turks] took them out of the hands of the knights, and since then they have been neither increased nor diminished, neither strengthened nor weakened".

Nor do we find in the *Observations* any of the usual lamentations about the fate of Cairo by other travellers, who speak of the houses, once so splendid, which have fallen into decrepitude. In most of their accounts everything preceding the Turkish conquest, even though the earlier rulers were Muslims, like the Mamelukes in Egypt, is presented as better, more "civilised", than it is now. Belon, however, finds no signs of decadence: true, he does credit the splendour of some buildings to the magnificence of the Circassian Mamelukes, but he does not report any decline since that period. On the contrary, he shows that the Turks could also be builders: in Cairo, for example, he notes that there were a number of "finely built" mosques dating from after the Ottoman conquest.

Similarly his visit to the Holy Land does not lead to any recriminations. He does recall associations with saints and apostles, but he does not express horror at seeing Jerusalem in the hands of the infidels as so many other travellers do, nor exhort Christians to undertake a new crusade. The sight of tombs and chapels does not distract him from the observation of the riches of nature.

Finally, Belon does not seem to be troubled by something that roused the indignation of other westerners: the absence of any stable social hierarchy in the Ottoman world. He notes that the highest dignitary after the Grand Signior himself may be a man of whom it is not known where he came from or who his father and mother were, but finds nothing wrong with this. The man who enjoyed Suleiman's highest favour, his grand vizier Ibrahim, was the perfect illustration of a social promotion that took a former slave to the highest offices in the empire by the will of the Sultan and in recognition of his personal merits. Belon draws attention to this difference from European societies, and concludes soberly that nobility "is as men wish to judge it" and that "nobility is not judged in the same way in every country, since the nobles of Florence and Venice were happy to go in for trade, which elsewhere was considered beneath a nobleman's dignity.

The portraits of other nations confirm Belon's qualities as an observer. He finds no one beneath his notice, not even the gypsies who were then universally reviled, finding them to be particularly skilled metal-workers. He never throws ridicule on other people's religious beliefs, except perhaps, and then only in a light tone, in the case of the Jews ("the cleverest nation in the world, and the most artful"), who do not eat any fish that has no scales. He takes a certain sly pleasure in relating how he involuntarily gave rise to a memorable dispute between Jews in a village in Macedonia when he proved to them that a fish which they believed they were allowed to eat had no scales.

The religion of the Greeks, the subject of much critical comment by other authors, some of whom attributed the decadence of the Greeks to their errors of dogma, is discussed by Belon without animosity. Far from ridiculing the monks of Mount Athos, whom he had seen at close quarters, he praises their austere life and describes the economy of the monasteries, in which each man contributed by his labour to the wellbeing of all. "As for the monks whom I have called caloyers living on Mount Athos, you are not to think that they lead an idle life, for they leave their monasteries in the early morning, each with his tool in his hand and carrying some biscuit and a few onions in a scrip slung over his shoulder – one a hoe, another a mattock, a third a billhook. Each one works for the domestic needs of his monastery. Some work in the vineyards, others hew wood, others again build boats. ... Some are tailors, others builders, others carpenters, others of other trades, all working in common, spinning the wool from which their shifts and other garments are made".

Belon's attitude to the Muslim faith is more ambiguous. Although he regarded the Koran (to which he devotes a long disquisition in his third book) as a tissue of "follies", he knows it better than other travellers. He knows that Mohammed is not buried at Mecca, but in Medina, and avoids any suggestion that Turkish baths are anything other than a hygienic practice. He gives a minute description of circumcision, without showing any disgust; and if he is critical of the dervishes whom he encounters in the streets of Constantinople it is not so much on religious grounds as in the name of reason. As a good physician, he cannot approve of the practices of these "fantastics", whose "arms and breast are covered with scars, some across and some up and down, which they cut with their knives".

Of all the nations which appear in the *Observations* Belon seems to be most in sympathy with the Egyptians. Of all the peoples living in the territories of the Ottoman empire they were the least known and least regarded by western travellers. Belon distinguishes them very clearly from the Turks, but perhaps less so from the Arabs; and he sometimes confuses the issue by calling them "Moors". They are, he says, "the most recreative of peoples, ever ready to leap about or dance, or indulge in some caper". This lively and light-hearted nature, in which he recognises characteristics already noted by the ancient authors, is a quality he admires, while the Turks seem to him melancholic, slow and lazy. He also admires the remains of Egyptian civilisation more than Greek and Roman ruins. Of all the monuments which feature in the three books of the *Observations* it is the pyramids that get the most detailed and most enthusiastic description.

Daily life of the peoples

Belon's portraits of the various "nations" within the Ottoman empire differ from those of other travellers, which gradually develop into stereotypes. Instead of giving minute descriptions of the dress of the Turks, the colours of their turbans and the finery of their women, he is more interested in their manners and way of life. He has relatively little to say about their dress or their physical characteristics, on which some of his observations are delightfully naïve, showing that the science of anthropology had not yet been born. In Arabia, he notes that "the people of this country are quite happy to live in the open under palm-trees, which is why they are olive-coloured". On the other hand he is interested in everything related to human activities, whether it is a question of agriculture or of amusements. He is constantly concerned to distinguish what is peculiar to each region. Thus he notes the Cretans' skill at archery, attributing it to their "antiquity", and remarks on the continuing popularity of a traditional dance, the ancient *pyrrhica saltatio*.

He observes different methods of catching birds and fishing, and does not disdain to record recipes for local dishes. Thus he sets down the best way of cooking "scarus", a kind of fish whose liver, beaten up with salt and vinegar, makes a delicious sauce. Similarly, he describes how the peasants of Lemnos eat cucumbers raw and without any seasoning, first taking off the skin lengthwise. "I know no butchers more skilled in preparing fresh meat than those of Turkey", he says. He also describes a simple dish like oxygal (a kind of soft white cheese made from sour milk), of which Turks both old and young were particularly fond, as "a dish fit for a great lord".

Belon shows none of the prejudices of a westerner convinced of the superiority of his own way of life. On the contrary, he never misses an opportunity of learning, and noting with admiration, some particular technique, like the way in which Turkish muleteers can so rapidly load and unload their beasts, or the marvellously simple method by which the craftsmen of Constantinople print patterns on fabrics. He also praises the talents of Turkish musicians, who play an instrument which sounds exactly like a German flute in spite of its rather rustic appearance, The whole of the third book is devoted to the customs and manners of the Turks, of most of which he speaks in favourable terms, and some of which had not been remarked on by other western travellers.

Thus Belon was practically the only traveller to take such a close interest in the education of children. Children do not generally feature in other travellers' tales, since they were kept out of the way of visitors, but also because they were not regarded as of great importance at that period. Belon, however, devotes a long chapter to the preparation of pap for infants and to their swaddling clothes and cradles, omitting no smallest detail.

Among human activities trade occupies an important place. Although Belon was not a merchant, he was interested in everything concerning daily life, and he regularly mentions the trade carried on by land or by sea in the regions through which he is travelling. He is interested in the price of mastic from Chios, and when he is in the port of Silivri, two days' journey from Constantinople, he observes: "Large ships commonly come to Seliurée to load up with goods which are brought from Adrianople and from Thrace and Bulgaria. As an example of this, when I was there a Venetian ship was just completing its cargo of goods which had been brought not only from the countries mentioned above but also from Anatolia, such as wool, leather and cotton".

Finally, Belon, like all travellers since the Renaissance, showed some interest in "antiquities", that is, Greek and Roman remains. As soon as he arrived in Constantinople in August 1548 he organised an expedition to the ruins of Nicomedia, where he collected medals. He frequently describes ancient remains, and in his concern for accuracy transcribes the Latin inscriptions on tombs. But it is evident that he is more interested in the riches of the living present than in dead ruins. Thus on his visit to Nicomedia he soon turns to describing with wonder and in much greater detail the riches of the sea, the multitude and abundance of fish in the Propontis and the different ways of catching them[13]. Similarly, he begins a circumstantial description of the ruins of Troy, but the enumeration of walls and arches soon gives way to more modern subjects, such as the fruit-trees and the saline baths in the surrounding area.

This attitude extends to the descriptions of towns, and even of Constantinople itself. The chapter devoted to the Ottoman capital begins with a description in laudatory terms of its site, which guarantees it both safety and abundance; but this presentation, which was then becoming a standard feature of the writings of travellers, is the only point of similarity between the accounts of Belon and other travellers. The picture he paints is more personal, reflecting his own particular preoccupations. Thus he writes in abundant detail about the city's great market, describing not the building itself but the extraordinary variety of the wares on sale, particularly products of the sea. He seems to be less interested in St Sophia – we may note in passing that, far from deploring that it has fallen into the hands of barbarians, he considers it much superior to the Pantheon in Rome, with which it was generally compared – than in the Sultan's collection of wild animals.

It can therefore be said that in general Belon is less interested in the past than in the present. Thus he does not adopt the approach common to cosmographers and other travellers, who in presenting a particular people described their ancient manners and way of life before their life in modern times. Although Belon does make reference to antiquity, to some of its heroes and to particular events, he does not do so in systematic fashion. Nicolay perpetuates this approach in his *Quatrième livre des Navigations*, describing in successive chapters "The ancient religion and manner of life of the Armenians" and then "The modern religion of the Armenians", distinguishing between "The ancient religion of the Greeks" and "The modern religion of the Greeks" and between "The ancient religion and ceremonies of the Persians" and "The modern religion of the Persians", and so on.

In sum, throughout a long and very full account of his travels, in which he devotes more space to the customs of peasants than to the ceremonies of the powerful, Pierre Belon presents an extraordinary fresco, rich in information on the history of the sciences, from botany to ornithology and mineralogy, and rich also in racy and sometimes naïve details on the everyday life of the peoples of the Ottoman empire. His successors were quick to realise this, quoting him, copying him, sometimes shamelessly borrowing whole paragraphs. His reputation spread beyond the frontiers of France, for many foreign authors, seeking reliable information, looked to him. In the annals of geographical literature his name ranks with those of the most celebrated cosmographers and travellers of the Renaissance.

HISTORY OF THE TEXT

The *Observations* were published in Paris in 1553 by Guillaume Cavellat and Gilles Corrozet, two booksellers who had formed a partnership for the publication of several of Belon's works. They also published in 1553 *De admirabili operum antiquorum & rerum suspiciendarum praestantia* and *De arboribus coniferis*, then in 1555 the

Histoire de la nature des oiseaux. Each time two different title pages were printed, bearing the respective addresses of the two partners[14]. This first edition of the *Observations* was illustrated with woodcuts which, according to Paul Delaunay, were by a certain Arnold Nicolaï, of whom we have found no trace in works on the history of engraving and printing in the 16th century. It is true that all the engravers of that period have not been listed. Engraving was a free craft, unlike other crafts which were closely regulated and hierarchically organised. Moreover the attribution of the woodcuts is made more difficult by the absence of any monogram or other mark[15].

The second edition of the *Observations* and the third (Paris, 1554 and 1555, "freshly revised and augmented by figures"), still published by Cavellat and Corrozet, contain a map of Mount Sinai and a portrait of Pierre Belon at the age of 36, with a legend in Greek, which was later included in many editions of his various works. It is a head and shoulders figure of Belon in three-quarter-face, looking to the left and wearing a cap. The attribution of this portrait presents a problem: according to some sources it was the work of an engraver from Lorraine named Claude Woeiriot, but this attribution has been strongly contested. It rests on the presence in the portrait of a cross of Lorraine, which also appears in some figures in the *Histoire des oiseaux*. Claude Woeiriot was the son and successor of an engraver and goldsmith in the service of the Duke of Lorraine, Jacquemin Woeiriot, who had practised his trade in Nancy and later moved to Paris. But the opponents of this theory have shown that the cross of Lorraine was very widely used by French engravers and printers in the 16th century.

These are not the only differences in the later editions. Chapter 12 in Book III, "The manners and diverse fashions of Christian religions in Turkey", is omitted, and there are additional illustrations (which Paul Delaunay also attributes to the mysterious Arnold Nicolaï):

- Portrait of the crayfish, which the Greeks call carabus and the French grasshopper
- Portrait of the crocodile, a fish of the Nile
- Portrait of two women of Cairo, variously clad, as when they are in their houses

- Another portrait of an Egyptian woman, dressed to go about the town of Cairo
- Portrait of a citizen of Cairo on horseback, going to a festival with his wife
- Portrait of an Arab villager
- Portrait of a Circassian or Arab lord on horseback, one of the richest lords in Egypt when it was ruled by the Soldan
- The pipe for males and the pipe for females
- Portrait of a Turkish woman of Asia

The figures of people are more perfunctory than the representations of fauna and flora. They show less concern with detail and accuracy. The bodies and faces are barely sketched, and even the clothes, which generally form the centre of the composition (since it is the dress that characterises the person), are rather crudely drawn. Nicolas de Nicolay's illustrations, which are later than Belon's and sometimes depict the same subjects, are undeniably more polished. The comparison is particularly striking in the case of Belon's "Portrait of a Turkish woman of Asia going about the town", which is closely similar to Nicolay's "Turkish woman going about the town"[16]. The general attitude of the figures is identical – the position of the body, of the feet and hands, down to the very folds in the outer garment, which is half open to show the richness of the inner dress. The figure in the *Navigations* reveals a floral pattern of great delicacy and an elegance in the fall of the garment, following the curves of the body, producing a harmonious effect which the naïve and rigid figure in the *Observations* totally lacks.

There is also an edition of the *Observations* published in Antwerp by Christopher Plantin in 1555. This is the rarest edition. The format and pagination are different (VIII + 376 + 33 folios octavo instead of 224 folios quarto). Serge Sauneron notes that some of the illustrations in this edition are reversed. Paul Delaunay suggests that Plantin had used the original woodcuts and that these were dispersed in a sale by order of the court in 1562, so that it was later necessary to have a new set of illustrations engraved (according to Delaunay) by an engraver called Peter van der Borcht). This theory does not seem to the present editor to hold water; for what proof is there that the engravings dispersed at Antwerp were the original engravings? This seems doubtful, if only because of the reversed figures in the Antwerp edition of 1555. Moreover Philippe Renouard's study of 16th century Paris booksellers[17] refers to a deed of 27th June 1556 dissolving the partnership between Cavellat and Corrozet and recording the purchase by Cavellat of the rights of privilege and the "figures" used in earlier editions of the *Observations*. These were the engravings used by Cavellat in the following year to illustrate a book entitled *Portraits d'oiseaux, d'animaux, serpents, herbes, arbres, hommes & femmes d'Arabie, d'Égypte, observés par Pierre Belon du Mans* (with a dedication to Henry II signed by Cavellat and not by Belon). This compilation of material from Belon's works, made in his absence, re-uses the engravings from the Paris edition of 1555. It seems, therefore, that these engravings never left Paris and would continue to be used by Paris printers.

Serge Sauneron lists other editions, which, however, he knows only from bibliographical references. They are dated 1557 (Paris), 1558 (Antwerp) and 1585 (Paris). The first is mentioned in the catalogues of several American libraries. The third are listed in bibliographies (respectively those of Jolowicz, Paulitschke and Tobler and of Jolowicz, Paulitschke and Röhricht), but none of the three is listed by Atkinson or Brunet[18]. It goes without saying that there are no copies in Paris libraries. There are thought to have been two other editions (regarded by Sauneron as uncertain): Paris, 1558, and Lyons, 1567.

The Paris edition of 1588 (XXIV + 470 p., two of which are unnumbered, quarto, in a Roman and no longer an italic font) was published by Jérôme Marnef and the widow of Guillaume Cavellat, "au Mont Saint-Hilaire, à l'enseigne du Pélican". The date of completion of printing is given as 24th February 1588. Jérôme Marnef, who had been authorised to practise as a bookseller since 1546, was the uncle of Denise Girault, Guillaume Cavellat's wife. A partnership between these three had been established by a contract of 1st May 1563. After Cavellat's death it had been continued between the widow and Marnef, under a contract dated 26th June 1577[19]. This new edition of the *Observations*, "freshly revised and augmented by figures", follows the text of the Cavellat–Corrozet edition of 1555 and contains the same illustrations, to which were added maps of Mount Athos and the island of Lemnos[20].

Plantin's Antwerp edition of 1589 is a Latin translation by Charles de l'Écluse, under the title *Petri Bellonii … Plurimarum singularium & memorabilium rerum in Graecia, Asia, Aegypto, Iudaea, Arabia, aliisque exteris provinciis ab ipso conspectarum observationes, tribus libris expressae* (XVI + 495 p. quarto). Some of the illustrations are different, which corroborates Paul Delaunay's hypothesis that a new set of engravings had been made in Antwerp.

The same Latin text was republished at Antwerp in 1605, following the publication of Charles de l'Écluse's *Exoticorum Libri X*.

There were no further French editions of the *Observations* until Serge Sauneron's edition of the part of the work covering Belon's travels in Egypt (in the first volume of the series *Voyageurs occidentaux en Égypte*, Cairo, Institut français d'archéologie orientale, 1970). There were, however, a number of translations: into English, though only in much abridged and often merely summarised passages from certain chapters (in 1625, in Samuel Purchas's compilation *Purchas his pilgrimes…*, and in 1693, in John Ray's *Collection of Curious Travels and Voyages* and *Travels through the Low Countries*), German (in 1755 and 1792, in Paulus's collection *Sammlung der merkwürdigsten Reisen in den Orient)*, and Bulgarian (in 1953).

THIS EDITION

We have chosen to reproduce in this edition of the *Observations* the text of the first edition of 1553, which differs from later editions in several respects. In the first place, Belon usually speaks in the original version in the first person singular, but in later editions prefers the plural "we", which is more solemn but also more neutral. He also, in general, moderates the vigour of his judgments, no doubt for reasons of prudence, and includes a number of additional Latin quotations, overloading a text which is already dense. Finally, as we have already noted, the 1553 edition includes a chapter (Book III, chapter 12) which does not appear in later editions. For all these reasons we have judged it preferable to present Belon's work in all the spontaneity and freedom of its first version[21], but including in notes certain additions in later editions which seemed worth including. We have also used the illustrations from the Paris edition of 1588, which were available and were identical to those in the first Paris editions; we have not, however, included a small number of illustrations added in the Antwerp edition of 1589, which are clearly by a different hand[22].

We have sought, so far as possible, to identify the plants and animals referred to by Belon, following, in the part relating to Egypt, the notes in Serge Sauneron's edition. In order to avoid an excessive proliferation of notes, however, we have brought all this information together in two copious indexes (Botanical, p. 539; Zoological, p. 580), which together with the onomastic, geographical and thematic indexes (pp. 550-579) will, we hope, make this a useful work of reference for historians, naturalists and the general reader.

OBSERVATIONS OF MANY SINGULARITIES

and memorable things found in Greece, Asia, Judaea,
Egypt, Arabia, and other foreign countries, in three books,

by Pierre Belon of Le Mans

To Monseigneur le Cardinal de Tournon

*The Catalogue containing the most notable things in this present book
is on the other side of this page*

AT PARIS
In the shop of Gilles Corrozet, in the great hall
of the Palace, by the chapel of
Messieurs the Presidents
1553
With privilege from the King

THE CATALOGUE CONTAINING
the most notable things
in this present book

*The ancient names of trees and other plants, snakes,
fishes, animals, birds and other terrestrial beasts,
compared with the modern French names;
and many true portraits of them drawn from nature,
never previously seen*

*The manners and way of life of various nations
in Greece and Turkey*

*The antiquities and ruins of many illustrious towns in Asia and Greece,
as also the description of Cairo, Jerusalem,
Damascus, Antioch, Bursa, Alexandria
and other towns in the Levant,
with their modern names*

*The description of many mountains celebrated by
ancient poets and historians*

*Many discourses on the roads on various journeys
in Egypt, Arabia, Asia and Greece,
containing various matters of the ancients compared with the moderns*

*Ample discourse on the true origin of fine gold,
and on the principal gold and silver mines
of the Grand Turk*

To the Most Illustrious and Most Reverend Lord, François Cardinal de Tournon,

singular and liberal Maecenas of men studious of virtue,
to whom Pierre Belon, his most humble domestic and servant,
addresses greetings and wishes for entire prosperity

Monseigneur, it is most fitting that learned men hold you in admiration, and that foreign peoples well affected to our republic, as also the French people, have greatly praised and esteemed the excellence of your good judgment and magnified your prudence and virtue; for among all other illustrious prelates you have singularly loved and honoured letters, advanced men of letters and by your special favour inflamed and promoted their studies, causing many children and older men of good intelligence to be selected and maintained and taught and indoctrinated in all the arts in universities and your colleges in Tournon and others which you have built and well supplied with expert and learned men.

The sciences and disciplines which are now familiar and common in our nation are right to acknowledge you as their patron, since while bearing the heavy burden of our republic you have taken pleasure in starting them off in their studies, training up noble minds, advancing them according to their qualities and also in employing them in work for which they have been found to be disposed and capable of serving the common benefit. From this it has resulted that the minds of men who had been previously been, as it were, asleep and sunk in a profound slumber of ancient ignorance have begun to awaken and emerge from the darkness in which for so long they had remained buried, and in so coming out have created and displayed all kinds of good disciplines. Which disciplines, in their so happy and desirable rebirth, just as new plants after the harsh season of winter recover their vigour in the heat of the sun and are consoled by the sweetness of spring, having similarly found an incomparable Maecenas and favourable restorer so propitious to them, have not ceased to flourish and produce new shoots. Then, gaily spangling their suckers and covering their shoots with verdure, they come into the grace of their summer, when each

3

one is decked with the fairest flowers. And having then engendered a delectable fruit of inestimable goodness, there is not one of them but presents its first fruits to its sovereign adorner, the gracious Sun whose benign aspect had given them fresh vigour. It was the magnanimous king, most wise, most puissant and most prudent, Francis the first of that name, to whom, as to a liberal Maecenas of men studious of virtue, to whom each of them employed himself with all his power to present something of value, but particularly fruits gathered in the delectable garden from exquisite grafts on the plants of Minerva which he loved with a singular affection.

And he was of such a benignant and liberal nature that whenever a man, whether a foreigner or one of his nation, presented something to him, however small, he received it in the most friendly way, repaying him who presented it most generously with a royal gift and honourable guerdon. Wherefore all men in general followed the example of this most virtuous and incomparable prince, father of the sciences; so that his court seemed some great Academy or ancient school of philosophy in which was taught the theory and practice of every virtue.

Therefore, Monseigneur, since the Muses have known you, singularly among all others, as leading enemy of all ignorance, being assured of the many sciences which are infused in your divine spirit, and all by common consent knowing well your noble heart, presented you with the palm, and then, having chosen you as their leader, desired to appoint you as a sovereign Phoebus over the harmony of their resounding instruments and over the sweetnesses of their well tuned songs, so that in this excellent music the handsome royal theatre should be adorned by your presence.

Knowing also that Greek and Latin letters are so familiar to you that all that you read of the best authors in theology, philosophy, astrology, cosmography or history you read in the actual language of their authors. In which Greek sciences and letters you are the more excellent that since your early years you have worked diligently to learn them, and have become well versed in them; and now the greatest pleasure that you can experience is to employ your time as may be convenient in reading the most excellent ancient authors. And following the natural excellence of your divine spirit, which has always delighted in the contemplation of natural things, of which you are a sovereign admirer, on learning of my desire to arrive at the understanding of matters concerning medicines and plants (which I could not properly acquire save by long journeyings), it pleased you to command me to travel to distant regions to see them, and seek them out in the places where they grow, a thing that I should not have been able or would have ventured to undertake without your help, knowing that the difficulty would have been the costs and expenses that I have had to incur. And so having, with God's help and the aid of your liberality, completed the journey, which has not been less useful and delectable for me than difficult and laborious, and not wishing to waste the repose and leisure which I at present enjoy thanks to your benignity, I have recorded in writing in our language the memorable things and singularities as I observed and selected them in various places, so far as they seemed to me worthy of being described, in order to demonstrate to you that I have not failed to carry out your intention.

Moreover in order that our nation, which knows what affection you bear for the public benefit, may enjoy something of the fruit of my travels, of which you are the author, and since any good thing is the more laudable when it is common to many, I have written of my observations in our ordinary French tongue. I have set them down in three books, as faithfully as possible, and using no artifice or elegance of speech, but in simple terms, telling of things truly as I found them in foreign lands, giving each thing its French name in so far as it was possible for me to find one in the vulgar tongue. The knowledge of these things is no less useful and pleasant than the ancient errors resulting from ignorance of many things of which I learned the truth were harmful and pernicious.

And in taking liberty to carry my discourses farther I resolved not to omit certain topographies and particular descriptions of places which seemed to me memorable, representing them as well as I could and putting them, as it were, in front of readers' eyes, just as I myself saw them. I shall touch on the manners and way of life at the present day both of Turks and Jews and Greeks. And this small work of a man still young I have ventured to present to you, Monseigneur, not claiming that with such a small thing I can discharge my debt to you, but hoping that with the aid of Our Lord, and since it has pleased our most magnanimous, most fortunate and most clement king to maintain me among his scholars, and thanks to the benignity and liberality of Monseigneur Chancellor Olivier in giving me the means to carry on my studies, you will see another short work of mine in the translation of Dioscorides into out language[23] and commentaries on it in order to satisfy your very laudable desire to learn about foreign plants in Europe, Asia and part of Africa, as well as snakes, fishes and other terrestrial animals which I observed both on land and sea and in the ports of the Levant, resolving in all that I write not to set down anything that I have not first seen for myself; in order that, following your command, having written about everything truly as nature has produced it, anyone can persuade and assure himself that he is reading of it as it really is.

Monseigneur, I most humbly beg the Creator of his grace to give you entire prosperity.
From your house in the Abbey of Saint-Germain-des-Prés-lez-Paris, 1553.

Preface

Just as men are made up of body and soul, so their works and enterprises follow either the nature of the body or that of the spirit. And if the works of the body and the spirit are excellent, then they are of durable memory. For since men are naturally inclined to covet reputation and renown, for their glory and praise, they study to acquire it in divers fashions, some by the power of the body, others by liveliness of spirit. The labours of Hercules are celebrated in history; Alexander and Pompey have been dubbed great, and Caesar is famed for valour and boldness. But Plato, Aristotle and other contemplative philosophers have acquired reputation for the subtlety of their understanding and their profound erudition. Others by the same means having followed some worthy aspiration, not hesitating to expose themselves to divers perils, feeling it more reasonable to seek glory by the faculties of the understanding, have similarly gained immortal renown. To this Democritus bears good witness, who for the great desire that he had to acquire the practice of the sciences, that is to say both experiment and theory, and principally of astronomy and geometry, sold his patrimony to his brothers in order to employ the money from the sale in distant peregrinations in the countries of Egypt, India and Chaldaea in order to become acquainted with the gymnosophists[24], and then returned to Athens with great reputation and was honoured for his learning. Many others have achieved fame by much lesser matters, which however have brought great public benefit. Similarly many kings who have merely left their names to certain plants or other things which they discovered or devised have made their renown immortal. Did not Mithridates, king of Pontus and so many other provinces, make himself more renowned and more illustrious by a single medicament which he devised, to which he left his name, than by the opulence and grandeur of his kingdom, although he had won many victories in divers battles, and spoke and understood twenty-two languages, in which he heard and replied to all the nations that were subject to him? So long as the earth shall produce centaury the name of Chiron Centaurus, who was the teacher of Aesculapius, will remain imprinted in the memory of men. Has not gentian made Gentius, king of Sclavonia, more renowned than all his riches? Have not Lysimachus, king of Macedonia, and Eupator[25], who ruled in Thrace, perpetuated their names by plants? Have not Juba, king of Mauritania, the Greek Achilles, Teucer, King Clymenus[26] and many other great personages who gave their names to certain plants, by this means gained eternal renown?

Many others striving to overcome all difficulties have by a similar desire carried out distant peregrinations. Neither the terror of shipwreck in the perilous sea, nor the turbulence of the boisterous winds beating on ships and breaking them up amid the waves whipped up by storms, nor the fear of losing their freedom at the hands of inhuman pirates, nor dangerous passages through harsh rocks, nor the intemperance of excessive hear or extreme cold, nor nights darkened by rain clouds with lightning and fearful thunder, nor the danger of crossing uninhabited deserts in fear of wild beasts have been able to repress the ardour of their noble courage, already aflame in their generous hearts, and lead them to abandon their undertaking.

Ulysses was esteemed and judged by everyone the wisest and most prudent among other illustrious princes because he had observed the diversity of manners of many different men and had seen the diversity of foreign towns and countries. Herodotus, Diodorus, Strabo and many other ancients have left us accounts of their distant travels, from which men have received inestimable benefit, since all their works conduce to the comfort and repose of posterity. For since we are at ease and in safety, having no perils and dangers, we can read works of history which inform us of an infinity of things acquired by the innumerable labours and incredible sufferings of other men.

And since the singularities of plants, animals and minerals are for the most part known to us thanks to such peregrinations, without which it is difficult for us, and indeed quite impossible, to have a share in the gifts and riches of foreign lands, I resolved to go and see them in their native places. And since it would otherwise have been difficult for me to get to know them I decided first of all to get some idea of their likenesses from the books of our ancestors, in order to impress it on my mind; and then I ventured to go and look for them in distant foreign lands, hoping for no other reward for my labours than to see them as they are. Since it was my deliberate purpose and desire that drew me to travel in order to see them, whether on mountains or in valleys, on plains or in shady forests, in many parts of the world, my intention was completely fulfilled; for in looking for them and identifying them many other things were offered to me in Asia and Greece worthy of being communicated to our nation, which it has seemed to me fitting to observe and describe in writing thus succinctly. For if I had described in detail all the things that I shall mention I should have feared to tire the reader with my prolixity. Which observations I propose to write down in three books, the first of which will include some singularities of Mount Athos, the island of Lemnos and many other things in Greece.

The second book will contain a description of the ruins of Troy and many other illustrious towns in Asia; and I shall add a description of a journey by sea from Constantinople to Alexandria, and from there to Cairo and on to Mount Sinai, and from there to Jerusalem, and so back to Constantinople.

The third book will describe the present way of life of the Turks as I was able to observe it during my residence in the very heart of Turkey. And in order to leave the reader in no doubt about when I made my observations, I have thought it well to say that we departed in 1546, in the time of King Francis, and returned in 1549, so that the journey lasted three full years. In addition, after considering that men grow in knowledge on each others' shoulders, and that anything that we say, having only the authority of ourselves, is not greatly esteemed, it has seemed to me right on occasion to cite passages from good authors to give authority to what I shall say hereafter.

First Book

1

*That nature leads each of us in this world on different paths, so that
the aims of all of us tend towards different ends*

Although I have undertaken to set down in writing in this book
the memorable things and singularities of foreign countries as I
have observed them, nevertheless I do not wish on that account to
debar anyone who can do better, but rather to incite him pursue his
task. And although many, both ancients and moderns, have already
written on such or similar matters in their travels and navigations,
nevertheless since I have observed the whole content of this present
treatise I have ventured boldly to write it down, without fear of
calumny from others. For I am confident that anyone who compares
this work of mine with the writings of those above mentioned
will not be able justly to reproach me with taking anything from
other writers, except from the good ancient authors, whom I have
frequently called to my aid in giving the names of animals and
plants and other such things, called by their proper names rendered
into our ordinary French tongue.

And since such things had never before been examined nor
rendered into our tongue, nor brought into agreement with the
ancient authors, my task has been the more laborious. Those who
undertake a distant journey in foreign lands for their private affairs
are more curious to look for things necessary for carrying out their
purpose than to employ their time in other observations with which
they are not concerned, as appears from the business of a merchant,
who, despite having made many journeys to India and Newfoundland
nevertheless, having no other aim than to employ his money to
advantage in the purchase of goods, is not interested in acquiring
the infinite singularities which a curious man might observe.

The excuse in such a case is that such things are of no use to him,
and also that the minds and dispositions of men are so different that
if a number of men are travelling in company through a foreign land

it will be difficult to find two who observe the same thing; for one man will be inclined to note this, and another that, besides which there is no man, however diligent, who can sufficiently examine everything in detail, for memorable things must be considered carefully before reaching an assured judgment on them. For it is necessary that the characteristics noted in a description should be in accordance with the thing described. I have resolved to avoid writing about things seen in countries nearer home, as it were at our very gates, resolving rather to write about strange and foreign matters. For such was the intention that stimulated me to undertake my travels. On arriving in the country of the Turks, therefore, I began to write about all things that aroused my curiosity; for I found that what I was looking for, and could not have found anywhere but there, still bore the same name used by the ancient authors.

And since I see many things very common in our usage with names so familiar that there is not a man or woman but will use them in referring to the things that bear these names in the vulgar tongue, though the names are wrongly attributed to them, I have determined to make it my duty in this book to show that the names given to many very common things are wrong.

2

That we should not be too ready to accept the names of things, even though they are in common use, unless they match the descriptions of the ancients and agree with the thing described

I shall take as examples a number of common plants and familiar animals, in order to demonstrate that their ordinary names are wrongly applied to them. It may be that in doing so I shall displease some people. But if anyone is offended by what I say let him declare it, if he thinks fit, and we shall reply to him as seems appropriate.

I will now maintain, therefore, that our nation and many in other nations who obey the Roman church, have not hitherto known the herb thyme, since the thyme that we grow in our gardens is not thyme, nor any species of thyme, but is a species of mother-of-thyme. Hyssop, too, and savory, which we have in common use, are not the herbs that the ancient Greeks used in medicine. I say, therefore, that if the things to which we give such names do not agree with the descriptions of the ancients we must conclude that they are not the plants meant by the ancients. As an example we may take our thyme, the name of which is so familiar to all that there is no one, of whatever condition he may be, who does not give it the name of thyme; and yet that name is wrongly given to it. The herb that we call thyme is not the one to which that name properly belongs, but another plant which is common in the country of Greece. The herb properly called thyme, following the accounts of Theophrastus and Dioscorides, must be covered with small heads ending in a point, and narrow at the foot, like those of *stoechas*, with which they are compared, similar to the hanging warts which grow on some people, either on the neck or on the shameful parts, and were called by the Greeks *thymia*, as Celsus bears witness. But the herb that we call thyme does not have these characteristics and is therefore not properly so called: that is to say it is not the plant from which bees gather excellent honey near Athens on Mount Hymettus and in Sicily on Mount Hybla, and which the authors for that reason call *atticum* and *hyblaeum*.

For the same reason, although the herb that we commonly call thyme grows wild in abundance in the garrigues of Provence and Languedoc and resembles the herb in our gardens, nevertheless since it does not have the characteristics above described it cannot be true mint[27]. True thyme, however, is so common and abundant throughout Greece that no other wild plant is more commonly seen on the mountains, with flowers which vary in colour from place to place, sometimes pure white, sometimes sky-blue or purple, or sometimes a mixture of the two. But since we are not accustomed to grow it in our gardens, it is unknown to us. And since thyme has given its name to hanging warts, so it is also the name of a fish in Ticino called *thymus*, which the people of Lodi in Lombardy call *themero* or *themelo*[28]

As for savory, which the Greeks call *thymbra*, and in the vulgar tongue *tribi*, it ought, to earn that name, to be laden with ears; for so it is described by Dioscorides. But since we see that the savory of our gardens is not laden with ears, it must be confessed that that this is not the plant that the ancients used in their medicines. I do not say that the herb in our gardens is not the one that has long been known as an ingredient for pottages and accordingly is used in cooking; but it is not the one that was mixed into medicines and grows wild in Greece, which is not found anywhere in our countries, although it is common all over Greece.

Similarly with hyssop, of which there are two kinds. One is a field plant which grows indifferently all over the countries of the Levant, both on hills and along the main roads, in Cilicia, Thrace, Phrygia and many other countries. The other kind is a cultivated plant, which we know and grow in our gardens, but it is very different from the wild variety, which is the one formerly used by the Greeks in making up their medicines.

I have chosen to cite the example of these plants, which are very common and known to everyone, in order to make clear that I have not always accepted the vulgar names which the inhabitants of the various provinces gave me when they were speaking of things that I wanted to write about unless I had first diligently considered them; for otherwise I should frequently been led into error. For just as the name in the French vulgar tongue of the *plane* has led many people to think that it is the *platane*[29], though this is a species of maple, so there may be a similar confusion in another nation. And this name of *plane*, although there is not a single tree of this species in the whole of the king's dominions, either cultivated or wild, is nevertheless wrongly used throughout France; and even scholars and other men of authority, seeing that the *plane* has leaves like those of a vine, and that the description of the *platane* is that it has such leaves, have concluded on the basis of this single characteristic that the *plane* is a *platane*. And yet that is false, for the *platane* has round seeds the size of a walnut, hanging in bunches, as our *plane* has not, which bears its seeds in the fashion of a falconer's lure. And in order to show by experience that we have none of these trees in the whole country of France, I set here its portrait drawn from life.

Figure: Portrait of the platane

Moreover the plant which we call houseleek has been hitherto been held to be a *sempervivum,* but I maintain that this is not so. For *sempervivum* grows copiously in Crete and Corfu as a small shrub a cubit in height, and sometimes two, with a stem the thickness of a man's thumb, the top of which is covered with leaves surrounding it on all sides, corresponding in all respects with Dioscorides' description. And I wonder that those who in describing and portraying such things are not aware of this; for what the moderns have painted as houseleek is the *cotyledon alterum* of the ancients.

This has happened also with the white mulberry-tree and another plant, a kind of maple, which many by common consent have said is the sycamore. And yet the sycamore is so rare that it has never been seen, either wild or cultivated, either in Greece or in Italy. Is it not difficult, therefore, to believe that it can have been seen growing in France?

I will say the same about birds, snakes and other terrestrial animals, minerals, stones and metallic substances. Our goldfinch *(chardonneret)*, whose name comes from the thistle *(chardon)*, seems to be the bird that the Greeks called *acanthis;* but *acanthis* is not the goldfinch. And if the French vulgar tongue calls certain snakes asps, it is in error, for there are no asps in France. Nor are there any moray eels, which in our vulgar tongue are called lampreys, nor any fresh-water crabs, a name which has been wrongly given to our crayfish. It is generally believed also that saltpetre is nitre, but that is false[30]. And just as we impose false names on things that are common among us, so we have some very common things of which we do not know the true name. There is not a peasant in Gascony but will call the salamander a *mirtil,* in Savoy a *pluvine,* in Maine a *sourd,* and yet none of them knows that it is a salamander. Accordingly we must not take on trust the common names given to things in the provinces unless we have first compared and carefully examined the writings of the authors.

And in citing these examples I mean to say that we must look for the truth about things unknown to us by way of those that we do know. But just as men who feel themselves to be great-hearted, generous and well born, when reproaching the infamy that they find in a man who thinks much of himself because he is a nobleman, say in their common proverb that there is nothing in common between a villain and a nobleman, so I will say that there is no comparison between a man of good understanding and an ignoramus, nor between a man of generous heart and one consumed by envy. And so I will refute the calumnies of certain men of ill grace, in order that that he who has been most forward in trying to damage me may find himself to be a great fool for so strongly blaming my curiosity.

Such a man cited ancient custom, saying that our fathers lived happily without seeking out so many unnecessary petty subtleties; saying also that since they did without them we can well do likewise, and that without them they still managed to remain healthy and to recover when they were ill, and that such things should be left to men with more leisure, or to those who seek out such things more out of curiosity than for their utility. To such an ignorant person I can most suitably reply that the men of past times who had not discovered how to make bread remained healthy and recovered when they were ill, even though they lived on acorns, like the ancient Arcadians[31].

I should therefore like to see such ignorant persons contenting themselves, in accordance with ancient custom, with living only on acorns, or on figs like the Athenians, or on wild pears like the Tyrrinthians[32], or on canes or reeds like the Indians, or on dates like the Caramanians, or on millet like the Sarmatians, or on terebinth seeds like the Persians, and leave us to eat good wheaten bread – blaming, if they wish, those who discovered how to make bread as over-curious. I should likewise like to see them, despising architecture as a work of curiosity which the ancients were able to do without, leaving their houses and going to live in caves or under the trees in forests.

And if they do not feel sufficiently confuted by these considerations I should expect them also to blame the curiosity of Aristotle, who in teaching us the difference between animals was not content to describe only their external characteristics but, iexamining their internal anatomy, made it his business to count the ribs of snakes, the entrails of fishes and birds and the different parts of the bodies of all animals. Similarly Hippocrates and Galen were content with what their ancestors had been accustomed to do. But such ignoramuses have voluntarily blindfolded themselves, deliberately ignoring matters that they do not want either to see or to know, seeing that custom and time renew and improve all things for the common benefit. For men in the course of their life are well able to accommodate themselves to circumstances in accordance with what nature teaches them, leaving what is worse and choosing what is better for their utility, and so from wild and rustic they have become docile and domesticated, and have variously changed their dispositions. Some of them, taking singular delectation in understanding natural things and desiring to assure themselves of the native perfection of such as are legitimate, have set to speculating and discerning the true from the false; so that if a man seeking to counterfeit artificially a precious stone, a metal or other such thing had come so close to nature that he had rendered it so like the natural object, not only in form but also in all other qualities, nevertheless a man of lively and ingenious mind will keep contemplating, examining and testing it until satisfied whether it is false and adulterine or true and legitimate.

For that no man could with just cause reprove him or blame him, or say that this was mere curiosity without any utility. And so I conclude that the ignorant cannot reasonably accuse me of useless or unnecessary curiosity. But leaving the ignorant with their frivolous and idle allegations and returning to speak of the singular things to be seen in foreign countries, it has seemed to me not amiss, before proceeding to my account of things in Turkey, to say a few words in passing about the island of Crete, which is now called Candy, since it is one of the halting-places on my journey where I stayed longest.

3

Brief discourse on the singularities of Crete, and particular observation of the manners of the Greeks

The authors of all good sciences and disciplines whom we revere today came for the most part from Greece, which (since fortune permits that things change suddenly) from being rich and opulent as it was anciently, and well provided with men learned in all disciplines, and dominant by its virtue over great part of the world, is now reduced to such a state that that there is not a foot of land but is under the yoke of the Turks or the servitude of the Venetians.

The Turk holds the largest part of its territory, both on land and on sea, but what the Venetians hold is only in the sea[33]. The Greeks who are under the Venetians are somewhat better off, in regard to religion, than those who are tributary to the Turk. And, comparing the two, I find that just as those who are subject to the Turks are governed in the manner of the Turks, so those who are under the yoke of the Venetians are governed in the Venetian way. All Greeks, both in one party and in the other, are in such a marvellous state of ignorance that there is not a town in all their country which has a university; and they take no pleasure in learning letters and sciences. All indifferently speak a language corrupted from its ancient state; though that language is closer to good Greek than Italian is to Latin. Those living in towns which are under the Venetians speak Italian as well as Greek; but the villagers speak only Greek. It is the same with Greeks in countries under Turkish rule, for in the larger towns they speak Turkish and Greek, but in the villages only Greek.

The Greeks have not abandoned the ancient appellations of things called by their proper names, except in places where they have been most in contact with other nations. and much more in towns on the coasts than inland. For having long had dealings with foreigners, both Turks and Italians, they have borrowed from them terms which they have incorporated in their vulgar tongue. I shall prove this to be true by citing a number of fishes that are commonly caught off the shores of Crete. The fish that the ancients called *sphyraena* and the people of Smyrna and Mitylene call *sphyrna*, and in Marseilles, because it resembles a rowlock, is called *pesescomé*, is known in Crete by the vulgar Greek name borrowed from Italian, *luceo marino*. that is to say, sea pike; but this differs from the hake, anciently called *asellus*, which they now call *haidero psaro*. It is the same in the Greek lands subject to the Turk, which have similarly changed the ancient Greek names and replaced them by new names in the Turkish language. As an example I take the fish that we call barbel, whose ancient name was *mystus*, and which they now call *mustachato*, which is part Italian and part Turkish. Similarly the carp, formerly called *cyprinus*, is now *sasanbaluk*. The Turks have done the same, borrowing from the Greeks many names for things that they have found in Greece previously unknown to them, for which they had no names; thus in referring to certain fish found in Greece they say in their language *glanos baluk* or *chella baluk,* that is to say, catfish-fish or eel-fish; for *baluk* in their language means fish.

This does not seem to me to be too unnatural; for a nation, coming to a place where it finds something that has no name in its own language, and having no authority to invent a name, is surely entitled to borrow and use the local people's name for it: just as we do with animals and drugs brought to us from the Indies, which we call by the same names that they have brought with them from their country. as appears from a small animal brought from Brazil which is called an armadillo. It is a sort of hedgehog which was not known to the ancients, but since it is kept filled with stuffing (for it is covered with hard skin) some have called it an ichneumon; but that is wrong, for this animal has nothing of the nature of an ichneumon. Have not the French themselves borrowed some names from the Arabs? They call the *cedria* of the ancients *cotran* or *catran*[34], and there is no builder of boats or ships who does not know the word, for it is used to caulk pseagoing vessels, and there is no iron merchant who does not sell it in his shop, which everyone knows to call *cotran*. And although the Greeks do not always use the same names for things in one place as in another nevertheless they do to a great extent approach the ancient appellations, particularly in the case of proper names.

4

That the Greeks, , now under the yoke of foreign lords, behave in accordance with the ways of their masters

It must be understood, too, that all Greeks do not speak the same vulgar tongue; for in one place they speak it better, in another worse. And since their accents differ from one another I remember having frequently heard the street urchins of Pera[35] in Constantinople making fun of the speech of the foreigners who come there by sea; and grown men too mocked each other's manner of speech, as Frenchmen do when they imitate the dialect of Picardy or any other language that is not French.

In describing the manners of men living in the Greek fashion I think it well to make a distinction between tradesmen and villagers on the one hand and noblemen and respectable citizens on the other. For those who have most money to spend and are concerned to maintain their reputation for greatness wear garments following the custom of their lord and master.

Those of them who are under the Venetian are dressed in the Venetian manner; and if they are under the Turks they dress in the Turkish fashion; but the common people, whether under the Venetians or under the Turks, whether on the islands or on the mainland, preserve something of the ancient fashion; for they ordinarily wear their hair long, shaven in front above the forehead, and wear large double caps.

I found the inhabitants of the islands to be preserving their religion and their own way of life; and likewise the people of Cyprus, Rhodes, Lemnos, Chios, Imbros, Thasos, Patmos, Cos, Mitylene, Corfu, Zante, Naxos and Crete and other islanders have remained in the Christian faith, although they are under the Turk, as have the others on the mainland of Europe and Asia. All of them in general have few domestic utensils, any more than the Turks; nor do they sleep on feather beds. They have counterpoints or mattresses called *estramats,* made of stuffing or of wool, to sleep on. They all regard it as abhorrent to put water in their wine; and nowadays they still drink as much of the one as of the other, and principally the wines of Crete. They differ from the Germans, while drinking the same amount, in this respect, that the Germans drink in large draughts, while the Greeks drink their strong malmsey in frequent small sips.

But since there are certain ceremonies to be observed in drinking in the Greek fashion I think it right to describe them here. It must be understood that Greek tables are ordinarily very low, and they are accustomed to drink one after the other in a certain order; and if anyone asked for wine outside his turn he would be regarded as uncivil. The one who is quickest at serving wine holds the jar and pours it out for the whole company. The custom is to drink from a small glass without a foot, and to empty it in one draught, not leaving a single drop of wine. They sometimes invite one another to drink, in the manner of the Germans, and then they embrace one another, each touching the other's hand, then kiss the other's hand and put it on their forehead and finally kiss one another on the right and left cheeks; but in such a case they do not observe the regular order of drinking. And since they drink the strong wine in small sips and this makes them thirsty, they always have a jug of water at hand, from which they drink in great draughts: for otherwise their thirst would not be quenched.

Women do not take part in their banquets, and are not present when they eat and drink in company. This has in all times been their custom. The ancient author Macrobius bears witness that this was the custom in his time in Rome, as it was also in Plato's time in Greece. In his second book, chapter 9, referring to what Plato had said, Macrobius writes: *Et non magis inter minuta pocula*[36]. When eating (he says) they do not utter a word, but when it comes to inviting one another to drink everyone starts talking. His actual words are *Primis mensis post epulas iam remotis, et discursim variantibus poculis minutioribus, solet cibus quum sumitur tacitos efficere, potus loquaces*[37]. A little later he says that the Parthians[38] when banqueting did not permit their wives to be present, but only their concubines; and also when drinking would not discuss serious matters.

The ancient pagan custom of weeping for the dead still prevails in Greek lands, as also in the countries of the Albanians, the Bulgarians, the Croats, the Circassians, the Servians, the Sclavonians, the Dalmatians[39] and others who share the faith of the Greeks. But it is the most fantastic thing that can be conceived; for when someone has died the women gather at an appointed place, and in the early morning before daybreak they begin to wail and beat their breasts, scratch their cheeks and undo and tear their hair, so that it is great pity to see them. And in order the better to perform such a mystery they hire a woman who has a good voice and sings louder than the others to mark the pauses and stresses; and they mourn thus, beginning with praise of the dead man from his childhood onwards and continuing the tale until his death.

It very frequently happens during these mourning ceremonies that the women beat themselves in earnest; and the girls scratch their whole faces. And although the signoria of Venice, which rules on many islands where the inhabitants have this custom of mourning the dead, as in Corfu, Cyprus and Crete, sometimes forbade the practice the inhabitants still did not give it up; for men too were concerned in the matter. The custom is that Greek women do not show themselves in public; and yet if there is some beautiful woman in the towns where the dead man is being mourned she will be most happy to have found an occasion to show her beauty, accompanying other women as they go in company about the town, with dishevelled hair and bare bosoms, displaying all their charms. While this is going on the men of the town are also present, having at least the pleasure, on this occasion, of seeing at their ease the wives and daughters of their neighbours; for at other times they have little opportunity of seeing them; although the men may have different reasons for their interest, some affected by jealousy, others by other motives[40].

5

Observation of the principal places on the island of Crete

The three principal mountains in Crete have changed their ancient names. Those which were formerly called Leuci are now called the mountains of Madara or of Sphachia. Mount Ida is now known as Psiloriti, and Dicta as Sethia, and in some places as Lasti[41]. They are so high that they are covered with snow throughout the winter, although cypresses grow here and there between the rocks in the valleys.

The island has a total perimeter of 1520 miles; and since there are so many mountains there are very few plains. There is, therefore, much uncultivated land, though this brings no less profit to the lords of the island than fertile land by providing good pasturage for stock. They keep large flocks of sheep and goats, which bring in great sums of money from cheese and wool.

Standing on the top of Mount Ida, I could quite easily see the sea on both sides of the island. It was with good reason that the Cretans were anciently devoted to Diana; for in our day they still follow antiquity, being led by a natural instinct from childhood onwards to the practice of drawing the Scythian bow. Even a small child in the cradle, in a rage and crying, calms down when he is shown a bow or given an arrow into his hand; and so they are more expert in its use than are the Turks. And just as anciently they fought valiantly at sea, so today they are so dexterous, skilled and bold on the little ships they call squiraces that they defend themselves with great courage against their enemies. I say this as one who was there when they showed their mettle under attack by pirates between Zacinthos or Alzante and Cerigo or Cytherea, acquitting themselves so well that two fustes[42], in calm weather, did not dare to close on one small squirace from Candy.

This island of Crete is difficult for a hostile force to attack. Since it can be reached only by sea and has few harbours, it is thus sufficiently well fortified. It is true that the inhabitants of some towns and castles that are fortified and defended by walls have good harbours, like the towns of La Canée, Candy, Setie, Voulismeni, Chisamo, Selino and Sphachie[43]. But apart from these towns there are few harbours along the coast, and these a long way from towns: indeed I know only one good one, called La Sude [Souda], beyond the town of La Canée, which is where Barbarossa's galleys put in when they landed on the island during the last war of the Turk against the Venetians. But, as I have said, they achieved nothing on the island, for the inconvenience of the place and their small numbers constrained them to reembark at once without striking a blow.

There are now only three towns of any great repute on the whole island of Crete. The principal one is Candy, anciently called Matium, from which the whole island of Crete has taken its modern name. The second largest after Candy is La Canée, anciently called Cydon, which produced quinces known as *cydonia*. The third is Rhetymo [Rethymnon], which the ancients called Rhythymna; it has only a poor harbour, which cannot be entered by ships and galleys and can take only small boats. But La Canée and Candy have very good harbours for all kinds of vessels, and are very well enclosed and protected from all winds.

So much for the principal populated towns; but as for the rather poorly built castles situated here and there on the island, I propose to touch on them only lightly. The one at Voulismeni, which was anciently called Panormus, is still preserved entire, on a hill on the coast between La Cytie [Sitia] and Candy, with a fearful gulf of the sea on its left side.

La Cytie, anciently Cyteum, is the fourth strong place in Crete, a small populous town situated at the lower end of the island, opposite Rhodes; and it is a voyage of only a hundred miles from one island to the other, that is to say from the town of Rhodes to the town of La Cytie.

There are two other small castles at the upper end of the island. One is on the side facing the Aegean Sea, looking north, called Chysamo, anciently Cysanum, which is almost wholly ruined but still preserves its ancient walls entire. It is not situated on a hill but low down, within a bowshot of the coast.

Half a league from Chysamo in the direction of Cano Spata, or Capo Spada, are the ruins of an ancient town on a hill half a mile from the sea. which still preserves remains of its walls and such a great number of handsome cisterns that anyone contemplating them must think them a great wonder; the local people call this place Paleo Helenico Castro [Palaiokastro]. The harbour walls, which are now almost completely covered by sand, bear eloquent witness that this was anciently a mighty town.

On the other side of the island, opposite Chysamo, is another castle called Selino, situated on a low hill on the shores of the sea. There is also another town called Sphachie, which is not walled but is a large scattered village on the slopes of the very high mountains formerly known as Leuci Montes, and now as the mountains of Sphachie. There is only a small castle to provide a defence against corsairs, containing only scant lodgings for the castellan. The inhabitants of this village are the most warlike and the best archers on the whole island, and they like to have stronger bows than the inhabitants of other regions. Whatever was said anciently about the rivers of Crete is insufficient to persuade us that there is a single river on the island that is navigable, or could carry even a small boat. It is true that there are a number of large streams in which dasheens grow freely without being cultivated; and it seemed to me a great novelty to find them growing in such great quantity, and also fresh-water crabs. The temperate nature of the climate of Crete and the abundance of water in the streams enable the inhabitants to have many very fine gardens and orchards of excellent beauty, which bring them great profit. Some of them are in such pleasant country that a man would never tire of contemplating them, principally in the possessions of a Venetian nobleman called Juan Francesco Baroczo[44], who always arranged for me to be honourably received in all his places and houses and to be shown the singular things in the country.

The orchards are for the most part planted with almond-trees, olive-trees, pomegranate-trees, jujube-trees, fig-trees and other such fruit-trees, including very large orange-trees, lemon-trees, Adam's apples and citron-trees. The Greeks extract the juice from their fruits, fill barrels with it and load them on to their squiraces, and then send it to be sold in Turkey, either in Constantinople or elsewhere. The Turks make great use of it in their pottages instead of verjuice; it is also much sold by retail in the same shops that sell salt fish and *garum*[45]. There are some places in Crete where palm-trees, both large and small, grow, mainly along the coast or by a stream which flows from a spring on the sea-bottom, which the Cretans call in their vulgar tongue *almiro*. But they bear no fruit, for the climate of Crete is too cold for palm-trees.

6

Of the false labyrinth of Crete, and of the ruins of some towns on the island

The labyrinth which can be seen today in Crete is not the one mentioned by the ancient authors; for the one that is shown today is situated at the base of Mount Ida, called Psiloriti in the vulgar tongue. This labyrinth is nothing more than a stone quarry; but the inhabitants of Crete still point it out under the false name of labyrinth. It was a quarry of very fine hard stone which was extracted in ancient times when they were building the town of Gortina [Gortyn][46], which anciently was one of the principal towns on the whole island, as appears from its ruins. And just as visitors to the great pyramid in Egypt called Busiris must have guides from a nearby village to show the way and provide light inside the pyramid, so here it is necessary to have guides from a village anciently called Gnosos [Knossos] near the quarry, to show the way to those who want to visit it. It is true that there are a number of changes of direction, this way and that way, in the quarry, but these are merely because stone has been hewn from the quarry at these places. This can be proved by the remains of ruts left by cart wheels and by the small stones lying here and there by the side of the road.

The ruins of Gortina are very extensive, and there are still a few columns standing erect, set in the ground, and a small village called in the vulgar tongue Metaria. At some places stones have been removed from the walls, since they were of finely dressed stone from the quarry, and could easily be transported elsewhere, for the place is not far from the sea. There is also a stream flowing down from the mountain, and I believe that it is the one that Strabo and Solinus called the Lethyus[47], which can be forded without either plank or boat. There is also a channel which is still entire, borne on large arches, carrying water which drives a number of mills. There are likewise great numbers of plane-trees in the valley in which the spring emerges; but they all lose their leaves in winter. There are also a number of arches and walls belonging to a well-built church among the ruins that are still standing, and several vaults of strong cement and brick above the river Lethyus which (in my opinion) were designed to level the ground and make the square in which the town market was held.

7

How the Cretans make ladanon

Among the notable things to be seen in Crete is the manner of making ladanon, which is one of the most renowned drugs used in our perfumes. Here it is not made from the plant called ledon, as the ancients thought, but from another small shrub called cistus[48], of which there is such a great quantity that the mountains are covered with it. Its nature is such that, being green in all seasons, after it has lost its spring flowers and leaves and its winter leaves it grows new leaves which have a lanuginous feel in summer. In the heat of the sun these are covered with a kind of moist dew; and the greater the heat, the more of this dew there is on the leaves.

There is a species of cistus which grows wild in the country bordering the Oise in Maine[49], chiefly round the village of Fouletourte, near La Soulletiére (which was my birthplace), which matches in all respects the Greek plant except that it is not covered by dew like the cistus of Greece and is much smaller.

The Greeks who gather this ladanon have a specially made instrument which they call in their vulgar tongue an *ergastiri*. This has a shaft rather like a rake without teeth, to which they fit a number of thongs of untreated leather which hang down from it. They rub these thongs gently against the shrubs, and the dew sticks on to them. This is an almost intolerable labour, for they must spend the whole day in the sun on the mountains on the hottest days of summer. This work is commonly done by caloyers, that is to say Greek monks or hermits. And the place in Crete where the greatest quantity of ladanon is made is near the foot of Mount Ida, at the village of Cigualinus, and round Milopotamo[50].

8

Of a fish called Scarus very common in the waters off Crete, but rare elsewhere

There is a fish very common in Crete called *scarus* of which the ancient authors make much mention; for it was in past times one of the principal delicacies of the Romans, holding the first place in dignity among all fish. We are not accustomed to see it in our waters, either in the Ocean or in the Mediterranean Sea, and I am assured that it is not found in the Propontis or the Hellespont or the Pontus Euxinus or the Adriatic. And yet it is so frequent in some places off the shores of Crete that no fish is more commonly caught there. And since it is found in the same country and almost at the same time of year as ladanon is made, and also because the main fishing season is at the time when ladanon is gathered, I was able to observe both of these things on the same journey, more by chance of fortune than of deliberate purpose.

28

I had already spent quite a long time on the island, but, not being present at the right time, had never seen either one or the other. Then when I took ship to go from Rhethymo to the town of Candy, it happened that corsairs who encountered us out at sea forced our ship to make for the coast between Milopotamo and Cigualinus. The seamen abandoned their vessel and fled inland to seek safety in the mountains; and since it is not the custom of corsairs to leave their ship to pursue those fleeing inland they pillaged only clothing and suchlike things, leaving the vessel with what they could not carry off. But, fleeing in terror into the mountains, I came to a monastery of caloyers in the valley running down to the shore, where they were taking in the nets that they had set to catch the scarus. And since I stayed there several days I had leisure to enquire why these fish are so common here and so rare elsewhere.

I found that *scarus* is a fish that lives among rocks and requires food that suits its stomach. This is a small plant which grows nowhere else; and the *scarus*, being fond of this plant, likes to stay in this part of the island. The caloyers and other local villagers, knowing the nature of *scarus* and that it is fond also of beans, sow these in their fields and use them as bait to catch the fish, putting the leaves in the nets in the sea and keeping the pods for themselves; and the scarus, entering the nets, remain prisoners. Otherwise they would be difficult to catch, for they cannot be taken on the line and very few are caught in dragnets. And since they grow beans on purpose to catch scarus, they call them in the vulgar tongue *scaronotano*. The scarus swims in large companies. like the saupe, and is hardly larger than the red mullet. I do not wish to set out here all the characteristics of the scarus, for I have amply described it elsewhere along with all other fish[51], where I also give its portrait.

I must also add one notable thing: after I had been fleeing from the corsairs until very late in the day without eating anything, the caloyer brought me a scarus cooked on a spit after their fashion, and I saw that they stick a skewer through its mouth and along its body to roast it over charcoal; and so, spitted in this way, it looked exactly like a person laughing, for the scarus has teeth arranged like those of a man, and with its lips drawn back by the heat of the fire it looked just like the mouth of a man laughing. It is of the colour of a red mullet, but not so bright; but the most notable thing about this fish is the plants that it eats, great quantities of which are always found in its stomach. It also has a very large liver, which is used in making a sauce for it. When beaten up with its guts, salt and vinegar it gives a good taste to the whole fish. And in order to make clear what fish I have been talking about I set here the portrait of the scarus.

Portraiɛt d'vn poiʃʃon de Crete, nommé Scarus.

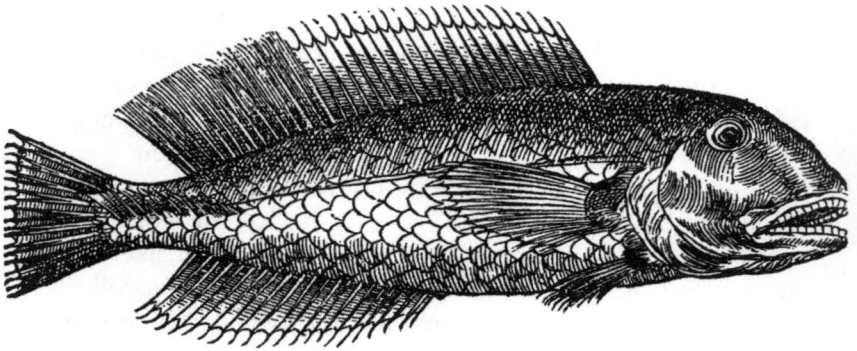

Figure: Portrait of a fish of Crete called the scarus

9

The French names of several species of birds observed in Greece, compared with their ancient appellations

What leads me now to speak particularly of birds is that, finding myself on a small ship sailing in spring between the islands of Zacynthos and Cytherea, various species of migrant birds, tired by their flight, landed on our vessel, whose names in the vulgar tongue I then got to know. But having amply described them in another book[52], it will suffice me to say only a few words about each of them. Since I know that many people doubt whether the animals that live in other countries in the Levant are of the same size and appearance as those that we know in our countries, I have been moved to explain that all kinds of animals, birds, snakes, fish and plants in these countries are just the same as those that we see in our provinces; and if there is any difference it will be found in the whole species. It is true that there are many kinds that we do not see in our countries, to which the ancients gave names, and we have trouble in learning what they were. For how can a German, a Frenchman or a man of any other nation find the right name in his language for a strange bird if it is not seen in his country?

I shall take the example of the bird that the Greeks called *merops* and the Latins *apiaster*, which is so common in Crete that there is no place on the island where it cannot be seen flying, and yet is so rare elsewhere that even the mainland Greeks do not know it. It is scarcely ever seen flying in Italy. The French, the Germans and other peoples in Europe have thought that our tit was *merops;* but that is an error, for *merops* is a bird of the size of a starling and is not good to eat, and is very similar to the halcyon, which we call the kingfisher. It is no longer called *merops* in Crete, but *melissophago* or honey-eater, which name seems to correspond to the Latin *apiaster*, for it feeds on bees while in flight in the manner of swallows. It does not usually fly on its own but in flocks, particularly along mountains on which true thyme grows, to eat the bees from which it takes its name. And although the tit, which the Greeks call *parus* and the Italians *sparnoczolo*, consumes many bees and the robin, called *rubecula*, which the Venetians call *pettorosso*, also feeds on bees, neither of them has been given the name of *apiaster*, as had previously been thought. And in order to dispel the error I give here its true picture.

*Figure: Portrait of the Merops, which might well be called the
bee-eater*

This bird is of the most beautiful colouring that can be imagined, with the hues of a parrot, and is scarcely larger than a starling. Its cry can be heard from a great distance, making a sound like a man whistling *grul gruru ururul* with his lips rounded, high-pitched like an oriole. Its exquisite beauty leads the small boys of Crete to capture it with cicadas, as they do the large swallows called *apodes*. And to do this they put a pin bent to form a hook through a cicada, and to this they attach a net of which they hold the end. The cicada, thus attached, is still able to fly. Then the *merops*, seeing it flying, swoops down and swallows the cicada in flight; the bent pin holds it to the net, and so it is captured.

The bird which we call *coqu* (cuckoo) and the Greeks called *coccyx* is now called by the Cretans *decocto*, which means eighteen. They so name it because the cuckoo's cry sounds like *decocto*.

The bird which we call *bergeronnette* (wagtail) and the Latins *culicilega,* and anciently *knipologos,* is now called by the Greeks *susurada.*

And here *attagen* is called *taginari.* Some call it *attagas,* as in Constantinople. And having seen that the *attagen* is very similar to our little bustard, I looked for some feature that should distinguish them for me. The little bustard's legs are not covered with feathers, but those of the *attagen* are feathered in the upper parts, and it has a short, black and very strong beak, and is smaller than the little bustard. But otherwise the two are very similar in colour and body form, though the *attagen* is variable in colour; for some of them are quite white, which I took for the birds that in Savoy are called white partridges, and were called by Pliny *lagopodes,* because they are all white and have legs covered with feathers like the *attagen.* When I was in Venice, staying in the house of Monsieur de Morvillier, I did indeed see white *attagens;* but the Italians call both species francolins. The bird which the Romans called *tetrao* and the Italians now call *galo cedrone,* and in Savoy a *coq de bois* (woodcock), is frequently to be seen in the high mountains of Crete, twice the size of a capon, and with a red spot on each side of the temple close to the eyes, like a pheasant; and it is black, with shining feathers, like the neck of a wood-pigeon, with no touch of white except on the wings, and feathered legs like the *attagen.*

10

The Greek names of some other birds compared with the French appellations

The birds which the ancient Greeks called *ciclae* and the Latins *turdi* and we call thrushes, *mauvis* (redwings), rails and *tourets* (redwings) are here called *schynopoulli,* which is as much as to say lentisk birds. And since they also feed on myrtle berries, they are in other places called *myrtopoulli.*

The bird which Aristotle calls *viscivorum* is called in French a thrush, which is the first in its genus. It is larger than any of the others. The second, which Aristotle called *pilarem,* is commonly called in our language a fieldfare. It is of the size of a blackbird. The third, which he calls *iliacum*, is commonly called a redwing, which is the smallest of all, and the yellowest in the fold of its two wings and on its underside; it is of the size of a starling.

The bird that we call a goldcrest is called in their vulgar tongue *trilato*, which corresponds to the ancient *trochilos*; and they distinguish this from another, smaller bird which they call *tettigon* and the Latins *tyrannus*, and the French *poul* or *soucie* or *sourcicle*; for it has yellow feathers on either side of its head like a crest, which shade its eyes as eyebrows shade ours; hence its French name[53]. It is scarcely larger than a grasshopper.

The owls, called *craves* in Picardy, which have a red beak and red feet, and which Aristotle calls *corakias* and Pliny *pyrrhocoraces*, are very common on the summits of the high mountains on the island; the Greeks now call them *scurapola*.

The bird which Aristotle called *kianos* and Pliny *ceruleo*, which, because it frequents the rocks on the high mountains and resembles a blackbird, has changed its name and is now called *petro cossipho*. It is smaller than a blackbird and is totally blue, and is an exquisite bird to keep in a cage and sing. Its song is similar to a blackbird's. We have no name for it in French, for we have none of them in our country, nor in Italy, except any that have been brought into the country in a cage; for young birds are sometimes taken out of the nest and taught to speak. They have also both black and white blackbirds, which they call, like the ancient Greeks, *cociphos*.

There is also a third species of blackbird, called the white-collared blackbird because it has a white line round its neck between the throat and the breast, which is to be seen in great numbers in the Maurienne valley and the valleys of Savoy.

The bird known in many places in France as *dix-huit* ("eighteen") and in Paris as a lapwing, which the Romans anciently called *parcus*, and the Italians call *paoncello*, is called in the vulgar Greek tongue by its ancient appellation *aex* because it has a cry like the bleat of a goat. Others call it *taos agrios*, that is to say wild peacock, for it has a crest raised above its head like a peacock, in the manner of the crested lark.

They have no grey partridges in Crete, but they have red ones of the size of a hen, which they call in the vulgar tongue *coturno*, a name which seems to have been borrowed from the Italians. The bird which was anciently called *curuca* and which we call the brown warbler is now called *potamida* in Crete. I was assured that it commonly feeds on the young of the cuckoo; there are several other birds which also do so, but this one eats more of them than other birds.

There are some who maintain that *potamida* is a nightingale, and to tell the truth I thought so too; but I have since found that the nightingale is called *adoni* or *aidoni*. The French know two species of nightingale, the common nightingale and the redstart, which is the one that the Greeks anciently called *phoenicurus* and the Latins *rubicilla*. But *potamida* is a different bird from the nightingale, with feet and beak of a leaden colour tending towards ashen. It is known in France as the brown warbler or greater whitethroat. The bird that the Greeks anciently called *aegotilax* and the Latins *caprimulgus* is also commonly known on the island of Crete; and because it flies about in towns at night and utters a most fearsome cry we call it *fresaie* or *effraie* (barn-owl) [54]. Like the little owl and screech-owl, it does not come out in daylight. Some people call it an *orfraye* (white-tailed eagle), but that name properly belongs to another bird called *ossifragus,* of which I shall speak later. The barn-owl is much the same colour and size as a cuckoo, and makes its nest in our country in tall towers and crevices in churches. But those that live in Crete nest in the rocks on mountains along the coast, where they do great harm to the goatherds, who are not accustomed to putting their goats into sheds at night, since they suck milk from the teats of the goats. Ovid refers to them in these words: *Carpere dicuntur lactentia viscera rostris. Est illis Strigibus nomen, sed nominis huius causa, quod horrenda stridere nocte solet*[55].

11

The ancient and modern names, both French and Greek, of some other birds

Among all the birds that I have known there are none that do not have four toes on their feet but the plover, the guillemot, the little bustard and the oystercatcher, which was anciently called *hoematopus*. This is a bird rarely found on our coasts, though it is occasionally seen. It is of the size of an egret, with wings like those of a gull and the body of a flamingo, which the Latins call *phoenicopterus*, a beak four fingers long like that of a woodcock, for which reason some call it a sea woodcock. But its beak is different from the beaks of all other marsh birds, which are round, whereas the oystercatcher's beak is flat with a pointed tip and a touch of black at the end; but all the rest is red. The whole of the head and neck are black, while the upper sides of the wings are white: which has given it its French name of *pie de mer*, or sea magpie. It is white under the wings and on the underside of the body. The tail is as long as a duck's tail, with a black tip. It has two toes that are joined; the one in between is separated. It does not have a small spur to the rear, as all river birds have, and also it has delicate, soft feet, not dry and hard like the others. Its legs are three fingers long. Its toes are short, with curved nails, like the nails of bustards. Its meat is not good to eat, being hard and very black; and it has a very large, wide and robust throat.

The woodcock, which was anciently called *ascolopax*, preserves something of its ancient Greek appellation, for it is still known as *xilornitha*. that is to say wood hen, which matches its Latin name, *gallinago*. They call larks *chamochiladi*, and wood-pigeons *phassa*. They have no better name by which to call curlews than *macrimiti*, that is, long-nose.

The Greeks have no names in their vulgar tongue to distinguish river birds as well as we do, for they refer indifferently to teals and tufted ducks as ducks, which they call *pappi*. There is a particular species of sea diver in Crete, seen swimming at half-tide, which differs from the cormorant and the other divers called *mergi;* it is the bird that Aristotle called *ethia*. On the coasts of Crete it is known as *vuttamaria* or *calicatzcu*. It is about the same size as a teal, white on the underside and black on the head and back, the wings and the whole of the tail. Alone among flat-footed birds, the feathers with which it is covered are of fine down. It has no rear spur on its feet. It is also the only flat-footed bird to have no rear spur on its feet. The feathers with which it is covered are of fine down, lying close to the skin. Its beak is sharp-edged, hollow and almost flat, covered with down for much of its length, black on top and white underneath; and the top of the head is wide. The small river diver called in France *castagneux* (little grebe), is not known in Greece.

The greenfinch, called in Greek *chloris* and in Latin *lutea*, is called in the vulgar Greek tongue *assarandos*, which corresponds to its name in Maine, where it is called a *serrant*. The birds which the Latins called *fringillae* and we call chaffinches are called *fringilari* by the Greeks, abandoning the practice of their ancestors, who called them *spisae*, and those which were anciently called *orospisae* and we call *montains* or *pinsons d'Ardenne* are not distinguished by separate names but are both called *fringilaro*, which is pure Italian, from *fringuella*. Our buntings are also common in Greece, but they have forgotten their ancient Greek name *anti*; for, having learned the Latin names, they call them *flori*. They also call a sparrow in their vulgar tongue *sporguitis* and a gull *laros*. A goldfinch, which was anciently called *pikilis*, and in Latin *carduelis*, is called *guardelli* or *stragalino*. Although the name goldfinch is right for the bird known to the Greeks as *acanthis* and to the Romans as *spinus*, which is our canary, nevertheless they now call it *spinidia*.

There is nothing commoner in Crete than the bullfinch, which can be seen flying about over small bushes; and since it is a small bird with its head, tail and part of the body black, it is often called in the vulgar tongue *asprocolos*, that is to say black-arse. But this name is wrongly given to it, for there is another bird that is particularly called white-arse, which the Latins called *vitis flora* and the Greeks *oenanthi*. Other people call the bullfinch more properly by a name which suits it equally well, *melanocephali*, that is to say black-head. The ancient Greeks called it *melancoryphos* and the Latins *atricapilla*, which is the same as *zikalis*, which the French have named *papafighi* or *becafigui*, and the Latins *ficedula*.

The bird which the ancients called *ortygometra,* that is to say mother of quails, is rarely seen in Crete, but in other places in Greece it is as common as in Italy or France. It is a bird similar to a quail in some respects; and, since it has the defect of being a poor flyer, nature has compensated for this by making it a swift runner. The French call it a rail, and in Italy it is called "king of quails". And since it is always found on water it resembles a water hen, which the Italians call a *foulica;* but it is much smaller and is not so black, having patches of white under its wings and on both sides. It has a short tail, like all other river birds, with a reddish underside. Its beak is two fingers long, but in comparison with the woodcock, sandpiper and curlew, which have very long beaks, it could be called short.

Vultures, eagles and falcons make their nests in Crete not in oaks and other trees, like other birds, but on cliffs overhanging the sea, falling almost vertically down, in places that are precipitous and difficult of access. It is scarcely possible to see them except from a ship out at sea. In order to take them from their nests, therefore, it is necessary to have a long rope which is attached to a stake set in the ground at the top of the cliff and hangs down its face. A man then climbs down the rope until he comes to the vulture's nest, and then climbs up again on the rope by which he went down. And sometimes they put a small boy in a large basket, which they lower from the top of the cliff, and when he comes to the nest he puts the birds in his basket and is then hauled up again.

The vultures, both the brown and the black kinds, live on the mountains in Crete where the herds graze their stock, carrying off lambs and kids, as well as any hares that they find in the open. And so the herds try to catch them and turn them to profit; for they skin them and sell their wings to the makers of arquebuses, who use them to feather arrows; and they sell the skins to furriers, who curry them to make furs which are sold for high prices. They call falcons in the vulgar tongue *falconi,* although a falconer is called *hieracari,* from *hierax,* which is a general term covering all birds of prey. Nor do they distinguish birds of prey by particular names, as do our falconers; for the saker, the goshawk, the gyrfalcon, the lanner and the tercel are confounded with the falcon, without any distinction of species.

The kite, which was anciently called *ichtynos,* is now called *licadurus.* And since I have treated of them in another work of mine[56] I shall say no more on this subject for the present.

12

Description of a small animal; common in Crete called the phalangy

The Cretans call the phalangies[57] *sphalangi,* which are small venomous beasts somewhat larger than a spider, with eight feet, four on each side. Each foot or leg has four joints, and there are two very slender nails on each leg, curved into the form of a hook; the two front legs on each side are for walking forward, and the two rear ones for going backwards. They always live in a slanting hole two feet deep, which they enter backwards, drawing their food after them; and they put wisps of straw at the entrance to keep it always open, and there they ordinarily stay. The upper part of their body is ash-coloured, with two reddish spots towards the front; and if you turn them over you will find a black spot at the point where the feet are attached to the body. Their underside is yellow; and if you want to see what makes them dangerous you must look at their mouth, where you will see two small black stings like those of the centipede, with which they bite and hold on to their prey. They spin webs like those of spiders and live on flies and butterflies. They lay some sixty small eggs which they brood in their breast, from which the young are hatched; and they carry them under their belly until they are large enough. They have a hairy body; but since they are not all of the same corpulence, they dig their hole according to the size of their body; and I have observed that they differ from one island to another.

13

Of a species of wild goat common in Crete which the French call ibexes

There are no wolves on the island of Crete, and so they can safely leave their animals to graze in the fields at night without any fear, and particularly their sheep. If the inhabitants of the country catch any fawns of the ibexes (of which there are great numbers) wandering about on the mountains they rear them along with the tame goats, so that they too become domesticated. But the wild goats belong to anyone who can catch them or kill them. Their size does not exceed the normal corpulence of a tame goat but they have fully as much meat as a deer, and they have the same short tawny hair, not like that of a goat. The males have a large brown beard, unlike any other animal with the skin of a deer. They turn grey when they grow old, and have a black line along their back. We also have ibexes in our mountains, mainly in precipitous places that are difficult of access. It is a great wonder to see such a small animal with such heavy horns, some of which I reckoned to be four cubits long. They have as many stripes round their horns as they have years of age. I have observed two different kinds, as I demonstrated by the difference between horns brought from Cyprus and Crete, which I presented to the bailiff of the mountains of Lyons[58].

I sometimes had the opportunity of seeing them caught and hunted with dogs by the inhabitants of Greece. There are peasants on the tops of the high mountains of Crete, particularly round the mountains of Sphachie and Madara, who are such good bowmen that they can hit them with their arrows from a distance of 25 paces; and to do this they take females which they have reared and tamed as kids and tether them at some place in the mountains where male ibexes are accustomed to pass. The bowman stands a little apart, hiding behind some bushes, down wind, being well aware that the ibex has such a strong sense of smell that he would be scented at a distance of a hundred paces. The male, finding the female in his path, stops, and the peasant shoots him with his bow. And if by chance the ibex is not badly wounded or the arrow has remained in his body, it knows how to medicine itself, for it looks for the herb *dictamnum,* which grows on rocks in Crete, and eats it, and by this means quickly cures itself[59]. And since I was in a convenient place to take a true picture of it, I show it here as it is in nature.

portraict du Bouc eſtain.

Figure: Ibex

14

Of a sheep in Crete called Strepsiceros, with a discourse showing what a unicorn[60] is

There is a kind of sheep in Crete, particularly on Mount Ida, which the shepherds call *striphocheri*[61], which differ from our sheep in having quite straight horns, and are as common as the others, being found in large flocks. This sheep is no different from the common sheep except that in the latter the rams have twisted horns and this kind of sheep has horns sticking straight up, like a unicorn[62], which are spirally-twisted.

When I saw such large flocks, knowing that the ancients had made no mention of them, it occurred to me to enquire whether they had anything to do with the unicorn. This sheep led me into a discourse on the unicorn, which I see nowadays in such high esteem and price that it is great cause for wonder, since it was anciently in no repute; for if it had been we must suppose that the authors would not have kept silent about it. Aristotle, indeed, does say that there is an animal called *orix*, cloven-footed, which is called a unicorn, but he says nothing about the virtue of its horn. Columella was also familiar with the *orix*, saying that it was kept in walled pastures and parks along with other animals. And if the Romans, who so much valued things that were rare, had heard in their time of such a great virtue as the unicorn is said to have they would not have failed to interest themselves in it.

And so, desiring to speak clearly about it, concealing nothing of what I think of it, I find that the unicorn horn which the ancients knew must have been black; and yet the one that we have is white. Which ancient author, either Greek or Latin, is there who would have believed that a small piece of unknown matter, which I know is frequently of rohart[63], could be worth 300 ducats? I have been shown pieces of it, to see whether I recognised it, which had been bought as unicorn at the price of 300, and were in fact fragments of rohart.

Only one ancient author, Aelian, writes that unicorn horn has virtue in medicine, but he believes that it is black. And seeing that our unicorn horn is of a different colour, I will say that it is different from that of the ancients, since he says that it is an Indian ass[64] with a horn on its forehead, coloured reddish on the outside, white underneath and black inside. Pliny, speaking of the unicorn, quotes Aristotle's words: *Unicorne, Asinus tantum Indicus, solida ungula.* Then later he says: *Unicorne bisulcum, Orix*[65]. It appears from these words that there are two kinds of animals with a single horn: the *asinus indicus,* which is not cloven-hoofed, and the *orix,* which is.

I know that the wild asses which are called in Latin *onagri* have no horns. This means that unicorn horns come from some other animal of which we have no description. But since they are to be seen in many places it cannot be denied that they exist; for there are some twenty of them in Europe, and as many others broken into fragments, including two in the treasury of Saint Mark's in Venice, each about a cubit and a half long, thicker at one end than at the other, the thicker end not exceeding three fingers across, which are well marked, agreeing with what the authors have written about the horn of the Indian ass, though other features are lacking.

I know also that the horn belonging to the king of England is spirally twisted, as is the one in Saint-Denis, which is believed to be the largest ever seen. It is a thing worthy of greater admiration than any other that I have ever seen in my life produced by any animal. It is natural and not artificial, and has all the characteristics of any animal's horn, and since it is hollow inside it is to be supposed that it does not fall off the animal bearing it, as is the case with the horns of gazelles, chamois and ibexes, whereas the horns of fallow deer, red deer, roe deer and giraffes do fall off.

No man, however tall he may be, but will have difficulty in reaching up to the tip of the king's unicorn horn[66], so long it is; for it stands fully seven feet high. It weighs only thirteen pounds and four ounces[67], though when held in the hand it seems to weigh more than eighteen. It is as straight as a candle, wider at the base and tapering towards the tip. The base is beyond the grasp of a man's hand, being five fingers in diameter; and when surrounded by a rope it measures a palm and three fingers. It has a somewhat rough surface at the part nearest the head but is smooth and polished elsewhere. It is surrounded by shallow flutings twisting spirally from the base to the tip, turning from right to left like the shell of a snail or a tree ringed by honeysuckle. Its colour is not quite white, for the ravages of time have somewhat darkened it. It is hollow up to more than a foot from the base, that is, in the place into which fitted the bone that held it firm on the animal's head. This is what allows us to conclude that it did not fall from the creature's head.

Since it is such a heavy burden on an animal's head, we must suppose that the animal from which it came cannot have been of lesser size than a large ox[68]. But the *strepsiceros* of which I have spoken above, which also has straight horns, fluted and spirally twisted, does not exceed the normal size of a sheep. I give below its true portrait, not taken from any author, for no one has previously written about it or given any other figure than this.

Portraict de Strepsicheros, ou Mouton de Crete.

Figure: Portrait, of Cretan sheep

15

Of a stone in Crete mentioned by Solinus, called Dactylus idaeus

I think right to add here that the stone called by Solinus *dactylus idaeus*, and otherwise *belemnites*[69], and by us wrongly called *lapis lyncis,* took its name from Mount Ida, where it was originally found. But in addition to its occurrence in Crete we have also seen it on a mountain near Luxembourg called the Mont Saint-Jean, when King Francis[70] caused the hill to be fortified[71]; for when the pioneers dug ditches three feet deep most of what they excavated was *dactylus idaeus*. Merchants sell it in their shops, calling it *lapis lyncis*. But this name is wrong, for *lapis lyncis* is yellow amber, of which I speak later.

16

Description of the highest mountain in Crete, which the Greeks call in their vulgar tongue Psiloriti, anciently Ida, and the plants that grow there

Finding myself on the summit of Mount Ida, I described it as follows. The peak is pointed, like a pine-cone situated on top of other mountains. And although the whole mass of this mountain reaches down to the sea on both sides of the island, and is called by the name of Ida, the name applies particularly to the peak which is higher than the others. It is true that Mount Madara extends over a greater area than Mount Ida, but it does not rise so high into the air.

The Cretans have changed the name of Mount Ida and now call it Psiloriti. On the peak which is the highest point on the mountain is a small chapel, but it is only a little house built of stones laid one over the other, without lime, to form a vault which serves as roof. It lies so high that the winds frequently blow so violently that they carry away small stones from the building. Lower down, below the chapel, is a level area surrounded on all sides by mountains, on which there is great abundance of pasturage where sheep and goats are brought to fatten during the summer. Anyone who climbs to the summit of the mountain and looks round in all directions can see almost the whole circuit of the island, and also other islands surrounding Crete like Melos, Cérigo, Cicérigo, Cytherea[72] and others in the Archipelago. The temperature of the air is so low on this mountain, as on all others of great height, that at midday on the hottest summer days, even if there is no wind, a man cannot stay here for long without enduring extreme cold. No one lives here, therefore, either in winter or in summer. Although the shepherds bring their sheep to graze here during the day, they take them back to the valley in the evening. To the east of the mountain can be seen wide plains reaching to its base, on which there are many pleasant cold springs.

The side facing the town of Candy is well covered by forests, in which are finely veined maples, many holm oaks and other trees called *acillacas*. The side looking south has no tall forests, but many trees which should properly be called shrubs, like strawberry-trees, andrachnes, *aelaeprini*, that is to say *phillicae*, called in Latin *alaterni*, *cisti*, and other such trees that we do not have in our country; and this is where ladanon is made.

The other side looking towards the Mesara, that is to say the plain in which Gortina is situated, has great numbers of cypresses, spruces, which the Latins call *piceae, chamaeleae, thymeleae,* thuyas and dwarf cedars. This is the side on which visitors are shown the false labyrinth. There are great numbers of wild goats living in herds on the mountain. There are also many hares. I was on the mountain at three different times of year and on three different paths, but never found *rubus idaeus* growing anywhere. White-flowered oleander blossoms in April half-way up the mountain near a village called Camerachi on the road to Candy. The track up the mountain on the west side is very steep and difficult to climb, running almost as straight as a ladder. There is a village at the foot of the mountain from which it is a seven miles' climb to the summit.

It appears that the side of the mountain looking east is more temperate than the others, for all round the base of the mountain the soil is rich and humid, and there are many villages. Here all the land is well cultivated, with fruit-trees, vines and olive-trees, and all kinds of vegetables and corn are grown in the fields. All this land, of such great extent, belongs to Antonio and Mateo Calergi[73], two brothers who have held the first place in dignity and nobility throughout the island for a thousand years. Of this I shall have more to say later.

17

The names of the exquisite trees and plants that grow wild round Mount Ida, and the manner of gathering scarlet-grain

I cannot speak of the plants growing on the territory of Mount Ida without acknowledging the great courtesy and good nature of the Calergi, who are lords of this area and enjoy the greatest credit throughout the island of Crete. For just as Signor Joan Francesco Baroczo of the town of Rhetymo arranged for me to be safely guided by his people on the mountains of Sphachie and Madara, so Monsieur le Chevalier Antonio Calergo of Candy, a Venetian nobleman, gave me people from his household to guide me and sufficient provisions to spend some days on the mountain; for when we were looking for plants we slept at night in shepherds' huts, in which they make their cheese. The sepulchre of Jupiter, as described by the ancients, is still shown today, preserved entire.

It must be understood that the mountain is of very great extent, that its roots reach down to the sea on both sides of the island, and that its territory is wide and spacious. For its roots begin close to the town of Candy, and it is situated right in the centre of the island, so high that there is always snow on the summit, and even in the full heat of summer it is so cold that a man cannot endure it, although down in the valleys it is very hot. Among other notable plants that grow in the valleys are wild pear-trees, which bear fruits that are good to eat; the peasants fill their bags with them and carry them round their neck to sell in nearby towns. They find them attached to the leaves in early May. They are about the size of a gall, covered with hair, and are sweet and pleasant to eat. In the same month of May they also gather the flowers from spiny caper-bushes and similarly carry them to market, prepared only by being boiled and

47

slightly salted. Male and female mandragoras and both kinds of peony, called in the Greek vulgar tongue *psiphedile,* grow in all the humid valleys, with white flowers. The plant called *tragium,* with yellow flowers and seeds like ceciliana, is found along the banks of streams. The herb called *leontopetalon,* which has very deep roots, also flowers in winter, like the mandragora.

The aromatic herb melilot grows on grass-covered hills, very like rest-harrow, which is called *ononis.* The marjoram that we grow in our gardens is found here growing wild, producing red flowers at the end of June, which the peasants call *matherina.*

There is nothing more common here than clover, which is called *menyanthes.* The herb *heliochryson* flowers at the end of June; it is so abundant on the mountains that there is little else in the areas where it grows; and since it is a favourite haunt for hares the local people call it *lagochimithia.* By *heliochryson* I do not mean our *stoechas citrina,* for, as Hieronymo Hungaro, a doctor, showed me in Crete, it is the one called *ageraton.*

The white-flowered oleander is not found in Crete except in the valleys on Mount Ida, near the village called Camerachi. The wood of the maples which grow on the cold mountains, called *asphendannos* by the peasants, is more veined on Mount Ida than anywhere else.

Andrachnes have retained this name, and also *acillaca* and *philica,* which are very tall trees bearing acorns. As for cypresses, they do not grow here in forests, as some have thought, but one here and another there at certain places in the mountains, although they have not been sown there; but they prefer the south side, and are of such a nature that even though they have been cut down at the base new shoots still grow from the trunk.

Cypresses do not grow to a great height here, but prefer to grow thicker; and large boxes are made of cypress wood in Candy. They also grow in the mountains of Sphachie, called the Leuci, as well as on Mount Ida, now called Psiloriti.

The herb *tragacantha* also grows here in very great quantity, but only on the summit of the mountains. We observed both species; but here they do not collect the gum, although some writers have ill-advisedly asserted that they do. And if I wished to prove what I say I would cite only the authority of the principal lord on the island, Monsieur le Chevalier Antonio Calergo, to whom I remember having put this proposition.

Stavesacre grows wild almost everywhere in Crete. The herb called *coris* is also very common; it has the most ill-tasting root that I have ever eaten, so much so that it made me vomit, which nothing else has ever done.

The shrub called *anagyri,* which has such a foul smell as to make a man's head ache, grows along almost all the main roads, and still keeps its ancient name. In the vulgar tongue it is called *anagyros.* It has such a bad taste that even hungry goats will not eat it. I also saw the tree spurge, surnamed *dendroides,* growing to the height of two men and as thick as my thigh. The herbs *thapsia, ferula, libanotis* and *seseli* are also very common.

There also grows here a small shrub called in the vulgar tongue *agriomelea* because it bears small fruits resembling pears. It is a shrub not found anywhere in France except on the rocks at Fontainebleau, where it grows very freely. The shrub called *malaucier* in Savoy is called *codomalo* in Crete. Having particularly looked for black hellebore on the island of Crete, I never found any, and I am of opinion that hellebore does not grow there, either the black or the white form. But I did find there a fourth species of *aristolochia,* in addition to the three others described by the ancients, climbing on trees and weakening them like *ephedra* and *smilax,* but otherwise agreeing in leaves, seed, root, taste and smell with *clematitis.*

Scarlet-grain, called *coccus baphica,* is a source of great profit in Crete, and since gathering it is the work of shepherds and small children, older people take no part in it. It is found in the month of June on a small shrub, a kind of holm oak which bears acorns, at which time it range between white and ashen, joined without a tail to the trunk of the shrub. And since the leaves are prickly like holly leaves the shepherds hold a small fork in their left hand to bend them to one side and a small sickle in their right hand with which they cut off the small branches, and then pull off the little bladders or excrescences which I have above called scarlet-grain. These bladders are round, the size of a small pea, with a hole on the side touching the wood. They are full of small red living animals scarcely bigger than mites or the eggs of lice, which emerge from the bladder, leaving it empty. It is the custom for the small boys who gather them to take them to a man who buys them, sorts them out and takes them out of their shells, and then forms them into small balls the size of an egg, handling them gently with the tips of his fingers; for if he pressed too hard they would dissolve into juice, which would be of no use as a dyestuff. And so there are two kinds of dye, one made from the shells and the other from the pulp; and since the pulp makes a better dye it costs four times as much as the shells.

18

Brief account of several other wild plants that grow in Crete

Notable among other plants in Crete is *dictannum*, which does not grow well in soil, and so is mainly found in gaps and crevices in the rocks and in no other places. It is found only in Crete, but *pseudodictannum* is found elsewhere. It is called *cromido filo* in the vulgar tongue. Sow-thistles are called *zucho*, the alder *schlitro*, lettuces *maroulla*, honeysuckle *agioclima*, viburnum *clemaczida*, chicory *pycra*, the nettle *zuchnida*, the lotus-tree *cacavia*, jujube-trees *zinziphia*, giant fennel *artica*, polium *denaida*.

Three different species of *origanum* flower at the beginning of June, but particularly *onitis*, which prefers to grow among rocks on the driest sides of hills facing south, while *heracleoticum* likes humid places and *sylvestre* differs from both of these and is more at home along hedges in fields than in open country.

There is a kind of thistle very common in Crete which is called in the vulgar tongue *ascolimbros*. The Latins anciently called it *glycirizon*, although it is different from liquorice. It grows wild everywhere, with yellow flowers, and is milky. Its roots and leaves are eaten before it has grown any shoots. When I was in Ravenna I saw it being sold in the market along with other herbs, and in Ancona, where the women who pull them out of the earth told me that they were called *riuci*. I have also seen it being gathered in the territory of Rome, where it was called *spinaborda*. It is the herb of which modern Greek authors speak, calling it *ascolimbros*. Pliny in several places, and in book XXI book, chapter 16, speaking of the thistles, and distinguishing the artichoke from *scolimus,* says: *Scolimus quoque floret sero, & diu.* Then he adds: *Scolimus carduorum generis ab his distat quod radix eius vescendo est decocta*[74].

The thistle, which the Greeks anciently called *acanon,* has now borrowed a rustic name derived from *acanou* in *aconochia,* which is an entirely fitting name; and since it is pricklier than all others the prickly group of plants is called *acanaceae.*

Daphne, as described by Dioscorides, is found growing in Crete, different from the one which the Germans have depicted. The plant called *gladiolus* or *xiphius* grows on fallow land and, coming out in spring, produces only one narrow leaf eight fingers long, ending in a point, with seven veins, from which emerges another smaller leaf, and then a third; and then the stem appears, with flowers, arranged in order, of the finest scarlet colour, so that none can rival them in redness. And if you pull it out of the earth along with its root you can throw it like a quarrel[75], for the root is thick and round, like the head of a matrass[76], with its leaves, of which there are only three on the sides of the stem, serving as feathering.

The herb *tithymalus mirsynites* grows both on the mountains and on the coasts of Crete, as also does *paralios.* The herb *securidaca,* which they call *peleki,* is common in the fields. Terebinths, laurels, strawberry-trees, lentisks and dwarf cedars still keep their ancient names, as do *aspalathos* and another plant much resembling it which they call *achinopoda.*

The shores of the sea are white with the herb *gnaphalion;* for the one which the herbalists have depicted is bastard. The roots called by Theophrastus *bulbos littorales,* which our French druggists sell as squills, also grow in abundance along the coasts.

Wild cabbages grow in the rocks round the harbour of Souda. *Chamaesyce* and soldanella flourish in the sand along the shores. The ivy-leaved *dracunculus* is found only in humid areas in Sphachie. But the other kind which we know grows indifferently in many places on the island. The shrub *halimus* is now called *halimatia,* and is so common throughout the island that most of the hedges consist of it; and the tips of the plants are good to eat. The shrub that we call *agnus castus,* anciently *agnos,* is called *lija.*

51

The houseleek grows into a shrub in Crete. True thyme is so common that they burn it in place of wood. The herb *thymbra,* which the Greeks call in their vulgar tongue *tribi,* that is to say wild savory, grows in thin and barren soils, mainly in the territory of Rhetymo; on which two plants, and mainly on thyme, grows *epithymum.*

The plant *tribulus terrestris* often does great harm to crops, mainly to vegetables, which they call in the vulgar tongue *atrivolo.* Here I must say that those who interpret Holy Writ, where it refers to *tribulus ficus,* and say that *tribulus* is a thistle, are in error; for *tribulus* is a plant that does not grow in France, at least in the terrestrial form, while the aquatic form is what we call water chestnut. The herb *heliotropium* is called *heliocorta; atractylis, ardactila;* broomrape, *lycos.* There is no hyssop anywhere on the island, either wild or domestic, but in its place the apothecaries use a spurious little substitute herb.

Stoechas grows wild in many places. Among other notable plants I must mention some singular things in the garden of the Minorite friars in the town of Candy, like scammony and *apios,* which also grow wild in the mountains, as does the styrax tree.

The *ricinus* plant, because it does not die back in winter and continues growing for many years, becomes a tree so high that a ladder is needed to climb it. Cotton and sesame are a source of great profit; they are sown in the month of April. Tar and pitch are made in Crete, mainly in the Leuci mountains, otherwise called the mountains of Sphachie, where there grow great numbers of wild pines, otherwise called *piceae.*

One of the things in Crete that I found most memorable is a plain called Sethie [Sitia] or Lasti [Lassithi], of very great extent, on the summit of high mountains a little above Voulismeni, in the middle of the island near the town of Sethie. The land is arable, with great quantities of corn, vegetables and *orobus,* which is a kind of vegetable that has not yet been given a French name. What makes the plain so fertile is the water of the streams flowing down from the hills which surround the plain on all sides.

In Crete there grow small wild pears different from ours, which they call *achladas.* Wild pears are called *agusaga.*

Polium is called *denaida* in the vulgar tongue. The kind of asparagus that we grow in our gardens is scarcely to be found in Crete, for they have only the wild kind that they call *corruda*, which grows everywhere. In addition to this they have another kind called *polytricha*.

The anemone, a flower variable in hue, is transfigured in Crete in more than ten colours. The inhabitants of the island call our hawthorn *coudomalo*. Cicadas are called *symphogna*, which is also their word for an old woman. Comfrey is called *stecouli*.

Above the castle of Chysamo, on the side of the mountain on which is a monastery of caloyers called Saint John of Predermos[77], there grows a kind of wild artichoke which the shepherds call *agriocinara*, in the shape of a pear, with a root a cubit long, as thick as a man's leg, black outside and inside, which I believe to be the one sold by the druggists as *costus indicus*. I mean the black root that they call *costus*, and I believe that it was in use in ancient times. It has a head like the artichoke, which the shepherds prepare and eat raw. Its flower is commonly white, though there are some that are purple, and has a pleasant smell. Its roots are similar to those of the white chameleon, and its leaves to those of the black chameleon. It is different from the wild artichokes which grow in many places in Italy.

The black and the white chameleon have never been depicted among our other plants by anyone, since neither of them grows in either Germany or France or Italy, and so these three nations (saving their honour) have been misled; for neither the carline thistle nor any other such thistle is either the black or the white chameleon. Of the black chameleon I shall speak elsewhere. The white chameleon has a root as thick as a man's thigh, a good foot long and sometimes a cubit, with such a strong smell that if it is in a room it makes everything smell of violet powder, so strongly that it has an intoxicating effect. The shepherds of Crete and small boys in the villages, particularly in Rethymo, gather the gum from it, which the women are accustomed to chew, as they chew mastic in Chios, and in Lemnos the gum of the pine thistle. They call the white chameleon *cola* or *cameleons*.

Acanthus mollis grows in many humid areas in Crete, but *acanthus spinosus* grows in fields and along paths. The practice of preserving shoots of *ononis* has not died out in Crete, nor of eating the tips of eryngium; but it must be understood that this eryngium is the marine species which grows on the shores of the sea, different from the one that grows in the Mediterranean area.

In sum the island of Crete produces many plants and other singularities not found elsewhere. In all times, therefore, it has had the reputation of being a generous nourisher of plants. Macrobius bears witness to this in the 5th chapter of book VII of the *Saturnalia: Sed nec monstrosis carnibus abstinetis, inserentes poculis testiculos Castorum, & venenata corpora Viperarum: quibus admiscetis quicquid nutrit India, quicquid devehitur herbarum, quibus Creta generosa est*[78].

As for snakes, I have observed only three kinds in Crete, one of which is called *ophis* by the peasants, the second *ochendra* and the third *tephloti*. I can confirm what was said anciently, that there are no venomous beasts in Crete; for when we were looking for the snake which I have said is called *ophis* our guide lifted a stone under which one of them was hiding and was stung in the hand, drawing blood, but he suffered no other ill than the scratch.

19

Of the malmsey of Candy, called "pramnium vinum", and that it is not made anywhere else

The wine that we call malmsey is made only in Crete, and I can affirm that the wine which is carried farthest, for example to Germany, France and England, has first been boiled. The ships that come to Crete to transport malmsey to other countries are particularly concerned to load up with the malmsey of Rethymo, knowing that it stays good for a long time, and that the more it has been treated the more excellent it is. In the town of Rethymo, anciently called Rhythymna, there are large boilers along the shore which are used at the time of the vintage to boil their wines. I do not say, however, that all malmseys are boiled, for those of La Canée and the town of Candy, which are transported only to Italy, and about which there is no fear of their turning sour, are not boiled. They refresh their wines each year, improving the old wine with the addition of the new and strengthening the new wine with the addition of the old.

The wines of Crete in ancient times were sweet, as they still are today. Malmsey was called *pramnium*, as appears from the words of Dioscorides, who says: *Creticum cognomine aut Pramnium, aut Protropon*[79]. Homer too expressly and greatly praised the wine of Crete, which he called *pramnium*.

The island of Crete also produces excellent muscatel, some made early, before the main season, and some at the time of the vintage, though they rarely travel beyond the Straits of Gibraltar. It is to be noted that there are two kinds both of muscatel and of malmsey, one which is sweet and the other which is not sweet, which the Italians call *garbe*, or as the French would say green or rough, which is not brought to our country since it is not boiled like the sweet wine and does not keep so long.

20

Of the ancient manner of dancing with weapons, called "pyrrhica saltatio"

While in a country village, in the house of Signor Joan Francesco Baroczo, near the town of Sphachie, I saw peasants from surrounding villages gathering for a festival, some with their sweethearts and others with their wives, so that there was a very great company. And after they had had a good deal to drink they began to dance at the hottest time of the day, not in the shade but in the full heat of the sun, although it was the hottest day in the whole of the month of July. And although all the peasants were laden with weapons, they continued dancing until night fell. These peasants almost always wear a white shirt, girded by a broad belt with a large buckle, and cloth breeches, but the shirt is not enclosed within them. Instead of chausses and shoes they wear boots reaching up to their belt, to which they are attached. Their shirt hangs out in front and behind. Thus accoutred, and laden with a wallet in which are a hundred and fifty arrows or thereabouts, well ordered, which they wear on their back, a bent bow hanging from their arm or over their shoulder, and a rapier at their side, they strive to make their finest leaps. And they would not think that they were properly dressed unless they had all this on them.

This Cretan dance with weapons seems to resemble the dance of the ancient Curetes[80], which the Latins called *pyrrhica saltatio*[81]. In the Greek dance there are three steps: the first is a simple step forward from one foot to the other, as the Germans do; the second is somewhat like the branles[82] danced in French villages; the third is strange, for the dancers move one foot forward and then back, then the other one likewise, and they sing to each other, dancing in time with their songs, in a ring, then again in a ring, and sometimes two by two, with mighty leaps.

The custom is for the women's headdress to be simply thrown over their head like a veil, without being attached. Their bosom and shoulders are always bare, so that they are dark and tanned by the sun, and they wear no stockings. I am talking here of village women, who go about quite freely in public; but in towns Greek women are always enclosed, and do not usually go out except at night, to go to church or to visit one another.

And since our purpose draws us to other matters I shall abstain from writing more fully of things in Crete, since it is such a short distance away that we see every day people coming from there or going there, and will now speak of things in Turkey.

21

That any man with an order or passport from a Basha, or from the Turk, being dressed in the manner of the Turks, and having a guide with him, to serve as interpreter or dragoman, can travel safely throughout the country of the Turks

Although the Turks ordinarily assemble in large companies, which they call caravans, to travel more safely about the country, nevertheless a man dressed in their fashion, with a safe-conduct from the Porte[83], that is to say a passport from the court of the Grand Signior, and a dragoman to serve as guide, can go wherever he wishes in all the countries ruled by the Turks, except in deserts and at dangerous frontier crossings. And so in case anyone else moved by the same desire should wish to try and do what I have done, I have thought it right to say a little about it here.

When I arrived in Constantinople for the first time, in order not to waste time idly I crossed the harbour which separates Pera from Constantinople[84] every day, so that, seeing in the shops the things that the Turks are accustomed to sell, and find out what they have that we have not.

To do this conveniently, after finding a Turkish man of education who knew Arabic, I agreed with him on a price for giving me a table of all the goods, drugs and other matters sold in shops in Turkey, which should contain also Avicenna's table, written in the Arabic language, containing all the things that are brought to them from other countries.

And to speak briefly of it, it was one of the things that taught me most and helped me to learn what I wanted to know. For when the table was finished the Turk read out the words to me one after the other, and as he read I wrote down in my script the word which he had written in his vulgar tongue as he had written it in Arabic. Then I asked him to show me the thing that he had named, so that, having seen it, I could write down in my own language, below the word he had written, the thing that I had seen, desiring by this means to be able to ask for it elsewhere when I wanted it; and wherever I went in Turkey I made great use of it among the Turks. For if I were asked to give help in some malady, when I wanted to get something in a druggist's shop (for there are no apothecaries), if I could not ask for it in their language I showed its name in writing, so that the merchant selling it could understand better what I wanted. This was a most useful means of getting them to show me the simples[85] which are no longer sold in the way of trade and which our merchants who trade in Turkey have not been accustomed to send us.

I wish to give this honour to the trade in merchandise. that we owe to it all the singular things that we have from distant parts of the world. Were this not so, should we have spices, cinnamon, cloves, nutmeg, pepper and other such things? Why are many singular drugs and excellent things that were so well known to the ancients now unknown, except because they are no longer dealt with in the way of trade? Has the earth ceased to produce *amomum, calamus odoratus, ammi, costus,* acacia and other similar things which anciently were in such great use? It is certain that it has not, and that these things do not come to us because there is no one to ship them to us across the sea. When I was in the Levant I mentioned many of them to the merchants, which because they were unknown to them were not sent to us, and which are now beginning to be commonly on sale in Venice and other places, in particular true nitre, cardamom, true turpentine and other such things, of which I shall speak more fully elsewhere. And I am sure that if I wanted to prove that I was the first to bring back many such drugs which we do not have, and which we should not have been able to get for any money, I should not lack sufficient witnesses.

22

That the Turks write the same word or term in their script in more than twenty ways

The ancients had a kind of earth which was in great repute in many medicines and is still as much used as it ever was. The Latins called it *terra lemnia* or *terra sigillata,* and the French sealed earth[86]. This earth is so singular that ambassadors returning from Turkey commonly bring some back with them to give to great lords. For among other things it is effective against plague and all kinds of defluxions[87].

It is sold by druggists under the name of sealed earth, but is for the most part adulterated; and the only place in the world where it is found is the island of Lemnos. Since I intended to go to Lemnos I enquired carefully before leaving Constantinople whether the merchants were able to get some, and managed to find seals with eighteen kinds of impression. Having thus acquired seals of all kinds which were then on sale in Constantinople, I showed them to a Turk who knew Arabic, to find out why there were so many different kinds. The Turk, after reading all of them, replied that they all contained the same two words in Arabic, *tin imachton,* which means sealed earth, and that the seal which had most writing on it meant the same as the one which had least. The earth is formed into small tablets weighing up to four drachms each, some more and some less.

The characters on these tablets had different forms of writing, and I was told that the reason for this was that the Turks can use different letters or characters to express the same meaning. There is also another reason: that the various lords and governors of the island had different seals. There are numerous counterfeiters who make such skilled imitations that they resemble the genuine ones. And to show the great diversity of the characters imprinted on seals, here are portraits drawn from the seals themselves illustrating the diverse characters.

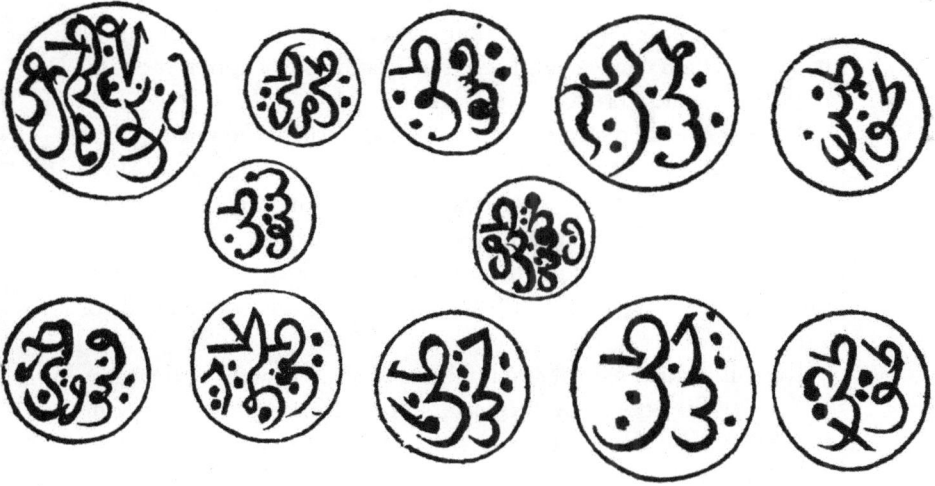

Figure

23

*Description of the different kinds of sealed earth, and of the seals
imprinted on them*

After I had got all the seals and different kinds of earth that
I could I decided to go to Lemnos to discover the truth of the
matter, and learn to distinguish the genuine ones from the false;
and I described them as follows. The most ancient seal among the
earths, according to the Greeks and the Turks, is a sort which is
scarcely wider than a man's thumb and has only four letters in all,
of which those at the sides are like two hooks and the other letters
in the middle are twisted like the character ⊠, which is the symbol
for a medicinal ounce. In the middle of the seal there are only four
dots; and the earth is so fatty that it seems like tallow and can be
broken up when chewed, and is not of a sandy consistency. It colour
ranges from pale to reddish and dark.

There is another sort, which is in small tablets the same size as
the first, but the characters on the seal are rather larger, and there
are only three letters in all, with seven small dots; the earth of this
seal is somewhat more reddish than the first, and has a slightly
bitter taste, and when you chew it there are always some grains of
sand. It is less fatty than the first kind but is no less esteemed for
its goodness.

There is a third sort of small tablets of sealed earth, of the same
size as the first two, but the letters are different; for it has one
resembling a hook for catching fish, which is between two other
letters resembling the symbol for an ounce, which is like the letter
⊠, and its colour is different from the first two, being dotted with
small spots of white earth mingled with the red.

The fourth sort is of a lighter red and paler than any of the
others; and in this sort I observed three different kinds of seal in
the same earth.

The sealed earth which is commonest in Constantinople is for
the most part falsified. The tablets are larger than the others and
are of a different colour; for the others are reddish, but these are
straw-coloured. And since they are false they are found in greater

quantity. There are two other sorts differing both in the form of the letters, which are thought to be among the more genuine, and in the type of earth, one containing more sand than the other, and they have almost the same taste; and they are rarer. There is still another kind which is adulterated with *bolus armenus*[88] soaked in water and then sealed, with a seal using different characters from the previous two, but of the same size; and it has only two letters in all, which are very twisted. There is still another sort, formed into ill-shaped tablets, which are rounder than any of the others, of the size of a walnut, which would be like the stones thrown by an arbalest, were it not that they are slightly flattened when they are sealed. I found them to be more clearly stamped than the others.

There is another sort of seal less common in the shops, which I found only in two shops in Constantinople. Its price, therefore, is higher than any of the others; and it is more aromatic, so that it might seem when tasting it that some substance had been added to it to give it such a taste; but it is of the nature of the earth from which it is made. It is one of the seals with the greatest number of characters. The earth is somewhat sandy, ranging in colour from reddish to dark. Thus it can be seen that all sealed earths are not of the same colour, for they are frequently found in a seam of a whiter colour, another time redder, and sometimes a mixture of the two. Those who approve the quality of sealed earth by tasting it have a surer judgment of it, finding it aromatic in the mouth, and somewhat sandy, than others who try to make it hang from their tongue.

All of these differences I wrote down and depicted in drawings when I was in Constantinople, and took them to the island of Lemnos, on which are the place and the seam from which this earth is extracted. But they extract it only on one day in the year expressly dedicated to that purpose, which is the sixth day of the month of August. Before leaving Constantinople I enquired of all the seamen on a bark which had just arrived from Lemnos if they had brought any of this earth; but all of them replied that it was impossible to get any except at the hands of the subashi[89] on the island, and that if I wanted to see it in its natural state I must go there in person; for the inhabitants are prohibited, on pain of losing their head, from taking any away. They also said that if any of the inhabitants had sold even a small piece of it, or was found to have any of it in his house without the knowledge of his governor, he would be condemned to pay a large sum of money, for it is not permitted to dispose of any of it except to the subashi who holds the farm and rent of the island on payment of tribute to the Turk. All of this increased my desire to go and see it in the seam from which it came. I had first of all to get a safe-conduct, which they call an order, which would enable me to travel in Turkey more safely; and this I obtained easily by the favour and credit of Monsieur de Fumel[90], who was then ambassador, for Monsieur d'Aramont was absent.

24

Voyage from Constantinople to Lemnos, an island in the Aegean called
Stalimene in the vulgar Italian tongue

Having found a brig going to Salonica, which is a large town anciently called Thessalonica, and sailing by way of Lemnos, and made the necessary preparations for my journey, I went on board, and we set sail. If the wind is favourable it takes less than four days to go from Constantinople to Lemnos. We sailed through the Propontis[91], and came to Gallipoli, where we stayed only one day.

Since we are talking of sailing in the Propontis, I will say that it is the easiest of all seas to sail on, and also give the reason. The reason is that the sea in the whole of the Propontis and the Pontus Euxinus neither rises nor falls, nor does it increase in the course of the moon, as do the Ocean and much of the Mediterranean Sea; and also that they have vessels suitable for such seas that neither ebb nor flow.

The Propontis, the Hellespont and the Bosphoruses[92] are in constant flow, as are the islands of the Cyclades and much of the Aegean Sea. The result is that if a vessel is in the open sea in calm weather, with no wind, the length of its journey will be reduced by more than ten miles a day, by reason of the great flow of water from the Pontus Euxinus to the Propontis, and from there by way of the Hellespont and the Cyclades to the Mediterranean Sea. I find that anciently several authors marvelled at this. Thus Pliny writes in the 13th chapter of book XIV: *Non est omittenda multorum opinio priusquam digrediamur a Ponto, qui maria omnia inferiora illo capite nasci, non Gaditano freto, existimavere, haud improbabili argumento, quoniam aestus semper e Ponto profluens, nunquam reciprocetur.* That is to say, we must not fail to mention, before we leave the subject of the Pontus, the opinion of many that the lower seas began at that cape[93], and not at the Straits of Gibraltar. Their argument is not improbable; for the tide, that is to say the perpetual flow of water from the Pontus, is never reversed. As for myself, I am of opinion that this place is the source of all seas, since such a great quantity of water flows down and never turns back, and must necessarily have passage out of the Mediterranean through the Straits of Gibraltar, which is called in Latin *Gaditanum fretum.* Otherwise it would overflow on to the land and drown all the neighbouring countries.

When we had emerged from the mouth of the Hellespont and come into the Aegean, being three brigs in convoy, we were becalmed, and it was already very late when we sighted three sail of pirates, which constrained us to make for the harbour of the island of Imbros[94], where because of contrary winds we were forced to stay for two whole days. On the third day we put out to sea and with the aid of oars soon came to the island of Lemnos, and then passed between two points, one on Lemnos called Blava and the other on Imbros called Aulaca, which faced one another 18 miles apart.

After I had landed and explained to the government of the island that I had come to see the mine of sealed earth, they gave me no hope of seeing it unless I came back on the sixth day of August. But since I stayed for some considerable time in a number of villages on the island, and was frequently called to see Greeks and Turks who were ill, I had good opportunities of seeing the various things of interest on the island, and principally in the town of Lemnos. For one of the principal men on the island, living in the castle in the rock, who had fallen ill, enabled me to see all the kinds of sealed earth that there were on the island, after I had given him to understand that I must choose for his medicine the best of all those that they might show me, most of which were not stamped with any seal.

25

Description of the towns and ruins of Lemnos

I find that Lemnos is called in Italian Stalimene, a name corrupted from two words in the Greek vulgar tongue, Sto and Limni. Sto means "at", and Limni Lemnos[95]. The town which is now called Lemnos was anciently called Myrina. It is of small esteem, but is still preserved entire. It is very similar to the castle of Corfu or the town of La Cavalle [Kavala], formerly called Bucephala; for it is situated on a hill projecting into the sea, with two bays, one on either side, so that the entrance from the sea is very narrow. The rocky hill on which the town lies is surrounded by old walls, and there is a castle on the summit, on which there are ordinarily guards; not because the town or the castle is held as a fortress, but to resist corsairs in galleys or fustes, if they should come to attack it without warning. It must be said that the guard maintained here by the Turks is by way of a precaution, to keep the island in obedience and in fear of rising in revolt or handing it over to the Christians.

As for the town called Ephestia, now called Cochyno, it is now totally uninhabited and ruined everywhere; for the towns which anciently lay in difficult country and were poorly provided with the conveniences necessary for the inhabitants, particularly supplies of fresh water, declined and were not rebuilt. I found that six pounds of good wine cost no more than one asper, that is, three pints in the measure of Paris for one carolus. The inhabitants of the town sought better accommodation, building houses in the plain just outside the gates of the town, where there is now a large and pleasant village with great numbers of vines. The whole island is dotted with low hills, but in between them are fine plains of good fat soil. All the other islands in the sea, round Lemnos have higher hills, like Thasos, Skyros, Tenedos and Imbros[96].

The castle of the town of Lemnos has only two gates. The one leading into the lower town is difficult of access, since it is cut out of the rock; there is a bridge, and when it is drawn up the lowest part of the town falls sheer down to the sea. The other gate is on the summit of the hill, and the path is so steep that a horse cannot climb it. The town and the castle contain very few houses, and there is no large fortress that could resist an attack by force of arms. Both the harbours, one on either side of the town, offer poor shelter, for vessels in them are exposed to the winds.

The town of Lemnos or Myrrhine is less populous than it used to be; yet the land on the island is more fertile and abounding in all things than it was in past times. And although the island is of no great size it has seventy-five villages, which I myself counted, inhabited by men who are all hard-working and wealthy, cultivators of vegetables and all other things, like peas, beans, chickpeas, lentils, corn, wine, meat, cheese, wool, linen and hemp.

It must be understood that on all the Greek islands in the Mediterranean Sea on which Greek is spoken live in safety under the rule of the Turk, thinking only of living their own lives, with no concern for guarding the fortresses, for the Turks relieve them of that trouble. Hence they prefer to live in the country rather than in the town, and devote themselves to tilling the soil. Their language has not changed because of the coming of the Turks, nor have they changed their religion. Of the seventy-five villages on the island I found no more than two or three that did not speak Greek and were not Christian. It is true that those who live in the fortresses are Turks; but the people in the villages are Greeks.

An old man who was a native of the island told me that it had never been so well cultivated and so rich and populous as it is now; and this must be attributed to the long period of peace that they have enjoyed without being molested. The island abounds in tawny-coloured horses, which are commonly small; they are amblers by nature, as in England, and none of them are trotters; and they are so small that scarcely any can be found that would be worth the price of ten ducats. They are sturdy and of stocky build.

The island is longer than it is wide, from east to west, so that when the sun sets the shadow of Mount Athos, which is more than eight leagues away, falls on the harbour and the end of the island, which is on the left-hand side of Lemnos, as I observed on the second day of June. For Mount Athos is so high that, although the sun was not particularly low nevertheless the shadow touched the left-hand end of the island.

I followed the course of a small stream which passes close to the village, in the plain near the harbour, coming from a rock which is only half a league from the town. The spring, which falls from a considerable height, is called in the vulgar tongue *cataracti*. The commonest plant on the island is black chameleon, which has flowers of such a pure sky-blue that, without fear of being defeated, it could challenge azure as the paragon of excellence and beauty. It is so high in colour that, compared with it, the sky and cornflowers and cyan-blue would seem pale. The herb that we call the blessed thistle grows freely in the plains without being constrained thereto by the industry of the gardener. The Greeks call it by the corrupt name *gaideracantha*, which is as much as to say ass's thorn.

Asphodel is common on all the mountains. The herb that on Crete is called *ascolimbros* is called *scombrovolo* here, that is to say mackerel's thistle, which yields milk like chicory, has yellow flowers and is sweet to eat. I do not know any root cultivated in gardens which tastes better than *ascolimbros* except skirrets and parsnips. And since Pliny wrote that the people of Lemnos worshipped the birds which the Romans called *gracculi*, because they ate the island's grasshoppers, I was moved to enquire what bird was called *gracculus*, but I found that *gracculus* was what we call a jay[97], as I shall show in the book in which I give the portraits of all birds.

26

The names of plants that are common on the island of Lemnos

We saw *psilium* growing in the fields, and *thlaspi, draba*, nutgrass and galingale. Spikenard grows along the streams. Nipplewort is a herb which grows neither in France nor in Italy, and is therefore unknown to us. There are also several species of reed, pennyroyal, apparitory, cotyledon and *appe*, greater and lesser, which the Greeks now call *pattimendilla; atractylis, scorpiodes, scorpiurus, chrysanthemon*, which they eat raw, *mentastrum*, wild marjoram, *aspalathus, synonis*, all species of heather, pimpernel, *bruscus, capillus veneris*, goat's beard, spurge, chicory, germander, alkanet, snakeroot, several kinds of corn-cockle, the herb called *millegrana*, otherwise *hernia*. Wild lettuces. wild cabbages, which hang from the rocks along the coast, soldanella, *chamaesyce, daucus,* rest-harrow, scabious, sainfoin, which they call *atrivolo,* or *atrivolo,* by the same name as *tribulus terrestris;* sorrel, horned poppy, docks, oleander, *hipposelinon, ascyron, ilex,* lesser burnet, wild cucumber, *phalaris,* Roman nettle, polypodium, *apocynon, peplis,* white and black poplars.

There are many other plants on the island to which I cannot give either Latin or French names, or names in ancient Greek; but I have described them and given their names in the vulgar tongue, in order to show what kinds of plants are to be found in these countries but not in ours. Among them is a kind of herb which the Greeks of the Archipelago, Crete and Nicomedia call in the vulgar tongue *sarcophago;* but the inhabitants of Lemnos call it *phrocalida,* those of Phrygia *mauronia,* as in Lesbos, and the Italians *crabonella.*

There is another herb which they call *andrayda,* another *agurupes,* another *coutuzusonnada,* which is not *papaver rhoeas,* another *achinopoda* or *cachynopoda,* which the inhabitants gather for burning. They also gather in summer dried stems of the herb called *agurupes* in the vulgar tongue, and do the same with the dried stalks of asphodel, since they are short of wood and their land is unsuitable for trees, except cultivated trees.

The part of the island farthest east is the driest and least suitable for trees. But the western and southern parts are wetter and greener. The places where trees grow and the wetter areas between the low hills produce fruit-trees, such as fig-trees, walnut-trees, almond-trees and some olive-trees. There are also two kinds of jujube-trees, one of which is quite well-known in France, although it is wrongly called in many places, both in Paris and elsewhere, the olive-coloured kind, whereas it is in fact the white kind, mentioned by Columella, of which there are large numbers in Paris and other surrounding towns, though it bears no fruit, or, if it does, it never ripens completely.

The people of Lemnos have the custom of gathering oleander flowers and attaching them to the branches of pomegranate-trees, believing that these flowers have the virtue of preserving the pomegranates and preventing the trees from losing their flowers; and they maintain that this can also prevent the pomegranates from splitting.

All the inhabitants of the island, lacking oregano, are accustomed to gather a herb from the hedgerows and keep a quantity of it in their houses, which they eat along with fish, calling it in the vulgar tongue *lagochymeni,* that is to say hare's form; its taste and smell are similar to those of oregano, and it has leaves like those of yarrow. Its seeds are in small clusters like those of a Roman nettle. I examined it carefully and tasted it, and I have never found anything that was more like the true *ammi* than this. They are, therefore, quite right in taking it with both fresh and salt fish, accompanying it with fenugreek to make a good sauce for the fish.

The Greeks give the name of *paliurus* in the vulgar tongue to the tree which many have thought to be the third species of *rhamnus,* as I can confirm is true; for one of the inhabitants of the island told me that he had been painfully stung by a thorn which he called *apaluira.* I went with him to the mountain to see the tree, and found that what he called *paluira* was the same thing as this *paliurus.* Their hedges are made of the *rhamnus* shrub, which grows freely on Lemnos, and has preserved its ancient name, for it is called *rhamnos* in the vulgar tongue. The highest hills on the whole island are on the side facing Macedonia, looking west, on the left-hand tip of the island, and were called Soace by the ancients.

When I was getting roots of black chameleon pulled up, near a village called Livadochorio, a number of Greeks and Turks who had nothing better to do came to see the plant and the root being pulled from the earth. I had them cut into pieces and strung up to dry. The Turks, seeing us thus engaged, wanted to do likewise; and since it was very hot and everyone was soaked with sweat, those who had touched the root of the chameleon and then wiped the sweat off or scratched their face with the hand that had touched the roots felt such a violent itch on the skin that they had touched that it seemed like a burning fire; for the root of the black chameleon is of such strength and virtue that if it is applied to the skin it inflames it so much that all the squills[98] and nettles in the world would not inflict a hundredth part of the pain. The itch is not felt immediately; and so it came about that an hour or two later we all began to have our skin so inflamed at various places on our face that our faces were redder than blood; and the more we rubbed our faces the worse became the itch. We were near a fountain under a plane-tree, and at first we merely laughed about it as something of a joke. But in the end they were very angry, and had I not excused myself by saying that I had never found the plant to have such an effect it would have gone ill with me. My excuse to them was accepted, for I had suffered just as much as they. It was a remarkable thing that such a small root should have the power to cause us so much distress.

White chameleon grows in as much abundance in the part of Corfu called Leschimo and in the plains of Crete as black chameleon on Lemnos. French and German physicians have never given themselves the trouble to depict black and white chameleons, for they have never seen any; and indeed they do not grow in Italy; for in addition to saying that I have looked for the plants all over Italy, I can cite in my support the *herbario* Messer Aloisio, gardener of the signoria of Venice in the garden at Padua, who will not contradict me, for he himself says that he has also looked for them and has never found them.

27

That the great lords of Turkey, living in their way, eat mechanically, taking no delight in it

The officer who was lieutenant to the subashi on the island of Lemnos was called the voivode[99]; and it was necessary to get his permission to go to the part of the island where sealed earth was extracted. And having invited me to his dinner, and treated me in the same way as himself, he gave me the opportunity of describing how the Turks are accustomed to entertain the guests whom they invite to their private feasts. It is not to be doubted that if they wanted to treat an ambassador or other such person more delicately they would contrive some other means of preparing the meal than was offered to me; but I desire only to describe what they do without on ordinary occasions. The first course was raw cucumbers without any vinegar or oil, which they eat without any other sauce. After that we had raw onions and raw *mouronne*, and then soup of boiled flour, and honey and bread. And since among the company there were some Christian Greeks, we drank wine, which had been brought by caloyers who lived nearby. In such a fashion do the Turks treat one another in their banquets, and there is no question of having napkins or a white tablecloth.

The Turks make no difficulty about consorting with Christians, preferring beyond comparison to associate with them rather than with Jews. The Turks are extremely avaricious, but it is not without reason, and it displeases me to have experienced it so often. For on the following day, when I proposed to leave Livadochorio and go to the place where sealed earth is extracted the voivode prohibited me from going there and my guides from taking me there until I had paid him two ducats, and I had perforce to pay them to him.

The order which I had from the Porte was of no service to me in this case, for without mincing his words or otherwise excusing himself he gave me to understand that if I wanted to see the place where I proposed to go I must give him the two ducats, or otherwise I must not go. I have desired to write this down in order to show what robberies the Turks resort to when you are at their mercy. They will do nothing for you but for ready money, and are greedier for money than any other people in the world; and if there is no more than a penny to be got they will have it, and not let you off a single farthing. They do that because a man may be governor of a province for a longer or shorter period, perhaps only for a month or a year, and will then have to leave it and take up another post a thousand leagues away; and so if they have any occasion for plunder they will not let it pass them by.

28

Description of the place on Lemnos where earth is extracted for sealing

After the voivode had given me permission I set out for the mountain; and in recompense he gave me a number of seals in sealed earth, and gave me a janissary to accompany me. We went to lodge in a nearby village called Rapanidi, which is not far from the harbour called Hecatoncephales. It is not more than three leagues from the village of Livadochorio to Rapanidi; and, being five in our company, we went first to see the ruins of Ephestia, where there is still to be seen the old castle, now almost completely ruined. The sea comes right up to the walls, and there is not a single house; and yet the harbour is better than the one at Lemnos, and offers better protection against all winds at all times of year. Ephestia lies directly opposite Samothrace, which is only four leagues away.

We left the ruined castle and took the track from the left-hand corner of the walls towards the hill, which is scarcely more than four bowshots away. Between the hill and the harbour is a small chapel called Sotira, in which the caloyers of Lemnos assemble on the sixth day of August, which is the day set for extracting earth from the seam[100]. The chapel consists only of four low walls supporting a stone roof.

Leaving the chapel and making straight for the hill, we found two paths, one to the right and the other to the left, leading to two springs a bowshot apart.

The spring to the right does not dry up in summer, while the one to the left dries up completely; but since there is still some moisture in the soil a few reeds grow there. We rode up the right-hand path, on which there are no trees but a carob-tree, an elder and a willow, which give some shade over the spring, where there are steps made of stone going up towards the place where earth is extracted for sealing.

The path leads upward and comes to the other humid area; and a little higher up on the left can be seen the place where earth is extracted on the sixth day of August. And since it is taken from a seam which comes to the surface there is nothing to be seen but a slanting hole covered with earth. And if a stranger were there, even if he were shown the spot, he would be unable to guess where the mouth is, for it is stopped with earth, and it was impossible for me to have it opened. The reason is that it cannot be seen except on one day in the year, when it is opened with great pomp and ceremony.

29

That things which are base and of little esteem are made precious by ceremonies, and that things of little value acquire authority when ennobled by superstition

I shall show by the example of this earth how ceremonies give authority to base things which in themselves are of little value; for although the earth of which I speak is of very great virtue, nevertheless if it was so common that any who wanted it had only to go and take it, the merit that men attribute to it for its virtue would be cried down were it not rendered precious by great ceremonies. So much so that if a seam of the same earth as at Cochino had been found in some other part of the island I am in no doubt that the Greeks would make difficulty in using it if the caloyers had not been present when it was extracted and the accustomed ceremonies had not been performed on the occasion; and even if they had some from the same place at Cochino they would scruple to use it or give it to others if it had not been extracted on the sixth day of August, believing that some of its virtue must come from the things done by the art of the men who were present and took part in this sacrifice; and they would consider it as having no virtue if they had not seen it being extracted.

I shall show by some other examples that ceremonies and superstitions have the power that I have described. And since people of other countries know nothing of the matter I shall take iris root as an example. Although it is found growing in abundance in the mountains of Macedonia and can be bought at a modest price in merchants' shops, nevertheless it was not considered permissible for anyone to gather it but a man who was chaste and had watered the earth with sugared water three months in advance, wishing by such ceremonies to appease and pacify the earth. And other superstitions, which are described by Theophrastus, had also to be performed.

That is why this root was anciently regarded as having a consecrating power. It was so too with the mistletoe which the druids gathered from oak-trees with a silver sickle, and with several other great ceremonies described by Pliny. It is manifest that the ceremonies connected with sealed earth were performed in different ways, and that at different times there were different ways of sealing the earth. For in the time of Dioscorides, who wrote long before Galen, the custom was to mix the blood of a he-goat with the earth in making the tablets; and consequently they were accustomed to perform certain ceremonies when killing the goats, which were dedicated to Venus; and this, as the fables tell us, had the result that the women of Lemnos had the unpleasant smell of a he-goat and were therefore disdained by their husbands, whereupon all the women by common consent killed all the men on the island.

The priestess then stamped the tablets with a seal which had the figure of a goat, and so they got their Greek name of *sphragida aegos*, which means goat-seal. For since goats both male and female were commonly regarded as sacred on the island their blood was mixed with the earth. Galen, desiring to know the truth of the matter, when coming from Troy (then called Alexandria, a colony inhabited by Romans) and going to Rome, travelled by way of Lemnos and enquired whether it was still the custom to mix he-goat's blood with the earth before sealing it. But when he was in Lemnos, at the very place of which I am speaking, he found that they no longer did so. And in describing the practices that were then in use he writes that a priestess scattered wheat and barley on the earth and performed other ceremonies in accordance with the custom of the country. And then they filled a cart with the earth and took it with them to the town of Ephestia.

This was related by Galen, along with much else which for brevity's sake I will not describe. It is a remarkable thing that sealed earth has been in use and in high repute among men since such ancient times: indeed in the time of Homer and Herodotus, who lived long before Dioscorides and Galen, it was in such high honour that it was rendered august by ceremonies.

But in this present time, from what I saw and heard on the island, these first two ceremonies are no longer performed, and they now have a different one, which I was unable to see since I was not on the island on the sixth day of August. Now the greatest personages and the chief men on the island, both Turks and Greeks, priests and caloyers, go to the little chapel called Sotira where mass is celebrated in the Greek fashion with prayers, and then, accompanied by the Turks, they all climb the hill which is only two bowshots from the chapel, where fifty or sixty men dig away the earth until they reach the seam of sealed earth. And when they reach it the caloyers fill a number of basins or small bags made from animal skins with sealed earth and give them to the Turks there present, that is to say to the subashi or the voivode, and when they have taken as much as they need on this occasion the seam is closed and covered with earth by the workmen who are still there. The subashi sends most of the earth that has been extracted to the Grand Turk in Constantinople. He then sells the rest to the merchants. And in order that no one should be able to get any except at their hands they hold the inhabitants under such close control that it would be impossible for a man putting twenty workers to work for a whole night to reach the seam of earth without being discovered. Those who are present when it is extracted from the seam are allowed to take a small quantity each for their own use, but they would not dare to sell it without being found out.

The Turks are less strict than the Greeks and many other nations: they allow Christian Greeks to say their prayers over the sealed earth in their presence, and themselves assist and aid the Greeks. And if what the oldest inhabitants told me is true, the rule that the sealed earth could be extracted on only one day in the year was introduced when Lemnos and the islands in the Aegean Sea were under Venetian rule. The soil on the hill is not so sterile as to prevent the wheat that is sown there from flourishing.

There is no inhabitant of the island of Lemnos who does not know about Vulcan. And just as small children on the island of Corsula[101] can tell the story of the dolphin as if it had taken place only the other day, so the story of Vulcan is told on Lemnos, but in different ways; for some say that when he and his horse fell they broke their thighs, and that he was cured on the spot by the virtue of the earth, while others maintain that it was only one hip and that he was compelled to stay there until it was healed. The latter opinion seems to contain a slight scintilla of its antiquity. There are no men appointed to guard the earth and no trace of any wall built to guard it.

30

When we had made the circuit of the mountain we returned to the village of Rapanidi, which was only six arbalest shots away, near the mountain of Cochino. I call it a mountain, though it is not a high mount but rather a hill or mound. It is not so difficult to climb, nor half as high, as Montmartre, near Paris, but merely a low hill on which oxen could draw a cart to the top.

When we reached Rapanidi they brought us a number of fish that had been caught in the harbour, which is only three arbalest shots away. Some of them are caught on lines, like a fish which they call *cano*, anciently *cana*, and at Marseilles a *serran*, at Genoa a *bolasso*. There was also another called *ropho*, anciently *orphus*.

The fish caught in dragnets were *blenni, glini, atherinae, sargi, gobij, merulae, turdi* and those that the Greeks anciently called *sgourdelles*, the fish to which on account of their beauty the Venetians give the name *donzelles*, and which at Genoa are called *zigurelles*.

I could not find any Greeks in the village who were prepared to show me any sealed earth, from fear of the Turks, except one man who got me a bag of it and delivered it to me in secret, and then travelled the whole of the following night to take it to Lemnos for me; for if he had been caught the subashi would have taken much of his property.

I found many different kinds of earth in various villages on the island, but no one ever showed me any sealed earth, except in a few houses in Myrina, which is the name of Lemnos. I was also told that that the place where they were accustomed to extract earth had always been the same.

It was not for lack of diligence that I found no remains of the labyrinth on the island of Lemnos, and I believe that if there had been any I would have found them as I did for other things. The island of Lemnos is very poorly supplied with trees, for there are none growing wild in any number save round the village of Rapanidi, where there is a forest of *esculus*, which are not cut down for burning because they yield a drug which the Greeks and Italians call *velonia*. They use the calyces and acorns of *esculus* (which is an evergreen tree) in the preparation and currying of leather. They do not export velonia from the island but keep it for their own use and profit. From the place where earth is extracted on the hill to the town of Lemnos it is only 12,000 paces.

After seeing all the places on the island I returned to the village of Livadochorio and took leave of my janissary.

On the following days, while waiting for a boat to take me on my way, I walked about on the island, and met a man from Chios who had set up as a doctor on Lemnos, a man most ignorant in the art of medicine, but in spite of that he had made more than 300 ducats in two years, for I believe that there have never been any people more eager to medicine themselves than the inhabitants of Lemnos. They do not pay in ready money but give what they have, some barley, others cheese, others garlic and onions, and others linseed; from which things we also profited as if they had been money, for we should have has in any case to buy them for our use.

31

Of pine thistle gum and other singular things, with the names of snakes known to live on the island of Lemnos

While I was going about the island I gave orders to obtain by various means living examples of all the different kinds of snake that live there, which I cut up carefully and anatomised. And since they are known in the vulgar tongue by names peculiar to the country I wrote them down as follows: *cenchriti, laphiati, ochendra, sagittari, tephliti* or *tephlini, nerophidia*.

Although all these appellations are in the vulgar tongue they nevertheless retain something of their ancient names; for what they call *cenchriti* is what the ancients called *cenchris*[102]. Having had its true portrait drawn, I set it here.

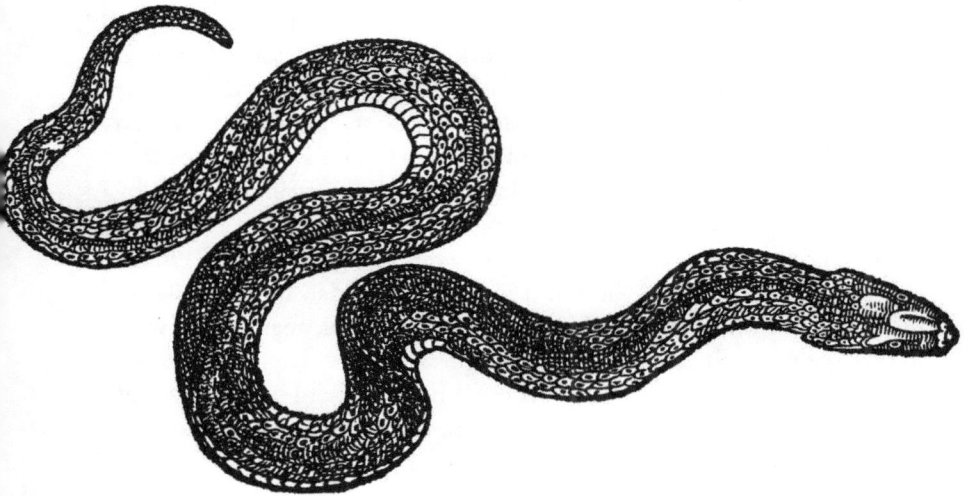

Figure: Portrait of the snake called Cenchris

Laphiati is what the ancients called *elaphis. Ochendra* is what they called *echis* or *echidna,* although that is not the true viper. The snake called *amphisboena* has kept its ancient name. The one called *sagittari* is what the ancients called *jaculus;* but the inhabitants of Lemnos do not agree with the people of Andros and Paros in the name of this snake, for the *jaculus* has black spots on its back, somewhat in the form of an eye, like the spots on the back of the fish called *torpedo,* which Pliny called *oculata,* but different from *melanurus.* The one called *tephliti* or *tephlotis* matches the ancient name *tiphlini.*

The phalangies of Lemnos are all of one colour, differing in that respect from those of Crete and Zacynthos. While I was in Lemnos, having seen so much black chameleon, I thought that I should have no difficulty in getting some of the gum from the white chameleon, and in order to get it more easily I asked the inhabitants if they had any glue; for chameleon gum, and also the white chameleon plant, are called in Greek *colla* (gum). And when I applied to a carpenter he replied that he would be able to find some, and he brought me what he called *colla*. This, however, was not the gum of the white chameleon but gum from the herb that is called *chondrilla*. They use it for gluing lutes and other works of marquetry; which gum is engendered in the root of the herb called *chondrilla,* by the benefit and virtue of a worm which feeds on the root, enclosing itself in a small bubble the size of a bean made from the milky substance that comes out of the root. The people of Lemnos know it and call it by the name of *colla* in the vulgar tongue.

The wax which the ancients called *propolis* is yellower on Lemnos than it commonly is, though it is usually blackish in other places. The plants that grow on the east side of the island, near the hill with the sealed earth, are *thapsia* and *centaurium minus.* The peasants also sow much cotton and sesame. There is none of them but knows that the herb *andraida*, administered in the form of a drink, is good for treating pains in the stomach and breast.

The peasants in the villages are diligent in surveying the rugged and hilly country where wild fig-trees grow. They cut branches of these trees on the eve of Saint John's day and put them on their cultivated fig-trees, hoping that by this means the fruit will be protected from any attacks that may be directed against it.

All springs are carefully preserved, since they are great gardeners, and among other things cultivate garlic and onions and also grow great quantities of cucumbers, which have the finest taste that can be imagined. They eat them with bread but without salt, oil or vinegar. And when some friend comes to his garden the peasant will pick a cucumber, hold it straight in his left hand, remove the skin along its whole length and let the skin hang from his hand in the form of a star. Then he will cut it in four and distribute it to those present, who eat it without any other sauce. I have written about this because to us it seems strange, though with them it is a token of good manners, as it would be with us to share a good pear.

32

Of the oysters that are commonly fished on the shores of the island of Lemnos

There are no rivers on Lemnos, and so the inhabitants could not give me the name of a single fresh-water fish. But since they have very good fisheries round the coasts they have a great abundance. And since I saw them fishing for oysters, which they call *gaideropoda*, I will describe here their manner of fishing.

The fisherman holds a long rod with an iron tip, the end of which is flat, and with it strikes hard on the oysters, which are attached to the rocks, and after he has dislodged them he scoops them up with an iron hand which is fixed to the other end of the rod; and he uses the same method to fish for sea-urchins. These oysters are very different from ours, for the shells are held so tightly together by two clamps that that it is very difficult to prise them open. And since they resemble an ass's shoe the Greeks call them in the vulgar tongue *gaideropoda*, that is to say ass's foot. There are no small crabs feeding on them, as with the common oyster.

Leaving the town of Myrina and following a small stream called Solinari, on a path leading to a windmill, which is off to the right on a low hill in the direction of the harbour of Condée, I came to an area barren of vegetation apart from a few black chameleons, with some white ones here and there, growing in red soil. I dug into it and discovered a vein of earth, of which I took a small quantity. Comparing it with the earth from Ephestia and examining it carefully, I found that it agreed in all points with the earth which the peasant had brought me from Rapanidi. As I have said, all sealed earths are not of the same colour, for it happens sometimes that the seam is whiter and another time redder, and sometimes a mixture of the two.

The shoemakers of Lemnos use fatty earth to glue the leather in place of glue. I do not mean to say, however, that the earth from the hill at Cochino is fatty, for it is particularly thin, almost like marl.

33

Of the hot baths of Lemnos, and of the monasteries of the Greek monks

There is no island in the whole of the sea of the Archipelago on which there is not a monastery of caloyers, and so it is also on Lemnos. The monastery on Lemnos is not far from the village of Livadochorio, and is called Agio Paulitico.

There is a spring on the island supplying hot baths, which the Greeks call in the vulgar tongue *thermes*. The water is not so hot as in many others, for it is possible to plunge into it when it emerges from the spring, which cannot be said of all the other baths that I have seen, either in Phrygia, Cilicia, Arabia, Macedonia, Italy, Germany or France. So there is no grand building, but merely a little room in which anyone can take his clothes off, and from there enter a vaulted room in which there is only a large trough hollowed out from stone which had anciently served as a sepulchre. The spring has no great flow of water, and so only one man, or perhaps two, can bathe at the same time.

34

Voyage from Lemnos to the island of Thasos

I decided to go to the island of Thasos, which is very close to Lemnos, accompanied by two caloyers. We had left the harbour before daybreak, and when it was full day we had sailed so far that we were almost half way between Lemnos and Thasos; but then there sprang up a contrary wind of such violence that there was nothing for it but to put in at the island of Scyros, which is 50 miles from Lemnos. We ran before such a violent wind for the space of four hours that we reached harbour on Scyros before nightfall. On this island there are very high mountains.

On the following day we set sail for the island of Thasos, and had fairly good weather for the voyage. I stayed there for three days, wandering this way and that, and then I had to take the boat that was going to Montesancto, otherwise called Mount Athos. It is no matter for wonder that the Romans held the marble of Thasos in reverence and esteem, for the mountains and rocks on the island are of the finest marble and the whitest to be found anywhere. The harbour of the town shows that it was once a much greater place than it is now.

There are large numbers of firs and spruces on the mountains on the island, and also large numbers of *thapsia* and *ferula*. At some places there are still to be seen great mounds of slag, that is to say mineral waste, which show that much metal had been extracted, which seemed to me to confirm what Herodotus says about Thasos being a town illustrious for its gold and silver mines. I was shown some silver medals, which had written on them in Greek letters something which was as much as to say king of Thasos. The Greek author Thucydides wrote that that he presided in his time over the mines of Thasos. The Thasians were ruled by Alexander the Great, for although the island is near Thrace it is close to Macedonia, very near the port of Bucephala; and from the port of Thasos it is not more than two and a half leagues to the mainland of Macedonia[103]. The mines of Thasos in ancient times yielded 80 talents every year to Philip and Alexander, but now they are no longer worked and yield nothing.

Leaving the island of Thasos to go to Mount Athos, it took me only four hours to reach Liato Pedi[104], which is one of the principal monasteries on the Isthmus, on the whole of Mount Athos.

35

Description of Mount Athos and the memorable things to be found there

The mountain that I am about to describe is called Athos in Greek and Montesancto in Italian. I do not think I have written about anything more worthy of being described in detail than this mountain, for the ancient historians have said so much about it that their writings make it most justly to be wondered at. And indeed it is an extraordinary place.

The earliest account by Herodotus, concerning the Persians on this Mount Athos, which tells us that Xerxes cut a canal across the narrow point at the head of the isthmus to allow his ships to pass across it, seems to me to be totally false; certainly I cannot confirm it. When I passed that way I examined the area very particularly; for, having set out from the town of Hierissos [Ierissos] to see if there was any trace of a cutting or excavation, I found nothing; or at least if there had been any such thing it must have been filled in by now.

Although there are many nations in various parts of the world following the Christian law in different fashions and believing in Christ, there are none that have not set up a head to be sovereign in their church. I believe that those under the obedience of the Greek church are more numerous than the Latins. The Greeks, in separating themselves from the Roman church, chose another manner of worship very different from the Latin form. And just as the Latins recognise one sole head of their church, with his seat in Rome, to whom all nations following his faith obey, similarly the sovereign heads of the eastern church are called patriarchs, whose seats are diversely assigned, for there are several nations, although they do not speak Greek, who are subject and obedient to their patriarchs.

Poets and historians have greatly contributed to making this mountain famous; and it has in all times been dedicated to Greek monks; indeed I believe that in the time of the pagans there also dwelt there priests worshipping idols. There is throughout the whole of Greece only one order of monks, who are called *caloyers,* and *calogria* for the females. Which name, rendered into our language, represents what the common people call father-in-law. *Caloyer,* however, properly means "good old man", and *calogria* "good old woman". Mount Athos was anciently dedicated to them, and they enjoyed the privilege which still endures today, that no other Greek or Turk can live there except he be a caloyer. These caloyers never marry, although priests in Greece do. They abstain all their life from eating meat, and most of the time from eating sanguineous fish, principally during their fasts. They live most austerely, and have nothing in more common use than preserved olives, which are different from those that we are accustomed to preserve in this country, for theirs are black and fully ripe, and keep without the addition of any sauce, like baked plums.

And since there are fully 6000 caloyers living in various parts of the mountain, on which there are some twenty-four large and ancient monasteries, well established and fortified by high walls, scattered here and there, both on the coast and inland, which I have visited, and since all who come to visit them are fed without paying anything, it has seemed to me worth while to describe them and take them in order according to their situation, and to add their proper names, knowing well that it is here that the Greek ceremonies are well maintained and regulated in their churches, and that for that reason these caloyers are held to be more religious than those who have not been nourished on Mount Athos.

The nations which follow the faith of the Greeks are Circassians, Wallachians, Bulgarians, Muscovites, Russians, many of the Poles, and the peoples of Mingrelia, Bosnia, Albania and Sclavonia, with some Tartars and also the Serbs and Croats. In sum, all the nations living round the Pontus Euxinus, both on the coasts and inland, have followed the faith of the Greeks, who along with those above mentioned hold the caloyers of Mount Athos in the greatest veneration, and esteem them in their various countries, attributing to them some quality more than they do to others who have not been on the mountain. And the Turks themselves, who rule over all the countries I have mentioned, give them great alms for their good life and strict observance of the ceremonies which they maintain.

The monks in the monasteries on Mount Sinai and Mount Lebanon, in the deserts of St Anthony, the town of Tor [Al-Tur] and other places on the shores of the Red Sea, in Antioch, Alexandria, Jerusalem, Bursa and Damascus, and numerous other monasteries scattered here and there in Asia, in territories ruled by the Turks, are much more highly esteemed by Christians for having dwelt on Mount Athos.

All the monasteries, and the religions of Asia which I have named, although under the rule of the Grand Turk, say their services in the same language as they do in Greece. And although the sovereign of the Greek church, named the patriarch, has his seat in the city of Constantinople, nevertheless there are several others of the same name and of equal power in the countries in which they preside.

The patriarch of Alexandria has absolute command over all men of the faith of the Greeks living in Egypt and Arabia, and has a large house in Cairo which is scarcely less than the house of the patriarch in Constantinople, and is also called patriarch.

Another patriarch has his seat in Damascus, with absolute command over all the monasteries and people of the Greek religion living in Syria, and is required to be in the monastery on Mount Lebanon on the fifteenth day of the month of August to celebrate mass there. And there is another in Antioch who has command over the monasteries and other Greek Christians in Beirut, Tripoli, Aleppo and other places in Asia.

The Grand Turk does not interfere with these patriarchs in the exercise of their religion, subject to their payment of tribute. It is said that the patriarch of Constantinople pays 12,000 ducats, covering both Mount Athos and other monasteries in Europe.

When one of these patriarchs dies the bishops and metropolitans, who are like our cardinals, meet to appoint a new one. And it is to be noted that no one can become a patriarch unless he has been a metropolitan, just as it is with the papacy.

As for the 6000 religious whom I have called caloyers living on Mount Athos, you are not to think that they live an idle life, for they leave their monasteries in the early morning, each with his tool in his hand and carrying some biscuit and a few onions in a scrip slung over his shoulder – one a hoe, another a mattock, a third a billhook. Each one works for the domestic needs of his monastery. Some work in the vineyards, others hew wood, others again build boats. And I can think of no better comparison than the household of a prince, all contributing to the common economy; for some are tailors, others builders, others carpenters, others of other trades, all working in common, spinning the wool of which their shifts and other garments are made; though indeed they are very poorly clad, almost resembling those whom we call hermits or black robes, otherwise called the poor friars. I would have called them monks in accordance with our common usage, which is a misuse of the term; for a monk or *monachos* is properly a solitary, as it might be a hermit, nowadays called on Mount Athos by the name of *phileremos*.

To get a good idea of this mountain and how it is shaped, you must imagine a man lying on his back in the sea, extending from west to south. If you do this you will have a picture of Mount Athos. From end to end it is three days' journey. It is like a man swimming on his back in the sea, with his feet touching the shore; the place where his feet met would be narrower than any other part of the body, and then the body would grow wider up to the shoulders, where it would narrow again to form the neck; then would come the head, round and rising higher than the body. Similarly, there is a very high mountain at the end of Mount Athos, which can be seen from the sea at a distance of over thirty leagues; this is the point which forms the head of the mountain. And it could properly be said, looking at it from a distance, from the mountains of Macedonia, that you can see the form of a man lying on his back.

For just as the chin and the nose of a man lying on his back on the ground rise higher, and from there a short distance farther an interval can be seen between the chin and the breast, represented by the space of the cavity which descends from the chin to the throat, so the mountain is seen to grow wider, figuring the hills of the shoulders, and then becoming lower and narrower, and thus representing the middle of the body at the level of the navel; then growing in size again to the position of the hips; then continuing to the position of the knees, where it rises again, as if a man lying on his back had drawn up his legs. Then, continuing down the legs from the knees, the mount grows narrower again to join the mainland, so that the body of this peninsula of Mount Athos seems to have been expressly counterfeited by the industry of man to represent the body of a man lying on his back.

36

There are nowadays some 5000 or 6000 caloyers living on Mount
Athos, scattered here and there in the monasteries

The whole body of this mountain is difficult of access both
for people travelling on foot and for those on horseback. On the
mountain you could count five or six thousand caloyers living in
monasteries, of which, if they arelisted in detail, there are up to
23 or 24. And there is no monastery, taking one with another, but
has more than 200 religious; for in one there are 300, in another
200, in yet another 100, and so on with the others, some more and
some less.

37

That all the monasteries on Mount Athos are strong in order to resist
pirates, and that pirates do them no great violence

Of the twenty-three or twenty-four monasteries that are on this
mountain there are none that are not strong and securely enclosed
by walls, both to withstand the violence of enemies if they were to
be attacked and to resist sea corsairs if the need should arise. For
since they are on the shores of the sea the pirates could do them
some mischief if they were not well defended in their monasteries.
However the pirates, though they are Turks and enemies of all
mankind, commonly do not demand anything from them and make
no great effort to cause them any displeasure.

Justice prevails among brigands, and the law of reason can
be debated between evil people. For although they are the most
pernicious of men, and contrary to all religion, they still have some
discretion and remorse in their consciences and they wreak no
violence on the caloyers of Mount Athos; for they, who would not
spare father or mother, brother or sister, parent or friend, if they
could sell them for ready money, have some obscure instinct that
leads them to support the caloyers.

These sea pirates pursue men not only for their bodies, but to sell them, making them slaves; for they can get 50 ducats for each slave.

38

That Mount Athos is held in as much reputation among the Greeks as Rome among the Latins

There has never been a time since the earliest writings of the Greeks that this mountain has not been greatly renowned; and this is indicated by the name it bears. For the Greeks it has now the same reputation for sanctity as has Rome for the Latins. The Greeks call it in their vulgar tongue Agion Oros.

Those who go about on the mountain, either as travellers or on business, are supplied with food by the monasteries without charge, but they give them only what they eat themselves, that is to say preserved olives, raw onions, beans soaked in water and salted, biscuit, rarely fresh bread, and sometimes fish, either fresh or salt, for they are on the shores of the sea. Not all the monasteries are close to one another, and the principal monasteries on the whole of the mountain are only two in number, one called Vatopedi and the other Agias Laura.

The sea is of great advantage to them, both for the shipping which supplies them with all goods from outside the mountain and also because it provides them with fishing grounds which are of great benefit to them. Fishing in the sea is a pastime which they enjoy and from which they draw great profit. And to do this more conveniently they make boats from the large trunks of plane-trees, and without great difficulty or expense make each boat out of a single trunk. They fell the tree at the base and then hollow out the trunk, fashioning it in the form of the boats used for crossing the Saône or the Seine. They also put two pieces of hollowed-out trunk together, joining them with dowels, to make boats which in quiet and calm weather can go as far out to sea as is necessary to catch the fish. And they float their nets on gourds for lack of cork, just as the fishermen of the Pontus and Propontis use the bark of pine-trees.

The monastery called Agias Laura is one of the principal monasteries on the whole of the mountain, and is situated at the foot of the highest peak, which is the true Mount Athos, looking out towards the island of Lemnos. In this monastery there are fully three hundred caloyers. I will now name the monasteries scattered about all over the mountains facing the mainland of Macedonia.

39

The names of all the monasteries, naming them in order, beginning at the mainland

Leaving Macedonia, and entering the peninsula by way of the first large village named Hierizos [Ierissos], which is a little above the strait, and from there going along the coast, when you have left the village of Hierizos, you come on to the isthmus named Aladiefna. Beyond this you come to Prulacas [Provlaka], and from there you climb a hill called Megalivigla. This is the place where watch is kept day and night, particularly when pirates are suspected to be at sea. Not long ago Hierizos was no more than a large village, but eight years ago the Grand Turk had it enclosed by walls and fortified, for fear of pirates.

Continuing beyond Megalivigla, you come to the first fountain above the road, then when you enter the territory of Mount Athos and have left the isthmus which joins the mountain to Macedonia, and have passed the fountain, which the Greeks call Protonero, you find the monastery called Sguraf [Zographou].

Beyond this, going east along the coast, you come to another monastery called Chelandari. Then after this is the monastery called Simeon, which is a most handsome and admirable monastery; but the next one, which is called Vatopedi, is still larger and more admirable and rich. Continuing beyond Vatopedi, you come to Pantocrator, and from there to Yuero [Iviron], which is situated on a low bluff on the coast. From Yuero you go on to Philotheou, and from Philotheou to the monastery of Caracoul [Karakalou], which is almost the last of the monasteries, for the one which is at the end of the mountain, at the foot of the tall peak of Mount Athos, is called Laura.

After leaving the monastery of Agias Laura and continuing round to the other side of the peninsula, you find another series of monasteries, both on the coast and inland, just as on the side which I have described. Continuing the circuit of the mountain beyond Laura, the first monastery is called Agiou Paulou, which looks out on to the island of Skyros. The next monastery is Dionisio. Beyond this is the monastery of Glygoriou [Grigoriou], and from there you come to Russio [St Panteleimon], which is dependent on Russia. Then after this come the monasteries of Xenopho [Xenophontos], Archangelos, Diocherio [Dochiariou] and Castamoniti [Konstamonitou], which are round the mountain on the sea. Those which are farthest from the coast in the plains and valleys, and which are in the forests, are Castamoniti, Simon Petra [Simonopetra], Ichares [Karyes] Protato, Cothleomuz [Koutloumousiou] and Philotheou.

No one should marvel that so many monasteries have been built here, for the territory is three days' journey long and more than a half-day's journey across. These monasteries have holy relics in their churches, and have great pilgrimages. The churches are very well furnished and well built, to which the caloyers go every day to sing the service. All that they say is in the Greek language. Formerly there were good Greek books written by hand to be found on the mountain, for the Greeks in the monasteries were in past times much more learned than they are at the present time. Now there are none who know anything, and it would be impossible to find in the whole of Mount Athos more than a single caloyer with some learning in any of the monasteries. If you wanted books on theology written by hand, no doubt you could find some, but they have nothing in poetry, history or philosophy.

40

*Why numbers of books have been ruined and destroyed in Greece, and
of the foundation of the monasteries on Mount Athos*

We must attribute this ruin of Greek books to the carelessness
and ignorance of the peoples living in Greek lands, who are totally
bastardised. And not only within our memory, but also in times
long past, there has been no one of learning in the whole of Greece.
No doubt there have been some with knowledge of the Greek and
Latin languages, but I am talking of knowledge acquired by study,
such as is found throughout the countries of the Latins.

Among all the 6000 caloyers who live on the mountain in such great
multitude you could scarce find two or three in each monastery who can
read and write, for the prelates of the Greek church and the patriarchs,
enemies of philosophy, excommunicated all priests and monks who
had books and wrote or read books other than books of theology;
and they indicated to other men that it was not licit for Christians
to study poetry and philosophy. Thus churchmen suffered the penalty
of excommunication, from which they could not be absolved except
by great fasting and the payment of certain sums of money and other
corporal punishments by way of penance before being absolved.

All the monasteries which I have mentioned were anciently
founded by various nations, both foreign peoples and the Greeks
themselves, and have incomes from various parts of the world.
There are still a number of them today which receive their revenues
sent from Russia, others from Wallachia, others from Trebizond,
others from other places in Italy and from Rome. The caloyers of
Vatopedi told me that their monastery had been funded by some
church in Rome, from which they now received nothing; and that
although the Russians and Wallachians and the peoples of Bosnia
and Mingrelia and Circassia and Muscovy are now required to pay
tribute to the Turk, and speak various languages very different from
Greek, they still receive some money from them, but they have lost
any income from the Latins.

All the monasteries I have named are conducted in the Greek
fashion and are not governed in that of the Latins. By the Latin

fashion I mean all those which obey the command of the pope. And since there is no diversity of habit among the caloyers, they almost all know one another. Their life is very strange. The shifts they wear are not of hemp or linen but of wool, which they spin themselves, and the habit is of the same colour and fashion as that of the religious whom we call the poor friars.

There is no monk in any of the monasteries but practises some mechanic trade, and they never hire any workmen to carry out work for them; but when there is anything to be done for the monastery they will do it all together, or it will be done by individual monks – as for example pruning vines, tilling the soil, bringing in wood, gardening, fishing. – all together they will dispatch the business of the monastery. Some are cobblers, who make shoes for the others and repair them when they are worn out. Others are tailors, who cut out and sew robes. Others are carpenters, who make boats and carry out other carpentry work. Others work the mill, others are builders, and so on with all the other trades. It is an economy concerned with the profit of the monastery, which, being governed in this way, is very different from the manners and way of life of the monasteries of the Latins.

The Greek religion is so regulated among them that if some poor widower, or perhaps some younger man, wants to leave the world and become a caloyer, if he chances to have some little property, it will come in common to the monastery. They do not call themselves by the name of brother, but of father and son. Some are taken in to work the land, or to dig or to hoe, and will be employed in the work in which they are most skilled. And if they can read Greek, or if they have some little learning, they will sometimes have more authority than the others, for they will be employed to sing before the others; particularly since they have this custom in their churches that one of them reads publicly what the others have to say in their singing.

You will find few caloyers who are priests and who say the mass. And if they are priests in the monastery they are not thereby excused from carrying out manual work like the other fathers, and each one is required to set his hand to the task. Hence it comes about that they do not spend their time studying or writing, and cannot even learn to read in their own language; and thus they are in a marvellous state of ignorance.

41

Of some ceremonies in the church of the Greeks, and of the ignorance that there is among churchmen in Greece

I have already said that generally all the Greeks, and those who follow their faith, obey the command of the patriarchs. Each country has its own, and there is one in Alexandria. though his dwelling is in Cairo, one in Damascus and one in Constantinople. All the caloyers on Mount Athos give entire obedience to the patriarch in Constantinople and do everything in accordance with his commands, being in his devotion, as we are in that of the pope.

The caloyers of Mount Athos who go to live in other monasteries in Greece, or in other parts of the world, are esteemed more than those who have not been there; and similarly those of Jerusalem, Mount Sinai, Mount Lebanon, Cairo, Damascus, Bulgaria, Russia, Bosnia, Wallachia, Muscovy, Albania, Sclavonia and other countries in which languages other than Greek are spoken esteem the caloyers of Mount Athos. The reason is that they make profession of better observing the ceremonies than the others who live in the Greek fashion.

They also have candles and lamps lit in their churches, and statues in relief and painted images, as do the Latins, and also use bells. But the Greeks who are under the Venetians have more liberty than those who are slaves of the Turk. Both have an iron rod three fingers thick, as long as a man's arm and slightly curved, hanging from a nail at the door of the church, which produces a sound almost similar to a bell, with a clear metallic ring; and they have no other form of bell-ringing on the mountain than this iron bar. When it is time to come to the church for prayers the caloyers are called by the sound of this bar. In the whole of the mountain they keep no hens or pigeons, nor any other domestic fowls, nor any cows or goats or sheep, for they eat no meat. They know birds only from hearing them named among themselves; and since they eat no meat they do not try to catch them.

I have observed, however, that the bird which in Maine is called the royal finch and in Paris the hawfinch, and which Aristotle and the Greeks called *malacrocanefs* and the Latins *molliceps*, has taken on the same signification in their language; and the little bird that lives in bushes which the French call *terco* or *turcot* and was known in Latin as *torquilla* and in Greek as *jynx* is as common here under the name of halcyon. There is no place anywhere in the world better suited for monasteries than Mount Athos.

42

Of the singular plants on Mount Athos, growing naturally without being cultivated

I found Mount Athos more densely covered with vegetation than any other place where I have ever set foot, and there is no plant of any importance but is known by the same ancient name recorded by Theophrastus, Dioscorides and Galen. The herb producing a small root which the ancients called *apios,* is now called *chamaepidia,* and there is no caloyer anywhere on the mountain that does not know that it has laxative properties. And since I see that several great personages have been deceived, taking another plant for this one, I have thought it right to present a portrait of it, drawn for me from a specimen which I had preserved for some months out of the ground, and when I replanted it produced leaves, flowers and seeds, such as can be seen in the figure here presented.

Le vray portraict de l'herbe nommee Apios.

Figure: The true portrait of the herb named Apios

The caloyers of Mount Athos have this privilege, that no one can live anywhere on the mountain but themselves; and so they have cultivated it with fruit-trees, vines and olives. This place is meant for them, for it is suitable for solitaries, and is worthy to be compared to a paradise of delights, for men who like to live in the fields.

A very common plant here is *hippoglosson*, which they call *coraco votano*, that is to say crow herb. Black hellebore grows in a number of valleys.

There is no one living anywhere on the mountain but knows the name of the tree that Pliny calls *alaternus* by its true ancient name as used by Theophrastus, *philica*; but on Corfu and in Crete it is known as *alaeprinos*, for it has leaves between the holm oak and the olive, as Pliny said. The tree which we call the beech is very common on the mountain, but they all call it *oxya*; of which *oxya* I shall have more to say below at greater length, since I walked much about the mountain thinking that the *oxya* was different from the beech. The tree which the ancients called *ostria* still retains its ancient name there. It is the one that we call beech, which is very common all over the mountain. I wonder that some men of our nation, learned and well informed, have fallen into the error of thinking that the *cerrus* of the Latins was the tree that our common people call beech, seeing that the beech bears no acorns and that *ostria* is so well described in Theophrastus.

Aria also retains its ancient name on the mountain, although the inhabitants of Mount Ida in Crete call it *acillaca*. Thanks to the great abundance of streams flowing from clear fountains which are so common here, wherever you choose to walk in the shade you find yourself in such a great profusion of delightful plants that no mind, however ill-tempered it might be, but will at once be refreshed by such a great number of excellent trees, providing shade with perpetual verdure, as if it had been expressly constructed as a rural garden. And since this seems the right time to speak of the plants which provide the verdure on this mountain, I will now name them one after the other.

43

The names of the evergreen trees growing wild in the valleys on
Mount Athos

The tall laurels and wild olive-trees repress in all seasons the excessive ardour of the sun, and here the strawberry-trees which elsewhere are usually mere shrubs grow into large trees. The andrachnes which are common here serve to form arbours.

The mountains are covered here by *aria, philica* or *alaternus,* and holm oaks growing to a great height, as well as by spruces and firs. Broad-leaved myrtles, of both the sterile and the fruit-bearing species, and red oleanders grow to an excessive height, with trunks which are equal in height to fig-trees. *Smilax laevis* rises to the top of the highest plane-trees, falling back on to their branches and shoots, forming a shade of perpetual verdure against the assault of the cold, the violence of the winds and the vehemence of the sun.

But since there are several other evergreen trees on Mount Athos, in addition to those that I have named, I take occasion to add them here.

44

The names in general of the trees and shrubs that I have observed in
various countries as being evergreen

Since, therefore, I have thought it appropriate to describe the evergreen plants, it has seemed to me reasonable to begin with the tallest trees on the earth, which are the cedars. I do not propose to describe them with particularity, but merely to name them succinctly here.

In addition to the tall cedars of Syria there are dwarf cedars in Lycia, which have sharp pointed leaves and for that reason were called by the Greeks *oxycedri,* contrary in this to the other species of cedar in Phoenicia, which have round-edged leaves.

The myrtles are of this number, although they are of different kinds: some are white and others are black, some have narrow leaves and others have broad leaves. Then there is a fifth species, which is common in our country, but is found only as a cultivated tree in cold regions.

All coniferous trees, also called resiniferous, except the *larix*, are also of this number; desiring to specify them by French names, I shall refer to them by the names which were given to me by the inhabitants of towns and villages in Savoy and Auvergne. And in order that they shall be properly understood I shall match them with their ancient names. What the French now call *alevo* was named *pinaster*, a tree not known to the Greeks – different, however, from the wild pine. Those which we call *suiffes* are of the genus of the firs, some of them being male and others female, which I shall call *sapini* or *abietes foeminae*. For the tree which anciently was called *abies* is different from *sapinus*. It is true that *abies* has three French names, for some call it *sapin* (fir), others *vergne*, others *sap;* but *sapinus* in Latin is called *suiffe* in French. And in order to distinguish better I have set the portrait of it here.

97

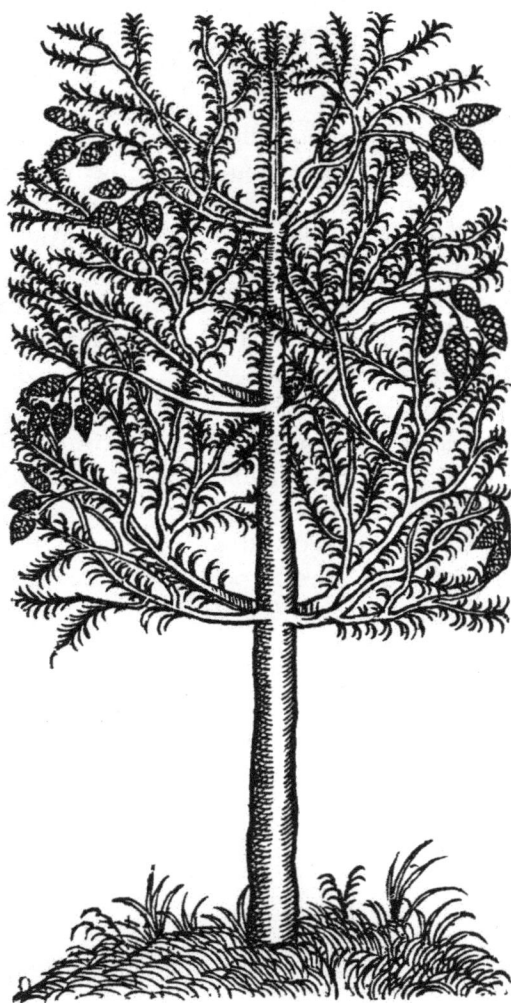

Figure: Portrait of the suiffe

The tree so common throughout Greece which the ancients called *picea* has several French names, for I find that the inhabitants of the Lyonnais on the hill of Tarare call it, some of them *pignet*, others wild pine; but the people of Savoy and Auvergne more commonly call it *pignet* than wild pine.

The larix tree does not grow in Greece. The French call it the larch; it alone among the conifers loses its leaves in winter.

Orange-trees, Adam's apples, citrons and lemons are also of this number. There are also several sorts of caper-bush which are evergreen, including those that grow on the rugged rocks of Crete, some of them spiny, others without spines.

Holly, acacia, *aria* or *acillaca*, cassia-trees, palm-trees, senna, tamarind, the trees common in Greece called andrachne, *phylica*, the balm-tree, box, cypress, a tree of Trebizond which bears cherries, *esculus* and *cerrus*, otherwise known as *valagnida*, *ephedra* or *anabasis*, heather, *phana*, the *cillus* shrub, ledum, and the species called *glans unguentaria*, are evergreen trees. White and black ivy, *halimus*.

The henna tree which grows in Egypt, otherwise called *alcanna*, differs in this respect from *cyprus* or *ligustrum*, which the French call privet, since it loses its leaves in winter, while the henna retains them. The tree called *ilex* or holm oak, the shrub bearing *coccus* or scarlet-grain, the junipers, both large and small, and five species of laurel, one of which has no scent; the tree called lentiscus from which mastic is made, *licium*, the tree that bears wool, rosemary.

The sebesten-tree, sycamore, a tree peculiar to Egypt, and the *sabina*, both first and second, the thuya, the tree which produces cork, the yew. The carob-tree, the oleander, *oenoplia*, otherwise known as *napeca*, which grows in Egypt and Syria; *percea*, *polemonia*, and a species of broom which grows in the deserts of Arabia.

The plant called *tragium*, which grows in Crete; *acacia altera*, myrobalan trees, and also the salvias of Crete, which bear apples good to eat, and the tree called *anapala* are green in all seasons.

I know this not from having read it in other men's writings, but from having observed it; for I have written about none of these plants that I have not myself seen. I have still to note several small plants which do not lose their leaves in winter, like butcher's broom, the true thyme, the savory of Greece, and other such things, desiring to name only trees and shrubs. Some others, like the terebinth, have been numbered among evergreen trees, but I have not named them here, having found by experience that it was not so.

45

Observation of surrounding places which can be seen from the summit of Mount Athos

There is a kind of cantharides[105] on Mount Athos different from our common species, which the Greeks called *buprestis*. They would be similar to our cantharides, save that they are yellow, with a strong smell, and larger, feeding indifferently on brambles, chicory, nettles, spikenard and other plants. The caloyers know them by their ancient name as *voupristi*. They have wings for flying like flies. They gave me sufficient reason for the term that they use, They have suffered great harm from them; for when horses and other ruminant animals browse on grass which they have touched, they swell up and die. And as the bite of the viper called *prester* is a pernicious venom for men, similarly the species of yellow cantharid which I have mentioned is an immediate poison for cattle; and I believe that it would also be a poison for men. The reason why the Greeks anciently called it *bouprestis* is that if a bull or cow, which the Greeks call *bous,* in grazing swallowed one of these flies it would die immediately; and they frequently die merely from eating grass which they have touched. You will also find other etymologies for the ancient name diversely proposed by different authors.

The plane-trees of Mount Athos can be compared in height with the cedars of Mount Lebanon, and with the tall firs of Mount Olympus and Mount Amanus.

Smilax aspera also likes to grow on the bushes and in the hedges of the mountain. So too does *smilax laevis,* which I distinguish from the sown or cultivated form which bears beans of different colours. It particularly likes to grow at a great height on Mount Athos, reaching up to the summits of the tallest plane-trees, and clings on to the trunk over the branches. It is of the nature of the wild vine, which climbs rapidly upwards, particularly if it finds something to give it support, as likewise does the *ephedra.* If the *smilax* of which I am speaking by chance finds a shrub which of its nature does not grow to any great height, the *smilax* also will not grow so strongly as to weigh down the shrub which gives it support. But on the other hand, if it finds a tall tree it will keep growing until it reaches the top of the tree, were the tree to reach up to the sky.

I did not expect to hear from the mouth of a countryman whom I asked for the name of this *smilax* a term so correct as the ancient name; for in his Greek vulgar tongue he called it *smilachia*.

The tallest point on the whole of Mount Athos, and the most celebrated, is at the end of the peninsula. And since it is raised highest into the air, there is almost always snow there, which lasts into summer. The summit is completely barren, and consists of very rugged and difficult rocks. Standing on the highest summit of the mountain looking northward, which is the side where the snow lies longest without melting, I found it more fertile and abounding in trees; and there are more plants in the valleys.

The part of the mountain looking south is arid and treeless, particularly near the summit. The summit of the mountain is in the shape of a pear, being pointed and round. There is a chapel on the highest point, in which the caloyers of Agias Laura (which is a monastery situated at the foot of the mountain) come to hold a service with singing on a certain day in the year. The day is fixed among them, and is well known to all the monasteries, and I believe that it is on the feast of Our Lady in August.

When we were on the summit of Mount Athos, we could see clearly the islands and countries surrounding it, like Cassandria, Schiato [Skiathos], Scyrus, Lemnos, Tassos [Thasos], Samothrace and Imbros; which we saw almost as clearly as if they had been quite close to us. It is always extremely cold up on top of the mountain. Although we were there with the sun at its highest on one of the hottest days of summer, with no wind, it was extremely cold, so that we could not stay there long.

Descending from the summit on the south side, we approached the foot of the mountain, where we found forests of firs and spruces, which are somewhat different from those that are to be found in the forests of Crete, and those that grow in the mountains of Auvergne, for the cones are so firmly attached to the branch that when you use force to pull them off you also remove a splinter of wood; also they are smooth and not rough as ours are. We also found giant fennel, great quantity of *peucedanum* and *centaurea major*.

There are no paths on the mountain, wherever you go, but you must climb up or down, for the whole country is uneven.

46

The caloyers or monks of Mount Athos practise the mechanic arts

I have written earlier that the caloyers spin their own wool; and so I have thought it appropriate to describe the manner in which they do it, seeing that their distaff, spindle and spindle-whorls are not the same as ours. Their distaff is made of cane or reed, called *donax,* and is cut only between the knots of three joints, so that the distaff is only two feet long. They pierce the cane between the joints to make a hole in which they insert three fingers of the left hand, that is to say, the little finger and the two fingers next to it, reserving the thumb and the finger next to it for drawing the wool and distributing it to the thread and managing it on the spindle. The upper joint of the cane serves as a fork which catches the wool so as to hold in firmly on the distaff.

The caloyer spinning in the manner of this country does not fix his distaff against his side, but holds it erect with his three fingers. They do not make large frames for their wool, for it suffices them to wash it in hot water and card it somewhat. And so the spindle must be made like the distaff, and matching it in size.

It is not to be marvelled at, therefore, that the ancient Greek authors named some plants after the distaff, the spindle and the spindle-whorl; for still today the plant called *atractylis* serves as their spindle, its stem being as straight and smooth as if it had been planed by a craftsman. And if they do not use the stem of *atractylis,* they use a small slender rod or wand no thicker than a man's little finger, of the same width at both ends and in the middle, fixing to it a piece of iron in the form of a fishing hook, to catch the thread and attach it to the spindle. The spindle-whorl must match the distaff and the spindle; and so it is very different from the one women use in our way of spinning. And since the spindle-whorl was invented for the greater convenience of spinning, and to give movement and weight to the spindle, I desired to show that the spindle-whorl of the Greeks is still just as the ancients described it; and it has given its name to a plant and poison called *sphondilion*[106], which I know to be commoner in England than in France. The spindle-whorl of the Greeks resembles a pear cut in half transversely, with a hole in the middle, having no teeth. When spinning they hold the spindle-whorl upwards, and the tail of the spindle downwards, and twist the thread round in the fashion of this country.

I believe that there has never been an enclosed town in the whole circuit of Mount Athos, for there are no traces of any. It seems, therefore, that Vranopolis, Paloetriun, Thyssus, Apollonia and Cassera, which Pliny mentions, were merely small villages in the places where now are situated the monasteries.

I found a caloyer who had newly come from the town of Sofia to live on Mount Athos, a good workman at making wicker bottles from willow twigs or the bark of the lime-tree or osier wood, or the top shoots of chestnut-trees, or other such wood that is easy to bend, like the bark of elms. After he had completed the body of the bottle and covered it with wicker, it had to be made watertight; and for this purpose he took the resin of the *picea* called *pefkine* and in Latin *spagas*, a term used by Pliny, and since it is viscous and slow to melt he heated it a little and threw it into the bottle. Then the resin, filling the holes in the osier and stopping up the cavities in the wicker, hardened and thus made the bottle watertight. Such bottles of wicker coated with resin are of the best fashion that can be desired for people who have to walk on the paths of Mount Athos, for they are not liable to split in the sun like wood, nor to break like earthenware bottles, and are not heavy like pewter bottles. And since they are light and long-lasting, and since the workmen who make them live in Sofia, those who sell them in the islands of Greece call them Sofia bottles, after that town in Greece in the country of Servia. These wicker bottles are much used by the Wallachians, Bulgarians and Circassians.

47

Of the fresh-water crabs which live in the streams in the mountains, different from our crayfish

As we walked about on the mountain our guide led us astray off the known path. We had no victuals with us, and could not hope to reach that evening the place that we were going to. Leaving the right road in the mountains of this territory, whether travelling on horseback or on foot, is to be avoided, except out of carelessness or a deliberate decision to undertake intolerable labour. Finally we found ourselves in the evening at a little stream, in which there were so many crabs, not resembling crayfish, that you could catch a thousand of them in an instant.

The caloyer ate them raw, and assured us that that they were better raw than cooked. We ate some along with him, and I do not recall ever eating any meat which seemed to me more delicious and flavoursome than this, whether from the urgent necessity of hunger or the novelty of the meat. When I saw that these river crabs were unlike crayfish, I thought that they must have come from the sea. But turning round and looking down at the coast, I found that the place was so high and so difficult of access that it was not possible for the crabs to have found there way up from there, and on looking closer, I found that there was much difference between them and sea crabs, and concluded, therefore, that there are river crabs which differ from crayfish.

We found a kind of plant in the valley named *elegia*, from which they take branches which they use for writing; for neither the Turks nor the Greeks write with a quill from a goose feather.

48

Of the strange way of life of Greek monks, and of their austere fashion, superstition and ceremonies touching eating and drinking

I wish now to write of the strange way of life of a caloyer, to show how different other people's lives can be.

On the following morning, having come to the monastery called Simeon [Simonopetra], one of the caloyers of the monastery, a man suffering from asthma, who was a smith or farrier, had a slow fever; and withal he had a very severe cough and was always thirsty. He invited me to his dinner, during a *saracosti*, that is to say one of their fasts, and gave me what he had in the way of delicacies.

The caloyers eat no sanguineous fish during their fasts, which is the reason why they must live on plants and other such meatless things when they are fasting. He brought us rocket, roots of ache, leeks, cucumbers, onions and fine little cloves of green wild garlic (all which herbs they have in the gardens of the community of the monastery, though some of them cultivate them privately); and we ate these plants raw without oil or vinegar; for such is the manner of life of these poor people. He also brought us pickled black olives, which they call *demarties*, some very black biscuit and wine.

These caloyers, not having occasion to heat the oven very frequently, are accustomed to eat biscuit. He called two of his companions, who brought some salt dried fish, cuttlefish, murex and octopus. At this season they can eat well on all species of crab, sea-slug and other shellfish, like mussels and oysters, because they have no blood.

The poor sick man complained of having no appetite. He said that, were it not that he had kept nuts to eat since the beginning of his sickness, he would long since have been in his grave, and thought that he could not keep alive on anything else, since they gave him an appetite to eat bread, which he soaked in water, and salted olives. These caloyers always begin their meals with raw onions and garlic, and the staple of their dinner is salted olives and beans soaked in water. They finish with rocket and cress; and whatever their state or condition, whether well or sick, they are not accustomed to put water in their wine.

When I saw the manner of life of this man, trying to persuade him to eat good fresh fish, knowing that he was very thin, and that his body was much emaciated, he replied that had he been on the point of death he would not have wanted to eat it, still less to eat meat. Such a manner of living is found not only among the caloyers or the priests and other churchmen of Greece but also in the common people, who if they were to die of it would not (during

105

their fast) eat sanguineous fish nor any other form of meat, so strict are they in observing such superstitions.

49

Journey from Mount Athos to Salonica, and of the rare fish that are caught there

The monasteries situated on the coast, like Laura, Yuero [Iviron], Vatopedi and several others, do not leave their boats either in harbour or anchored offshore at night – mainly, of course, those which have not their own harbour; but haul them out of the water, and then shut them up in some place with doors made of iron, in order that they can withstand the fire of the pirates.

There are not many good harbours round the mountain, except at Vatopedi and at Laura. The monasteries do not sow much wheat; but those which cultivate vines, olives, figs, onions, garlic, beans and vegetables exchange their products with the seamen who bring them corn, or else buy it with money.

I saw mills grinding grain with so little water that the mill-stream was no bigger than a man's arm. They build a reservoir in a low-lying area, with the upper part of considerable width. The lower part is narrower, like a funnel, where there is an opening from which the water falls so steeply that, striking a small wheel constructed very differently from ours, it can drive a large mill of any size that they may desire.

They gather the berries of the laurels, of which there are large numbers in the valleys, and from them press oil, which they send to be sold in the towns of Wallachia, Bulgaria, Servia and other neighbouring places.

They fish for sea-bears, which the people of Naples and Messina call *massacara*, which are almost like lobsters, but they are no bigger than crayfishes, and also they are not covered with spines any more than is the lobster; for the crayfish is prickly all over its back, as is the spider crab. And indeed it was this fish that Suetonius meant, writing about the cruelty of Tiberius Caesar, who caused a poor fisherman to have his whole face scarified with the rough shell of a crayfish[107].

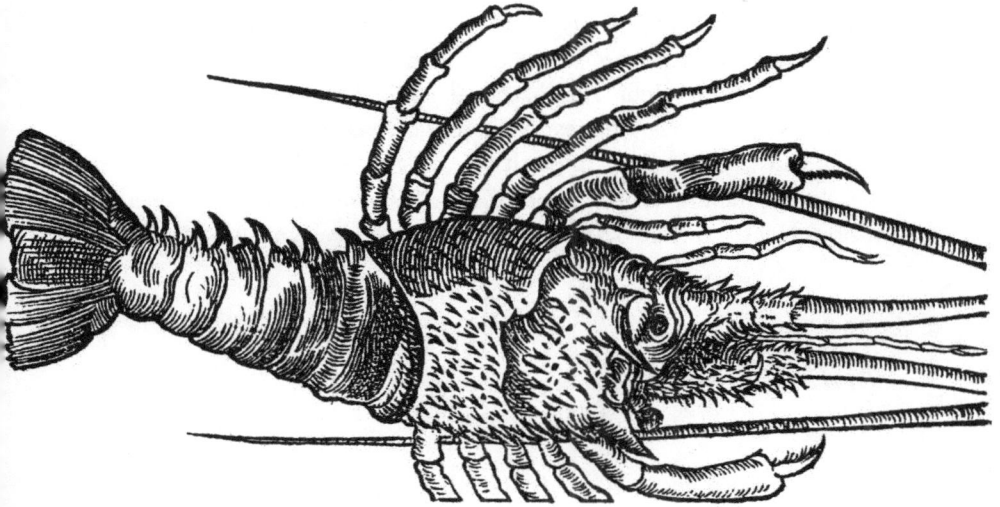

Figure: Portrait of the crayfish, which the Greeks call carabus and the French
sea-grasshopper

Having left Mount Athos to go to Salonica. I got there easily
in two days. Salonica is a large town, well renowned and wealthy,
anciently called Thessalonica, which is mentioned by Saint Paul. It is
situated in Thessaly, adjoining Macedonia, where the plague had so
ravaged the inhabitants that they left the town and abandoned their
property. The Turks among all other nations are the people who are
the least concerned about consorting with those struck down by
plague[108], as I noted in Salonica. I was only two days on the road,
going from Salonica to the mines of Siderocapsa [Sidirokastro] in
Macedonia, which is the place anciently called Chrysites[109]. It is
now a village which brings as much profit to the Turk, from the
great quantity of gold and silver produced there, as the largest town
in the whole of Turkey; and yet it is only quite recently that they

107

have begun to work the mine again to obtain gold and silver. The village was formerly poorly built, but it now resembles a town.

Siderocapsa lies in the valleys at the foot of a mountain, situated on a ridge on the slopes of a hill. I can find no better comparison for it than the town of Joachimstal in the country of Bohemia, called in Latin Vallis Ioachimica. The metals which are worked in Siderocapsa are the reason why the men who extract the ore have settled here and made the place more populous. They have laid out very beautiful gardens and orchards, and there is water everywhere, which is greatly to the benefit of the gardens; and vines in particular are very well cultivated. Those who live at the mines of Siderocapsa are "collected" men[110] and speak various languages, like Sclavonian, Bulgarian, Greek and Albanian.

50

Of the Grand Signior's gold and silver mines, and full discourse of the origin of fine gold

Siderocapsa lies in Macedonia, adjoining Servia. I believe that it is the place of which Diodorus wrote, saying that Philip, father of Alexander the Great, was the first to strike gold philippics, when Crenidas discovered the mines[111] and began to work them; and he said that thereafter the mines yielded every year 1000 gold talents, and much more.

The metal-workers in the mines are now mostly Bulgarians. The peasants of the surrounding villages who come to market here are Christians and speak Servian and Greek. The Jews who are in similar case have so greatly multiplied that they have made the Spanish language also very common, and when speaking among themselves speak no other language[112].

I stayed for some time at Siderocapsa to see the mines, and also because I wanted to know how gold is extracted from its seam. And since gold is the most perfect and purest of all metals, and is given such diverse names in Europe, I wanted to examine whether it acquired them in the mine; but I found that its impurity proceeds only from the perfidy of those who alloy it.

Goldsmiths and coiners give different kinds of gold a variety of names according to their estimate of their greater or lesser value. Thus one kind is called ducat gold, another crown gold, another copper gold, another pistole gold, being respectively equivalent to twenty carats or eighteen carats, and so on with the others, one worth more and another less. But such names and dignities arose in different countries, where the gold was adulterated, sophisticated and falsified by the perfidy of those who mixed it and multiplied it by the addition of other metals of lesser value and less pure. This multiplication was devised by those who increased it in various kinds of modern coins. For ducats, crowns, philippics, angelots and portagues are variously forged from either pure or impure gold. This debasing of the coinage is not a modern invention, for I find that as early as the great days of the Romans, when the republic was unable to meet the expense of its wars they sometimes reduced the weight of the coinage to make a profit on it, adulterating pure silver by adding an eighth part of copper to increase it.

Nature never made any more perfect elementary substance than gold, which is as pure and unmixed as are the simple elements of which it is composed. We are not wrong, therefore, in regarding it as more excellent than any other form of wealth and esteeming it in our judgment as more precious than other metals. For nature being pleased to compose it well proportioned and of equal quantity, well matched in the symmetry of the elements, has made it from its origin already purified, as are the same simple elements, and by this conjunction of elements, all of equal virtue, has engendered such a delicate and perfect mixture in indissoluble union, so faithfully contriving its mingling together that it has produced an incorruptible substance which is permanent for all eternity in its excellence and goodness. That is why it cannot be overcome by the ravages of age and cannot contain within itself or tolerate any excrescence or superfluity of rust. For even if it remains buried in water or in fire for a long space of time it is never stained, and does not acquire any different quality or any dross. It is a privilege which is peculiar to it above all other metals.

The mines of Siderocapsa yield a great quantity of gold and silver to the emperor of the Turks, for what the Grand Turk receives from them every month, not including the wages of the workers, amounts to the sum of 18,000 ducats a month, sometimes 30,000, sometimes more and sometimes less. Those who lease the mines told me that they did not recall that over the last fifteen years the mines had ever yielded less than between 9000 and 10,000 ducats a month for payment to the Grand Signior.

The metals are refined here by the labour of Albanians, Greeks, Jews, Wallachians, Circassians and Servians as well as Turks. There are between five and six hundred smelting ovens scattered about in the mountains of Siderocapsa, which ordinarily smelt the ore; and each oven has its particular masters, who employ the workmen as their own expense. The workers who dig out the ore underground and bring it to the surface do not have the use of the caduceus, called in Latin *virga divina,* which the Germans use to find the seams, but without any other kind of calculation pursue their digging according to what they find.

The pyrites and marcasites[113] found here are of different colours. They never find either gold or silver in the pure state except after smelting. There is no copper or cobalt ore, and they do not use charcoal. There are no fluors in the ores. They carry out the excoction[114] of metals in a different way from the Germans.

The rules for the distribution of work among metal-workers are well observed here, as in other countries, and the man who separated the silver from the gold by the use of aquafortis[115] was an Armenian Christian. The names that they now give at Siderocapsa to metallic substances are neither Greek nor Turkish, for the Germans who have recently begun to work in the mines have taught the inhabitants to call the ores and mining tools by their German names, which men of other nations, like Bulgarians and Turks, have learned.

Their ovens work differently from those in Germany. They are accustomed to work all week, beginning on Monday and finishing on Friday evening, since the Jews do nothing on Saturday. All the chimneys and smelting ovens are situated on the banks of streams, for the wheel which inflates the bellows must be turned by force of water. There are seven streams which turn the wheels. Their names are as follows: the first is called Pianize, the second Amerpach, the third Kyprich, and those to the east Roschets Isvorz.

The ovens in which the pyrites are smelted are poorly built, with sloping wooden roofs. The chimneys are wide, and set in the middle of the building, strengthened by stout masonry on the rear side but with only a light wall on the front, which is broken open on Friday evening; for being slightly vaulted they are coated with white smoke or soot, anciently called *spodos*[116], at the place exposed to the flames smelting the ore; which soot sticks to the chimney, deposited by the fumes from the metal. In the vulgar tongue of the Greeks it is called *papel;* others call it *papula;* they make no use of it, and hold it in no esteem. There is also *pompholix*[117], which is rather whiter. And anyone wishing to collect it could easily find ten pounds of either kind every week in the chimneys of the smelting ovens.

The bellows in the ovens are upright, with their nose on the ground, at the bottom of the chimney. They are raised and lowered by arms actuated by a wheel outside the building which is turned by the stream. The wheel has two intersecting ribs, with eight blades fixed transversely in the middle. The first four blades operate the bellows; the other four are not continually in use, for they are used for working other bellows separating lead from silver.

The chimney or oven has a large mouth into which they throw charcoal and ore for smelting, now one, now the other. There are two small openings in the chimney. One is low down, at the bottom, through which the smelted ore flows. The other is rather higher, half-way up the chimney, which is the vent for the wind that blows out here; and since the fire requires to breathe it gets air from this hole. The metal flows out of the lower opening, accompanied by dross, which is always on top and has to be continually removed from the metal underneath, into a small opening adjoining the oven. And since the dross, which is lighter, is of no use the workmen remove it and throw it away. As it cools it forms a crust on the metal, which they scrape off with an iron rod, while the gold and silver and lead which are mixed, and are heavier, remain below.

The fire which is used in separating lead from silver does not burn charcoal, but wood, which is blown to great heat by the bellows. For this purpose the bellows must be set differently from those described above, which stand erect, supported on their nose, while those used for separating out the lead are set at an angle, also worked by force of water and actuated by four arms, as described above. The lead which is smelted by a wood fire is different from that smelted by a charcoal fire, and does not look like lead, but rather metal waste. In the Greek vulgar tongue it is called *molivi*, which means lead in the form of litharge[118], called *molibdoena;* it is then smelted again to produce lead. And the more thoroughly the silver has been purified the finer it will be. The Latins call the dross from the silver *scoria*, which has the coarse name of silver shit, and is thrown away by the metal-workers as being of no kind of use. In the Greek vulgar tongue it is called *leschen;* which is a name that the Germans have taught them.

When they want to resmelt galena[119], that is to say to treat it by excoction, they first break it up and then throw it on a fire of charcoal and wood which they have made for the purpose. The galena, being as hard as marble, would be too tough for the oven were it not treated by excoction. They make a bed of galena, mixing it with much wood and charcoal, and then light the fire; and when it has changed colour they smelt it in the chimney.

Livy, in his description of the mines of Siderocapsa, anciently called Chrysite, says that the kings of Macedonia were successful in their wars because of their great profit from the mines, and were much renowned for the gold and silver of Macedonia. It seems, therefore, that but for this Philip would not have succeeded in his enterprises and that Alexander his son would not have undertaken such arduous tasks. But since it was this that enabled kings to carry out such great endeavours; we must attribute only to gold and silver the honour of carrying through many enterprises and great wars of which they had been the cause. The Roman general Aemilius Paulus, after conquering king Perseus[120], forbade the Macedonians to extract any more gold from their mines, in order to diminish the wealth of the Macedonians and increase that of the Romans. Solinus also tells us that the mines of Macedonia were rich in fine gold.

51

Other discourse of the gold of Peru and the Indies, and also the manner in which metal-workers refine the gold from which the ducats of the Grand Turk are forged, and that there is only one kind of ducat gold in the whole of Turkey

The Grand Turk has expressly commanded that the gold and silver of Siderocapsa should be faithfully purified and refined with great care. I have already described how they are accustomed to separate lead from gold and silver; but there are no great ceremonies about separating gold from silver. This is done only by the virtue of aquafortis, for which an Armenian is responsible. After he has separated silver from gold he causes it to be beaten into square sheets a foot wide and two feet long, of the thickness of the back of a razor. He puts these into a vessel to be sprinkled with powder, having first put in it a layer of a powder composed of salt, alum[121] and powdered tile, and then puts a sheet of gold on this mixture, covers it with powder, puts another sheet on top, covering this with powder, and so continues; then after enveloping all the sheets in the mixture pours vinegar over them. Then after they have been heated in a charcoal fire they are left to be calcined and purified for a whole day until the gold has been thoroughly purified. From this ducats are then forged, and when perfect are transported to Constantinople. This is how the governors of the country have sought to ensure that ducat gold is preferred to all others, since it is known that it is the purest and that other kinds of coined gold have commonly been adulterated.

Coined gold in Turkey is fine ducat gold, which is so pliable and delicate that it can be bent without effort. Its brilliance, like that of any other gold, is not contaminated even though it is handled by dirty hands, but always remains clear and beautiful in its natural colour. Other metals when rubbed against anything leave a stain of their colour; but this is not so with gold, which leaves no stain either of yellow or of black. It is no matter for wonder, therefore, if its colour alone makes us love it, since it seems to have something of the brilliance of the sun's rays, and has such virtue that since its beauty is pleasant to our eyes every man desires it and longs to have it.

When eaten in any form, whether entire, in filings or in leaf, gold is not harmful to life as other metals are, but rather greatly comforts the heart and the vital powers. And although the ancient Greek authors say nothing of this virtue the Arab authors found it out by experience. But, being aware of its virtue, some deceitful men have had occasion to commit great abuses; for, desiring to have a greater name than that of doctor, have called themselves healers, feigning to have found some new virtue in gold, and have made young children chew it in double ducats, feeding them in their own fashion and saving their saliva for use in treating the sick. But since these are such manifest deceits I am satisfied that they will not remain unpunished.

52

Whence came the occasion for the fables about the golden fleece

I have many a time heard disputes between men of learning, doubting whether gold was found in the sand in rivers, as has been thought; and this leads me to say a few words about the matter in this place.

It is certain that in all times men have searched for gold by whatever means they thought best. Experience having taught them that the gold which is mixed with sand in rivers, being heavier and in such small grains, sinks down to the bottom and is difficult to separate out, they devised an ingenious method of sifting it by collecting it in sheepskins which still retained their fleece.

This leads me to suppose that they had not yet discovered the use of mercury, as is the practice nowadays, for the method using sheepskins is no longer in use. But from this method of separating and sifting gold from sand arose the fable of the golden fleece. Jason and the Argonaut, sailing into the Pontus and coming to a river in which the peasants separated out gold with fleeces, had good reason to tell many tales on their return. But what can be said of them is much the same as I shall have to say of the Spaniards and Portuguese in speaking of the gold of Peru; for what gave the Argonauts such renown was not the skin or fleece of a ram but the gold that they brought back in their ship.

I do not know what river they came to[122], but, although Pliny has already named the rivers reputed to have gold mixed with their sand, I have thought it appropriate to insert their names here. The Tagus in Spain, the Hebrus in Thrace, the Rhine and Danube in Germany, the Ganges in India, Pactolus in Hungary, the Ticino, which flows out of Lake Verbanus, the Abdona which flows out of Lake Larius, the Adda and the Po in Italy[123] are renowned for carrying down gold mixed with sand. And since I know that there are many nations which believe that the fish in rivers reputed to have gold feed on it, this seemed to me to be the occasion to say a few words about it; and I thought it worthy of my observation to enquire into the truth of the matter.

The inhabitants of Peschiera on the shores of Lake Garda, and also of Salò, have persuaded themselves that the carp in their lake feed on pure gold; and, nearer home, the people of the Lyonnais firmly believe that char eat no other meat than gold. There is not a peasant round the Lac du Bourget but firmly believes that the whitefish that are sold every day in Lyons feed only on fine gold. Those living on the shores of the Lac de Paladru in Savoy also believe that char live only on gold.

Similarly the people of Lodi in the Milanese told me that the fish called *themolo* or *themero*, anciently *thymalus*[124], grow fat by feeding on gold; but having looked more curiously into their stomachs and observed everything while dissecting them, I found that they live on other things and not on gold, and that char, carp and *themeres* do not have stomachs which can digest gold. The local people say in their common proverb that fish which feed on gold are excellent above all others, meaning those above mentioned, which surpass all other river fish in goodness. Being ignorant of the truth, they assert this as if it were true.

It is generally accepted that wherever gold is found it is refined with great labour and great expense, not excepting the gold of either Peru or India. The Spaniards may say as much as they please about the marvels of the gold of Peru; but nevertheless it appears from a number of passages in their writings about sailing to the western islands that gold from the mine has to be smelted, as in all other places in Europe. But if you believe what they say, anyone arriving in

115

the Indies has only to dig, as when knocking down an old house, to find gold, which he has only to pack up ready for loading on a ship.

But it is clear that that is wrong, for most of the gold that merchants have brought back had been traded by the local people in exchange for other goods, particularly women's jewellery. Although the Spaniards brought back very great quantities of gold when they first went there, they cannot expect to get so much when they go back there now; for what they did when they first arrived can be compared to the exploit of a sergeant who relieves a poor man of any metal that he finds in his house which he had amassed over many years for his use. And if the sergeant has carried off all that he found in the man's house, what hope has the poor peasant of getting as much again except after many more years? The same is true of the Spaniards, who when they first arrived on the islands of Peru searched so successfully and worked so well that they pillaged all the gold and silver that the Indians had gradually amassed over many years. I suggest, therefore, that if they want to get as much again, will they not have to set a time by which the Indians must amass it for them? But in fact they will have to wait a very long time, or else set many men to work, and meet the expense required, for the Indians had won it from the mines by the force of fire, just as we do in Europe.

I believe that I can prove this from what they themselves have written about the matter. And since the Indians do not use money it is to be supposed that their silver and gold were used to make utensils. Although the mines of the Indies are more productive than they are elsewhere, easier to work and at lesser expense than in Europe, and their rivers yield gold mixed with sand of better quality than with us, it is still necessary in both cases to employ much labour and incur much expense to win it, and to spend much time in ridding it of its impurities, It is and not merely, as many people had thought, a matter of finding it already formed into ingots, parcelling them in dozens and packing them for loading on ships.

And as further proof of what I say, the same authors who speak of the king of the Indies whom they took prisoner recognise in their books that there are many buildings used for the smelting of gold and silver, that the mineral gold of the plains is much more difficult to amass than that of the mountains which rise above the richest parts of Peru, that the gold of the mountains is mixed with tin and sulphur, and that in order to separate it from the other metals they light a great fire, hot and glowing, which by heating up the sulphur releases the silver from the conjunction of the other metals and allows it to flow out purified. From which words, taken from the Spaniards' book[125], it is manifest that gold and silver are extracted from the seams and refined there in the same manner as with us; for it must be remembered that, wherever it is mined, it is a mineral and consequently accompanied by a number of other minerals. And so if they sometimes brought back a great quantity at one time it had come from the ransoms of kings and from the trade in which they exchanged their goods for gold.

I determined to say this because many people thought that gold was so common in that country that horses and carts and ploughs were shod only with pure gold.

The gold of eastern India is extracted from the mines in the same way as on the western islands of Peru. By the eastern islands of India I mean the country of Ethiopia, which is ruled by Prester John[126]. The letters written in Latin, which can now be seen in print, sent by Prester John not many years ago to the king of Portugal show that he promised him a thousand times a hundred thousand drachms of gold, which amounts to the sum of a million drachms, if he made war on the Turks[127]. And Prester John did indeed send soldiers and money to fight against them. A million drachms is a very great sum of gold to be given by the Indians to the king of Portugal in one lot; but this does not mean that it did not require great expense to extract it from the mines. Prester John sent another letter to the king of Portugal, four or five years after the first, in which he asked him to send men from the country of the Christians in all kinds of trades, particularly workmen skilled in producing gold leaf and in carving medals, good coiners and engravers of gold and silver.

He also wanted good printers, to publish books for him in printed characters; but above all else he asked for a large number of workers fully expert in mining, knowing the skills required of metal-workers, able to recognise the purity of seams of all metals and masters of the science of separating gold and silver from other kinds of metals in the seam. It is manifest from these letters that all the gold and silver of eastern India is extracted from the mines by the industry and great labour of the metal-workers, some of whom are more expert in the art than others, and that the level of skill is not equal for all, not only in Prester John's country but also in the countries of Europe and Asia. And indeed many metal-workers left the mines of Bohemia and Saxony, and also of Germany, to go and work in India, being transported there at the expense of the king of Portugal.

It appears, therefore, that they have been accustomed in both of the Indies to extract gold from the mines at great expense of money and time, as we do in Europe, and that the Spaniards were wrong in speaking so vaingloriously about the matter, knowing very well that they were not writing the truth.

And in order to be able to speak more to the point, I sought to prove that the gold extracted and refined from mines in the west is as fine and perfect as gold from mines in the east, both in the north and the south. For although the east is hotter and drier than the west, and the north is colder and wetter than the south, nevertheless the coction[128] of gold is as perfect in one area as in the other, for the gold produced in the coldest country in the world is as perfect as that produced in the great heat of Ethiopia. This can be proved by experience, since all the gold from mines, from whatever seam it may be, after being refined, is just as perfect in one part of the world as in another, without regard to the climate of the place, whether hot or cold, whether dry or wet. And that this discourse of mine may not seem too severe, I propose to demonstrate the truth by giving reasons for what I have said above.

I maintain that if someone brought us gold from Ethiopia, which is the hottest country in the world, extracted from the mine and then refined and purified, and compared it with gold brought from another country, the most northerly and the coldest that there is, and someone else did the same with gold from the east, and someone else again with gold from the west, all of them after being refined will be of the same quality and show the same colour on a touchstone[129]. For, being refined by the power of fire, it will be found that the substance of the gold from the north will be neither better

118

nor worse and in no way different from the gold from the south, and that all four will be of the same quality. Other metals, even the best refined, are of another nature. They are very easily damaged, but gold, even when drawn out into threads as fine as a spider's web or buried between such corrosive medicaments as sublimate and verdigris, salt and vinegar, even if left for two thousand years, would not be corrupted, but on the contrary would still be refined.

Now if by chance there was anyone who, contradicting this, put forward the example of some animals or plants, or their fruits, and denied what I had said about them, asserting that a fruit is more perfect in one country than in another, and also that an animal thrives better in one country than in another, saying also that iron, steel, copper, lead and silver are purer in one place than in another, I would confess to him that all the above-mentioned things are true, but I deny that there is anything in nature which lasts into eternity and resists all damage, as does gold. All the above-mentioned things are subject to deterioration and change, become corrupted very easily and acquire their qualities, either good or bad, when they first appear and when they come to an end. It follows from this that when they are in full vigour they are not all the same. But gold is incorruptible, is not subject to such changes and will be so as long as the world shall exist. And so it will be permanent, and neither air, nor the other elements, nor the winds, nor the sea will harm it, or either hasten or delay its decline; but it is its nature that makes it so.

Before leaving Siderocapsa I climbed to the summit of the highest mountain in the area, and from there I saw clearly the island of Lemnos and Mount Athos, which are in the Mediterranean Sea. Then, looking towards the mainland of Macedonia, I saw a hilly and mountainous region reaching as far as the eye could see. I also saw two lakes, only a short half-day journey away. Clearly visible, too, was the mining country, with its chimneys and all the smelting ovens, which are scattered here and there in the mountains, both to the east and to the west. Then I saw the two coasts at the base of Mount Athos, at the point where it is joined to Macedonia. They seem, when seen from a distance, to be not very far apart; but when I was there I found that it was more than a half-quarter of a league across.

Most of the trees growing wild in the mountains are beeches, which the Greeks call *ostriae*, another kind of beech, which they call *oxiae*, oaks and chestnuts. Trees cultivated in gardens are pear-trees, apple-trees, almond-trees, walnut-trees, olive-trees and cherry-trees.

The village of Siderocapsa is a place of great antiquity, but within the last twelve or fifteen years it has greatly increased in size.

Here I witnessed the practice of a superstitious form of medicine, and have thought it worth while to describe the treatment. A Turk medicining a Jew who was very sick of the spleen measured his belly with a strip of paper and then took the measurement to a young walnut-tree and cut a piece of bark the size of the spleen; then, after speaking many words in Turkish and performing other ceremonies, returned to the Jew and put the bark on his belly; after which he hung it in the fireplace on a thread and told the Jew that as the bark dried so his disorder would diminish. And since I was present at this treatment I desired to describe it. But the Turk seemed to me but a poor doctor, for he looked for the spleen in the middle of the belly above the navel, which was a sign that he was a poor anatomist.

I found two kinds of snakes here that I had not seen anywhere else. The Greeks called them in their vulgar tongue *sapidi* or *sapiti*, names which correspond to what the ancients called *seps* or *sips*. The pyrites or marcasites of Siderocapsa have changed their Greek name into a foreign one; for there are none of the inhabitants, whether Greek or foreign, but call them *ruda*. Others say *quitz* or *ritz*, in the manner of the Germans; it is the dross that the Latins call *scoria*. The metal-workers, whether Servians, Bulgarians, Albanians, Jews, Turks or Greeks, call it by its German name, *schlakna*.

There is another kind of dross different from *schlaken*, which they call *lesken*, which is heavier than *schlaken*. This name seems to me to be rather German than Greek. *Schlaka* or *schlaken* is a light, spongy dross, like dross from metal; it is found floating on top of the gold and silver ore after smelting and is thrown away. For wherever metal is smelted no use is made of this useless dross. But *lesken* or *leskena* is very heavy, and is of more use than *schlaken*, for the Germans and Bohemians use it to mix with other metals. And just as *stimmi*, which the Latins call *antimonium*, is a common

120

metal resembling *lesken*, obtained in the same manner and of the same substance and almost similar in all respects, produces gold and silver pyrites, which are much used by bell-founders and pewterers, and above all by those who make mirrors and cast type, *lesken* could equally well be used in a mixture with other metals. But there was no one at Siderocapsa who was prepared to make use of it; and yet I am sure that it could well be smelted with iron to make cannon-balls, and would improve them greatly and save much expense.

Although I said nothing about it to anyone in that country, since it seemed to me that I must be wrong in this, seeing that there is such a great quantity all over the mountains that two million pounds of it could be found without difficulty, not only in the areas where the mines are now worked but also at various places in the mountains where mines were worked in the past. I know it by no other name, not having been able to learn its ancient name; for the Greeks working in the mines have retained very few of the ancient names.

The inhabitants of the Siderocapsa area gather great quantities of leaves from the shrub that the Arabs call *sumac* and the Greeks *rhus*, which they find growing in the mountains. They use them to thicken skins and tan leather, just as the Egyptians do with pods from a tree which is common in Egypt called *acacia*, and as the Greeks and Anatolians do with the calyces and acorns of *esculus*, the Sclavonians with black myrtles, the French with oak bark and the people of Lesbos and Phrygia with the barks of the wild pines called *piceae*. And since they have abundance of this shrub they load it on to ships for transport elsewhere. They also diligently gather the fruit of this shrub for sale; first drying it somewhat, then skinning it, taking off only the thin red outer skin, and throwing away the hard stone; then they sell it in the markets for sprinkling on food, either broth, gruel or other such soups cooked after their fashion.

53

Description of other singularities found in the mines and in the mountains in this region

We went on purpose to see a mine shaft which had until recently brought great profit to its owner, who was a Jew; but he had been constrained to abandon it, although it had an abundance of metal, for in it there was a metal demon, which the Latins call *daemon metallicus*. And since it appeared frequently to the mine-workers in the shape of a goat with golden horns, they called the shaft *hyarits cabron*. It was above the village called Piavits in the mountains very near the stream called Rotas. This demon was so repulsive that no one would go there, either by himself or in company. Fear or fright did not generally prevent the miners from going into the mines, for there are other metal devils who I was told did no harm. There were others also which helped the men to work in the mines.

The machines that they use for bringing out the ore are not all the same, for sometimes the seam is so deep underground that two horses are required to pull them, but when the ore is not deep underground the machine can be pulled by four men. Sometimes too the mine is worked open-cast. There was a time when the metal-workers smelting the ore had great difficulty with their ovens, when the opening in the middle of the oven through which the air from the bellows is vented was continually being blocked by the dross from the metal and they had to stop work. But one day a passing stranger taught them a way of remedying this great inconvenience. They thought him simple-minded for teaching them this without charging them anything; for if he had thought of asking them for money they would readily have clubbed together and given him 6000 crowns for showing them how to do it. The method or secret of dealing with the problem was this. As I have said, the chimney is broken open on Friday evening and closed up again on the following Monday, when the oven and surrounding area have cooled down; then they throw a great quantity of charcoal into the oven, then on top of this a layer of ore, then a layer of charcoal, and so on alternately until the chimney is full. They do all this first, and then they set light to the charcoal and direct the flow of water over the wheel. This in turning blows up the fire, which continues to burn the charcoal and as it is consumed and diminished smelts the ore. The process thus continues day and night without stopping, and as the charcoal burns and the ore is smelted they throw into the oven a quantity of white stone broken down into small pieces, so as to prevent the vent through which the air is expelled from getting blocked.

This stone is shiny and gravelly, and is called by two different names in different nations. The Servians, Bulgarians, Wallachians and Turks call it *varouitticos* or *varouitnicos,* or by another Greek name, *assuest* or *asuest*[130]. This is the stone that was shown to them by the man mentioned above; and they need to throw some of it into the chimney three or four times a day, either more or less according to how much the vent through which the air passes is blocked by the metal while it is smelting.

There is a small village above Siderocapsa, situated on the summit of the mountain on the east side, called Piavits, which is very ill-provided, with only a few small houses roofed with planks of wood. Below, at the foot of the mountain, is a large village called Serine.

When I was on the mountain above Piavits I found large pieces of scoria or *schlaken;* and since it is a long way from any streams I wondered whether in past times wind rather than water was used to activate the bellows in smelting ovens. For seeing that there was no stream, and that nothing was more certain than that they had smelted metal there, it seemed to me that they could not have had the skill to adapt the wheels which are now turned by water power to inflate the bellows used to smelt metal ores, and that the bellows must have been worked by the labour of men. And certainly the ancients had some means of extracting and refining metals in great quantity.

I came upon some young Greek boys who were gathering a kind of heather which is known throughout Greece as *phana*. When I asked what was the difference between heather and *phana* they told me very readily, demonstrating the difference between the two by one single characteristic. This was that when they went out to collect *phana* for use as fuel they did not take any iron tool with them to dig it out, for it can be pulled out of the earth with all its roots with little force, whereas heather could not be uprooted without a pick. The roots of *phana* extend sideways through the earth and go no deeper than those of the shrub *cistus* or privet.

The sea which anciently was called Chalcis is no more than a quarter of a league from Serine; there is a safe harbour for boats at the head of the bay on the Gulf of Chalcis[131]. There are ordinarily more than 6000 men working in the mines of Siderocapsa, and since the village of Serine is almost on the sea and the smelting ovens are near it the workmen go there to get provisions, and the boats in the harbour bring supplies from far and wide.

After they have worked all week, and have recovered the metal and separated the lead from the gold and silver, and the gold and silver have been purified, it remains only to separate them with aquafortis. And although the gold has been rid of the dross it is purified yet again and refined in the manner that I have described; and then it is cast into ingots and drawn out into round strips the thickness of a man's finger and two or three toises long. Then small notches are cut in them and they are divided into small pieces with a hammer and chisel; after which they are weighed in scales and flattened, and then stamped to form ducats, and finally transported to Constantinople.

The lake called in the vulgar tongue Peschiac or Covios is only two days' journey from Salonica and half a day from Siderocapsa. In the lake are various kinds of fish, which I wanted particularly to see. They catch a kind of fish which the local people call *laros*, which has given its name to a bird called by the Greeks *laros*, by the Latins *gavia*, which the French call *mouette* (gull) and the men of Le Havre[132] *mauve*. And since gulls are fond of this small fish they have taken its name.

I brought back some of the fish called *claria*, and when I was showing them in public a number of Jews gathered round and told me that this fish had scales and so they could eat it; for the Jews, wherever they are, never eat fish unless it has scales. But I, not seeing any scales on these fish, put them into such a state of doubt and dispute among themselves that they almost came to blows. Those who had recently come from Spain accused the others pf practising a bad custom. The priests who were present among them, considering the matter in detail, examined the fish more closely and found some rudiments of scales. Then they agreed together, having concluded that they could eat the fish without any scruples. Nevertheless I find that *claria* has no scales, and that it is what in Lyons is called a *lotte* (burbot) and in Paris a *barbote*.

I also found a small fish which they call a *liparis,* that is, fat, of which the authors have left no description, and of which we have only the name in Pliny. The fish caught in Lake Covios are called in the vulgar tongue by the following names: *perchi, plesti, platanes, lipares, turnes, grivadi, chella, schurnuca, posustaria, cheronia, claria* and *glanos.* These are the names used by the villagers of Pischar, Redina and Covios, which are situated on the shores of the lake.

I also saw other small fish in the market, caught at the mouth of a small stream. The Greeks call them *gyllari,* which I took to be the fish that Euthydemus calls *gelariis;* but these fish are none other than small mullets, which the people of the Propontis call *cephalopola.*

In the humid valleys in this territory, which is also a mountainous region, all capillary plants[133], asplenon, *lonchitis altera,* cotyledon and plants which like damp conditions, grow freely. This cotyledon, otherwise called *umbilicus veneris*[134], is by no means so rare that it cannot be found in many places in France; but since I had it drawn with its flower and has not hitherto been pictured, I give its portrait here.

La figure du Cotiledon.

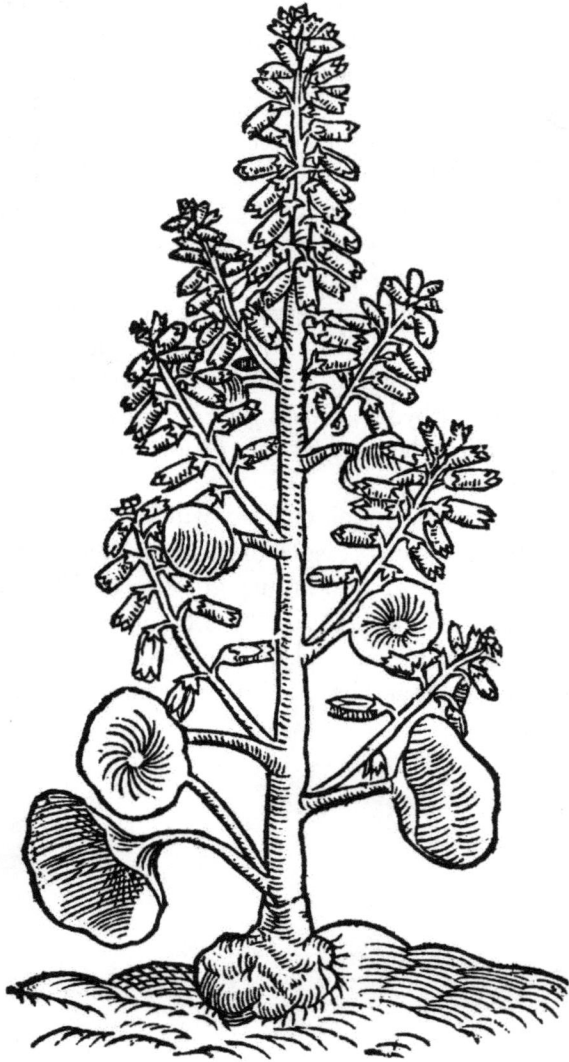

Figure of the cotyledon

I have named these particular plants, although there are many other kinds growing in this area; but when I was there I did not write down anything about the others, and accordingly I do not wish to add anything now. And wherever I was, you must believe that I wrote down day by day what I have noted in this book.

And when I wanted to remember the names of the plants that I saw each day I made a practice of putting a branch or leaf of each plant in a bag, and when I had leisure in the evening or in the shade I took the leaves out of the bag, one after the other, and wrote a description of them as I saw them; which is why I have named heretofore and shall name hereafter many very common plants known to all.

This enabled me to write about them as I have done and to show that they are found in these countries just as they are in ours; and I always had a pick with me to uproot them, and also to dislodge any snakes that I saw hiding in holes in the ground.

54

The names of many wild animals

When I enquired about the wild animals living in their plains and mountains they told me about them, giving their names in the vulgar tongue as follows: *platogni, gouvidia agria, agrimia, zarcadia, agriomochtera, squanzocheros, laphi, alopus, lycos, lagos.*

Platogni are our fallow deer, *gouvidia agria* are wild cattle, *agrimia* ibexes, *zarchadia* roe deer, *agriomochtera* boars, *squanzocheros* porcupines or hedgehogs, *laphi* red deer, *alopus* foxes, *lycos* wolves, *lagos* hares. And since I know that it is a matter of no small difficulty it seemed to me that it might not be amiss to say a few words about them here, beginning with the roe deer, which is commoner in mountainous country than in plains.

I find the name *zorcadia* to be related to *dorcus*. Solinus, writing *capream* in Latin, means the animal that the French call ibex.

Yet Theodore[135], imitating Plato in translating Aristotle, always rendered *dorcada* as *caprea*. Nevertheless it is manifest that the roe deer, which the people of Rome, speaking Italian, call *capriolo,* which is sold by the pound in Rome in winter, has small branching horns like those of a stag, which fall every year. It is of similar corpulence to a stag, except that it is smaller, but has the particularity that it has no tail, as Aristotle already noted. It is the animal that Aristotle called *dorcus*. I propose to prove that it matches the animal which Pliny calls *caprea*, except that there is some small difficulty about the text; but if it is read in the following fashion there will be no difficulty: *Capreis, ramosa dedit natura, sed parva*[136]. Then for *nec* substitute *et;* so that it reads *et fecit ut Cervis decidua*[137]. The text will then be in agreement with Aristotle, who writes of the roe deer in these terms: *Inter Cornigera omnium quae explorata habemus, minimum Dorcas est in cervino quoque genere numerandus, ut qui Cornua habeat omnibus annis decidua*[138]. The Greeks give it various names, some *dorcus*, others *zax*, or *dorx*, or *dorcalis*. Columella calls it *capreolus*.

This shows that the roe deer was known to the ancients; and it is now known by its name in the vulgar tongue to everyone almost everywhere. I bring in here a portrait of the chamois, which the Greeks called *cemas*. The king calls it an *isard*, but that is an old French term. The Latins called it *rupicapra*, for they live among hard and rugged rocks, both for sleeping at night and as a retreat during the day after they have eaten the plants in the valley. And in order that everyone shall know of what animal I am speaking I have had it represented from life.

Le portraiƈt du Chamois ou Yſard.

Portrait of the chamois or isard

If the horns of the isard or chamois were branched it could be said that that this was the animal that Pliny meant when, speaking of the *caprea*, he said: *Nec fecit ut Cervis decidua*[139]. For it does not lose its horns in winter, any more than do ibexes; but since the horns are not branched it cannot be *caprea*. It has indeed the habits of the roe deer and a similar coat, but it is of a different nature. Its horns are small, black and rounded, rising straight up from the forehead, between the eyes, and curling back at the tips. It often happens that in scratching its rear parts the horns enter so deeply into the flesh that it cannot withdraw them, and so dies, because they are turned back in the form of a hook.

It is smaller than a fallow deer or an ibex, with a black line running along its back. Its ears are smaller than those of a sheep. It has a tawny coat, with a black line along each side and another along the muzzle, starting from the root of the horns and passing above the eyes to end above the lips. It has a mark in the shape of a star on the forehead. The upper side of the tail is black, well covered with hair, and is round and as long as that of a fallow deer. The French name of the chamois does not seem to me to be modern, but to be derived from the Greek *cemas*, which is mentioned by Aelian.

I must also mention another animal of this species, which, not having found any French name that fitted, I have been constrained to call by its ancient name, as given to it by the authors, which is *tragelaphus*, a combination of goat and stag[140].

It is similar in coat to the ibex but has no beard. Its horns do not fall off; they are similar to those of a goat but are sometimes twisted like a ram's. Its muzzle, the fore part of the head and the ears are like those of a sheep, and the purse of the genitals is like that of a ram, hanging down and very large. Its four legs are white, resembling those of a sheep. Its thighs, in the part under the tail, are white; the tail is black. The hairs on its stomach and the upper and under sides of its neck are so long that they seem like a beard. The coarse hairs on the shoulders and breast are long and black, with two grey patches, one on each side of the flanks; and the nostrils are black and the muzzle white, as also is the whole of the underside of the belly.

Now since I have previously spoken of the *hippelaphus*[141], I will repeat that king Francis had a horse with the rear parts of a stag, and some thought that it should bear that name; but that cannot be so, for Aristotle says that the *hippelaphus* had horns. It is also said that it was engendered by a stag which had mounted a mare, which is not true of a *hippelaphus*. It remains now for me to give the portrait of this *tragelaphus*, since it has not been shown anywhere else.

Portraict de Tragelaphus.

Figure: Tragelaphus

I have already mentioned that the Greeks call the fallow deer in their vulgar tongue *platogna*, and anciently *platycerotas;* however Aristotle does not use the term *platyceros*, but always says *prox*, which the translators render as *dama*. It is almost of the corpulence of the stag; it is thus larger than the roe deer, but different in colour. A fallow deer has a smaller head than a stag. Its horns fall off every year like those of a stag, and are farther forward than in other kinds of deer. Its back is tawny-coloured, with a black line running along it. It has a long tail reaching down to the hock, as in a calf. It happens frequently that their sides are dappled with white spots, which they lose as they grow older; and it also sometimes happens that the females are white all over, so that they could be taken for goats were it not that they have very short hair. Examples of their horns, of notable size, are displayed in various places, like those to be seen on the way up to the château of Amboise.

Also to be seen there is an effigy cut in stone of another animal of this kind, on which horns have been put from another animal which had worn them; it has seemed to me worthy of mention; for I believe that it is the one that Aristotle called *hippelaphus*, since it has a beard like the ibex. However that may be, it was a very rare animal, which I think must have been seen in France; for otherwise it would not have been represented in effigy in relief with its horns.

55

Journey from Siderocapsa to Bucephala, and of the river Strymon, and of the fish caught in it

It takes only half a day to go from Siderocapsa to the town of La Cavalle [Kavala], anciently called Bucephala, by sea, but by land it takes two long days; the road runs close to the sea for long time, turning and twisting, for it is a deep gulf, in which are both the Gulf of Chalcis and the Gulf of Strymon[142].

It has an abundant growth of plants and shrubs. Androsaces, *chamaesyce*, soldanella, otherwise known as *thalassocrambe*, tree spurges, *myrsinites* and *paralios* are so frequent along the coast that scarce anything else is commoner.

We had the sea to our right and the land to our left. We had sometimes to go over low hills, on which terebinths do not grow into tall trees, as they do on the island of Corfu; but in this rugged, rocky country they grow no taller than hazelnut-trees.

The tallest trees are *aria* and *phylica*, which because we do not have them in our country have no name in our language. Returning to the coast and then turning aside somewhat, we travelled through forests, passing under service-trees and ashes, which are scarcely less tall than firs.

We crossed the stream which flows out of Lake Peschar, otherwise called Covios, but since it was the height of summer we passed it close to the sea dry-shod, for the water had seeped away into the sand. We camped in the plain near the stream, in the shade of the very tall terebinth trees that grow near the coast, and when it was already evening came upon some fishermen who had caught in a line of nets tied one to another some sixty different kinds of fish, of which, after examining them, I wrote a description on the spot.

The gulf flanking Mount Athos, otherwise called *Strimonius sinus*, is so wide and deep that we continued round it for almost a whole day. Soon after leaving it, turning inland towards the town of Tricala [Drama], anciently called Trica, which is now the seat of a *sangiagnar*[143] or captain in Macedonia, and is now one of the finest towns in the whole country, where there is a great quantity of corn for loading on to the ships which put in at the mouth of the Strymon, quite near the town. On our way we came to the Strymon, called Marmara in the vulgar tongue, which flows down from Tricala.

We came first to Ceres [Serres], anciently called Cranon, which is another large town situated in a beautiful plain in Thrace, almost in Macedonia. The river Strymon is now called by several other names in the vulgar tongue, for in the part where it forms lakes it takes the name of the villages lying near it. There are large numbers of swans and other river birds of similar size, which Aristotle called *pelecanes* and Pliny *onocrotali*, which feed in the river.

It flows slowly, has low banks and is not deep, and accordingly has a rich growth of plants, and there is such an abundance of water chestnuts that the ancients were not wrong in saying that in their time the local people fattened horses on water chestnuts, otherwise called *tribulus*.

At some places the river is broad and at others very narrow. It is frequently dammed by weirs constructed to supply mills, as on the rivers in our country. The wheels are not turned by water passing through a trough or a millstream, but in the fashion of the floating mills on the Loire, except that the blades are not so wide. The millers on the river Strymon speak Greek, and from them I learned the names in the vulgar tongue of the fish which they catch in the river, as follows: *cheriscaria, cephalos, glaignon* or *glanos*, that is to say *silurus*, otherwise called *hiena, platanes, chelli, turnes, grinadies, moustacatos* or *mystos*, which is a barbel. The eels here are of very great size.

The river is also called Marmara, because there is a large wooden bridge below the village called Marmara built by Abrahin Basha[144], and a large lake in front of the village which also bears that name. Many ships from Ragusa, Chios and other parts of Greece, from Venice and sometimes from Egypt, put in at the mouth of the river and can in a short time obtain as much corn as they want for their cargo. The ships bring goods from their various countries for sale and sail a good league up the river, sometimes staying there for two months during the winter; and when they have sold all that they brought with them and loaded up with corn, wool or leather they return home in spring.

At the mouth of the Strymon can be seen the ruins of a town, now totally uninhabited, which the local peasants call Chrysopolis. Pliny, however, puts Chrysopolis very near Chalcedon.

Continuing on our way, we went to see the town which is called Ceres in the vulgar tongue, and anciently Cranon, where we stayed only two days. And from Ceres we went to the town of Tricala, anciently called Trica, and then on towards the town of Philippi, skirting a large mountain called in the vulgar tongue Despota.

We were now in level country, in a very large plain, fertile in corn and watered by canals, with many villages. We passed on the left Mount Pangeus, where silver ore is still extracted from mines on the side of the mountain. It is called Malaca or Castagna. All the inhabitants of Tricala and Ceres speak the Greek vulgar tongue, but the Jews who live there speak Spanish and German. The villagers speak Greek and Servian.

When I was in Macedonia I found that the peasants in every town or village gave what we call parsley the name of *macedoniki* or *macedonico*, as they do in other parts of Greece except Cyprus, where they call it *coudomalo*. But celery is generally called in all parts of Greece *selino*, which is diligently cultivated in wet areas and eaten raw. When we passed by way of the mines of Castagna on our journey from Philippi I learned that they yield only silver and lead, and sometimes gold; but I saw them only in passing, without stopping. In all my previous travels I had never seen mistletoe growing on oak-trees, but when we passed through the forests in the plain at the head of the Gulf of Chalcis I saw it in abundance.

There is not an oak-tree between Mount Athos and the towns of Ceres and Tricala but has mistletoe growing on it, which is entirely different from the mistletoe that we see growing on our apple-trees, pear-trees and other fruit-trees; and there is not a villager but calls it *oxo*, for they make a very strong birdlime from it. The arable fields in this country are much spoiled by the shrub *paliurus* and the *rhamnus* tree; for they invade and occupy much arable land.

56

Description of many antiquities and ruins in the towns of Macedonia, and in Philippi and Philippopolis

It is only two days' journey from Trica or Tricala to the remains of Philippi, which is now totally ruined. It is somewhat less than three whole days' journey from Philippi to Philippopolis[145], which is another large town in Macedonia. But since Macedonia is encircled by the river Strymon the authors put it in Thrace.

Philippopolis was formerly called Peneiopolis, but when Philip, father of Alexander, took pleasure in enlarging it he named both towns after himself, one Philippi and the other Philippopolis. Philippi was and still is situated on the great road from Rome to Asia and Constantinople, and is not far from the sea, but Philippopolis lies inland. The great road from Rome to Constantinople, in the time of the Romans, ran by way of the town called Brundusium, crossed the Adriatic Sea to Valona or Durazzo[146] and continued by way of Philippi to La Cavalle [Kavala], and thence by ship to Alexandria Troas.

I spent two days seeing the ruins of Philippi, which is now no more than a village, with only five or six houses built outside the circuit of walls, near the water. Philippi is in the same situation and built in the same fashion as Philippopolis; for it encloses and contains a large area of plain and part of the nearby mountain, up to its summit, where the walls take in a well-built castle; and it has cisterns which are still entire. The walls of Philippi are almost totally ruined, built of brick and cement and at some places of dressed stone, but without any moat or ditches. It is the town of which

Galen speaks, when, having set out from Troy to go to Rome (but in those days Troy was called Alexandria), he travelled on the road that I have described. For after he had been on Lemnos he had to pass through Philippi, in the plain on the east side, with the mountain which serves as its fortress to the west. The plain is so wet that it almost seems to be a marsh. The marshmallow which grows on it has yellow flowers, like those which according to Theophrastus grow near Athens on Lake Ochomenus.

The plant *cytisus,* which we do not have either in France or in Italy, is very common in the plains of Thrace and Macedonia.

There is no place where larger marble sepulchres are to be seen in the fields than Philippi. The marble was quarried in the mountain enclosed within the town's circuit of walls, which are built of pure white marble. A number of inscriptions recording the deeds of the Romans are still to be seen, cut in Latin letters on marble at several places on the mountain.

The island of Thasos, which produced the whitest and the finest marble in the world, lies only a half day's sail away; and I believe that these handsome marble tombs in the fields along the great road came from Thasos. Of all the tombs the one that has remained most entire is that of Alexander's doctor, which still bears his epitaph written in Greek, but in part corrupted by Servian letters, which cannot be properly read.

And just as the sepulchres were hollowed out of a single stone two toises long, half a toise across and the height of a man, so the lid was also carved from a single block. The excellence and grandeur of the town can be judged from the large number of sepulchres, for in ancient times wealthy Greeks were buried in tombs outside the town in the country, so that the inhabitants of the towns were not troubled by the bad smell of the bodies; for they were not accustomed in Greece to burn the bodies of the dead, as in Italy, or to cover them with earth, as we do now. And, nearer home, the Italians have now another manner of burying bodies, differing from ours, for they make vaulted caverns at various places in churches, with an opening on top like the mouth of a well, which they close with a round stone with an iron ring attached to it, with which they raise the stone when necessary. And when a body is brought for burial they drop it in without covering it with earth, and then they close the opening with the stone and plaster all round it. There is a village in the plain, a quarter of a league from Philippi, called Bolisce, where I saw a large block of marble bearing these words: *Neviae musae in testamento*[147], now in use as the trough of a well.

A little way beyond Philippi on the great road there is a large square stone standing erect, like the base of an obelisk, inscribed in Latin letters, which is the tomb of C. Vibius Cor. Quartus. The local people have a fable about it, saying that it is the manger of Alexander the Great's mare. But by the mare they must mean his horse Bucephalus. They took me to see it as a great curiosity. It is of great size and height, standing erect with the upper part hollowed out. The town of La Cavalle[148], which is quite close, was named after Alexander's horse; we shall have more to say about it below.

The ruins of Philippi are more worthy of admiration than those of any other town. I attribute that to the abundant supply of stone, since there is a seam of marble within the town. There is a very fine amphitheatre, reaching up from the level ground to its highest point, which so far has remained entire and would last for many years if the Turks refrained from carrying off its tiers of seating, which are carved from marble. It is not oval in shape, like the theatre at Otricholi or the one in Rome, but round, like those of Nîmes and Verona; for it is not closed in on all sides. The place where you enter looks south, and is open from ground level to its summit. It was built in a place very convenient for the purpose, for at several points it is hewn out of the mountain, in marble carved into steps.

The most ancient things that have remained standing in Philippi are three massive pillars of enormous width and height, which are remains of the temple of Divus Claudius[149], in which there are still an infinity of statues and large marble columns carved in the Doric and Ionic manners, marvellous in structure and of great art. Having found a caloyer from the mountain called Castagna, we left Philippi to see the monasteries on the mountain, which are four in number.

The trees that grow on the mountain are planes, beeches, strawberry-trees, andrachnes, holm oaks, *aria, alaternus,* firs and wild pines and *esculus.* The tree which the Macedonians anciently called the female dogwood and which the French now, in imitation of the Latins, call *sanguin,* are scarcely smaller on this mountain than are our tall male dogwoods.

57

Description of the town of Bucephala, formerly called Chalastrea, and now La Cavalle

After I had travelled about on the said mountain for the space of two days, I came in a day and a half to the town of La Cavalle [Kavala], which anciently, before Alexander named it Bucephala, was called Chalastrea. I did not have to return to Philippi, but left the road on the left.

La Cavalle is a town which was so called after Alexander's horse Bucephalus[150]. Many, reading Pliny's writings, have been in doubt about which country Bucephala was situated in. For when he describes the river Indus he says that the town of Bucephala was the chief town of three inhabited by the Azenians[151], which was so called because Alexander's horse had been buried there. But this same Pliny, writing about Greece, says at the end of the chapter on Achaia[152] that Bucephalus was a port, which he conjoins with Anthedon. And Mela, writing of Greece, and principally of Macedonia, mentions Anthedon, and soon afterwards the gulfs and promontories of the Peloponnese, including the gulf of Bucephalon on the east side, and from what he says it is manifest that Bucephalon was either a promontory or a gulf.

It must be concluded that Bucephala in Greece is a town situated on a promontory projecting into the sea only two leagues from Philippi[153]; and it is now a very handsome place, although not so long ago it was deserted and almost wholly ruined. But since the Turks returned from the Hungarian war, bringing with them all the Jews that they found in Buda, Pest and Albaregal or Albereal [Székesfehérvar], and sent them to live at La Cavalle, Tricala or Trica, and Ceres or Cranon, it has always been inhabited[154]; and there are now more than five hundred Jews among the Greeks and Turks.

The situation of the town is almost the same as that of the town of Lemnos, for it is enclosed by the sea on all sides except the rear part, which is very narrow. There is a large harbour, but it is not safe, so that when galliots and frigates put in there they are beached, and also fustes and barks, for the harbour is not well protected from all winds; though if need be they can ride out a storm, but not without some damage. There are still many cisterns within the circuit of the town, which are all still entire: which recalled to us another ancient ruin in Crete called Helenico Paillo Castro[155], which is on the mountain a little way beyond Quissamus. These ancient cisterns are made of such strong cement that they will last as long as hard marble. La Cavalle is one of the keys of Macedonia, just as Philip called Magnesia[156] one of the keys of Greece.

58

That the walls still to be seen on Mount Hemus show the separation between the forces of Macedonia and Thrace

There was formerly a fortress wall above La Cavalle, which still remains entire, almost a quarter of a league long, situated on the highest summit of the nearby mountain, and there is nothing more certain than that this marked the boundary between Thrace and Macedonia, that is, between the forces and powers of the two kingdoms. For the cosmographers expressly excluded the towns of Philippi and Philippopolis from Macedonia, although they were the capital cities of the Macedonians, and on the hither side of the river Strymon.

This wall which prevents passage above La Cavalle is vaulted, and has two corridors within it somewhat similar to the wall which runs from Saint Peter's in Rome to the Castel Sant'Angelo, constructed in the form of a gallery. At the end of the wall, on the highest point in the mountain, there is a large tower designed to assert its strength in the direction of Thrace.

Some years ago Abrahin Basha[157] restored an aqueduct which had been constructed by the kings of Macedonia to bring water to La Cavalle from a spring more than three leagues away. It comes from a high mountain, and runs along the coast until it comes to a valley; and to enable it to cross the valley he had to build great arches of sufficient height to carry it from the mountain to the town; and these arches are more than 30 toises high. And because of the abundance of water coming from the spring the town, which had been uninhabited, became very populous.

The island of Thasos, which was anciently the base of Alexander's galleys, was only two leagues from La Cavalle. The said Basha also enclosed the town within new walls, on which I found a Latin inscription which had been written in the time when the Romans ruled Greece. I noted it down, as follows: *P. Hostilius. P. S. L. Philadelphus petram inferiorem excidit, titulum fecit, ubi nomina cultor scripsit & sculpsit. Sac. Urbano S. P.* All these letters were at the base of a massive wall.

59

That there are no hostelries in Turkey, but that there are hospices in which to lodge

To show that there are no hostelries in Turkey, I shall speak of a large building which Abrahin Basha caused to be constructed in La Cavalle, which the Turks call a *carbachara*[158]. He also built a mosque adjoining his hospice, to feed and lodge all travellers. And being one of a company of three, with our mounts, we were fed there for three days without complaint and without its costing me anything.

I shall have to speak often of these carbacharas, and so I shall take this one as an example of the others. I know no other name for it in French but carbachara. And in explaining what it is, it should be remembered that there are no hostelries in the countries ruled by the Turk and no places to lodge but these public institutions called carbacharas. They are built in different fashions, but the commonest is that the great lords who have become rich in the household of the Turk, or in some other way, desiring to do some good work in this world and thinking that this will be profitable for their salvation, build such establishments out of charity, not having any relatives to whom they wish to do good. I shall explain the reason elsewhere.

Thinking, therefore, to gain merit by such benefactions, they carry out various works for the public weal, such as a handsome bridge, a fine caravanserai and, adjoining the caravanserai, a mosque and, adjoining the mosque, a bath-house. And in order to maintain all the officers required to serve in these institutions they donate money to meet the necessary expenses, such as paying for the wood burned in them, paying priests to say prayers and conduct the services, paying for the oil burned in the mosques and other things necessary for the kitchens and for those who prepare food for travellers.

Those who lodge in a carbachara or caravanserai must bring their own equipment with them, such as blankets or esclavines[159] and mattresses to sleep on, linen and other requirements, for in the caravanserai they give you nothing but a small empty room, and each traveller must use what he brings with him. When he arrives in the caravanserai each man lays out his belongings, and if he wants water he must fetch it in the jar that he has brought with him. And when the pottage of the caravanserai or hospice has been cooked anyone who wants it must take his own dish to get it. The caravanserai also gives meat and bread. And since the Turks call their pottages by various names I have thought it right to specify the dishes that they give travellers by way of alms. No one who comes there is turned away, whether Jew, Christian, idolater or Turk. Principally they give liberally pottages made from *trachana* or *bohourt*, or *afcos*, or rice.

The inhabitants of the island of Metelin[160] are skilled in baking flour, which they mix with sour milk. They first boil the flour, then dry it in the sun and with it make a mixture which is called *bohourt*. This *bohourt* is transported from Metelin and sent throughout Turkey, where it is much used for making pottages. The people of Metelin make another kind of substance from flour which they call *trachana*, which is in no less demand than the first. It is, in my opinion, what was anciently called *maza* in Greece and Italy. The usage of these two substances, bohourt and trachana, is so great throughout the whole of Turkey that it could hardly be greater; for they cannot enjoy a good meal unless they use them in their pottages.

They are so fond of rice that at least six boatloads of it coming from Egypt are discharged in Constantinople every year. There is also another kind of vegetable of which great quantities are brought from Egypt by sea, called by the Greeks *afcos,* a corrupt form of *aphace.* They bring in a supply of it each season, for distribution as required.

The Turkish fashion of eating is very different from ours, for when the meat is cooked they take it out of the pot and add to it whatever they want to thicken the mixture. And since they make a quantity of it at a time they mix it with a long wooden spurtle. They have no tables to eat off, but sit down on the ground and lay out a round piece of leather to serve as a tablecloth, which is laced like a purse. There is no one in Turkey, however great a lord he may be, but carries his knife in his belt. Each man has his own spoon, and by this means is able to avoid getting his fingers greasy, for they are not accustomed to have napkins. They do, however, have large handkerchiefs, with which they wipe their fingers.

No Turk, who ever he may be, is ashamed of lodging in this kind of hospice, or of accepting alms in the manner that I have described, for it is the custom of the country. A foreigner will be treated no worse than the most eminent personage. What I have said must be taken as applying only to places where such charitable institutions have been established, as at Bucephala.

The said Basha did great works for La Cavalle. In addition to bringing water from a spring to the highest point in the town on arches built at great expense he also directed the water to his mosque and his bath-house and all the squares in the town. He also had three marble sepulchres brought from a field a quarter of a league from the town and set under fountains to serve as troughs for watering travellers' horses.

These four sepulchres bear inscriptions, as follows: *P. C. Asper, Atriarius Montanus, Equo publico honoratus, item ornamentis decurionatus, & iniuraliciis pontifex, flamen divi Claudi Philippis. Ann. xxiij. Hic S. E.* The second is the same size as the first, inscribed with these words: *Cornelia P. fil. Asprilia fac. divae Aug. Ann. xxxv. H S. E.* The third sepulchre is thus inscribed: *Cornelia longa Aspriliae mater. Ann. lx. H. S. E.* They are each eleven feet long, five high and six wide.

Sometimes Turkish women who have some little property have such public works and buildings constructed or in their will bequeath what they have for the benefit of soldiers, so that they will strive more vigorously to fight against the Christians, for they have the false opinion that this is the means of saving their soul by the death of Christians killed by the hand of those to whom they have left such alms. When I was preparing medicine for a man sick of the spleen at La Cavalle I found the manner of making what the ancients called an *elatorium*[161], as was done in times past, that is to say light and white, and of such a nature that it burns in a fire like grease. I believe that in our day there is no one who can boast of having seen such a thing on sale. I shall say more about it elsewhere, when I describe plants in detail.

60

Of the great road from La Cavalle to Constantinople

Taking the road from Bucephala to Constantinople, we found on the summit of Mount Emus, two leagues from La Cavalle, walls similar to those on the hill at La Cavalle, closed against coast of Thrace and controlling the passage into Macedonia over the mountain. From there we made our way down into a plain of great extent, close to the shores of the sea, with the island of Thasos on the right and the high mountains of Emus on the left, which we had already traversed without seeing a single cypress there. We crossed a river which the Greeks call Mestro in the vulgar tongue; the Turks call it Charasou, that is to say Black River. That name would well suit the river Meclas, which gave its name to the gulf called the *Melanicus sinus;* but it is not the same.

I shall speak of it later. This present river is the river Nesus[162], which flows down from Mount Emus, as also does the river Strymon; and Mount Emus is like a fortress wall between Thrace and Macedonia, with one end of the mountain lying between the river Strymon and the river Nesus.

The river Nesus is very sluggish, but nevertheless carries down much gravel, and is only a little smaller than the river Strymon. It flows straight towards the island of Thasos; that is, it is nearer the end that looks towards Samothrace than the point that faces Mount

Athos. The river Strymon, of which we have already spoken, flows into the sea between Mount Athos and the island of Thasos, from which the sea takes its name of *Strimonicus sinus*. The bridge over the river Nesus is of wood, like the one over the Strymon, but is not so long.

At the end of the bridge we found some shepherds roasting whole sheep, except for the head, to sell to travellers. They had spitted them and were roasting them in a fire of willow branches, after removing the entrails and sewing up the belly. No one who had not seen it would ever have believed that such a large mass of meat could be roasted.

However, this is no new thing for the Turks, for when they circumcise a boy in Anatolia whose parents are sufficiently rich they roast a whole ox, spitted on a long iron rod. Inside the ox they put a whole sheep, and in the belly of the sheep a hen, and inside the hen an egg. Then, after sewing up the belly of the ox, they roast it on a great fire, so that all these viands, down to the egg, are cooked. All the meat thus cooked is eaten by the relatives of the circumcised boy at a great feast. The shepherds that I have spoken of cut the sheep into pieces when it is roasted and sell it to passing travellers. We camped under willows at the end of the bridge in order to rest our mounts, and bought some of the roast mutton, which we judged more flavoursome than if it had been roasted in separate pieces.

After we had dined we set out on our way again and made a good day's journey, reaching the town of Bouron [Lagos], which still retains its ancient name, where we lodged. It is situated near the lake called *Bistonius lacus*[163].

Our road took us over a fertile plain of meadowland covered with *cytisus, halimus* and *rhamnus* (which, however, is not the currant-bush). As for *halimus,* although its natural habit is to grow into a substantial thornless shrub, as in Crete, here it spreads over the ground in the fashion of a spiny caper-bush.

We found the plant called *scordion* near the town of Bouron, which can be compared in size with Aigues-Mortes and is similarly situated in a large humid plain close to a salt-water lake. Lake Bouron or Bistonius brings great profit to the country, for there are excellent fisheries. The sea here never grows or diminishes, any more than do the Pontus Euxinus, the Propontis, the Hellespont and much of the Aegean Sea.

They catch in the lake great quantities of small fish resembling the bleak, which the Greeks in Bouron call *lilinga*, and in Constantinople *licorini*. It is the fish that Galen called *lentiscus*, and is called *vandoise* in Paris and in other countries chub. They prepare it as we do with herrings, salting it, smoking it and drying it, and then sending it in cartloads and boatloads to many parts of Greece and to Italy. They prepare it in the same way as the people of Boiana do with *scourances*. I find no difference between the *scourances* of Albania and *licorini* except that they are smaller.

Most of the men of Bouron are fishermen; for, having a lake so rich in fish close by, they are active in catching them. The asparagus of Greece has sharp pointed leaves, which they call *corruda;* and the cultivated variety grown in gardens, which has rounded leaves, finding the soil in this plain so much to its liking, was so common that no other plant was to be seen. We came to a small township called Commercine [Komotini], which is half a day's journey from Bouron, where there were all kinds of viands which we were glad to buy. There are the ruins of a small castle, in which is the church of the Greek Christians; for the village is inhabited by Greeks, with very few Turks.

61

Of a very ancient place in Thrace called Cypsella, with the manner of making alum

After staying encamped for some time at the town of Commercine, under trees of *esculus* and *aria*, we set out again over the plain, with the mountains on our left, and came to another village called Cypsella [Sapes]. I had resolved to travel by way of Cypsella on purpose to observe the making of rock alum. I stayed for three and a half days at the place where it was mined. Wherever alum is worked it is almost always by open-cast, that is, when the seam of ore is near the surface; although at Cypsella there are places where the rock is extracted from a depth of six toises.

The village of Cypsella is in Thrace, and is called by that name in Greek, and Chapsylar in Turkish. Most of the inhabitants are Turks, with only a few Greeks. There are also some Jews, one of whom had the farm of the revenue from alum. I lodged with him in order the better to learn the truth about the manner of making alum.

I found that the alum which is made at Tolfa in Italy, in the territory of the pope, is similar to that of Chapsylar, as I was able to see when, travelling from Civitavecchia to Rome at the time of the creation of Pope Julius III[164], I had only to deviate a little way from the main road to go to Tolfa. The alum made at Chapsylar is perfected and refined at the place where the rock is extracted from the mine, and is thus made at less expense than the alum of Tolfa, which has to be transported from the seam in carts to the place where it is smelted. And although the alum is concentrated only by lixivium[165] from the ashes of the rock extracted from the mine, which must first be burned, no one is permitted to make it but the man who has taken the farm of the revenue from the mine. The rock is extracted at the roots of the mountain, which I believe to be Mount Serrion.

The village of Cypsella is beside the great road that runs from Durazzo to Constantinople, situated at the point where the path goes off to the summit of the mountain. The mines lie a little off to the left. The rock is extracted from the mine with very great difficulty, and is so hard that it has to be broken up with great blows of hammer and chisel; and then it is smelted, in the same way as in the making of lime or plaster. And since there is an abundance of wood, and the rock does not need to be taken any distance from the mine, the workmen smelt it at the place where the ore has been extracted. They work by task, and each of them has his own little lodging or house, in which, set in the ground, are four wooden troughs, into which the lixivium is poured until the alum is congealed and reduced to rock as we see it.

The rock which contains the alum is first built into a vault and burned in a light fire, as is done in making plaster; for if it was over-heated the substance of the alum which it contains would evaporate through the heat of the fire. It thus remains hard, and when exposed to rain for two or three months resolves itself into powder. For just as marl, with which fields are fertilised, is not softened and broken down into powder immediately it had been quarried but is left for some time exposed to the air and gradually dissolves through the action of the dews of night, rain by day and the frosts of winter, making up for the lack of dung, so this hard stone is roasted only in a light fire and remains entire, as if the fire had not made any change in it, and after being left for some days in the open is so much softened by the dews of night and rain by day that in a short time it is all converted to ash.

Rock from the alum mine which has not been roasted, when built up into walls or other masonry remains unchanged, like all other stones. After the rock is reduced to ash, either by natural rain or by rain produced by art, it is finally baked with the water from which lixivium is made, which is put in square troughs or earthenware or wooden jars, and there congeals in ten or twelve days. Such is the manner in which alum is made at Chapsylar, which when transported to Italy is called alum of Metelin [Mytilene].

But since there is both red and white alum, I will venture to say that the mine producing white alum can also produce red; for the colour results only from the method of making it, according to whether the ash has been well or ill treated. Alum produces a dross which some of the workers keep and make into a red dye which in France is known as earth of Macharon, though it is not preserved at Chapsylar. The valleys are red with this dross, which is carried down by mountain streams along with rainwater.

62

Of the great road made anciently from Rome to Constantinople

Continuing on our way to Constantinople and beginning to climb the mountain, when we were some way up we looked back and could clearly see the road that we had taken from Lake Bistonius, which is now called Lake Bouron, and the village of Commercine, which is situated in a very large plain. The road over this plain was the ancient great straight road from Rome to Constantinople, which was paved with very large stones hewn in the antique fashion, for between Bouron and Commercine, and between Commercine and Chapsylar, where there was difficult going on heavy soil, the Romans paved it, and it still remains entire today.

I can prove by this that the Romans anciently made this road from Rome into Asia, and also that this paving shows that it was not mere prentice work, for it is perfectly straight. And to go to particular places you must leave the paved road either on the right or on the left. At some points the road runs through woods, and there are tall trees which have grown between the stones of the paving since those days.

We climbed Mount Serrium, which is steep and difficult at many places. It can be seen in many places that the rock was cut with chisels and other tools, which cannot have been done without great expense.

This great work makes me think that the road from Rome to Constantinople was much frequented. And it is also notable that Pliny, writing of the distance between places in Greece, always counts from Dirrachium, which is a town near Valona, now called Durazzo, and the port at which travellers coming from Italy landed in Greece after crossing the Adriatic Sea; saying that from Constantinople to Durazzo he makes the distance 711 miles. And he takes this as being the distance from the Propontis to the Adriatic Sea.

We came to a village inhabited by Greeks on the summit of the mountain, where we had for greater security to take two men on foot to guide us on the mountain, on which there is a great quantity of the herb miscalled in French winter savory, which we found growing in abundance among the rocks, and which I had already seen in Crete, and a few days earlier in the amphitheatre at Philippi, and later saw on the mountains at Spoleto in Italy, in the march of Ancona. But since it is now grown commonly in our gardens, I will note its ancient name as I learned it from the inhabitants of Crete and the island of Cytherea, who call it in the vulgar tongue *tragarignani*, which is the same as *tragoriganum*[166].

63

Of the river called Marissa, anciently Hebrus, and of the pillaging of the Turks

There is no bridge over the river Marissa [Marica], and so it must be crossed by boat. The custom of the country is that a man and his mount pay only one asper for the crossing; but I was compelled to settle for fifteen for my guide and myself, for the avarice of the Turks is such that when they find themselves at some advantage over foreigners they pillage them of all that they can, and the person must perforce pay what they demand. Their desire to exact ransom is such they would not spare even their own father if they have some small occasion to get money from him.

A quarter of a league from the port we passed a small township called Vire situated in very beautiful country on the slopes of a hill and surrounded by ancient walls.

This river, now always called Marissa in the vulgar tongue, was anciently called the Hebrus. The inhabitants of the villages round the river Hebrus have the practice of drawing great mounds of sand from the river in summer, when it is low, knowing that the sand will contain some small quantity of grains of gold; and they make sure that the mounds are at some distance from the banks of the river so that when it overflows it will not carry them away. For the purpose of separating the gold from the sand they assemble wooden planks with holes in them to wash out the gold with water from the river. If they find some small portion of gold it is at the cost of great labour and expense and much time; and in any case without quicksilver they cannot much profit from it. The rivers Strymon and Nesus flow into the sea near each other, the one below the island of Thasos and the other above it. But the Hebrus reaches the sea opposite the island of Samothrace, as Pliny noted. The river flows so slowly that it seems not to move at all. The water is turbid, but very sweet, and so cold at the height of summer that it seems icy. There are many tamarisks growing along its banks. It has many bends, and turns back on itself as the Seine does between Paris and Pontoise. So much water comes down from the mountains in winter that it carries all before it, flooding a great expanse of meadowland, called Doriscus, where Xerxes mustered his army on his way to Greece.

Since the meadowland is flooded every year and turned into marshes there are no villages on it, though in summer it is grazed by large numbers of horses. The Grand Signior himself has more than 1000 horses grazing here in summer, and I believe that the inhabitants of the local villages have scarcely less than 500. The meadowland is so clean that there a no moles, snakes, mice, rats or fieldmice on it; for the winter flooding drives them all away. The plant *cytisus* can be seen growing in many places. The villages round the meadows are situated along the hills, for the land, being surrounded on all sides by hills and mountains with many streams, is very suitable for ploughing and provided with all necessary things. The country people here have multiplied greatly.

In some places the banks of the river are quite high, where river halcyons, commonly called kingfishers, and swallows make their nests in the earth, as also does the bird called *merops* or *apiaster*, which the inhabitants of Crete call *melissophago*. Having had occasion to observe these halcyons, I find that they are no different in any respect from those that live on the banks of our rivers, for their nests are also made from the bones and scales of small fish, like ours.

The villagers living near the river Marissa have gardens in the meadowland along the course of the river, for, having an abundance of water and very good soil, they cultivate melons, *copous*, pumpkins, gourds, cucumbers and other such summer fruits. They told me that dasheens also grow here in some places, but this I cannot confirm.

We now came into hills at the end of the plain and entered a region of low mountains, in which I observed a species of maple different from all those that I had previously seen. It was the sixth species among all the others that I have noticed. It grows into a small shrub, of which I shall speak elsewhere at length, when I come to describe trees.

We came upon some natural hot baths some way inland opposite the island of Imbros, when we were at the river called Melane and the bay of the same name, which encloses Gallipoli on its peninsula, on which is Sestus, lying opposite Abydus[167]. There are two hot springs in these baths, one which has been set aside for men, the other for women; and as it costs nothing to bathe in them, there is no one to clean them and so they are very dirty.

Here can be seen the ruins of a town and walls of great extent, which the authors call Macrontichos[168], which lie close to the baths, and provided protection against enemies threatening harm to Thrace.

64

That some nations leave their country at certain times of year, and then return at another season

Continuing on our way to Constantinople, we encountered large bands of poor Albanian peasants, otherwise called Ergates, who were returning to their country from working in Turkey. Like the Lombards and Savoyards who leave their country at certain times of year and return at some other time, these poor Albanian peasants leave their country in troupes to live elsewhere, for their own country is barren. They go to Turkey in summer to harvest corn and earn some money. When they come to countries fertile in corn, like the plains of Macedonia and Thrace or Anatolia, they are employed by the Turks to gather corn and extract the grain. And when the season is over they return home to live with their wives. They have a way of cutting the corn which is more laborious than the French way; their sickles are somewhat different, being flat, broad, without teeth and less curved. When cutting the corn they hold it in their right hand, with a wooden implement in their left hand, which is slightly curved and pointed at the end, with three holes in which they put three fingers of the left hand, the little finger, then the second and the third. They keep the thumb and the finger next to it free to grasp the corn; then, opening their hand and grasping the corn, they cut a much larger handful. After that they thresh the corn, not with flails as in our country but with oxen, as is the practice throughout Greece; and in doing this they draw after them wooden boards in which are fixed chalcedonic stones[169], which cut up the straw and crush it.

And since I have compared these Albanians with the Savoyards and Lombards, I will add that I have seen them setting out in troupes, like flocks of starlings. The Savoyards go to Italy to cut down poplar trees along the Po and holm oaks, that is to say *ilices*. in Friuli, and other kinds of hard wood in Tuscany and Romagna; but the Savoyards are different from the Albanians in this respect, that the Albanians leave their country at the height of summer and return home in the autumn, while the Savoyards leave home in autumn and return in spring. For since they live in the mountains, snow prevents them from doing anything all winter, and also because the timber which they cut in Italy during the winter is hard and laborious to cut, which is a task that they could not do in summer, while if they stayed at home they would be idle all winter. But when they return to their country in summer they find firs, wild pines, larches and other like soft woods which give them less labour to cut in the heat of summer.

The Lombards do the same as the Albanians and Savoyards, for they set out in bands, keeping together in large troupes until they are out of their country; but when they reach Germany, France, Flanders, Denmark and other more distant countries they separate, each one going by himself to the place that he has in mind, sweeping chimneys here and there during the winter. But when they return home they are like the storks, which come each one by itself. And this is the way in which men of different countries are constrained to go and seek a living at certain times of year in countries other than their own.

The Albanians, anciently called Epirots, are Christians, and speak a language of their own different from Greek. They are, however, of the religion of the Greeks, and since they live on the confines of Greece they also know the Greek language. And when they return to their country they live all winter on the money that they have earned in Greece. They almost all go barefoot, and are extremely poor, as people of little expense and great labour. And so they never fail to find work all summer in the fields in Turkish villages, for the Turks are lazy, little given to the labour of tilling the soil, slow, tardive and very dilatory in their business. Continuing on our way, we found stones of jasper and many colours about the countryside, and also stones of chalcedony; and the walls of houses in villages in this country are sometimes built of jasper and chalcedony.

65

That the trees called terebinths bear a kind of gall that is in great usage in Turkey

The peasants of Thrace and Macedonia, knowing the great usage of the galls on the terebinth trees which grow in the hills, and having abundance of them, do not let slip the occasion for the profit that they can get from them; for they go out towards the end of June to gather the fruits under the leaves at the foot of the branches which bear the seeds in clusters, and there they find a small gall which is hollow within, the size of a hazelnut, which if it was left to increase in size would grow longer in the fashion of a small horn; but they gather it while it is still small and sell it for a high price to dye fine silks in the town of Bursa. .

We continued on our way through Thrace, and encountered a caravan or company of muleteers from Salonica who were going to Constantinople; and we lodged in a village called Aignegic.

Since the Greeks do not eat tortoises or either marine or freshwater turtles, they are so numerous in the countryside of Greece, and particularly of Thrace, that they are commonly seen on the main roads, of very large size. And were it not that gardeners are much afraid of them, since they eat plants which bring them profit, and are particularly fond of melons, pumpkins, cotton and sesame, no one would kill them. But when gardeners find them in their gardens they kill them and then impale them on a hedge.

66

That the Turks when travelling about the country incur little expense

On the following day when we continued on our journey, I found that birthwort was very common in the fields. We also saw true hyssop, two kinds of *polium* and *chamaedrys*.

We found all things necessary for our sustenance in the villages, such as butter, eggs, poultry, bread, cheese and milk. All the carters and muleteers in our caravan made provision of a kind of sour milk called oxygal[170], which they carried in cloth bags hanging from the packsaddle of their beasts. And although this milk is very liquid it remains enclosed in the bags, without leaking through the fabric.

The Greeks and Turks are accustomed to take husked garlic, beat it up in a wooden vessel and mix it with oxygal. It is a dish fit for a great lord, so pleasant it is to eat, and it is eaten not only by carriers but also by the great ones at the court of the Turk. And for anyone who does not believe that it is a dish as exquisite as I say, it is easy to try it. The Turks have it in common use, for they believe that it refreshes them in summer and warms them in winter.

We left the road to Gallipoli on the left and took the road to Rodosto[171], which anciently was called Perinthus.

We rested during the day under walnut-trees to refresh our mounts and then continued on our way. In the evening we camped in the plain, and replenished our provender from the supplies carried by the caravan to be sure that we had enough; and there we slept.

67

That the Turks know better than any other people how to load and unload their baggage when travelling through the country

I think it worth while to describe here a thing that I observed among the Turks, which they practise in both peace and war. It is their manner of loading and unloading their baggage on horses, camels or mules. Five or six men had so skilfully unloaded in the evening and loaded again in the morning all the beasts in the caravan, which numbered a hundred and fifty, that it was done before I knew. Three men without any other aid can load a hundred horses in less than a quarter of an hour, provided that the load is trussed up after their fashion. It is necessary for each bale to be tied up with crossed ropes at each end and for the ropes to be attached in the manner following.

After two men have lifted one of the bales on to the packsaddle the third muleteer must tie the rope round the other bale which is still on the ground to one of the crossings of the ropes on the bale that is already loaded on the packsaddle, which one man can easily hold in place against the packsaddle. The ropes on the upper bale must also be tied in the same fashion as those on the lower one, and one of the men who helped to lift the first bale must now help to lift the other one; for one man is enough to hold it on the beast, and the other two each take one end of the rope, of which each bale has only one, and pass it through the higher of the crossed ropes, pulling it tighter or looser according to whether they want the load to hang higher or lower, and leave it as long or short as they want. They tie the ropes on the outside so that they can be more quickly undone in the evening. The two bales then lie across the packsaddle in the form of a Saint Andrew's cross.

When the caravan arrives at a halting-place one man can unload all the horses in the company in a moment, undoing each end of the rope, letting it fall so equally on each side that both sides go down in balance. The man who is holding the rope and letting the bales down can stop them at the same time and the same height, half a foot above the ground. A child could unload a hundred horses in less than a quarter of an hour without letting a single bale drop.

Of the town which was anciently called Perinthus, now Rodosto, and of Heraclea

We were between Perinthus and Gallipoli when we came to a river, which I believe to be the river Arzus, and crossed it on a bridge. The Turks call it Chiaurlic, and it is certain that it flows into the Propontis between Gallipoli and Rodosto. Rodosto is a town on the shores of the Propontis which anciently was called Perinthus[172]. It is very ancient, without walls. Following the great road to Constantinople, we left the town of Heraclea on the left, which is not on the road but is an arbalest shot off it.

Heraclea has retained its ancient name, which led me to enquire why the honey of Heraclea, called *heracleum*, was poisonous. It must be understood that there are several Heracleas, but this one is in Thrace[173]. I could discover no other reason than that there is much black chameleon growing in the region, which develops an excrescence on its roots called *ixia*, which is a pernicious and dangerous poison and kills those who eat it all in a moment. And if bees take the matter for their honey from the flowers I make no doubt that that is a poison pernicious to man.

We continued on our way, passing near the town of Seliurée [Silivri], which anciently was called Selymbria. When we were two days' journey from Constantinople, half a league from the town of Seliurée, I saw slag from metal-working beside the road along the coast, which showed that there had been mines here in ancient times; and although I carefully examined the slag I could not determine from what metal it came. The remains and ruins of buildings are evidence that there were formerly furnaces for smelting metal here, and there are great piles of waste, which is called in French metal shit, to be seen in many places. In times past metals were smelted with bellows worked by men, and not by water as we do now. Yet there are a number of streams in this area which in my opinion could have been used for the purpose if they had been in the habit of using water to turn the wheels and work the bellows, as is the practice with us.

When looking for the plants that grow on the territory of Seliurée I saw a lactescent plant similar to the oleander, and flowers likewise, but smaller in all points. Seen from a distance, it resembled the *tragium* of Crete, but close up it seemed to me more like *lysimachia purpurea*. I also saw some *cytisus* and collected a great quantity of their seed.

Leaving these ancient mines, which are on the main road running along the coast, we came to lodge in Seliurée, which has a very handsome little castle on a hill. Seliurée cannot properly be called a town, since it has no walls. The houses, the baths and the mosques are below the castle. The whole town lies on a slope, and is very similar to the town of La Rie[174] in England, as also is Gallipoli. To reach the great road to Constantinople from Seliurée it is necessary to go over the hill and continue on the plain. Most of the houses in Seliurée are at some distance from the harbour.

Large ships commonly come to Seliurée to load up with goods which are brought to them from Adrianople and overland from Thrace and Bulgaria. As an example of this, when I was there a Venetian ship was just completing its cargo of goods which had been brought not only from the countries mentioned above but also from Anatolia, like wool, leather and cotton.

Anatolia or Natolia is on the other side of the Hellespont, and the Turks call it Anatoli, which is a Greek word meaning the east. The country in Asia which is ruled by the Turk is commonly called by this name of Anatolia; for Europe being separated from Asia by the strait of the Bosphoruses, the Propontis and the Hellespont, all the country that is beyond it is called Anatolia, so that when the Greeks speak of Anatolia they include many other provinces, that is to say the whole of Phrygia, Galatia, Bithynia, Pontus, Lydia, Caria, Paphlagonia, Lycia, Magnesia, Cappadocia and Commagene[175]. And if they wish to speak of some special business or wares from one of these countries it suffices them to say that it is from Anatolia.

69

Of the great silence and modesty of the Turks in travelling about the country

When I was in Seliurée there was a company of Turks, some 4000 in number, who were lodging both in the caravanserais and other places in the town and also outside the town under the trees. All of them were horsemen, who were going to the Grand Turk's camp against the king of Persia[176], and were all in one band; but they left long before daybreak in such silence that we, who in similar case had intended to leave before daybreak, heard nothing, although they were quite close to us. This seemed to me a thing worthy of remark, hat such a large troop should be able to leave without making any noise.

It is only one day's journey from Seliurée to Constantinople, all through open and treeless country. There are two wooden bridges to be crossed three leagues on the hither side of Constantinople, the first of which is very small, but the second is much longer, and is called Buikchegmegy [Büyükçekmece].

The whole country of Thrace could be compared to Picardy, for it is treeless, with very large plains, and no hills anywhere. There is a village between the two bridges, and since there is much traffic on this road victuals can be bought there at any time. Both bridges, the first and the second, are built of wood over brackish ponds which reach inland from the sea like a gulf, on which there are many boats for going from one village to another, and also for fishing. There are several windmills on the shores of the lake, which we passed on the left; they have eight wings or arms, like all other windmills in Turkey, and not four like ours. And since there are two bridges to cross, so too there are two lakes which are joined into one, and the profit from the fish caught in them is very great. Beyond the village of Buikchegmegy is a pleasure palace of the emperor of the Turks, situated on a hill within a wood of tall trees and enclosed by walls.

The trees in this wood are hazels, oaks, elms, ashes, willows, planes and lotus-trees. Finally we arrived in Constantinople for the second time and ended this journey, at the beginning of the month of August.

70

Of the town of Pera, and of Constantinople

Before speaking of Constantinople I think it well to write first of the town of Pera[177], which is separated from Constantinople by a channel of water, like other towns situated opposite one another on the banks of a river, as for example the two parts of Carcassonne or Beaucaire and Tarascon; so that to go from Constantinople to Pera it is necessary to cross the harbour.

It is from this that it gets its name, for Pera means "over" or "beyond". Any strangers coming to Constantinople or Pera either by sea or by land will find no hostelries to lodge in; and so everyone must bring with him the wherewithal to spend the night.

Nevertheless when any foreigner arrives in Constantinople or Pera he will be able to find lodging in one fashion or another, since caravanserais, which are public lodgings in Turkey, are never lacking in the towns, and also because there is no man of any nation, at least for the most part, but will find some lodging to stay in, for commonly everyone goes to someone whom he will have heard to be of his nation. Accordingly, knowing that all the republics and great lords of Europe have their ambassadors in Constantinople, particularly when peace is universal among princes, and that the ambassadors both of republics and Christian rulers, like those of France, Venice, Ragusa, Chios, Florence, Transylvania, Hungary and others, commonly reside in Pera, except the ambassador of the Emperor, who lives in the city of Constantinople, all strangers apply to them.

Frenchmen in particular commonly do better than other nations, for they are better received by our ambassador and better treated than men of other nations by their ambassadors; and also because Frenchmen finding themselves in a foreign country support one another and love each other better than men of other nations. The liberality of Monsieur d'Aramont[178], the king's ambassador to the Grand Turk, bears witness to this, for he so loved to do pleasure to all men of the French nation, or who were of the French party, that no man ever came to Constantinople, of whatever condition he might be, and applied to him but he received them in the most friendly way and entertained them in his house.

His liberality is also shown by the great number of Christian slaves whom he liberated from the hands of the Turks at his own expense. And when any Frenchmen come to Constantinople, in addition to seeing that they are given all that they need, he arranges for them to be clothed if they have no suitable garments. And his house is open to everyone. When a Frenchman is anxious to get away from this country he gives him money according to his condition, sufficient to take him back to France. And if he knows him to be of noble race, after treating him as honourably as himself, he arranges for him to have mounts and other things necessary. And just as he has never baulked at the expense which he has had to incur for the arrival of the greatest personages, so he has never disdained to do pleasure to the humblest persons. And having experienced this in my own person, I should be worthy of being deemed ingrate if I did not bear witness to it, for I am well assured that there is no man who can contradict a single word of what I have said, unless he be malignant and refuse to admit the truth.

71

Description of the ruins of Nicomedia, and of what is to be seen there now

After staying for some time in Constantinople, I set out to see the ruins of the town of Nicomedia, which has preserved its ancient name. Nicomedia was situated on a hill. The extent of its walls was very great, reaching from the harbour at the foot and taking in the whole summit of the hill. The town is now totally ruined, but the walls of the castle, situated on the top of the hill, are still entire. There is no more than three toises of distance between one tower on the castle walls and the next, such a great fortress it must have been. The walls are built of baked bricks joined with strong cement.

The town has a pleasant situation on a low hill. There is an abundance of water from springs, which has made the town populous, being inhabited partly by Turks and partly by Greeks. The capitals and sections of pillars and great columns in the castle show that Nicomedia was once a powerful city.

I also found some very fine antique medals, both Greek and Latin. On the seashore can be seen the fish that the Latins called *pinna*, sticking upright in the ground, very much in the shape of a ham. The Latins also called it by another name, *perna*[179].

Having spent some time on the little islands in the Gulf of Nicomedia, in the Propontis, I observed that there are nine of them, which can be clearly seen from Constantinople. They were anciently called the Demoneses. The first is now called Proto by the Greeks; the second Bergus; and the third the Isula del Corbo[180]. The others are small islets which have no name of their own. There are many other islands lower down towards the Hellespont, but some of them have changed their ancient times: thus the one that was anciently called Proconesus is now called Marmara, and Besbicus is now Calomino[181].

72

That the nations of the Levant prefer to eat fish rather than meat

Before concluding my account of the riches of the Propontis, knowing that it abounds in all kinds of fish, I must remark that it derives no less profit from them than any country with good pasturage derives from its livestock, for all the people of Turkey and Greece are fonder of fish than they are of meat. Those who hold fish in such great horror seem to me to do so from prejudice rather than otherwise[182]. We find from the ancient authors that meat was anciently considered inferior to fish. And the monks of Egypt abstained from eating fish all their life, desiring to show by this that they were depriving themselves of a delicacy, just as it would be with us to eat no meat.

This dislike for eating meat and esteem for fish had the result that the ancient Greeks and Latins knew less about birds than about fish. Thus their physicians had more to say about fish in their books on foodstuffs than about terrestrial animals, and we do not find that Roman emperors and great lords esteemed birds in their banquets as men do now, except perhaps thrushes and francolins; for they delighted in fish more than in any other kind of game, so that partridges, pheasants, woodcocks, plovers and other birds which stand high among the delicacies prized by the French, were not esteemed in their meals by the most gluttonous Roman emperors. I will add that the Grand Turk himself, his predecessors and his whole court prefer to eat fish rather than flesh, and that little game is to be seen in the market in Constantinople. And so, since the place abounds in fish, they set out to catch them in various manners, as will be seen hereafter.

73

That fishing in the Propontis is of very great profit

The time, therefore, now seems opportune to speak of the manners of fishing in the Propontis, and in the first place of the one that brings the greatest profit. The sea at Constantinople is more abundant in fish than other seas, and accordingly the inhabitants are industrious in catching them. The fresh water which flows down from the great rivers into the Black Sea and is then mixed with the water of the sea is most proper for feeding the fish of the Pontus and Propontis.

The water then flows into the Mediterranean. In passing through the Propontis it neither increases nor diminishes, for there are no tides there. The fish have their fixed season for passing from one sea into the other, and their times for not moving and for going about. This being well known to the inhabitants of the Propontis, they are commonly more accustomed to eating fish than flesh. And so they choose the places in the sea where the fish are most commonly to be found, particularly near the shore, where the water is not very deep. They set up two posts in the sea, about the length of a ship's mast, some 40 or 50 paces apart, and construct small cabins on top of them from which one or two men keep a lookout for fish. On the posts are cross-pieces forming a ladder on which the men can climb up and down. The cabins serve to protect them from the heat of the sun and from rain.

The men perched up there act in the same way as the men who keep a lookout on vineyards. If they see a band of fish approaching one man tells his companion to keep a good watch, and when they see them entering the catching area each man pulls a rope attached to a net lying under water, thus raising the net and enclosing the fish within it.

Now in order to understand how matters are arranged, it should be explained that the net is square and has ropes attached to the four corners, that the two corners farthest from the high posts are farthest out to sea, attached to the tops of two stakes set in the sea bottom and only just emerging from the water, and that the two corners of the net, being attached to the stakes, are immovable. The other two corners of the net have ropes attached to them which are held by the men in the cabins. The net being thus held by its four corners half-way down in the sea, as soon as the men see the fish coming towards their net they warn one another; then, when the fish have entered the trap, they pull up their ropes, and thus the fish remain imprisoned in the net. Then one of the men ties up his rope so that the net remains suspended, and climbs down the post on the cross-pieces that serve as steps. At the foot he finds his boat, tied up to the post, and at once rows towards his companion, who lets his rope down a little; then he rows over the net and pulls it up, starting at one end and continuing until he has hoisted the fish out of the water in one corner of the net, loads the fish into his boat and climbs up again to his cabin to look out for more fish. They catch all kinds of fish indifferently by this means, like sphyraena, which Provençals call *pesescome,* sea-bream, blackfish, bonito, *cholios,* gilt-head, dental, saupe, white sea-bream, mullet, perch, *sur, menes, giroles* and other such fish, which they catch at different times of year, mainly in summer in calm weather, when the sea is peaceful and there is no wind; for during a storm the look-outs would not be able to see so clearly into the water as they can when the sea is calm.

74

Of other manners of fishing in the Propontis

There are several other manners of fishing in the Propontis which are also common to all peoples. One such method is fishing with a drag-net, which is the surest way and is known to other nations.

The fishermen in this sea do not use cork to support their nets as they do in the Ocean and the Mediterranean. Some commonly use light bark instead of cork, like that of pines and wild pines, which they bring from the Black Sea. Some use gourds, as on the lakes of Macedonia. When I was in Constantinople I went out many times in the boats of the fishermen of Pera for the purpose of seeing what fish were caught off the islands of Marmara and Besbico and in the gulf of La Montanée [Mudanya], After they have caught many fish they return at once to sell them in Constantinople.

The manner of fishing with drag-nets is thus: there must be two boats sailing in company, and they must have plenty of rope for their nets. The bay in which they fish must be clear of rocks, and the place where they take the fish out of their nets must be level. They cast their nets into the sea to their full extent; each boat ties its ropes to one end of the net; and then they make for the shore, pulling the nets behind them. If they cannot get the ropes to the shore they take to the oars. Both ropes must be of the same length, and one rope must never be pulled without the other. When the ends of the two ropes reach the shore they get out of their boats, which are some twenty paces apart, and begin to pull them in, watching the knots in the ropes to make sure that one is not farther in than the other, so that they pull at the same rate. And when the net draws near land the fishermen come in also. Then they take the ends of the ropes and pull them in at the same rate; and when they come to the net-bag they take care that the fish do not escape from it. And if they have caught any octopuses they open the arms and break the beak with their teeth; for if they were not killed they would escape from the boat.

If they have caught any moray eels they seize them at the back of the neck with pincers and break their jaws with a stick, and batter their whole body; otherwise they would bite them if they took them in their hands, for they have teeth as big as a cattle-drover's goad in a long beak. And if they have caught any sting-rays they cut off the tail at once, just as do our fishermen in the Ocean, who send them to us in Paris or in Rouen along with the sting. And although these sting-rays have no French name nevertheless Parisians call them rays, since they resemble rays.

They also catch indifferently almost all species of fish, although I am able to say that they catch no *scarus*. There is also another particular manner of fishing with a square net[183], which is practised only by fishermen on the coasts round Constantinople. particularly those living to the left of the road to Barbarossa's tomb[184].

All the Spanish slaves whom he liberated and who became Turks settled on the shores of the Propontis, where they made fine buildings and gardens along the shore; for the Grand Signior granted certain liberties and privileges to any who built houses on the coast. By the same token they also built houses on piles set in stones gathered from the sea. For, as I have already said, the sea in the Pontus, the Propontis and the Hellespont and in much of the Aegean never grows or diminishes, but is in perpetual flow.

It must be understood that this kind of net is used only for catching small fish, like sand-smelts and *cabassons* and all kinds of small fish that frequent the shore and grow no larger. Accordingly the meshes of the net are very small. It would resemble a hoop-net, were it not that the mesh is much larger than that of the nets used in rivers. It is suspended at the four corners from two curved sticks crossing one another, attached to a long rod which is supported on a pole set erect in the ground and notched at the top, on which the shaft of the net balances, in such a way that when the net is lowered into the sea the other end of the rod is raised into the air; attached to this end is a short length of rope, which is pulled down to lift the net out of the sea, when the fish in the net are suspended in the air.

The abundance of the fisheries in the Propontis and the profit to be had from them have led to such an increase in the population of Constantinople that villages have been built all along the coasts. Conger eels are not so common here as they are in the Ocean, and accordingly the manner of fishing for them is not the same; for when the Ocean withdraws from the land the fishermen go among the rocks along the coast, where they find small fish called *exoceti* under stones left dry by the tide, in which they insert hooks on short lines fastened to the rocks before the sea returns.

When the returning tide covers the rocks the congers, rays, dogfish and catsharks[185], finding this bait of small fish, swallow them together with the hook and are thus tied to the rocks; then when the sea has receded the fishermen return to their bait and find the fish stranded on dry land. Nature has made this small *exocetus* well suited to serve as bait, for since it likes to stay on dry land and live out of water under stones the fishermen can find them and use them for their purposes. That is why the Greeks anciently called this fish *exocoetus*. The modern Greeks call them *glinos,* some of which in the Propontis have a crest on their head like a cock. And since they have large teeth and a sharp bite the inhabitants of Comasco, at the mouth of the Po, call them *vulpe,* and at Marseilles *havecque;* but in our Ocean they have not yet been given any name.

The other manner of fishing common to seamen, particularly on seagoing galleys and ships, is that they are never without their nets, of which they have two kinds. Those of one kind, which are sometimes double, are cast into the sea, supported on cork and not tied to anything, and fish coming and going in the sea are entangled in the meshes and remain caught.

75

Of the manner of fishing at night with fire, using a trident. and of other manners in the Propontis

The seas of Pontus and the Bosphoruses and Propontis are always of the same height, and the inhabitants have a manner of fishing at night with fire that is greatly profitable. It is as follows. They have a light boat with two men in it, one of whom rows with two oars, one on either side, while the other kneels in the bow of the boat, with a flaming torch of *tede*[186] wood beside him, in a sconce fixed to the side of the boat, over the water. And since this *tede* wood is in such common use for fishing it is sold in village markets, and is called in the vulgar tongue *dadi*.

Those who fish with a trident do not want moonlight, for the darker the sky the better for the fisherman. If the man kneeling in the bow with his trident and looking attentively into the water sees a fish lying asleep he raises his hand to tell his companion to steer the boat forward or back, making a sign with his hand either open or closed, by which signs his companion knows whether to direct the craft this way or that way. They must not talk to one another, for the sound would be conveyed through the water to the gills of the fish lying asleep, which would awaken them and cause them to flee; for some fish have sharper hearing than others. And so they steer the boat very skilfully, putting the oars into the water so quietly that the fish hear nothing. Also there must be no wind, the sea must be calm and the water not too deep. The fish do not like to sleep in places where it is too deep, for when sleeping they lie on the sea-bottom or on some stone. And fish do sleep neither more nor less than terrestrial animals; indeed some fish have sometimes been heard to snore.

And just as all animals that have a brain cannot live without sleeping, so all fishes that have a brain cannot do without sleep. Pliny, following the authority of Aristotle, noted this in his writings; although the Greek author Actuarius attributed the appetite for sleep to the stomach. The fisherman, seeing the fish sleeping, thrusts his trident swiftly down to the left or the right, depending on where the fish is lying, so as to strike it in the back, and the trident, which has hooked prongs, clings on to the fish, and the man then lifts it into the boat.

This manner of fishing at night with fire, using a trident, is also well suited for catching octopuses, *totenes,* cuttlefish, and all kinds of fish with scales, such as bass, maigre, mullet, dental and pandora. They also fish with hooks, in this manner. They tie two or three hundred hooks on a long line supported on gourds, bait them with meat or fish and take them in the evening about a league and a half out to sea and leave them all night, so that fish in quest of food, such as moray eels, angelfish, catsharks, rays, dogfish and other like species are caught on the hooks. On the following morning, if there is no storm, they go out to pull up their hooks, which they can see from a distance since they are marked by the large gourds to which they are attached, and bring back the hooks and the fish that they have caught.

There are some towns in Italy where one man can fish with four or five lines at the same time, fixing them between the timbers of a bridge; and while he is baiting one line the others are just as if he were holding them in his hand; so that if a fish takes one of the hooks he can wait to pull it in until he has put fresh bait on the others. The manner of fishing for mackerel in the Propontis is very different from that practised by fishermen in the Ocean; for there they let out long lines which trail behind their boats in a rough sea, and the rougher the sea and the faster the boat sails, the more fish they catch. The Greeks do not practise this manner of fishing, but use only drag-nets or other kinds of net.

There are no fishes commoner in the market of Constantinople than the silurids, but the Jews do not eat them because they have no scales. Also commonly found there is the swordfish, which the Latins called *gladius*. The Turks, Greeks, Jews and all other nations of the Levant do not eat the dolphin, which with us is a special delicacy on fast days, called in the vulgar tongue porpoise. There are two kinds, but the one that is called a goose is the true dolphin, as I have sufficiently proved in the book on fish.

It is well established that our *célerins* are what other nations call sardines. I diligently examined them in the Propontis, and also in the Ocean, but found no difference except in size. There was a liquor called *garum*[187] which was anciently in as great usage at Rome as vinegar is now with us. I found it in as great demand in Constantinople as it ever was in the past. There is not a fishmonger's shop in Constantinople but offers it for sale.

Fishmongers were named *cetarij*, but they have not yet gained any French name, except for those who call them herring-merchants; but they have found a name in the vulgar tongue in Italy. The Romans call them *piscigaroli*, which seems to me to be derived from the words for fish and garum. The piscigaroles of Constantinople, who are for the most part in Pera, cook fresh fish every day and sell them already fried. They take out the guts and the gills and soak them in brine to turn them into garum.

It can, however, be a matter of great importance what kind of fish is used to make it, for it is really only the *trachurus*, which the Venetians call *suro*, that serves them for making it. This liquor was anciently so much esteemed that Pliny calls it a most exquisite liquor, saying that there was nothing dearer than this garum. He says that there were several kinds; and I believe that it can also be made from scaled fish. And to show that the Jews have in all times maintained their austerity in their manner of living I will cite the words of Pliny, speaking of garum: *Aliud vero ad castimoniarum superstitionem etiam sacris Iudaeis dicatum, quod fit e piscibus squama carentibus.* That is to say, the other kind of garum, which is dedicated to the chastity of superstitions, and also to the most devout Jews, is made from fish that have no scales[188]. Did I not know that they still maintain in our own day the practice of not eating ordinary garum I should not have said this; for there are certain particular ways of making it expressly designed for their use. There is a kind of drug made from sturgeons' eggs, which we call caviare, so common in the meals of Greeks and Turks throughout the Levant that there is no man who has not eaten it except the Jews, knowing that the sturgeon has no scales. But those who live at La Tana [Taman], who catch very great quantity of carp, put aside their eggs and salt them in such a way that they are better than might be thought, and make a kind of red caviare from them for the Jews, which is also sold in Constantinople.

76

Of the antiquities and many singularities of Constantinople

The city of Constantinople is situated in a place more suited for the grandeur of a prince than any other town in the whole world; for it has such a great advantage from the sea that no man could find a more convenient place. There is nothing more antique to be seen than what the Roman emperors and later the Greeks built. Constantine alone despoiled Rome of more of its ornaments of antiquity to transport them to Constantinople than twenty other emperors had built in a hundred years. And so all that we now see there that is beautiful and antique was brought from Rome[189].

Among other things there is a porphyry column, at no great distance from the church of Saint Sophia. There is also a Hippodrome, which is a most sumptuous and magnificent structure, within which are two obelisks. One of them was clad with gilded sheets of brass, and was built of blocks of marble tied together with iron and lead. The other obelisk, which is not quite entire, was brought from Egypt. There is also a serpent of cast brass, of prodigious size, standing erect in the manner of a column[190]. Constantinople also encloses seven hills within its walls, just as does Rome[191]. It is ringed by three circuits of walls, but it appears that they were built at different times[192], for fragments of marble pillars can be seen built into the masonry, showing that the work was done in great haste.

The church of Saint Sophia is the finest building among all others that have remained standing, and very different from the Pantheon in Rome[193]; for the whole interior of the church is built in the form of an openwork vault supported on pillars of fine marble in various colours, and there are almost as many doors as there are days in the year. Since it is now a Turkish mosque Christians dare not set foot in it, though Christians and Jews are permitted to enter it as far as the door and look at it from there. Anyone who has seen it will no longer admire the Pantheon in Rome, now called Santa Maria Rotonda. And I wonder that the Pantheon has been so much cried up, since it is by no means a work of such great art as has been claimed. Any ordinary mason could conceive in a moment the manner of building it, for with such a massive base and such thick walls it did not seem to me a difficult task to add the openwork vault.

But Saint Sophia is a very different matter. Like the Pantheon, it has an exterior built of brick and an interior faced with marble; but while the Pantheon is massive and solid everywhere Saint Sophia is open, spacious and delicate in all its parts. It provided a pattern for the Turks to build their mosques in its likeness, so that of the half-dozen most excellent mosques built in the last hundred years there is not one that was not made on the model of Saint Sophia.

There are the ruins of a very ancient palace, called by the common people the palace of Constantine, in which the Turk keeps his elephants and other tame beasts. There is also a place in Constantinople where the Grand Turk keeps his wild beasts, which is an ancient church[194] close to the Hippodrome, and to each pillar in the church is tied a lion: which I could not see without marvelling, for they untie them and handle them and tie them up again as they will, and even sometimes walk them about the city. And since all the Grand Signiors, however barbarous they were, took pleasure in seeing singular and rare animals, when anyone in any nation ruled by the Turk caught a wild animal he sent it to Constantinople, and the emperor had it most carefully kept and tended. There were also wolves chained up, wild asses, hedgehogs, porcupines, bears, lynxes and ounces, which are also called lynxes. Even the smallest animals, such as ermines, which are called in Latin *mures pontici*, that is, rats of Pontus, are looked after most attentively. There were also two small animals so strongly resembling cats that they seemed to me no different but in size, whose ancient name I could not discover. At time I thought that they were lynxes, for I took the ounces to be panthers; but I was unable to establish what animals they were.

It is a great wonder how they treat these animals so gently and make them half tame, as also they do with jennets, which they allow to move freely about the house, being as tame as cats.

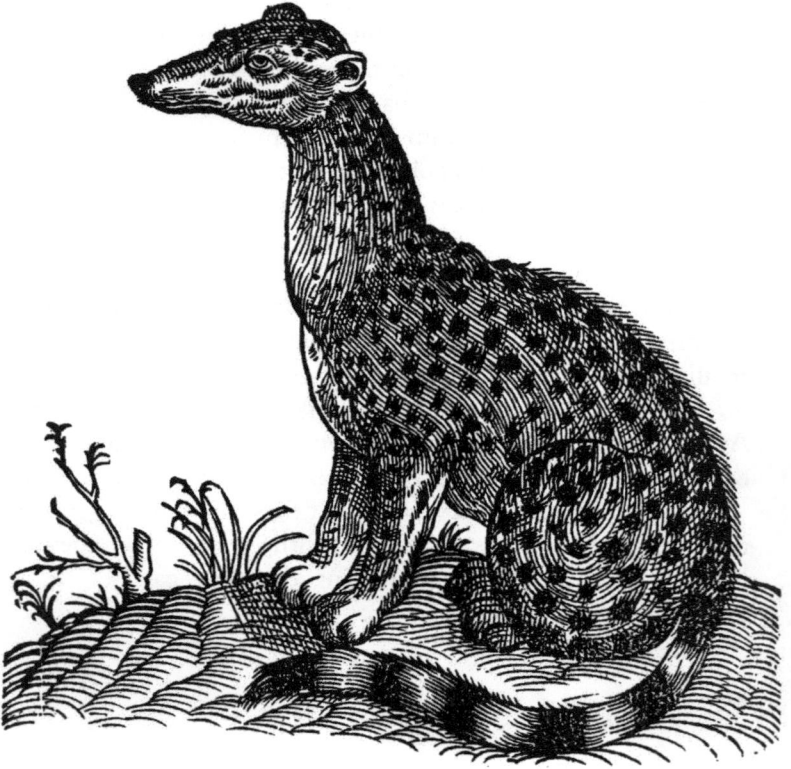

Le portraiƈt de la Genette.

Figure: Portrait of the jennet

And since Pera and Constantinople are almost the same thing, with only the harbour between them, which people have frequently to cross, there are ferrymen with boats almost as flat as our fly-boats, who are commonly poor slaves. The men who carry the cargoes of ships to the warehouses are for the most part Egyptians, and work in gangs of not less than eight or ten men. For having to unload large and heavy bales and other great loads such as are commonly carried on ships, and vessels full of wine, they carry them all together, all walking at the same pace and chanting in unison to keep time.

There are many in Constantinople who work in various trades unknown to us; for since they have not the art of printing it is a general practice to write on paper which has been specially smoothed. They do not make paper in Turkey, but buy it from Italian merchants who bring it to them by sea, Those who smooth it have a board made of pieces of boxwood closely fitted together and hollowed out on top, on which they put the paper, so that by rubbing it will become smooth; and for this purpose they use a piece of chalcedony or jasper fixed on a stick a cubit long, which they hold at both ends and rub the stone on the paper.

The Turks like to have their swords, which they call scimitars, not so shiny as ours, but damascened, that is to say dulled on both sides; and so the armourers have the art of soaking the point of the scimitar in a basin containing sal-ammoniac, verdigris and vinegar and then holding it erect and allowing this mixture to flow down the blade all day, so that it eats away a little of the iron or steel, following the pattern on the blade, which gives it a good appearance, the more particularly because it is then polished to make it more pleasant to look on. The workmen who make the sheaths for knives and scimitars have also the art of graining the leather very beautifully, of which I shall speak elsewhere.

The Turks hold precious stones in as great or even greater esteem than we do in ours country. And indeed they have more kinds of stones than our jewellers. Among them are one that is wrongly called *achryma* and another called *soultan meheure;* but I shall speak of them at greater length elsewhere. There are many shops which live by no other trade than by making paintings on coloured fabrics. And since they do such beautiful work quickly and without great labour I shall describe the manner of doing it. They begin by starching cotton or linen cloth, either yellow or blue or some other colour, which they stretch out stiffly and then smooth and polish. And they have a wooden stamp carved with some pleasant pattern, to which they apply colour, like those who imprint something in a mould, and they press this on the cloth and rub on top of it, and thus the painting remains on the cloth, and, continuing in this way, they produce fine paintings with little labour.

There is a kind of musical instrument made from canes, which when played by a Turk skilled in its use produces sounds as beautiful as a German flute. And indeed when a Turk passed by in the street playing this instrument all of us who were in Monsieur d'Aramont's house at the time thought that it was a German flute; but when we looked out of the window we saw that the instrument was made in the same manner as haymakers' pipes, with twenty-four reeds; others have only eighteen. Anyone who had not heard it would never have believed that from an instrument which to us is so mean could proceed such great sweetness of music.

Anyone visiting the shops of the workmen who make the handles of knives will find great numbers of animals' teeth and horns; and I myself have seen those of *bubalus*[195], gazelles and several other kinds of animals, brought from countries round the shores of the Great Sea; and in addition to two kinds of teeth from hippopotamuses and elephants there are others which have no name in the vulgar tongue. Anyone who wants to get the true *calamus odoratus* must go to the merchants' shops and ask for *cassabouserire;* for acacia he must ask for *akakia;* for acacalis, *kesmesen;* for amomum, *hamama;* for ammi, *ameos;* for napellus, *bisch;* for sugar, *alhasos* or *tigala;* for armala, *harmel;* for roots of ben albun and rubeun, *behenhamer* and *behen abias,* for the herbs which we believe to be *ben albun* and *rubeun* never resembled the description of them[196]. They sell the seeds of *hebulben,* which is not in use with us, and also a nut the size of two fists, full of small seeds that are good to eat and as sweet as hazelnuts, which they call *coulcoul,* that is to say coulcoul nuts. To get what our apothecaries call *calamus aromaticus* you must ask for *acoron.* They do not use colocynths peeled, but entire, which is a great error. All the merchants sell the green seed of terebinth and its resin, which is hard. They sell a kind of moss very different from ours, for we are wrong in thinking that moss is *usnea,* and they call it *usnech* when they sell it.

The authors praise Roman wormwood, which I saw on sale in the shops of Constantinople and in use, resembling in all points the kind that grows in our gardens, except that it grows wild in this country. I have had occasion to wonder that many people in Europe, having doubts about this wormwood and refusing to use the true herb, take in its place a wretched little herb, a species of southernwood, which has no virtue, and make no use of our common cultivated form, which is the true Roman wormwood. This seems to me an error similar to that of the Venetians, who take some little herb which grows in great profusion in the mountains of Friuli to be the true hyssop and have given up using the cultivated form, making a small error grow into one twice as great as it was before. The people of Constantinople, who have such a diversity of drugs in their shops that it creates confusion, use hyssop in either the wild or the cultivated form, but by mistake, for they call it and take it for thyme, and in its place use some useless little herb unknown to the ancients. And consequently they do not use the thyme of Greece, for they gather the true hyssop, calling it in error thyme, and thus find themselves without true hyssop, substituting something else in its place.

Anyone who wants rhapontic should ask for rhubarb, for they do not distinguish between the two, but call them both rhubarb; and they should choose long roots, black at the upper end, which are similar to centaury inside. It is manifest that there is a great difference between rhubarb and rhapontic.

And since I shall speak of both these plants, and also of all kinds of animals, plants and medicinal substances, in the commentary on Dioscorides which I have written in this language, I shall say no more about them for the present, and bring this first book to an end.

The Second Book

of many singularities and memorable things observed in divers foreign countries

To the reader

Having read infinite discourses on the peregrinations of many men, both in our own time and in the time of the ancients, who have travelled by land and sea, we find that those who sought to concern themselves with things which were outside their knowledge and which they did not understand, have frequently been convicted of lying. I take the example of what is now called *mummy*[197], of which some writers, presuming too far, being ignorant of good letters and natural things, have pronounced that it is made from human bodies submerged in the moving sands in the deserts of Africa or Arabia. But when I specify the things that I have observed in Egypt I shall prove that mummy is a very different thing from what the common people think, and that the Greeks and Latins were not ignorant of this.

And so, in writing this second book, I propose to set down only what I have observed with my own eyes, or else, taking the authority of the ancient authors, I shall prove from their writings what I say about many matters of which I propose to speak. And feeling free to write down in full the things that came to my notice, which I desired to examine, I have made ample discourse, concealing nothing of my opinions of them.

But since the favour and credit of Monsieur de Fumel, a gentleman of the king's bedchamber, has been of great assistance to me in doing so, I should deserve to be accused of ingratitude if I did not confess freely that I am much in his debt: for I gained knowledge of many things while travelling in his company, when he showed me much courtesy.

I met him in Constantinople, where he was then ambassador for King Henry II to the Grand Signior, with whom he was in great favour: for he gave him men from his court expressly to escort and conduct him in safety in all the countries and provinces to which he desired to go. And being accompanied by honourable French gentlemen, and also by janissaries, attendants[198] and dragomans, he honourably carried out many great and laborious travels in the territories of Turkey, as will be seen hereafter.

1

*That travels by sea are exposed to uncertain weather, and the voyage
from Constantinople to Alexandria*

Men proposing to travel by sea can in truth never have any surety
about the weather. Since all voyages are subject to the winds, it
most frequently happens that vessels both large and small, whether
driven by oars or by sail, whether galleys or other kinds of ship,
which in prosperous weather, with the right winds, will complete
their voyage in a week, in other weather will take more than two
months. A mariner, talking of the voyage on which he is about to set
out, may well compute the time it will take, but he will not regard
it as a certain thing; for only if the winds are right for sailing in the
direction he proposes can he hope to achieve his objective.

It so happened that I sailed from the strait of the Propontis
at Constantinople to Venice in thirteen days, a voyage on which
travellers have sometimes spent six months at sea. Now that I am
about to describe the voyage from Constantinople to Alexandria,
a city in Egypt, I must explain that the ships of the Arabs,
and principally of Egypt, have a fixed season for sailing from
Constantinople to Alexandria; they commonly leave towards the
end of the month of August, for the northerly winds are usually of
longer duration in September than at any other time of year. And
in order not to miss such a good occasion for sailing, many vessels
leave Constantinople at that time to go to Alexandria. But to sail
from Alexandria to Constantinople they leave in spring, for the
southerly winds in this region continue steadily in spring longer
than at any other time.

We spread sail when it was already vespers, continuing night
and day with a good northerly wind, and took only a day and
a night to pass through the Propontis. This is the name of the
sea round Constantinople, which is enclosed between the two
Bosphoruses[199] and has two deep gulfs, the Gulf of La Montanée
[Mudanya], anciently called the Gulf of Nicopolis, and the Gulf
of Nicomedia, anciently called *Astacenus sinus*[200]. On the following
day, being now in the open sea, we had the country of Phrygia on

the left hand, and the country of Thrace on the right; we passed through the whole of the sea of Propontis, which is not wide, and is surrounded by mountains, so that when you are in the middle you can see land on all sides, and a number of islands which I have mentioned above. On the following morning we came to Gallipoli, where we stayed, and anchored off the shore.

2

Of the ancient cities situated on the shores of the Propontis, on the Thracian side, and of the town of Gallipoli

Gallipoli is four good days' sail from Constantinople, which may be reckoned at around 36 leagues. There are no harbours for large ships on the way, though there are plenty of accessible beaches; and indeed almost the whole of the Propontis and the Hellespont could be called such, for there is sufficient depth everywhere. Going by land from Constantinople to Gallipoli, following the coast of Thrace, you pass four ancient towns which still retain their old names, and they are not walled, like all other towns in the countries ruled by the Grand Turk.

The first town is Selimbria, now called Seliurèe [Silivri], where there is a harbour for small boats and beaches for larger ones. The second is Heraclea [Ereğli], which has a very fine harbour, large and spacious, for ships and galleys. The third is Rodosto[201] [Tekirdağ], anciently called Perinthus. The fourth is Gallipoli, which is a large village without walls, situated on a low hill; and this is the place where the Propontis ends and the mouth of the Hellespont begins, for the whole stretch from Gallipoli along the strait, a distance of around two leagues, as far as the Aegean Sea, is called the Hellespont.

The Turks now have the custom that all seagoing ships, large or small, from whatever country they come, which wish to pass through this strait are required to stop and report to the men on guard at Gallipoli, and take their passport and present it at one of the two castles in the Bosphorus. A vessel which has shown its passport at Constantinople will be exempt from showing it at

Gallipoli, but to leave the strait passports must be presented at one of the castles.

Every large ship which desires to leave Turkey by this strait, of whatever nation it may be, must remain at anchor for three days, so that the Turks may have time to make a search of the whole ship; and no ship is excepted and is not visited. The Venetians, Anconitans, Genoese, Neapolitans and Ragusans[202] sail there commonly. And since this is a key point, and one of the most important places of passage in Turkey, by which slaves could flee, for this reason they keep a careful watch on it. When a foreign vessel enters the strait, having a good wind in its sails, it does not ask for permission, for all ships can enter freely; but it is not similarly free to leave, for if by chance there was hidden in the ship some fugitive slave, or any other thing which it is forbidden to take out of Turkey, it would have to pay a large sum of money.

We stayed at Gallipoli for two days, and went to an Augustinian monastery which has still its church in the fashion of Latin Christians. In the countryside round Gallipoli there are a number of ancient sepulchres of kings and emperors of Thrace, constructed in the form of large round mounds, resembling small hills, with which the whole of the country of Thrace is studded. Several others can be seen at a distance on the hills, so that you might call them little hills on great hills, made by the artifice of man, as indeed they were.

The harbour of Gallipoli is very small for ships, but it is big enough for fuste*s*, galliots, brigs and mahones[203], which are the kind of vessels that the Latins call by the Greek name of *hippagi*, and are used to carry horses and camels from Europe to Anatolia.

Great numbers of these mahones, which customarily are commanded by the janissaries of the Grand Signior[204], can be seen coming into Constantinople every morning. The rear part of these galleys is open, so that the horses or camels go on board as if into a stable, without any difficulty. The galleys can be seen drawn up on to the beach in the harbour of Gallipoli, lining the whole shore on piles, under roofs of merrain oak, as if in an arsenal. Here, as in Constantinople, all kinds of foodstuffs can be found in the market.

The town is inhabited by Greeks, Jews and Turks, and is a very important place of passage from Europe into Anatolia. When we had been two days in Gallipoli, we set sail to continue on our way, and when we came to the castles we anchored for the second time. For no ship (as I have said), whether foreign or Turkish, passes through this strait unless it has anchored at Gallipoli, and it must stop again in the strait at the castles. If a vessel, ship or galley laden with merchandise is foreign, it must stay three days waiting here; but if the vessel is Turkish, and the wind is right, it is despatched on the first day, in order not to.waste time.

3

Description of the Bosphorus of Thrace, and of the castles named Sestus and Abydus, and of the ruins of Scamandria.

This strait with the castles is a little less than a half-quarter of a league wide. It was anciently and still is the place where the castles of Sestus and Abydus are situated; and it is the place of which the poets have told the fable of Hero and Leander. The castle on the Asian side, called Abydus, which is situated in a marshy area, has been rebuilt in a square form. The circuit of the castle walls encloses a tall square ancient tower which still stands to its full height, and which the Turks have heightened still further and equipped with artillery on the top. At the four corners of the walls are four small and rather weak bastions, and it seems to me that this castle, although a key of Turkey, is not particularly strong. The stone with which it was fortified was taken from the ruins of a nearby town , which I believe to have been anciently called Scamandria[205]. It is situated on the mainland of Asia Minor, and is only half a league from the sea, and a short half-day journey from the castles. There are to be seen the sumptuous ruins of magnificent buildings in very beautiful white marble, and of columns carved with all sorts of devices, and also some large and handsome square capitals. It is situated on a hill, and surrounded on two sides by a wide expanse of spacious and beautiful meadowland. The place is marshy in winter, but in summer is quite dry.

I saw here a large stone carved in relief, depicting a figure clad in a hauberk in the ancient style, with armour on his breast, a plumed morion fastened under his throat, a long buckler held high, a curved sword in the fashion of a scimitar, not hanging from a sword-belt but from a sling round his neck, very beautifully worked. I believe that this building was a magnificent temple, dedicated to some god; and now the Turks carry the stones to the sea to convey them to their castle, which they have made a fortress.

The other castle of Sestus is in Europe, situated on the peninsula of Thrace near a very large village called Maito[206], inhabited by Greeks. Sestus is situated at the foot of a hill and is built in the form of a trefoil. The first tower in the middle of the castle is in the shape of three semicircles joined together. The second surrounds the first one in the same shape, so that one encloses the other. The circuit of the walls forms a triangle, one corner of which looks towards the hill, with a tower on top of it, which defends the castle against attack from the hill. From this tower two sides of the walls run down to the sea, enclosing the tower within. The walls of the castles which extend along the shore, both on one side and on the other, are equipped with good pieces of artillery, ready to fire if need be to stop any ships that might try to flee without permission, or enter the Hellespont by force. The castle on the Asian side is similarly equipped with artillery; but because it is of greater importance it is stronger and much more carefully guarded. The one which is in Europe is weak in face of the hill which dominates it.

Figure: map of Hellespont

When passing through the Hellespont, you see hills covered with fine forests of wild pines, called in Latin *piceae*. The inhabitants use their timber, called *teda*, which when lit gives light like a candle, to make black pitch and *cedria*[207], which the French call by the Arabic name of *quodran* or *quatran*, and in Avignon *cade cerbin;* and since it is sold cheaply, foreign ships coming here take great quantities of it, and sometimes load up with it. The Turks put it in sheepskins or goatskins, for it is very liquid. A full skin costs no more than half a ducat. It is much more liquid than the pitch produced in the hills round Bordeaux and sold in barrels. This is the substance that the people of Egypt used in ancient times to preserve dead bodies, from which is made the drug that we call mummy, of which I shall speak at greater length later. Seamen now use *cedria* to tar ships' ropes. They mix it with the pitch found in the soil, called *pissasphaltum*[208], which is extracted above Ragusa, and then melt them together so that the *pissasphaltum* becomes softer and more ductile, for of itself it is very dry and could not be used without being mixed with the *cedria*, which, as I have said, is made in Phrygia. And in order to make clear what tree I mean by wild pine, I give its portrait here.

Figure: Portrait of the wild pine

Great quantities of *alga latifolia*, which is a plant growing in
the sea, like hay in a meadow, are cast up on the shores of the
Hellespont and the Propontis. The inhabitants, finding it on the

shore, gather it and dry it so that they can make use of it. They mix it with clayey soil, in order to roof their houses with it, for it is long, wide and pliable, making a good mixture of cob, so that their houses have roof terraces. This mouth of the sea flows most impetuously, and as a result it casts ashore various waste substances which are of great utility, like the fifth species of *alcyonium*, which is mentioned by Dioscorides, and which the inhabitants of Samothrace, Imbros and Lemnos call in their vulgar tongue *arkeilli*. There are great quantities of this on the island of Besbico, one of the islands in the Propontis, a little way below Marmara[209], with which whole ships could be laden, though it is sold very dear by the druggists of Venice and other nations. But they no longer call it by its ancient name, for since it is light and looks like foam , they call it in the vulgar tongue *spuma maris*[210]. Here too I found *antipathe*[211].

4

Particular description of the castle of Abydus, which is one of the keys of Turkey

The castle of Sestus, in Europe, which I have described above, is of lesser importance and is not very strongly fortified, but the castle of Abydus is stronger. And since we entered this castle, I will tell briefly what we saw there. It is square in form, and surrounded by ditches, but they are not deep. Its walls are weak, and do not enclose a large area. There is a tall tower in the middle, in the manner of a keep, which is the very wall that stood there when the Turks took the castle from the Greeks[212]. The artillery in the castle is not mounted on wheels, but stands on the ground, backed by a strong wall to the rear, so that it can neither retreat or advance. The guns, 27 in number, are ranged in a line pointing down at the level of the sea. There is a village adjoining each castle, both at Sestus and Abydus, but the one at Abydus is larger.

Here, on Tuesday the 28th day of August, I saw a great band of storks, which in the judgment of some of our party numbered between three and four thousand. They were coming from the direction of Russia and Tartary, for they crossed the Hellespont in the form of a St Andrew's cross. When they were above the island of Tenedos they wheeled slowly round, following one another, to form a circle, and then broke up into small bands before leaving the mouth of the Propontis. Thus separated, they formed more than twenty bands, flying one after the other and heading due south; and thus they had travelled from the north.

Black chameleon is plentiful in the fields at Abydus and on the shores of the Hellespont. The people of this region make their brooms from the plant called *lépidon*, which the Greeks call in the vulgar tongue *sarapidi*.

There were more than a hundred Turkish passengers on our ship, travelling from Constantinople to Egypt, for the journey is much quicker by sea than by land, as I shall show hereafter. Each passenger pays a ducat for his passage. Egyptian merchants, having sold their merchandise in Constantinople and not wishing to return to their country empty-handed, take a great number of passengers travelling to Cairo or other places in Egypt. Our ship lay at anchor in the harbour of Abydus until we were given clearance to leave.

During this time, while walking along a number of small salt streams I found a species of terrestrial snake which normally feeds all day in the sea, just as the grass snake does in fresh water, but it comes in to sleep on land. It is almost red in colour, but there are some that are grey.

5

That the ruins of Troy can be clearly seen from the sea.

We left the castles in the morning with a good favourable wind, which seamen call the mistral or tramontane[213], and passed out of the strait of the Hellespont into the open waters of the Mediterranean Sea, which is more than three leagues from Abydus. We left the peninsula on the left, on which is a promontory called by the ancients Mastusia, where were the tomb of Hecuba and the sepulchre of Protesilas[214].

Soon afterwards we saw the island of Imbros, which is slightly smaller than the island of Lesbos, though its mountains are higher, and left it on the right, for it is very close to the coast of Thrace. Then when we had sailed farther and were quite far out at sea we saw the island of Lemnos, which is farther from the mainland than Imbros. Lemnos is called in Italian *Stalimine*, and in the Greek vulgar tongue *Limno*. Since it is low-lying and has no high mountains, we saw very little of it.

Sailing farther into the Mediterranean with a good wind, the mistral, we continued on our course closer to land, with the coast of Asia on the left. For if we had followed a course to the right we should have missed the Chios channel, through which we had to pass. Approaching the point on the mainland called the Cavo di Genissari, anciently named Sigaeum[215], we saw quite close up the ruins of a castle anciently called Caput Gymneseum, which show that it was very ancient. We could see it from a fair distance, since it stood high above a promontory. The walls of this castle were made of brick and strong cement. Within the castle are some very large cisterns and large cellars, which I saw when I went to Troy. Our ship passed between the island of Tenedos, which we had on the right, and the ruins of Troy on the left.

6

Description of the ruins of Troy

The ruins of Troy can be seen from a fair distance, for the walls of the city are still standing at certain points. Since I went to see them by land, I shall say what remains are still to be seen; and following our course by sea I shall also say what can be seen from the sea.

To go there from Constantinople by sea, you would have to land at Abydus, in the strait with the castles, from which it is only a half-day's journey. And after visiting the ruins, in order to see some beautiful country, you would have to return over Mount Ida and over Mount Olympus and Orminium, following the ordinary main road to the town of Bursa[216]. Mount Olympus is almost as high as the Mont Cenis, but there is no path so difficult. A traveller who did not want to take this route could take the road to Gallipoli and return to Constantinople by land along the coast of Thrace.

Troy lies on the slopes of a hill, and can be clearly seen from the sea, for it also extends along the shore. Between Tenedos and the ruins of Troy we sailed between two points. One was low down beyond Troy, opposite the island of Metelin [Mytilene], and was called Cavo Sancta Maria, and anciently Iarganum. The other was at the end of Tenedos[217]. Between these points our vessel found itself becalmed. We could see some arches which are still standing, built of cement and brick in the ancient manner, at the foot of a low hill or promontory. Lower down, below the promontory, on the shores of the sea could be seen the ruins of two castles within the town. The people who live round Troy are partly Greeks, partly Turks and partly Arabs; all of them call the territory in the vulgar tongue Troada.

It was not without reason that the magnificence and grandeur of Troy, being so great as it was, was celebrated by the ancient poets. The ruins of the buildings still to be seen there today are so admirable to look at that it would not be possible to express their greatness except by a long discourse. The circuit of the walls bears sufficient witness to the greatness of the city. They are built of large stones, coarse-grained and very spongy, blackish, hard, square-cut, from quarries on a nearby promontory called Assos[218]. The ruined towers on the walls can still be seen. Those who say that all the ruins have been demolished are not to be believed.

The foundations of the walls encircling the city still appear, reinforced at some points by pillars and spurs two toises wide. I spent four hours going round them, either on foot or on horseback. Outside the circuit of the walls can be seen large marble sepulchres, made in the antique fashion, all of a single stone, like great chests whose lids are still everywhere entire, lying open on the busy main roads. The ruins of the two castles, built of fine marble, can still be seen in their entirety, and it would not be possible to ruin or destroy them by any means. The one which stands on the sea at the lowest point of Troy extends along the shore in the form of two platforms, the walls of which are built of alternating red and white marble blocks. The other castle is on the summit of the hill on the other side of the wall encircling the city.

From the upper castle, looking down, you can see almost the whole of the city, and almost the whole of the surrounding country.

The walls of the castle extend for some distance outside the city walls. After I had made the circuit of the remains of these walls I looked round the interior of the city, which is but a confusion of ruins. Among them is the large base of a square platform, built of hewn stones of very great size; and I believe that this was the foot of some tall lighthouse or beacon, which gave light to seamen at night. There are also several cisterns, still preserved entire, in which rainwater was stored, since in all this territory there was very little spring water, There are also to be seen the ruins of churches, built when the place was inhabited by Christians, great parts of the walls of which are still standing, and in them are to be seen crosses carved on the marble stones.

The city was ruined so many times that no building has remained entire; and so it is now completely uninhabited. No one can live there because of the barrenness of the soil and the great lack of water. There is not a village or a house for more than a league round; so barren and sandy is the soil. Few fruit-trees grow here. The *esculus* trees bring in a fair revenue for the territory; their acorns are gathered when the shells are still soft by the inhabitants of the surrounding area, who knock them down with sticks just as people knock down nuts. They then leave them to dry out under the tree, having no fear that pigs will eat them, since they do not keep any, and when they are dry they gather them and carry them in bags on camels for sale in nearby towns, like Bursa and Gallipoli.

They use the acorns to prepare leather, just as we tan leather with pounded bark, as they do in Egypt with acacia fruits, in Italy with myrtle leaves and in Greece with sumac. Within the great area of these ruins, there is a fine spacious expanse of land, now sown with cotton and sesame, which is a plant bringing in a good revenue, for from sesame they make their oils in Egypt. In addition they have a species of melon which grows without being watered and is of such a nature than it can be kept all winter without going bad. I believe that nevertheless they are true melons, which can be eaten like any others when they are picked, but they are different in this respect that they keep all winter and almost all the following summer. And as proof that they are true melons, I am quite satisfied that the plant is similar in form to those that we have; and the taste little different. They also have many of our kind.

They have another kind of fruit, with the Arabic name of *copous*, which is common throughout Turkey and Greece; but the Greeks, following antiquity, call it *chimonicha*, the Latins by a kind of Greek name, *auguria*, and the Arabs *napeca*. This term *auguria* is given to it improperly, for *auguria* is none other than the cucumber which we know.

Also to be seen in Troy are large colossi lying on the ground, carved in antique fashion, and there is a place quite close to the castle and to the sea where there is a great accumulation of marbles; and I believe that someone must have put them there out of curiosity, for this could not have been done without great expense. There are also a number of gates in the circuit of walls, which today are almost entire, and principally one on the hill beside the castle which gave access from the city to the plain. There is also a long stretch of very high walls, reinforced by buttresses to the rear, which leaves the circuit and runs into the open country in the direction of Mount Ida. The other gate on the landward side, leading down towards the hot baths, is still entire. The other gates on the seaward side are much ruined, and there are only a few remains. I found a pillar of white marble set in the earth, but now half lying, which had this inscription on one side and the other: *Imperator Caesar Mar. Aur. Antoninus Pius Felix Particus Maximus, Germanicus Maximus. Trib. P.i. Imp. Po.xv. Maximus Imp. Cos.iii. provinciam Asiam per viam & flumina pontibus subiugavit.* All these words were on one side of the pillar, so much consumed by antiquity that I could scarcely read them. On the other side of the pillar were written other words, of which the beginning was *Imp. Caesar Aug. Diocletiano regnante.* I could not read any more.

As for the rivers Simois and Xanthus[219], so celebrated by the poets, which watered the plains of Troy, I have nothing to tell save that they are now small streamlets, which can scarcely provide sustenance for loaches or minnows, for they are dry in summer, and even in winter a goose would have great trouble in swimming in them.

The road from Troy to the hot baths looks west towards the island of Lesbos, which is no more than two leagues distant. Tenedos is also quite close to it, so that you have only to cross the channel between the two. The baths, which are naturally hot, are only half a league from Troy; there are a great many sepulchres on the road, which is lined with them: many more than on the road from Philippi to La Cavalle [Kavala]. The sepulchres seem to be of Greeks, for they have Greek letters on them, although there are also some of Latins, as appears by the Latin letters. Nearer the hot baths we saw sumptuous buildings magnificently carved in the antique manner, on one of which I read *Julio,* on another *Magistratus.*

This length of wall, which, as I have said, reaches out from the circuit of the walls, extends for a considerable distance, though I followed it only round Troy. My guides, however, said that it was twenty miles long. However this may be, it is a very great work, and I believe that it was a fort which provided defence against attack by land. It extends in the direction of Mount Ida, which is only two or three leagues from Troy. They told me also that it ended only at the Gulf of Satelie. It does not, however, continue all the way at its full height, for it has been pulled down at a half-quarter of a league from Troy, but they say that farther away it is as high as it is near Troy.

These hot baths have three salt springs, from which salt could very well be made, as is done at other salt springs. This could easily be seen from their streams, which in summer are crusted with salt by the sun. It is these springs that Pliny speaks of in book XXXI, chapter 7, where he says: *Larissa Troade,* for the place where they are situated is called Larissa[220]. The vaulted rooms, built of cement and brick in the antique fashion, are still standing. In one of them people do not bathe, for the wall has fallen and blocked the spring; but there is a small lightly built house at one of the springs in which people can bathe. This is not such a sumptuous building as the one at the baths on Mount Taurus.

7

Of the island of Metelin and the promontory of Sygaeum

To return to the place where I had left it and resume the course of my voyage, it is to be remembered that we were at sea opposite the point called Cavo Sancta Maria, anciently Sigaeum, where we saw the ruins of an ancient castle, which I believe to be the castle of Achilles[221]. There is still to be seen there a large mound in the form of a low hill, which may be the tomb of Achilles, erected by the people of Metelin in his honour.

We made no further progress all this day than from the strait with the castles to opposite the island of Metelin [Mytilene, Lesbos], for the wind drove us slowly. That night was also without wind, either for us or against us. On the following day our ship was still opposite the castle of the town of Metelin, the largest town on the island of Lesbos, from which the whole island has taken its name. It is inhabited by Turks, but the country people who cultivate the fields and vineyards are almost all Greeks. The wine of Metelin is much favoured among all others in Constantinople, and is almost all red. In order to give it more colour they add elderberry seeds in accordance with the doctrine taught them by the Jews. The other wines which are brought to Constantinople from Chios and other islands in the Cyclades are not sold at such high prices as the wine of Metelin, the taste of which can be distinguished from the others.

Metelin is a very fertile island off the coast of Phrygia. It breeds stout horses, low and stocky in build. It draws great revenue from the cheeses made here and from its good wheat, from which they make great quantities of two kinds of drugs that they use in their pottages, one called *trachana* and the other *bouhourt*, which were anciently called *crimnon* and *maza*. The Turks now use them both in peace and in war, as the Roman armies used *maza*[222].

We did not have a good day's sailing, and were only opposite the rock in the Aegean Sea between Chios and Tenedos which when seen from a distance looks like a goat (called by the Greeks *aega)* and has given its name to the whole of this sea.

On the following day a Greek wind from the tramontane quarter began to favour us, but it was slow and carried us only past the island of Metelin, which we had on the left. We saw its castle from a great distance, for it had been newly whitened, and besides it stands on a hill. It is situated on the west side of the island, facing the island of Tenedos, and is built in the antique fashion, and consequently is not very strong. The town is near the harbour, which is very large and handsome, and very safe for all ships. The wind did not change all day, and we were already at some distance from Metelin when we saw the island of Psara[223], which we left on the right. It is a small island near the Cavo Mastichi, on which wild asses live, different from those found in the country of Assyria; they cannot live anywhere else, for they die if they are carried elsewhere. Now we could no longer see the Cavo Mastichi, anciently called Phanae[224], for the same wind, now rather brisker, grew stronger towards evening, which brought us at nightfall very near Chios.

We passed through a strait in the channel between Chios and the point of Magnesia, to which we were so close that we could have thrown a stone from our ship to the land. This Magnesia is not the one which is watered by the river Meander in Thessaly, some 15 miles from Ephesus[225], but is close to Chios. It was now on our left, with Chios to the right. On the side of the island facing us was a very high hill called Pelleneum [Pelinaion]. We came to Chios and anchored in the channel as night fell, waiting for the day.

8

Succinct description of what we observed in the island and town of Chios and that mastic is found only here

It can be seen from the account that I have given above that it takes two days of good weather to sail from the castles in the Hellespont to Chios, for we arrived there on the third day of our voyage. As soon as it was daylight we left the ship to go and see the town, which is small. It is situated at the foot of a hill on the shores of the sea, on the side facing Anatolia, looking east. The people of

Chios pay tribute to the Turk, amounting to 12,000 ducats a year, in order to preserve their liberties; but they are not permitted to fortify the town[226].

The harbour is small, but sufficiently good for galleys and other kinds of lesser ships, and large barks. Larger ships can anchor in the channel without entering the harbour. Chios is the only one of all the islands that produces mastic, although Galen in the second book of Glaucon[227] praises Egyptian mastic[228]. I know, however, that at the present day it is found only on Chios, where the lentisk trees are cultivated with such diligence that the people of Chios devote no less expense and labour to their cultivation than do our wine-growers to the cultivation of their vines. And since the main wealth of the inhabitants of the island comes from mastic, this is a great inducement to take great care in the cultivation of the lentisk trees. And as olive-trees and other such fruit-trees must be watched and cared for, so the lentisks would not yield their gum if the necessary care was not taken. The lentisks which grow in Languedoc, Provence and Italy are the same as those in Chios, but they do not yield mastic.

There is a particular mine of green earth on the island of Chios, very much like the colour of verdigris, which is known in Turkey as earth of Chios, though this is not the substance known in antiquity as *terra chia*, for this green earth was called by Vitruvius *theodotion*.

There is no other town whose people are more courteous than those of Chios[229]. It is also, from my own experience, the pleasantest place to stay that I know of, nor is there any place where the women are more courteous and more beautiful. They bear infallible witness to their ancient beauty, for as a nymph on the island of Chios, surpassing snow in whiteness, was known by the Greek name of Chione, that is to say snow, so the island, taking the name of the nymph, was named Chios. The men also are very friendly. And although it is a Greek island, for the most part the people live in the Frankish manner, that is to say in the Latin fashion. Nevertheless many of them are Greeks, and desire to live in the Greek fashion, so that it is open to each man to choose and to say what manner of life he prefers.

The observances of the two religions are much different. Those who are true Greeks, if they see any one of their people eating sanguineous fish during a fast, are greatly scandalised. How (they will say) are you not a Romeos?, which is as much as to say, Are you not a Greek? For those who govern themselves in the Greek fashion are called Romei, and those who obey the Latin church, that is, are subject to the command of the pope, are called *Franqui*. And since the Greeks are forbidden to eat sanguineous fish during their fast, they think ill of one of their faith who does eat it. Religion in their nation is very strictly observed.

But the people of Chios, being partly Genoese and Italians and partly Greeks, and tributary to the Turk, live with all the accustomed liberties which the Turk allows them. Before the signoria of Chios fell under the power of the Turk, it was absolutely in the power of the Genoese. But since it has belonged to the Turk, it is not so subject to the Genoese as it was before, for it now has its own rule and government to its taste, and not as the Genoese would have it. So also it is with the lordship of Ragusa, which is similarly tributary to the Turk. The language of the Chians is partly Greek, partly corrupt Italian, as is the Genoese tongue; also their clothing and manner of life are in the Genoese fashion. The island's revenue from mastic is so great that they pay the Turk 4000 or 5000 ducats a year, by way of deduction from their tribute, and sell it to them at the price of 105 ducats a quintal. The rest they keep for themselves. French merchants, seeing that it is always the same price, commonly think and say that when they have gathered a certain quantity they throw away the rest. But that is false; for, as I have said, they go to great expense in caring for and maintaining the lentisks.

After the southerly wind which had been against us had ceased for some time, we set sail, left Chios and continued on our way to Alexandria with a favourable Greek wind. The first island that we saw from a distance was Icaria, now called Nicaria, which we left on the right, and had sailed only a little farther when we saw the island of Samos, which was visible from a distance, for there are some very high hills on it. It is a small island belonging to the signoria of Chios, which is not wide but of some considerable length. It has few high hills, and so has little timber, but it has much corn and good pasturage for sheep, from which they make much cheese. This island has good harbours, and were it not for the fear of corsairs

Chios, like many other islands now uninhabited, would be better cultivated. For when the least sea corsair comes here, he has little difficulty in taking them slaves and putting them in the galleys by force. A little farther on we saw the island of Ios[230], between Icaria and Naxos, on which it is said that Homer was buried.

9

Of the island of Samos

The island of Samos, although it is large, is now almost uninhabited. It is a great matter that an island like Samos, which has a perimeter of 588 miles, should remain deserted, seeing that it was anciently so celebrated and powerful that it withstood the power of the Athenians. It is uninhabited because of the fear of pirates, so that now there is not a single village, and consequently there is no livestock. It is more round than long or wide, and is separated from the mainland of Asia by a channel of no great width. The part of the island which looks north and west has a very high hill, called Cercerius [Mount Kerkereas], of most rugged rocks, which are almost inaccessible. We had on our ship a Greek seaman who had been on Samos, who said that he had seen a number of streams on the island; but we saw it only from the sea, though we were not very far off it. Samos has a great abundance of very tall trees, from which the corsairs can very quickly build fustes to pillage and rove the seas.

10

Discourse to define what a corsair is

But since this word corsair is not well understood in the Mediterranean regions, and since I have been in their hands, I want now to give some information about them. It is all the same whether you call them corsairs or sea pirates. And to explain briefly who becomes one, and how he begins, we must suppose that three or four daring men trained for the sea set out on a venture, who when they begin are poor, having only some small bark or frigate, or some ill-furnished brig; but have a box with a dial for navigating, called the *bussolo,* and also have some small stock of war material, that is to say a few light weapons, for fighting at a distance. For their subsistence they have a sack of flour and some biscuit, a goatskin of oil, honey, some strings of garlic and onions and a little salt, sufficient to last a month.

They then set out, sailing wherever they hope to find profit. And if the wind compels them to stay in harbour, they will draw up their bark on land, cover it with branches of trees, cut wood with their axes, light a fire with their flint and steel and make a loaf with their flour, baking it in the same fashion as Roman soldiers did in time past when at war, who carried with them a tile or sheet of copper or beaten iron, which they laid on two stones and then lit a fire under it, after laying the dough on it, and when the sheet was hot it heated the dough and baked their bread. Then, having thus equipped themselves, they are likely within a month or two to take some good booty. And if chance allows them to find some good encounter, they will in a short time be greatly rewarded. But whatever they gain, however small, will raise them very high.

And since this is a plague so contagious that in a single day it spreads from Asia to Africa, there is no man who does not fear it greatly and seek to avoid it. It is a public evil which constrains people on land to keep a lookout for the corsairs out at sea and watch for them in the manner which I shall describe. There is not a hilltop on the islands or on the coast of the mainland but has posted on it all day long men keeping a lookout, watching to see any such corsairs sailing on the sea. And if they see any vessel they will judge and easily recognise from the look of the vessel whether it is a corsair or not; for however good an appearance the corsairs present people will be wary of them. And so they always sail about hiding and concealing themselves, in order to take their victims by surprise.

If the watchers see such vessels out at sea, they light a fire with their flint and steel; but since the fire cannot be seen by day, they have material ready prepared that makes a great deal of smoke. And if there are several vessels, they make smoke at different places, for a plurality of smoke signifies that they see a number of ships. By this sign all the inhabitants of nearby ports are warned, and keep a good lookout. And the watchers on other hills, although they have only seen the smoke, will not fail to do the same. When night begins to fall, they make bright fires, which all will see. For the custom of seamen is such, that when the light begins to fade in the evening, they look towards the places where a lookout is kept, knowing that the watchers light a bright fire every evening as a sign that all is safe; and they know then that the coast or the sea is clear; and in the contrary case, when there are several fires, they know that the coast is in danger. And if the lookout on the hill has lit two fires, that means that he has seen two enemy vessels; and similarly with three or four, and so on with other numbers. But if he lights fires without number, this means that the vessels which he has seen are so numerous that he has been unable to count them.

These warning signals are a common practice everywhere in time both of peace and of war. They are as good a contrivance as anything that has ever been devised for the public benefit, for it needs only one watcher to warn a whole countryside, which is not a new invention. Also the watchers communicate with one another, so that one who is at some distance from the first watcher warns another who is still farther away, as if he himself had seen it, and so the message can be passed on within a day to a distance of over 150 leagues.

Herodotus tells us that the inhabitants of Schiro [Skyros][231] were able to inform the Greeks, over a distance of more than 30 leagues, about three galleys which Xerxes had captured from them. Fires of this kind are also used in England, principally in time of war, as in the islands of the Aegean Sea. For at the sight of a single fire they will raise all the surrounding countryside in arms in less than three hours, and, each district knowing where to go to repel the enemy, they can prevent them from landing in their territory.

The corsairs are well aware of these arrangements, and so they commonly sail by night, land at some place which they know is suitable for their purpose and cover their frigate with branches. While their frigate is beached they have time to look out for anyone coming from the villages either to guard livestock or go for water, or on some other business, whom they will capture and make a galley slave.

If they know their business, they will have made poor use of their time if, after being at sea for no more than two months, they have not taken some dozen or so men as slaves, and if they continue in this course will move up from a frigate to a brig, from a brig to a fuste, from a fuste to a galliot and from a galliot to a galley. And if by chance two bands of corsairs come together, then, joining up, they are greatly strengthened. They are enemies of their friends as well as of those who are completely strange to them, and if they come upon their own relatives, they will not spare them. If only two corsairs sail together, they will attack a squirace, a marciliane, a lute[232], and other such small seagoing vessels. But they will not dare to attack a large ship if it has even a few guns.

This is how the corsairs pillage at sea, and gradually make themselves more powerful and formidable to all the people of the islands, to such an extent that the poor peasants are in greater fear than the bird on the bough; for when they are least thinking of them they find them on their tail. And so the fishermen round the coasts and all small vessels, wherever they are, are almost always in a state of fear. To give an example, when I was on the island of Paxo[233], anciently called Ericusa, near Corfu, and was with my guide, looking for plants, the corsairs carried off the ferrymen who had taken me there.

On another occasion, when I was on a large Venetian vessel named *La Priola* which was lying at anchor in a harbour on an island in the Archipelago called Zia, and anciently Cio [Kea], waiting for a good wind to go to Constantinople, I saw a bark coming from the island of Andros with a good wind and entering our harbour, where it arrived very late, followed by another bark manned by pirates, which would have entered the harbour along with it, but that the corsairs saw our ship also there; and so they went to hide in another harbour on the other side of the island, for it was already night. On the following morning before it was light, the pirates, of whom there were eight in company, came and hid in the reeds, waiting for daylight, hoping to board the bark which they would find on the shore and to carry it off by force along with all who were on board. And certainly they would have done this, but for the help which we were able to give. When those who were on the bark saw that they had been taken by surprise, the strongest of the men threw themselves into the sea to save themselves by swimming, but the others who had stayed with the women and children were taken prisoner. These corsairs were so bold that they set out to carry them off while we were there, although we were in great number. The master of *La Priola* loosed off a falconet, drew up his arquebusiers along the side of the ship and fired a culverin at them, which compelled them to leave the bark alone; for in order to get out of the harbour they would have had to pass fairly close to our ship, and so they were forced to return to their own bark.

These poor folk who had come from the island of Andros would have been made slaves of the Turks but for our help. The Turks never kill the people whom they capture, either at sea or on land, but sell them. If it is a handsome young woman, they sell her for 80 or 100 ducats; an old woman would fetch 30 or 40 ducats, a young boy of good appearance 40 or 50 ducats. A stout, well built young man will fetch 60 ducats. This is why ships are always armed, and why vessels that are not armed are always in a state of fear.

Having spoken sufficiently of the corsairs, I shall return to speak of our voyage. The Greek wind which was in our favour continued throughout the night, so that we left Samos on the left and passed through the strait between Samos and Nicaria [Icaria]. It was already broad day when we passed near two small rocks, which are much renowned among seamen, called the Stoves, because it is a very dangerous passage. They have taken their name in the vulgar tongue from the Greeks who anciently called them Ipni, that is to say Furni [Fourni]; but the ancients did not mean these ones, but other rocks which are at the mouth of the river Peneus [Pinios], near Thessaly. These rocks are greatly to be feared, particularly when you pass them at night. The chart names them the Fourneaux [Stoves]. And since it is necessary to pass by these rocks, or else take a very long way round, all of us were in great fear; for it has often happened that ships have perished there in a storm.

Continuing on our course, we passed near another island called Gaideroniso[234], which is as much as to say Donkeys' Island; it is uninhabited and of no renown.

11

Of the island of Patmos

We had the island of Patmos, where Saint John the Evangelist lived in exile and wrote his Apocalypse, on our left. The hills on this island are very high and can be seen from a great distance. It is called in the vulgar tongue Parmosa, and is inhabited by Greek Christians. It lies well out to sea beyond the island of Icaria. The inhabitants of this island live in full Christian liberty, in the Greek fashion, as do all the other islands of Greece which pay tribute to the Turk. The magistrates and heads of the towns, however, are commonly Turks.

The harbour of Patmos is large enough for fustes, galleys and small ships. The whole island is fertile in grain, and there is an abundance of all kinds of vegetables. There is also a monastery of Greek caloyers, in which is to be seen the hand of a dead man on which the nails grow like those of a living man. Although they are regularly cut, they grow long again after a certain space of time. The Turks say that this hand belongs to one of their prophets, but the Greeks say that it is the hand of Saint John, who wrote the Apocalypse in the monastery.

Continuing on our course with the Greek wind, we saw on the right, fairly far out to sea, the island of Lipsos [Leipsoi], which is small and deserted. Soon afterwards we passed the island of Pharmaco [Pharmakonisi], anciently called Pharmacusa. It was near this island that corsairs took Caesar slave, when he was going to Rhodes to study under Apollonius Molo.

After passing Pharmaco, we came to an island which was anciently called Irion, now called Lero [Leros][235]. It is inhabited by Greek Christians, and is directly opposite a point in Asia, reaching well out to sea, which the chart names Cortolo. Here are to be seen ancient castles situated on hills and low mounds. The hills on Leros are much higher than those on Samos, and the land is very well cultivated by Turks and Christian Greeks.

We passed Leros and came to another large island called Calimno [Kalymnos], inhabited by Christian Greeks. Beyond this we came to another island called Psermo [Pserimos], on which there are two or three towns and a number of villages. The land is cultivated by the labour of Greek Christians.

We had the town of Smyrna on the left, now one of the richest towns, and with the greatest trade in merchandise, in the whole of Anatolia, which was anciently called Smyrna. We had to pass a point opposite the island of Psermo, which juts well out to sea from Anatolia, named on the chart Cavo Rosso [Fener Burun], and anciently Erithris, which means red cape. We had great difficulty in passing it, for the weather was dark, and besides it was about midnight. The bad weather, which was contrary to us, took us so much by surprise that we were using only one side of the sail on the port side. It was a north-westerly wind so impetuous that it had made the sea violent and angry.

On the following morning we entered the channel between the island of Cos and the mainland, the district of Halicarnassus[236], which is no more than five leagues wide. The sea between Samos and the island of Cos is so full of small islands that they could not be counted accurately except with great trouble; they were all anciently called the Sporades.

12

Of the island of Cos, the country of Hippocrates

When it was day, being well advanced into the channel, we had a clear view of the whole of the island of Cos, which was the home of Hippocrates. The Turks call it Stancou. Its hills seemed to us higher than those on any of the other islands that we had yet seen; for they are scarcely less high than those of Crete.

The town of Cos is entirely inhabited by Turks, and on the whole of the island there are only two villages inhabited by Greeks. The castle and town of Cos are also called Stancou. The castle lies high, with round towers larger than those of the castles of Metelin [Mytilene] and Tenedos. The town lies low, situated on the coast below the castle. This island is very fertile and abundant in animals, and is longer than it is wide. We skirted it for a long time with a favourable wind, hoisting all our sails, for the tempest had ceased. Then we put on all the auxiliary sails to increase our spread of canvas.

Leaving the island of Cos on the right, we entered the channel of Rhodes. We were still a long way from the town, which we could see situated on a low hill on a long promontory; and since it has tall towers, and lighthouses or beacons which give light to direct ships safely into harbour, we were able to see it from a distance. When we drew closer we could see what is said to have been the ancient city of Rhodes, situated on a low round mound near the coast, two leagues from the present town. It is said that there was a convent there for the knights of religion[237]; and certainly there are handsome mansions here and the place is strongly fortified. It is carefully guarded by the Turks. Having finally arrived at Rhodes, we anchored, disembarked and went to see the town.

13

Singularities observed in Rhodes

The town of Rhodes is partly situated on the slopes of a hill, partly along the coast. Most of the inhabitants of the villages on the island are Greeks, who can enter the town during the day to work there and sell their crops in the market, and are allowed to stay there all day, but the Turks do not permit them to sleep there at night, because of their suspicion of revolt or of treason. I do not mean that no Christians at all spend the night in the town: for many of their slaves are Christian.

The Venetians keep a factor in the town for the trade in merchandise, and he does not leave the town at night, although all his family are Christians. The Grand Turk ordinarily maintains five galleys worked by slaves here, and their captain is charged to purge the sea of the corsairs who have been in the habit of carrying out raids in the Cyclades, Sporades and other places in Greece belonging to the Turk, and thus to keep the Mediterranean Sea in subjection and all the rest of Greece in safety. For he carries out regular courses with his galleys, and if there is any word of corsairs in his area he will not rest until he has found them.

All the buildings of the knights of Rhodes, both French and of other nations, still stand entire everywhere, for the Turks have not removed any of the coats of arms, paintings, sculptures or carvings and signs that they found there. And numbers of inscriptions both in French and in Italian can still be read today. I must say also that the Turks have always had this custom, that any castle or fortress that they have taken is left in the state in which they found it, for they never demolish any buildings or carvings.

On the following day we went to see some nearby villages outside the town, and attended the mass of the Greek caloyers, and saw their gardens, which were very well cultivated with pomegranate-trees, orange-trees, jujube-trees and sebesten-trees, of which they have great numbers, and they make birdlime from its fruit. There are also fig-trees, almond-trees and olive-trees.

The inhabitants of the villages on Rhodes live according to the Greek religion, and still preserve the old names of things. The watch which the Turks keep at night in Rhodes and other castles in Turkey is done by voice, for the guards pass the word from one to the other, and not by bells as in the towns of Italy and at Ragusa. The walls of Rhodes are in the same state as they were when the Turks took them out of the hands of the knights, and since then they have been neither increased nor diminished, neither strengthened nor weakened. Here you can buy fine silk needlework, particularly bed curtains. This work is produced in various colours, in cross-stitch. The pattern is of foliage, and is different from Turkish work and the work produced on Chios and Cyprus.

14

Modesty of Turkish soldiers. And of a snake called jaculus, and of the bird called onocrotalus

Here we saw a tame bird called *onocrotalus*, which flew about the town. Observing its size, I found that it was by no means as big as a swan. It is all white, and much larger than a goose. Its legs are like those of a swan, and its feet likewise, but of an ashen colour and covered with hard leather. It is a gay bird, robust and vigorous, which holds its head straight and high. Its beak is broad and fluted, pointed and turned up at the tip. It has feathers on the back of its head, forming a kind of crest like a lapwing's, and when it flies it beats its wings like a swan. It feeds both in salt water and in fresh. I shall prove in another work of mine, in which I have given portraits of birds, that it is a pelican, but of this I say no more at present, for the sake of brevity.

Among the singular things on this island I saw the snake called *esculus,* speckled with small spots on its back resembling small eyes, like the spots on the back of the electric ray, the fish called in Latin *torpedo.* I found it under a spiny caper-bush outside the town, at the spot where the Turk set his artillery when he was besieging Rhodes. The Greeks now call it in their vulgar tongue *saetta,* that is to say *sagitta,* and the Turks *ochillane,* the ancients *acontias.* It is three palms in length and no thicker than a man's little finger. It is ashen in colour tending towards the colour of milk, and its underbelly is totally white. It has scales on its back and broader scales on its belly in the manner of other snakes. It is black on the upper part of the neck, and marked with two white lines which begin at the head and continue all the length of its back to the tail. Its spots are no bigger than lentils; but, its back being ashen colour, the black spots are round, surrounded by a white circle. I shall speak more at length about its anatomy elsewhere, when describing all snakes in detail. But having a true portrait of it, I set it here[238].

Le portraict du Iaculus , autrement dit Acontius.

Figure: Portrait of the Iaculus, otherwise named Acontius

I also saw a brig on the shores of the harbour discharging its cargo of a drug used in medicine called red storax[239] The Greeks now call it *maurocapno,* and I was told that it grows on the island.

But since those who travel by sea cannot be too long away from their vessel, I had no time to go off and look for the tree; for when seamen have the right weather, they would not wait for any man alive. This means that those who have sailed in a galley or a ship have not been able to see much of the land, since they must always be ready for their ship.

Having observed the Turkish soldiers on guard duty at the gates of Rhodes, I have had occasion to write of the great continence and obedience of the Turkish troops; for although there were twenty or thirty men at the gates of the town, guarding them carefully, it was with such great silence and modesty that there was no more noise than if there had been no one there, and they seemed more like ordinary craftsmen than men of war. And indeed they are so peaceable in all their affairs that none of them had any arms, not even a sword. There are now only two great gates open in Rhodes, one facing the harbour and the other on the landward side, as well as a false door opening into the grand master's garden.

The peasants of the island coming to the market to sell their kids, cheeses, butter and other such provisions, are dressed in the same fashion as the peasants of Crete. They are black and wrinkled of face, having long hair, hanging down to their shoulders, and wear large double caps. Their doublet is of leather without sleeves, their shirt hangs down in front and behind, and they wear leather boots which come up so high that they fasten them to the doublet. They have cloth breeches over their shirts. Anyone not accustomed to seeing them would think that they were wearing masks, like street dancers, for they are accoutred like the masked men who go around playing the clown at Shrovetide in Rome and Venice. They sell their old clothes to the Turks, who pay them in cash without cheating them.

It is easy to see by the ruins outside the town that there were formerly large faubourgs round Rhodes, which were totally destroyed during the siege by the Turk and have not yet been rebuilt. However there are a few villages scarcely more than a bowshot from the gates which are inhabited by Greeks and Turks, and where the caloyers have a monastery.

15

Voyage from Rhodes to Alexandria

Having stayed for some days in Rhodes and done our business, we returned to continue our voyage. We had a north-westerly wind, and we had to sail for a long time to port, that is to say to the left side of the ship, for we had to reach a point called Cavo del Bo [Cape Zonari], some distance up from Rhodes.

This is the place where the Turkish galleys first came when the Turk landed on the island and laid siege to the town. When we reached this point we had a very favourable following wind, a tramontane, that is to say a northerly wind, and headed directly for Alexandria, choosing a straight course; and having a suitable wind, put on extra sail. This is what the Italians call the French rig, apparently to distinguish it from the lateen sail, which is triangular, while the French sail is square.

The good wind remained favourable for us all night, and at daybreak we had sailed so far that we were out of sight of the island. The wind continued until midday and then ceased. The sea being now smooth and the weather calm, we tried to establish where we were. We knew from the chart that we were already half way, for with a good wind the passage from Rhodes to Alexandria takes less than three days and three nights.

When seamen find themselves in the open sea with no wind, the vessel moves no more than if it were in harbour. Then each man begins to play, to fish, to bathe, making no difficulty about throwing himself into the sea and diving, passing from one side to the other under the ship. This is when seamen are afraid of the corsairs; for in calm weather a large broad-beamed vessel is in great fear of even a small narrow ship driven by oars. But when there is a wind, small vessels have no fear of galleys, for with sails they can always escape.

A sirocco wind now began to blow up, and grew stronger towards evening, until it became very violent. This compelled us to furl all the sails and content ourselves with one small sail, which we had to lower to half-mast and strengthen with good ropes and stout cables.

The wind veered to westerly, blowing quite gently and continuing so all night. Then at daybreak the tramontane wind returned to favour us; and we were able to make good speed, sailing at least four or five leagues an hour, which is the fastest that boats can sail except in a storm. Sailors call it going with fortune.

The course of our voyage was such, that we had to follow a straight course from the strait of Constantinople with the poop of our ship facing north and the prow pointing south; for the course from Constantinople to Alexandria is a straight line from north to south.

Now since I have said so much in this discourse about our voyage, it seems proper not to leave the matter until I have first spoken of the navigation of the ancients, which was much more difficult than it is now, as will appear in the following chapter.

16

That seamen navigated anciently without the needle and quadrant.
and without the use of the lodestone

The ancients had greater difficulty in their navigation than we have now; for then, neither in peace nor in war, had they any means of determining their direction, save by conjecture of the position of the east, the west, the north and the south, the stars by night and the sun by day; and most commonly they kept within sight of land. But now that everyone knows the virtue of the lodestone, navigation is so easy that two men can venture out whenever they want with a small bark ready to face all kinds of hazards and the most violent winds, and cross the open sea, which the ancients would not have ventured to do in full daylight, lacking as they did the quadrant and the needle which has been rubbed on a lodestone.

This is the stone otherwise known as *lapis Herculeus,* or *magnes,* and *sideritis,* and in Italian *calamita,* in which are found contrary virtues: for one of its ends causes the needle to point north, and the other south. I find that the man who first devised the use of this stone was called Flavius, but the first to describe its virtue was Albertus Magnus, who having found that it was in use in his time, thought that the practice was ancient, and that Aristotle had understood this virtue. But neither Aristotle nor those who came long after him ever learned the lodestone's virtue, nor that one end of it caused the needle to point north and the other the contrary way. Aristotle knew well that it attracted iron, but he did not realise that it could serve in navigation.

The qualities of the lodestone gave some alchemists the idea of contriving various deceits, promising certain subtleties in matters of love, claiming that since it attracted iron it also attracted the amorous desires of men and women; but that is false. And they spoke more highly of the white form, knowing that it is rarer and more difficult to find than the ordinary kind, which is the colour of iron. Great quantities of this lodestone are now to be found on an island in the Mediterranean Sea called Erba [Elba], anciently Ilua, situated opposite Plombin [Piombino], where it does not cost much.

17

That there are only two large navigable mouths of the Nile that large round-bottomed vessels can enter

Between Rhodes and Alexandria a saker, tired from flying, perched on the lateen yard of our ship, where it stayed for a good two hours. Several quails, coming from the north and heading south, were also captured on our ship. For me this confirmed that quails are migratory birds, for I had already observed others in spring, when I crossed from the island of Alzante, otherwise called Zacinthus, to the Morea, otherwise named Negroponte[240]

There I saw that quails coming from the south were flying north to stay there for the whole summer; then I saw a great number of them being caught along with various other kinds of migrant birds which had landed on our vessel, tired by their flight. We also saw another bird unknown to all who were on the ship, which was about the size of a cock and roughly of the colour of a redwing. We also saw some onocrotals flying from north to south: birds that are rarely known in France or Italy, save that they are sometimes seen on the lake of Mantua, but from there they go back south in winter.

There was no wind all day and for much of the following night. On the next day we had quite a good wind from Greece, and continued on our way, coming into a part of the sea that the water of the Nile from the Damietta mouth had disturbed and given a different colour from its normal hue, so that the sea was white with it. It was a sign that told the sailors that they were not far from the mainland of Egypt, which was not yet in sight; for the whole territory of Egypt lies low, having no hills that can be seen from the sea.

It was already very late when we entered this disturbed water, and there was not much wind; so we anchored in the open sea, with 90 toises of water. The custom of the Moors, that is to say the Egyptians[241], when coming from Constantinople, is that if they arrive very late at night in these troubled waters, not knowing whether they are short of or beyond Alexandria and the mouth of the Nile, they anchor in the sea until the following morning, so that when there is enough light they can see where they are and in which direction they must go to reach harbour. And if they see that they have gone too far, they will be able to turn back towards harbour.

We spent the night on board, the sea being calm, and in the morning, drawing up the anchors from the sea-bottom and spreading the sails, we left the area of troubled water. We had sailed only a short distance before we entered another stretch of water affected by a Nile current from the direction of Rosetta. These two streams are the main currents from the Nile. The Rosetta current stained the sea in colours ranging from green to straw yellow, but this lasted for no more than half a league, and we came into an area of blue water. The first thing that we saw in Egypt was the castle of Rosetta, which is a day and a half's sail from Alexandria.

While we were still in the open sea, watching for the first thing to appear in Egypt, we saw only palm-trees and sycamore-figs, and the tall column of Pompey which is on the promontory above Alexandria; for since the country is so low-lying and without hills, it is not seen from a distance. It was already late when we entered harbour, and so we did not leave the ship that evening.

18

Summary of the route from Constantinople to Alexandria

It can be seen by considering the days spent on this present voyage that it can conveniently be completed in fifteen days, provided that the wind is favourable, as it was on our voyage. And to repeat our course day by day, if we had not stayed at Gallipoli in the strait with the castles, otherwise called the Bosphorus, and in the town of Chios and in Rhodes, we should have covered the distance in eight days. For from Rhodes to Alexandria took only three days and three nights, from Chios to Rhodes two days and two nights, and from Constantinople to Chios only two days and three nights. This shows that you can travel a long way in few hours, provided that the wind is favourable.

19

Of the two towns of Alexandria, one in Egypt, and the other which was a Roman colony in Phrygia

On the following morning we left the ship and went to the town of Alexandria. Before speaking of Alexandria I shall say first that there have been several Alexandrias, but among them all two are renowned. The Romans rebuilt the town of Troy the Great, sent Roman colonies there and named it Alexandria, as Pliny mentions. This is the town of which Galen frequently speaks; for he had never heard of any other than this Alexandria on the site of Troy, and knew nothing of Alexandria in Egypt, as can be sufficiently seen from his writings. It is enough for my present purpose to treat succinctly of the magnificent things that I observed, for to write in detail of the city of Alexandria after so many great personages would be mere useless repetition.

It is situated on sandy ground on a point, with the Mediterranean Sea on one side and the large expanse of Lake Mareotis on the other. The very walls that Alexander the Great built in ancient times are still entire, but the interior of the town consists merely of the ruins of ancient buildings. It was deliberately ruined when the king of France, with the king of Cyprus[242], forced the Soldan to leave it, and, seeing that he could not hold it, caused it to be demolished But since then the houses have been rebuilt little by little, according as people wanted to live there. And were it not that western merchants keep some people there to carry on trade, it would be but a poor place.

All sorts of foodstuffs are brought to the town, both from Egypt and from Cyprus and other neighbouring places. The bread which is made here, and also in Syria, is formed into flat loaves like pancakes, on which they scatter wild cumin seeds; and so these seeds are on sale in large bagfuls in markets and merchants' shops.

All kinds of wines are brought here by sea from various places, for Cyprus is only a little way away. The meat, both of sheep and kids, veal and beef, is very flavoursome. They have large numbers of a kind of goats, they call gazelles and the Greeks anciently called *oryx*. They shoot them with arquebuses in the countryside, where they roam about in herds. Here too they have hens and eggs. Alexandria is situated in a place abounding in fish, where I have seen sea-bream, bass, maigre, dentex, mullet, ray, angel-fish, dogfish and gurnard; and there are many others which are brought from the Nile, either fresh or salted. They also have pomegranates, bananas, lemons, oranges, citrons, figs and sycamore figs, carobs and other kinds of fruit which we do not have. They also have all kinds of vegetables, which are much renowned, and they are rich in all kinds of corn, like rice, barley, and far, otherwise called spelt.

The plant called by the Greeks *dolicos* here has yellow flowers. They also have great quantities of a species of pea called *latyri* by the Greeks, *manerete* by the Venetians and *cicerchie* by the Romans. Anyone who wants to know what things are most abundant in a town has only to walk about the squares on market days, where game, fish, vegetables, fruit and other wares are sold, and he will quickly see what the inhabitants have in most plentiful supply: as was made manifest to me in Alexandria. The Egyptians scarcely ever have a meal without a kind of root, called dasheen, which they cook along with meat. It produces great profit throughout Egypt, and so it is the thing most sold in the markets of towns and villages. I set here a figure of Alexandria, drawn from my observation, so as to show a true representation of the city.

VRAY PORTRAICT DE LA VILLE D'A-
LEXANDRIE EN EGYPTE.

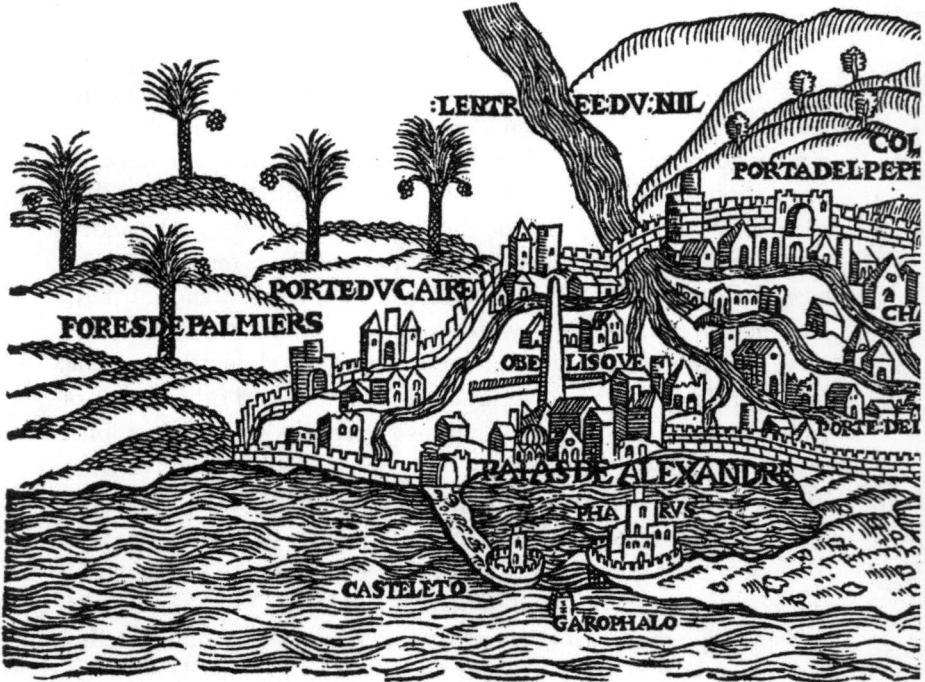

Figure: True portrait of the town of Alexandria in Egypt

Lac d'eau douce de moult grande estendue,
& de grand reuenu en poisson.

,A VILLE D'A-
GYPTE.

LAC MAREOTIS

EE DV:NIL

COLONNE·DE·PONPEE

PORTADELPEPE

MO SAVFE

CHATEAV·NEVF

CHATEAV·VIEIE

LISOVE

PORTE·DE·LA·MARINE

S·DE·ALEXANDRE

PORTO·VECHIO

PHA RVS

GAROPHALO

TERRE FERME D'AFRIQVE.

MEDITERRANEE.

20

Of the animal anciently called hyaena and now civet

The consul who was then in Alexandria for the business of the Florentines had a civet which was so tame that when playing with men it would bite their nose, ears and lips without doing them any harm, for it had been fed since its birth on milk from a woman's breasts. It is rare indeed to see an animal so wild and difficult to tame becoming so domesticated.

The ancients were familiar with the civet, and I shall prove, with their authority, that it should be called *hyaena,* although they had never perceived that it voided an excrement with such a strong smell: yet it seems clear that there was a species of odoriferous panther. The authors speak of *hyaena* as a wild beast living in Africa, which leads me to think that in those days civets were not kept in cages. But now that they have been tamed they are of greater value than they were anciently. The name that we call them by is borrowed from African authors, for we have abandoned their old name.

The civet is squat like a badger, but of greater size; and many people, reading the accounts of *hyaena* and knowing that it has an orifice, in addition to the one for the purposes of nature, from which the substance called civet is extracted, have thought that it was a badger. But the ancients and Aristotle called the badger *throchus.* The *hyaena* has black hairs on its neck and along its back, which it draws up when it is angry, just as does a pig. Hence the fish called *glanis* has also been called *hyaena.* Its muzzle is more pointed than a cat's, and it also has a beard. It has red, gleaming eyes and two black spots under the eyes. Its ears are round, similar to those of a badger. It has a speckled coat, with black spots on a white ground; and its legs and feet are black, like those of an ichneumon. Its tail is long, black on the upper side, with white spots on the underside. It feeds on flesh, and has a body of great agility. Here is a picture of the civet. If it is compared with the description of the *hyaena* it will be seen that what we now call civet is the *hyaena* of the ancients.

Figure: Civet

21

Discourse of various things in Alexandria, and of the obelisks and great colossi of the Egyptians

On the following day we went to see the tall column of Pompey, on a small promontory outside the town, a half-quarter of a league from Alexandria. The column is of admirable width, and of inordinate height, taller than any other that I have ever seen. The columns of Agrippa[243] at the Pantheon in Rome fall far short of its width and height. The whole mass, the column, the capital and its cubic form, is of Thebaic stone[244], the same stone as all the obelisks which have been brought out of Egypt. It is said that Caesar had it erected here for his victory over Pompey[245]. This column is so large that it would now be impossible to find a workman who could contrive means of moving it elsewhere.

From this promontory there are wide views over the sea and on land. To the south is the wide and spacious lake of Mareotis, surrounded by forests of palms. It is less than half a league from Alexandria to this lake. The country is for the most part of shifting sands, which would be entirely barren were it not that there grows there a plant called *harmala,* and also caper-bushes bearing the large smooth capers that are brought to us from this country. The small capers come from spiny caper-bushes, which lose their leaves in winter, but the caper-bushes bearing smooth capers which grow in Egypt and in Arabia do not lose their leaves. Tamarisks grow freely in the sandy soil of this territory, though elsewhere they seek out only damp places.

The plant named *harmala* is very similar to moly. It is a species of wild rue for which the Arabs, Egyptians and Turks have various uses. They perfume themselves with it every morning, and persuade themselves that by this means they drive away all evil spirits. This has led to such great usage of the plant and its seed that even the smallest merchant will have it in his shop, as if it were some precious drug. The ancient author Apollodorus[246] attributes to galingale what I have said of *harmala,* saying that the barbarians never leave their houses without being first perfumed with galingale. This has sometimes led me to think that the usage of this plant is ancient.

Among the singular things that we saw in Alexandria are two needles[247], otherwise called obelisks, near the palace of Alexandria. One stands erect and entire; the other is broken and lying on the ground. The one still standing is much larger than the other which is lying on the ground. It could be compared in size with the one that stands in Saint Peter's Square in Rome. When I speak of an obelisk, I am speaking of one of the things in this world that is most worthy of admiration, and we can but wonder why they were carved in such a strange fashion. If there were only three or four of them it might be thought that they had been carved out of curiosity by some king: but seeing that there are a great number of them, some of them very large, like those to be seen behind the Minerva in Rome, in a square near the Pantheon and up at the Ara Coeli, and that there are other smaller ones, like those to be seen in the Populo[248] and in the pope's palace; and, knowing also that they are carved with Egyptian characters or hieroglyphic letters, I conclude that they were carved anciently to be put over the sepulchres in which bodies were preserved in Egypt, and not to be dedicated in temples.

Many men seeing a stone hewn from the rock in one piece, so

large, so long, so wide and so well polished, are led to believe that it is made from a mixture of different stones; for all the obelisks are hewn from Thebaic stone, which has a variety of different grains, in two or three colours, like a starling's breast. This is why the Greeks formerly called it *psaronium*, for *psaros* in Greek means a starling. But they were wrong in this, :for the thrush-like grain is due to the nature of the rock, which is of these different colours. What makes the obelisks so worthy of admiration is that they are made from a single block of stone, as one might imagine a turret made all in one piece.

I believe that all the obelisks now to be seen in Rome had been carved in Egypt before Romulus set foot in Rome. The rock from which they were taken is so homogeneous, without any veins in it, that stone could be found suitable for hewing out a tower in a single piece, larger and longer than the towers of Notre-Dame in Paris, if it were possible to move it; for there is a hill two leagues long, all of solid stone, without any veins, where matter could be found for hewing colossi or obelisks of any length or size desired.

There are three low hills within the circuit of Alexandria's walls, which are called the "hills of sweepings"[249], like the refuse dumps of Paris. The handsome aqueducts, the great cisterns and the wells which are supplied by the Nile are truly things worth seeing, made of such fine material and so sumptuous that they are still entire; and indeed they were very necessary. The inhabitants of Alexandria fill them once a year, when the Nile floods Egypt, and can then drink the water throughout the year. It comes into the town in a large channel which first fills the cisterns where it is purified and clarified. The whole town of Alexandria is built over handsome cisterns and vaults. It was anciently built of stout masonry of hewn stone[250], since there is little timber in Egypt, except the wood of the palm-trees which are common there; but that is no good for carpentry work.

The Egyptian peasants go about the countryside looking for dead palm-trees; then they cut off the tops and find in them a white pith, which they sell in Alexandria. It is eaten raw, and has the taste of an artichoke. It is what the ancients called palm marrow or brain, and the Greeks *encephalon*. But it must be understood that there are different kinds of palms, for I observed another thorny species in Crete, different from the kind that mariners bring from Spain by sea, called *cephaloni,* which are the small palms that the grocers of Rouen and Paris sell fresh in their shops, costing only four or five sous each.

22

That a tame ichneumon is still kept in many houses in Egypt, and the fight between another creature also called "ichneumon vesper" and a phalangy

The inhabitants of Alexandria keep an animal called the ichneumon, which is principally found in Egypt. It can be tamed in the house like a cat or dog. The common people have given up using its ancient name, for they call it in their language "Pharaoh's rat". I saw peasants bringing young ones to the market in Alexandria, where they sold readily to be kept in houses, because they hunt rats, just as does the weasel, and they are also fond of snakes, which they eat indifferently. It is a small animal which is little trouble to keep. Those who have had pictures made of it for their own purposes without having seen it have not given a good idea of it, as can be seen from this present portrait, for the pictures that have been previously made of it give no impression of what the animal is really like.

Figure: Portrait of the ichneumon, which the Egyptians call Pharaoh's rat

The first one that I saw in Alexandria was in the ruins of the castle, which had caught a hen and was eating it. It is cunning in spying out its food, for it rears up on its hind legs and when it has found its prey it creeps up and swoops on the animal and strangles it, feeding indifferently on all kinds of live meat, like snails, lizards, chameleons and generally all species of snakes, frogs, rats and mice and other such creatures. It likes birds, particularly hens and chickens; and when it is angry it bristles, raising its hairs, which are rough and hard, like the hairs on a wolf, and of two colours, whitish or yellow alternating with grey. It is longer and more thickset than a cat, and has a pointed black muzzle like a ferret, and no moustache. It has short round ears, and is greyish in colour, tending towards straw-yellow, like the monkeys called *cercopitheci*. Its legs are black, and it has five rear toes with short spurs on the inner side. It has a long tail, thicker at the base; and its tongue and teeth are like those of a cat. It has a particular characteristic not found on other four-footed animals which has led the authors to think that males as well as females have it. It has a very large orifice surrounded by

223

hair in addition to the vent for excrement, resembling the shameful member of the females, which it opens when it is very hot. But the orifice for excrement is always closed, so that there is a cavity in it. It has genitals like a cat, and is much afraid of wind. Although it is small it is so dexterous and agile that it is not afraid to risk an encounter with a large dog; and if it finds a cat it will strangle it in three bites. But since it has such a pointed snout it has difficulty in biting a large mass and would not be able to bite a man's hand if the fist was clenched. The authors have many other things to say about this animal, particularly about its war with the asp, and also that it destroys crocodiles' eggs and that it is very watchful, attributing to it many singular virtues which I have not set down here to avoid prolixity, thinking it sufficient to give its description.

But since there is another small beast, which is a kind of wasp, also called *ichneumon vespa*[251], which is at mortal war with the phalangy, and since I have seen them fighting I think it right to describe it here. It is a species of bloodless insect, with the body of a bee or wasp, which is very like a large winged ant, smaller than a wasp, and lives in a hole in the ground like the phalangy. And when it comes across a phalangy it can get the better of it; but when attacking it in its hole it frequently withdraws without doing anything.

It happened in one such fight that the *ichneumon vespa*, finding a phalangy outside its hole, dragged it away by force, as an ant does a grain of corn, carrying it wherever it willed: although this was not without great difficulty, for the phalangy, digging in the hooks on its feet, put up a stout resistance. But the ichneumon stung it in various parts of its body with a sting which it draws like a bee, and, tired with the effort of dragging it, began flying hither and thither, about the distance of an arbalest shot; then returning to its phalangy. Then, not finding it in the place where it had left it, followed its tracks, as if it were on its scent, like a dog following a hare. Then it stung it again more than fifty times, and, continuing to drag it away and taking it wherever it would, finally killed it.

Among the goods, drugs and other singularities in the shops of Alexandria we found ostrich skins and great quantities of their feathers; for when the Ethiopians kill them they skin them. They eat the meat and barter the skins with all their feathers for other goods, which the merchants bring to Alexandria for sale. From there they are distributed to various places in Turkey; for the Turks also use them to make panaches and wear them on their turbans, as in France on caps, morions and other headgear.

The gardens of Alexandria and the whole of Egypt are difficult to maintain, for it is necessary to carry water in ox-carts to water the soil. Their jasmine is different from ours, for it has strongly smelling yellow flowers. Roses also are yellow, but have no smell.

23

Of the manners of the Alexandrians and of the deserts of Saint-Macario, and of various other things in Alexandria

Five days' journey from Alexandria in the direction of Africa are the deserts of Saint-Macario[252], which were the dwelling-place of Saint Anthony, where now live Arab caloyers, who share the Greek faith; and there are a number of monasteries occupied by both Arabs and Greeks. When we were in Alexandria we met some Venetian gentlemen who had recently returned from there, some of whom out of curiosity had brought back branches and flowers of the tamarind trees which grow there. There too are found such great quantities of eagle-stones[253] that they are loaded into ships and in ancient times were transported by merchants to Rome. Pliny tells us that the aquiline stone called *cissites* was found in Egypt near the town of Coptos.

The ancients have left us accounts of a secret means of testing a thief with eagle- stone, which still prevails among the Greeks today, and of which Dioscorides makes special mention; though he does not wholly confirm it. When the Greeks want to find a thief, they bring together all those who are under suspicion of the theft and agree to come for this purpose. There are then great ceremonies, in which the caloyers take part. They make a dough without leaven and form it into small rolls of bread the size of an egg, and each of those gathered there is required to eat his three rolls, each one in a single bite, and to swallow them without drinking. I was present on one such occasion, when the man who had committed the theft was unable to swallow his third roll, and in trying to force it down almost choked; but being still unable to swallow it, spat it out again. The monks preserve this as a secret, and are unwilling to disclose it; but I heard that it was due to the eagle-stone, a little powder from which was put into the dough when forming the rolls.

The place that Caesar called Pharus[254], which was then an island, is now attached to the mainland, and there is a castle which is difficult and inconvenient to maintain, for water has to be carried there every day, drawn from the cisterns of Alexandria. All the buildings in Alexandria have roof terraces, as commonly do all buildings in Turkey, Arabia and Greece, where the inhabitants sleep in the coolness of night throughout the year, in winter as well as in summer. The Egyptians and Arabs above all other nations sleep in the open at all times of year without any beds, and with no more than a small cloak or some other covering over them they are quite easy; they have no use for beds, believing that the feathers would be very dangerous for them. It is no marvel, therefore, if the people of this country have been able to observe so exactly the course of the stars, for they see them at all hours of the night, both when they rise in the morning and when they go to bed; and besides the sky is never overcast here.

The usual habit of the Alexandrians is to speak Arabic or Moorish; but the Turks who are mingled with them speak a very different language. And because there are many Jews, Italians and Greeks, various other languages are spoken. There are caloyers, both Jacobite and Greek, who have a house for the patriarchate of their church, at the place where anciently lay the body of Saint Mark[255], before the Venetians carried it off to Venice. The Latins and the Jews also have their own churches. Among the singularities which the consul of the Florentines[256], seeing me looking for druggists' shops, showed me was a root called *bisch* by the Arabs which he let me taste, and which caused me such great heat in the mouth, lasting for two days, that it was as if there was a fire in it. Several moderns have greatly abused the Arab authors over this root, and have so often corrected them, and wrongly maligned them, that it is quite shameful; and yet they themselves had never seen it. It is quite small, like a small turnip. Others have given it the name of *napellus*.

24

Voyage from the city of Alexandria to Grand Cairo

After spending some days in Alexandria we made our preparations to go to Cairo. There are two ways to go there, one of which is longer, by the Nile, and the other shorter, by land. But since the Nile had flooded Egypt, we embarked on the Nile at Rosetta. When we were half a league from Alexandria we came into a wide sandy plain, in which grow various plants, among them one called by the Greeks *anthillis* and by the Arabs *kali,* which the people of this country dry for burning, since they have very little wood.

By baking lime with this plant, they have a double gain, for they sell it in Alexandria, and they are careful to preserve the ash of the plant, which they sell to the Venetians. The ash grows as hard as stone, forming large masses which can be loaded into the ships of the merchants who buy them and take them to Venice, to make crystalline glasses. Those who make the glasses in Maran de Venise [Murano] mix the stones with pebbles brought from Pavia on the river Ticino, which mingled in due proportion with the ash makes the paste for the finest crystalline glass. But the French, who began not so long ago to make crystalline glasses, use the sandy soil of Étampes instead of the Ticino pebbles, which the craftsmen have found better than the pebbles from Pavia. But they have not yet been able to find anything that can serve in place of the ash, and so they have to go to Provence to buy it. This leads me to think that it is the same as what they bring from Syria by sea. It is called in French soda, taking its name from another plant called soldanella, which when burned leaves ash with the same virtue, which they can use in place of the Syrian ash.

25

Of the singular things found between the city of Alexandria and the town of Rosetta

On the roads through the fields, two leagues from Alexandria, we found shepherds with flocks of goats, which have such long ears hanging down that to save them from trailing along the ground they have been looped up three fingers' width. The shepherds, seeking to make good use of their time in the country, sift the sand, looking for antique coins; for it sometimes happens that they find medals and coins of fine gold and silver. The country on our right consisted of spacious expanses of sand, in which nothing grew but a few caper-bushes and the plant mentioned above called *kali* or *harmala*.

The country on our left was somewhat higher, with some large villages scattered here and there between the forests of palm-trees. When we had travelled about three leagues we found fresh water good for drinking, which seemed like a spring but was in fact a jar filled with water from the Nile, brought in goatskins carried on camels, which some Turk kept filled for the love of God; for they esteem it a great charitable deed and merit to provide water along the principal roads to satisfy the thirst of travellers. There can be no thought of finding wine here, and even in towns it is as much as you can do to find fresh water.

The palm-trees here and throughout almost the whole of Egypt are very tall. Some of them bear on a single trunk twenty large trees separate from one another, all stemming from the same root.

Night overtook us on our way, and so we travelled for a long time in the dark, following the shore of the Mediterranean Sea, which we had on our left, and did not stop until we reached the fresh water of one of the first streams of the Nile, which we forded close to the sea. Here we found only a fishermen's hut, in which there was only salt for salting fish and salt mullet roe, which the ancients called *cephali*. We camped here, and spent the night in the open with our camels and mounts.

This first stream of the Nile is not the one that was called *Canopicum Nili Ostium;* but I could not learn what name it had anciently. It is not very deep, for we were able to ford it, even in the season when the Nile had flooded Egypt. We set out again next morning, following the stream of the Nile and travelling through sandy plains in which there were no trees but tamarisks. They grow to a great height and bear galls, which the Arabs call by the modern name of *chermasel*, and which in past times were much used in medicine and in trade[257].

Continuing along the coast of the sea, we found small black myrtles, which are of low growth, for the sea wind torments them constantly. They like to grow along the sea, which is why they were sacred to Venus, according to the fable of the poets, who say that she was born in the sea. After following the sea for a long time, we came into a region of drifting sands, where we saw small hills of fine sand formed by the wind. This plain was so barren that not a single plant of any kind grew there. That evening we reached the town called Rosetta, which the Moors call Raschit, situated on the shore near one of the main mouths of the Nile. The inhabitants of this town are diligent in cultivating their gardens, in which there grow banana-trees, papyrus plants, sugar-cane, dasheens and sycamore-figs. The sycamore-figs are trees of such exquisite greenness that indisputably they surpass all others in verdure. They also cultivate a kind of root which the Italians call *dolceguini*.

Chameleons are frequently found on the species of shrub which is called *rhamnus altera*. They can change into different colours. Ordinarily they are green, verging on yellow or sometimes on blue. Because of this they cannot easily be seen, for when a chameleon is sitting on a branch covered with a similar green, however curiously you look, you will have difficulty in finding it. They feed on flies, caterpillars, snails and grasshoppers, living in the manner of snakes and eating all kinds of small insects, which I have often found in a chameleon's stomach when I was carrying out an anatomy of it. Some have said that chameleons live only on wind. Now it is true that a chameleon will live for a year without eating anything, which is not a thing difficult to believe, for I have seen snakes of different kinds living for the space of ten months, without giving them anything to eat. They must, however, sometimes have a little water to drink.

26

Of the town of Rosetta at the mouth of the Nile called Ostium Canopicum

Rosetta is a handsome town, without walls. The Venetians have a consul here, otherwise called a bailiff, who looks after the trade in merchandise. Large ships can moor in the Nile, coming up close to the houses of the town. There is no town in the country of the Turk with a harbour, however small, but the Venetians have someone to inform them of the goods in the harbour, whether on a river or on the sea, and on land. This is a great advantage for them, since they have information from all parts of the world.

They also know the prices of goods in distant nations, which is why they surpass all other republics in matters of trade; and if they learn that there is some merchandise to be obtained from some harbour they send their people so that they may have the profit on it. There is a small castle near the sea, adjoining Rosetta, situated on the side towards Alexandria. It is not quite two leagues from the mouth of the Nile to Rosetta. Arabic is spoken there, as it is throughout Egypt. There are many Jews in the town, for they have so multiplied in all the countries ruled by the Turk that there is not a town or village but they live there and have multiplied. They speak all languages, and they did good service to us, both in interpreting for us and in telling us about things in this country.

We found the same kinds of foodstuffs in the markets of Rosetta as in Alexandria. Forests of palm-trees give the town shade. The houses are built in the same fashion as in Cairo. They have great advantage from the timber which they bring from Constantinople in their ships, for when sailing to Constantinople they are always laden, and in order not to come back empty they load up with timber for building in their country: for there is no good timber in Egypt. The animals of Egypt, thanks to the abundance of pasturage and the good fodder provided by the plants watered by the Nile and the temperance of the climate, are of good size. The buffaloes, oxen, camels, horses, asses, sheep and goats are very large. The sheep are fat, with large, thick tails trailing on the ground and a fold of skin hanging from their neck, like the dewlap of cattle, called in Latin *palearia*, and they are covered with blackish wool.

27

Of the fishermen of the Nile

There are many men in Rosetta who make their living by fishing in the Nile, and they have one peculiarity, which is that they use the bags under the throat of the birds that Pliny calls *onocrotali*, which are attached to the bird's beak in the shape of a racket, for bailing water out of their barks and small boats. When the beak is on the bird's head, it is round like a circle, for when the bird was alive it used this bag as a second stomach, so that when it had swallowed many shellfish and mussels, and these, feeling the warmth, had opened, there was more room in the bag, and after vomiting them up again the bird could eat the meat separated from the shells. These bags are of such substance that humidity does not corrupt them, so that they last for a long time in use by the fishermen. By *onocrotalus* I do not mean our bitterns, which are called in Latin *boves tauri*, and have a cry like an ox, nor spoonbills, whose beak is wide at the end, but the bird that Aristotle calls *pelecanes*. They swim on the water like swans and geese, and are fat and corpulent, of the size of a large swan, and are all white, with broad legs and feet, between ash-coloured and black.

28

Voyage from Rosetta to Cairo, and of several things that are on the Nile

We boarded a boat on the Nile to go to Cairo, and with a favourable tramontane wind blowing on our poop had soon completed our journey. The Nile flows from south to north, and we had to go against the current of the water. When we had travelled some distance and had crossed to the other bank, we all landed and continued our journey along the banks of the Nile. It was a very great pleasure to see the countryside with so much vegetation. Those who travel from here to Cairo on the Nile have a longer journey, because of the windings of the river.

Most of the handsome villages of Egypt are built along the Nile, both because of the abundance of the fresh water that floods the country and is used for watering the gardens. There are also some villages at some distance from the Nile, but they suffer from shortage of water for most of the year. We came to a village called Anguidie and beyond this to another, larger village called Mahatelimie; then to Dibi, and from there to a small town, half a day's journey from Rosetta, called Nantubes, which lies on both banks of the Nile, like Beaucaire and Tarascon on the Rhône. At this point the Nile is no wider than the Rhône at Lyons. Farther on we came to a village called Elminie. On this day we covered a considerable distance, for we had a good wind to help us on our way. The gardens of this place and the surrounding ountryside were flooded by the Nile and surrounded by forests of palm-trees. The fields were divided up by hedges of the shrub called *rhamnus,* which is different from our currant-bush.

We also saw tamarisks laden with their galls. In many places the fields were sown with rice, papyrus and banana-trees, and at other places with dasheens. And since dasheen is also called lotus[258] or Egyptian bean, and since I had been unsuccessful, in spite of my diligent efforts, in finding any seeds of this plant, and had been laughed at for my pains by people in Cairo, who told me that it had no seeds, I took occasion to enquire why the ancient authors called it Egyptian bean, knowing very well that it produces no beans.

For my part I maintain that this plant grows along the rivers in Crete, for I have seen it growing wild; but the Egyptians cultivate it diligently. And finally I found the source of the error. Herodotus, the very ancient author, speaks of two kinds of plants that grow on the Nile, one of which has a round root, which is the dasheen, and the other bears a head containing seeds resembling olive-stones. Other authors coming after him follow in his tracks, one after the other, writing about it whatever they think fit. For similarly, when Theophrastus says that its root is thorny, the matter is otherwise. Dioscorides also uses almost the same words as Theophrastus in describing the Egyptian bean; and Pliny, borrowing from them, speaks in similar terms. And so I am of opinion that by *faba aegyptia* we must understand true edible beans grown in Egypt. Galen too seems to me to mean ordinary beans, in his book on foodstuffs, when he speaks of the Egyptian bean. And to clarify what Pliny says about the Egyptians making various kinds of cups and other vessels with its leaves[259], it must be understood that the leaves are broad, and are pressed together and folded into a cone, so that they can draw water from the Nile and drink it; and after they have drunk, they throw it away.

Finally we came to a large village called Berimbal. The countryside was all covered with water, save that there are dykes at some places, built up so that they can go from one village to another. The inhabitants, to avoid the flooding of the Nile, are compelled to build the houses in their villages on higher ground Many such villages are to be seen, for the country is flat, and the houses, built of the heavy soil of the region, with pointed roofs in the manner of a beehive, can be seen from a great distance. Some houses are also built with a roof terrace, in the fashion of a platform, which is a kind of roof common throughout Greece and Turkey.

They have such a great lack of wood and stone that their houses are no more than small huts, for there is no more space within them than in a small hutch for housing geese. The reason is that they ordinarily sleep, drink and eat out of doors under trees, either to avoid vermin, or for the sake of coolness, for there is no rain here in winter. And in summer they do not seek coolness in their houses, but under the palm-trees. Tamarisks grow in Egypt indifferently either in damp places or on dry ground, so that small forests of them can be seen both in dry places and on damp ground on the banks of the river. These tamarisks are so heavily laden with the growths that I have called galls that the branches almost break under their weight. It seemed unusual to us to see, in this month of September, a river bird, which the French call a *bièvre* because it causes damage in ponds as a beaver does, and the Latins *vulpanser,* swimming with its new-hatched chicks on the Nile[260]. The river birds commonly leave the northern countries in winter, fly to Egypt, where they hatch their young, and return in summer, fleeing from the violent heat of the sun, which would be intolerable for them.

29

*Of the large Egyptian towns and villages situated on the banks of the
Nile because of the abundance of water*

As we sailed past Berimbal a number of small Egyptian
boys dived into the Nile to catch the bread which was thrown
to them from the boat, in order to have the pleasure of seeing
them swimming so well. They think no more about jumping into
the water than would ducklings. Continuing on our way with a
tramontane wind, we came to a large village called Sindou, and on
our right Diuruth. We made such good progress that we reached a
large town called Foua where we found lodging for the night. It was
anciently a town as big as Cairo, and still today there is no town in
the land of Egypt, after Cairo, that is larger than Foua. It is much
larger than Rosetta. Opposite the town is a large island on which
sugar-cane, sycamore-figs, palm-trees, dasheens and all kinds of
vegetables and corn are grown, as well as rice, which among many
other things brings great revenue to Egypt.

We spent the night at Foua, waiting for daylight; and although
we had a good wind the sailors would not venture to sail during the
night, because there are several bends in the Nile where it is fast
and dangerous. It flows almost as fast as the river Loire. There are
places where it follows a straight course and it is possible to sail at
night with all sails set and a good wind without any fear, for it is
slower there than where it has bends.

30

That the Nile in comparison is much like the river Po

It would scarce be possible to find in our Europe any river more
resembling the Nile than the Po, at least between Ferrara and the sea,
for there it is possible to travel upstream under full sail against the
current of the water, which can also be done on the Loire, as on the
Nile as well as on the Po. The Loire, however, is of no great depth.

All the kinds of barks and vessels on the Nile are different from the barks and boats on other rivers; and indeed it is generally the case that boats are everywhere different, depending on the nature of the rivers, for men try to adapt their vessels to the nature of the place so that they will follow the course of the river properly. Thus on a river which is fast and dangerous, with a very deep bed and high banks, they could not leave the bank of the river or come in to moor unless the ends of the vessel were as high as the bank, for otherwise would need to have a ladder; and so vessels on the Tiber are narrow and crescent-shaped, with very high prows and poops ending in points turned upwards. The rudder must also be worked by a long bar and the steersman must be high up; or else he would not be able to see where he was going. But the Nile, with its banks at water level, carries boats which are low, wide and flat.

The boats on the Nile are short, deep, roofed over, rounded, and have the rudder on one side, like those on the Tiber and the Po, which can sail down to the sea and on to Venice. Boats which are long in body and have no great depth of water to sail in, as on the Loire and the Seine, have the rudder to the rear. The boats on the Nile commonly are not very large.

Those who say that some waters can carry larger boats and heavier loads than others of the same depth, citing as an example the river Oise, which although narrower than the Loire carries loads three times heavier, and attributing this to the water rather than the depth, have not, I think, made their case; but since this is a matter of experience the doubt can very easily be resolved. When the Nile is high, flooding the whole country, it carries very large boats, which sail on it only during the inundation; for when it is low there are certain places where it can be forded by a man on horseback. The Nile is navigable by sailing boats, for neither hills nor forests keep the wind off it, any more than on the Po; although just as there are poplars on the banks of the Po which keep the wind off at certain places, so it is with palm-trees on the Nile. The fishermen on the Nile have this in common with those on the Po, that they both have water in the bottom of their boats, with a hurdle over it to walk on, so that their fish can be kept in the bottom of the boat, alive, and they can walk on the hurdle without getting their feet wet.

235

Continuing on our way, and being now some distance above the village of Sindou, we passed on the left[261] the mouth of the channel which Alexander cut to convey water to Alexandria, to fill the cisterns, wells and fountains in the town. The soil that was removed to make the channel can still be seen on either side of it, and the mouth of the channel is no more than a quarter of a league from the village of Sindou. The land on our right was somewhat higher than the land on our left and is of sandy soil, and consequently, since the Nile does not reach it, it is more barren. But the land on the left, which is low-lying and flat, and flooded by the waters of the Nile, is fertile and covered with vegetation. The river birds withdraw here in winter, so that the fields and meadows are white with them. They are mainly storks, of which the Egyptians are fond: with good reason, since frogs multiply there in such great numbers that but for the storks there would be no creatures more frequently to be seen there, and also because they kill snakes, swallowing them whole.

On the higher sandy land on the other side are to be seen vultures, Egyptian sakers, kites and other kinds of carrion-birds, the commonest of which is the bird that I call a saker, with the body of a crow, the head of a kite, a beak between that of a crow and an eagle, slightly hooked at the tip, and legs and feet between those of a crow and a bird of prey. I find a bird of this name in the writings of Herodotus and other ancients, and it seems to me that it is what they call *accipiter aegyptius*[262]. It is of the colour of a saker, but some are to be seen of other colours. I shall show their portrait in my book on birds.

During the inundation the buffaloes of the Nile are up to their bellies in water feeding on the plants on the ground, putting their heads into the water up to their shoulders, and when they have finished feeding, they draw their head out of the water, then chew the plants and swallow them in the sir, for no animal with lungs, neither birds and four-footed beasts nor whales, dolphins and all others that chew can swallow their food in water. And in such a manner they feed during the inundation.

There can be no better swimmers than the Egyptians; and they have to be so, for they often have to swim from one village to another during the flood for business that they have with one another, and for this purpose they are all clad in the same way, with a long white shift, which is a very simple garment, and a kind of seamless woollen cloak, like a long, light carpet, which they wind round their shoulders and part of their body. They wear no other clothing when they go about the country, and if they have to cross an area of deep water they wind their cloak and shift round their head, in the manner of a headdress, and so, swimming, they can cross the flood of the Nile. If they have to travel any great distance they pull some reeds after them, and when they come to the end of dry ground they take to swimming, supporting themselves on the reeds.

The same tramontane wind enabled us to make good progress, and when we were still more than forty miles short of Cairo we caught our first sight of the pyramids of which the authors make so much mention, for they are on high ground well exposed to the view of those sailing on the Nile, which is what Pliny means by these words: *sane conspicuae undique annavigantibus*[263]. The Egyptians, not knowing the word pyramid, call them pharaohs. They are still more to be wondered at when seen close up than they are described by the authors, as I shall show hereafter.

31

Some particularities of Egypt and the Egyptians

There is no nation that preserves more of its antiquity than the Egyptians, for still today we see them in the towns wearing the same garments as are described by the ancients. Throughout Egypt it is not the custom to leave chickens to hatch under the wings of their mother; instead they have specially constructed ovens, as we saw, in which they put 3000 or 4000 eggs at a time, and they are so skilled in managing them and tempering the heat that they all hatch at the same time. These ovens are common to many villagers, who bring their eggs to be hatched from different parts of the country.

They make embankments, from fear that the Nile will overflow, which they reinforce with faggots of straw, sugar-canes, *halimus* and *rhamnus,* and tamarisks, in order to keep the Nile in its bed.

Continuing our journey on the following day, with the wind astern, as favourable as we could have wished, we came to some

237

places where the Nile had frequent bends, and since we were in an area where palm-trees prevented the wind from filling our sail the boatmen had to disembark and haul our bark by main force, and were forced to cross to the other side to avoid the force of the current. And since the wind was weak, and we were now on the other side, we left the boat, and stayed there only for a short time until we had a good wind.

32

Description of birds and other animals observed on the Nile

The country of Egypt, being warm in winter and marshy, has numbers of river birds, and among others the one that the Greeks and Aristotle called *crex*. I recognised it from its cry, which is harsh; and just as the lapwing cries *aex,* so this bird cries *crex, crex* when it is flying. I wrote down its description as follows.

The bird called *crex* is of a size between a curlew and a sandpiper, with beak and legs also between the two. Its legs, thighs and feet are black, as also is its head, but the upper side of the neck, breast and shoulders is white, while the upper part of the body is ash-coloured, with a white line running across each wing. It takes its food on the ground and in the air, in the manner of the lapwing, which the ancient Greeks called *aex,* and thus makes a great deal of noise with its wings when flying. I believe that it has no French name, although I formerly thought that the barge-bird[264] was the *crex,* since Herodotus compares it in size with one of the species of the bird called *ibis.*

I had previously described this black ibis, thinking that it was *haematopus;* but having since then observed its habits, I have concluded that it is not *haematopus,* but rather the black ibis, of which Herodotus was the first to write, and after him Aristotle. It is the size of a curlew, or somewhat smaller, totally black, with the head of a cormorant, a beak more than an inch long, but pointed and bent, and somewhat curved, and all red, as also are the thighs and legs. It stands as tall as a bittern, which Pliny called *bos taurus,* and Aristotle *ardea stellaris,* and has a neck as long as an egret, so that when I saw the black ibis for the first time it seemed to me in habits and appearance like a bittern.

The Egyptians, Moors or Arabs, are more superstitious and ceremonious in their religion than the Turks, although both are of the same law, following Mahomet and subject to the Grand Turk, who conquered them in battle. Nevertheless the Turks attribute greater sanctity to the Arabs than to themselves. The reason is that the Alcoran was written in Arabic and later translated into Turkish, and also that the more learned Turks do not profess to speak the Turkish language, but rather Arabic. Their characters are the same, but the language is different. And so the Turks have no letters but those that came from the Arabs.

When we left the boat on the banks of the Nile to visit the villages we heard the Moors singing in their mosques, that is to say churches. They respond one to the other in alternate voices, in the manner of Latin priests, with almost the same accents and long sounds as those who sing the psalms in Latin. This is not the manner of the Turks, who have a rough and rude language in comparison with Arabic, which is very suitable for words composed in rhythm; and the Alcoran is written in rhythmic verses.

When we were near Cairo, four leagues before the town, we saw the place where the Nile divides into two branches, the one to the left running down to Rosetta, which is *Ostium Canopicum*, from which we had come; the other, going off on the right, goes to Damietta, which is *Ostium Pelusiacum*[265]. Thus we can say that the Nile has only two main mouths navigable by large vessels, or at most three in all. I do not deny that it has many small streams, but it has only two large ones that are navigable. It may well be that some are navigable at certain places during the flood, but at other times they are small streams which can be forded at the point where they reach the sea, as we did when we crossed the small channel between Alexandria and Rosetta. Our wind continued up to Cairo, where our voyage ended. We disembarked at a large village called Boulac [Bulaq], which is close to Cairo, situated on the banks of the Nile.

Before I finish speaking of the Nile, I shall first say something about some of the animals to be found there, and among others the one which the Latins and also the Greeks call *hippopotamus*, that is to say river horse. I find that the Latins, following in the footsteps of the Greeks, did not change the Greek name, which means in Latin *equus fluviatilis*, but always called it *hippopotamus*. I believe that they preferred to use that name because when they saw that this beast bore no resemblance to a horse they did not wish to give it a name in their language, bur retained the Greek word. And for this the reason must be, either that the Romans did not know the *hippopotamus* of the Greeks, or else that the animal which they thought to be such was not the one that the Greeks called *hippopotamus*. And if the one that was brought to Rome when Caesar triumphed over Cleopatra, as Dio writes, and also the others which were shown in the games of M. Scaurus[266]and in the triumphs of Pompey, were hippopotamuses, I make no doubt that I gave true portraits of them in the book which I published on all fishes, for the animal that I saw alive in Constantinople, brought from the Nile, matched in all respects those to be seen engraved on various medals issued by Roman emperors. I shall for the present say no more about it, having written about it elsewhere in French and Latin[267].

The river Nile has many other much renowned fish, which however I do not wish to specify in this place, except to say that since the pike is common and we have difficulty in finding an ancient name for it, I wish to show that it was anciently called *oxyrinchus*. They also fish for two kinds of round fish, the size of a man's head, the skins of which are filled with stuffing or hay and are brought to us by the merchants. The Greeks call them *flascopsari* in their vulgar tongue, and the Latins *orbis*, or else by the Greek name *orchis*, for they are as round as a bottle. There is also one whose skin is made not of scales but of bone, and so they keep it, just like the skin of the other one. Crocodiles are also particular denizens of the Nile, and their skins are to be seen almost everywhere.

Figure. Crocodile

33

*The difference between the boats which sail on the Nile, and the
names, of the commonest trees in the gardens of Cairo*

Having completed our sail up the Nile and landed at the village
of Boulac, which is where gerbes[268] and barks and other kinds of
vessels on the Nile put in to discharge what they have brought to
Cairo, I observed the vessels called gerbes, which are of three or four
different kinds. Some are low, flat and wide, very short in relation
to their width, Others are larger and wider, but so squat that they
are almost round. The largest would be almost like the boats on
the Seine, but that they are much shorter. They carry heavier loads
than the others, particularly straw from the Grand Signior's sugar-
canes, and sail only during the flood, and no lower than the village
of Foua. They have lateen sails. The smallest of all are flat, low and
wide, with a square sail, and do not travel far from Boulac, serving
only as ferries across the Nile, carrying provisions from the villages
to Cairo and carrying livestock from one bank to the other. The
gerbes which go to Damietta and Alexandria have lateen sails and
can venture out to sea when the water is calm and the weather fair;
but if the sea became rough during a storm they would not hold out

long. Accordingly when they want to put out, they choose a time when the weather is calm and the wind favourable. I also observed the trees in the gardens, which were sycamore-figs, palm-trees, cassias, pomegranates, oranges, acacias and tamarisks.

34

That some have mistakenly thought that chameleons lived only on wind, without eating anything

When I saw no coppiced trees to make faggots, or forests to cut down to make charcoal – and they need a great deal of it for use in smelting metals (of which there have always been great quantities in Egypt) – I looked to see what wood they had most of. They use branches of cassia, tamarisks, *rhamnus,* sycamore-figs, *napeca,* reeds and palms; but finally I found nothing in greater use than sugar-cane straw. I found also that this is in agreement with the authority of the ancients, who, knowing that they needed material to smelt their gold, said (as also is written in Pliny): *Pineis optime lignis aes ferrumque funditur, sed & Aegyptio papyro, paleis aurum*[269]. For the principal metal of Egypt has always been gold.

The hedges of the gardens round Cairo are everywhere covered with chameleons, and principally along the banks of the Nile, so that in a short time we saw great numbers of them. It is not without cause that they live in the bushes, for vipers and horned vipers swallow them whole when they are able to catch them. When chameleons want to eat, they shoot out their tongues, which are almost half a foot long and round like the tongue of a woodpecker, resembling an earthworm, and at the tip of the tongue they have a large spongy knot, as sticky as birdlime, with which they catch insects, that is, grasshoppers, caterpillars and flies, and draw them into their mouth. They dart out their tongues as swiftly as an arrow from an arbalest or a bow.

35

Of our arrival in Cairo, and of what we saw there

When we were at Boulac, waiting for mounts to go to Cairo, we heard something that was quite new to us and worthy of being recorded. A troupe of women to the number of ten or twelve passed along the street, singing all together a greeting in the Egyptian fashion. It was a sound that I had heard before in villages on the banks of the Nile, but I had been unable to think what it was, for women never go about the town but with their faces covered, not for any exquisite beauty that they have, but in order to observe Mahomet's commandment.

For even Ethiopian women, who are blacker in colour than a coal-man, cover their faces with a mask, just as do the fairest Turkish women of Asia. Because of this it was difficult for us to hear how this sound was produced, so new it was to us; and having heard such a cry several times, which seemed to be a confused harmony, we learned that the women open their mouths as wide as they can and sing in falsetto, moving their tongue between their teeth and then drawing it back towards the palate, so as to produce a high note, in the way that village women selling milk in Paris end their cry.

They mask themselves differently in different parts of the country. The form of mask worn by the village women of Arabia and Egypt is the ugliest of all, for they wear only a cotton cloth, black or of some other colour, in front of their eyes, hanging down in front of their face and ending in a point at the chin, like the face-covering worn by a noble lady, and in order to see through this cloth they cut out two holes for the eyes. Thus accoutred, they resemble the men who castigate themselves on Good Friday in Rome or Avignon. In the larger towns the women follow the fashion that they have learned from Turkish women, who cover their face with a small veil woven from the hairs of a horse's mane, and women of higher station wear a veil of fine linen in front of their face.

[We would compare a man who set out to write of Egyptian women's dress to one who undertook to depict the clothing of women in France, Italy or Germany: for there is an infinite variety of headgear differing within the same country and in no way resembling those of their neighbours; and similarly Egyptian women are very different in their dress from Turkish women. They are not accustomed in Egypt or Turkey or Greece to tailor the garments of either women or men. Nor is there any requirement to distinguish people of different faiths by wearing garments of different colours, for, as we have said, there is such a distinction only in the turban. Christians wear turbans of various colours, now blue-green, now red, and Jews yellow, for only Turks are permitted to wear white or green; and green is allowed only for those who claim to be of the lineage of Mahomet.

The headgear worn by Egyptian women is particularly worthy of note, for it is antique, as can be seen portrayed on many medals. The authors call it *turritum capitis ornamentum*, or *turritam coronam* or *vittam turritam*, meaning a high head-dress in the form of a tower. Some women wear high pattens and others ankle boots with hobnailed heels, in the manner of Turkish women. Since this manner of head-dress so clearly shows its antiquity, we were moved to observe it, considering also that our Latin poets seem to mention it. And so, desiring to show more clearly how they are attired, we display their portraits here, and thereafter those of Turkish women in Asia][270].

Le portraiĒt de deux femmes du Caire diuerſement veſtues, ſelon qu'elles ſont eſtans en leurs maiſons.

Figure: Portrait of two women of Cairo diversely attired, when they are in their houses

*Autre portraiɛt d'vne femme d'Egypte, ſelon qu'elle eſt
acouſtree allant par la ville du Caire.*

*Figure: Another portrait of a woman of Egypt, dressed
for going about the town of Cairo*

On that day we walked into Cairo, since a stranger is not permitted to enter the town on horseback, unless he is a great lord, or in the company of one who is, but it is not counted wrong for either local people or strangers to enter on an ass. The noblemen of Cairo and the soldiers of the Turk are finely mounted on horses with short horse-cloths just as in France, and have reserved horses for themselves, being unwilling to permit this privilege to the common people. Women too commonly go about on asses with packsaddles covered by a carpet. [And so, knowing that each nation preserves its native character, in order not to confuse the character of the Egyptians with that of the Turks, we show here a citizen of Cairo on horseback, going to a tournament with his wife mounted on as ass, according to the manner of the country.][271]

Figure

From Boulac to Cairo is only half a league. Passing through orchards, we saw many fine fruit-trees. There are no tamarinds in Egypt except those that have been sown out of curiosity. I found another among the poor houses outside Cairo, near Boulac, and some wild lemons, which never produce a fruit larger than a pigeon's egg. Cassia-trees, sebestens, palms and sycamore-figs grow very tall here. When we arrived in Cairo all the members of our company were permitted to go about the town without a guide, for at whatever time of day I wanted to enter or leave the town I met with no hindrance, nor had any fear of coming to harm. Moreover I want to say that if a stranger clad in a long cloak desires to go about any of the towns of the Turks, no one will harm him, any more than an inhabitant of the country.

Towards evening a kind of small lizard can be seen creeping along the walls, eating flies. The Greeks call them in their vulgar tongue *samiamitos,* the Italians *tarentola,* the ancients *chalcidica lacerta;* but since the moderns confuse this name *tarentola* with the phalangy, and the Italian word *tarentola* or *terantula* is derived from *terra,* and since in any case these are not ancient names, it would require a long discourse to give a description of this little lizard, *chalcidia lacerta,* of which I shall speak more fully in another place.

It has often happened that a man writing about a country that is strange to him thinks that he is the first to discover it, but if he reads the ancient authors he will find in them accounts very similar to what he has observed. Thus when I saw that each of us was so persecuted by the little flies that we call mosquitoes, while we were asleep at night in Cairo, that it seemed in the morning as if we had measles, I had set this down in writing, adding that it is necessary to keep your face covered when sleeping under a tent, or else to sleep in the open air on a roof terrace. On reading Herodotus, however, I found that he had already written about similar experiences. The Egyptians, he says, use the nets with which they catch fish to make a tent at night, from fear of flies.

When the Egyptians prepare leather they do not use the bark of oak-trees as in France, nor the calyxes of *esculus* as in Asia, nor the leaves of lentisks, terebinths or *rhus* as in Greece, but use the fruits of the acacia tree, which are sold in large bags in the shops of Cairo, and also *kali* or *antilis* for dyeing. When in Cairo, searching diligently for various drugs mentioned by the ancient authors, I discovered that many are still used which are not brought to us by merchants, such as nitre, acacia, *calamus odoratus, amomum. costus, benalbum* and other similar drugs.

36

Of the houses of Cairo, of the gardens, and of the tower which shows the rising of the Nile and the fertility of the year

The buildings of the castle of Cairo, the fine rooms and halls, and the paintings they contain, bear witness to the magnificence of the Circassians, who ruled in Egypt not many years ago, until they were vanquished in battle by the Turk[272]. The walls are faced with marble to the height of a man round the doors and windows, in a band of damascening and marquetry more than a foot wide, with mother-of-pearl, ebony, crystal, marble, coral and coloured glass. Similar work is also to be seen in some of the houses of Cairo.

Most of the houses are two-storied, with roof terraces. The doors are so small and low that a horse cannot go through them, and a man has to bow his head when he enters. The locks are commonly made of wood, with as much art as an iron lock. It is common throughout the territories ruled by the Turk for the doors of houses to be very low, so as to avoid the obligation to lodge horses in time of war. The doors of the houses of great lords, however, are much the same as in the countries of Europe.

The birds which I have called Egyptian sakers are very common in Egypt, and stay in the country throughout the year. Kites too make their nests here at a time when they are absent from our region, and are so tame that they come up to the windows of houses and are fed there on dates. They spend the summer in Europe to avoid the great heat of the sun.

Cairo is very large and spacious, and is not completely surrounded by walls, since most of the city is enclosed by a branch of the Nile which serves it as a wall. It is a small channel devised by the Roman emperors when they ruled Egypt, and on its banks is a building in the manner of a strong tower which makes it possible to estimate the fertility of the soil and the charge to be levied on the country's revenue in the current year. And, knowing that the Nile is the source of Egypt's fertility, those who are appointed for the purpose come here on a certain day each year to see how much the Nile has risen. When the water reaches a certain opening in the tower they can judge what will be the fertility of the soil of Egypt; and since it does not rise to the same height every year there are different points which indicate approximately what the soil will yield in the coming year.

The revenue of Egypt was very great when the Romans were masters of the country, but it has diminished greatly since then; for the Romans in their day spared no expense to make it fertile. I marvelled greatly to see such great numbers of cassia-trees in the gardens of Cairo and throughout Egypt, although the ancient authors make no mention of them; and Theophrastus, who wrote about almost all the other plants of Egypt, does not mention them. And Theophrastus, writing about plants, was well informed, as was Aristotle, writing about animals; for just as various peoples under Alexander's rule took various species of animals to Aristotle when he was writing his account of them, similarly various peoples had to bring plants to Theophrastus when he was describing them; and it appears from his account that he had to incur great expense and send men to various parts of the world to observe them. And so, finding no passage in any of his works referring to cassia, I concluded that he had nothing to say about it, except perhaps in the third chapter of the fourth book, where he says that it had been reported to him that there are such large trees round Cairo that three men could not join hands round them. Indeed the cassia-trees are as large and tall as our walnut-trees, with similar leaves, as it appears from the present figure, in which the tree is represented as it is in nature.

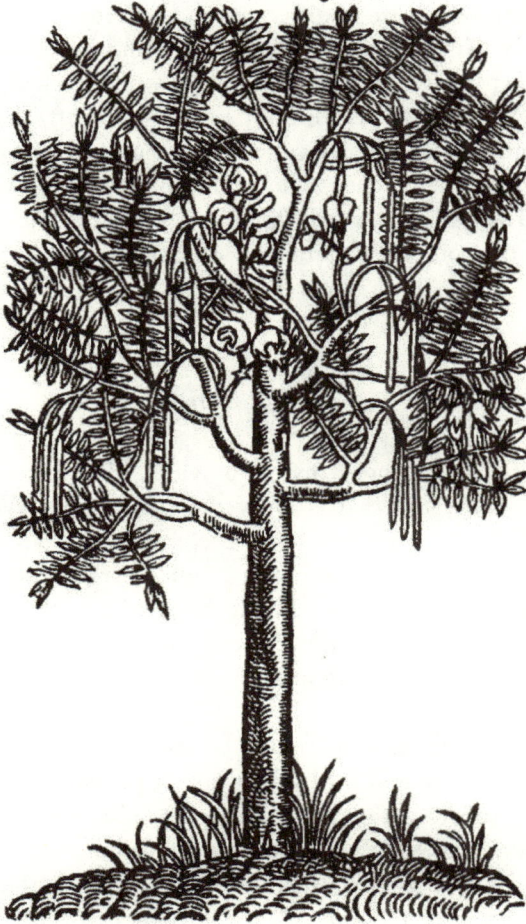

Figure: Portrait of the cassia-tree

It is not to be wondered at that Egypt abounds in garden plants, for they have very great heat and no difficulty in watering their plants, and are careful to sow at the right time. When the Nile is high they have no need to do any watering, but both before and after the inundation they have to take great care. Since the water channels coming from the Nile are not deep, they have machines for drawing water, which are of different kinds. There is one which can be used only when the water is very high and is not difficult to make. They set up two straight lengths of wood, forked at the top, to support a pole in the manner of a gibbet, and attach to it a two-handled pan or a wooden vessel which hangs on two ropes. It is held by two men, one on each side, who stand in the water up to their navels and by pulling strongly on it draw up water, which they then cast on to the soil of the garden.

37

Description of the city of Cairo and its castle

The city of Cairo is longer than it is wide. All business in it is carried on by men, just as it is everywhere in Turkey. Women, girls and small children seldom leave their houses to appear in public. And I believe that if the common people were accustomed to going out and showing themselves about the town, and the women bought and sold as in our countries, the city would not appear to be much more populous, for the population is not so large as common report has it.

The city is in the form of a triangle, with the castle, which is on its highest point, situated on a hill at one of its corners; so that if a man started out from the castle and followed the walls down towards the south he would come to another corner of the city. Setting out again and going north, he would come to the third corner, in the manner of a Greek Δ. Then, leaving this third corner and going up towards the castle, he would have completed the circuit of the city. There are almost as many houses outside the walls as there are within the city, many of them having made the mistake of thinking the city would not be walled.

The castle is situated on hard rock, in which steps have been cut to make it easier of access, much as in the château of Amboise, for the castle of Cairo is similarly set high. It is almost round, and has a number of large round towers built in the antique fashion, but of small blocks of stone. And since it stands so high, there is a square spiral staircase on the side facing the garden, with sloping steps, like the one in the palace of Saint Peter's in Rome, so that horses, camels and asses can climb the staircase with their loads. The courtyard of the castle is large and spacious, and the living quarters are very pleasant and handsome, with wide views in all directions from the windows, so that you can see almost the whole country of Egypt from here, just as if you were standing on the highest point of one of the pyramids. The castle of Cairo, if compared with other fortresses, cannot be considered particularly strong.

Some, comparing Paris with Cairo, assert that Cairo was anciently called Is, and that being of similar size it was called Par Is, that is to say, like to the town of Is. And indeed there was a town of great renown called Is, which Herodotus mentions, but it was not Cairo, for he says that Is was eight days' journey from Babylon[273], named after a river of that name which flows through the town and from there goes on to join the Euphrates. The inhabitants of Cairo, being much troubled by the heat of the sun, are constrained to seek the shade of leafy trees; and so they cultivate and rear sycamore-figs in many places in Cairo, at crossroads and in public squares. And I would say more about it were it not that I have amply described it along with other trees which are perpetually green; and so I have preferred to give a picture of it here.

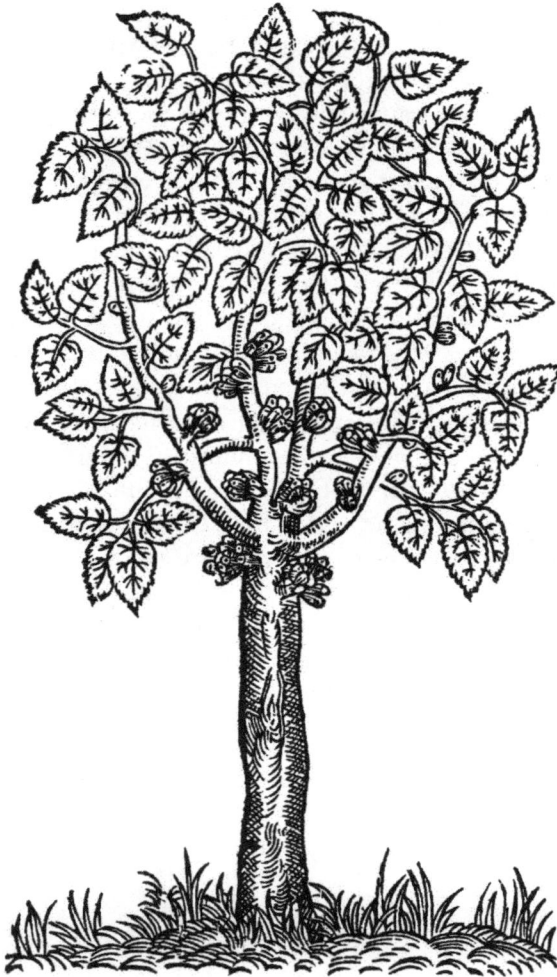

Figure

They also have a small kind of plant special to this country, which grows up and covers arbours with greenery, and is made to climb up on poles to the windows of the houses. The most notable thing in Cairo is the Basestan[274], an enclosed space in which silver and gold wares, silks and certain kinds of precious drugs are sold; where there is ordinarily a great multitude of people assembled, for they come here to carry on their trades, as in the Palace in Paris or the Bourse in Antwerp or the Exchange in Lyons. And if there is anything new or fine in the city, people flock to see it. One of our company expressed a doubt whether there were as many mosques as there are great churches in Paris; but several of us, having considered the matter, decided that Cairo fell very little short of Paris in this respect.

38

Of a great water channel between Babylon and the city of Cairo
which carries water from the Nile to supply the castle

We left the city to go to the old town of Cairo, which anciently was called Babylon, situated above the city; although there is another Babylon in Assyria, now called Baghdad, situated in Mesopotamia.

There we saw the ruins of many ancient buildings, constructed of brick and cement, which seemed to have been of great magnificence. There is now a small village inhabited by a few Armenian and Greek Christians, who showed us a beautiful and finely built chapel which a Christian doctor had built in honour of Our Lady. In this church there is an underground vaulted chamber[275], in which Our Lady hid with Our Lord when he was small and they were fleeing from Judaea to escape Herod's tyranny.

On our way we saw a great water channel[276], with more than three hundred arches, which is situated a little way above Cairo, built of fine masonry of dressed stone to carry water from the Nile to the castle of Cairo, with a device consisting of a large wheel turned by oxen which raises the water and conveys it to the castle.

The Moors or Egyptians are the most recreative of peoples, ever ready to leap about or dance, or indulge in some caper. This is not a new thing for them, for Flavius Vopiscus writes that the Egyptians were great versifiers and actors in farces, and ever ready to leap about. In this respect they are very different from the Turks, who are naturally gloomy, slow and lazy. The Moorish women of

Cairo play an instrument called *cinghi*[277], which is also known in Constantinople. It is little less harmonious than a harp, and although it does not produce great music, nevertheless it is agreeable to the ear when it is accompanied by singing. The Moors or Egyptians play more music than the Turks, principally with oboes and viols; and I venture to say that the Turks knew nothing of music except what they have learned from the Moors.

39

Description of the balm-tree

We went to see a garden in a village where balm-trees grow, which is no farther from Cairo than from Paris to the Lendit fair[278]. And since the balm-tree[279] is a famous plant, precious and rare, I want to record all that I have learned about it. I know that some people believe that the balm-trees at La Materée [Al-Matariya], near Cairo, were brought there from Judaea, and I shall show now that this is not so. They are in a large garden within a small walled enclosure which is said to have been made since the Turk took Egypt from the Soldan, and it is also said that it was a basha, a lieutenant of the Turk, who deemed them worthy of having their own enclosure.

When I saw them, there were only nine or ten trees, which yield no resin. Among the characteristics which the ancients have taught us for recognising the balm-tree is that it is green throughout the year. Nevertheless the trees at La Materée had very few leaves in the month of September, which seemed to me unusual, for other trees which remain green in winter do not lose their leaves until spring, when the new buds have appeared. Such trees are greener in autumn than they are in spring. But other trees which lose their leaves drop them in winter, to renew them in summer. And so it seemed wrong to me that the balm-tree should lose its leaves in summer and recover them in winter; for when I saw these shrubs, such leaves as they had were newly produced. I cannot truly say what is the proper size of the balm-tree, for all the trees in this garden had only small, slender branches, with only a scanty covering of leaves, and the stems were only a foot high, and barely thicker than a man's thumb.

Everywhere that balm-trees grow, they scarcely exceed two or three cubits in height, and at a foot from the ground they send out spindly branches, which commonly are no thicker than the quill of a goose's feather. The shrubs at La Materée had been recently pruned, so that they had only the stumps from which the rudiments of the branches would later spring. For the balm-tree follows the nature of the vine, which must be pruned every year, or else it deteriorates. The shoots of the balm-trees that we saw had reddish bark, and bore green leaves arranged in the same manner as the lentisk, that is to say on either side, as we see the leaves on rose-bushes or on ashes and walnut-trees; but they are no bigger than the leaves of chickpeas, and are so arranged that the last leaf at the tip of the branch makes the total number of leaves odd, so that there will be three, five or seven, and I have rarely seen more than seven. The leaf at the end of the branch is larger than the others which follow, for they grow steadily smaller, as happens with the leaves of rue.

I find that Pliny followed in every detail what Theophrastus had written, as did Dioscorides, and, following in his tracks, they wrote that the leaves of the balm-tree are similar to those of rue, which I found to be true. But since I had passed too lightly over the balm-trees at La Materée, and had not properly observed them on my first visit, I returned to see them again, and having found means to pick a small branch, which I tasted, and also its leaves, I found them to be somewhat astringent, with an oily taste, and aromatic, but the bark had an even stronger odour. The branch is covered with two barks: the first has a reddish exterior and covers the under one like a parchment, and this in turn is green and overlies the wood.

When tasted this bark has a flavour between incense and a terebinth leaf, similar to the flavour of wild savory, which is very pleasant, and when rubbed between the fingers has something of the odour of cardamom. The wood is white, and has no more odour or flavour than any ordinary wood. It has straight and very spindly branches, mere slender shoots round which the leaves emerge in no regular order, appearing now on one side and now on the other, and so on at some distance from one another, seldom completely surrounding the branch; and (as I have said) each leaf is so disposed that on one shoot there may be three or five or seven. Having dried my balm branch and compared it with the *xylobalsamum* which is sold in the merchants' shops, I found that it matched in every respect.

The opinions of the authors who have written about the balm-tree are so diverse that if I had not seen it for myself I should not have ventured to write another word after them, and would have believed that it was never cultivated in the plain of Jericho, as has been written. But since I have seen the shrub and examined it carefully I have thought it right to make such description of it as I consider appropriate for a matter which requires close observation. I have found by experience that the wood commonly called *xylobalsamum* which is sold by the merchants, brought from Happy Arabia, matches the Egyptian shrub grown at La Materée. So either the wood called *xylobalsamum* and the fruit called *carpobalsamum* which we can buy in the shops must be false, or the shrub in the garden at La Materée, which is thought to be a true balm-tree, must be false. But having seen that they match in all points and convinced myself that they are the same, I conclude that the one sold under the name of balm-wood is the one which in all times has been in use.

The balm-tree is now grown only in Egypt near Cairo, and although Theophrastus was of opinion that it is never found growing wild, nevertheless I venture to assert firmly that it has existed in all times and is still found in Happy Arabia, whose wood and fruit have been brought to us since remote antiquity by the same merchants who bring other wares from Arabia. And I will show that they were known to the merchants, as were the other drugs; which I can easily prove by the composition of the medicines in which it had been customary in all times to mix them. Did not Mithridates put them in his medicines? This is proved by Dioscorides, who complained that in his day balm seed was adulterated: *Carpobalsamum adulteratur semine hyperico simili, quod a Petra oppido defertur*[280]. By Petra we are to understand Mecca. Of the wood he says: *E ligni genere quod xylobalsamum vocant, probatur recens, sarmento tenui, fulvum, odoratum, quadantenus, oppobalsamum spirans*[281]. From this it is manifest that it was in common use along with other drugs. It is also manifest in the words of Diodorus

Siculus, the very ancient historian, describing the riches of Happy Arabia, saying that it produced balm in areas bordering the sea. He does not mean, therefore, that it is a cultivated variety of balm, but that it grows wild.

Pausanias also says that balm was an Arabian shrub. The authors disagree in speaking of balm: Strabo writes that it grows in Syria near Lake Gennesaret, between Mount Lebanon and the Antilebanon. Other authors assert that only the region of Judaea produces it, and that the branches must not be touched to extract the resin except with implements of bone or glass, saying that if the trunk of the balm-tree were cut by iron to get the oil it would die at once. Cornelius Tacitus writes that when iron is put close to it, it is put in a great fright, and that therefore it must be cut with other instruments than iron, or else it would not yield any resin. When I asked the merchants of Cairo about balm when I was comparing my branch, they said that all the *xylobalsamum* and *carpobalsamum* that they had ever sold came along with the other drugs brought from Mecca, and that they recollected having seen the balm-bushes now at La Materée brought from Arabia Felix by the Soldan at great expense. And since so many people had assured me of the facts I decided that I could write without any hesitation and without dissimulating anything of what I thought.

40

Of a great obelisk still standing near Cairo, and of the trees growing in the garden at La Materée

There are many sebesten-trees in the garden at La Materée, and also sycamore-figs, which they call Pharaoh's figs. Their figs would be very like ours, but that they are red on top, the size of an egg and almost always split. They are no good when dried, for they are meagre and hard, full of seeds, and taste bad and savourless, particularly for those who are not accustomed to eating them. When fresh they taste somewhat better, but at their best they are still not worth much, although they bring in great revenue to the whole of Egypt.

Basil is sown all over Egypt, growing to three times the height of our basil. They eat it as we eat other herbs. Aubergines, which we call love-apples, are grown in great numbers in sandy soils; they have two or three sorts, white and red, long and round. I think that it is what Theophrastus calls *malinatalam*, for, speaking of things in Egypt. he says: *Locis autem arenosis haud procul a fluvio nascitur terrenum, quod Malinatalam appellant*[282]. They eat it at almost all their meals, cooked under ashes, boiled or fried.

In the garden at La Materée we were shown the place where Our Lord and Our Lady stayed for a long time when they came to Egypt, fleeing from Judaea for fear of Herod. Here too is a window at which Our Lady laid down Our Lord to rest. There is a fountain which waters the gardens containing the balm-trees, in which they say that Our Lady frequently bathed Our Lord and washed his swaddling-clothes.

It is now known that obelisks were carved to mark the sepulchres of the kings of Egypt, as were the pyramids and other great colossi. There is one such obelisk standing erect in a field a little way beyond La Materée, which is much taller and larger than those in Alexandria and in the Hippodrome in Constantinople. When we had seen it we turned bridle towards Cairo, going off our road on the right to see another garden, only a league from Cairo, in which is a large and spacious hall built by the Circassians when the Soldan was master of Egypt. This is a large building paved with large square stones and roofed with a kind of terrace as protection from the sun, the openwork roof being supported on pillars of dressed stone. The Nile comes close to the walls, not in its normal course but during the inundation. On the east side of this hall is a beautiful little garden, in which are many cassia-trees, henna-trees, rose-bushes and yellow jasmine. On the north and south sides are two small tanks like fishponds which serve to store drinking water. The whole building is painted on top. The beams and planks are of palm-wood. Since Egypt has become tributary to the Turk the building has been falling into disrepair.

41

That the kind of people of stocky build whom we call Egyptians are found in other countries as well as in Egypt.

There is no place anywhere in the world without the kind of poor people of stocky build whom we call Egyptians or Bohemians; for even between La Materée and Cairo we encountered large companies of them, and also in many villages along the Nile, camping under palm-trees, as much strangers in this country as they are in ours. Since their place of origin is Wallachia or Bulgaria they speak several languages, and are Christians. The Italians call them *Singuani*. They have a privilege from the Turks allowing Singuan women to prostitute themselves to any man, whether Christian or Turk, and they have a house in Pera at Constantinople, with several rooms which any man can enter freely without committing any offence. Ordinarily there are at least a dozen women in this establishment. These people find work in Greece, Turkey and Egypt in the iron-working trade, and make excellent workers in that trade.

When we had been in Cairo for some days we decided to go and see the pyramids, and after making the necessary preparations we left the town by the south gate and made our way to the boats which ferried us over the Nile. People go there only in a large company, for otherwise they would be in danger of being robbed. Accordingly a sanjak[283] with a party of spahis provided an escort for Monsieur de Fumel and all the company travelling with him.

42

Observation of the pyramids

With all respect for Roman works and antiquities, they have none of the grandeur and pride of the pyramids[284]. The Egyptians, looking forward to the resurrection of the dead, were accustomed to preserve their bodies so that they might endure into eternity. They did not want to burn them like the Latins, for they believed that fire is an animating force which devours and consumes all things, and that after it has fully satisfied its thirst both the fire and what it has devoured perish. Nor did they want to bury the bodies like the Greeks, lest they should be eaten by worms. And in order to avoid all these inconveniences they preserved them with tar and nitre, and after they had preserved them they put them in sepulchres, under a great mass of stone. They chose the most barren places that they could find for the burials; and so the place where the pyramids are is in the heart of the desert. They are about four leagues from Cairo on the other side of the Nile.

We crossed the Nile on a boat driven by both sail and oars, below the island which lies opposite Cairo; and this was not the only stream of the Nile that we had to cross, for when we reached the other bank we went along a long causeway with stone arches and at some points small wooden bridges, on which we crossed the stream without a boat. But then, near the village of Busiris, where the water of the Nile had broken the arches of the stone bridge, we had to cross by boat; and from the village of Busiris there is another long causeway which ends at the pyramids.

The course of the Nile splits up for the first time well above Cairo, forming a channel which flows into Lake Mareotis, always following the desert side of this part of Africa. This led me to wonder whether this branch separates Egypt from Africa, for it passes close to the foot of the pyramids, between the fertile and the barren parts of Egypt. Thus the Nile which flows past Cairo is not the whole river, for it has already divided into two branches much higher up, where one branch goes off on the left to flow into Lake Mareotis.

When we had crossed the Nile and were on the same side as the pyramids we now had the whole of it between us and Cairo. And so, from whichever side you take Egypt, it always has the form of a delta, for if you set out to go round it, starting at Lake Mareotis and going upstream in a straight line to above the pyramids, and then going down from there to Damietta, which is Ostium Pelusiacum, would you not have reached one corner of a triangle? And if you went down from Damietta to Alexandria would you not have completed the other two sides? This would be the end of the triangle, like a Δ.

When we were going along the causeway at Busiris, which was broken at one point, the lake named after the Nile had overflowed and destroyed the causeway. Those of us who were well mounted had no difficulty in fording the river, following our guides, but the others who were poorly mounted had to wait for the boat; though some of them took off their clothes and, leading their mounts, forded the river on foot, with the water up to under their armpits.

The Moors of the next village accompanied us in our ascent of the pyramids, showing us the way. They are situated at a great distance from the sea but are only three stone's throws from the water of the Nile. When you first see the pyramids, they seem like mountains of enormous size and indeed they must have been assembled at the cost of great work and labour by men. The place where they are situated is very sandy and barren. Pliny said of it, following Herodotus: *Arena late pura circum lentis similitudine*[285]. The largest pyramid, lying on slightly lower ground than the second, appears to be smaller when seen from a distance, but close up is seen to be without comparison much larger. Indeed they are more admirable than they are described by the historians, the largest of them having an exterior built up in steps. I measured the base, which is 324 paces long from one corner to the other, which I counted extending my stride somewhat. Beginning to count from the foot of the pyramid to the top, I made it some 250 steps, each step being of the height of five soles of a nine-point shoe[286].

From the top of the pyramid I could clearly see the city of Cairo beyond the Nile, on the side on which is Desert Arabia, and on the other side, turning to face north, I could see the whole country of Egypt as if submerged, resembling a great sea. Then, turning towards the south, the side on which Africa lies, I saw nothing but barren sand. Examining the north side of the pyramid, I found it to be much more ruined than the other sides. The reason is that the humidity of the night dews and the Nile, stirred up by the northerly winds, causes great destruction, while the other sides, both on the east and on the south, not being affected by the humidity, are not ruined.

So much for the exterior of the first great pyramid. Now I will speak of its inner parts. We entered the pyramid by a square passage, having to stoop to walk through it, for it runs across the pyramid, sloping downward. It seems that there was a good reason for this, for if it had been built obliquely no light would have been admitted to the pyramid. As we went into the pyramid we each carried a lighted wax candle, and we could enter only one at a time, for when we came to the lower doorway we could enter the cavity only by lying flat on our bellies and crawling like snakes, and even so we could get through only with difficulty.

Within the pyramid we came to an empty space. Running up from this on the left was a square passage or gallery, finely carved, in which we could walk erect, for it is both wide and high, with no steps, paved with large flagstones which are highly polished and slippery. But there are arm-rests on both sides to help in the ascent. Then, after climbing fifteen or sixteen paces we entered a fine square chamber measuring six paces long by four paces wide and between four and six toises high containing a black marble casket hewn from a single piece of marble, twelve feet long, five feet high and as much in width, without a lid. This was the sepulchre of a king of Egypt, for whom the pyramid was built.

The black marble sepulchre was put in the chamber while the pyramid was being built. Returning from the chamber and walking down the spacious passage, we were facing north. When we emerged from the pyramid we turned left and came to a well which is now almost completely filled with stone. The whole history of these pyramids is to be found in Herodotus, Diodorus and other Greeks, following whom Pliny, writing in Latin, says that this well is very deep; and it is certain that water was drawn from it for use in building the pyramid and for drinking by the workers, for it is faced with a strong cement of lime and sand, which means that it must have contained water.

Returning to the first passage and continuing beyond it, we came to a small cavity on the left which must have been deliberately broken open, for elsewhere the masonry is quite solid. In it we found bats differing from ours and from those that I had seen in the labyrinth on Crete, for while our bats do not have tails longer than their wings, those in the pyramid had tails four fingers longer than the wings, about the length of a mouse's tail. We now left the pyramid and went to the second one.

43

Observation of the second pyramid

The other pyramid is second in size, with no steps on the exterior; and so it is not possible to climb it. Since it is situated rather higher than the previous one it appears from a distance to be the higher of the two, and when seen close up it is the other way round. It is square in shape like the first one, and complete to the top. The previous one has a space on the summit two paces in diameter on which fifty men can stand, but this one has a pointed top, without space for even one man to stand. It has an outer facing of cement, on which the part facing north has been consumed by humidity carried by the winds from the water of the Nile and the night dews, as on the great pyramid.

The lizards called stellions, which the Greeks call *colotis*, are very common round these pyramids and in the cavities of the sepulchres which are to be found in many places in this country. They lodge in between the stones and catch flies, as I was easily able to observe. They would resemble the geckos which frequent houses were it not that they have stronger legs and a flatter head. They produce the drug that the ancients called *crocodilea*[287] and our druggists now call *stercus lacerti*, which does indeed come from their excrements. Turkish women paint their faces with it. It is sold in all the druggists' shops of Turkey.

44

Of the third small pyramid

The third pyramid is much smaller than the other two. It still stands entire, with only one ruined patch, and is a third larger that the one called Monte Testaccio in Rome, on the way to Saint Paul's on the road to Ostia[288]. This third pyramid had no more openings in all its mass than if it had just been built, for the stone of which it is made is of a kind of marble which called *basalten*, otherwise *lapis aethiopicus,* which is harder than fine iron. This strong stone is the one used for most of the figures of Egyptian sphinxes, like the one on the Capitol in Rome, which were carved by the Egyptians in ancient times.

This third small pyramid is a good bowshot farther from the second than the second is from the first. I call it small in comparison with the two larger ones, for although the one in Rome is faced with fifty tiers of stones of white marble, smoothed and polished, like the one in Egypt, it is still but a poor thing compared with the least of the pyramids of Egypt, of which there are more than a hundred scattered here and there throughout this country; and there is not one of them so badly ruined as the one in Rome. Then, too, compared with the others, I can call it modern, for in the interior there is only cement, made from brick, lime and sand. It has sunk into the ground, and this has strained the marble facing, so that the structure is ruined at the four corners, where a number of trees and plants – terebinths, capers, brooms, brambles, laurels with no smell, *teucrium* and Roman wormwood – have found space in the gaping joints to establish their roots; and were it not that the stones are bound together with iron and lead they would long ago have fallen to the ground.

45

Of certain other pyramids in Egypt

In addition to the three pyramids described above we saw a great number of other small ones scattered here and there about the country on the same African plain, among which are a number of smaller ones built of small stones, and sepulchres of different kinds, built for the burial of those who were preserved with tar and nitre in Egypt and with bitumen in Judaea. The historians tell us that the Egyptians built their sepulchres according to their wealth, for the richest of them built more sumptuous monuments, like obelisks, colossi and pyramids, and those built by others were of poorer quality; and there were none so poor but had a few small stones assembled for their burial-place. These sepulchres are situated is such an inhospitable expanse of desert that no one would think of living there or of growing anything. It was such a place that Plato had in mind when he directed in his laws that barren country should be dedicated to the sepulchres of the dead. This is still the practice of the Greeks and of the Turks, imitating the Arabs, for they bury their dead in stony places on hilly ground which could not produce any crops. And since the sphinx or androsphinx which the ancients so frequently mention still stands entire in the same barren country as the pyramids, I do not think that I can pass on without saying a few words about it.

46

Of the great colossus, called by Herodotus the androsphinx and by Pliny the sphinx, which lies in front of the pyramids

After carefully examining a very large stone head to be seen close to the Nile, some distance above the great pyramid, I had occasion to admire the works of the Egyptians. Although Plato greatly exaggerated the size of the pyramids, he was more reasonable in his description of the colossal sphinx which lies to the right of the great pyramid, towards the east. I do not propose to give a long description of sphinxes, for in truth all that has been pictured or written about this animal, both by the Ethiopians and the Egyptians, is mere fable.

Diodorus too, in his description of them, has no more to say about them than that they resemble the pictures that have been made of them, but that they are rather larger and are of a gentle nature. He believed that we could recognise sphinxes from pictures of them, as did Herodotus with the phoenix. But it must be said that men have long been accustomed to see sphinxes and phoenixes in paintings, since in past times phoenixes and sphinxes were known only from pictures. And so, seeking to recognise sphinxes from pictures, I looked in many places where they were engraved or carved, to see what they were like. But finding that they were so diversely portrayed in various sculptures and medals, as well as in ten or twelve antique works in Rome, some on the Capitol carved in basalt or Ethiopic stone, others in a gallery in the Belvedere garden in the pope's palace in Thebaic stone like the needles and obelisks, none of them agreeing with any other, and that those portrayed on medals of Augustus and Hadrian are different from those carved in stone, I felt free to conclude that what had been said about them was pure fable, as I shall show hereafter. King Francis[289], restorer of letters and father of all virtue, caused two sphinxes to be cast in dark-coloured iron, imitated from those in Rome, which are still to be seen at Fontainebleau in the king's collection of antiquities, and which again bear no resemblance to Augustus's medals. Moreover I have never seen any with the characteristics that Pliny attributes to them. Some have breasts along the belly, others have them on the chest, like the sphinx under the arm of the great marble colossus representing the Nile, both on coins of Hadrian and on the one in the Belvedere garden in Rome. Others have no breasts at all, like those in basalt and Thebaic stone to be seen in Rome.

I desire now to speak of the Egyptian sphinx, which Herodotus called androsphinx, and which is mentioned by Strabo, Pliny and other authors. Pliny, speaking of the pyramids and the sphinx, says: *Ante has est Sphinx, vel magis miranda, qua sylvestria sunt accolentium.* Nevertheless, though he calls it a sphinx, he means a head of enormous size, as appears from these words: *Est autem saxo naturali elaborata & lubrica. Capitis monstri ambitus per frontem centum duos pedes colligit, longitudo pedum centum quadraginta trium est. Altitudo a ventre ad summum apicem in capite sexaginta duorum*[290].

This stone, set on a cubic base, is a large carved face, looking towards Cairo. The proportions of the face, as of the nose, the eyes, the mouth, the brow, the chin and other parts, are so well devised that it cannot but be deemed a work of great art; but it has no likeness to the other engravings of sphinxes.

King Francis, a great admirer of large monuments, had considered having a figure of Hercules cast, and indeed he would have done it had he not been prevented by death, for the model of the figures was preserved for a long time in the Hôtel de Nesle in Paris. It stood between 52 and 53 feet high, and if it had been completed it must have surpassed all such figures erected by Roman and Egyptian emperors. Those who saw it expressed great admiration for it, but

I should like to put forward another figure for comparison with it. This is the figure of the Sun in fine marble erected by Nero in Rhodes, which was exactly twice the size of the king's figure of Hercules; for while the king's figure was 52 and a half feet high the one in Rhodes was 105 feet. But this stone of which I am speaking is a still greater marvel, for, hewn from the solid rock, it is 63 feet high. Pliny says that it is 143 feet long. It is not, however, the exact measurements that concern me in the sphinxes. It is the grandeur and sublimity of this colossus, which is no less a marvel than a great obelisk. I will maintain that the Romans never made anything from a block of stone that can be compared in sublimity and magnificence of workmanship with a pyramid, an obelisk or the sphinx of which I am speaking. And indeed all the great works they made were in imitation of the Egyptians, and the effigies of sphinxes to be seen on the Capitol were brought from Egypt. I believe that this has been so since the time of Pliny, for they have none of the characteristics described by him, not one of them having either breasts or wings; for those to be seen with wings are pictures of chimeras[291] and not sphinxes.

I would not call the statues of the Romans antique in comparison with Egyptian antiquities. Among the relics of ruins and antiquities to be seen in Rome there is nothing more ancient than what they brought from Egypt. It now remains to say whence the sphinx came to the Egyptians. It is under the signs of Leo and Virgo that the Nile waters the lands of Egypt[292], and the Egyptians, desiring to signify their wealth, conceived a monster in sculpture with the fore parts of a virgin and the rear parts of a lion and called it a sphinx; and since it is a thing than can be made as a man pleases, it is to be seen in different forms in sculpture. Witness of this is the sphinx's head described above. And it is certain that it served as a burial-place in the same way as the pyramids and obelisks; for Pliny says: *Amasium regem in ea conditum*[293]. And since *funus conditum* is what we wrongly mummy, I wish now to show in what manner this mummy was made.

47

Of mummies, and of the ancient manner of preserving or embalming and burying bodies in Egypt

The Egyptians, looking forward to the resurrection of the dead, considered it a grave misdeed to have human bodies consumed in the elements, air, earth, water or fire. As I have already said, the philosopher Zoroaster taught them that fire is an animating force which devours all things and then itself dies along with what it has swallowed up. Accordingly the Egyptians did not want bodies to be burned in the fashion of other nations, but wanted them to be preserved, so as not to be eaten by worms. Thus Pomponius Mela, speaking of embalmed bodies in Egypt, calls them in Latin *funera medicata,* while Pliny speaks of *servata corpora.* And indeed they preserved them so well for eternity that they still last, and will last for ever, as what we call a mummy. There were different manners of preserving bodies in Egypt, for those who could spend more were better treated, and those who could spend most lavishly had the most sumptuous burial-places; but no man died who was not preserved, in whatever manner it might be. We give these preserved bodies the name of mummies, although the Arabic authors who wrote about mummy meant by that name the drug called in Greek *pissasphalton*[294], of which I have already spoken in the first book. The use of bodies embalmed in Egypt, that is to say the drug that we call mummy, is so widespread in France that wherever King Francis, restorer of letters, went his stewards carried mummy along with rhubarb in their saddlebags, and he himself had some on his person.

Those who, to give colour to their lying accounts of what we call mummy, have painted a picture of a sea of sand blown up by winds burying people travelling in the deserts of Africa and Arabia, have deceived many people; for although bodies do perish in these sands and are subject to putrefaction, they can yield only the substances of which they are composed. Those who have drawn maps marking the places from which mummy was obtained have shown thereby that they had little judgment or knowledge of the matter. In order to show that they lied about it I propose to prove this on the authority of Theophrastus, Dioscorides, Galen, Herodotus, Hippocrates, Diodorus, Strabo and Pliny, who in speaking of Egypt tell us that bodies were preserved with the drug called *cedria*, of which, while we were in Cairo, three lots were brought in which had recently been found in the sepulchres above-mentioned. We went into a number of sepulchres in the plain where they lie, some of which were vaulted chambers and others small rooms, such as are to be seen in infinite number in the country round the pyramids.

There were such great numbers of flies in the area round the pyramids that when we disturbed them as we passed the air was filled with their noise. I found the plant called *tithymalus platiphyllos* growing in this area. We went down to dine on the banks of the Nile below the pyramids, where the food that we had brought with us for the purpose had been prepared. We returned by the same route by which we had come. When we reached the banks of the Nile we found a number of Arab noblemen encamped there in their tents, waiting to welcome Monsieur de Fumel. They had prepared a banquet for him, and they had two players of viols with them, who sang together in the Egyptian fashion while they played. I found the harmony very pleasing, and I think it worth while to describe them here.

48

Of the viols of the Egyptians

The viols of the Egyptians have only a single string, or two at most, which is of horsehair, and is not twisted; and the strings of the bow and of the viol are the same. The neck of the viol is long, so that the player must make long strokes. The bridge is not set on a wooden base, as ours are, any more than on their lutes and gitterns, but on the skin of a fish caught in the Nile called *glanis*[295], glued below the wood. The rest of the body of the viol is like a flat box, ending in a long iron spike which supports it on the ground; for they do not hold the viol on their shoulder. They sing together in the same voice, which was pleasant to hear, for what they sing is in rhythm.

We arrived back at Cairo the same day, and stayed there for some time without going anywhere. The merchants who have shops in Cairo are of different nations, like Jews, Turks, Greeks and Arabs. The Jews for the most part speak Spanish, Italian, Turkish, Greek and Arabic.

49

Of the giraffe, which the Arabs call "curnapa", and the Greeks and Latins "camelopardalis"

There was no time when the Grand Signiors, however barbarous they may have been, did not like to be presented with strange beasts. We saw a number of such beasts in the castle of Cairo, brought from many countries, among which is one that they call in their vulgar tongue *curnapa*. The Latins anciently called it *camelopardalis*, a name made up from leopard and camel, for it is spotted like a leopard and has a long neck like a camel. It is a very handsome animal, with a disposition as gentle as a lamb, and more friendly than any other wild beast. It has a head almost like that of a stag, with small blunt horns six fingers long, covered with hair. As a distinction between the male and the female, the male's horns are longer; but both the male and female have ears the size of a cow's, the tail of an ox, black in colour, a jaw with no upper teeth, a long, straight, thin neck, a mane of slender round hairs and thin legs, the front ones long, the rear ones so short that the giraffe seems to be standing erect. Its feet are like those of an ox. Its tail hangs down to above the hocks; it is round, with hairs three times as thick as those of a horse. It has a very slender body, with reddish spots on a white ground. Its movements are like those of a camel; when it runs the two forefeet go together. It lies down with its belly on the ground, and has hard skin on its breast and thighs like a camel. It cannot graze on the ground when standing except by extending its forelegs widely, and then only with great difficulty. It is easy to believe, therefore, that it gets its food from the branches of trees, having such a long neck that its head can reach the height of a half-pike[296]. And having had it drawn from nature, I give its portrait here[297].

Portraiƈt de la Giraffe.

Figure: Portrait of the giraffe

50

*Of a handsome small African ox which the ancient Greeks called
"bubalos"*

The pleasure which a curious man can receive from encountering
a strange and singular animal is to discover its ancient name, so
as to be able to describe it; for a man who has sets out to describe
something without giving it its proper name seems to me to
undertaking a useless labour. And so, seeing a small African ox,
small in body but well formed, stocky, fat, with a smooth skin, it
suddenly occurred to me that this was the animal that the Greeks
had anciently called *bubalos*. Care must be taken, however, not to
be misled by the similarity of the names into confusing this beast
with the buffalo.

I found in this animal all the characteristics of the *bubalos*. It had
been brought to Cairo from the country of Asamia[298], although it is
also found in Africa. It was already old, of lesser corpulence than a
stag but stockier and larger than a roebuck, so well made and well-
proportioned in all its members that it was pleasant to see; for its
coat, being tawny in colour, seemed to have been turned browner,
so polished and shining was it. It was more reddish, verging on
tawny, on the belly than on the back, for it was almost brown. Its
feet are like those of an ox. Its legs are short and squat. Its neck is
short and thick, with a small dewlap (called in Latin *palearia*). It
has the head of an ox, with horns, rising from a bone ridge on top
of its head, which are black and much curved into the form of a
crescent, like those of a gazelle; but they would not be of great use
in defence, since the ends are turned down towards the head. It has
the ears of a cow. Its shoulders are slightly raised, and solid. Its tail,
like that of a giraffe, hangs down to the hocks, and also has black
hairs twice the thickness of the hairs in a horse's tail.

It bellows like an ox, but on a lower note. In sum, if a man were to
imagine a small ox, stocky in build, with a smooth, shiny, tawny skin
and crescent-shaped horns, he would have the picture of this animal.
And since I have called it *bubalus,* the name of the buffalo, I must
confess freely that I do not know the ancient name of the buffalo[299];

for although we have none in our region they are so common in Italy, Greece and Asia that no others are more commonly to be seen. And so it would seem to me strange if Aristotle, who expended 750,000 crowns of Alexander's minting in his search for animals, had made no mention of it. He speaks of the bubalus in several passages, and I am prepared to believe that he means the buffalo; but other authors lead me to wonder whether he did not mean the small animal of which I have spoken above. Pliny says: *Insignia tamen boum ferorum genera Bubalos bisontes, excellentique & vi & velocitate Uros, quibus imperitum vulgus Bubalorum nomen imponit, cum id gignat Africa, vituli potius cercive quadam similitudine*[300]. Solinus says the same. Pliny's description of the *bubalus* matches exactly what I have said of this small ox. And so I had no difficulty in concluding that in speaking of the *bubalus* Pliny and Solinus did not mean the buffalo. And having had my little *bubalus* drawn from nature, I give its portrait here.

Le portraïct du Bœuf d'Afrique.

Figure: Portrait of the African ox

51

Of another kind of deer resembling a fallow deer, anciently called "axis", and of the gazelle, anciently "orix"

There were also a male and female of a kind of red or fallow deer in the courtyard of the castle which I did not know, though I thought that it might be the *axis* of which Pliny speaks in his eighth book, chapter 20, where he says: *In India et feram nomine Axin, hinnuli pelle, pluribus candibiorusque maculis, sacram Libero patri*[301]. Both were without horns, and had tails of the length of a fallow deer's hanging down to the hock. And indeed when I saw them I thought that they were fallow deer; but having examined them more closely, and being well aware of the characteristics of fallow deer, I decided that they were not. The female was smaller than the male. Their whole coat was covered with round white spots on a tawny ground verging on yellowish, with white spots under the belly: differing in this from the giraffe, which has scarlet spots on a white ground, fairly large on the upper side but not tawny as on this *axis*. They have a more silvery, clearer and higher voice than the stag, for I heard them bellowing. And so, having seen by many signs that they were neither fallow nor red deer, I thought that they could properly be called *axis*.

There were also some tame gazelles, captured in the wild, which resembled roe deer, about the size of a chamois, with short fore legs and long hind legs, like a hare. They have a black line above the eyes like a chamois, and bleat like a goat, but have no beard. They have a reddish coat, verging on straw yellow, smooth and shining. The fore parts and rear parts are white, as on fallow deer. The tail, which is white on the underside and brown on the upper side, hangs down to the hocks, like that of a fallow deer. The gazelle runs more rapidly uphill than downhill, and rather stiffly on level ground. Its ears are erect like those of a stag, and it has slender legs with cloven hoofs. It has a long slender neck like a chamois. The male's horns are larger than those of the female, and would be quite straight but that they are slightly hooked at the tip, giving them a crescent shape, and they are longer than those of a chamois. They are tamed, for their natural habitation is in barren and waterless country.

52

Of the tumblers and mountebanks of Cairo, and of a species of monkeys called "callitriches"

There are many tumblers and mountebanks in Cairo that are not seen in Constantinople, who accompany their tricks by beating a tambourin with their fingers and singing in unison to the beat of the tambourin as the fancy takes them. Only one end of it stands on the ground. The wicker frame is only six fingers wide, and on it are several pieces of copper which jingle at the same time. They hold it with their left hand, striking it with the right. They are highly skilled in teaching various kinds of animals to perform tricks. They train goats, which they saddle, and then put monkeys on them, and teach the goats to leap about and kick up their heels like horses. They also train donkeys to tumble to the ground, feigning death, and pretend to kick the monkeys mounted on them. They also have trained monkeys, which is a rare thing to see, for usually monkeys are wayward creatures. They also have large baboons, which the ancients called *cynocephali*, so clever and well trained that they go from one person to another among those watching the performance, holding out their hand and inviting them to put money in it; and then they take the money they have been given to their master. There are several kinds of monkeys taught in this manner, and some of them are different from our monkeys, including the one that Pliny, for the great beauty of its hair and skin, called *callitriches*. It is yellow all over, like thread of gold, and belongs to the genus of *circopitheci*[302], which Aristotle called *cebus*, for it has a long tail like that of these monkeys.

53

Of the preparations to be made by those travelling from Cairo to Mecca

A caravan sets out from Cairo every year to go to Mecca, and many Turks come to Cairo to join this caravan. It is a journey taken out of devotion to Mahomet (although Mecca is not his burial-place), but is a duty required of believers. And since it passes through much desert country with no towns or houses, they make the preparations necessary for the journey. Among other things they take chickpeas cooked without water but merely roasted in a large oven, and there are many shops in Cairo that make their living solely from grilling chickpeas. So they have no difficulty in getting supplies, and each man buys as much as he needs for the journey. The Turks travelling to Mecca make two journeys: one is to Medina, where Mahomet's body lies, and the other to Mecca, to trade and bargain; for they bring back from Mecca many drugs and other wares. This is the town that the ancient authors called Petra, of which we shall speak more fully in the third book.

54

Description of our journey from Cairo to Mount Sinai, with a singular receipt for preparing meat for those going on a long journey

After we had provided ourselves with the things necessary for such a long journey as from Cairo to Mount Sinai we left the city by the north gate and found a caravan encamped near Cairo, outside a mosque, waiting until the whole company was ready; for men do not venture to travel through the lands of Arabia except in a large group. And so Monsieur de Fumel, with twenty janissaries as his guard, came to camp on the banks of the Nile, where we filled our vessels and goatskins with water from the river, taking supplies for three days, both for our mounts and ourselves. We were to pass through desert country where there are no fountains or streams and had brought provisions from Cairo sufficient for the journey there and back. One camel was laden with biscuit for those who were travelling in Monsieur de Fumel's company, who were very numerous, and another with meat prepared for the journey in the fashion to be described.

A large number of sheep were killed, chopped into pieces and boiled. Then the meat was separated from the bones, cut into small pieces the size of the tip of a man's thumb and boiled in fat, along with stewed onions, until the watery liquid in it was all consumed; then it was salted, spiced and put into kegs. This meat can keep for a long time, for although we carried it with us for two weeks, reheating it and adding an onion, it still tasted like a fricassee made that day, which seemed to us excellent meat for travellers in the desert.

It was an extremely hot day, for there was no wind. We spent the night under our tents on the banks of the Nile and set out again just after midnight so that we could travel in the coolness of the night. We passed through soft, barren sandy country where nothing grows but a species of black henbane, in such great abundance that no other plants are to be seen here. From its seeds the Egyptians make oil for burning, and also use it for several other purposes.

On the following day there was a light wind which refreshed the whole day, reducing the vehemence of the sun. Our route took us due east. I found a species of rat in this country which fed only on the seeds of henbane[303], with an ash-coloured back, a white belly, a long body, a long tail and a pointed muzzle. It was easy for me to observe them, for wherever I went I always had my pick with me and could dig in the earth and pull them out, as well as all kinds of snakes. We travelled only until midday, when we camped under our tents in order to rest our camels and our mounts. We watered our mounts in the evening with water from the goatskins which we had brought from the Nile. The camels did not take any, for they can go three or four days without drinking[304].

We stayed encamped until midnight. We felt cold, for the wind was cloudy and cold. They have damp mists in Egypt in September as we have dews in Europe in May. , though the days are still excessively hot. We then set out again in order to travel in the coolness of night. This was the third night since we left Cairo. We travelled for many hours during the night, and came at daybreak to well at Suez, where we stayed the whole day. This well is only a league and a half from the town and is enclosed in a little house. The water is brackish, but for want of anything else travellers and the people of Suez are compelled to drink it; for there is no other water unless they have brought it from the Nile. There is a very large and handsome cistern in the castle of Suez, which is filled once or twice a year with rainwater; for although it does not often rain here, yet when it does rain it is good water. The water from the well is mainly used to water camels and horses, for travellers usually carry their own supplies.

In my quest for the plants that grow in this country I went about on the plain at some distance from the road and found *ambrosia,* senna, the roses called roses of Jericho, gourds, acacia, the *paliurus*[305] of which Agathocles speaks and which Theophrastus describes, a particular species of broom, two kinds of *rhamnus* and the tree which the Greeks of Cairo call *oenoplia*. I caught a viper and two horned vipers, male and female, anatomised them and described them in detail, and stuffed their skins; and although I have written at greater length about this horned viper along with other snakes I am unwilling to pass on without mentioning that it has two small eminences above its eyes, like small barley-corns, seemingly the two small horns of which Aristotle speaks, calling them *colubrus thebanos*. But since all the authors, following one another, fall into error when the first one errs, so Solinus, following Pliny's words, wrongly said that the horned viper had eight horns, for we saw the contrary. It has teeth similar to those of a viper, similarly arranged. I am well aware that there are great differences between vipers according to where they live, for my great desire to learn about them led me to find them in England, France, Italy, Greece, Asia and Egypt, differing in body form and colour. The horned vipers, like vipers in many countries, produce their young alive, as does the salamander. And since Aristotle, in a passage in the last chapter of book V of the *History,* speaking of the viper, says: *Parit catulos obvolutos membranis, quae tertia die rumpuntur. Evenit interdum, ut qui in utero adhuc sunt, abrosis membranis perrumpant. Parit enim singulis diebus singulos, & plures quam viginti*[306], this gave me the desire to see the admirable works of nature and to observe vipers when pregnant. But it seemed to me, saving the truth, that they produce their young without any membrane. I desired to mention this here so that someone, aware of my uncertainty, might be able to observe it and perhaps give us some certainty in our doubt.

Ceste est la figure d'vne Vipere.

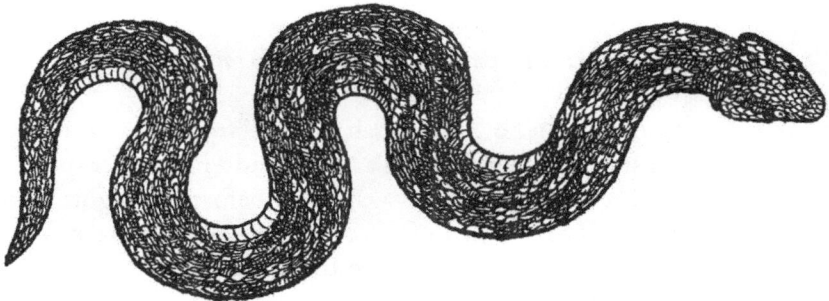

Figure: This is the figure of a viper

I found a number of other plants in this plain, of which I know neither the ancient nor the modern names. We camped and rested for the whole of the day in this place, on a level area adjoining the well.

55

Description of a very deep well in Desert Arabia

This well of which I have spoken merits a description, for indeed it is curious. It was made at great expense in times past, when the Soldan ruled in Egypt, in order to give Suez a better supply of water, and also so that those who travel through this country may be able to water their beasts. It is a small building enclosed by walls, square like a small fort, with a device enabling water to be drawn from the well, which is very deep, with a wheel turned by two oxen, from which hang two ropes a foot apart, and on these ropes are numbers of small jars; so that when the oxen turn the wheel the ropes turn too, drawing up water from the well in the jars, which are filled at the bottom of the well and at the top discharge their water into a basin below the wheel, from which the water runs in a channel outside the walls into cisterns outside the little fort, which is fortified so as to keep the people within it in safety along with their cattle.

56

Of the plants that grow in the sandy soil round Suez

It takes only an hour and a half to travel from the well to Suez, for the distance is no more than a league and a half. After spending a whole day there we set out again well before midnight, having decided to visit the town of Suez only on our way back. When daylight came we were already on the coast of the Red Sea, with Suez only a half-quarter of a league away. We passed through a barren desert in which there grew not a single plant, apart from acacia-trees, whose gum is diligently collected by the Arabs; it is the same as the gum we use in Europe to give body to ink and dyestuffs, called in Latin *gummi arabicum*. Its leaves are so small that if you take up a branch you can cover it with your thumb, and if you count the leaves you will find that you have covered three hundred and fifty of them. The inhabitants strike the branches with long poles, causing them to fall to the ground to provide fodder for their sheep. I have set here the portrait of this tree, drawn from nature[307].

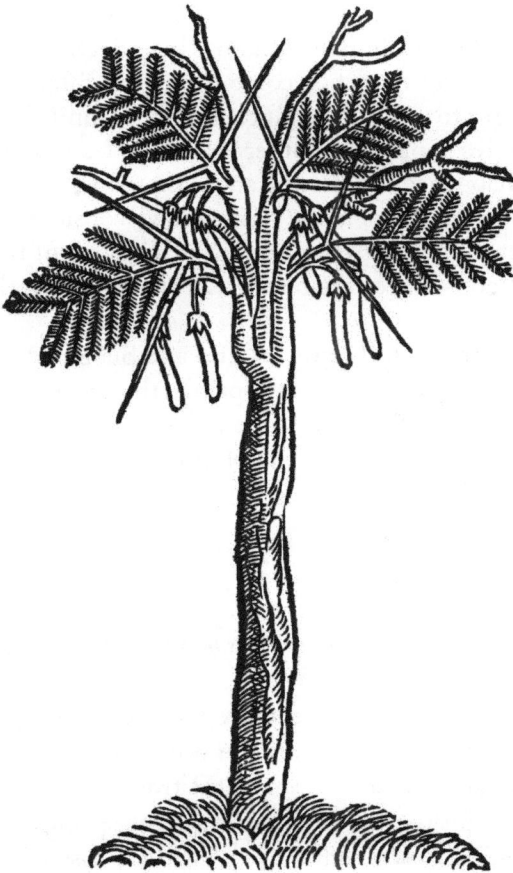

Figure

When we were some way beyond Suez we came into a spacious plain green with senna-trees, which grow wild here, producing the senna which is brought to us by merchants. The senna which is sold in the shops of drug merchants or dealers is of two very different kinds, as appears from the names given to them. One of them has seeds in flat pods curved in the manner of a scythe and pointed leaves. The other[308] also has flat pods, but they are much broader and less curved, and its leaves are rounded, not ending in a point like those of the first.

The first is the better of the two, and is called Levantine senna. The other is called medium senna, and is less effective. This diversity arises from the fact that they come from two different countries and are brought to us by different routes. This affinity between two things which resemble one another is liable to lead us into error, as has already happened with senna and false senna[309], which is now common in our gardens. Some writers have considered it to be a species of senna, but this is wrong, for it has none of the qualities of senna, which is one of the plants that remain green throughout the year.

We made three halts between Cairo and Suez. The first was on the banks of the Nile, under date-palms, the second in the plain described above, and the third at the well of Suez. It is necessary in following this route to stay at the places appointed, which I have called halting-places.

57

Of the twelve bitter springs mentioned by Pliny

Continuing on our way, we arrived at the bitter springs quite early, and set up our tents there. The water of the springs is very salt and bitter, and they are said to be the twelve springs mentioned in the Bible[310], for they are still known as the springs of Moses[311]. They lie in barren, sandy country, in a great expanse of nitrous soil. They are more than fifty paces distant from one another, though not always the same distance; for one is a hundred paces from the others, another fifty paces, sometimes more and sometimes less. All the springs emerge from the ground at a low mound or promontory, from which the water flows in a number of streams, which are soon lost in the sand. The sun had made us very thirsty, so that we were constrained to drink the brackish water. Although it was very bitter because of the nitre, everyone in our company drank it and found find it good, because we were all so thirsty.

58

Of the Red Sea

The end of the Red Sea is at the village of Suez, where there is an arsenal for the Turk's galleys, which are beached during the winter, for the shore and the harbour are not safe in all winds. This Red Sea is a narrow channel, no wider than the Seine between Harfleur and Honfleur, in which sailing is difficult and full of peril, for there are many rocks. Some who have heard talk of this sea think that its water is red, but that is not so. The sea runs from north to south, beginning at Suez and extending in a straight line for some 30 miles, but some distance from the twelve springs it curves a little towards the west.

The plain though which we were travelling was on almost the same level as the shores of the Red Sea, but on the other side there are very high rocky mountains surrounding the sea. It is only two bowshots from the bitter springs to the sea. When the tide receded I observed several kinds of small fish, shellfish and other excrements of the sea[312], among which I saw a fifth species of sea hedgehogs which I had not seen elsewhere, although I had already observed four kinds all different from one another. All kinds of shellfish of marvellous size live here, either because of the climate or the temperature of the air or the food that they find here.

59

Of a rhamnus tree that grows on the shores of the Red Sea

We found a shrub resembling *rhamnus altera* growing along the sea, with very thick, salt, white leaves. Its branches are thorny, but with blunt thorns like those of the buckthorn of Europe.

We also saw the tracks of the wild roe deer called gazelles, imprinted in the shape of a heart in the sand over which they had passed, for here the sand is level. They come down from the nearby mountains to drink at the springs that I have described, and also to browse on these shrubs. Pliny has gives a full account of the springs, which he call *fontes amari,* in the passage where he writes that Ptolemy constructed a canal[313] linking the Red Sea with the Nile, which was 100 feet wide, 30 feet high and 37,000 feet long. And when he reached the bitter springs he carried the sea no farther; for if it had mingled with the Nile the land of Egypt would have had no fresh water to drink. Or it may have been because the territory of Egypt is less than three cubits higher than the sea. We now camped for the fourth time since leaving Cairo and the third time since the Nile.

Having filled our goatskins with water, we continued on our way over stony, arid country, with no trees except a few brooms which grow here. The great heat lasted throughout the day, for the northerly wind which had refreshed the previous days had quite died down. And although the water in our goatskins, taken from the bitter springs, was brackish and stinking, being heated by the sun and almost boiling, we still had not half enough to drink on our way; for because of the heat and because drinking it hot made us thirstier we could not satisfy our thirst.

60

Of several trees of Arabia, and of those that bear wool, and of chameleons

I saw chameleons here which were different in several respects from the Egyptian chameleons, and of smaller size; for they have red stripes on a white ground, with nothing of the colour of the others. I shall describe both kinds at greater length in the book on snakes; but I have thought fit to give its portrait here, to show what it looks like.

Le portraiĉt du Chameléon.

We saw wild gazelles grazing in this country, travelling in large bands. We halted about midday to rest our mounts and avoid the great heat under our tents. When night fell we loaded our baggage on the camels, in order to travel in the coolness of night, and came into a region of small mountains and hills; then, at a small spring, we encountered some shepherds driving their beasts from one place to another and obtained some meat from them for our meal. We camped there for the fifth time, lit fires with wood from tamarisks, the trees that bear wool and acacia-trees, and cooked the fresh meat. While walking about in the low hills I found caper-bushes which had reached the height of small fig-trees, so that I had to climb the tree to get at its fruit, which is the size of a hen's egg and contains the seeds; its capers are the size of walnuts. The seeds taste as hot as pepper, as also does the caper.

I find that Herodotus was the first to mention the tree that bears wool; and following him Theophrastus, Pliny and other authors wrote about it. It is one of the trees that remain green throughout the year. Its wool is finer than silk, and from it the Arabs spin very beautiful fabrics, lighter and finer than those made from fine silk, and whiter than those made from cotton. This can be proved from the fruits of this tree, which I brought back and showed to contain a great quantity of wool.

We now left the plain and came into hilly country, more barren and treeless than the other deserts through which we had been travelling. And now, turning away from the sea, we left Desert Arabia and entered Stony Arabia. We camped that evening in a level area in the form of an amphitheatre, entirely surrounded by mountains except at one point. This was our sixth night's lodging. After we had rested and the heat had abated we travelled on for the rest of the day and the following night. At daybreak we came back to the sea, for at the point where we left it it turned in the form of an arc. We had to travel along the shore in the water for about three bowshots, and then left it, coming to a large estuary between hills of sandy soil, where we again found wool-bearing trees and tree-sized caper-bushes.

Continuing on our way, we passed out of the mountains and came into a plain where we saw large troupes of gazelles, which live so far away from water that I concluded that they do not drink, or at any rate drink very seldom. This is by no means unusual, for many other beasts can live without drinking, like sheep in England which never drink anything, just as vipers and horned vipers among all species of snakes live without drinking. So too do chameleons, which can live for more than a year without eating anything.

When we had travelled for many hours and it was beginning to be hot we halted to avoid the heat of the day, and when it was cooler we reloaded our baggage and continued throughout the night in coolness, and then came into very difficult rocky country. This was the beginning of the rocks of Stony Arabia.

61

Of the first village that we encountered on the way to Mount Sinai

By daybreak we had come into a broad pass between very high mountains both to right and to left, where we found a fine stream of clear, fresh spring water flowing down from a distant mountain. This was the first stream of real fresh water that we had encountered on the journey from Cairo. At the entrance to the pass was a large village inhabited by Arabs called Pharagou [Pharan], in which there were only three or four houses; for the inhabitants of villages in this country do not live in proper houses but under palm-trees in the open or under rocks[314].

The village of Pharagou seemed to us a pleasant place compared with the countries through which we had passed, for here good shade is provided by pomegranate-trees, palms, olives, fig-trees, pear-trees and other fruit-trees. This was the first village we had come upon since leaving Cairo, except Suez. After we had refreshed ourselves with the sweet water and had drunk our fill, and filled our goatskins and renewed our supplies of fresh meat in the form of chickens, goats and sheep, and also of fruit, that is, apples, pears, pomegranates and fresh grapes, and each of us was sufficiently rested, we set about loading our baggage and continued on our way.

The people of this country are quite happy to live in the open under palm-trees, which is why they are olive-coloured. And since it hardily ever rains here it is sufficient for them to have dwellings built of palm-branches against the trunks of palms, to give them some protection against the vehemence of the sun. The asses, horses, camels, sheep, kids, oxen, cows, goats, chickens and other animals of this country are much smaller and of lesser body than those of Egypt.

I climbed up on to the rocks, where I found the tree called *balanus myrepsica*[315] growing between the rocks to the height of a birch-tree. It also had similar branches and a white trunk, so that when I saw it from a distance I was convinced that it was a birch. The inhabitants of Pharagou are diligent in collecting its seeds, from which they make a great quantity of oil. I realised this when I saw outside the village a large heap of the seeds, with the pods, which split into three, collected by one of the Arabs.

Observing the plants which grow in the stream, I found the same plants that are found in streams in Europe, like balsam, pennyroyal, spikenard, pimpernel, water-cress and reeds.

We followed the stream up the valley, passing under forests of palm-trees. All that day we continued up the valley between the foothills of Mount Sinai, and halted to rest until night. We then travelled through the night and came to the foot of the high mountains of Sinai as day was breaking, slept for a little at the foot of the mountain, and soon continued on our way up a difficult ascent to reach the summit of Mount Sinai. The path has been made artificially, with steps of hewn stone, sometimes cut from the native rock, so as to make it easier to lead camels and other animals up the mountain. Horses are seldom taken up Mount Sinai, for the climb is too difficult for them. The ascent lasted a good half-league.

After we reached the top we had to travel more than two leagues between the mountains, which have a number of rounded peaks at some distance from one another on the summit of the highest mountain; for some are higher than others. It was after midday before we reached the monastery, although we had begun the ascent at daybreak.

62

Of Mount Sinai

I now desire to speak of Mount Sinai, since there is no place more famous than the monastery, and I will begin by saying that the monks in the monastery are Maronite Christians who live according to the Greek rule. Having been long informed of our coming, they came out to meet us and gave us a friendly reception.

The monastery is similar to the monasteries on Mount Athos in Macedonia, and is very like the one called Agias Laura. The church of this monastery is situated on lower ground, as is the case with the monastery of Ivero [Iviron].

There are ordinarily some sixty Maronite caloyers, some of whom are Greeks, others Syrians and others again Arabs, though all of them bear the name of caloyers and live according to the Greek rule. It as if German, Italian and Spanish monks lived with French ones; for they speak different languages but are all of the same religion. Similarly the Maronites, who are Arab Christian monks, and the Greeks are of the same religion and are all called caloyers.

The pilgrims who go to Mount Sinai are lodged in the monastery, for there are no other lodgings. It is situated in a valley at the foot of Mount Oreb. There is a great abundance of water, for a stream coming down from the mountain runs through the monastery, filling their cistern with water, which is very clear, cold, sweet and perfect in all qualities.

The monastery lies in the valley, surrounded by high walls. so that they can withstand any enemies who might wish to attack them. There is also a mosque within the monastery for Arabs and Turks, and lodgings set apart for them; for Christians cannot come here except when they are accompanied by Arabs or Turks.

There are very fine orchards in the valleys on Mount Sinai, in which they cultivate vines and vegetables and grow various plants, such as cabbages, lettuces, beets, onions, garlic, leeks and such other common plants. They also cultivate fruit-trees of various kinds, particularly almond-trees.

63

Description of Mount Sinai and Mount Oreb

After we had dined in the monastery and the heat of the day had abated we resolved to climb Mount Oreb. We had caloyers to guide us, so that as we climbed they might tell us about all the singular things on the mountain, and we followed the stream which runs down to the monastery. A caloyer aged 70 travelled in our company, a man better fitted for the ascent than anyone else in our party; for we were travelling on foot, ad this was a great sign of the good health of those living on the mountain. We were looking east as we climbed the mountain, and when we were somewhat higher up, at a place below the summit of Mount Oreb, we found a space in the valley where there was a church built on the spot where Elijah stood.

Continuing up from there, we came upon steps of hewn stone and a gateway which anciently was closed at the foot of the steps so as to shut off the farther side if it should become necessary to resist an attack from higher up the mountain. We climbed to the highest summit, where we found another church on Mount Oreb. This mountain was inhabited, as Sinai was not; for Sinai was arid, while Oreb has abundance of water from a spring. Diodorus, writing of the country of the Jews, speaks of this mountain, calling it the region of the Abbateans, in Latin *Abbataeorum*. He says that there is a well defended rock here which can be held by a very small force, for there is only one way up, which is steep and difficult to climb. I believe that he is referring to this place, for there is no other place in all the country of the Jews which matches this description than Mount Oreb.

The guides showed us all the sacred places, particularly those mentioned in the Bible. On the walls of the chapel on Mount Oreb were the names of a number of Frenchmen who had desired to leave a record of their passing here. On the way down from there we saw a large cistern constructed between two rocks not far from the chapel to store rainwater, of which we drank, for one of our guides had brought a cauldron and a rope to draw water from it. We had climbed the mountain on the east side, but descended on the west side; at the foot of which is situated a small monastery called Saranda Pateres[316], in which we lodged that night.

64

Of another monastery situated at the foot of Mount Oreb, and of the rock from which water gushed for the children of Israel

This small monastery is a dependency of the first one, and has a church. We saw gardens in which were many kinds of fruits, and in the monastery we found bread, wine and preserved olives.

We set out next day to climb Mount Sinai on the east side, looking towards the south. Sinai is much higher than Mount Oreb, and just as Mount Athos casts a shadow on Lemnos when the sun is setting, so Mount Sinai casts a shadow on Mount Oreb when the sun rises. When we were on the summit of the mountain I observed that it was of very hard rock, of the colour of iron, but not without vegetation, for there is great quantity of *absinthium seriphium,* which bears the small seed that we call wormwood, and *panaces asclepium,* fleabane and the agrimony of the Arabs. It is besieged on all sides by mountains all round, and is much higher than Mount Oeta in Greece and Mount Ida in Crete; but in my opinion it is not as high as Mount Olympus.

Nevertheless it is so high that when I looked south I could easily see the two sides of the Arabian Gulf, otherwise called the Red Sea, and I saw it curving in the form of an English bow; and I could also easily see the mountains on which is situated the monastery of Saint Anthony or Saint Macarius[317], which is in the deserts adjoining Ethiopia beyond the Red Sea, where there still live some Christian and Armenian caloyers, otherwise called Maronites. Then, turning towards the east, as far as my eye could reach I could see nothing but a mountainous region of high, rugged crags: this was Stony Arabia, adjoining Mount Sinai. Then, turning north and looking beyond Mount Oreb, which is only a league and a half away, I saw another region of crags and many mountains, extending towards the east, in which area is situated Jerusalem, lying in mountainous country contiguous to the territory of Mount Sinai.

Looking towards the west, I saw nothing but Desert Arabia, a barren, sandy country, through which we had passed on our journey from Cairo; and from there, looking between west and north, since the weather was clear and serene, we could discern the Mediterranean Sea, which is five days' journey from there: though I do not wish it to be understood that I could see it absolutely clearly. There is also a spring which emerges on the same side of the mountain and runs down to the monastery of Quarentapadri and waters the valley and the gardens of the caloyers.

The level area on the highest peak of the mountain is scarcely larger than the summit of the great pyramid, that is to say only four paces. But a little lower down there is more space, and the rock can be climbed only with great difficulty. for it is very steep and there are no steps. We went down to the monastery of the Forty Fathers, where we supped and spent the night; and then we returned to the

Le mont Oreb.

La chappelle de ſaincte Katherine.

ORIENT.   Ce mont eſt ſecond apres le mont.   en haulteur Sinaï.

Tout ce paiſaige eſt, du tenant du mont Sinaï.

En tout ce coſté n'y a que païs de mõtagne de lõgue eſtéduë, cõme auſsi eſt le païs de l'Arabie, pierreuſe ſterile & deshabité.

S. Helie.

Les degrez.

Le ru...

Monaſtere.

Logis des Caloieres.

La Moſquee.

Legi...

Fõtaine.

Mont de Moyſe.

Le chemin du mõt.

Rocher de dure pierre.

Le iardin.

noſtre Seigneur bailla ſa Loy à Moyſe.

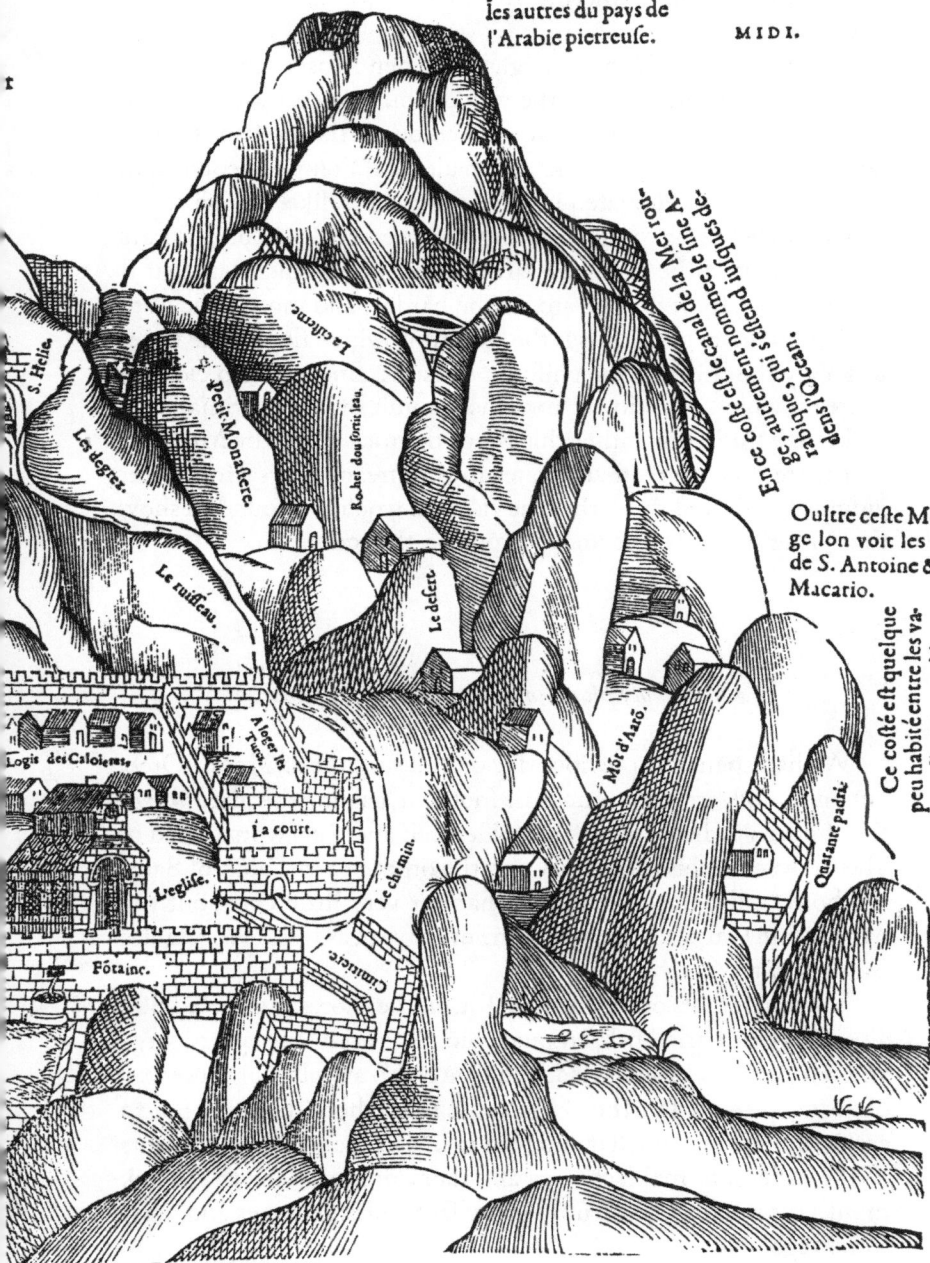

Le mont Sinaî.

Ceſte montagne eſt plus haulte que toutes les autres du pays de l'Arabie pierreuſe.

MIDI.

S. Helie.

Les degrez.

Petit Monaſtere.

Le ruiſſeau.

La chaire.

Rocher dou ſortit leau.

Le deſert.

En ce coſté eſt le canal de la Mer rouge, autrement nommee le ſine Arabique, qui s'eſtend iuſques dens l'Ocean.

Oultre ceſte Mer rouge lon voit les monts de S. Antoine & de S. Macario.

Logis des Caloiers.

A loger les Turcs.

La court.

L'egliſe.

Le chemin.

Mör d'Auio.

Quarante padri.

Ce coſté eſt quelque peu habité entre les valées d'autant qu'il y a quelque humidité.

Fötaine.

Cimetiere.

Figure: Portrait of Mount Sinai, on which Our Lord gave the Law to Moses monastery of Saint Catherine, from which we had set out on the previous day.

The rock from which water gushed when Moses struck it with his rod was shown to us on the way down. It is a massive vertical block of stone, of the same grain and colour as the Theban stone of which the needles or obelisks are made, like Pompey's column in Alexandria. It is granulated in different colours, like Theban stone. which has led some to think, seeing that the needles or obelisks are so massive, that the stone was artificially put together; but that is entirely false, for it is of all stones the hardest and most difficult to work with metal tools. This is the rock from which flowed the water to satisfy the thirst of the children of Israel. But it is also close to a stream which runs down from the summit of Mount Sinai. This makes me think that either this is not the rock struck by Moses or that there was not then any water in the stream; but saving better judgment I should think that the caloyers would be bound to show the spring that emerges under a rock on the mountain.

65

Of the holy places on the mountain of Sinai

We had spent the previous day on the summit of Mount Oreb, but on this day we went round the foot of it, passing the place where the children of Israel made the golden calf and then worshipped it. The caloyers of this monastery and the other deserts, both of Saint Anthony and Saint Macarius[318], harvest very little corn, but the patriarch in Cairo sends them some every year, as well as vegetables from Egypt.

The inhabitants of the town of Tor, on the shores of the Red Sea, also send them dried fish, among which I noticed sea-squirts, sargs and sea-bream, already dried. They have also supplies of preserved olives and vegetables. They keep cattle in the humid valleys, not to eat their meat but to sell it and feed their slaves and the inhabitants of the valleys, to make cheeses and dairy products, for the Greek monks eat neither cheese nor butter. They cultivate vines and grow some vegetables.

The land which is watered in the valleys and humid areas is of good quality, for this high mountain is not so cold as the high mountains of Europe, nor so hot as is the low-lying county. These mountains are so barren and dry that very little can be cultivated but in areas where there is some humidity.

We spent that night in the monastery of Saint Catherine. On the following day they showed us the shrine containing the relics of the bones of Saint Catherine, which is ordinarily hung in the church. They celebrate mass in the Greek fashion most honourably. There are a number of fine paintings in the church, and other relics of saints. The Turks who go to Mount Sinai also have a mosque within the monastery, which is not connected with the Christian church.

The caloyers are accustomed to provide food for visitors, but the meals are very simple ones. They cook rice, flour, beans and peas, which they put in a wooden dish in the middle of the courtyard, without any tablecloth, with some bread, crowning the dish with spoons, and those who come to the meal sit in the Arab fashion on their heels, supported on their forelegs. This fashion is common to all Arabs. The Turks do otherwise, for they sit on the ground in the manner of tailors. The schecarab[319] accompanied by his noblemen sat in the same way as the other Arabs in his party. The caloyers had a liquid manna gathered in their mountains which they called *tereniabin,* differing from the hard form of manna; or what Arab authors have called *tereniabin* is kept in earthenware pots like honey, and they take it to Cairo to sell, which is what Hippocrates called cedar honey and other Greeks dew of Mount Lebanon, which is different from dry white manna. The kind that we have in France, brought from Briançon, gathered from larches on the summits of the highest mountains, is hard and different from this kind. And so, there being manna of two kinds, both kinds are to be seen on sale in merchants' shops in Cairo. One is called manna and is hard; the other is called *tereniabin* and is liquid; and since I have written at greater length in the book on evergreen trees I shall say no more here.

66

Journey from Mount Sinai to Tor

Before we left the monastery the caloyers gave us long stout sticks, polished and quite heavy, which they told us came from the tree from which Moses' rod was made, with which he struck the rock to bring out water for the children of Israel. This tree would have been like the acacia, save that it has no knots. We took the road for the town of Tor, leaving the one by which we had come, with only two days' journey to Tor. We saw large herds of gazelles in the mountains of Sinai, along the rocks; and since they are not hunted they multiply in great numbers, like flocks of sheep.

We rested for the night in open country, and on the following day, having loaded our baggage at an early hour, we made for the mountain over which we had to pass in that day's march in the very difficult country between Tor and Mount Sinai. The vegetation on the mountains in this area consists for the most part only of *absinthium seriphium* or *ponticum, ambrosia, eupatoria, papaver corniculatum,* trees of *balanus myrepsica* and a species of Arabian broom different from ours. There are also caper-bushes growing between openings in the rocks, very different from those which grow into trees and also from those found in Greece.

We passed over this mountain, which is more difficult to descend than to climb, for we had more frequently to descend than to climb, since we were already at such a height. When we were already some way down we came upon a fine spring running down beside our track, and followed it for a considerable distance.

We found a number of acacias and *heliotropium magnum,* which was a small shrub, some three cubits high. There was also a kind of henbane, highly odoriferous and oily, which grows almost into a bush. There are also wild gourds and cucumbers, of a different species from those that we see in the countries of Asia and Europe.

After we reached the foot of the mountain it was just after midday when we entered a spacious expanse of country between the mountain and the Red Sea, in which we camped and rested that evening a good four leagues short of Tor. We set out again soon after midnight and reached Tor before it was light. Gourds grow wild in this country in such great abundance that there is no plant more common.

67

Description of the town and castle of Tor, and of the singularities on the shores of the Red Sea

After reaching Tor and camping under our tents in the plain, we went to see the town. We call it a town, but it is only a small village; for Tor, although it bears the name of town, nevertheless, since it is famous and of great renown as a place of passage, and is a port on the Red Sea, and since the country is so inhospitable for the inhabitants, it is a great thing to see such a village in such a barren place. Half a league from Tor they showed us the forty palms of which there is mention in the Bible, where there is a small natural hot bath, hardly larger than a small spring; the stream flows for some distance, but then is at once lost in the sand.

Because of the great inconvenience of the place where Tor is situated very few people live there, for they have neither wood nor fresh water except by travelling a long way to find it; and moreover the harbour is not safe, for it is much exposed to all winds. It is not really a harbour at all, but rather a beach.

The village is situated on rather higher ground, for the sea sometimes swells so much as to flood the countryside and surround the village. There is a small fort of dressed stone with four towers at the four corners, rather poorly built. It stands on sandy ground near the village of Tor, which has no defensive ditches nor fresh water, apart from a nearby well of salt water, which can be drunk if need be for want of any better. The area of this castle within the walls is only 60 paces by 80 paces long when walking quickly; and so I find it to be of the same length and width as the great hall of the Place in Paris.

A great part of Tor is inhabited by Jews and Christians, who are Greeks, Arabs and Armenians. There is also a church of caloyers, called Maronites. We went to their mass, which they sang honourably, partly in Arabic, partly in Armenian and partly in Greek. It is not their custom to sit down during the service of the mass. And since the mass lasts a long time they give everyone crooks and crutches to provide support under their arms.

There is a great market for dried fish, whose bellies they split open, add a little salt and dry in the sun. Among the fish that I recognised were bass, which the Latins call *lupi* and *umbrae* and we call meagre, sea-bream, called *canthari,* and tooth-shells. They also fish great quantity of sargs, sea-bream and *orade.* I say *orade* and not *dorade,* for what is called *orade* at Marseilles is different from the *dorade* or sea-bream of the Ocean. The sea-squirts found here are larger and commoner than in the Mediterranean.

There grows here a kind of coral which the Arabs call *chavein*[320], which is spineless and hollow within, having an infinity of small tubes; and since it is handsome, and is found in quantity everywhere, pieces of it are hung on the doors of both the mosque and the caravanserai. They are two cubits long and about the thickness of a man's thigh, partly white and partly red in colour.

I also saw a kind of stone which the ancients called *lapis arabicus.* I had no hope of knowing what it was until a caloyer showed me some balls of this stone which he said that he had brought from Saint Macarius, which is on the other side of the Red Sea, opposite Tor, in which place there is also great quantity of it, like pebbles in other countries. The stone is round, heavy, resembling gold marcasite, with grains of the same structure as androdamas[321].

Tor is a halting-place for caravans carrying drugs from Mecca and Happy Arabia. I know that pepper, ginger, nutmeg, cloves, lac, dragon's blood and mace[322] are brought here, some of which we saw being loaded on to a caravan which left Tor with us. It also included twenty camels carrying nothing but the round shells used to make key-ring pendants in Europe; but in Cairo they are used to polish paper and coloured fabrics, of oily substance, with which they clothe themselves, as men did in time past.

68

Of the boats and barks of the Red Sea

The barks, skiffs and other kinds of vessels belonging to the poor people of the towns on the Red Sea and of Tor are lashed together with palm ropes; and although they are not so firmly joined as they would be if they were nailed with iron nails, nevertheless they have no fear that of the sea entering, for the planks are so skilfully fitted together, caulked and made watertight with pitch that they navigate in complete safety.

Those who thought that boats were not built with iron nails in some countries from fear of lodestone were mistaken; for although lodestone has the natural virtue of attracting iron to itself it must not be thought that it has power to hold back a ship because it is built with iron nails, or to draw it to itself from a distance. It is because they have not the kind of wood that endures being fixed with nails, and also because the people of the country are poor and cannot afford the expense, they have no nails available to them and have no metal from which to forge them; and even if they have nails, not being accustomed to constructing boats using iron and being skilled in using rope to tie them together, they build their bots without incurring any expense.

This is why their boats are very small; and they are content with such small craft, both for fishing and for carrying on trade, and in summer for plying up and down the Red Sea. It is true that there are also large hookers[323], ships, galleys and other vessels of all kinds, but these are foreign vessels. But whatever the kind of ship navigation in the Red Sea is very perilous because of the multitude and frequency of rocks.

I found a kind of oyster on the shore at Tor which the Greeks anciently called *tridachna* and now call *aganon* or *agano* in the vulgar tongue. They are much larger than those of the Illyrian or Mediterranean Sea, and different from those which the people of Lemnos and Euboea call *gaideropoda* or *acynopoda*[324].

We found good wine at Tor, for the Christian, Arab, Armenian and Greek inhabitants cultivate vines, from which we filled our kegs and goatskins. The water drunk in Tor is transported from half a league away,, but is not good, being nitrous and saline. There is a street in the village which is roofed over, as in other places in Egypt, and the inhabitants stay under it to escape the vehement heat of the sun.

The palm-trees in this area produce fat, soft red dates which are very moist and of a different nature from those of other regions; and so the inhabitants are constrained to press them together in baskets woven from palm leaves and tread them underfoot as is done with bags of figs, forming a solid mass which keeps well, as is also the practice with tamarind fruits. These dates are the staple food of the inhabitants.

They catch very large and handsome turtles with shells the size of a house door. There was a time when Christians did not dare to eat them, because the patriarch of Alexandria had excommunicated any who ate them; but since then they have been absolved and now eat them.

We left Tor to return to Cairo, travelling through the country described above, with Mount Sinai on the right, the Red Sea on the left and the Tramontane[325] ahead of us. Passing through the country round Tor, we saw beautiful and delectable gardens near the spring, enclosed by a wall built of earth and straw, which could be entered only through the gates. Continuing on our way, we found a small kind of lizard, about the size of a skink, running about in the plain, which the Arabs call *dhab*. We also found stellions, whose excrements, called in Greek *crocodilea,* are collected by the Arabs and taken to be sold in Cairo. From there they are brought to us by merchants.

Our way took us through a region of barren, stony sand, where we found a small animal resembling a phalangium, with eight feet, four on each side, running about in the sand and climbing up the horses' legs, tormenting them and making them jib; but the drivers of the camels, knowing what was wrong, have a switch ready to brush them off at once.

We left the channel of the Red Sea to turn inland, where we found a spring of water, half sweet but somewhat saline, at which the camels were watered that evening. We camped there and then continued on our way before daylight along the shores of the sea. And to make a detour round a mountain we had to enter the water. We now had the land to the right and the side of the channel to the left. Then we returned to the open country, and we had to ensure that our party was well organised and prepared, for the fear that we had of the Arabs; for we had been warned that they had gathered to attack us and pillage us. The twenty janissaries, the secharab and the Arabs, with the company led by Monsieur de Fumel and the other people who were following him were ready to receive them if they came and attacked us. It was already very late; we travelled for a long time in good order, and for the fear we had of them we camped at a fairly early hour. And although we had made great diligence that day, nevertheless after filling our goatskins with water and reloaded our baggage we travelled on for a good two hours until it grew dark, and then camped in the open country, where we spent the night.

On the following day we continued on our way through a region of soft and arid sand. In the evening we came to a soft, humid place and rested between mountains on which grew tamarisks, brooms, acacias, a kind of reeds called *holoschoeni* and round galingales. There too we saw some small birds perching on the tamarisks, which I observed attentively to see if I could recognise them; for it is matter for some surprise to find birds living in such barren country. Among them I observed sparrows, buntings and linnets. On that day I also saw vultures and crows flying.

69

Computation of the days' journeys between Tor and Cairo

Setting out from there, we returned to the route which we had left when we went to Mount Sinai, following the road round the Red Sea where it opens out into a beach. We had to go through the water up to the camels' girths, being the second time that we had had to do this.

That evening we drew near to the twelve bitter springs where we had previously stayed; but not being able to reach them we camped half a league short of them, for our beasts were tired and night was beginning to fall. On the following day, having set out while it was still dark, we came to the springs and filled our goatskins with water; then we continued on the road by which we had come, leaving it to go to Suez, where we arrived at midday. If I computed the distance in days of travel, as we did in the journey from Tor to Suez, I would make it only five and a half, though indeed we travelled in great diligence.

Neither the water of this sea nor the sand on its shores is red, so the origin of its name must be looked for elsewhere. There was a king called by the Greeks Erythra who ruled in Egypt and gave his name to this sea, which was called in Latin *Erythraeum mare*, that is to say the Red Sea. It ebbs and flows like the Ocean, but is no more than an arm of the great sea running into the lands of Arabia, forming a channel which was originally called the Arabian Gulf but later was known as the Red Sea. It was King Erythra who introduced the practice of building boats, for before his time men sailed on rafts built of wood, as is still the way on the Durance[326] and other violent rivers.

69

Of the port of Suez on the shores of the Red Sea

Several modern authors maintain that Suez is the place anciently known as Arsinoe; and this seems to me to be probable. since it is the first port on the Red Sea and the one nearest to Cairo. It took this name from the time of Alexander the Great, for I find that Ptolemy Lagus had been ruler of Egypt and married his daughter Arsinoa, of surpassing beauty, to Lysimachus, king of Macedon; and for her Ptolemy Philadelphus her brother built this town, naming it Arsinoe[327] after her.

Suez is a most inhospitable place, and accordingly has only a small population; for there is no good sweet water for more than two leagues round the town. All that is to be seen there is a small, weak castle built in the antique fashion on a low mound. The great expense incurred by the Turk has improved Tor but little, for there is such great lack of all things that the place is barely habitable. The galleys which the Grand Turk caused to be built here are drawn up on shore, which we saw, between thirty and forty in number. They were brought from Constantinople by sea to the Nile, and on the Nile to Cairo, where they were taken to pieces and transported in separate parts on camels and in carts to Suez, and there rebuilt. The harbour here is not safe, being nothing but a beach which is exposed to all winds. It is difficult to navigate on the Red Sea, for the channel is full of rocks which do not appear above the water. All the expeditions and sea armies sent by the Turk against the Indians are mounted at Suez. And so when we were travelling on this road we encountered forty or fifty camels in their leather harness, sent to fetch water from the well at Suez, two leagues away, to supply the galleys which the Basha who was lieutenant or viceroy in Egypt was sending to India to make war on a town called Zibit[328], which had recently revolted. Although the water is salty and bitter, seamen drink it for lack of any sweeter water.

We continued on our way towards Cairo. And when we were half-way between the well and Suez we came upon watchmen on scaffolds like those used for keeping a watch on vineyards, several of which were to be seen in this country. On each scaffold were two or three men, so that if they saw anyone lying in wait some distance away they could warn the inhabitants of the town to be on their guard. Arriving at the well of Suez for the second time, we rested on the platforms until late in the evening, , then reloaded our camels at two o'clock in the morning and so, travelling in all speed throughout the night and the whole of the following day without resting, when we reached the banks of the Nile it was very late, and we spent the night at the same place from which we had set out on our way to Mount Sinai.

Here ended our journey to Mount Sinai, which we completed in twenty days; and of the nine or ten horses which we had taken with us there returned only three, the others having died on the way. The Arabs fed them only on beans and barley, just like the camels, most of which also died. On this day, about midday, one of the Arabs driving the camels, seeing a viper some distance away and crying out in his language to his companions, "Viper! viper!", they at once ran up and beat it to death with stones; suggesting to me that they have a great horror of vipers. The vipers and horned vipers of Egypt have a very flexible skin, as I observed when stuffing them; for after I had skinned them and filled the skins with stuffing they were twice their natural size, as does not happen with vipers from other regions. There are several other snakes in Egypt, of which I have not spoken; for the most dangerous are those that I have mentioned.

And since I had the opportunity of seeing the embalmed bodies, still entire, of certain winged snakes, which also have feet, and are said to fly from Arabia to Egypt, I set their portrait here[329].

Portraict du Serpent ællé.

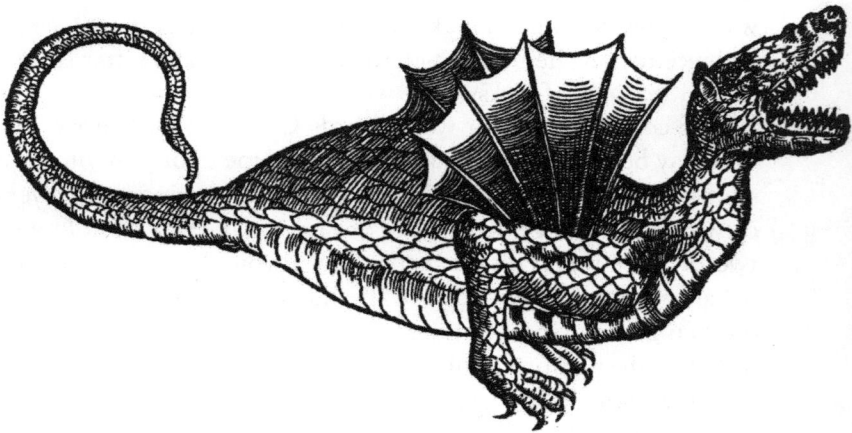

Figure: Winged snake

As we continued on our way we encountered a troupe of Arab or Egyptian peasants who had been impressed on the Basha's orders to row the galleys in the expedition mentioned above. When the Basha in Cairo, who is lieutenant for the Turk in Egypt, is arming his galleys he causes men to be taken by force indifferently throughout the country; for they would not dare to refuse, since it is for the service of the Grand Signior. They are put in the galleys at Suez, though they are not chained to them, for they are allowed to return to their homes when they return from the voyage. The obedience of the subjects of the Turk is so great that no on dares to resist his will. They take men without any concern for person; and Christians living in Cairo stay in their houses without going out during these periods, for they take any man whom they find in the streets.

The Turkish soldiers attached to Monsieur de Fumel throughout the journey carried enough biscuit to eat on the journey from Cairo to Mount Sinai and back and still brought some back, which seemed to us very great continence in their manner of living, which men of another nation would be unable to achieve.

We camped for part of the night on the banks of the Nile, and on the following morning loaded up the camels and returned to Cairo for the second time, staying there for some considerable time without leaving it. The journey from Cairo to Suez is the burial-ground of the camels of Egypt and Arabia, for they remain there when they make that journey, as appears from the bones to be seen lying along the road, and also from the large numbers of vultures which gather along the road, great companies of which we had seen on the previous day, fully fifty of them in each troupe; and I venture to say that among birds with hooked nails only vultures fly in bands.

71

Of the porcelain vases sold in Cairo, and of nitre

There is great quantity of porcelain vases which merchants sell in public. And seeing them called by a modern name, and seeking their etymology, I find that they are known by the name of a species of shellfish called *murex*[330], in that its shells are called porcelains. The similarity between the term *murex* and *murrhina* has led to them being called porcelain vases. But the vases called porcelain now sold in our countries have not a jot of the nature of the ancient vases. And although the best craftsmen of Italy do not make any such vases, nevertheless they sell their products under the name of porcelain vases, although they are not of the same matter. This name of porcelain is given to several kinds of shellfish. And since a beautiful vase made from a sea-shell could not be better described, following its ancient name, than by being called porcelain, it has seemed to me that these polished, shining shells resembling mother-of-pearl have some affinity with the matter of ancient porcelain vases; the more so as ordinary French people call paternosters made from large winkle-shells porcelain paternosters.

These porcelain vases are transparent and are sold at high prices in Cairo; and they are said to have come from the Indies. But that does not seem to me to be probable, for they would not be in such great quantity, or so large, if they had to be brought from so far. A ewer, a jar or any other vessel, however small, costs a ducat, and if it is a large vase it will cost more than that. I find great stubbornness in many persons in Europe who maintain that our saltpetre is the nitre of the ancients; and yet there is not a single grain of nitre in any Christian land but is brought from elsewhere. Yet nitre is so common in Cairo that ten pounds of it cost less than one *maidin*[331]. They use it to make dyestuffs, to tin pots and to dress leather, mixed with acacia pods.

We saw the fine mosques outside the city of Cairo built in recent years by great lords; for a basha or sanjak or other officer of the Grand Turk, desiring to leave something that will make his name memorable, erects such buildings for the love of God, and adjoining the mosques build cisterns for storing water so that passers-by can water their beasts and men can wash themselves according to their custom by plunging into them; for they believe that they are absolved of all their sins, according to Mahomet's promise, if they wash their bodies. The Arabs commonly provide water in public places, and have it brought by men who give it to all who pass that way, without asking anything for it but what those to whom they give it offer of their own free will. There is not a street crossing in Cairo or in any other town in Egypt or Syria, as also in Turkey, but has a large jar of water, which is filled every day, to satisfy the thirst of passers-by. From this follows that they feel no shame in dining in the street or eating in public. They buy what they want to eat in the market and then sit down near some jar of water, taking off their shoes to squat on the ground, and eat their meal in the presence of all the world.

The hay that is sold in Cairo is not cut from meadows, as is our hay, nor from couch grass like that gathered between rocks in the islands of the Cyclades, but is harvested from clover sown for the purpose, which has hollow stems; it is tied in bundles and then distributed in armfuls. Horses are very fond of it.

72

That yellow amber is not a mineral, as some have thought, but resin from a tree

The yellow amber used to make amber paternosters is no less esteemed among Arabs, Syrians, Egyptians and Indians than among Christians, for the Turks carry it with them in paternosters just as is done in our countries, and also tell their chaplets after their fashion; and in addition to making paternosters with it they use it or various other purposes, as for example to decorate the packsaddles, bridles and saddles of horses, mules and camels. We saw great sackfuls of amber in Cairo, not yet cut, in lumps the size of two fists; and sometimes the bark of the tree from which it came was still attached. It is to be supposed that the tree on which it grows is very tall, which can be imagined on seeing the bark, which is thin, smooth, well polished and fine: I saw some pieces that were broader than a man's hand. Some have thought that yellow amber is a fluid terrestrial liquor, which flows into the sea, where it hardens, and is then cast by winds on to the shores of maritime countries. But this opinion can be shown to be false by trying to make it float on water; and if the amber does not float, how can what they say be true? And therefore, having so often found the resin attached to its bark, I will hold with Diodorus, who says specifically that it is resin from a tree which has the property of attracting iron to itself, like lodestone, if it has first been rubbed: which Diocles and Theophrastus and some others had already observed, and which I have found to be true[332].

73

Of our departure from Cairo for Jerusalem

Meanwhile we had been making our preparations for our journey to Jerusalem, finding mounts and obtaining provisions, as we had done before going to Mount Sinai. The road to Jerusalem is more commonly travelled with horses and mules than on camels. Turks and Arabs setting out on a long journey in summer buy tamarinds, which are much used in Turkey, so that more than 3000 pounds of them are sold every year in Cairo, not for medicinal use but to quench their thirst.

Passing through the streets and looking through the grilles in the mosques of Cairo, you see very large and handsome vases in all kinds of marble made in the antique fashion, and I believe that they were anciently used for the burial of certain animals which were salted and preserved in them; for since they regarded these animals as sacred they preserved them and put them in such large vases to serve for their burial. Men were preserved in a different way, as I have already described.

The people of Cairo, referring to the lords who ruled Egypt in the time of the Soldan, called them Circassians, which seemed to me a novelty, hearing such an ancient name remaining modern.

The Basha of Cairo rules over his household in the fashion of the Turks, and not in the true manner of the Arabs or Egyptians. And having seen the manner of his dealing with Monsieur de Fumel, when he went to make his bow on taking leave of him, I think it fit to be set down here. He had all his janissaries drawn up in order, richly dressed , some in cloth of gold and coloured silk, others in other kinds of figured velvet, and all without sword, pistol or any other weapon, and holding their hands clasped together; for they do not want weapons except for war. The Arabs are accustomed to carry daggers, but the Turks have not yet adopted this practice; they have, however, other weapons more profitable in time of peace or war, of which I have spoken above.

When our preparations for the journey were complete we resolved to return by land, taking the road to Jerusalem.

74

Of a small evergreen tree in Egypt which produces a red dye

On Saturday 29th October 1547, at nightfall, we left Cairo and slept in a building attached to a mosque only a quarter of a league from the city. On the following Sunday we set out before daylight on our journey to Jerusalem.

On our left we had the land of Egypt, flooded by the Nile, in which we saw villages situated on higher ground amid the forests of palms. We found a small shrub called henna or *alcanna*, which they prune and cultivate diligently, producing handsome little clipped bushes. Latin writers interpreting the Arabs have said that it is our privet, called in Latin *ligustrum*, but this is wrong, for privet is a different tree from this one. This henna grows to the height of a pomegranate-bush, but, being pruned, throws out only small shoots, as do osiers. It is a very profitable plant for the Egyptians, for they dry the leaves and powder them to produce a yellow dye. This powder is sold for such a high price throughout the countries ruled by the Turk that it brings in more than 18,000 ducats in tax; for women in all the Turkish territories are accustomed to dye their hands, feet and part of their hair yellow or red, and men dye their nails red with this powder. Also, adding alum, they dye the hair of small children, both male and female, and the mane, feet and tail of horses. The women of this country believe it to be fitting and becoming to have part of their thighs and from the navel to the shameful parts dyed yellow, which they contrive by using this powder after taking their bath; for their skin takes on the colouring better after a bath than at other times. The practice is so widespread that the powder is not only used by the Turks but is also carried to Wallachia, Russia and Bosnia. And because people cannot do without this powder the tax on it amounts to a very great sum. It frequently happens that ships come from Alexandria to Constantinople laden with the powder, which is at once carried away and sold.

On leaving Cairo we followed the channel of the Nile which runs down to Damietta for a long way. And since we had set out at midnight we reached the road which we had taken on our way to Suez before daybreak.

75

Of certain villages in Egypt on the way to Jerusalem

We passed through great expanses of soft, sandy country, in which the peasants cultivate a species of pumpkin, which is so sought after in Cairo that during the months of September and October camels can be seen coming in every morning from all parts of the country laden with this fruit. It is a very profitable crop, for it costs but little to grow during the flood of the Nile. It is the fruit that Avicenna and Serapion call *batega*, but is now known to the Egyptians as *copus*, and is mistakenly called *anguria* by some people; but this is an error, for *anguria* is the name of the cucumber[333]. They sometimes grow so large that four or six would make up a camel's load and that a man could carry only one.

We slept that night in the open country. On the following day, continuing on our way, we came to a large village called Caucq, where we stopped to get provisions for the barren stretch of country through which we had to pass. We found rice, peas, beans, eggs, apples, pears, grapes, dates and figs. The only plant that grows in this sandy soil is black henbane, which covers the land with green.

We left Caucq late in the day and travelled all night to the village of Cataro[334], which lies only a little way from the Nile on higher ground. We arrived there during their fast, when the tops of the high towers or belfries of the mosques were surrounded by lighted lamps which illuminate them all night. This is the custom throughout Turkish territory where the people are Mahometans[335]. Their fasts each last for a moon, and on their fast days they neither eat nor drink until they see the stars or until it is quite dark, and then they banquet all night. Cataro is as large as Caucq, situated on the verge of the Nile and surrounded by palms. Here they cultivate very beautiful gardens, for there is an ample supply of water; and so the village is of great renown. Continuing on our way, we came to another village called Bilbez where we rested our mounts, dined and remained for the rest of the day, to avoid the heat as well as to rest our mounts. Here we found provisions in the market as we had at Caucq. Leaving the village and going east and north, we saw nothing on our right but barren country; but on the left we saw land watered by the Nile, which is fertile and well cultivated, with several villages and forests of palms and sycamore figs, which we could see from a great distance. We saw large bands of gazelles running about the countryside, in which we rested that evening, at our third halting-place since Cairo.

76

Of the strange and difficult road between Cairo and Jerusalem

On Tuesday, which was All Saints, we travelled only as far as the village of Salatia, where we rested all day. This is a village in which the houses are constructed of palm branches fitted against the trunks of trees; but nevertheless it is of great renown. There are also some small properly built houses, but very few. The peasants make small square enclosures with reeds in which to keep their geese, hens and ducks. Here we could buy camels, kids, hens, eggs, barley, bread, wine and other provisions. And since we had to pass through a large expanse of open country which was dangerous because of thieves, although we had janissaries with us, nevertheless we hired ten well equipped Arabs to accompany us. The Arabs commonly carry long pikes over their shoulders.

Leaving Salatia, we entered a barren stretch of country which lasted for more than five hours, part of which was green with tamarisks and *rhamnus* bushes with red seeds, different from the species that grows in Greece, which has black seeds.

On our journey from Cairo we had not carried supplies of water, for we had always found it in all the villages through which we had passed, but on this day we were constrained to fill our goatskins, since the country which lay ahead of us was quite without water. During the day we crossed the current of the Nile three times, with the water up to the girths of our mounts; and the water, being mingled with seawater, is bitter and salt. We also found bridges, which were wide but not very long. After crossing the salt streams we stopped and spent the night behind the ruins of a caravanserai.

On the following day travel was more difficult than we had expected, for we came into another region of soft, sandy soil, constantly melting and shifting. The muleteers had to wrap up the pasterns of the mules and horses, which otherwise would have hacked one another. After passing through the sand we came into a valley, where we saw a cluster of palm-trees round a well of sweetish water at which caravans water their beasts. Water is drawn from the well by a wheel in the Egyptian fashion. We continued on our way and came that evening to a village called Belba. There is a small, square castle situated in the region of Palmira, which is not far from the Mediterranean Sea, between Egypt and Syria. We were now in very desert-like, sandy country, but abounding in forests of palms. Belba is almost two days' journey from Salatia. The walls are poorly built, and the buildings within them are scarcely larger than small stalls for calves; but nevertheless we found here many kinds of provisions to buy.

The people of this country are small, dark, tanned by the sun, and do not sit down as the Turks do, who squat on the ground cross-legged, in the manner of our tailors, with their heels serving as a seat; and they will spend days like this without tiring, any more than we do sitting on a stool. For, being accustomed to this from their youth, they so continue throughout their life. And since they live in sandy country, if they sat down on the sand in the manner of the Turks it would be uncomfortable and they would spoil their garments.

Most of the Arabs, Armenians and Turks wear shifts dyed blue, and seldom white; and yet they are not much troubled by lice, for they go frequently to hot baths where they bathe and clean themselves. These Arabs always sleep on the ground, having only mats of reeds or palm-leaves to lie on, without any sheets. There was a caravan going to Jerusalem which waited for us at a well in the plain two leagues from the village of Belba. The water in the well is nitrous, for the soil is also nitrous; but we drank it for lack of any other. The caravan left at midnight; we let it go ahead of us, and left three hours later.

We had the Mediterranean Sea on our left, and skirted it for a long time. Our road ran due east. We made good speed and caught up the caravan, which we then accompanied until the evening. We camped near the shores of the sea, but did not stay there long. A quarter of a league from there, between two low mounds of sand, we dug down into the ground and at a depth of half a toise found fresh water, cloudy and white, with which we filled our bottles and goatskins. On our right we had the mountains of Mount Sinai, which we could see very clearly. Those who want to take the direct road from Cairo to Jerusalem do not go by way of Belba and Salatia; but we took a longer route, seeking the convenience of the Nile and good villages. But those who go the other way have to carry water and provisions for the whole journey. We found *ambrosia, thapsia,* some species of *libanotis,* tamarisks and *apocinon* growing in this region.

77

Of nitre, and of a small crab Of a more marvellous complexion than any other thing in nature

All that day we stayed under our tents, and then we followed the caravan, coming into another plain which lasted for six hours of travelling. At daybreak we came into lower country, all covered with nitre, which I thought was salt when I saw it gleaming in the footprints left by the horses and camels. I should not have recognised it so quickly had I not seen it previously in Cairo. It is not, however, saltpetre, for it comes naturally, and can be known by the characteristics described by the ancient authors: when it is burned it leaves a great deal of ash, but when saltpetre is burned it leaves none, and so it is not nitre.

This country lasted for a good half-league, and then we came back to the sea and travelled along its shores for a long time, seeing large numbers of sharks and dogfish, which find their food in the waters off shore. Here too I found a particular species of crab of very strange character; for in the greatest heat of summer, when the sun is at its hottest, they come out of the sea in such great numbers that the land is covered with them, and scurries along the sand for the distance of three bowshots, although it is scarcely larger than a small chestnut. It runs so fast that a man has difficulty in keeping up with it; and then, having spent the day on dry land in the vehement heat of the sun, it withdraws into the sea at night. Aristotle calls it *cancer cursor*. It is the most remarkable animal that I have ever seen. Some authors have wrongly classed it among the cetaceans, calling it *dromon*, that is, *cursor;* but, as I have said, they are of small size. I have given a sufficient description of them in the book on fish.

The nights were not so dark during the whole of our journey as to prevent us from seeing what was on our way. This evening, being at some distance from the caravan, a sanjak who was going to Jerusalem raised a false alarm, claiming that there were Arabs in the neighbourhood. But when we realised that the alarm was false we took no great account of it, for the janissaries accompanying Monsieur de Fumel were stout fellows and well equipped.

We had set out well before daybreak, leaving the shores of the Mediterranean Sea, and when it was full day the caravan and the sanjak halted to oblige some Marrano Jews[336] who were of the company and had given him some present to wait for them. Having managed the thing very shrewdly, they took the opportunity on Friday evening of getting ahead of the caravan and resting, for it is their custom to do no work on Saturdays. On the following day, which was Saturday, we were well accompanied and got ahead of them; and lodged in a walled caravanserai near a large village, built in the form of a castle. We bought some provisions in the villages. That evening we left the sandy country and came into an area of richer soil. Here we found the plant called *smyrnium,* which grows abundantly in this region, and also *ambrosia, alga tertia, anchusa* and *ligusticum.* Between Cairo and here the only trees were palms and the wool-bearing trees, with fruits full of slender threads of wool, of which I have spoken above.

78

Of certain trees, birds and other singular things produced in the land of Palestine

While we were still on higher ground, before coming to the caravanserai, we found the tree called *balanus myrepsica,* which is much taller than those of Arabia, resembling a birch, otherwise called *betula,* near which there was great quantity of *smyrnium,* whose seeds are round like corianders and highly odoriferous. As we drew near the caravanserai we saw, some distance away, some green trees but were in some doubt what they were; and seeing that they had branches at the summit in the manner of a crown and a stout trunk, gave good shade and had leaves packed close together, we concluded that they were sycamore-figs which had been planted in regular order, as we do with walnut-trees. There were also trees which the Greeks told me were *oenoplia* and others call *napeca,* growing round the well of the caravanserai.

This caravanserai marked the boundary and the first beginning of the fertile land of Palestine. Most of the gates of caravanserais in Egypt and Syria are of iron, and have within them a courtyard in the middle of which is a platform on which travellers camp; and all round the inside of the walls are porches to which they retire at night when it is raining, and also during the day when it is very hot.

We spent the whole night in this caravanserai, keeping a watch for fear of Arab thieves, for it had been reported to us that they were not far away. The caravan which had been behind us travelled through the night and got ahead of us before daybreak; but we could hear it from a great distance, and so we prepared at once to move away along with it[337]. The custom is, when some sanjak or other caravan of larger size is travelling through these countries, that a large bell is hung from one of the camels, which can be heard from a great distance, to warn the whole company to follow them.

Between Belba and Gazaro [Gaza], the first town in Palestine[338], we found expanses of fallow land in which there was such great quantity of rats and field mice that, were it not that nature sends here large numbers of the birds that Aristotle calls *percnopteri* and the French buzzards to destroy them, I believe that any grain sown by the inhabitants would be at once eaten. There grow here squills, *thapsia, ferula, polium, hastula regia*. We passed well cultivated fields of corn, vegetables and fruit-trees. The hedges between the fields were made of *rhamnus* and *halimus,* on which I saw flying some birds similar to those that we call shrikes, which eat mice as kestrels do. We saw also numbers of vultures and other carrion-eating birds, such as those I have described above as Egyptian sakers, called in Latin *accipitres aegyptii*. Some of our company called them pelicans, thinking them similar to those that are represented in paintings giving their blood to their young.

But since this word pelican has led me to enquire what bird it is, I want to make it clear that the bird properly called pelican is the one described as having two stomachs, a characteristic of *onocrotalus,* about which Albertus was in error, taking it for *ossifragus*. The bird which the Greeks call *phinis* has led many people to speak of the phoenix; and it is also the one that the Latins called *ossifragus,* which is depicted on a nest, tearing up its breast to feed its young, as appears in Aristotle's account of his *phinis*[339], and Pliny, after him, in describing the sea eagle attributed to his *ossifragus* all the same marks as did Aristotle to his *phinis*. It is larger than an eagle and is of the next genus, having hooked nails; and it feeds on flesh. It is ash-coloured verging on white, and has poor sight. It makes its nest and lives religiously; and being of benign nature and a good provider, feeds the young of the eagle when it abandons them. It takes them in and feeds them conscientiously, and looks after them until they are large enough. The French have a bird which they know by the name of *phinis,* calling it an osprey; but that is not its proper name, for it is *haliaetus,* which is included in the fifth species among the eagles. It is commonly to be seen on rivers and ponds, catching fish, hurtling steeply down like a stone from the air into the water and feeding on the fish which it catches. This bird, though called in French osprey, is not the bird known to the ancients as *ossifragus*.

We travelled for four hours over treeless plains. Finally we came to Gazaro, which is the first town in Judaea, and camped under a palm-tree in a garden close to the town.

79

Of the town of Gazaro

Gazaro is not walled. There is a square castle in the antique fashion standing on a hill, by no means a strong place, which is the seat of a sanjak. It is situated in a fertile region, with fig-trees, olive-trees, jujube-trees, pomegranate-trees and vines. There are some palm-trees, but their fruits ripen very late, for the climate is not warm enough. In Egypt and Arabia the dates had been ripe these three months, but at Gazaro they were still green.

There is a species of black lizards called stellions, about the size of a small weasel, with a much swollen belly and a large head, which are found in great abundance in Judaea and Syria. We saw also a bird which in my opinion surpasses all others in the charm of its song; and I believe that it is the bird called by the ancients *venatica avis*[340]. It is rather larger than a starling. Its plumage is white on its belly and ash-coloured on its back, like that of the bird called *molliceps*, in French hawfinch. It has a black tail, which is longer than its wings, as in a magpie, and flies in the manner of a woodpecker. We found all kinds of provisions for sale in the market in Gazaro, as bread, wine, hens, eggs.

The Greeks, Turks and Arabs living in Gazaro are very diligent in cultivating their vines. We camped there until the evening, and then set out very late and travelled all night towards Rama [Ramallah] through beautiful country. When daylight came we saw villages situated on hillsides along fields growing all kinds of grain.

We saw pelicans flying in large bands towards the sea as we continued on our way due north, with our backs to the south. And since there was a strong sirocco wind we heard the sea in turmoil, for we were not far from it.

The *oenoplia* and *napeca* trees grow here to the height of our pear-trees, with fruits the size of wild apples, and so similar to them that one could be taken for the other. They are sweet, with an agreeable bitterness, and contain a small stone of the size of an olive-stone. This tree is common in Egypt, Syria and Armenia, though there are none in Greece, nor anywhere in Europe. We also found fields planted with dasheens and sugar-cane, irrigated by water drawn from a well. From there we came to Rama, where we stayed all day.

80

Of the town of Rama

Rama was anciently a large town, as appears from its ruins; for the cisterns and vaults to be seen there are larger than those of Alexandria, though not in such great number. Rama is situated in rich and fertile country; but since the town is now deserted, with barely a dozen houses still inhabited, most of the land remains fallow. Many of the inhabitants are Greeks. They cultivate corn, barley, vegetables and a few vines. We were able to buy meat, bread, wine and other provisions. The second species of acacia grows here in abundance, and also a thorny shrub which I do not think was described by the ancients, although I suspect that it was the myrrh-tree[341]. It is twisted and thick-stemmed, with sharp thorns and leaves similar to an acacia but rather larger.

We left Rama before daybreak, travelling through large expanses of fertile land in which it would be possible to grow good grain; but the inhabitants of this area are lazy and unconcerned for their profit and work the land only negligently. It was beginning to be light when we entered the valley between the mountains of Jerusalem. When we had advanced some way into the valley, having precipitous mountains on either side of us, we saw some Arabs descending the hills on both sides, making a great noise, who as soon as they saw us came down to ask us for money, making as if to attack us by force; but since we had been warned that such rogues held passing strangers to ransom when they were stronger, we were not greatly alarmed by them. To cover themselves they made pretence of being guards protecting the territory of the Grand Signior, but were content to accept a small sum of money. They would not in any case have dared to use force, for in addition to those accompanying Monsieur de Fumel we had been reinforced by ten janissaries given to him by the sanjak at Gazaro. And they are wise enough never to attack pilgrims who are in sufficient number to resist them.

81

Of Jerusalem, which is situated between mountains

These mountains contain such an abundance of all kinds of wild and aromatic trees and plants that they can be compared to Mount Ida in Crete, to which they are also similar in climate and other respects. The cultivated land above the rocks is laid out in terraces, showing the diligence of the Jews in times past in working the land, making their territory, which in itself is stony and infertile, cultivated and abounding in fruits.

The same diligence in cultivating stony mountain country is seen in the Greek islands of the Aegean, among which we saw several, now uninhabited, which can scarce feed a hundred men but in time past fed more than six thousand, as can be seen from the hills and small mountains which were terraced in ancient times with walls of large stones to retain the earth on the slopes so that plants could be grown in it. The islands of Zia [Kea], Melos, Andros, Naxos, Paros and several others were laid out in this way by the ancient Greeks and made more fertile than the land in a plain. Similarly the Jews, with barren land ill suited to growing vines and fruits, made the hills fertile at the cost of great labour, with masonry which has lasted since the time when they were absolute masters of Jerusalem, which shows their great diligence and effort and is a reminder of the land's ancient greatness.

The trees which we saw growing wild on the mountains in this territory were andrachnes, spruces, *aria*, holm-oaks, terebinths and lentisks. The plants were *cistus, ledon, thymbra, smilax aspera,* pimpernel, *origanum heracleoticum, Tragoriganum,* sage, *stachys,* wild rue, *asphaltites, trifolium, cyclaminus, umbilicus seu cotyledon, thymus.* Also found here is wild hyssop, differing from our garden hyssop, which is not found in Crete. The slopes of the mountains facing west are very rich in vines, fruit-trees, olives, figs and pomegranates, compared with the other sides where only barren trees grow.

82

Brief computation of the journey between Cairo and Jerusalem

It is clear from the computation that I have made that the journey from Cairo to Jerusalem takes only nine days, or ten at most. We made fairly good speed on our way, for we arrived in Jerusalem on Tuesday 8th November, having left Cairo on 29th October. After travelling for four leagues through the mountains we came to a spring below the ruins of a church which had once been a monastery, as appears from the paintings, and I believe that it belonged to Latin Christians. There are some remains of a cloister. We dined there, and then went to spend the night in Jerusalem.

Pilgrims arriving in Jerusalem find lodging according to the religion that they follow, for if they are members of the Roman church, whom the people of this country call Latins, they lodge in the monastery of the Cordeliers[342], which is outside the town on Mount Sion; but if they are of the Greek religion they lodge with the Greek caloyers, who have their houses within the town; and if they are of the country of Prester John they lodge with the Indian religious; and similarly with other Christian nations like the Georgians and Armenians.

There are commonly thirty or forty Cordeliers in the monastery, among whom there are men of several nations; though most of them are Italian. They take pilgrims to all the holy places round Jerusalem; and so they ordinarily maintain an interpreter at their expense, whom they call a dragoman, who can speak Turkish, Arabic, Greek, Italian. and other languages to speak to the people of the country and reply for the pilgrims and conduct them to all the holy places. The Cordeliers keep guard every night in their monastery, each one being on watch on the walls at a particular hour, since the monastery is outside the town. They are in great fear of robbery by the Arabs; for although their walls are high they are afraid that the inhabitants of the surrounding low country may try to scale them with ladders.

83

Succinct description of the holy places of Jerusalem

The territory of Jerusalem is quite well cultivated, particularly round the town. They grow vines with great diligence. There are also olive-trees and fig-trees, from which they derive much oil. But the olive-trees have a particular characteristic which makes them different from others: they support red-berried mistletoe[343] with red seeds, to the great harm of the inhabitants, for it makes them sterile.

The gold and silver which the Cordeliers spend is sent to them from all over the Latin countries, for alms are assigned to them in various countries in Europe and collected by the guardians of the order, mainly in Cyprus, France and Italy. They told us that they used to have some in Germany and England but now receive nothing from them. There are no other monks of the Latin faith in Jerusalem but the Cordeliers.

On the following morning at daybreak a number of Cordeliers took us to see the holy places round Jerusalem. We began as follows. The first thing shown to us on leaving the monastery was the place where Our Lord celebrated the Last Supper with his disciples, quite close to the monastery of the Cordeliers; but the Turks had usurped it from the Cordeliers, making it into a mosque dedicated to Mahomet. Later, however, Monsieur d'Aramont persuaded them to return it. Then, at some distance from the monastery, they showed us the place where the Jews who sought to prevent the disciples from carrying away the body of Our Lady lost their arms, which is near the town gate. Farther on, following the walls of the town, we saw the place where Saint Peter wept after denying Our Lord, near the valley of Jehoshaphat. Farther round the walls is the temple of the virgins, situated at one corner of the town, which is now a Turkish mosque. A little below the same corner is a triangular stone, of which mention is made in Holy Writ in the psalm *Lapidem quem reprobaverunt aedificantes.*

Descending from there into the valley of Jehoshaphat, we crossed the brook Kedron, which is only a stone's throw from the town. There is no water in the stream except after rain, and there is a stone bearing the footprint of Our Lord when he fell from the bridge. Close by are two sepulchres hewn from the rock in the shape of a pyramid. Some believe that these are the sepulchres of Jeremiah and Isaiah. Following the hill and going uphill, we saw the place where was the tree from which Judas hanged himself. When we had circled the hill so as to lose sight of the town, we saw a chapel which is said to have been the house of the Magdalene, near which we found the stone on which Our Lord sat when she spoke to him about raising Lazarus from the dead; this place is only a quarter of a league from Jerusalem.

Farther on we came to a small village in which is the sepulchre of Lazarus, whom Our Lord raised from the dead. To see it we had to go down into a vault as large as a room, in which is a tomb the height of an altar, where pilgrims often have a mass said. On the way back to Jerusalem we saw the place of the fig-tree which Our Lord cursed. This is the place called Bethany.

Going uphill towards the territory called Bethphage, which is rugged and stony, we took the path to the right, which runs up to the Mount of Olives; and from there, continuing along the tops of the hills, we had a view of the whole area for a great distance round, for we were on the highest spot round Jerusalem. We passed by the way which Our Lord took when he made his entry into Jerusalem, and where he mounted the ass which he had caused to be untied and brought to him along with its foal. On our way down from this high place, going south, we saw the plain of Jericho, and also the Dead Sea, otherwise called Mare Asphaltites, in which Sodom and Gomorrha were engulfed.

On the same mountain, turning left, the Cordeliers showed us the place where the disciples did several things. Being on the Mount of Olives, we saw Jerusalem very clearly, since we were on higher ground than the town. From there we passed by the place where Our Lord said *Vae tibi Jerusalem*.

84

Of the sepulchre of Our Lady in the valley of Jehoshaphat

There is a chapel on the summit of the Mount of Olives built by Christians in which can be seen a footprint left by Our Lord when he ascended into heaven, near which is another low mound of the same height with another chapel, now falling into ruin.

Returning towards Jerusalem and descending the Mount of Olives, we passed along a path on which Saint Paul was when Saint Stephen was stoned[344]. Lower down we saw the three stones on which the disciples fell asleep when Our Lord was praying. Also where Our Lord was arrested, and where Saint Paul cut off Malchus's ear. All these places that I have mentioned are only two or three bowshots from one another.

Returning over the bridge on the brook Kedron, which we had crossed on the way out, we saw the place in the valley of Jehoshaphat where Our Lord sweated blood and water, where a chapel has been built. Beside it is the sepulchre of Our Lady and Saint Anne. This sepulchre is an underground vault built of large dressed stones and supported on large stone columns. The steps leading down into it are very large, for the chapel is underground. It is believed to have been built by Saint Helen, mother of Constantine[345], together with the wall surrounding the Holy Sepulchre. We left the valley of Jehoshaphat and made our way to the Golden Gate, where we were shown the place where the Romans breached the walls when they captured Jerusalem after a siege by Titus and Vespasian[346]. The gate through which Our Lord entered Jerusalem is the Golden Gate, through which we did not enter, for it was not open, but skirted the walls as far as Mount Sion. We completed the journey described above before dinner, for it was no great distance.

The rest of the day was devoted to seeing other places round the monastery, including a place where there are cavities in which bodies deposited there are consumed within twenty-four hours. Close by, lower down, we saw the Probatic Pool[347], which waters the valley of Jehoshaphat. From there we went to see the sepulchre of Our Lord, which is in the town, in a large church built by Saint Helen, mother of Constantine. Everyone entering the sepulchre is required to give 9 ducats, and no one is exempt, neither poor nor rich. Those who take the farm of the tax on admission to the sepulchre pay 8000 ducats to the Grand Signior, and so they hold pilgrims to ransom, for they cannot enter without paying. The Cordeliers and Greek caloyers, and other Christian monks, pay nothing to enter. The Turks hold it in great reverence, and enter it with great devotion. It is said that the Pisans[348] imposed this payment of 9 ducats when they were masters of Jerusalem.

85

Of the sepulchre of Our Lord, and of the ruins of Jerusalem

Jerusalem has recently been surrounded by high new walls, but they are of built of small stones and very weak, and could not hold out against cannon. The houses have roof terraces. The shops in the main streets have vaulted roofs like those in Alexandria; but they are not really comparable, for the vaults in Jerusalem are superbly built of dressed stone and have remained entire since the time when the Jews ruled here. The merchants selling drugs in Jerusalem speak several languages, as in Cairo.

Most of the Christian nations send men, more or fewer according to the country, to live in the town and serve in the sepulchre; and so there are reckoned to be twelve languages in the Christian religion – though I myself could find only eight. Among them the Latin nation, which they call Frankish, is pre-eminent before all the others, and includes all those in obedience to the Roman church. The second is the Greek nation, who are called in their language *romaeos*, whose obedience is not to the Pope but to their own various patriarchs. The third nation is the Armenians, who are closer to our ceremonies than the Greeks. Then follow the other nations, like the Jacobites, who come from the region converted to the faith by Saint James the Greater[349]. Others are Georgians, who are governed by their own laws, and are neighbours to the Persians, who in turn are bounded by eastern India and, never having been subjugated by anyone, are absolute masters of themselves. Others are called

Christians of the belt[350], who have taken the name of Copts, who were brought to the faith by Saint Thomas. Others are Indians, who are sent here from the land ruled by Prester John and are very black, called Abycini[351]. And since they are baptised in fire, they bear three burns, one between their eyes above the nose and the other two near the temples, and are not so black as the Ethiopians[352]. Others are Nestorians[353], others again are called Maronites[354], who are the same as Arabs. These various nations have each a chapel of their own, since they all differ on certain points, and are maintained by money sent to them by the princes of their provinces.

The Greeks occupy the choir and guard the site of Calvary, and the Latins have the guard of the Sepulchre. Monks of all the above-mentioned nations enter and leave when they will without paying anything. The church of the Holy Sepulchre of Our Lord includes the whole circuit of Calvary, which is a level area and not a hill as some have thought. It is tall and circular in form, an open rotunda; and in the middle of this rotunda is the Holy Sepulchre of Our Lord, under the middle of the nave, within a small chapel with a round vaulted roof, all in fine marble. The guardian of the Cordeliers of Mount Sion gives a certificate to pilgrims who have been sent by someone, to serve as witness that they have been there. It contains many other things, which I have not specified here for the sake of brevity.

86

Of the wilderness in which Our Lord was tempted, and of the river Jordan

We prepared our mounts, so that we should be ready next morning to go to the river Jordan, and then went to spend the night under olive-trees outside the town. We started early in the morning, before daybreak, travelling between east and south, leaving the Pole Star to the left. It was beginning to be light when we descended into the plain of Jericho, but before we reached it we saw in the distance a band of camels feeding on the leaves of cherry-plum trees to our left, at which some of our company were in great fear, thinking that they were Arabs watching us; and the janissaries whom the sanjak had given to accompany Monsieur de Fumel kept very quiet, saying in their language that the Arabs had been warned of our coming. They were in such pusillanimity and great fear that they extinguished the fuses of their arquebuses, in the hope that when the Arabs attacked us, not finding them in a state of defence, they would not ask anything of them and would do harm only to the Christians. But Monsieur de Fumel, a man truly bold, well accompanied by half a dozen honourable French noblemen, of the houses of Rostin, Saint-Aubin in Picardy, Perdigal in Gascony, Le Val and several others, with the rest of his people, each man with an arquebus, was the first to dismount, and commanded every man in his company to follow him. The janissaries, however, would not go down into the plain, but remained behind to await the issue. When we had travelled on a long way we mounted our horses again; and then the janissaries, who were still on the mountain, seeing that we had found no one, came down into the plain and followed us, for they now saw that what had so frightened them was only some camels feeding in the countryside.

We came to the village situated where the town of Jericho had once stood, where now there is nothing but a wretched square tower, scarcely stronger than a pigeon-house. Observing the plants growing in this plain, I was reminded to speak of a small plant which some deceiving monks have called rose of Jericho, and since it opens when the root is put into water, have devised a very specious deceit to rouse wonder in those seeing it, saying that it opens only on Christmas Eve or when women are in labour.

Those ignorant of its nature think that it cannot open at any other time; but this is false. They base their belief on Holy Writ, which says: *Sicut plantatio rosae in Iericho*. But the Bible refers to the common red or pink rose and not to this plant, about which some other writers have been deceived, having its portrait drawn and calling it *amomum;* but it is not *amomum*. We had already seen it in Desert Arabia on the shores of the Red Sea, growing in the sand; but there are none in Jericho. The plain of Jericho is surrounded on all sides by mountains, and adjoining it on the south is the Dead Sea. which has no outflow but seeps away into the ground.

To the north we could see the country in which the river Jordan rises, flowing down from there through the middle of the plain of Jericho. To the east we could see the mountains of Stony Arabia, which are not far away and also form part of its roots. To the west were the mountains of Jerusalem. The trees which bear *licion*[355] grow in this plain, and also the trees which bear the cherry-plum, from whose stones the inhabitants make oil. The shrub *acacia altera* also grows here in great profusion. The river Jordan flows from north to south, and its bed is scarcely too wide for a small boy to be able to throw a stone across it, for it is little more than seven or eight toises wide. Nor is it very deep, and pilgrims are accustomed to bathe in it. It is so shallow that a boat could not sail in it. Along its banks are black willows, tamarisks, *agnus castus* and many kinds of canes and reeds, of which the Arabs make use for many purposes. There is one tree from which they make their javelins and spears and light lances, and another from which they make arrows, which sell for five aspers each; and it is only great lords that shoot with the bow. The Turks, Greeks, Armenians, Arabs, Persians, Jews and Egyptians do not write with a bird's quill, but with a species of reed called *elegia,* which they gather diligently. We also found it in the streams on Mount Athos.

After we had seen the river and the Dead Sea we passed close to a ruined castle situated on a low mound. From there we went to see the spring which Pliny calls Calliroe, which is said to come from Elysium. In my opinion it is the spring called by Aeacus *fons solis*[356]. The water is very clear and cold and flows in a large stream. If it is true that the balm-tree was ever cultivated in this plain, it must have been near this spring.

I cannot agree with some great personages who are of opinion that such excellent dates grow in this plain; for having seen that the palm-trees that grow here now never ripen their fruits to perfection, I believe that they were never any good, unless it could be shown that the climate has changed since then; and that is not possible. In the stream flowing from this spring there grow cress, balsamine, rushes and other such plants, as in our countries. Here we ate in the shade of plum-trees and fig-trees.

From there we climbed up on stone steps to the place where Our Lord fasted, only a short way from the spring, where there are three vaults hewn from the rock, each in the form of a room. We then continued up to the top of the mountain, where the devil sought to tempt Our Lord. There are still remains of a chapel built on the spot. Then we came down and took the road back to Jerusalem. The Christians built a chapel in the wilderness where Saint John preached and baptised; now in ruins, it can still be seen near the river Jordan. It is easy to believe that when Saint John was in the wilderness he lived on grasshoppers, for the Greek writers tell us that there is a kind of grasshopper called *aphros* or *onos* on which the Africans live; and since it is of the same kind as those that Saint John lived on I have thought it right to mention it here, since the Africans ate it and enjoyed it not as medicine but as food.

We then returned to Jerusalem and prepared to go to Bethlehem.

87

Of Bethlehem and Hebron

On the following day, having returned to dine at the monastery of the Cordeliers, we made our preparations for going to Bethlehem, which is only two leagues away. When we had travelled half a league we came to a large terebinth tree, where Our Lady was accustomed to rest when going from Bethlehem to Jerusalem, which stands on the road near a field covered with small round stones, of the size and shape of a small chickpea. The common people say that there was a man sowing peas, and when Our Lady passed that way and asked what he was doing, he replied, I am sowing stones; and since that time the land has remained stony, as if his peas had been transmuted into stones. Here too, alongside the road, a stone's throw from the terebinth tree, is a large cistern hewn from the rock, which fills with water when it rains, which is good to drink.

Going thus at a walk, we took only two hours to reach Bethlehem, which is a small village of small, poorly built houses; and there is nothing handsome but a large and sumptuous monastery of the Cordeliers which was faced all round with marble, with a church built by Saint Helen, also magnificently clad with marble and supported on large marble columns. But the Turks have taken all these facings to decorate their mosques, and the temple that is called Solomon's temple is now a mosque of the Mahometans. The Cordeliers showed us the place in a vaulted chapel where the Virgin Mary gave birth to Our Lord, which is under the great church. We were also shown the sepulchres of Saint Jerome and his disciples, and of the Holy Innocents, within the church.

After dining in Bethlehem we walked down a little farther, where there are fine olive-trees and fig-trees. Near here is the place where the angel announced to the shepherds that Our Lord was about to be born, where there was formerly a small chapel, now ruined, with nothing left but a vault with pimpernel, *tragoriganum, zygis, thymbra, onitis* and *origanum heracleoticum* growing on it.

We returned to the monastery quite early and made our preparations for going to Hebron to see the sepulchres of Adam, Abraham, Isaac and Jacob. Mounts can be hired in Jerusalem – mules, asses or horses – to go wherever you wish. It is only seven or eight leagues from Jerusalem to Hebron.

We left Bethlehem before daybreak, and passed through a region of rugged mountains. We arrived in Hebron quite early. The sepulchres of Adam, Abraham and Isaac are in a Turkish mosque to which Christians are not admitted, but they can see them through an opening in the wall. The Jews told us that there is a district beyond Hebron inhabited by Jews, of whom they can get news not from Jews but only from other people; for there is a river between them which flows all the time except on Saturdays, when it dries up completely; but since the Jews on this side, who do not go out on Saturday, cannot leave home, and also because the river is not navigable, they have to remain where they are, and so they cannot see one another. It is manifest that that is a lie, and not a new one, for Pliny writes in the first chapter of his thirty-first book that there is a stream in Judaea which dries up on Saturday. But we, being in Judaea, could see that the story is false, as also is what some think, that Jews lose some of their blood on Good Friday. We were with them on Good Friday, but did not observe that they lost any blood then, any more than on any other day of the week.

The place where Abraham was when he saw three men and worshipped one of them, *Tres vidit, & unum adoravit*, was shown to us outside the village of Hebron, at a ditch in the field in which Adam was created; and it is marked by a terebinth which has three trees growing out of one trunk. The ruins of Hebron show that it was formerly more populous than it is now. We returned to Jerusalem and went to see the spring called *fons signatus*. On our way there we saw the same plants as between Rama and Jerusalem. On our way back we passed through the village in which Saint John[357] was born, and saw a ruined church formerly built there by Christians. The village is inhabited by Arabs, and in it are cisterns built in the manner of fish-ponds, with a small spring flowing into them. Here too is the place where Saint Anne came to visit Saint Elizabeth[358], a hill on which there are great number of olive-trees.

We came that evening to the monastery of the Cordeliers in Jerusalem, where we slept. On the following day we visited many places in the town, and that night slept in the Holy Sepulchre of Our Lord; for pilgrims are allowed to have food taken in, and to stay there for up to three days if they wish, or to go in as many times as they desire, provided (as I have said) that they have paid the 9 ducats which all who wish to enter the Holy Sepulchre are required to give.

The streets in Jerusalem where the merchants have their shops are roofed over, as in other towns in Turkey. They are reinforced by large buttresses and on the outside by stout flying buttresses.

Jerusalem is the seat of a sanjakate. and accordingly there is a sanjak, with a number of spahis, who are a kind of mounted soldiers. A sanjak is the governor of a region. The spahis are not stationed here and there in the villages round Jerusalem, as in Greece or Asia, for the peasants will not suffer them; and so they are stationed with the sanjak in the town. It is strange that the sanjaks are so frequently moved from place to place in Turkey; for when one of them has spent no more than half a year in one place he will be required, at the command of the Turk, to move elsewhere. Sometimes he will go from Africa to Europe or to Asia, and will spend fully six months on the journey before he and his company reach the place where he is to be stationed; and if soon afterwards he is sent to another place he will not refuse to go there, and so he will spend his life now here and now there, in perpetual movement, like all officers and soldiers of the Turk[359]. There are some twelve sanjakates in the territory of Syria, Judaea and Damascus, which are given to the favourites of Bashas residing in Constantinople. It is to these that the Turk sends those whom he desires to promote, and they are moved from place to place according to the will of their superior. I could compare this with the granting of offices and governments of provinces, but that such offices are perpetual, while the sanjakates are given, changed or withdrawn at the pleasure of the ruler, for each of them, seeking to increase his status, solicits and gives presents to the Bashas to have his sanjakate changed to a better one. Thus they rise from degree to degree according to the favour that they enjoy; of which the sanjak then in Jerusalem was an example, for after he had spent a year at Tana[360], which is a town on the Black Sea, his office was changed and he was sent to the Morea, which formerly was called the Peloponnese; and when he had been there for half a year he was sent to Jerusalem. I have given this as an example, but it is the same in all the other sanjakates.

88

Journey by land from Jerusalem to Damascus, and what thorny trees are common in the territory of Jerusalem

I walked round the walls of Jerusalem looking for plants and examining them carefully, for I wanted to know what thorns I should find, so as to discover what thorns Our Lord's crown was made of. When I found no thorny plants commoner than *rhamnus*, it seemed to me that his crown must have been made from that tree, for I found no brambles or other thorny plants growing there – although there are some spiny caper-bushes. Since the Italians call rhamnus in their vulgar tongue *spina sancta*, particularly round Macerata and Pesaro, where I found that the hedges consisted of no other trees, as is the case also in Jerusalem, I think it right to mention this here. I have in mind also that the ancient Arab writers say that the tree from which the crown was made was *alhansegi*, which interpreters turned into Latin as *corona spinea*.

The fruit-trees in the territory of Jerusalem are figs, olives, pomegranates, jujubes and plums. And so, knowing that merchants in the towns always sold wood from various kinds of trees in their shops and yards, as they still do today, it is difficult to think what matter the cross was made of but the wood of these trees.

We made our preparations for going from Jerusalem to Damascus, which is only five short days' journeys. We left Jerusalem on Monday evening and arrived in Damascus early on the following Sunday. It was already late when we left the town, and we spent the night in an almost ruined caravanserai near a spring in a village called Elpire two and a half leagues from Jerusalem. The ruins of this village show that it was once a place of some size. It is the place from which Our Lady returned to seek Our Lord when he stayed in Jerusalem to dispute with the doctors in the temple. This territory is fertile in vines, fig-trees and olive-trees.

Our road ran towards the north. Continuing on our way, we set out again at midnight, passing through country planted with sesame and cotton. The mountains round us were green with *esculus, aria, ilex* and small *costus* trees, from which the local people gather the scarlet-grain that they sell to Venetian merchants, who buy it in all parts of the world. We also found trees of *eleprinos* or *alinterna, terebinthus* and andrachne and saw plants of *tragoriganum, zygis, onitis,* pimpernel and some kinds of *libanotis.* Let me not be blamed for not calling *libanotis* rosemary, for it is but a fifth species.

We were still travelling somewhat downhill, for Jerusalem is situated on high ground, so that from whatever direction you approach it you have to climb. We made good speed, for our mounts had been rested in Jerusalem. We reached Napolosa [Nablus] at midday, which I believe was anciently called Shechem, situated in the territory of Samaria, and later called Neapolis. Nearby can be seen the ruins of a small church, in a valley a half-quarter of a league away, at which was the well where Our Lord asked the Samaritan woman for water. Now there is only the place in a field on the right of a road coming from there.

We stopped at Napolosa and spent the rest of the day there, encamped under mulberry-trees. The hills of Napolosa are well cultivated with fruit-trees. The olive-trees have stout stems, and are laden with red-berried mistletoe, as in Jerusalem, but are not so fertile as those which produce slender shoots. They cultivate mulberry-trees to supply food for the worms from which they spin silk, and also small fig-trees to feed the worms with their leaves. The figs grown in Egypt and Arabia are meagre and almost as dry as sycamore-figs.

89

Description of an Arab man, and of Nazareth, where it was announced to Our Lady that she would conceive Our Lord

On the following day we left the town of Napolosa, which is situated on the slopes of a hill, with a small castle in the antique fashion. It is a place of passage where all men going to or coming from Jerusalem must pay two ducats. We travelled for a long time before daybreak, passing through mountains and valleys. We arrived in the evening at Nazareth, which is a small village, and saw the place where the angel hailed Our Lady. The country is watered by streams flowing down from the mountains and by springs which are distributed in channels running in all directions, so that the land is made fertile.

The village of Nazareth is inhabited by Arabs. The chapel built on the spot where the Annunciation took place is small and vaulted, and you go down into it on steps, for it is underground. Here can be seen the ruins of a church built in the times when Christians ruled in the Holy Land. We spent the rest of the day visiting places in Nazareth, which is situated amid low mountains with an abundance of water. The inhabitants are of small and slender stature, as are all Arabs.

Portraict d'vn villageois Arabe,

Figure: Portrait of an Arab villager

Their garment is a loose-fitting coat woven from goats' wool, striped white and black, simply cut and with no more shape than a sack, which hangs down to their calves. Over it they wear a broad leather belt, four fingers wide; and the larger the buckle, the finer they feel themselves to be. They carry a curved dagger, not hanging from the belt but held tight against their body by the belt. Their shift hangs below their coat down to their heels. Its sleeves are very wide and extend beyond the sleeves of their coat. They wear pointed hats folded back like the headdress of the duke of Venice, coloured black, unlike the hats of the Egyptians, which are red; and they are surrounded by a wide band of cotton fabric. They wear no breeches and have no stockings or boots, although their women do wear them, as also do Turkish women. Their shoes reach up to their ankles.

When they go about the country, whatever the weather, whether in company or alone, both in peace and in war, in winter or in summer, their right arm is always bare and free of its sleeve, and their shoulder and half of their chest are also bare, so that if necessary they could draw their bow, and also so that, having their arms bare, they are readier to fight: desiring in this way to show that they are stout fellows.

Their bows and quivers are different from others in Turkey. The Arabs' bows are more like Greek than Turkish bows, for the Turks in Asia carry a small, well-made bow, much curved, hard to draw, but the Cretans' bows, which are of two kinds, those made in Sphachie with ibex horns and those made in Candy with buffalo horns, are larger than the Turkish bow; and since they are larger than Turkish bows they take longer and thicker arrows, just like those of the Arabs, which are larger and take large arrows. And the bows of the Tartars and Wallachians surpass all of these in breadth and length, though they are weak. All of these bows do not require the archers to have jackets or gloves, as do English bows and those of Brazil, and others who have wooden bows. The Turks, Cretans, Arabs and Tartars, using bows that are glued together, have no gloves for drawing their bows with, but instead have a small ring of ivory, horn or boxwood. The most sumptuous are of gold and silver, set with shining stones; though this is no modern invention, but very ancient; for the ancient Greek doctors, like Galen, desiring to describe the shape of the part of the throat that the Latins call *larinx* and the French uvula, say that it resembles the ring that the

Thracians put on their right thumb when they draw their bows; and indeed the uvula is entirely similar to the ring that the Turks wear on their thumb when they draw their bow.

90

Of Lake Gennesaret and the Sea of Tiberias

We travelled only a short way until we came to the shores of the Sea of Tiberias, a lake in which carp, pike, tench and chub are caught. We passed the foot of the hill where Our Lord fed five thousand men with two small fishes and five loaves of barley bread. All that day we travelled through barren country except in some humid places where the inhabitants cultivate dasheens, cabbages with good hearts, large beets, onions and garlic, and also some bananas. The plain in which the Sea of Tiberias lies has tall thickets of *napeca* trees, which are thorny and bear fruits that are sweet and good to eat. Since they are so thorny they have spoiled these arid regions, and are not sown along with crops. In any case the local people, seeking land to till, cultivate only easy and humid soil.

We passed through the village of Capernaum, where there are some very fine springs. Looking round Lake Tiberias, we could see the land of Galilee and the village of Bethsaida, where Saint Peter and Saint Andrew were born, and also Chorazin, which Our Lord cursed.

The villages are now inhabited by Jews, who have recently built houses all round the lake and, having established fisheries here, have populated this land which was formerly uninhabited. The lake is not so large but that the land all round it can be seen.

Continuing on our way, we spent the night in a caravanserai near the river Jordan, which we crossed on a stone bridge. The Arabs sought to do us some violence, but we resisted them vigorously and strongly. There were villages near the caravanserai, and the peasants brought poultry, eggs and bread for sale, and also figs, grapes and white and red jujubes.

Next morning we set out from the caravanserai, travelling through very stony country, as is indicated by the name it bears;

for since the country is so harsh and rugged it is called *Regio Trachonitis*. Here grow *coccus* and *esculus* trees, which the Greeks anciently called *platyphyllon*, and now *velaguida*. They bear acorns the size of a pigeon's egg, on which men could live in time of famine, for they have something of the taste of chestnuts. Since they do not rear pigs here, the acorns go to waste.

About midday we came into a region where we were overtaken by rain, which lasted until the evening, when we arrived at a caravanserai, a good three leagues from Damascus. We camped under our tents near a village adjoining the caravanserai, for many travellers had stopped here early and the rain had prevented them from leaving.

On the following day we came into well cultivated and fertile country, with many villages. To our left we had the mountains of Tripoli, which were already covered with snow, and the land of Phoenicia. When we came into the plain of Damascus, as we were still on a hill, we could see the town at a great distance, for it is situated in low-lying flat country.

Willows and tall white and black poplars grow in this country, so that it seemed to us to be surrounded by forests. There are many orchards here which are watered by streams coming down from the mountains which make the land fertile. It is only six days' journey from Jerusalem to Damascus, so that it costs only two or three ducats per mount for each person. We arrived in the town at quite an early hour.

91

Observation of things in Damascus

There is such great abundance of water in Damascus, from the river Chrysorrhoas, that almost everyone has a fountain both in his garden and in his house. The streets of the town are narrow and not straight. The bazaar, that is to say the market, is very handsome, and is roofed over. The houses are well built; but what is finest about them is the openwork porches, which give them coolness. The walls of the town are double, as in Constantinople. The ditches are not

339

deep, and in them they grow mulberry-trees to feed the worms which produce silk. The towers on the two walls are close together, with a large square tower between two small round ones, and they are of different sizes. There is a small square castle outside the circuit of walls, and yet it seems to be enclosed within the town, for the outer districts are twice the size of the town, and so markets are held in the outer districts.

The bazaars and basestans[361] are within the circuit of walls. The gates of the town are faced with sheets of iron, unlike those of Cairo, which are faced with leather. On the east side is a square tower, on the top of which is an inscription in Arabic characters, said to have been put there since it was recaptured from the Christians, for a little lower down can be seen two lilies carved on marble, which are the arms of France or Florence. Beside them is a lion, which has led some to think that they are indeed the arms of France or Florence. The shops of the tradesmen are the same as in Cairo.

The doctors in this country, when they are called to see a patient, make it their business to obtain the drugs that the patient requires; for they bargain with their patients, and according to their malady undertake to cure them, and the money will not be paid to them until the patients have first been cured. It seems to me, therefore, that they have the same fashion of medicining as was practised by the ancient Greek and Arab doctors when they served both as surgeon and as apothecary. I do not, however, mean to say that they were not held in as great honour as they are today; but there were not so many of them, just as there were not so many judges and lawyers, nor so many men of justice as we see now. But since men have in this world three principal things of value in their life, their soul, their body and their possessions, and since the soul is the divinest part of man, so all men, thinking of their salvation, even if they are pagans, have always held their men of theology in sovereign dignity. So much, therefore, for the soul. After their soul, having nothing more dear than their body, and desiring their health, they have held doctors in great honour; and also desiring to preserve the possessions that they have acquired by labour and industry and to enjoy their own in peace, they have held lawyers and men of justice in veneration. In ancient times as still today, well governed republics have been unable to do without these three professions, which have always existed: though I do not believe that they have so much multiplied in other countries as in ours.

There is no need of a sergeant in Turkey to take a man to court. Anyone who wants to bring a someone before a judge must himself go to him and ask him to come before the justice of God; and if there are other Turks present he will not dare to refuse. Then, going to the judge, who sits all day under a sloping roof adjoining his house, they argue their case before him, and he will at once decide the matter as seems good to him. And so they need no solicitors, procurators or advocates.

Those who sell simple drugs also sell composite ones, among which I observed in their shops ancardine, metridat and theriac, philonium[362], hamech[363], rose and violet honey, rose preserve from the Stechades[364], lobes of foxes' lungs[365], oils of absinth and aspic, and mint. Goods are sold in Damascus and in Syria in a weight called a *rotulo*, as in Egypt.

What we call damask plums or damsons are not the same as those gathered in this country: that name I apply to our small, sweet, black ones, which are the most common and the best that we have. Those of Damascus are dear even in the country where they grow, and are larger than a walnut, firm-fleshed and sweet with a touch of bitterness. I saw them only dried, for I was not there at the time when they are green. The stone is large and flat rather than thick and round.

There are workshops in Damascus which do nothing else but clean cotton of its seeds. They have a square iron rod a foot long and two fingers thick, with which the cotton is pressed against a board, so that the round seeds are driven out and thus are separated from the cotton. They feed horses and camels on *ervilia* and *ervum*[366], which are small seeds that are also sown in France, although they have no French name. And since I saw them hulled, and they appeared red, I could not have recognised them without seeing them whole. The sugar called *alhasur*[367], which grows on a plant in Egypt through the agency of a small worm resembling a snail which settles on the plant and builds its house, is in such general use in Damascus, and throughout Turkey, that everyone knows

knows its Turkish name, *tigala*. It is in small balls the size of a filbert, and, unlike white sugar, quenches thirst when eaten or drunk. The Arab authors bear witness that white sugar increases rather than quenches thirst. Alhasur when fresh has the property of quenching thirst at once and curing a cough in a brief space of time.

There are great numbers of Jews in Damascus, who are enclosed within a separate part of the town, as in Avignon. Armenians and Greeks have houses in the town but are not enclosed. The Venetians have an officer in Damascus for the purposes of trade, who is like a consul or bailiff. He has craftsmen from Venice in his service; for, being a man of reputation, he keeps a tailor, a cobbler, a barber, a doctor and an apothecary, dressed in the manner of his country, as well as several other tradesmen.

There is a Basha in Damascus, as in Cairo, who has a house outside the town. He does not live in the castle for feat of rebellion, for one of his predecessors had so won the love of the people that he sought to make himself an absolute ruler, and went out with his men to do battle with the force that had been sent by the Turk against him[368]. He had promised his men that he would allow them to pillage the Jews. But as fortune had it he was vanquished and defeated in battle, at which the Jews were greatly rejoiced; and they still glory in it today, saying that the victory of the Turk over the Basha was because he had planned to pillage them. In memory of this they celebrate a festival every year on the day on which the Basha was defeated, and say that they have inscribed this victory in their records. There is no Jew living today but hopes to see Jerusalem return to their hands. That is why they keep these matters in their records of all that takes place.

Syrian sheep have a shorter tail than Egyptian sheep, but it is just as thick. Much use is made of condrilla gum[369], and it is commonly sold like other drugs. Women use it to chew in place of mastic. This gum is made by the art of a small worm which encloses itself in the gum from this root, which it gnaws and pierces; and from this there flows a kind of milk, which hardens in the form of a small hazelnut and is then gathered by the local people, who sell it to merchants in the towns. And as the women of Crete, not having condrilla gum, use the gum of white chameleon[370], and the inhabitants of the island of Chios use mastic gum, so the Persians use terebinth gum, which can be chewed without harming the teeth and without being consumed in the mouth, like those above-mentioned.

92

Of the display of those who set out in large companies from the town of Damascus to go to Mecca

While we were in Damascus we saw a caravan making its display in preparation for travelling to Mecca for the love of Mahomet. This caravan is a great company of men which leaves Damascus twice every year. There are sometimes a thousand men in the company, sometimes two and at other times three. But before leaving they make their display, which is a fine thing to see, with great pomp and parade.

Turks living in Europe who want to make this journey can go by either of two routes. Some embark at Constantinople and sail to Cairo, for there is likewise a caravan leaving Cairo for Mecca once a year. But those who live in Asia find it much more convenient to make the journey from Damascus rather than from Cairo. They begin by arranging for the provision of camels, which are essential for the journey, since they can go on for a long time without drinking and are accustomed to travelling in deserts; and so they do not take horses, which cannot suffer thirst so long.

The finest thing in the display is a shrine with a beautifully fringed canopy, accompanied by several prophets of Mahomet and carried on the back of a camel, in which, resting on a cushion, is the book of the Alcoran, which contains the law given to them by Mahomet. The great lords and inhabitants of Damascus, the spahis of the sanjak and basha, and other Turkish gentlemen lend them horses to carry this display throughout the town. Among other ornaments and finery on the camels are hairs from the tails of Indian oxen, which are white and delicate. It is reckoned that the tails sell sometimes for four ducats, sometimes for five, for they are delicate and fine; and so it is only great lords that have them.

[They hang them under the horse's throat. It is a brave sight to see a great Turkish lord on horseback; for since they have short stirrup leathers and very wide stirrups they have no rowels on their spurs, and carry their scimitars between the saddle and their thigh, and have a small whip in their hand. Accordingly in order the better to show what such a lord is like we here include a portrait of one of them on horseback with the finery worn in their country][371].

They take players of oboes and tambourins to accompany them on their journey, and they also take with them some twenty falconets for the safety of the whole caravan, for fear of being robbed by Arabs when travelling through desert country. The general display lasts two or three days, but they have another month in which to obtain supplies of the provisions required for their journey. Accordingly there are many shops in Damascus, as in Cairo, which sell only roast chickpeas, which they call by the vulgar Greek name of *ervithia*, which when roasted and dried in large brass pans are very suitable for those making a long journey. They also take supplies of biscuit, dried salt meat, cooked grapes, rice, bouhourd and tracana, which are types of grain cooked with milk and then dried.

Portraict d'vn des seigneurs Circasses, ou Arabes à cheual,
qui. estoyent des plus riches seigneurs d'Egypte, lors
que le Souldan y dominoit.

Figure: Portrait of one of the Circassian or Arab lords on horseback. who
were among the richest lords in Egypt when it was ruled by the Soldan

93

Of the buildings and other singularities of Damascus

I saw no game in Damascus more notable than the partridges of this country. They are smaller than the red ones and are grey. The back and neck are of the colour of a woodcock, but the wings are of a different colour; those of the part nearest the body are white, brown and tawny, while the ten main feathers are ash-coloured. The underside of the wings and the body are white. There is a band round the breast like the one round the neck of a blackbird or a little bustard, which is red, yellow or tawny. The underside of the neck and head, the beak and the eyes are like those of a partridge. The tail is short. I should have written it down as a species of corncrake or plover but that its legs are covered with feathers, as in a white partridge of Savoy or a feathered pigeon.

There is a very large, beautiful and magnificent mosque in Damascus, finely built, and also a basestan, which is a place appointed for the sale of the most costly and richest wares in the town, such as silks in all colours, goldsmiths' and silversmiths' work, oriental stones, scimitars, saddles, bridles and other such high-priced articles, and also male and female slaves. All things are sold in Turkey as at auction. There is not a town in this country, however small it may be, but has a basestan, and not a village but has its market, called the bazaar.

The buildings in Damascus are in the same style as in Cairo, being well designed to give coolness. And just as in northern countries they have hot baths to keep warm in, so in Damascus the baths are built in the fashion of a porch, with low windows on two sides, so that, being seated on the ground, they have a flow of air at this low level to keep them cool. The large grapes which are brought to us in large boxes of plane-wood are true Damascus grapes, which the Arabs call *zibeben*.

There is no iron ore in the territory of Damascus from which steel is smelted, as many people have thought; for what we call damascene steel is merely refined and purified here. I enquired whether there were any mines, but was told that there were not.

Iron, steel and copper are brought here from elsewhere and are given the tempering and preparation which renders them more perfect. And indeed there are men here who are highly skilled in engraving and chasing steel and brass. The brass, steel and copper wares produced in Damascus are at once bought up and taken to Cairo and Constantinople. And so you will find more damascene work in Constantinople, and at lower prices, than in Damascus itself; for when the craftsmen have produced some fine work they sell it to the merchants, who then transport it elsewhere.

Following the little river, anciently called Chrysorrhoas, which runs through the town and serves to water the surrounding country, you come to the gardens outside the town. Those who have said that this river is the source of the river Jordan are wrong, for it is not so.

I have frequently said that there are no hostelries in all the countries ruled by the Turk, which is why there are many handsome caravanserais to be seen in the town of Damascus, in Cairo and in towns throughout Turkey. The Arabs call them khans. They are built in the form of large halls, in which all travellers, whether strangers or local people, are lodged free of charge.

94

Journey from Damascus to Mount Lebanon

We now made our preparations for continuing our journey to Constantinople. Leaving the town very late in the day and travelling north, we went only as far as the foot of the mountain from which the stream runs down through the town and camped there that evening.

Next morning we had a steep climb up the mountain, and when we reached the top we had a view of the town, which is of great extent and seemed to us very large. The gardens, verdant with trees of many kinds, are almost incorporated in the town in the beautiful level plain; and they are well watered by the stream, which flows so impetuously that it can be heard all round the town. But when it reaches the plain it is tamed, and can be conducted and distributed in an infinity of small channels, as the inhabitants desire.

Accordingly they have had the reputation in all times of being great gardeners, as Pliny well knew, saying *Syria in hortis operosissima.* It is the fairest and most fertile plain that I have ever seen. And indeed the inhabitants go to great trouble to make it fertile.

Coming down from the mountain, we found ourselves amid low hills in which are several villages which cultivate the land most diligently; the land is very fertile, and they channel water with great art round the little hills. The vines are of sturdy growth, with vigorous branches. They are skilled in tending them, planting them at such a distance from one another that a cart can be driven between them. It is no great marvel, therefore, if the grapes are so fine and the wine so strong, as compared with other countries where it is scarcely stronger than water, because the inhabitants plant the vines so close to one another that there is scarcely room to walk between them to tend them.

The ploughs used in the lowland country of Syria are different from ours. Two small asses, failing oxen, can draw a plough without wheels made of poplar wood with two very light shares. Ploughing is no great labour, for they only scratch the surface of the earth; and since their plough has a very small share without a coulter they carry it back on their shoulders when going home, as Pliny had already noted: *Syria tenui sulco arat.* The vines of Syria are different from those of Jerusalem, for they stand almost four cubits high, supported on .stakes planted in regular order, with space to plough between them, and bear five or six shoots arranged in order on either side. But in Jerusalem most of the vines grow without support and are not arranged in regular order.

We travelled on until we came in sight of Mount Lebanon, which was already covered with snow. Here we found Mesue's *eupatorium,* Pontic wormwood, lesser centaury, white and red jujube-trees, poplars and two kinds of dwarf cedars, with sharp and with rounded leaves. The inhabitants cultivate pear-trees, apple-trees, apricot-trees and almond-trees. We came that evening to a small village called Calcous and lodged in a caravanserai hewn from the rock with a vaulted roof. The houses in the village are in the same fashion.

Next day, taking the road for Mount Lebanon by way of Tripoli, we had the Antilebanon on our left between us and the land of

Phoenicia, which adjoins Syria. On the summit of Mount Lebanon is a monastery of Maronite and Greek caloyers, who show travellers the tall cedars like those with which Solomon built his temple, as being most durable. This is the only tree (with the exception of the fir) whose fruits always point upwards towards heaven. It bears large, hard cones, like those of the pine but smoother.

95

Of the antiquities of the town of Caesarea, now called Balbec

We turned bridle for Balbec, an ancient town of Phoenicia, of great renown, situated at the foot of Mount Lebanon. Nearing Balbec, we saw a sepulchre in the open country, supported by massive short, round pillars of Thebaic stone, which had a vaulted roof built of large stones and ending in a point.

The town of Balbec lies in a beautiful situation, but is now almost wholly ruined. Its ruins show that it was once a place of great magnificence. There is a castle which is almost entire, with nine tall columns of greater girth than those in the Hippodrome in Constantinople. There is also another column above the town still standing erect, like Pompey's pillar near Alexandria, with a square capital topping the column. There are several platforms of dressed stone, built in the fashion of sepulchres and inscribed with Arabic letters. The inhabitants are for the most part Jews, who say that the town was built by Solomon. But in fact it is the town anciently called Caesarea Philippi, which Saint Paul mentions having visited; and it is here that are the sources of the Jordan[372]. The walls are not of great height, but are of the most finely dressed stone of any town in the world. It is a most sumptuous place, with no surrounding ditches.

A man curious of antiquities could not see all that there is to be seen in Balbec in a week, for there are many antique and notable things, which I was unable to observe because we did not stay long enough. Here we found wine, and got supplies of provisions, and dined, and in the evening we continued on our way. We found a platform built of large stones on the slopes of a hill, twenty-five paces long and fifteen wide, with a spacious interior and walls of no great height but extraordinary thickness. That evening we came to a village called Lubon, where we found an ancient building erected by the Romans, which is still entire, built of massive stones two toises long. This village is well shaded by elms and walnut-trees and watered by a stream running down from the mountain.

Leaving the village, we came into a plain. After we had travelled some way we began to climb a hill, on which we found Arabs coming towards us as if determined to attack us, with their arms out of their sleeves the more easily and vigorously to throw stones and the better to wield their bows. The Turks who were in our company were not prepared to defend themselves, and withdrew apart; but Monsieur de Fumel, accompanied by several French noblemen, faced up to them and drove them off most valiantly, though not without some being wounded on both sides.

We continued on our way and soon came into a great plain like the one round Damascus, over which water is led in small channels so as to make the land fertile; for they have fields as level as the sea in which they can channel water wherever they wish so as to make them fertile. There are many villages on both sides of the road where trees are cultivated most diligently, but principally mulberries, both black and white, which we wrongly call sycamore-figs, and which supply food for great numbers of silkworms. They coppice black mulberry-trees and fig-trees, for the leaves are then tenderer on the new shoots. We also found *absinthium seriphium,* Mesue's *eupatorium,* growing by the roadside.

It is very rare in Syria and Asia to see any fine buildings in the fields. This is because most men in the Levant and the whole of Asia are slaves, and so do not build any large buildings in the fields, as they do in Europe. From this it results that the country is for the most part uncultivated. And just as they do not build in the fields, so the buildings in the towns are also poorly built. The reason is that the noblemen in the lands of the Turk are not the same as those in Christian countries, who live there from father to son. The Turk who holds the post of highest dignity after the Grand Signior will not know where he comes from nor who his father and mother are; and any man who is in the pay of the Turk considers himself to be as much a nobleman as the Grand Turk himself. But this does not come to him from father to son, as it does to Latin and Greek noblemen.

Nobility is not judged in the same way in every country, for most nobles in Italy, like those of Florence, Venice and many other republics, carry on trade and other practices that a man in our country cannot exercise without losing his claim to nobility. This I find to be in agreement with what Herodotus says about the ancient nobility of the Egyptians, who regarded themselves as more than other men because they did not practise the mechanic arts and were the first to be called to war: which dignity they inherited from father to son. And since republics have had diverse judgment on the nobility of men, I conclude that nobility is as men wish to judge it. The greatest honour and quality that a man in Turkey can have is to declare himself a slave of the Turk, just as in our countries we say that we are servants of some prince. And since part of the property of slaves returns to the Turk after their death, those who have any money do not employ it in building; and so the houses of the Turks are small in comparison with ours[373].

Continuing on our way, we had the mountains of Lebanon on the left, close to our road, verdant with terebinths, andrachnes, strawberry-trees and *aeleprini*. We now lost sight of Mount Lebanon, which we had passed on the previous days. We began to travel through mountains, which extended out on either side of us, surrounding a large plain in which we descended into Cilicia[374].

After travelling some distance over the plain we rested for a little in a caravanserai. The caravanserais of the Turks in Asia are organised differently from those of the Arabs, for the doorkeepers of the caravanserais commonly sell barley to travellers to give to their camels; for they have no oats in this country. Those who sell this barley pay tax on it to the Turk.

On this day our journey was a short one, for we stopped before midday for the sake of the wounded men.

96

That the ancient manner of eating terebinth seeds is still practised today in Cilicia and Syria

I must not to mention here a matter which seems to me strange. In the next village I saw an Arab peasant leading a camel laden with terebinth seeds; for the nearby mountains are covered with these trees, from which they collect a gum that they take to Damascus to sell. The gum sold in Cairo, however, comes from the country of Asamia.

The country that the Turks call Asamia and the Latins called Chaldaica, with Babylon as its capital, included Mesopotamia and Assyria; and so the Turks also include Mesopotamia and Assyria in Asamia.

I have the witness of authors worthy of being believed that men have been accustomed for more than 2000 years to eat terebinth seeds, and that the Persians lived on them before bread came into use. These seeds are of such an exquisite blue that it surpasses all other azure colours; it is called by all the ancient Arab authors *granum viride*, meaning a hue between green and sky-blue.

97

Of the town of Hamous [Homs], anciently called Emissa

At daybreak we continued on our way over the great plain, in which we found plants of *smyrnium* and *leontopetalon*. We passed through the town which the Arabs call Hamza, the Turks Haman, and which anciently was called Emissa.

This town was anciently surrounded by good walls of dressed stone which are still standing; and within the circuit of walls is a very high mound, easily seen from all over the plain, on which is a castle anciently built by the Romans. Outside the town there is still a two-storey sepulchre in the form of a square pyramid, made of strong cement, inscribed in Greek letters with an epitaph of Caius Caesar[375].

There is a busy trade in silk in Hamous; and accordingly they rear silkworms most diligently, for they have gardens that are abundantly watered by streams flowing down from the mountains and making the plain fertile. They grow fig-trees and mulberries in the well watered fields, and also many fruit-trees. Their principal industry is making handkerchiefs and many-coloured headdresses, mingling silk and gold thread. They also make handkerchiefs coloured white, red and yellow intermingled with gold thread, which are known throughout Turkey as Hamous handkerchiefs.

The town is situated in a level and spacious plain, through which flow fine streams. The circuit of the walls is almost entire, but the interior of the town is ruined, and there is nothing worth seeing but the bazaar, that is to say the market, and the basestan, which is built in the fashion of Turkey. The walls show clearly that the town was once a magnificent place, and it is situated in beautiful country. We found all kinds of provisions here; and since Greeks, Armenians and Jews live among the Turks in the towns in this country we were able to find wine in all the towns to which we came.

98

Of the taverns of Turkey, in which the Turks drink a beverage called "posca" or "zitum", different from beer

The first thing that I observed in Hamous was that the practice of making the beverage anciently called *posca* is not entirely abolished, and I will go farther and say that there is no town in Asia but has taverns selling this beverage. They call it in the vulgar tongue *chousset*, which is what the ancient Greeks called *zitum* and the Latins *posca* or *pusca* or *phusca*, the same names that Suetonius and Columella used, and which is mentioned by Serapion and Avicenna.

It is a white drink like milk, thick and very nourishing, and goes to the head of those who drink too much of it, so as to make them drunk. It has been thought that posca was *oxycratum*[376], but it is something very different, for *oxycratum* is the substance that is now in common usage in Greek and Italian ships. The guards in Venetian vessels and galleys also ordinarily drink it; for when at sea they have to keep water for a very long time, so that it goes bad and begins to smell. To take away the bad taste that it has acquired after being so long in the ships they add a little vinegar, which gives it a very agreeable taste; and that is *oxycratum*.

But *posca* or *posset* or *chousset*, a drink different from beer, is what the ancients called *curmi* .which is very different from *oxycratum*. *Curmi*, that is to say beer, is made from whole and sometimes ground grain. But *zitum* or *posca*[377], now called *posset*, is made from flour formed into dough, which is cooked in a large pan; then a ball of this dough is thrown into water, which at once boils up and becomes hot without any fire, so as to make a thick drink. It produces a light white foam which Turkish women use to paint their faces, since it makes the skin delicate and tender, and they take it to the baths to rub themselves with. This is a characteristic of *zitum* of which the ancient authors were aware. It is therefore wrong to think that *oxycratum* is the same as *posca;* but *zitum* and *posca* are the same thing. To prove that *posca* is not *oxycratum* it is sufficient to cite a single passage in Suetonius, who says that a fugitive slave of the emperor was found in the town of Capua selling *posca*, and if there was nothing more in this drink than in *oxycratum* it is manifest that his tavern must have been ill stocked and cannot have made great profit.

99

Of the town of Tarsus, from which came Saint Paul

We left Hamous long before daybreak, and during the night passed a place situated on a hill which was said to be the ruins of the town called Sebastopolis, where many columns still stand erect, said by some to be remains of Herod's palace and by others of Herodian's. But the common opinion of the local people is that they are pillars from a church of Saint John; they say that it was here that he was beheaded. From there we descended into a valley and crossed a river on a stone bridge. Many people believe that this river is the Orous, others the Iris, others again the Martia. It flows down impetuously and turns many mills. Then we had to climb again to reach the plain, which I believe was anciently called *Sabaeus campus*, and is wide and spacious, a good day's journey across, and totally treeless. Sesame and cotton are grown here.

And so, continuing on our way, we came to the town of Hama or Hamsa, which was anciently called Tarsus[378]; it is half a day's journey from Hamous. I know that some moderns think that Hamous is the Apamea of the ancients. That town was also in a valley; it was anciently very populous, as appears from its extensive walls and the ruins within them. There is a ruined castle on a hill like the one at Hamous. Here too are to be seen several large high antique towers. I can find no better comparison for this part of Cilicia, in which Tarsus is situated, than the Beauce district in France. Along the banks of the river Cidnus, which flows through the centre of the town, grow fig-trees, mulberries, walnut-trees and other fruit-trees, but the fields are treeless. Thanks to the great abundance of the river, which waters the gardens with the aid of very high wheels, the town is well populated. Since the bed of the river is very low the water is raised by these great wheels and conducted in channels, which also serve baths and hot baths in the town. There are also large and well built mosques, but the houses are poorly built, scattered here and there on hills. The river can be forded without too much difficulty. It is dammed by small weirs to drive mills. There is also a small wooden bridge. Hama or Tarsus was the home of Saint Paul: not that he was born there, for he was a native of a village called Giscalis in the land of Galilee, near the Sea of Tiberias. We did not stay long in Tarsus, for after our mounts had been fed we continued on our way.

100

*Of the plains of Cilicia, and of the cisterns hewn from the round
which are filled with rainwater*

Pursuing our journey over a region of clayey soil and wide
waterless plains, we could imagine ourselves to be travelling through
Beauce or the Laudun region, for you could not dig an ell of land
in this part of Cilicia without finding rock, like the tufa at Laudun..
The inhabitants of Cilicia, concerned for their livelihood, have
devised a means of saving rainwater for their use and for watering
their stock: they have hewn underground cisterns from the rock,
leaving a small opening at the top through which the water enters.
And if on occasion the water in the cisterns runs short they have
to fetch it from more than four leagues away.

Continuing over the plain, we saw no other plants but asphodels
and giant fennel. Although this region is similar to Beauce, the
cultivation of the soil is very different, since there are plenty of
farmers in Beauce but very few in Cilicia; and they also have to fetch
wood from the nearby mountains, more than two days' journey away.
To make up for this lack they sow the land with a kind of grain
that is unknown in Italy and France, very similar to the sorghum
of Lombardy but differing in colour; for sorghum is reddish, while
the other is white. I find no mention of it in the Greek and Latin
authors, but the Arabs call it *hareoman*.

The inhabitants store the straw from this crop, which is as
thick as a man's thumb, and make their fires with it in place of any
other wood. They have millstones in their houses with which they
grind the grain; then with it they make a hard dough, spread it out
very thin and bake it in the heat of the sun, or else in the manner
practised anciently by Roman soldiers, who heated a tile in the fire,
laid it on two stones, put the dough on it and baked it in the heat
of the tile. The peasants of the villages bake their bread in this way;
but in the towns they bake it in an oven. I had previously seen this
corn growing in Epirus and Albania, where the peasants take it in
large sackfuls to the market in Corfu, and the islanders feed it to
their pigeons.

We did not camp that evening in a caravanserai, for rain compelled us to stay in a village, where we found bread baked in the manner described above and other kinds of provisions, along with cheap eggs and hens. We left early on the following morning to make up for the previous day's journey, which had been short, and continued over the plain until evening, where we came into a region of low hills with an abundant growth of shrubs with scarlet-grain. We arrived at the ruins of Marat quite late in the evening.

101

Description of the ruins of Marat

Marat was once a large town but is now all in ruins. I am inclined to believe that it was anciently called Maronia, but I am not prepared to assert that it was. It is surprising that it is not more populous, for it has springs and streams of water. There are only a few mosques and very few houses still with roofs. The ruins show that it was once a fine town.

Here we found a man impaled in the manner of the Turks. Such is their system of justice that when some delinquent or criminal has been convicted they tie his hands and legs to four stakes set in the ground and drive another up his fundament, and strike it with mallets until it emerges from his body somewhere near his head, and then raise him erect. The poor man then remains impaled with his feet tied and his arms stretched wide. This manner of impalement is not modern, for Herodotus says (speaking of the burials of the Scythians, from whom the Turks are descended[379]) that when the king of the Scythians died, among other ceremonies which they practised, they strangled fifty young boys, whom they impaled with a stake driven up their spine to the head, and then set the stakes in the ground round the king's sepulchre. I say, therefore, that this was an ancient custom practised by their ancestors – referring only to the manner of impalement; for it is no longer practised at burials.

Marat is half way between the town of Tarsus[380] and Aleppo. The fields in this area are sown with wheat, barley, cotton and sesame, but there is not a single tall tree, nor any small shrubs. We slept in a caravanserai. On the following day we continued over a plain as level as a smooth sea, on which we travelled all day. The land is ploughed here in the manner that I have described in speaking of Syria.

The main revenue of the country comes from cotton and sesame, which they sow in the month of June. I make no doubt that if it were sown in France it would grow as well as in Asia. The land of Italy bears witness to this, for in the time of the Romans it was sown with sesame and cotton; but now there is not a single plant of either. Cotton spends less than half a year in the ground, for it is sown in May or July and harvested in September, but it has to be sown afresh every year. Nevertheless I have seen it growing in gardens in Cairo, where it exceeds the height of a man and does not die down each year. There is also another kind of cotton which is brought from the Indies or from Brazil, very different from the cotton that grows in Asia; for Brazilian cotton has large black seeds assembled in clusters of ten or twelve grains together, unlike the cotton that grows in Asia, which bears seeds grain by grain.

It was already very late when we came to a stream flowing towards Aleppo. After crossing it we left the rich soil and entered a stony country of mountains and rocks. We now saw olive-trees, apple-trees, pear-trees, plum-trees and almond-trees. It is only three leagues from this stream to Aleppo, which we reached at a very late hour. We lodged with a Venetian nobleman, maintained there by the signoria of Venice for the purposes of trade.

102

Of the town of Aleppo, anciently called Beroea, and of rhubarb and rhapontic

Aleppo has been renowned since ancient times as a great city, for of all the towns in the East it has the busiest trade; and it is also the capital of Commagene. It is thought to have derived its Arabic name from *aleph,* which is the first letter in the alphabet, just as Aleppo is the first town in the region in which it is situated. I know that there are some modern authors who believe that it was anciently called Hierapolis, although Gillius is of opinion that it was called Beroea.

The caravans from Persia, the Indies, Mesopotamia and other countries in the east discharge their wares at Aleppo. Those who want to go India, Persia and other parts of the Levant will always find merchants travelling to and from Aleppo. And since it is a town to which the wares of the Levant are brought the Venetians maintain a consul here as ambassador in order to buy goods and send them to nearby ports on the Mediterranean like Tripoli and Beirut. And to enable them to play a greater part in the trade in wares from the East they keep many of their young people here and in other foreign countries to learn the language of the country and the manner of life of the inhabitants. When a caravan laden with goods arrives in Aleppo they are taken up at once, for there are wealthy merchants who buy them on the spot.

Most of the rhubarb brought to Europe is bought in Aleppo, where the inhabitants are accustomed to seeing sometimes a dozen camels in a caravan arriving laden with rhubarb, brought from the country of Asamia, where it is diligently cultivated. I could find no one who had seen the rhubarb plant of whose virtue the Arab author Mesue has so much to say; but he makes no mention of rhapontic, which the Greeks held in such high esteem. Mesue, who lived in either Damascus or Aleppo, says that in his time rhubarb was brought from the Indies and Seni, that is to say from Asamia or Assyria, in the third place from Barbary and fourthly from Turkey. He says also that the people of the country put the rhubarb to soak in water in order to draw the substance out of it; then with this, when it had thickened and dried out, they made trochisks[381]; and then they dried the rhubarb and sold it to merchants. In my view that could well be so in his time; but nowadays, knowing that they can make great profit from rhubarb, and that it is in great demand in every nation, they cultivate it with great care and produce it in such great quantity that at the time when we were at Aleppo ten pounds of it were sold for 12 ducats.

However it is not always at the same price, for when the caravan brings only a small quantity from Asamia that makes it dearer in the following year. It is cultivated in Asamia, that is to say Mesopotamia, where they sow its seeds. It grows roots of the size of a wild cherry's roots, which when they uproot it they cut into slices to dry; then as it dries and loses its moisture the pieces become wrinkled. This has led some to think that this results from the pressing out of the humidity, although experience shows that that is not so. To be more certain about this I enquired of the merchants who come to Aleppo whether an infusion is made from it, and found that few people make use of it in the area where it is grown, and that they use few medicines taken from rhubarb,

When I read the authors of our time disputing about rhubarb, I find some who doubt whether the ancients knew it; for we regard the Arab authors as modern compared with the Greeks. And so, seeing that Mesue distinguishes four species and makes no mention of rhapontic, and knowing that the caravans from Asamia bring only rhubarb, I concluded without difficulty that when Mesue refers to the fourth species of rhubarb from Turkey he means rhapontic. And indeed rhapontic is very similar to rhubarb, and although I do not mean to say that they are the same thing it is manifest that their virtues are closely similar.

The principal gums and spices, like *galbanum*, opoponax, styrax, asafoetida, *serapinum*[382] and other such things, are brought to us by way of Aleppo, as well as scammony. Hard dates are brought to Aleppo from Asamia, for Egyptian and African dates are so soft that they stick together in a mass and cannot be kept separate. It is only three days' journey from Aleppo to Tripoli, where the Venetian ships put in to load the goods that they buy in Aleppo.

The whole of the following day was devoted to seeing the town, which can be compared in size to Orleans. In the centre of the town is a circular mound on which is a castle surrounded by a moat filled with water. There is also a sanjak with his soldiers. The walls are built in the antique fashion; and since the town stands high it can be seen from a great distance. Enclosed within the moat was a wild ass called an onager, but it was different from an Indian ass. There we also saw a bird very like a crane, but having a smaller body, with red-rimmed eyes, the tail of a heron and a weaker cry than a crane; and I believe that it was what the ancients called a Balearic crane.

103

Special description of the form of the streets in towns and villages in Turkey

Carts never pass along the streets in villages and towns in Turkey, nor through the markets; for there is a track in the middle of the street expressly designed to drain water and for the passage of horses. On either side of this the street is raised in the form of benches, which have small sloping roofs to provide protection from rain and the heat of summer. And since the Turks wear long trailing robes reaching down to the ground, if they did not build their towns in this fashion they would always be covered with dirt. This fashion is generally observed not only in Aleppo but also throughout Turkey. Thus the streets in towns are not paved; and in order to avoid the dust raised by people's robes in markets and basestans in summer all the shopkeepers pay one asper a month to have water sprinkled in front of their shops. This is done by men who go round every morning carrying water in a goatskin. The Turk holds all the shops and workshops in towns in his hand and lets them to the merchants. He does not allow people to set up house in the place where the market is held; for Mahomet prohibits women from selling or buying or showing themselves in public. Workmen, whatever their trade, content themselves with what they earn during the day and do not work at night.

We stayed for some days in Aleppo. We made the circuit of the walls, which are of greater extent than those of Damascus, with corners at certain points, as in the walls of Jerusalem. The towers round the walls are at some distance from one another. Aleppo has eight gates, and great numbers of vineyards and orchards and beautiful gardens round the walls in which they grow white cabbages, lettuces, beets, leeks and onions to sell in the market.

The Turks use ancient coins and medals as weights for weighing out ounces, half-ounces and drachms, so that in many places I was able to get Greek and Latin coins. When I set out to look for them I went round the shops asking for *giaour manguour*, that is, Christian money; and, hearing this, they showed me what they had. The Turks,

Arabs, Egyptians and all other nations in the Levant under Turkish rule have no coins other than of gold and silver. The gold in their coins is fine ducat gold; the silver is fine silver, neither mixed nor purified. There are other coins in Turkey called *mangoures,* which are of pure copper. Sixteen of them are worth only one asper, and since they are heavy men do not usually carry them. Their purpose is to provide change from an asper when a customer buys something in the market. The markings on their gold and silver coins are in Arabic letters, and they have in all only one kind of coin called an asper, which is worth a carolus in our money. The Arabs and Egyptians have a kind of money which they call a *meidin,* which is worth one and a half aspers.

104

Journey from the town of Aleppo to Antioch

The inhabitants of Aleppo speak Arabic and not Turkish, for the language of the inhabitants of Egypt, Arabia, Syria, Cilicia and other neighbouring regions is Arabic. We left Aleppo after midday to go to Antioch, travelling through beautiful level country, well cultivated and watered by fine streams. We found lodging that evening at an early hour in a village called Farrou, near which is a tall antique column without a capital, still standing erect in a field.

In the morning we took the road for Antioch, and after travelling for some time left the level country and entered a stony region, in which we had frequently to go over small mountains and sometimes to follow the slopes of a hill. We saw the ruins of a castle, with white ivy growing on the gate, which was a new thing for me, for I had not seen any since Corfu. I also found andrachnes growing on the slopes of the hills, and we all took several branches with their fruits to eat on the road, for they were now ripe. They are of such a beautiful colour that they invite people to eat them. They hang in bunches, of the size and colour of raspberries, and as soft as the fruit of the strawberry-tree or the cork-oak, with the taste of the fruit of the cork-tree. We also saw *aria* and *esculus* trees, terebinths and *eleprinos,* which the Latins call *alaternus* and the people of Terni and Narni in Italy call *alaterno.*

Continuing on our way through the valleys, we saw on our left an ancient building in ruins, in the manner of a monastery, with a fine tower in the centre. We also passed a handsome ruined mansion built of dressed stone on which were some Latin letters, showing that it had been built by the Romans. We crossed a stream which had such an abundant flow of water that our camels were in it up to their girths. We lodged for the night at the foot of a castle called Heirim, all in ruins, situated in an uninhabited region, which is a great pity, for if the land were cultivated it would be no less fertile than the best land in Italy.

The ruins of this castle of Heirim stand on a mound, like the castles of Aleppo and Hamous. I cannot believe that even ten thousand men would have been able to hew the castle and its moat out of the rock in two years. It looks as if nature had taken delight in fashioning this mound on the rock so that the castle might be built. It is the last place in Turkey where dasheens and bananas grow. Andrachnes and *alaternus* grow among the rocks on the nearby hill. We used no other kind of wood to cook our supper. We did not lodge in a caravanserai but in a house in the village. It is a rare thing to find people in this country providing lodging for travellers; and when they do it is only a matter of giving them some corner under a porch and no other part of the house, just as if they were lodged under a market hall. I observed one thing worthy of note about our host: he had a dagger, curved in the manner of Arab daggers, which was not enriched either by gold or silver, for which our dragoman offered him four ducats; but he refused, saying that he had paid six for it in Damascus. Yet I believe that you could get them at less than a crown a dozen in the best town in France. Our host was one of those who profess to provide lodging for travellers; but this means that he provides nothing but the bare walls of his house, without any utensils. He had a number of unguents, like *metopium*[383], *rosatum* and a number of others that are in common use in Syria and Arabia which I do not mention.

105

Of the town of Antioch

On the following day we came into a plain of great extent, in which we crossed the river Orous, which flows towards Antioch; and which we had skirted on the previous day.. We crossed it a good way above Antioch on a large and handsome bridge near a large lake, which I believe to be the one formerly called *Stagnum Meandriopolis*. We followed the river for a long way until it flowed into the lake. It is only two days' journey from Aleppo to Antioch; but because it had rained, making the going difficult for the camels carrying our baggage, we took two and a half days. The direct road to Constantinople did not go by way of Antioch, but we left it on the right in order to see the town, which is situated below the lake. The direct road headed straight for Mount Amanus, and from there to Adana; though, turning off it to go to Antioch, we still had to go by way of Mount Amanus, which because it appears black is called in Turkish and Arabic the Black Mountain[384].

The situation of the town of Antioch is such that it cannot be properly described in few words, for the structure of its walls makes it most admirable to contemplate, more than a town built in the plain. It bears assured witness that Antiochus was a man of magnanimous heart and of almost incomparable greatness. The circuit of the town's walls is of no less extent than those of Nicomedia or Constantinople.

The town has a large population of Greeks, Armenians, Jews and Turks. It has an abundant supply of water from springs which emerge from the rocks within the walls. One side of the walls encloses a mountain, while the other side runs over the summits of two mountains, which serve as bulwarks. There are thus three mountains included within the circuit of walls: not low hills as in Rome and Constantinople, but true mountains.

I know of no town in France with which to compare Antioch than Lyons; for just as Lyons has within it the high hills of Saint-Just[385], so Antioch encloses high mountains. On one of these is situated the palace of Antiochus, which is not entirely ruined.

Some parts of it are still entire, like large halls and rooms and also cisterns made in the same fashion as those in the palace of Philippi in Macedonia, of immense size. The masonry of the castle of Antioch and the circuit of the town's walls is still preserved entire. At intervals round the walls are very tall square towers, whose builders have not spared the stone to fortify them. The walls on the west side of the town are so constructed that loaded carts and horsemen can go from the lower part of the town up to the castle, with the help of two vaults on the inner side of the walls. Each tower has its own cistern.

The mountains round the town are covered with holm-oaks, *alinternus,* scarlet-grain, andrachnes, *stoechados* and *stachys.* The storks which spend the summer in Europe feed here for part of the winter, as in Egypt, and also pelicans and several other kinds of river birds, which feed in the lake above the town; among them I recognised one which people living on the banks of the river Somme call a *cotée,* and in Paris a tufted duck, and which the ancients called *glaucium,* as also is the one which in French is called the white nun. The sheep grazing on the mountains have short, very fat tails a foot wide. The people of this country, and indeed throughout Turkey, make bread day by day, insufficiently baked and insufficiently leavened. The silkworms which the Italians call *cavalieri* are a source of great profit in the territory of Antioch, and are fed on the leaves of fig-trees and mulberry-trees growing along the banks of the river. There are some very tall plane-trees at the entrance to Antioch, of which there are none in either France or Italy except a few that are grown in Rome and other towns for their singularity. There are small numbers of sugar-canes, dasheens and bananas, which are cultivated very diligently in some gardens in Antioch. The inhabitants speak Arabic, as in Syria.

106

Observations touching the singularities of Antioch

The whole of the following day was devoted to seeing the holy places of Antioch, such as Saint Paul's gate and the sepulchres of several saints. For those who take the trouble to look for them there are many other ancient things to be seen. All kinds of provisions can be bought in the market. The shops of the druggists and tradesmen are similar to those in Damascus.

Lotus-trees grow in the town in great numbers, and also on the nearby mountains. And just as white and black poplars and fruit-trees make the plain of Damascus resemble a forest, so here the planes and lotus-trees make Antioch look as if it were situated in a wood.

The packsaddles of the horses of the carriers of Antioch are so long that they reach from the horse's ears by way of its neck to its tail. The peasants of Antioch are not so skilled in loading their baggage as the Turks, for their packsaddles are ill adapted to the load.

We left Antioch after dinner and crossed to the other bank of the river Orous, which we followed upstream for a long way. The country round Antioch is so marshy that our horses sank into it up to their girths, because it had rained in the last few days. When we had travelled for some time we came to some streams flowing down from the mountains, on whose banks grow oleanders, agnus castus and very tall plane-trees. We lodged in Sarameli, a village situated at the foot of a high mountain which forms part of the Mount Amanus range, which rises out of the plain. On the following day we travelled only two leagues before camping at the foot of a very high mountain, where we stayed the whole day, waiting for a horse that Monsieur de Fumel had sent for from Antioch. Meanwhile, climbing some way up the mountain, I found forests of spruce, Latin *piceae*, similar to those that grow on the hill of Tarare[386].

Other trees that grow here are *esculus, ilex,* andrachne and *oxycedrus,* as well as *polium, tragacantha, chamaedrys* and the pine thistle, which many wrongly call the chameleon.

We saw the peasants in the plain, who are accustomed to carry loads of wood, corn and other similar things on the backs of their oxen. Sometimes they themselves ride on their oxen when they are tired; for those who are not in a hurry use them as we use a horse. They sold us hens, eggs and meat; and although they spend the whole summer camping under their tents in the fields, they are as well accommodated there as in a town or village.

107

Of the passage over the highest summit of Mount Amanus

On the following day our journey took us in a direction between east and north, skirting the high mountains. Mount Amanus is commonly called Monte Negro, that is, the Black Mount. Pliny, however, writing of *Mons aster*, did not know that name. We had to climb straight up the mountain on a precipitous slope, in the most difficult ascent that we had yet experienced. We found tall cedars, as on Mount Lebanon, tall junipers and savin junipers, as on the Taurus Mountains. The andrachne grows even taller here than on Mount Ida in Crete.

We took more than six hours to reach the summit of the mountain, and when we were on the highest point, looking back in the direction from which we had come, we could see the summits of the mountains of Syria and Caria, and in particular the peaks of what we took to be Mount Pierius, round the base of which we had travelled on the previous days. We could also see, at a great distance, the long range of the Taurus, the summit of which was already beginning to be covered with snow. The descent of this mountain was not so difficult as the ascent had been, for the way down was not so direct as the way up had been. Since we were travelling in the dark one of our company fell into a valley more than forty toises deep, without any injury either to himself or to his horse, which was a thing to be wondered at by the whole company.

This mountain is most abundant in all kinds of plants. I saw strawberry-trees scarcely less tall than those on Mount Athos, which grow in the mountains near the monastery of Agias Laura. I also saw some tall *alaternus* trees, which elsewhere are usually no more than shrubs. *Picea,* andrachnes and large-leaved laurels also grow here. Lower down I found white-berried myrtle, *thymelea, chamelea* and the herb which the Germans call *kellerkraut,* which is different from the two above-mentioned.

At the foot of the mountain we rested on the banks of a small stream. We dined on the shores of the Sinus Issicus[387], which curves in an arc to form a very large bay. This gulf is in the country of Pamphylia, which is bordered on one side by Cilicia. When we were on the slopes of Mount Amanus we had the sea rolling in at the foot of the mountain, and we could clearly see the place where the Taurus range begins on the coast opposite Cyprus. With the sea reaching the foot of Mount Amanus, a man could easily throw a stone from the slopes of the mountain into the water of the Mediterranean. We had to travel along the shores of the sea, round the gulf, for a long way, crossing a number of fine rivers.

Continuing round the shores of the bay, we had to climb another hill covered with wild pines on a very narrow and difficult path. Beyond this we came to a small castle at the foot of the mountain where there are regular guards, since it is a very busy place of passage. Here we found many kinds of provisions to buy, like bread, wine, cheese, meat and barley for our mounts. We stopped for the night a little way below the castle, under a white mulberry-tree, which the French take for a sycamore. We had a good fire all night, for we had as much wood as we wanted. We set out again before daybreak and travelled on in the dark through low-lying, level country. When it was full day we returned to the shores of the sea, where we came to a river, which I believe was the Issos, that we had to ford close to the shore. We passed through some very pleasant country, for the roads were lined in some places with tall laurels, holm oaks, planes, *smilax aspera* and many evergreen plants. We had the mountains on our right and the sea on our left.

After crossing the river we came into the great plain in which Alexander and Darius are said to have fought. Here there grows a shrub that I had never seen anywhere else, very similar to a myrtle. There is a great abundance of myrtles, but none with white seeds. We crossed a very ancient arch, which the authors have called *Portae Ciliciae,* built of brick and strong cement, which is harder than dressed stone. The plain seemed like an amphitheatre, for the tall mountains surrounded it in the form of a half-moon, enclosing the sea in the Sinus Issicus.

Passing under the Gates of Cilicia and seeing the andrachnes with their clusters of berries, already red and ripe, we all broke off branches and ate the berries as we travelled on. The country here is not populous, and such inhabitants as there are are not given to fishing or sailing on the sea, so that we did not see a single boat along the whole of this coast. Although the country is ill populated and has few inhabitants, it is well watered by streams, for in two hours we crossed more than twenty flowing down from the high mountains into the sea.

Some distance beyond the Gates we came into barren and stony country, and then through woods which were no more than thickets. Here there grows a small shrub of which I have already spoken, and which I can describe only by calling it *pseudomyrthus*. We found a caravanserai, not far from the villages, where we rested.

108

Of the town anciently called Adana, and of an animal of Asia called "adil"

There is a kind of small wolf in Cilicia, and indeed generally throughout Asia, which carries off and steals anything that it can find belonging to travellers who sleep outside the caravanserai in summer. It is an animal between a wolf and a dog which is mentioned by several ancient Greek and Arab authors. The Greeks call it *squilachi* in their vulgar tongue, and I believe that it is the animal called by the Greek authors *chryseos,* that is to say *aureus lupus*[388].

It is such a daring thief that during the night it comes up to people lying asleep and carries off whatever it can find, like hats, boots, bridles, shoes and other pieces of clothing. This animal is only slightly smaller than a wolf. When darkness falls it barks like a dog. It never goes by itself, but always in packs; and there are sometimes as many as two hundred in a pack, so that no animal is more common in Cilicia. When travelling in a pack they give a cry one after another, like a dog barking *hau, hau*. We heard them crying every night; and were it not that the dogs prevent them, they would make their way stealthily even into the villages. They have a very fine yellow coat, and the local people make furs from their skins, which are sold for a great price.

Next morning we left the caravanserai, pursuing our way to Adana, and came to a stone bridge on which we crossed a small branch of the river Pyramus. Here, on the right, was a castle situated on a rock very difficult of access. Then we followed the river until we came to the ruins of a town which was called Caesarea Ciliciae, where we found a bridge to cross the river.

The rivers in this country, although they are navigable, have no boats on them, for, the country being unpopulated, there is no one to travel on them. The domain of the Soldan of Egypt extended as far as here, and this was the boundary between the Arabic and Turkish languages and between the empires of the Arabs and the Turks. The first battle between the Arab and Turkish nations was fought here, as a result of which the Turk brought them under his rule and made them subject to him. In the ruins of Caesarea there are only a caravanserai and a few small houses.

After crossing the bridge we continued to follow the river, which we had on our left, and then came into a wide barren plain, which has no inhabitants but those who bring their stock to graze here. The myrtles here have white seeds, and are so common that they are like thickets. We passed under tall terebinths, which form forests here, and are scattered about, mingled with wild pines. This area supplies grazing for very large flocks of sheep and goats, which bring much profit to their masters, both in butter and cheese. And although the butters are different from one another in choice and goodness, whether because of the animal from which they come or of the pasturage or of the person who makes them, nevertheless they do not differ so much in character as does cheese; for when you taste the butter of different animals, like buffaloes, cows, mares, camels, sheep and goats, you do not find very great variety, but the contrary is true of cheeses, which can be distinguished from one another merely by smelling them and looking at them, and can be infallibly judged by tasting them.

Turkish peasants, wandering about in the country far from the towns watch over their flocks all summer in the fields; and, having no vessels of earthenware or wood, kill some sheep or goats, and turn and fashion their skins, which they fill with butter or cheese; and they carefully preserve the stomach, for they also fill it with butter, which they have previously boiled and allowed to cool before putting it in the stomach. Each stomach contains between 30 and 40 pounds of milk, and the skins hold more than 50. I do not say that butter is never treated in any other way, or salted as we do; but that is not done except in Greece. The same practice is followed by the people of Mingrelia, who take the skins of oxen and cows immediately after they have been flayed, without currying them, fill them with butter, and then send it by sea to Constantinople to be sold, just as oil is brought to us from Languedoc in goatskins.

I make no doubt that if these peasants had suitable vessels they would not keep their cheeses in skins, for they are not accustomed to keeping it in solid form. And when this cheese is distributed in Greece, where merchants go to sell it, the Greeks call it in their vulgar tongue *dermatisi hilatismeno;* and they do not say *tyri,* which means cheese, but simply call it "salted in skins", just as we say *salé* instead of pork. But they make a difference between this cheese and another kind which they call *cloro tyri,* that is, fresh cheese, which is what Columella calls in Latin *caseum viride*[389], not because it is green but because it is soft. The shepherds here do not strain the milk any more than they do in Crete; but the Cretans put a branch of *aspalathus* at the mouth of their jars, or else goose-grass, so that if any hairs are caught there the cheese will be purer. But this Turkish cheese "salted in skins" is usually full of the hair of the animals, because they do not strain the milk.

Continuing on our way, we travelled due north, and found huts and tents in various places on our route belonging to the poor peasants who go out in summer from the towns and villages into the country and stay there until the winter, running their households in the same way as in a village or town. And when they have stayed in one place for a week they move on to another place, taking with them their tents, which are made of wicker covered with felt. And when they return to the towns they fold them up and keep them carefully until the cold season is over. I am sure that the inhabitants of the countries of Asia endure just as hard winters as those living in the heart of France. They are lazy and do not cultivate the land properly; even rich peasants like to sit about doing nothing, and were it not that they have their land cultivated by their slaves there would be but little land cultivated at all.

We arrived that day at Adana, where we heard about the town of Anazarba, whose name was changed to Caesar Augusta, among others by Oppian and Dioscorides. The Jews told us that there is now a village at the mouth of the river which flows through Adana, called Tyberis, which has retained its ancient name. Adana is a large town, or rather a village grown large, and a busy place of passage. There is a handsome stone bridge, very wide and spacious. The river, which is called in Turkish the Schelikmark, comes from Armenia Minor, passes through Lydia and Cilicia and flows into the Mediterranean below Rhodes. It is not navigable, since it carries down great quantities of stones and earth in its water. The town of Adana is not enclosed by walls. There is a castle with four square towers, which are not particularly strong. Here we found all kinds of provisions as well as wine, for there are Greeks, Jews and Armenians in the town; and the Turks themselves grow vines for the sake of the grapes. We now found a change in the money used, for hitherto we had used *meidins* in Syria, Egypt and Cilicia, and those who had any left had to change them into aspers. The Arabic language was of no service to us in this place, and was replaced by Turkish.

We changed our mounts in Adana and took supplies of provisions for three days. The Turks sell their goods by weight or by measure, but do not increase the prices for travellers, so that local people pay the same as the greatest strangers. Bread is sold by weight, and as a result is ill baked. Salt meat is in great favour; after salting it they hang it up to dry and throw cumin powder on it. Those who have written that the Turks dry meat in order to reduce it to powder and use it in time of war seem to me to have misunderstood the matter; for when I enquired if this was true I found quite the contrary, and I have never heard that either in Greece or in Turkey or in Arabia it has ever been the practice to dry meat in this way and make it into powder. The meat of both oxen and sheep, larded with fat, is cut into very thin slices, salted and then dried. This meat is greatly esteemed both in peace and in war, and is eaten raw along with onions as they travel. It is true that in Crete and Chios the peasants are accustomed to dry a whole hare or ibex, or a sheep in pieces; it is first salted, then stretched out on a wooden frame and put in an oven to dry. I have frequently been in peasants' houses in the mountains of Crete and seen whole ibexes dried in this way, and also kids and lambs; but this method is not found in Turkey, for the Greeks do it during their fasts when they have killed a hare or a wild goat, desiring to preserve it for after Easter, for they are not in the habit of salting meat in salting-tubs, any more than in Turkey.

109

Journey over Mount Taurus

The Turks make various kinds of food for travelling about the country or in time of war, among them a kind of sausage which they call in the vulgar tongue *stopides*. They are made of walnuts strung together to the length of a sausage and then soaked in hot wine in the manner of those who make candles. They must be covered with must, little by little and not all at once, giving them a coating, which is repeated several times. Others add flour to thicken it more quickly. The same procedure can be used with figs, almonds, filberts and other hard fruits, which, made thicker by the application of hot wine, form something like a chitterling sausage. This kind of sausage is common in this country, and is a convenient form of food for travellers.

They make carpets at Adana, mostly by the application of heat, in the manner of hats and felts, so that properly speaking they are felts made in the form of carpets, which the Turks use to sleep on when they are travelling, for they are light and soft. Travellers going over Mount Taurus stock up with provisions for three days before leaving Adana, for it is three days' journey though barren country from Adana to Heraclea. Mounts cost 50 *meidins*, which is the equivalent of one ducat, and ten *meidins*. The men of this country wear caps shaped like a hippocras bag[390], the pointed end of which hangs over their shoulder, and since they are made of felt they can be easily used for straining jelly. Turks who are men of reputation living in towns and villages, like the rich, wear white turbans; but poor peasants wear the kind of caps that I have described. We saw this kind of cap all the way from Aleppo to Adana, but at Adana we saw others folded down in a different way. The inhabitants of the various provinces recognise one another by such signs, and also by their manners of dress.

110

Journey from Adana over Mount Taurus

From Adana our route lay between west and north. The plain continued until midday, and then we began to climb Mount Taurus. We camped and slept at the place where night overtook us, and since it was a calm night and was cold we cut down some small plane-trees, andrachnes, oleanders and strawberry-trees, and made a good fire with a dry carob-tree. On the following morning, long before daybreak, we set out to climb the mountain, which is a steep and difficult ascent. On the summit I saw juniper-trees growing as tall as cypresses, with sweet berries the size of a walnut, almost similar to a gall. The inhabitants of the country eat them, as I could see from the stones that I gathered along the roadside, thrown away by those who had eaten the berries. The stones are so hard that they can be broken only by heavy blows with a hammer. This, after the cedar, is the most singular tree to be seen on Mount Taurus; and it is evergreen. I also saw styrax trees and wild pines or spruces. It took us half a day to reach the top of the mountain, and when we were on the summit we found it covered with snow. Here I also observed a kind of savin juniper, of the species which Dioscorides described; or it may have been the thuya of Theophrastus and Homer. And since I had in previous years seen a tree at Fontainebleau in the king's garden which was called the tree of life, brought from Canada in the time of the late King Francis the first of that name, I examined this juniper on the mountain with great care and having described both trees in detail I found them very similar, but differing in

374

certain characteristics, which I shall describe when writing more particularly about plants. The planes grow on this mountain still taller than at Antioch, and are of such a nature that they lose their bark in winter, differing in this respect from the andrachne; for the andrachne loses its red bark in the greatest heat of summer and puts on an ash-coloured bark which is originally of a pale colour; but the plane loses its leaden-coloured bark in winter and takes on a grey bark. We also found tall cedars like those on Mount Lebanon, whose cones several of the company gathered, on my persuasion; they are very similar to the cones of fir-trees, but are larger and smoother, and point upwards. I do not wish now to spend time describing this tree, but instead I give here its portrait, to show what it is like.

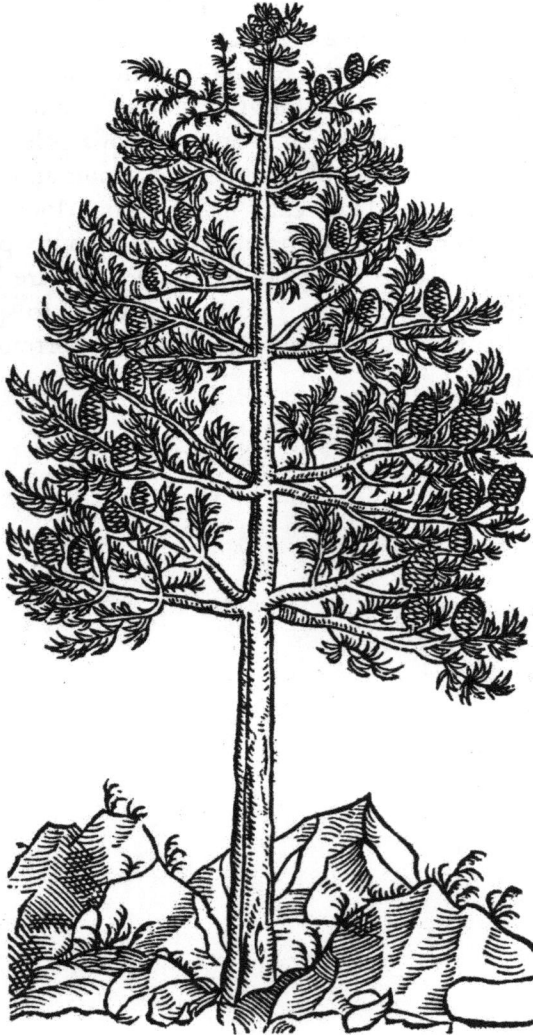

Figure: Portrait of the cedar

We travelled for a long time along the ridge of this mountain,
but we had not yet reached its highest point, for we had other

mountains both to right and to left of us. And when we came to a point below a castle situated on a crag above us we began gradually to descend. It was already late when we came to a caravanserai by the roadside situated at the foot of this high mountain. There are such great quantities of cedars on the summit of the mountain that we saw scarcely any other trees more common; and certainly there are no fir-trees, which the Latins call *abietes;* and yet they resemble cedars so closely that I could believe that they were cedars, or that the fir is a species of cedar. And so I have thought it well to give its portrait here, following that of the cedar.

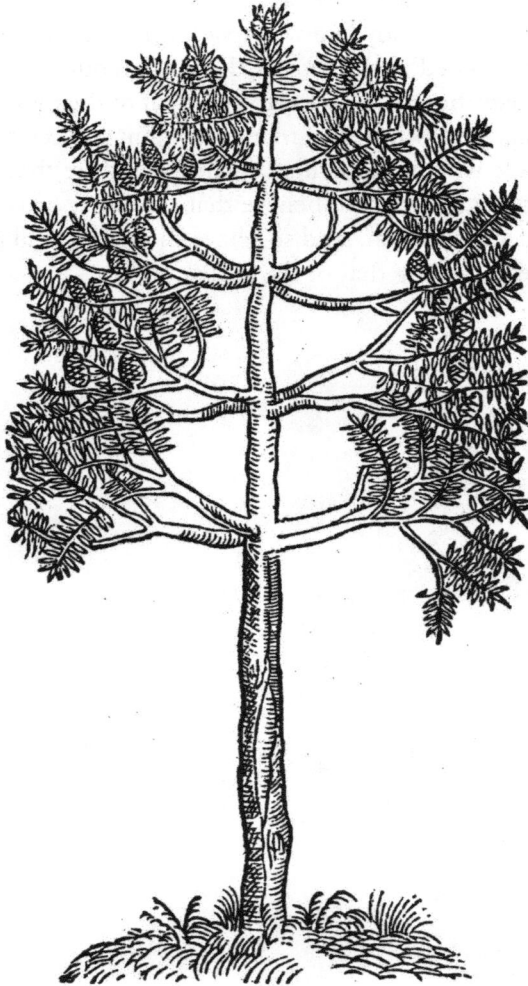

Figure: Portrait of the fir-tree

Other trees not found here are the larch, which the Latins call *larix, sapinus,* which the French call *suiffes,* and *alevo,* otherwise called pinaster. There is als0 an *alevo* at Fontainebleau, brought from Canada and presented to King Francis along with the tree of life.

111

Of natural hot baths that are on Mount Taurus, and of the town of Heraclea

That evening we came to a caravanserai near a natural hot bath. The bath is enclosed by brick walls similar to those of the saline bath at the ruins of Troy. The bath has a slight smell of sulphur, but its deposits of sulphur do not harden into stones as they do at Padua and Bursa. Next day we followed the stream which flows down from here into the plain. When we climbed to the top of a neighbouring mountain we found that no trees grew there. After travelling only a short way from the caravanserai we came into a region of arable land enclosed by hedges of a tree which Columella calls the white jujube-tree, with fruits resembling those of the red jujube-tree except in colour, which is sold in markets in towns. The Greeks call it in their vulgar tongue *ziziphia*, corrupted from the name of the jujube.

Travelling over the mountain until midday, we saw Heraclea clearly at a great distance, situated down in the plain. We continued downhill, passing several villages situated on the flanks of a mountain which protects them from the north winds and the mistral.

Here we found great quantity of absinth and *ambrosia*. The plain of Heraclea is very fertile and cultivated everywhere, and there are many villages; for the streams flowing down from the mountains water the soil of the gardens and orchards, in which they grow all kinds of fruits, like peaches, dogberries, plums, apples, pears, almonds, pomegranates, oranges and other such garden trees. There is a very large village near Heraclea which is inhabited only by Greek Christians speaking their vulgar tongue and is purely Greek; and there is another village of Armenian Christians. Both are highly diligent in cultivating their gardens. Their vines are very well tended; and since they have water at their command they grow all kinds of plants in their gardens, just as we do in ours.

We arrived at a very late hour in the town of Heraclea, which is the first town beyond Mount Taurus, situated just at the foot of the mountain, close to its roots. It is well known that there are several

Heracleas: I have already spoken of one situated on the shores of the Propontis, near Rodosto. And having said that Rodosto was anciently called Perinthus, I feel bound to mention here that some modern authors question whether Heraclea on the Propontis should be called Perinthus; but for myself I have resolved not to consider the matter, since it has been the least of my cares to restore the ancient names of towns which have changed them for modern ones. And so I leave the question whether Heraclea on the Propontis is Perinthus or Rodosto to any who may wish to consider it.

Here we found all kinds of provisions, bread, wine and meat. I was assured that on the plain of Heraclea there were stud farms producing more than 4000 horses a year, of which more than 600 are taken for the public services each year. Horses from here are much esteemed in Turkey, and are called Caramanian horses. The local people, having an abundance of sumac trees in the neighbouring mountains, gather their fruits, which we saw on sale in the market of Heraclea in large sackfuls. They use it to give a touch of sharpness to their food; after adding to it garlic beaten up with salt they sprinkle it on meat, whether stewed, boiled or roasted, which gives it a certain sharpness and an agreeable flavour. We stopped at Heraclea to allow our mounts to recover, and remained there for the whole of the following day. The plain of Heraclea is two days' journey across, and is inhabited only in the part which has abundance of water.

112

Journey from Heraclea to Cogne [Iconium], and of the goats that bear fine camlet wool

Having found mounts for going from Heraclea to Cogne, called in Latin *Iconium*, we set out on our way. The mounts cost one and a half ducats each. Here the plain was irrigated by water channels as at Damascus. Looking towards the foot of the mountains, we saw several villages at great distances from one another. The plant which the Greeks called *absinthium marinum* is abundant here; it is so called not because it grows near the sea, which is more than four days' journey away, but because our ancestors gave it this name, since it grows in some places on the Mediterranean. The country here is white with the smaller kind of sage and *polium*.

We crossed three wooden bridges, for there are many water channels and streams. A strong cold southerly wind now rose, which blew sand into our faces with great violence. We passed close to a round hill which seemed to have been made by human art, for it is high and surrounded by ditches full of water. Continuing on our way, we came into a very stony region, much like the country round Fontainebleau, but with no trees. We lodged in a caravanserai on the main road at a spring, and set out again before daybreak, coming into wide treeless plains. As we travelled we saw mountains at a great distance from us on either side, with no trees growing on them except on the summit. At the foot of the mountains we found only the absinth above-mentioned, called *seriphium marinum,* and the other Pontic kind, which differs in no respect from our garden plant, except that it is white.

The goats in this country have a wool so fine that it could be taken for the finest silk, and it surpasses snow in whiteness. These goats are not as large as our sheep; and they are not shorn like sheep, but their wool is torn off. Their flesh is as tender as mutton and has no gamy taste. All the finest camlets[391], whether watered or plain, of the greatest beauty, are made from the wool of these goats, which, or some similar kind, are mentioned by the Greek author Aelian, who says that the goats of the Caspian Sea are very white, without large horns, and that their wool is so soft that it can be compared with the finest Milesian wools[392], which are the most delicate and finest wools to be found anywhere. But Pliny, for his part, writes about another kind of goat: *Tondentur caprae quod magnis villis sunt, in magna parte Phrygiae, unde Cilicia fieri solent. Sed quod primum ea tonsura in Cilicia sit instituta, nomen id Cilicas adiecisse dicunt*[393].

It appears, therefore, that the goats are of different kinds. Those which produce camlet are tame, and are different from ours, for they are smaller and have short horns and wool whiter than snow, long, and finer than human hair. We found no plant commoner than *ambrosia,* so aromatic that we were intoxicated neither more nor less than if we had been in a cellar full of new wine. The inhabitants gather it and use it to heat themselves, since they have no other kind of wood. They also dry sheep dung, as do the people of Armor in Brittany. This plain of which I am speaking is very barren, for there are neither streams nor springs. We lodged at a fairly early hour in a large village called Sarameli[394], where I found that they had brooms made from the *ambrosia* plant. I took a handful of this and showed it in France as a great singularity, for it does not grow wild in Europe, at any rate so far as I have been able to discover.

113

Of the town of Iconium

On the following day we left Ismil and continued over the plain, which reached as far as Cogne, and lodged in a large caravanserai. The walls of Cogne are built of different kinds of stones, like those of Constantinople. It can easily be seen that the walls of Cogne are modern, for in them are pieces of marble from churches on which can be seen inscriptions in Greek, showing that the town was formerly occupied by Greek Christians. The crosses and remains to be seen here demonstrate this very clearly. The circuit of the walls is round, but the towers, few and far between, are square.

The town of Cogne, anciently called Iconium, lies quite close to high mountains, from which several streams flow down through the town. The part of the town facing the plain looks east. There is a marble figure of Hercules at the gate of the town which is between east and south, outside the walls beside a tower; but it has now no head, for the Turks knocked it off not long ago. Cogne, like Aleppo, has eight gates. It is inhabited by Greeks, Turks, Arabs and Armenians. The vines here are carefully cultivated, and so we found good wine, which was sold to us by the Jews. The finest buildings in Iconium are the mosques, the baths and the caravanserais.

The only wood that they burn here comes from the tall juniper, the second species of savin juniper, two dwarf cedars and the stems of ledon; but when I tried to distinguish them I was unable, despite all my diligence, to specify their individual characteristics, for they are all of the same colour and have the same smell and taste. None of the six are covered with hard bark like other woods, but have long strips covering them in layers, like vines, and the heart is red, surrounded by a white coating like the carob-tree and the yew; and when I burned them I found no difference in the smoke or in the ash, which in all of them is uniform as in the lime-tree and light as in the willow. All of them, except ledon, produce resin harder than that of the terebinth. Their wood is of the same hardness and splits in the same way when hewn. All of them ripen their fruit at the same time in winter and are green in all seasons.

114

Of the goldsmiths of Turkey

The Turks go to almost as much expense in the matter of gold jewellery as we do, and what they make is of very fine quality. They are fond of wearing rings, and like to have well fashioned knives, which they hang from their belts on a silver chain, in sheaths enriched by fine inlays of gold or silver. It is a common custom among both the Turks and the Greeks to have a knife hanging at their belt; they are usually forged in Hungary, with a very long shaft, and when the haberdashers of Turkey buy them they give them to craftsmen to put on a handle, which is commonly of rohart[395], of which there are two kinds. One is compact, straight and white, resembling the horn of a unicorn, and is so hard that steel cannot cut it, unless it has been well tempered. The other is curved like a boar's tusk, which I should have taken for the tooth of a hippopotamus, were it not that I have seen living hippopotamuses which had no such teeth.

They also give the knives handles of Indian tortoiseshell, which are gold-coloured and transparent; and a handle for a knife of this kind costs about a ducat. The goldsmiths squat on the ground at their work. Their furnace is on the ground in the middle of their workshop, without a chimney, and they use a single round bellows which they raise and lower when they want to blow up the fire.

We stayed in Cogne for two days to rest our horses and obtain supplies of provisions, and also because it was the Christmas feast. After we had rested and dined we set out again, making for the mountain which we had to cross. It began to snow, covering the ground and causing our guides to lose their way. When we reached the top of the mountain we travelled for a long time through forests of spruces and came to a village, where we lodged in a caravanserai. The following day was a difficult one for us because of the weather, and also because we had now to climb and now to descend. This country is well populated, and there are many villages. And although it was winter we found oxygal, which is a food common in Turkey, mainly in summer. They keep it ready prepared in large dishes which they sell in the shops at the price of one asper, and this is sufficient to satisfy four Turks. We had not travelled far that day when we emerged from the mountains and came into the plain of Pamphylia, in the region called Caramania, which takes in both Cilicia and Pamphylia. There are seven sanjakates in its territory. We travelled through groves of very beautiful small fruit-trees. We passed the town of Angouri, anciently called Encyra[396], on our right. It is now the most renowned town in all this country for its busy trade in camlets. For there is no town where so much camlet is made as here, more particularly because the goats which produce the fine wool from which they are made are found only in this part of Pamphylia.

115

Of the town of Achara

The towns of Turkey are not usually walled, and neither is Achara [Akhisar], which is a town in Lesser Armenia. Here we saw stones inscribed in Latin letters which formerly served as sepulchres but are now used as troughs under fountains for watering travellers' horses.

We lodged in the caravanserai. The town lies near a wide and spacious lake, which we skirted for a long time. I was told that several kinds of fish are caught in this lake, among others tench, pike, carp and bream. In this account I have measured the length of a journey in days of travel, since the Turks do not count in miles, as in Italy, or in leagues, as in France. We left Achara and continued over the plain, where we saw villages situated on the slopes of the hill, both to right and to left. We dined in a small village in which

384

we found a sufficiency of provisions. In the evening we lodged in another town called Carachara [Afyon Karahisar], that is, Black Castle. where this journey ended for the present.

Since I stayed there and spent the winter and much of the spring in the surrounding area, I had leisure to observe many things concerning the manners and way of life of the Turks. [A man who knows some trade is always better received by the Turks than another who does not. That is why some of the slaves taken by the Turks in war are freed from servitude sooner than others. Those who know a trade can quickly earn money to pay their ransom, while others who do not are forced to carry out mechanical tasks, for those in whose service they have to remain make them till the ground and guard their flocks. Most of the janissaries, too, have some particular skills, for, living in seraglios in their youth, they are taught some trade. In short, since knowledge of a trade can provide a living for persons of servile condition, it serves no purpose in this country to declare yourself a nobleman.

There are many tradesmen who sell only fresh-baked bread to be eaten along with must. But since there is some difficulty about the manner of their ovens I will explain what they are like. They have large earthenware vessels like the vats in which we wash clothes, which are half-buried in the floor of their bakeries. There is a hole in the bottom of the vat, connected with which is a round earthenware pipe; and the vat being set almost on its side, with the pipe close by, the wood or charcoal which is put under the vat lights easily and heats it on all sides. When the dough has risen the baker makes it into thin pancakes, which he puts on a wicker tray like the top of a basket, the size of a man's cap, and, holding the tray, lays them on the upper surface of the vat, where they hang down and are baked. When the baker lays one on to bake he takes off another which is already baked, for there are several thus lying on top of the vessel. To take them off he has a small fork in the shape of a hook to pick them off with his left hand, so that he can detach the bread and let it fall on to a long spatula held in his right hand. The baker must not, therefore, have too long a beard, for it might get singed by the flame which bakes the bread. The inhabitants send to buy the bread and eat it hot along with must, which to them is a great delicacy.

This is more popular in winter than in summer, when there are fruits and other things to eat. But since I shall have more to say about this in the third book, below, I shall say no more for the present.][397]

But before discussing such matters further I propose to give some account of the laws handed down by Mahomet, almost by way of parenthesis, in order to show more clearly how the barbarity and folly of this false prophet has led astray all this poor ignorant people to follow his law, which is a truly fantastic dream. And so I will end this second

The Third Book

of observations of many singularities and memorable things in divers countries in Turkey

To the reader.

Since I have found a fresh occasion, in writing this third book, to treat of the singularities of the manner of life of people in Turkey, as I observed them during my residence in Asia at its very heart, I have thought it fit, before anything else, after speaking and making particular discourse of the way of life of the various countries through which I travelled, to say a few words about the fantastic things that the false prophet Mahomet left them in his Alcoran. Although I do not give the date of the days, months and years in this work, like many others who have described their travels, anyone who desires to know it has only to read the preface to the first book, and there he will see the dates set out at length. I have already shown by the testimony of men of sufficient authority and knowledge that I have no lack of witnesses to approve my account of the travels which are mentioned here.

1

Particular discourse on the beginning and origin of the laws of the Turks

I had leisure to observe many things concerning the manner of life of the Turks, particularly when I was in Paphlagonia[398], where I stayed for some considerable space of time. Accordingly I have decided to include here a short account of Mahomet (such as no one has yet written in our language) before writing anything else, so that it will be easier for me thereafter to explain why the Mahometans have adopted such a manner of life. It was not so long ago that Mahomet was born in a town in Happy Arabia called Mecca and founded the sect of the Turks, in the year 620 after the birth of Our Lord, and died in the year 683[399]. The Turks have a book called

Asear [Sira] containing the whole of Mahomet's life, which they hold and observe as we do the Gospels. Included in this book is all that he did from his birth until his death; and it tells us that his father was called Abdola Motalip and his mother Imina, both of them idolaters. It relates that Abdola died before Mahomet was born, and that his mother Imina died two years after he was born, so that he was orphaned of both father and mother[400]. It also says that Mahomet was of the lineage of Ishmael, the son of Abraham, who had two sons, one to Sarah called Isaac and the other, Ishmael, to Hagar; and that Ishmael built the temple in Mecca, which was the first (so it says) built by men in the world. It also says that when Mahomet was four he went fishing with other small boys, and that when he was all by himself in a field the angel Gabriel, clad in garments as white as snow, appeared to him in the form of a man, took him apart behind a hill, opened his breast with a sharp razor, drew out his heart and took out of it a black drop, in which the Turks say that the devils tempt men, and which all men commonly have; and that the angel put his heart back in its place and thus cleansed his breast, so that thereafter he could never be tempted by the devil. Such is the tale told in the book Asear about Mahomet's early years.

The book Asear also says that at the age of sixteen Mahomet frequently travelled to Persia, Cairo and Syria with a rich merchant named Gadisa, the husband of his cousin german, whom he took in marriage after Gadisa's death. She was his first wife[401], by whom he had four children, three daughters and a son. Having taken over Gadisa's business, he traded in goods until he was 38, and then withdrew to a solitary life in a desert place, going every day to hide in a cave at no great distance from Mecca, in which he remained until night, practising such strict abstinence that he became weak. It also says that as a result he lost his understanding and began to have dreams and visions and hear voices when there was no one there, all of which he recounted each night to his wife; but she said to him that these were temptations of the devil, at which he fell into such a frenzy that he thought that he would become mad, and one day contemplated throwing himself down from the top of a mountain.

When Mahomet began his Alcoran he feigned that the angel

Gabriel had dissuaded him from his intention, saying that the angel had appeared to him in human form, with white wings, saying to him, "Rejoice, Mahomet, God sends thee greetings, for thou art to be his prophet. Thou art the most perfect of all his creatures". He also said that the angel showed him some letters, telling him to read them. When Mahomet said that he could not read the angel replied, "Mahomet, read the name of thy creator", and then disappeared and went away[402].

The Asear also writes that Mahomet returned to his house filled with joy, and that the trees, stones and animals which he encountered on his way did him honour and greeted him, saying, "Mahomet, thou wilt be the messenger of God". All which things he recounted to his wife; but she would not believe him, saying that it was a temptation of the devil, at which Mahomet was much afflicted, to the point of falling ill. The Asear also says that the angel then appeared again to Mahomet as he was lying in bed, bringing him the second chapter of the Alcoran, in which it was written, "Arise, magnify thy creator, cleanse thy garments and hold idols in horror"; and then Mahomet called his wife and recited to her what he had dreamed, but she said that it was no more than a vision and a temptation like the previous ones. At which Mahomet was much angered, and became more ill than he had been before; but he says that the angel returned to him at midnight, bringing him the third chapter of the Alcoran written down; whereupon Mahomet returned to health. His wife said that she would have liked to see the angel, but Mohammed replied that that would not be possible.

2

Of the devices used by Mahomet at the beginning in seducing the ignorant populace to attract them to his law, and of those who aided him

While Mahomet was preparing to establish a new sect he at first had good fortune; for he encountered two Christians in Mecca who had the books of the Old and the New Testament and knew something about them, and helped him greatly in making his Alcoran. And having had dealings with many nations in Syria, Judaea and Egypt, he was of shrewd understanding; and after he had caused some chapters to be written down (which he said had been sent to him by the angel Gabriel to be put into his Alcoran) he had them transcribed and gave them secretly to certain men in Mecca so that they could learn them by heart; for at the beginning he did not dare to communicate them to anyone except secretly.

After a relative of his, a powerful lord in Mecca named Homar, and another called Ubecar[403], with several of their relatives, had resolved to remain no longer hidden, they decided to declare the Alcoran in public. Then great numbers of people in Mecca were determined to kill Mahomet, but when they found that many people believed him to be a demoniac they were content to leave him in his folly. But soon afterwards they met together again and decided to put him in prison. Mahomet, being warned of this, fled immediately from Mecca and went to another town called Almedine[404], which is two days' journey from Mecca, and persuaded the men of his party to put a handful of ashes on the heads of their horses, and scatter another handful in the air, and tie the reins of their horses, and repeat a verse from the 18th chapter of the third book of the Alcoran, saying that thus they would make themselves invisible to anyone pursuing them. The whole story of his flight is written down in the Alcoran in the second chapter of the first book. And after he had stayed for some time in Almedine he recruited his strength with men who joined his party, made the Jews tributary to him, and then returned to Mecca with a great army and made himself master of the town, which he subjugated by force of arms[405].

3

That the whole faith of the Turks is contained in the Alcoran made by Mahomet

All the superstitions and ceremonies of the Turks come from the teachings of the Alcoran. And the term Alcoran means nothing more than a collection of chapters or assemblage of psalms. It is also called by the other name Alforcan. This Alcoran is all written in rhythm, ending in the consonance of verses; and it is so strictly preserved that if any Turk alters a single letter, or changes the style or an accent, the law prescribes that he shall be stoned to death within the hour. The Alcoran was not in the same order in the time of Mahomet as it is today; but after his death a son-in-law of his called Osmen[406], who was the third king after him, took his writings as he had made them during his life, which were kept in a chest, and put them into order, arranging them in chapters with titles, of which he made four books. The first book contains five chapters, the second 12, the third 19 and the fourth 65. All these chapters of the Alcoran have their own names and are numbered, to a total of 211. All Turks[407] hold the Alcoran in such great reverence that they kiss it and embrace it, and swear by it as if by God. And they call it the glorious book.

The Alcoran contains in their entirety all the laws that Mahomet gave to the Turks, both about what they have to believe and to do, and what they have to look forward to in the other world for good men and bad men, and also about the things that are prohibited to them in matters of eating and drinking. In doing so Mahomet stole part of the New Testament and part of the Old Testament, as appears from what he writes on the creation of the world; for he relates how Adam and Eve sinned, and left Paradise, and came down to earth, and how the angels sinned, and what was the cause of their sinning.

He tells also how God sent Moses to lead the Jews out of their captivity under Pharaoh, and how the Jews received the Law, and the things that happened to them on leaving Egypt, and how they adored the calf, and the manner in which they crossed the

Red Sea, in which Pharaoh was drowned, and how they sinned in counterfeiting false gods. He also treats of the New Testament and of Our Lord and Our Lady, and of the mystery of the nativity, life and miracles of Our Lord, and of the Gospels, and of the law which he gave. Mahomet says in the first chapter of the first book, and in several other places, things about Our Lord, as for example: we, God (he says), gave writing to Jesus Christ, and helped him with the Holy Ghost.

And in the first chapter of the second book he also says that God granted the Alcoran to Mahomet and the Testament and the Gospels to Jesus Christ, to be the law for many men; and in the second chapter of the first book he treats at length of the conception of the Virgin Mary, where he gives almost the whole story of the visitation by Elizabeth. The glossators of the Alcoran say on this passage that Jesus Christ and his mother were alone exempt from temptation by the devil, and agree that Our Lady was without original sin. He makes particular mention of the nativity of Our Lord in the first chapter of the third book, and of the angelic greeting and the mystery of the Annunciation.

He mentions three excellences of Our Lord in his Alcoran. The first, in the second chapter of the first book, is that Jesus Christ ascended to heaven in body and in soul. The second is that he calls him the word of God. The third is that he calls him the spirit of God, as appears from the third chapter of the first book. The Alcoran never attributes these excellences to anyone else, neither to Moses, nor to David, nor to Abraham, nor to Mahomet himself. He also writes in the second chapter of the fourth book that Jesus Christ knew the secrets of human hearts, and brought the dead back to life, healed men suffering from incurable maladies, gave sight to the blind and enabled the dumb to speak. He says also that his disciples performed miracles which were beyond nature. But the Turks, holding to their false creed, credit such things to the praise of their Mahomet and not to that of Our Lord.

4

Of various sects that have arisen among the Mahometans in the matter of their religion

The Turks, in addition to the Alcoran, observe the commandments of another book which they call the Zuna[408] of Mahomet, meaning the way or law, that is to say, to follow the counsel of Mahomet. This book was written by his disciples after his death. Thereafter it came into various hands, some adding to it and others taking things out, as seemed good to them, so that there is now great confusion and contrariety between the two books, what Mahomet said affirmatively being now stated negatively; and there arose such division within his sect that the alcaliph[409], that is, the king ruling in that generation, commanded that wherever there were to be found men learned in the Alcoran, who are called alfaquis, they should be sent to the city of Damascus to hold a council, and to bring all writings that they could find.

Then the alcaliph, of the two hundred who had come, chose six alfaquis, that is, learned men; and of the six the first to be chosen was one Muszlin, the second Bochari, the third Buborayra, the fourth Annecey, the fifth Atermindi and the sixth Dent. He then had them go into a room in which were all the books that had been brought from all parts of the country. Each of them composed a book selected from the writings of others and presented his book to the alcaliph, who gave it to the other learned men to examine, and commanded that all the other books should be drowned in the river at Damascus which is called in Latin Chrysorrhoas and in Arabic Adegele, so that of two hundred camels' loads there remained only the six books called the Zuna. All the rest were thrown into the river; and the king commanded all the alfaquis, that is to say, theologians of Mahomet, that they should not dare to cite any authority of Mahomet but what was contained in the six books of the Zuna. And later there was a learned theologian of Mahomet who took the six books of the Zuna, gathering all the passages, and made them into a book which is called the book of flowers.

The Turks hold the books of the Zuna to have the same authority as the Alcoran; for which reason they regard the above-mentioned alcaliph as a holy man. And although so many doctors of their theology had brought together in six books what was written in such a great number of others, nevertheless since there were still great contrarieties there arose many schisms among them. So it came about later that they were divided into four opinions, and the Persians are now still in disagreement with the Turks[410], each calling the others heretics. And were it not that the power of the Turk has much unified them by his conquests over the Soldan of Babylon[411], and that Syria, Egypt and Mesopotamia are tributary to him, there would be diverse opinions among the nations, because they are of different languages. The Turks believe that the Alcoran was made in a single night and the others say in a month, which has given great authority to the Alcoran. But their belief is false, for Mahomet himself confesses that he stayed for thirteen years in Almedine while making it, and ten years in Mecca[412]. And this the chapters show quite clearly, some being called Medenia and others Mechia.

5

Of the fear of the torments of hell with which Mahomet affrighted the Turks, and of their burials

When the Turks bury someone, after washing the body and wrapping it in a shroud, they do not sew up either the head or the foot of the shroud, following the commandment of Mahomet, who says that after the dead man is laid in his tomb there come two black angels called in Arabic Mongir and Guanequir[413], one carrying an iron mallet and the other an iron hook, who cause the dead man to rise and kneel and then replace his soul in his body, in the same way (says the Alcoran) as a man puts on his shift; and then the two angels interrogate the dead man, asking if he believed in Mahomet, and if he observed his law, and if he did charitable works in this world when he was alive, and if he fasted during the fast of the Turks which is called Ramadan, and if he performed the ceremonies of the Zala, and if he paid the tithe and gave alms[414].

If the dead man gives a good account of himself to the black angels, they will leave him and go away; but immediately there will appear two other angels as white as snow, one of whom will support the dead man's head with his two arms to serve as a pillow, while the other will stand at his feet, and they will guard him and keep him company until the day of judgment. But if the dead man gives a bad account of his life to the black angels, that is, if he did not believe in Mahomet, and other things as mentioned above, the book of the Zuna says that the black angel with the iron mallet will give him such a heavy blow on the head that the dead man will be driven five ells down into the earth, while the other black angel will continually torment him with his iron hooks, and the first angel will continually beat him with his mallet, and will continue this torment until the day of judgment. Accordingly the Turks write the dead man's name in saffron on his body, and leave enough room in his tomb for him to rise and kneel; and there are some who roof the tomb with planks, lest it should be filled up with earth. These things have so affrighted the Turks that in the morning when they perform their prayers they say in their language: Lord God, deliver me from the interrogation of the two angels, and from the torments of the tomb, and from the wrong way, Amen. The object of the prayers for the dead which are said by Turkish men and women over graves in the cemeteries is to deliver them from the interrogation of the two black angels.

6

Of many very strange things that Mahomet wrote about the Judgment

Mahomet, having translated his Alcoran from a number of passages in the Bible, included something about the creation of the world and the story of Adam, whom he says God made with his hand from pure earth and gave him the breath of life, but that because of Adam's sin all his descendants were doomed to die. As regards the day of Judgment, he says that when the end of the world is near a horn will sound, and that all men on earth and the angels in heaven will die, and then the horn will sound again, and at its sound both men and angels will rise again.

He also says in the fifth chapter of the first book that all the animals on earth and birds in the sky will rise again on the day of Judgment. The book of the Zuna says that the sheep killed on the day of the Turks' Easter, which they call Bairan[415], will enter Paradise on the day of Judgment, and that the sheep which Abraham sacrificed in place of his son Isaac had been fed in Paradise for the space of forty years, and that the angel Gabriel had carried it, and that the sheep was black. That is why the Turks kill several sheep as sacrifices on the day of their Easter, although they are not obliged to kill more than one; for the book of the Zuna says that all the sheep killed by the Turks as sacrifices on the day of their Easter will pray on the day of Judgment for those who were the cause of their being sacrificed.

The Alcoran says in the first chapter of the first book that there are two angels in a cave in Babylon, as judges of the men of Babylon, who are hanging by their eyebrows and will be thus tormented until the day of Judgment. The gloss on this passage says that God sent two angels to Babylon to be judges of the men of the city, who came down from heaven every morning and returned in the evening, and that one day it came about that they saw a very beautiful woman complaining about her husband; but she was so pleasing in their eyes that they begged her to grant them her favours, which she agreed to do if they would teach her the prayer which gave them the power to mount to heaven. This they agreed very willingly to do, and they taught her the prayer. But immediately she had learned it she went up to heaven, and the angels, because of the sin that they had committed, lost the virtue of the prayer, so that being unable to mount to heaven they remained on earth. Then God called on them to choose whether their punishment should be in this world or in the other; and when they chose punishment in this world he condemned them to be hung by their eyebrows until the day of Judgment.

The Alcoran also says that the two angels taught the art of necromancy every day to the men of that country. And in the 19th chapter of the third book the Alcoran says that God set the stars in the sky for the beauty of this world and to keep watch on every malignant devil, and that to drive him away when he seeks to listen to the secrets of Paradise each star pursues him with a flaming brand. The book of the Zuna says that the stars are held hanging in the air on golden chains, and that they are there to keep watch, for otherwise the devils would come to listen to the secrets of Paradise and reveal them to divine men.

7

The pleasant journey that Mahomet feigned to have made to Paradise one night while sleeping, and of the great follies that he relates about the paradise of the Turks

Mahomet, dreaming one night while he slept, had a vision which he recited on the following day and wrote down. In this he did great benefit to all his successors, in respect that the spoils of war were assigned to them. It is one of the articles which he said God granted to him when speaking with him. He had been lying that night with one of his eleven wives called Axa, whom he loved above all the rest[416], and when he awoke at midnight, thinking that someone had knocked at the door, he says that he got up to open it and found the angel Gabriel, carrying seventy pairs of wings as white as snow and as brilliant as crystal; and he had an animal with him, as white as milk, larger than an ass and smaller than a mule, which was called in Arabic Alborach[417]. It is written in the book called Asear that the angel Gabriel embraced Mahomet, and while embracing him said: O Mahomet, God has sent me to greet thee, and has commanded me to take thee this night with me to Paradise, to see the greatest secrets that ever son of man has seen. Mahomet said that he was content to do this. And the angel said to Mahomet: Mount, then, on Alborach, and let us go. But Alborach drew back, and the angel said to him: Why dost thou not want Mahomet to mount thee? I assure thee that never better man has mounted thee, or will mount thee, than Mahomet. But Alborach replied that he would not let him mount unless Mahomet first promised to take him into Paradise with him. Then Mahomet replied to Alborach that he would be the first animal to enter Paradise. And at once Mahomet mounted, and the angel took the reins, and they travelled all night to Jerusalem.
The book of Asear says that on the way Mahomet heard a

woman's voice saying: O Mahomet, Mahomet; and the angel said to him: Why do you not reply to this voice. Mahomet made no reply. And as they continued on their way he heard another voice saying: O Mahomet, Mahomet. And the angel told him not to make any reply. And when they were a little farther on Mahomet asked the angel who had been calling him, and what women these were. To which Gabriel replied that the first woman who had cried to him was the one who divulges the law of the Jews, and that if he had replied to that voice all the Turks would have become Jews, and that the second woman was the one who publishes the law of the Christians, and that if he had replied to her all the Turks would have become Christians.

Soon afterwards they arrived at the temple in Jerusalem, which Mahomet and Gabriel entered, and found all the prophets and messengers who have come to this world; who came to meet him at the door of the temple, receiving and greeting him in this manner: God keep you, O joy of the true messengers, honourable prophet. And then they carried him through the air in great solemnity into the great chapel, and begged that he would say a prayer for all of them, recommending themselves to him, and that he would remember them when he was speaking to God. It says also that when Mahomet left the temple he found a ladder made of the light of God which reached up to heaven. Gabriel took him by the hand, and when they came to the first heaven, which was made of fine silver, with stars hanging from chains of fine gold, which are as large as the mountain called Noho near the town of Almedine, Gabriel knocked at the door.

The doorkeeper asked who they were, and Gabriel replied: I am the angel Gabriel, and with me is Mahomet, the prophet and friend of God. And immediately the doorkeeper heard Mahomet's name he opened the door of the first heaven, in which they found a hoary old man, who was Adam, who embraced Mahomet, thanking God for giving him such a son, and recommended himself to Mahomet.

Passing on their way, they found angels in various forms, like oxen, men, horses and birds (among them a cock which had its feet in the first heaven and its head in the second), and Mahomet asked the angel what these things meant; and the angel replied that the angels prayed to God for their fellows on earth, and that those who had the form of men prayed for men, and those who had the form of oxen prayed for oxen, and similarly with the others. Those who were in the form of cocks prayed for cocks, and when this great cock crowed all the other cocks on earth and in heaven crowed. Then, coming to the second heaven of fine gold, they knocked at the door. The doorkeeper asked who was there, and Gabriel replied: It is I and Mahomet. Then they entered, and found everywhere the name of God and that of Mahomet, written in this fashion: There is no God but God, and Mahomet is his prophet. And they found Noah, a hoary old man, who embraced Mahomet and recommended himself to him. Then they found many angels of marvellous form, one of whom had his feet in the second heaven and his head in the third, and one hand in the east and the other in the west.

From there they mounted to the third heaven, made of precious stones, in which they found Abraham and a great number of angels, one of whom had eyes seventy thousand days' journeys apart and held a book in his hands in which he was writing and effacing all things, and was called the angel of death, writing down the names of those who are born and effacing the names of those who die.

From there they mounted to the fourth heaven, made of fine emerald, where they found Joseph, son of Jacob, who greeted Mahomet and recommended himself to him. There were also great numbers of angels, one of whom was weeping sorely; but it was for the men who because of their sins were going to hell.

From there they mounted to the fifth heaven, made of fine diamond, where they found Moses, who recommended himself to Mahomet, and still greater numbers of angels than in the other heavens. And from there they mounted to the sixth heaven, made of a carbuncle[418], in which was Saint John the Baptist, who recommended himself to Mahomet. From there they went to the seventh heaven, which was made of the light of God, where they found Jesus Christ, and Mahomet recommended himself to him. Here too they found great numbers of angels.

The angel now took leave of Mahomet. He began to mount through difficult country, where he found so much water and so much snow, and became so weary that he could go no farther. Then he heard a voice from heaven, saying: O Mahomet, greet thy creator; thou art very near to him. Then he saw such a great light that it troubled his sight. He says that God had on his face seventy thousand veils of the light of God, and that he was no farther from him than two arbalest shots. And Mahomet says that God put his hand on his shadow, which made him feel very cold. He says that God spoke to him in this place, and gave him many commandments of the Law, and revealed many secrets to him. And the book of Asear says that God gave him five things which he had never given any man.

The first, that Mahomet is the most exalted creature that ever was either in heaven or on earth. The second, that he is the most excellent and most honourable nobleman of all the sons of Adam on the day of Judgment. The third thing, that he is the general redeemer, that is, the pardoner of sins. The fourth is that he knows all languages. The fifth is that the spoils of battles and wars are to be delivered to him. The book of Asear then says that he now began to descend on the way that he had mounted, and that he related to the angel Gabriel all that had happened, and the angel said to him: O Mahomet, God had commanded me to bring you to this place so that you could be shown all his secrets. But now let us go to hell, so as to see the secrets to be seen there, how men are tormented by devils. Mahomet wrote all the above-mentioned things in his Alcoran, which show how little understanding he had. In describing the paradise which he promises to his Turks Mahomet mentions five things. The first is that there are houses. The second is that there are household goods. The third is that there are victuals for eating and drinking. The fourth is that there are garments. The fifth is that there are beautiful women to pleasure them[419]. Then he says that hell has seven gates[420], and that the devils are of different kinds. Some are chained with iron chains, others spitted on iron spits; and there are men who are forced to drink molten lead continuously and eat rotting meat and apples from a tree which is the true source of devils. All of which things I have written down to show that Mahomet was a man of little judgment to write such nonsense.

8

How it comes about that Mahomet's law allows Turks to enjoy the company of female slaves, without regarding of what religion they are

Nowadays Turks have converse indifferently with female slaves, having no regard for whether they are Jewesses or Christians or idolaters. This was granted to them by the law in Mahomet's lifetime. For it came about that although Mahomet had several wives believing in his law the king of the Jacobites made him a present of a very beautiful slave, a Jewish virgin, of whom Mahomet became greatly enamoured, and could not rest until he had known her. But his wives, becoming aware of this, could not bear it with patience, and told him that if he continued they would leave him. But Mahomet, being unable to contain himself, was greatly troubled, for two of his wives left him and spread the story throughout the town of Mecca.

Mahomet, who was a vigilant and careful man, thought how to remedy the matter by some device. Then he composed a chapter of his Alcoran making a new law for his followers under which it was permitted to all men of his faith to have converse, as he did, with their female slaves as with their wives: which law he put at the beginning of the chapter in the fourth book of his Alcoran which is still called the chapter of the Prohibition, the words of which are as follows: O Prophet, since thou soughtest to prohibit that which was permitted to thee to please thy wives, know that God hath permitted thee to allow men to have converse lawfully with slaves. The Prophet had committed the secret of this law to some of his wives, who published it everywhere. Notwithstanding this, you wives, if you repent to God, will find great comfort. But if you remain repudiated by Mahomet his creator will give him other wives than you, both virgins and widows, believing in his law, who will be devoted to him.

When the men of Mecca read this chapter they were well content with this law, and were grateful to Mahomet for it. Then the relatives of the wives who had left Mahomet came to beg him to take them back: at which he was greatly rejoiced, for he desired nothing better, although he feigned not to want to take them back. And from that time Turkish women have lived without jealousy with female slaves. It must be understood that a Turk can have a hundred of them if he wishes, but he may not have more than four married wives at the same time.

9

Brief account of the feigned paradise which Mahomet promised to the Turks, and of the fantastic things that he relates

Mahomet, speaking of the matter of which heaven is made, says that God created it from smoke, and that he established the firmament on the tip of an ox's horn, and that an earthquake is caused when the ox is troubled and trembles or moves, so that, having the whole of the earth on its horn, it causes it to quake.

The Turks now believe a thousand follies that Mahomet told them. Among other things they believe that there are seven paradises of gold and silver, enriched with pearls and precious stones, in which Mahomet says that there are palaces finer than those built on earth, and great rooms and halls, and gardens planted with fruit-trees, of two or three sorts in each kind, and that fountains and beautiful rivers flow by the palaces, some flowing with milk, others with excellent honey and others with sweet wine; and in the middle of the paradise is a great tree, which extends over the whole paradise, the leaves of which are of gold and silver, and the branches hang down to just above the walls, and that on each leaf the name of Mahomet is written along with that of God. It is from this passage that the Turks have taken the most singular of their prayers, which they say when on a journey, in these words: *Le illehe ille allach Mahomet razolollah*[421]. And if a Christian man pronounced these words he would have to die, or become a Turk.

They also believe, according to the teaching of the Alcoran, that in paradise Turks will live laughing and taking pleasure, without cares or sadness, being always joyful and content, sitting on carpets and curtained beds and sheets of brocaded satin, scarlet and silk; and the saddles and trappings of their horses will be of precious stones, and they will be served by pages as handsome as precious stones set in fine gold, clad in liveries of silk and green scarlet and satin laced with gold, who will serve the Turks with cups and goblets of gold and silver.

And after the Turks have eaten and drunk their fill in this paradise the pages, decked in their jewels and precious stones, with rings on their arms, hands, legs and ears, will come to them, each bearing a fine golden dish with a lemon or citron on it, which the Turks will take to smell and taste; and when each Turk raises it to his nose there will immediately emerge from it a beautiful virgin, splendidly garbed and bejewelled, who will embrace the Turk, and the Turk will embrace her, and they will remain thus embracing one another for fifty years, without rising or separating, taking together all the pleasure that a man can have with a woman. And after fifty years God will say to them: O my servants, since you have made great cheer in my paradise, I will show you my face. Then he will take off the veil on his face, and the Turks will fall to the ground, dazzled by the light that comes from him, and God will say to them: Rise, my servants, and enjoy my glory, for now you will never die or suffer any sadness or displeasure. And, raising their heads, they will see God face to face; and then each one will take his virgin and conduct her to his chamber in the palace, where they will find food and drink; and, making great cheer and taking pleasure with his virgin, he will pass his time joyously with no fear of dying.

This is what Mahomet has written about his paradise, with many other such follies, and it seems to me that the origin of the seraglios of the Turks comes from what Mahomet has said about the pages and virgins of paradise; for he says that these chaste virgins were created by God in paradise, and are well guarded and enclosed within walls. And Mahomet says that if one of them left the seraglio in paradise at midnight she would give light to all the world, as does the sun, and that if one of them spat in the sea the water would become as sweet as honey.

Before finishing with the paradise of the Turks I want to tell the fable of the banquet related by Mahomet which God gave to sainted Turks. In the first place Mahomet says that God commanded Gabriel to fetch the keys for opening paradise, and that the angel who kept them had seventy thousand of them, and that each key was 7000 leagues long. The angel Gabriel, finding himself unable to lift such a heavy key, told God, who said to him: Invoke my name, and that of Mahomet, who is my friend. And Gabriel, having invoked these names, carried the key on his shoulders and opened paradise, where he found a table of diamond seven hundred thousand days' journeys long and wide, surrounded by stools and chairs of gold and silver. He also says that the Turks who come to this banquet will find the tablecloth laid and napkins of satin embroidered with gold thread. Each Turk will have his own seat, on which he will sit, and that the pages will serve at the banquet, giving the Turks various kinds of viands and fruit to eat and wine and water from the rivers of paradise to drink. And at the end of the meal each page will bring the citron or large lemon of which I have spoken above. Mahomet also promised to give a banquet after God had given his. There is a fountain in paradise (he says) whose water is whiter than snow and sweeter than honey, which is seventy thousand days' journeys long and wide, where there are more glasses and cups to drink from than there are stars in the sky. This was given by God to Mahomet so that all Turks might come there too, and Mahomet will offer them water to drink, and those who drink it will never more be thirsty. And Mahomet will leave paradise and go down to hell and select all the good Turks there who have deserved punishment and bring about their redemption. He will take them to the fountain, and since, coming from hell, they will be black and burned, he himself will wash their bodies in his fountain and they will become as white as snow; and then he will take them to the paradise of the other Turks. Preachers in Turkey also say that Mahomet will transform himself into a sheep and have the Turks turned into fleas; and, leaving hell to take them into paradise, he will go in, so that the fleas may fall of there and take the form of the other Turks.

10

Of marriage among the Turks, and how it comes about that they are
permitted to have four wives

The Turks of today and those who follow the law of Mahomet cannot have more than four wives. This is not a new institution, for during Mahomet's lifetime he allowed those who followed his law to take four wives; but he also made a law for himself allowing him to marry as many women as he pleased.

It is said in the book of Asear that he had fifteen wives, not counting a great number of female slaves whom he had as well, and that he had eleven at the same time. He made a law which is still observed, that there should be equality between all women, so that they should all be treated the same, both in clothing, in eating and drinking and in sleeping. And if this is not done the wife concerned can appeal to the judge and take her husband to court. I find that for this reason it is still the case that the daughter of the Grand Turk or of a Basha will have no greater rights in this matter than the daughter of the poorest man in all Turkey. Accordingly a Turk can get rid of his wife on the slightest pretext; for if one of his wives complains to the cadi[422], and if he wants to leave her, the marriage is dissolved on the spot. Mahomet also made a law during his lifetime, that no other man might marry any wife whom he might repudiate. In this country repudiating a wife is almost as common as dismissing a chambermaid in France. Mahomet desired also that after his death his wives should not be able to remarry, although he had nine still living when he died. It is written in an Arabic book entitled "Of the good customs of Mahomet" praising him for his virtues and his physical strength that he lay with his eleven wives within a single hour, one after the other. He also made a law which is still maintained, that if a man has repudiated his wife three times she cannot return to him unless another man has first known her.

There are four things that the Turks are forbidden to eat: blood, pork, anything that has been offered to their idols, and animals that have not been bled. In the time of Mahomet and for some time after slaves were freed if they turned Mahometan. This was because the first man to believe in Mahomet was a slave, whom Mahomet had promised to free if he would believe in him: which he did, and then was given his liberty. The book of the Zuna says that there was a law under which any Jewish or Christian slave who became a Mahometan was freed without the consent of his master; but it is not observed at the present time.

Here I shall finish with Mahomet's laughable tales and will speak of the Turks. I know of no greater absurdity than the belief of our common people that Mahomet's coffin is suspended in the air by the virtue of lodestone; but this fable is not an invention of the moderns, for anyone reading Pliny will find the same thing in the 14th chapter of the 35th book, where he speaks of lodestone in these words: *Eodem lapide Democrates architectus Alexandriae Arsinoes templum concamerare inchoaverat, ut in eo simulacrum eius e ferro pendere in aere videretur*[423].

11

The manner of rearing children in Turkey

The Turks have a marvellous manner of rearing small children, but an easy one; for although they wrap up and swaddle the infant completely, they leave the rear passage quite bare. Thus they do not have to wash the swaddling clothes so frequently; for they have cradles made of stiff leather, in which they make a round hole at the place where the infant's buttocks will be when it is sitting or lying in the cradle; and they have a small pot, wider at the top, which is set under the hole in the cradle, so that when the infant does its business it is not scattered about but falls into the pot. Thus their infants do not need so many swaddling clothes as infants reared in our fashion, and they are less foul-smelling and there is not so much trouble or difficulty in rearing them; for as soon as they begin to grow, and are able to walk by themselves, they are required to sit above the hole in the cradle until they can control their bowels.

Small children completely wrapped up in swaddling clothes would piss in their clothes were it not that the Turks provide otherwise. They have small pipes made of boxwood which are sold in haberdashers' shops, made specially for the use of small children. They are hollow, bent up at one end, and no more than a finger thick and six fingers long. The turned-up end is put on the child's member. There are two kinds, one for male children and the other for female children. The one for males is round, as shown in the figure. The other, for females, is longer and has a wider opening, as is shown in the other figure.

La canelle pour les masles.

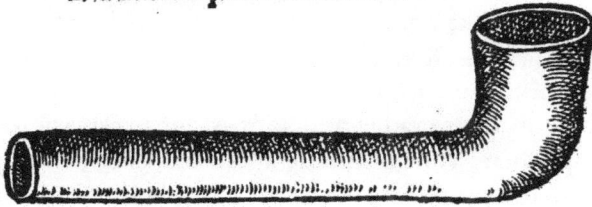

Figure: The pipe for males

La canelle pour les femelles.

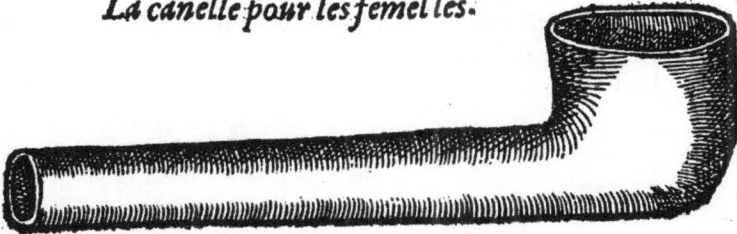

Figure: The pipe for females

If you did not know how they apply them you would find it difficult to understand their use. When they put a pipe on a male child they insert the end of the member in the pipe and pass the stem of the pipe between the child's legs so that the end is over the hole and the water falls into the pot below the cradle. They do the same with a female child, bringing the pipe between the child's legs so that the water may fall into the pot. This fashion is very convenient for the Turks, who are always sitting on carpets, and were it not for this device their children would be constantly soiling them.

They do not make pap or any such foods as we are accustomed to give small children in Europe. The women give them nothing but the breast until they are a year or ten months old. This is a practice common to all nations in the Levant, who are not accustomed to make pap or drink milk; and, without going so far afield, the Italians feed infants only with the breast until they are a full year old, and after a year the wet-nurses chew up whatever they are eating themselves, like walnuts and bread, and give it to them. They do not give them pap, but rather make some good soup or panada[424]. When the Turks want to lift their infants they always lift them over the hole in their cradle; and so it is not necessary to wash them or wipe them. When they are a year old, and are beginning to chew food, they give them food cooked in their fashion, and do not hesitate to let them eat onions, which they first chew along with bread or meat, and other foods. Also they do not mind what they lay them down to sleep on, for they make no use of feathers. Such is the custom throughout the country of Turkey, both among rich and poor; and the Turks do not so dote on their children as they do in the country of the Latins.

12

The manners and diverse fashions of Christian religions in Turkey

Although the Turks are not under any threat of war, and have castles affording security throughout the country, nevertheless they are always on their guard as if they were at war. I used to hear them beating their tambourins evening and morning, and making marvellous melody in time with oboes. There are two kinds of tambourin, small ones, which can be carried on horseback and are indented only at one end, and larger ones, indented at both ends. They do not use short drumsticks to beat them as we do, and do not carry them hanging from their neck, but lay them on the ground and beat them at both ends. They hold in their right hand a curved stick like a billiard-stick[425], with which they strike the right end, and in the left hand a short stick which usually beats twice as fast as the one in the right hand.

The tambourin that is double is much easier to carry on horseback. The body is of brass, and there is always one smaller than the other; and the tambouriner must bend down to beat them, unless he has supported them on something. The watch that they keep at night is not done with bells, as we do, but they speak to one another, shouting and replying one to another in a loud voice, as I had previously observed in Rhodes. The Arabs have taught the Turks to play oboes along with the tambourins, which is an excellent practice both in time of war and of peace. There is not a sanjak but has players of oboes and tambourins, particularly where there are castles to guard. The oboes are short, but wide at the base, and make a very loud noise. They can easily be carried on horseback, and are tuned to the two kinds of tambourin.

I was frequently present at services of the Armenian Christians who live in the towns of Turkey, and it seemed to me that they approach more closely to the ceremonies of the Latins than any of the other Christian nations. And although there may be several Christian nations in a Turkish town or village, nevertheless when some Armenian has died it is only the Armenians who accompany the body to its burial; the Greeks also accompany their dead; for one nation does not accompany another, and they have nothing to do with each other's affairs. This is why there are frequently five or six cemeteries in a Turkish town, belonging variously to different religions; for the Turks make no difficulty about it. When an Armenian priest reads from the Gospel the congregation are accustomed to kiss one another, to the right and to the left, as a sign that they pardon one another. The congregation understand the Armenian language when the priest speaks to them. All that is written in Armenian is almost all the same as the ancient language, which is similar to their vulgar tongue.

13

Of the Armenians and other Christian nations living in Turkey

In the early days of the Turkish conquest the Armenians were the first to be attacked when the Turks came out of Scythia; for since the Armenians, who then were Christians, were the weaker of the two they lost their kingdom[426]. Nevertheless they have always remained constant in the Christian faith, as is shown by the fact that they are still known as such throughout Turkey, for when they refer to an Armenian in this country it is taken for granted that he is a Christian, If an Armenian becomes a Turk[427] he loses his name of Armenian.

They are found living in towns and villages outside Armenia, in Asamia and in Adiabene[428], since the king of Persia suffers them to live in his country. They are peaceable and friendly people, and are usually poor farmers, good gardeners and skilled in tending vines. The priests of the Armenians are married, like those of the Greeks. They celebrate the mass with a chalice like the Latins; they are clad in the same ornaments of copes and chasubles; and they consecrate the bread not in large loaves like the Greeks but in small hosts like the Latins. The whole congregation responds to the priest, singing in Armenian.

All the Christian religions living in Turkey are allowed to have each their own church; for the Turks compel no one to live in the Turkish fashion, but each man is permitted to live according to his faith. This is what has always maintained the Turk in his greatness; for when he conquers a country it is sufficient for him to be obeyed, and provided he receives tribute he does not concern himself with men's souls. I saw many villages in Thrace, some inhabited only by Bulgarians, others by Wallachians, others by Servians, others by Bosnians, Albanians, Dalmatians and Sclavonians, all practising their Christian religion; for when the Turk conquers a province he carries off the peasants from the villages and sends them to formed colonies and cultivate land round Constantinople or elsewhere which was previously unpopulated. Sometimes when I was going about on the shores of the Pontus, visiting such villages, I would find five or six different Christian languages, varying from village to village.

The Turks are very careful to have their children taught the Arabic script, and to do this more conveniently they have built porches and public places to send their children to learn to read and write, and Arabic grammar. The girls too are taught by women, and there is no village, however small, but has such a porch or shed, where every day the boys of the village assemble. They squat on the ground while reading, a posture very comfortable for small children, for it is a very restful position. When the children say their lesson they sway their body forward and backward; and I believe that it is for emphasis, and for the difficulty of the language[429].

14

Of the Jews living in Turkey

The Jews driven out of Spain and Portugal have so firmly established themselves in Turkey that they have translated almost all kinds of books into their Hebrew language, and print the books in Constantinople. They also print books in Spanish, Italian, Latin, Greek and German, but they do not print in Turkish or Arabic, for they are not permitted to[430]. The Jews living in Turkey ordinarily speak four or five languages, and there are some who speak as many as ten or twelve.

Those who came from Spain, Germany Hungary and Bohemia had taught the language of the country to their children, and the children also learned the language of the country in which they came to live, like Greek, Sclavonian, Turkish, Arabic, Armenian and Italian. There are few who speak French, for they have no dealings with the French.

The Jews have always been great traders, and learned to speak all kinds of languages, as can be easily proved by the writings of the historians, and also because it is mentioned in Holy Writ; for when Jews came from all parts of the world to Jerusalem for the feast of Pentecost, the apostles of Our Lord had never left Galilee and could speak only the language of their country of Judaea, and yet on that day each of them could speak all languages under heaven, And the Jews who were present marvelled greatly at this; for those who had come from the country of the Parthians and others from the lands of the Medes and the Elamites[431], from Mesopotamia and all parts of Judaea, others from Cappadocia, Pontus, Asia, Pisidia, Pamphylia and Egypt and parts of Libya and others who had come from Rome, with many proselytes, that is to say people who of their own free will had become Jews, and those who had come from Crete and Arabia, hearing the apostles speak, were all astonished and asked one another: Those who are speaking, are they not Galileans?, and yet we each of us hear our own language, in which we were born. These words are written in the acts of the apostles, by which I deduce that from the most ancient times they were trafficking in all the countries in the world.

The simple wit of the Turks has become sharper from converse with the Jews than it was before they had any dealings with them, just as the French have somewhat changed from converse with outlanders, or at least their slumbering minds have become more alert. The Jews, in whatever country they are, are more cunning than any other nation. They have taken over the whole traffic in merchandise in Turkey to such an extent that the wealth and revenue of the Turk is in their hands; for they tender the highest price for the farm of revenue from the provinces, and have the farm of taxes and port dues and other things in Turkey. This is what leads them to take the trouble to learn the languages of those with whom they are dealing.

Jewish merchants have a trick, when they go to Italy, of wearing a white turban, hoping that people will take them for Turks; for men have more faith in the word of a Turk than in that of a Jew. Jewish travellers wear a yellow turban, and Armenians, Greeks, Maronites, Indians, Copts and all other nations of the Christian faith wear greenish-blue or many-coloured turbans; only Turks wear white ones[432]. And since I was frequently compelled to make use of the Jews and have dealings with them, I soon realised that they were the cleverest nation in the world, and the most artful. They will never eat meat cooked by a Turk, Greek or Frank, or eat any fat, either of Christians or of Turks, or drink any wine sold by a Turk or Christian.

They have so many differences and schisms among themselves that many of them are in disagreement with one another. Some of them have Christian slaves, both male and female, who are made to work at various tasks on Saturday, as for example in the printing office in Constantinople or in trade; and they use Christian women slaves, making no more difficulty about having converse with them than if they were Jewesses. All these things are reproved by others as a heresy in their law, believing that if a Jew has bought a female Christian slave he should not know her, as she is a Christian, and that he should not make a slave who works for him work on Saturday.

The others reply that this is not forbidden, since slaves are things bought with their own money. Within recent memory there was a Jew in Cogne who was physician to the son of the Grand Signior and had two beautiful young Spanish Christian slave girls, who also spoke Italian, in his service, by whom he had had children, and yet he wanted to sell them. But they, as I have heard tell, were sorry that they must fall into the hands of Turks; for when a Turk has had a young slave girl, and has had children by her, he sells her to the highest bidder to get money with which to buy another. And so it may happen that a woman will be sold in the market twenty or thirty times, and that men in similar case will be sold forty times, sometimes to Jews, sometimes to Turks. The stricter Jews believe that it should be forbidden to have converse with foreign women, but that it is lawful for them, if they have a female slave of their law, to use her as they wish.

Those who medicine the sick in Turkey, Egypt, Syria and Anatolia, and in other towns in the countries ruled by the Turk, are for the most part Jews; but there are also some Turks. The Turks are more learned, and are good enough practitioners, but they have few of the other qualities requisite for a good physician. It is easy for the Jews to learn about medicine, for they have an abundance of books in Greek, Arabic and Hebrew which have been turned into their vulgar tongue, like Hippocrates and Galen, Avicenna, Almansor, or Rhazes[433], Serapion and other Arab authors. The Turks also have books by Aristotle and Plato turned into Turkish. The druggists who ordinarily sell drugs in the towns of Turkey are for the most part Jews; but the Turks know more about the drugs, and have more medicinal substances, that is to say simples, on sale in their shops than we have in Europe, so that the best druggist in Venice, however well stocked he may be, will not have so many simple drugs in his shop as a druggist in Turkey. I am not referring to the quantity of simples that they sell but to their great variety.

When a physician has written his prescription he sends it to the druggist to obtain the drugs he wants, for there are none of those that we call apothecaries, and he must get the goods item by item from the druggist's shop and pay for them on the spot; for all business is done in Turkey for ready money. And so there are not so many papers and debts and bills; and in all dealings by retail they give no more credit between neighbour and neighbour, than they would to any stranger from Germany.

15

Of trafficking and markets in Turkey

The Turks do no more than is strictly requisite for their trade. I am speaking of the merchants who sell their wares in the true native fashion of the Turks and the Greeks; for the Jews who were driven out of Spain and some renegade Christians have set up shops in Constantinople, both as wholesalers and as ironmongers, in the fashion of the Latins; which enables them to cheat and take advantage of their customers, as in Europe, where great numbers of shops are to be seen in every little township and village, selling no more than ten or twelve kinds of things, and even these are old and rotting.

The Turks are a people who live long, for they are not demanding in their tastes, living most of the time on garlic and onions and drinking no wine but on rare occasions; but since in time of plague they take no precautions and are not afraid of catching it they often pay for their carelessness.

All the Turkey carpets that come to us from Turkey are made between the town of Cogne [Konya] and Carachara [Afyon Karahisar], a town in Paphlagonia. I have already said that fine camlets are made from goats' wool at Angouri [Ankara], which is the first town in Cappadocia, and carpets are also made from goats' wool; but those made in Cairo are not of good quality, for they are merely woven in many colours. The carpets of Adana are made of felt, and are very light and soft for lying on.

The Turks have markets in their towns and villages on a certain day in the week, just as in Europe. The peasants come in from the country and from one village to another to sell their produce. Some bring wood, others eggs, butter, cheese, silk, thread and other things. Jewish women, who can go about with their faces uncovered, commonly come to the markets to sell needlework; and since the law of Mahomet prohibits Turkish women from appearing in public to sell or to buy anything they sell their work to Jewesses. Yet the law is not so strictly observed as to prevent some Turkish women from selling their wares in the markets, wearing a veil over their face, through which they can see clearly; and when they want to speak they raise the veil like the visor of a helmet. They commonly sell napkins, handkerchiefs, head-coverings, white belts, pillowcases and other such things of greater value, like bed-curtains and bed-linen of various kinds, which the Jewish women buy to sell to travellers.

The Turks like to have white, finely worked linen, so they do not complain about spending money on it. You will sometimes see two small embroidered handkerchiefs selling for twenty aspers, for which we would not pay six sols in France. There are various ways of embroidering linen in Turkey, the commonest of which is that they first draw a pattern on the cloth and then follow the drawing with two threads so as to reproduce the pattern. We have none of this kind of embroidery, nor the way of stitching it; for the women go from one stitch to the next with a very slender needle, following the drawing, and do beautiful work in many colours of silk[434].

16

*A thing worthy of great wonder, that the Turks eat opium to make
them bolder in war*

There is nothing to be observed in Turkey more worthy of being
noted than the opium which is now made there, particularly at
Achara [Akşehir], Carachara [Afyon Karahisar], Spartade [Isparta],
Emetelinde and other neighbouring towns in Paphlagonia,
Cappadocia and Cilicia. They sow the fields with white poppies,
as we do with wheat, and are careful to ensure when sowing it that
each peasant sows as much of it as he has people to gather it. And
when the poppies have produced their heads they make slight cuts
in them so that a few drops of milk ooze out, which they then allow
to congeal. Some peasants will gather ten pounds of it, others six,
others more or less according to the diligence of the people whom
they have employed to gather it; for the great matter is not to have
sown much land, but to have people to gather it.

I believe that were it not that the Turks make much use of opium
there would no longer be any trade in it, like other drugs that are
now no longer used. There is not a Turk but buys it, and if he has
only a single asper in his purse he will spend half of it on opium,
whether in time of peace or in war. A Jewish merchant in Natolia
told me that there was not a year but fifty camels' loads of it were
transported from Paphlagonia, Cappadocia, Galatia and Cilicia
to Persia and India, to Europe and to other distant countries, and
also to all the lands ruled by the Grand Turk. I should have had
difficulty in believing this had I not been told in detail how much
is produced by each village round Carachara and the other towns in
Paphlagonia, Cappadocia, Lesser Armenia and Galatia. I was told
also that the Persians made even greater use of it than the Turks.
One day I decided to find out by experiment how much opium a
man could take at one time without suffering any ill effects, and I
found a janissary of my acquaintance who was accustomed to take
it every day, and who then ate in my presence a half-drachm of it[435].
And on the following day, finding him near a haberdasher's shop,

I had a drachm weighed out and gave it to him, and again he was none the worse, save that he behaved like a drunk man.

Eating opium in Turkey is not a modern habit. The reason why they eat it is that they have persuaded themselves that it makes them more valiant and less afraid of the perils of war, so that when the Turk assembles an army there is such excessive consumption of it that there is none left in the whole country. They have a common phrase for asking a man, Have you taken opium?, which amounts to as much as saying to someone in another country, You are drunk. A Christian Armenian with whom I lodged for a long time ate it frequently in front of me; and having tried opium myself, I found no other effect than a feeling of overheating in the breast, some disturbance in my brain and dreaming in my sleep.

I believe that if anyone wanted to cultivate the poppy in Europe, France, Germany or Italy he could do the same as in Asia, provided that he took the trouble to gather it in the right way, for the climate of Natolia is as cold as that of France. It is done in the same way as the authors have described. We have none of it in our country but what is mixed, for the merchants bring together great quantities of it before distributing it throughout the country; but since I have learned by what characteristics to choose it, I will now describe this. The best opium is very bitter, hot to the taste, so that it inflames the mouth. It is yellow in colour, verging on the colour of a lion's skin, and pressed together into a ball of small seeds of different colours. For when the seeds are gathered from the heads of the poppies they are squeezed together into a kind of cake. The smell is strong and unpleasant, and even if those using it are of a naturally cold complexion it still inflames their mouth. Before leaving Natolia the opium is formed into cakes, which weigh no more than four ounces, or at most half a pound; but the merchants, to get more profit from them, double them in size, so that the cakes which leave the shops in Venice are almost a pound in weight, and consequently are adulterated.

17

Of the signs that the Turks make to their mistresses, and of the dress of Turkish women

Since it is very difficult to see Turkish girls and women, it is still more difficult to speak to them. And so when a Turk wants to convey to a lady that he desires to be her servant he contrives to be in a place where he can see her from a distance. The women of Turkey commonly spend their time on the roof of their house, which is in the form of a terrace. It is not possible (as I have said) to speak to them, and when they go about the town their face is covered; but they can be seen from a distance. And so the Turk, having seen the woman whose servant he is, raises his head, puts his hand to his throat, pinches the skin of his throat and pulls it out a little, indicating to her by this sign that he is in chains as her slave in extreme servitude; for in this country a man cannot declare himself to be in any greater extremity than by making himself someone's slave in chains. And if the lady remains silent, or lowers her hand, he takes great hope from this.

It is a matter of great difficulty to see the face of a beautiful Turkish woman uncovered, and it is more difficult in one place than in another, for their husbands prevent them from looking out of windows. It is the custom for both married and unmarried women, whether old or young, to remain enclosed within their houses, unless it is to go and pray for the dead or to the baths, but they almost always go in the company of other women, and they go several times a week; and since Turkish women (Mahomet says) do not go to paradise, so they do not go to church, for Mahomet does not permit it because (he says) they are not circumcised as men are. Many are of the view that there is a place for Turkish women in their churches, but I can say with certainty that there is not; for I made enquiry into the matter, and all those to whom I spoke told me that women do not go into mosques[436].

All women, both in Turkey and in Arabia, wear long, wide pantaloons like those worn by sailors, which hang down over their shoes; and I found that the reason for this is a matter of which it is not licit to say anything more, even in covert words, for it is an observation of too great curiosity. It is not for nothing that there is a common proverb, *Other lands, other manners*[437].

Portraíct d'vne Turque d'Asíe.

Figure: Portrait of a Turkish woman in Asia

The robes worn by Turks have no collars and no sleeves, or only very short ones, almost always cut off above the elbow. Men and women wear the same robes. They commonly have stitching, mainly on silk; and before doing the stitching they press the cloth with a hot iron, leaving a crease which never disappears, any more than a crease in camlet. They never use camlet or silk without first taking out the creases, which is an easy thing to do; for since camlet is given a crease by the application of heat, so the crease can easily be removed by the application of heat.

Mahomet's law requires that women should be simply dressed; but when they go out, or to the baths, or in company with a new bride they all wear outer garments of fine white cloth. And since under this they wear handsome garments of fine silk, they kilt up the white garments so that those of fine silk appear. Their sleeves are very narrow, and so long that they cover the hands; for the law required that neither their hands nor any part of their skin may be seen in public.

Turkish men and women wear boots which are open in front, for both men and women wash their feet, their hands, their arms up to the elbow, and also the neck. When they go to do their necessary business they take water in a jar with a spout to wash themselves in front and behind, even if there is a hard frost. They teach this fashion to children, both male and female, and continue it all their lives; for Mahomet does not permit them to use for this purpose paper on which the name of God might be written. Their privies are arranged in such a way that they make a long narrow hole in the ground, over which they squat, and can easily wash themselves with their hand. This was the benefit that Mahomet gave them, that by frequently washing their shameful parts they purify themselves of their sins. Hence it is that they have troughs full of water at street corners in towns, in a small enclosure into which men go to wash themselves apart, and women likewise apart; but in their houses the privies are common to both men and women.

18

That the Turks have several wives, who live together without discord or jealousy with concubines and female slaves

The Turks are very avaricious by nature, and much devoted to money; and their greatest wealth and commerce lies in getting ready money. There are no legal agreements for buying and selling, and consequently no lawsuits; for when they buy or sell anything they pay on the nail. Men have the economy and management of the household, leaving no governance to their wives, who are responsible only for charge of the children and for living in peace. This is quite contrary to the manner of life of the Latins, among whom wives undertake not only the management of property but also authority and absolute power over the whole household, and are frequently its mistress. It is quite the contrary among the Turks, where the husbands are the masters; for one Turk may have three or four wives and six, seven, eight or more female slaves, all subject to his authority.

Nevertheless he will keep them all in such good agreement with one another that he will have no fear of jealousy between his wives and his slaves. The reason for this is clear; for although men are permitted to have four wives at the same time all the wives are equal in power, and it must be remembered also that both the wives and the slaves were bought with good ready money. When a Turk has a handsome daughter of marriageable age she is so much ready money in his purse, for daughters when they are married do not take away any money by way of a dowry, or any furniture from their father's house; but rather those who want to have them buy them by paying a large sum and clothing them, and the father will deliver them to the highest bidder, and having so delivered them will not be concerned to see them again.

Thus there is no such great concern with family relationships in Turkey as there is in Europe, and there is little amity between relatives. A man in Turkey who is the son of a slave girl will be no worse thought of than if he were the son of one of the lawful wives, for a slave girl is not considered to be adulterous; and similarly if a

Turk married the daughter of the Grand Signior and also had as a wife one of the poorest daughters of an artisan the artisan's daughter would be an equal companion to the Grand Signior's daughter. Female slaves perform whatever services the Turk requires of them, and if they have children they will be regarded as his in the same way as those of his wives. In consequence children have no great love for their father and mother, and a brother loves his sister no more than he would love a neighbour.

Wives. although they are all together in this way, agree very well among themselves; for, being all confined in one room, one wife has no more credit than another, and all of them concern themselves with nothing but what their husband has commanded them to do. It is not the custom in Turkey to say, The mistress has ordered this to be done, or to say, She wants it to be done thus. They carry no great bunches of keys at their belt to earn the name of good housekeepers, and indeed never have any keys.

Their housework does not take up more than a quarter of an hour a day, for the only household furnishings that a Turk needs are a carpet on the floor to sit on; they have no use for stools or chairs or benches or sideboards, and most often they have no bedstead. All that they have is a few cushions to lean on, and in the evening they lay out a blanket to spend the night, and in the morning they fold it up and put it on a shelf or hang it from a rail. Few people use sheets, for both men and women change into white linen trousers, like those worn by sailors, to wear at night.

They do not employ slaves to clean their dishes, nor do they have any great stock of dishes, for it is enough for them to have a porringer for all kinds of pottages and a bowl for all kinds of soup; and they have no glasses to rinse, for the whole party drinks from a vessel of leather or wood. Men lay great weight on having their turbans as white as possible, but they wash them themselves at the baths along with their trousers and shifts, or give them to slaves in the hot baths to make white.

The Turks do not define valour in the same way as we do; for in Europe, if a man is always ready to fight, and has a bold and challenging eye, and is scarred, a great swearer, hot-tempered, and has given the lie to another such, he will be regarded as valiant, and lauded as a man of high condition. But the Turks in time of peace are of modest demeanour, leave their weapons at home in their house and live peaceably, and are never seen wearing their scimitars as they go about town; but when they go to war their knives will be ready when required, and they will display their valour against the enemy, and will never be found fighting among themselves. And if a man were found to have fought with his companion he would not on that account be deemed valiant. They have a most admirable way of punishing delinquents by a beating, which is the true way to humiliate the overweening and punish those offenders whom they do not wish to kill; and they have ample means of punishing malefactors in more violent fashion when the case requires it.

19

Clear proof that the Turk can more easily assemble five hundred thousand men in a camp, and an army of two hundred galleys, than another prince one hundred thousand

Let us suppose that the king has assembled a camp of 100,000 peasants to lead to war in a distant country. Will it not be believed that they will better endure the hardship than an army of noblemen would? and that they will not die so soon from cold, heat, hunger or other accident as those who are more delicate? Leaving aside the question of valour, I venture to say that they will. Who will believe that the Grand Turk when going to war can lead such a great army? Many people wonder at it, for, hearing of such a multitude, they deem it to be impossible, both because of the difficulty of maintaining such a large troop in a camp and because even a king or emperor in Europe is hard put to it to supply an army of more than 50,000 men.

Nevertheless what I have said about the Turk will not seem so difficult to believe if a comparison is made between their manner of life and ours. For their manner of life in peacetime will make plain how such a large assembly of men can live in time of war, and how it is as easy for the Turk to have a camp of a million men as for a Christian prince to have one of 50,000. In brief, their manner of living in peacetime is so austere that it would seem to us like living in a war. Living as they do, they are neither more nor less content with their way of life than we are with ours, for they are accustomed to it from their earliest years.

Those who have been accustomed to sleeping between sheets and on feathers in a bed, to eating a hot nourishing meal every day and to drinking good wine at every meal would lose heart at once if they were deprived of this style of life; and if they could see their property only seldom during the year, or if they were three or four years without seeing their family or having any news of them, they would be much discomforted. But all these things would be nothing to the Turks, for the life that they lead in their houses is still more austere and meagre than what they endure in a war. The Turk does not recruit foreigners for his wars, but only such men as he pays and keeps in time of peace; as a result, being devoted to his service, they are content with their life and patiently bear the hardships of war, even more easily than the legionaries and soldiers of Rome. Accordingly the Grand Turk, unlike Christian princes, makes money when he goes to war from the selling of supplies. A Turkish soldier will not baulk at paying fifty crowns for a horse, were that all the money in his purse; but he knows that he will have it for his whole life, for the Turks are accustomed to keep a horse for twenty or twenty-five years. Both they and their horses sleep on the hard ground. The horses never eat from a manger or rack, whether at home or at the wars, and never sleep but on the ground without straw.

The wealth of Turkish soldiers does not consist of land or of houses, but of ready money, for if they bought any land during their life it would fall to the Grand Turk after their death. Consequently they are not given to building houses, and, wherever they go they carry with them the same copper pot that they use in time of peace and the same bowl from which they eat; and they never go without their gun, whether they are at home or away at war. They drink only water, and commonly eat garlic and onions. Thus how could they be any worse off in a war than in their houses? In short, they have as much advantage over us in the trade of war from living the life of countryfolk and peasants as we have over them in peacetime from living better and in a more lordly way than they.

And since nature has given them for their dowry to be brought up to country ways from their earliest years, so they have been taught to camp under tents and pavilions; and as they have very light and soft cotton cloth they make their pavilions and ropes much easier to use than ours of linen or hemp. Their cotton ropes are so delicate, soft and light that they never become stiff when wet, unlike those of our pavilions in Europe, which are inconvenient and dirty and get so twisted in rain that they are very difficult to handle. The Turks always have a small axe hanging from their belt, and it is the custom for all Turks, whether rich or poor, to have such an axe, both in peace and in war, which serves them in two ways: one side of the axe has a cutting edge, and the other is in the form of a hammer, with which they drive their tent-pegs into the ground. The other side is used to cut wood for making tent-pegs and for fires when they are in the country. This kind of axe is most ingeniously made, and I think it worth while to describe the manner of its making.

20

Of a small axe suitable for all purposes, both in war and in peace,
which is common among the Turks

Those who make such axes in Turkey take a mass of iron weighing about a pound and a half and pierce a hole through the middle of it with a large iron punch. One side of the axe is in the form of a hammer and the other side has a cutting edge. In piercing the iron they leave a hole large enough to take the haft of the axe. The punches are of different kinds. Some are round, others square. Since the hole in the axe takes the form of the punch, the punch must taper towards the point, so that the haft can enter the hole easily.

There are many turners' shops in Constantinople employed solely in turning wood brought by sea to make the hafts, for ships coming from the Great Sea are frequently laden with wood from the *asphendannos* tree, that is, the mountain maple, for making axe hafts, and also dogwood, which surpasses in hardness all other woods. Ships can also be seen arriving in Constantinople from

Mingrelia with cargoes of yew wood, both red and white; for since the Turks do not use wooden bows they make no difficulty about using yew wood with part of the heart to make such hafts. When I say red and white I mean that the outside is is white and the inside red. In Turkey turners work sitting down, and they do not have a rod hanging down to turn the wood, but a long bow held in the left hand; and in the right hand they hold the iron implement, supported and held firm by their foot, grasped between two toes, which does the work.

21

Of the Turks who preserve certain practices from antiquity

There are still many practices among the Turks which hark back to antiquity; among which I will mention a way of burning parts of the body which the Turks do themselves without a physician. When they have some defluxion[438] or disorder in the head or some other part of the body they burn the place with gunpowder or a rag. The practice was mentioned sixteen hundred years ago by the Greeks, who called it Arab ustion[439]; and it is still used by the Turks and the Arabs, so that many of them have their forehead and temples or other parts of the body scarred by such burns. I found that this manner of burning had great virtue; for when I was in Salonica, a town in Macedonia, I tried it on a Jewish woman whom I cured of a disorder in the head which had lasted for more than six years, during which she had taken the remedy used by Dioscorides to cure sciatica, namely applying roasted goat droppings to the fold at the root of the thumb at its junction with the arm; and it now took only five burns to cure her.

The Turks go about it very differently; if they have some disorder in the head or another part of the body they take some cotton cloth twisted up, of the thickness of a sol and about the size of a walnut, or if they have no cloth some powder from an arquebus, and then set fire to it and put it on the place where they feel pain, and leave it to burn until it dies down of itself and is turned to ashes. They have such patience in enduring the burning that they wait until the fire has been extinguished and grown cold of its own accord, without any action on their part. They do not put anything on the burn to heal it but a piece of cotton over the scar. The Turks in all the circumstances of life pronounce the word *Alavara*, that is to say, God will aid. For, believing that their fate is predestined, they are armed against all perils at sea, on land and in battle.

22

Of the religious of Turkey

The Turks have a certain kind of people among them called *dervis* or dervishes, a name very similar to that of the druids, the ancient Greek philosophers who were in the colonies of the Athenians who set out from Phocaea and settled at Marseilles, where they founded a town. These dervishes[440] commonly go naked both in winter and in summer, and their arms and breasts are covered with scars, some across and some up and down, which they cut with their knives; but they are careful to cut more often up and down rather than across, for this does less injury to the muscles. They live only on the alms which the Turks give them.

The opinion of the people on such fantastics is not modern, for Plato, speaking of such people, attributed this folly to a kind of mania or fury, saying that it came from an *ecstasis*[441], that is, from imagining things which came to them divinely in the manner of prophesy, as they came to vaticinators. For the ancients, speaking of such imaginations, attributed them to some divinity, as they did the sayings of the sibyls. This was also the opinion of Socrates, who says that the imaginations of the vaticinators came to them divinely in mania or fury. Accordingly the deceivers who feign to be mad have been given the name of prophets in Turkey and are deemed innocents and held to be true religious. They counterfeit madness, and deliberately cut their skin, both on the breast and the arms; and because they apply ointment to the cuts the scar remains swollen, as big as a man's little finger. Many of them are so cut about with such lines that it is pitiful to see them. Some prophetic fury or kind of madness, I know not what, has led them to cut up their skin and

427

burn their temples in this way. For my part, I do not hold them to be in their right mind.

There are sly fellows who amass much money to make the journey to Mecca and visit the place where Mahomet is buried; for when they return they are cared for and cherished by the Turks like the younger children in a family. The sign that they bear to show that they are religious of Mahomet is a sheepskin over their shoulder, and they wear no other garment but this one skin of a ram or a ewe and something in front of their shameful parts. There are many such men in various parts of Turkey, as in Constantinople, Damascus and Cairo, to be seen buried in wheat or millet, quite naked, remaining there all day, lolling about this way and that, chattering like children to make people laugh, saying impossible things which make no sense, as when children are talking to one another. They live in a little hut of some kind, never leaving it all day, and passers-by throw them something to live on.

23

The manner of preserving snow and ice all summer, as practised by the Turks

When I was in Mysia and Paphlagonia during the winter I observed at several places how they preserve snow and ice, which they sell in summer for cooling sorbets. Their custom is not to drink wine, and so there are some Turks who live by no other trade in summer than making a sweet drink, in their language called *cherbet*. They call wine *serap*. There are special shops for the sale of sorbets. There are different kinds of sorbet: some are made from figs, others from plums and pears, others from apricots and grapes, others from honey. And when travellers, and also the inhabitants of towns, feel very thirsty in summer they send to buy some, and the sorbet-seller puts some snow into them to cool them, or ice if there is no snow; otherwise there would be no pleasure in drinking them, for a decoction made in summer would never be cold enough without it. It costs only a mail[442] to have a drink at the shop, already cooled by the snow which has been put into it. And so doing, the sorbet-sellers make a double profit; for after they have boiled up the figs, hazelnuts, plums, peaches and other such fruits they do not throw them away but sell them separately, and the decoction likewise separately. There are Greeks and Armenians in Natolia who send a dozen camels' loads of fruit from their orchards to be sold in Constantinople or other towns inhabited by Turks, specially for making such drinks. I know that fruit is brought to Constantinople from the town of Heraclea on Mount Taurus, for the fruit gathered in the plain at the foot of the mountain is excellent for making these drinks.

The manner in which the Turks preserve snow is thus. After there has been a heavy fall of snow and hard ice, when the north winds, that is, winds from between north-west and north (which are the coldest winds of all), are blowing with their greatest force, the Turks gather the snow and store it in little houses with vaulted roofs or set into the ground which they have constructed for the purpose in places without a southerly aspect, perhaps on low ground, behind a high wall or in the shelter of a hill, The snow must be packed together as if building a masonry wall, with ice mixed into it. The snow will last for two years without melting. This fashion can be observed throughout the whole country of Turkey.

I am sure that this could be done equally well in France, for I have seen several regions with a climate warmer than France in which snow is preserved throughout the summer. There was never a time when the ancient Asiatics did not preserve snow into summer; and I maintain that there was also such a practice in Rome: which can be proved by several passages in Galen, particularly in the preface to his book entitled *The method of medicining*, from which it appears that in his time snow was in as great use in Rome as it now is in Turkey. Pliny also complains about this, observing the delicacies enjoyed by the emperors of his time, which corresponds to what Galen says on the matter. Suetonius says the same thing when speaking of Nero. *Heu prodigia ventris*, says Plato, *hi nives, illi glaciem potant, poenas montium in voluptatem gulae vertunt. Servatur algor aestibus, excogitaturque ut alienis montibus nix algeat. Decoquunt alii aquas, mox & illas hyemant*[443]. He also says in another passage: *Neronis principis inventum est decoquere aquam, vitroque demissam in nive refrigerare. Ita voluptas frigoris contingit sine vitiis nivis*[444].

The snow which the Grand Turk uses in his seraglio when he is in Constantinople is brought from Mount Horminium or Mount Olympus; for he has persuaded himself that the snow preserved in ice-houses round Constantinople is not so good as the snow from the mountain, and he prefers that it should be of the previous year. And so slaves go to the mountain during the summer and bring down great quantities of snow, which they leave there until the following year, when ships come to fetch it. There are two fustes which leave Constantinople every week, manned by janissaries, to take passengers to Bursa; and when they arrive at La Montanée, where the passengers disembark, they load up with snow for the return voyage, which is brought down from the nearby mountain by horses, and when they arrive in Constantinople it is carried to the seraglio, for the Grand Turk uses it to chill his sorbet. The ambassadors of France, Spain, Venice, Ragusa, Florence, Chios, Transylvania and Hungary, who are more particular about their drinks than the Turks, are unwilling to have snow mixed with their wine, but put the wine to soak in water that has been chilled by snow, and thus their wine is drunk chilled throughout the summer without their having to take snow or ice into their stomach. A piece of ice the size of a man's fist will chill half a tub of water in a moment and will not cost even an asper.

24

The manner of swinging in Turkey

The Turks have many amusements during their Easter, but none gives them more delight than swinging. It is marvellous how high they can swing into the air. Their manner of swinging was quite new to me, for they swing by themselves. They make a very high frame in the form of a gallows with two uprights, from which they hang two ropes some two feet apart attached to two wooden rings, so that the ropes will better obey the swinger. The lower ends of the ropes are attached to a wooden seat in the form of a small saddle, with ropes at the four corners, on which the swinger stands; and by pulling back he gives himself such an impetus that, without anyone pushing him, he swings as high or higher than the top of the frame. Standing on the board, he holds on to the ropes on either side of him. It is almost unbelievable how high they can go both forwards and backwards, for the swing is a good two toises high; and when the swinger is tired of standing he can sit on the board. They have other ways of swinging for small children, which are childish, but fantastic.

25

Distinctions of honour, both in the beards and in the turbans of the Turks

Turks who wear a green turban stand in high repute among the others, for this is a sign of higher religious standing; but it is not permitted in Turkey to wear green trousers or other garments. The colour green is reserved for the most noble in their country, as a sign that they are of the lineage of Mahomet. Those who have been twice or three times to Mecca venture, however, to wear the green turban, for which they are more honoured than other men. It is a matter of great ceremony whether they have a beard or not; for old men wear a beard as a sign of wisdom. Young men have long moustaches, for they would not consider it fitting for a young man to wear a beard. This was noted by the ancient authors in speaking of the Arabs, but they also say that the Arabs wore their hair long, which the Turks do not.

26

Accoutrements of feathers worn by the Turks

The pompous bravery and absurd ostentation of the janissaries at the court of the Turk, particularly those enjoying his favour, are extraordinary; for they deck themselves with ostrich feathers and the plumes of the bird called *rhintaces*, which are in a mass of very beautiful feathers the size of a capon, all coming from a small body consisting only of skin, for the Arabs who sell them remove the flesh.

Some moderns call the bird *apus*[445], but I believe that it is the phoenix, as I shall show more fully in the book on birds. These Turks, being thus bedecked with feathers, have all the look of Saint Michael as we see him in paintings. They are not ordinarily accoutred in these trappings, but only when the Grand Turk goes to war, or when they are on campaign in his company. They have great wings made of very beautiful feathers fastened to their shoulders, like those who play angels in morality plays in Europe.

The janissaries are accustomed from their youth to wear a tall diadem on their head, like the chaperon[446] worn by noble ladies in France, except that it is perched up high on their head and goes right round it. From it hangs an iron rod a foot and a half long to which is attached a ring. The ring is just large enough to take a thumb and forefinger, and has round it ostrich and other feathers; and from the middle of the ring another long panache of fine ostrich feathers hangs down his back, reaching almost to the ground but not touching it, for it is suspended from the top of his head. Anyone seeing such men, thus accoutred and disguised, would take them for giants, so fearful is their aspect. The ring which rises so high above their head simply rests on their headdress without being fixed to it. It is not permitted to every janissary or other Turk to wear feathers, but only those who have approved their valour by killing enemies in war can properly wear them. A man who wears many feathers shows by this that he has killed many men; and a man who cannot boast of having killed anyone has no right to wear any feathers.

A soldier going to war takes no servant with him unless it be a slave. The janissaries take none, for they themselves are in the lowest class of slaves, and they carry their own provisions and weapons. It is true that every five of them have a horse to carry all their baggage and a tent. The Romans did the same in ancient times, for we read that in the war with Jugurtha Metellus issued an edict requiring his men to carry their own provisions and weapons and prohibiting them from having any servants. I also know that the janissaries at the court of the Turk who are closest to his person have one servant among ten in time of peace and one among five in time of war.

It is easy to see from this what great obedience there is in the household of the Turk. There is no need to refresh the standards of the Turks, for their standards consist of hairs from a horse's tail, dyed in various colours and set at the end of a half-pike. It is an abominable thing in Turkey to see slashed garments, whether in velvet, satin, silk or stuff. The Greeks and all the subjects of the Turk dressed in their fashion never wear slashed accoutrements.

The Turks commonly dress and accoutre themselves in figured velvet of various colours, and also in satin and other kinds of silk. When they go about the country they carry their gun, and always have a tin lantern, and a candle in it, which is a very common fashion. Everyone has his spoon hanging from his belt, and also a small leather bag for salt, but it is composite salt, as was anciently that of the Greeks. It is made from garlic pounded along with salt, then dried and pounded again; and after filling their bag with it they carry it with them to salt their meat. It is a thing which marvellously stimulates the appetite and makes their food good to eat and comforts their stomach after they have drunk copiously of cold water.

27

Of the great exercise of those learning to shoot with the bow in the towns of Turkey

There are mounds or butts of soft earth in the towns of Turkey which are not allowed to harden, for they are used every day by men shooting with the bow. They do not shoot from a great distance, as men do with wooden bows, and their arrows are not so long, but they shoot from quite close up. The man in charge of the butt waters it every day, so that the earth remains soft and never dries out. They shoot from a distance of six paces, and strive with all their might to hit the butt with their arrow. There is a man behind a board next to the butt who pulls out the arrow after every shot and throws it back to the man who shot it. And when a man has been shooting long enough he hangs up his bow next to the butt and pays according to the custom. Such butts are ordinarily to be found in public places in the towns, where the Turks go to practise; and they will shoot more than a hundred times without paying more than an asper.

28

Of various dishes that the Turks cook

The Turks have excellent ways of preserving vegetables in brine, and such preserves are cheap and are sold in all the towns in Turkey,. Thus they preserve the roots of beets, which are the size of two fists, some white or yellowish, others red. Some have thought them to be raves[447], but that is an error.

They also preserve large headed cabbages and large roots of raves and the roots of *enula campana*. A man can eat at little expense on such things, which were also popular in Rome and other towns of the Romans. Those who practised this trade were called *salgamarij*. This makes a very cheap meal, for four companions can have a dish of it for less than a carolus. It is a food that does not need cooking, for, being preserved in brine, it is ready for eating. They also have preserved grape verjuice, which is a great delight to the Turks, for, mixed with vinegar and mustard seed, it makes a very pleasant drink with bread.

They also have shops which do nothing else but cook sheep's heads and trotters for sale; and when they sell them they are skilful at opening them and serving them hot on a dish with a little fat and vinegar, powdered with salt which has been pounded up with garlic and mixed with the barks and seeds of the sumac tree, anciently called *rhus obsoniorum*.

The Turks have no shame about eating in public, and even great lords ordinarily do so. All Turks are descended from cowherds and shepherds, and they still retain all the signs of this in their manner of life; for even if they can afford to eat other meat they prefer dairy products which cost little rather than spending money on something better.

There is a whole settlement in Constantinople, at the top of the harbour on the Thracian side, which is devoted entirely to making *melca* and *caimac* and oxygal. Caimac is made from cream, and is made in different ways. It is what the Greeks anciently called *aphrogala*. Also very popular is curds, which the Greeks call in the vulgar tongue *misitra*. There is no need to enquire further about the origins of the Turks, considering their manner of life.

29

Of the circumcision of the Turks

The Turks are circumcised, but they are not circumcised on the eighth day after birth, in the manner of the Jews, but in their eighth, twelfth or fifteenth year, according to what is thought right[448]. A boy is not circumcised until he can speak and reply to those who circumcise him. He must raise the finger next his thumb in the air, for this is a sign that he professes the faith of Mahomet; which finger he must hold straight up. It is not permitted to perform the circumcision in the temple, but in his parents' house, for it is not lawful for anyone who is not circumcised to enter the mosque or church. There is a great gathering of Turks for the circumcision, for they make a feast after their fashion, with the boy who has been circumcised in the company. The priest[449] takes a pair of clippers, and tells the boy that he wants to show him what he is going to cut off on the following day, and, taking hold of the skin over the end of the member, tells him that he will cut it off tomorrow. Then he goes away; but it is only to deceive the boy, for he comes back again, as if he had forgotten something, and then cuts off the skin, which he had previously tied up and selected, without causing the boy any great pain; and he does nothing more than wash the wound in salt water and bandage it with linen, and so it will heal.

And after the boy has been circumcised his name will not be changed from the one that he was given at birth, save by the addition of *mussulma*, that is, a good circumcised Turk. And after his circumcision there is a great feast, such as we have in France for a wedding. He is taken to the baths with great solemnity, and when he comes back to his home they beat tambourins and give him a white turban, sometimes spangled with little flowers. He is taken to the church in great triumph. Then everyone gives him a present according to the quality and dignity of his lineage; and if he is of a great family, and of great wealth, he will be given gold, silver and other gifts by those who have been present at the banquet and the feast.

No Christian becomes a Turk by compulsion, but if he desires to become one of his own free will he is much more esteemed.

Those who have become Turks by compulsion, like those who have become Turks to save their lives, will be less esteemed. If a Christian is found with a Turkish woman the rigour of the law requires that he must die, or else the remedy is that he becomes a Turk. And if a Christian man kills a Turk he can save his life only by becoming a Turk or by paying a large sum of money. For in this country there is no difficulty that cannot be resolved by money. If a Christian women is found with a Turkish man she must become a Turk. Few people in this country who have been found guilty of a crime which merits death but are able to escape by becoming Turks are actually executed; for many become Turks to escape death.

The Sophy[450], who is a Mahometan, regards the Turks as heretics because Turkish women are not circumcised as the women of his country are; and so they can go into mosques, as the women of Turkey cannot[451]. I know also that Christian Coptic women in the land of Prester John in Ethiopia, who believe in Christ, are circumcised; for since the law requires that women must receive some kind of circumcision they cut off those parts that are called in Greek *hymenea* and in Latin *alae,* which they regard as corresponding to the male foreskin. Those who blaspheme and speak ill of Mahomet must die, but the law absolves them if they are willing to become Turks; and for such people no other ceremony is required than to be circumcised and hold up their finger, and by such a sign they become Turks and in consequence will be freed from paying the *haraczi,* which is the tax to be paid to the Signior[452]. For those who are Jews or Christians pay it, while Turks or Muslims, that is, the circumcised, are exempt.

30

That a slave can require his master to give him the choice for his
ransom, either the time to serve him or the money that he wants for it

If a Christian slave or prisoner in Turkey, serving the master who bought him, wanted to become a Turk he would not be free to do so; for since he is a slave he must serve his master and do his work; but his master could give him earlier freedom by reducing the number of years of servitude if he became a Turk. This means that slaves can do as well by persevering in their Christian faith as by being circumcised and becoming Turks. Slaves in Turkey are as well treated as servants in our Europe, and are happy or unhappy according to the master whom they serve. If they are with a good master who is fond of them they will be treated as he is himself. A slave can require his master either to fix his ransom or tell him how long he will have to serve him; for he can go to the cadi, who is like a judge, and lodge a plaint, saying: I want my master to sell me to another master unless he fixes my ransom or tells me in writing how long I have to serve him. The cadi must then judge the case, and will summon the master. The slave will ask the master how much money he wants him to give him, or how many years he wants him to serve. Then the master will invite the slave to choose which he would prefer, to buy his freedom in money or in service; and if the slave has no particular skills and has no hope of earning his ransom soon, and can more readily pay in labour than in money, he will choose service. Then the master will say that he must serve ten years, or twelve, or fifteen, and will give him a letter to that effect, and when the slave has served his ten or fifteen years he will be free to leave; but if the slave has a trade he will choose money to earn his freedom and will ask his master to fix a time, and he will then pay him according to what they have agreed.

I found some slaves who had paid their ransom in a short time, some in two years, some in six, and others in longer or shorter periods. For if the slave knows a trade he has abundance of work, and pays his master every month or every quarter. But slaves who have fallen into the hands of pirates have no hope of earning their freedom except after many years; for a pirate needs men to work his galleys and will keep them in his service and prevent them from working on land. Slaves belonging to a man of lesser condition have more hope of freeing themselves than those belonging to a great lord, who cannot appeal to the cadi, for if the master is a basha, a beglerbe[453], a sanjak or the like the cadi has no power over him. Thus a slave with such a master must be patient; but if his master is a villager the cadi will compel him to act in accordance with reason and justice.

The Turks make as much use of sesame oil as the French do of walnut oil, and in Languedoc of olive oil; and since it is made with great labour the work is commonly done by slaves. It is made only in winter. They soak sesame seed in brine for twenty-four hours; then they lay it out on a cloth and pound it with wooden mallets until it has been husked, and then soak it again in brine, when the husks float to the surface and are thrown away. Then they take out the seeds, heat them in an oven and grind them; and the oil flows as freely as mustard, for there is little waste. Then, after slowly boiling it, they separate out the dregs. It is a very sweet and delectable oil, and is quite cheap.

The Turks eat and drink sitting on the ground with their shoes off, just as the Romans did in past times in their triclinia. The triclinia of the Romans were what we now call dining-rooms, as are taverns; and in them were raised platforms or daises, like those on which tailors sit when working. They mounted on to these and took off their shoes, for they did not put their feet under the table, as is the custom nowadays, but, like the Turks, they reclined on cushions under their elbows. Martial approved of this fashion, for he says in his fifth book: *Deposui soleas. adfertur protinus ingens / Inter lactucas oxygarumque liber*[454].

In order to prove that a triclinium was what the French call a tavern or dining-room it will be enough for me to cite the authority of Varro, who, speaking of Indian chickens, says: *Meleagrides novissime in triclinium genearium introierunt e culina*[455]. And also of Suetonius, who mentions it in more than twenty passages. Thus in speaking of Caesar he says: *Convivatum assidue per provincias duobus tricliniis, uno quo sagati palleativa, altero quo togati cum illustrioribus provinciarum discubuerunt*[456]. And in another passage he says: *in Augusto, Liviae nuptias obiecit: et foemina in consularem e triclinio viri coram in cubiculum abductam*, etc.[457]. And elsewhere: *Divus Claudius adhibebat omni caenae et liberos suos cum pueris puellisque nobilibus, qui more veteri ad fulcra lectorum sedentes vescerentur, nec temere unqual triclinio abscessit, nisi distentus ac madens*[458]. Pliny too, speaking of elephants, says that they walk so smoothly that the glasses held by those drinking on a kind of triclinium constructed on their back do not spill any of their wine. I conclude, therefore, that when Turks eat sitting on the ground and sometimes leaning on cushions under their elbows on a kind of table raised above the ground, or on carpets on the ground, this could be called a triclinium, for it matches the accounts of the ancients.

It is a common thing in Turkey, as it was in the time of the Romans, to employ eunuch slaves: which I find all the stranger because the practice originated with a woman, Queen Semiramis[459]. She was a queen most puissant in war, who had many young boys castrated to be employed in the governance of her women; and since then her posterity has continued the practice, particularly in the country that she ruled.

When the Turks began to make eunuchs they were accustomed to cut off only the genitals, as did the Romans, leaving the boys with their member, which was a practice common to all nations; but when they grew up those who were robust, although they had lost their genitals, were nevertheless able to have converse with women. Hence certain empresses liked them all the better for it, because they had not the power to engender issue. The matter is shameful, and therefore I shall say no more about it. Then the Grand Turk, having learned that men castrated of their genitals could still give pleasure to his wives and concubines, ordered that the castration should be complete, cutting off the member as well as the genitals – though it still happens that out of ten or twelve who are to be made eunuchs up to six will escape it. Some say, however, that the reason for the emperor's order was different: that he one day saw a castrated horse mounting a mare and thereafter resolved that castration should be complete.

Female slaves can serve the Turks only within the house, for they do not venture to go about in public. It is more fitting, therefore, that a man's wives should be served by eunuchs than by other females who cannot appear in public as males can; for since a man commonly has several wives, as well as female slaves, and since male servants are not allowed in their quarters, every wealthy great lord has a eunuch whom he greatly loves and puts great trust in. The Grand Turk himself has frequently made a eunuch slave head of all his forces, with a great army under his command, having no doubt of his courage and being unable to believe that there can be a scintilla of cowardice in his heart.

Did not a eunuch of the king of Egypt named Ganymede[460] withstand Caesar and all the power of Rome? We find also that there were eunuch kings of Persia, and many other eunuchs have been great lords, of whom the authors have much to say. And, without going so far afield, the Basha himself who was the Grand Turk's lieutenant in all of Egypt, Syria and Arabia when we were in Cairo was a eunuch. in whom the Grand Turk had as much trust as in the boldest captain in his empire. The Romans, however, did not give so much liberty and power to their eunuchs as do the Turks, and as the princes of the East have done since ancient times; for we read that several eunuchs held out against Roman forces. And still today eunuchs in Turkey are familiars of their masters and mistresses as if they were companions. Their masters have great trust in them, and allow them to keep company with their wives and sleep in their quarters during their absence, without any scruple, knowing that since they have deprived them of the means of converse with women they have deprived them of all appetite. Thus there is no trace of any cause for scandal, and all is as clear as the palm of your hand. When their masters are at war the eunuchs remain behind, looking after their wives and concubines and serving them in all things. And so their masters usually leave them in charge of the whole household.

Christians too may have slaves, both male and female, whom they buy with their own money, as also do the Jews; but neither Christians nor Jews may have a Turk as a slave. A Jew may have a Christian as a slave, either a man or a woman, and a Christian may have a Jew. But the Jews are so closely knit together and are so cunning that they never leave anyone of their nation a slave. If he is taken either at sea or on land, in war or in peace, they go to great trouble to recover him, paying money to ensure that he will not remain in captivity. Yet the Turks hold them in very great hatred and cannot endure encountering them without loading them with abuse.

31

Of the priests of Turkey, and of the sciences of the Turks

The priests of the Turks are little different from laymen. They do not need to have great learning, but require only to be able to read the Alcoran and interpret it according to the written text in the Turkish language. They marry and dress like other men, being in no way different from them, and must have a trade to make their living like other men. Some are shopkeepers, others cobblers or tailors or practitioners of the mechanic arts. Some make their living by copying books, for there is no printing in the Turkish language in Turkey. Their paper is well smoothed and rubbed down so that it becomes as bright, shining and polished as enamel. The Turks, emulating us, have made such great efforts that they are now intent on mastering the sciences of astronomy, poetry and philosophy; and they not only take pleasure in these things themselves but also do not grudge the expense of teaching their children, both male and female. But the boys' schools are separate from those of the girls, in which the teachers are women, while the boys are taught by men. They also learn to make poems or songs, in verses of different numbers of syllables, ten or eleven, or more or fewer, so that when you hear a Turk singing you would take him for a German.

When the Turks marry they buy their wives with ready money. There is no question of a dowry in this country, and the husband must pay for the clothing and apparel in which she will be married. If after their marriage they do not get on well together, or if the wife is barren, the husband will go to the judge, who is a cadi, and will be given permission to leave her; and since they had taken each other without swearing any oaths, so they separate without other ceremonies. If a Turk dies he is buried by male members of the family; a woman by women. First the body is washed and clad in fine white linen, and then carried out of the town with great ceremonies. No one is buried in their temples. Their prophets, whom they call druids, walk in front of the body, carrying candles; the priests follow the body, chanting, until they come to the place of burial. They are in the habit of visiting the tomb and praying for the dead. Women come in troops on certain fixed days, at times set apart for them; the men similarly, but each separately, and at different times.

32

That the priests of the Turks serve as clocks in Turkey, crying the hours from the towers of the churches

There are no clocks in Turkey, but in their default the priests climb to the top of the very tall towers of their churches, which are called mosques. Each of them has two towers, one on either side, at least if they are churches of royal foundation; for no one is allowed to build a mosque with more than one tower except great lords. When the priests are at the top of the towers they cry out in a loud voice like a street trader who has lost his basket[461], which reminded me of the shepherd-girls who sing in the fields of Maine at Christmas; for the Turks chant in falsetto. Their voices can be heard clearly a good quarter of a league away, and sometimes half a league away, and it would be impossible for a man who had not heard them crying to believe that a man's voice could be heard from such a distance. Sometimes two or three can be heard at the same time. The priests put their fingers in their ears and cry so loudly that they are heard over the whole town; and they say these words in the Arabic language: *La Illah Illellah Mehemmet Irred sul Allah.* They make this cry five times a day, an hour before dawn, at daybreak, at midday, at three o'clock and at nightfall[462]. All of these times have a particular name in their language. The Turks make assignations with one another at such times to do business or to meet at a particular place. They usually go to the mosques at midday; but before entering they must wash their hands, feet and the shameful parts both in front and behind, and then throw water three times on to their head, and they must take off their shoes and leave them at the door.

33

Continuation of the journey to Constantinople, and also of the manners of the Turks

After spending the whole winter in Turkey, when spring came I resolved to continue on my way to Constantinople. It is a general rule that the Turks never put their horses to a trot unless compelled to; but when necessity forces them to do so, principally in war, they spare neither their horses nor themselves. They take no meals when going about the country, except in summer, when they travel in the evening and early morning, avoiding the excessive heat of the sun. But they eat on horseback while travelling, and water their horses at every opportunity along the way. Hence it is important to have fountains along all the most frequented great roads. Since they do not stop to dine, and ride at a walk throughout the day, they need to supply themselves with provisions on the previous day for the morrow. They are not particular about what they eat, and are content with onions, bread and dried fruits.

It is a common thing among the Turks, both great lords and the most humble, to eat onions raw. The great lords of Turkey are so accustomed to this that they never have a meal at which they do not eat them; and that is what keeps them in good health. The reason is worthy of remark by an observer; for since they do not have to spend much on themselves they can afford to feed many slaves. A man, two slaves and three horses spend no more in a day, taking one with another, than six aspers, which is equivalent to six caroluses. Should it not therefore be great cause for wonder that they are not more frequently ill from drinking only water, and from changing it so often? But they have, by chance, a remedy for this, which acts in two ways: the first is that garlic and onions, which cost very little, preserve them from all troubles of the eyes; the other is that they stimulate saliva and appetite for eating great quantities of dry bread. If those who have such greatly swollen throats in Lombardy and Savoy from the disease that they call *gos*[463], which has not yet found a Latin name, and which we call *louppes*, were similarly accustomed to eat raw onions or garlic in their meals it is certain that they would not be tormented by this malady as we see them, for it comes only from drinking bad water, from which the Turks are preserved by their practice of eating them regularly.

I had two possible routes to Constantinople: one was over Mount Olympus, which was the shorter way; the other was to go round it, but that was longer. And since the snow had now melted we chose to take the road over the summits of the mountains of Phrygia, which are higher than Mont Cenis. Leaving the province of Paphlagonia, we entered the region called Gallogreece [Galatia] and came to a large town which was anciently called Contieum and is now called Cute [Kütahya]. Both the road which goes round the mountain and the one over the summit are in Galatia or Gallogreece; for when you leave Paphlagonia you come into Galatia.

The most renowned town in Paphlagonia is the one which is called Totia and anciently was called Theodosia Gangrorum. On entering Galatia, if you take the road to the left you come to the town anciently called Cute, but if you take the road to the right you come to Boli [Bolu], which anciently was called Abonimenia. All the inhabitants of the country of Natolia anciently spoke Greek; for all the ruins that we saw in the towns of Cilicia, Lycia, Paphlagonia, Cappadocia, Pamphylia, Bithynia and Phrygia always had inscriptions in Greek, for Greek letters are to be seen on their sepulchres and buildings. And since if you take the above-mentioned road you come to two gulfs, one of La Montanée and the other of Nicomedia[464] you must take a long way round and cross the river Sangari, called Sagaris by the ancients, which flows into the Pontus Euxinus, where there is a very fine stone-built harbour, and then go round the lake which can be very clearly seen from Nicomedia[465]; and from Nicomedia the road follows the sea of the Propontis along the coast of the Gulf of Nicomedia, of which I have spoken above. I find that some authors have called it Cutia in Latin, but Pliny calls it by its ancient name of Contieum. Cute was, and still is, a famous strong town. Its castle, on a low hill, is still preserved entire, and it has good walls. The castle lies on a slope, reaching down to very near the town. Usually one of the beylerbeys of Natolia has his residence in Cute, for it is now the principal town in this province; but anciently it was another town called Gordinus [Gordion].

Not so long ago the eldest son of the king of Persia, whose name was Ismail, came raiding and ravaging the country of the Turk as far as Galatia, having in his company only between 4000 and 5000 men very valiant in arms. He came to Cute and there encountered a Basha called Corague, who was viceroy, who opposed him with twice as many men as he had, and fought him in battle. But the king's son killed the Basha and had him impaled and his virile member cut off and stuffed between his teeth, and then left him there. Then he laid siege to the castle, but was unable to take it, for a eunuch came in forced marches with a great army to relieve the place, and compelled him to retire[466]

34

That all women in Turkey, of whatever faith they are, have the hair at their shameful parts removed by the virtue of a depilatory and not by a razor

All kinds of provisions can be bought in the market in Cute – bread, wine, meat – for there are Armenians, Jews and Greeks in the town. I found something here that seemed to me more singular than anything that I had seen in all my travels: it is the source of a mineral that they call *rusma*, about which I desired above all things to have information. It has this virtue that if it is reduced to powder and then soaked in water it makes an ointment with which the Turks remove hair without pain and without causing harm of any kind. This depilatory *rusma* is so popular that it is used all over Turkey, and there is no one in the countries ruled by the Turk who does not know its name and the great virtue that it has. Turkish men and women are accustomed to wear no hair on any part of their body, and they think it abominable to have any. Hence this metal is in such demand that the Turk (as the Jews told me) draws 18,000 ducats every year in tax, which is paid to him by the man who has taken the farm. It is quite new for a metal of such small consequence to bring in so much money to its lord. None of either the ancients or the moderns makes any mention of it. The owner of a seam of this metal who knew his business would find it as valuable as a mine of pure silver; for ordinary people have become so accustomed to using it that they cannot now do without it, and so its price increases from day to day.

I shall explain in the first place what *rusma* is. It is a drug which resembles iron slag, except that it is lighter, and it is black, like something that has been burned; and indeed it is a mineral drawn from the ground and slightly burned. All Turkish women accustomed to using it apply it when they go to the baths. Both young and old, married or to be married, at least if they have hair on their body, of whatever nation or faith they are, whether Turkish, Greek, Armenian, Jewish or Christian, use it to remove hair, and for a good reason; for those who prefer to get rid of it with a psilothre[467] or depilatory rather than a razor find it just right for the purpose. Many people in Europe have tried to make depilatories from lime and orpiment[468], but have found it to be unsuitable, because they did not understand how it should be used when going to the baths or steam-bath.

I will now describe the manner in which they use this *rusma*. After pounding it into a very fine powder they make a mixture of equal quantities of quicklime and *rusma*, which they soak in a vessel with water; and when women go to the baths they anoint the parts that they want to be without hair, leaving this composition on for as long as it takes to boil an egg, and then see if the hair is ready to come away. For when sweat begins to exude from the skin the hair will be loosened at the roots and will fall of itself when it is washed with hot water and removed by the hand. This psilothre is so gentle that it does not sting, and leaves the part smooth, polished and without any trace of hair, which when removed with a razor leaves the skin rough and stubbly; using *rusma*, however, it is as if an old woman is transformed into a young one. But men, thinking such matters to be for women and not proper for them, will not use it, and prefer to remove hair with a razor. This is the reason why this drug is in common use, both among the poorest people and the rich, in Egypt, Arabia, Syria and Turkey. It has already reached Greece, but has stopped there, for it is not yet in use among people of the Latin faith.

35

That the women of Turkey are of singular beauty, and as immaculate as pearls

There is no woman in Asia of labouring or rustic condition but has a complexion as fresh as a rose, flesh as delicate and white as milk and skin so firm and smooth that it feels like fine velvet. And among other devices for achieving this they make a kind of ointment from a clayey kind of earth that the Greeks now call *pilo*, of which I shall speak hereafter. This earth is the same that was anciently used for a similar purpose, called *terra chia* by the Latins. Dioscorides says these words about its virtue: *Extendit faciem, et erugat, atque splendidam reddit, colorem in facie et toto corpore commendat, in balnis pro nitro detergel*[469].

It is also found at various places in Phrygia and Turkey, and I myself saw a seam of it at Lampsacus, opposite Gallipoli. And since it is in such great use there is not a haberdasher but sells it in his shop. When this earth is soaked in water it forms a kind of ointment, with which when they go to the baths they rub the whole body and face, and wash their hair. It would be impossible to find anything better for Turkish men and women, who drink water and eat raw vegetables, than their habit of going frequently to the baths. This was a practice that was also well approved by the ancient Romans, for Columella says: *Quotidianam Laconicis excoquimus*[470]. What most moves women in Asia to use this earth, which is recommended for washing with rather than soap, is that their hair at the back of their head is tinted with henna powder, and could not take on its colour if they used soap. And furthermore, hair that was already coloured yellow would turn black or red if they put soap on it; for soap, which by its nature is acrid, being made from a mixture of oil and lime, would give it a different colour; but by taking the grease off their head with this earth, they make the hair readier to take on its colour. The hair on the front of their head is cut short and tinted black, and hangs down only to their cheeks and half-way down their forehead, in the way in which children's hair is cut in Europe. And the blacker a woman's hair, the more beautiful she is considered to be; for just as the beauty of a face can be increased by its whiteness, so in women of a white complexion their face is made more pleasing by being overshadowed by black hair. Avicenna bears witness that this earth was used from the most ancient times in Arabia and in Egypt and Syria for washing hair; and so he calls it *terra capillorum*. He also calls it "earth for eating", saying that women with child often take a taste for eating it in these countries. Women's eyebrows are also tinted in the same black colour as their hair in front; and the blacker the colour, the more beautiful is esteemed the face. This fashion is not only observed in the towns, but generally in all the villages of Turkey, for they have baths everywhere.

It is no cause for wonder that the women of Asia have such beautiful complexions, for they are preserved from both moonlight and sunlight, and never leave their houses except to go to wash themselves in the baths or to the cemetery to pray for the dead. They go to the baths two or three times a week, where they spend four or five hours painting and pampering themselves; and it costs them no more than an asper to do all that I have described. They go in great companies to the baths, where there will be no men, for women have their own separate baths; and if they sometimes go to the men's baths it will be on a particular day of the week, for there are places where women go to the baths in the afternoon and men in the morning. There are also some places where women go to the baths only on Thursday afternoon. Once when, by mistake, I went to a bath-house, as I had done on other days, and found the door open as usual, I went in and found a great company of Turkish women who were preparing to wash themselves; but if I had not made great haste to withdraw I was in mortal peril, for Mahomet's law is so strict in such a case that a man could have saved himself only by counterfeiting madness, for (as I have already remarked) the Turks believe that the mad, in their innocence, have some character of sanctity.

Just as in ancient times there were no buildings in Rome of greater magnificence than baths and temples, so there is nothing finer to be seen in Constantinople and other places in Turkey than the mosques and the baths. Were it not for the great abundance of baths that Turkish men and women have for cleansing their bodies they would be shamefully lousy and dirty; but as it is, with this great advantage, they are the cleanest people in the world. Their baths are great palaces, and cost them no more than the value of a carolus each time that they go. After bathing themselves they do not lie on beds as we do in France, nor do they warm themselves with switches of twigs. When they go to the baths to wash themselves they enter a large round vaulted room, in the middle of which there is usually a handsome fountain of cold water, where they take off their clothes, wrap them up in their robe and lay them aside on a bench. Then the bath attendant gives them two large pieces of coloured cloth, one of which is worn in front and the other over the head and back.

From there they enter the bath, where there are a number of fountains of hot water, and when they want to wash themselves they have only to turn on a tap. Then slaves come to wash them, and rub them and curry them and manipulate them. It would take too long to describe in detail, but in brief this is what they do. Since it is too immodest to expose the shameful parts, they are completely covered by their cloth. The attendants make them lie face down, and then knead the muscles of the neck, the shoulders, the back, the arms and the thighs. Then, after turning them over, they deal similarly with the chest, rubbing it on all sides. Finally they shave the head; for the slave does not shave any other part, but gives them a razor, and they go into a little room beside the bath and themselves remove the hair from the shameful parts. Having done all this, they go out and return to their bench. Then the master of the bath-house gives them two clean, dry cloths, and they dry themselves decently, and put on their clothes again and pay the charge of one asper for the use of the bath.

Such is the manner of bathing throughout the country of Turkey, which is very different from the fashion of France, where we are accustomed to lie on a bed after leaving the steam-room. It is with good reason that we call ours steam-rooms *(étuves)*, while I have called the others baths. It is also true that all the other nations of Europe differ in this respect from France, for I have seen that in all the towns of Italy they do not lie on a bed after leaving a hot bath, nor do they in all the towns of Bohemia and Germany. After the baths of Turkey I find no nation closer to the fashion of bathing in ancient times than the Germans. But I found it strange that when going to the baths in Switzerland chaste women go at the same time as men who are strangers to them. Although everyone wears a cloth covering the shameful parts, nevertheless, since it is the custom of the country, seeing the women naked, they commit no lewd acts[471].

36

The receipt by which women colour their hair and eyebrows black, and old men their beards

The manner of making up the mixture with which Turkish and Greek women colour their eyebrows varies, but I learned the one which is commonest, and the receipt for which is known to the women. They take a small piece of burnt-brass, which is called *aes ustum,* and in the vulgar tongue *feretro d'Espagna,* weighing about one or two drachms, and by rubbing it lightly on an iron shovel reduce it to powder; then they take a gall of *istria,* called *omphacitis,* and put it on the powder. Then they take an iron rod, not quite red-hot, and lay it on the gall, which melts in the heat, and sprinkle three or four drops of water on it. Then they reheat the iron rod and lay it on the gall again until it is completely melted and mixed with the powder of burnt-brass. The mixture will now be in the form of a fairly thick ink, which the women pick up with a wooden implement like tweezers and brush on to their eyebrows, looking in a mirror, and leave it to dry. By continuing in this way five or six times they make their eyebrows blacker than the skin of a mole. Finally they wipe off the black from the skin round their eyebrows with a wet cloth. Many women of Pera, the wives and daughters of Greeks, remove the hairs of their eyebrows with *rusma* and then paint the skin over the roots of the eyebrows with the mixture in the shape of an arc, so that it appears as if they have high crescent-shaped eyebrows. This looks well from a distance, but seen from closer up it appears ugly. But this is not a modern usage, having been practised from the most ancient times.

37

Praise of most excellent beauty according to the fashion of the Greeks

When the Greeks want to praise beauty of particular excellence they raise their hand and incline it to one side, showing the thumb and first finger joined at the tips to form a circle, meaning that the eye of the person of whom they are speaking is as large as that. This is an ancient proverb much celebrated in the writings of the Greeks as judges of feminine beauty, who referred to women of excellent beauty in the single word *platyophthalmos*, which is as much as to say wide-eyed. But it is the high eyebrows that give a special grace to women with broad faces. In a similar case, when they want to praise the beauty of a particularly lusty man they show the same ring as I have described for women; and to add greater force to their opinion they commonly say that he has eyes as large as those of an ox. Anyone observing the statues and antique medals and paintings of the ancient Greeks will find that the eyes are unusually large compared with those on Latin medals. Turkish women get little exercise, since they rarely leave their homes, except when they go up to the roof terraces of the houses, where they stay all day, singing after their fashion in company with their neighbours. Greek women, principally in Pera of Constantinople, have more liberty than in other towns subject to the Turk; for they go about the town finely dressed, and, particularly if their husbands are rich, will be so painted and bedizened that their fingers will be laden with rings to the very tips of their nails, and will always have a thousand little trinkets hanging from their necks, with necklaces both false and real, and four or five girdles, some of fine silk, others of gold, others bordered with gems both genuine and counterfeit; and they are richly clad in silk. Thus they carry all their wealth on them to show it off. But they are to be seen in such garments only on feast days, dressed almost the same as on the day of their marriage, so that anyone seeing them going about the town would take them for new brides.

38

Of things difficult to believe that Turkish tumblers do in public

The Turks have conjurers and tumblers just as we have in Europe. Those who do such things have been taught them from their youth and have no other trade throughout their life. They do things that would be difficult to believe by anyone who had not seen them performed. It is a great feat to break an iron rod with blows of the fist, as a man can do after giving it a hundred or so blows within an hour.

I once saw a man with a large block of wood on one shoulder who, without touching it, made it jump to his other shoulder, and so to and fro, always making it move without touching it. Such tumblers go about the country in troupes of half a dozen to towns and villages where they know that they will find people gathered in the markets, and there they perform a thousand tricks in public, like walking barefoot over sharp scimitars, breaking up the legs of an ox with their teeth without using a knife and then taking the bones and striking them on their legs to break them. If I had not seen it done I should not have believed it; but I cannot think but that there is some trickery, for after they have taken the flesh off the bones they strike their arms and legs so violently with them that I wonder that they do not strike fire from them They continue striking until they have broken the bones, and so they break half a dozen, one after the other. If such things had not been done in the presence of great personages of our nation, who are still alive, I should scarcely have ventured to describe them; but I have made no difficulty about it, knowing that I should have no lack of witnesses. Had I not seen other tumblers of no great corpulence performing such feats I should have thought it possible only for a man of unusual strength, more powerful than others; but having seen it done by many men I cannot but think that there is some trickery.

These tumblers take up their stance in some place where there is a great assembly of people at some market, and while some of them perform their tricks the others ask the lookers-on for money. Money is given only by those who wish to give it, but the tumblers importune them so much that people do give them some. They ask for it for the love of God; for they have no shame about asking it for the love of God.

39

Of Turkish wrestling

The manner of wrestling of the ancients is still practised by the Turks, as it was anciently in Greece and Rome. It is one of the finest pastimes to be seen in this country. The wrestlers are completely naked except that they wear breeches of stout leather, smoothed, oiled and polished so that they cannot get a grip on one another. And if by chance there is some young man present while they are wrestling (for many people gather to watch them) who has the reputation of being stout and robust and wants to match himself against another man, one of them will invite him, doing him due honour; and if he accepts the challenge they will give him leather breeches, and then both of them will undress. The bystanders will offer to help them to undress, and will hold a robe or other piece of cloth round them while they are taking their clothes off.

When they are ready they take up position opposite one another, and since they are naked and their breeches are closely fitted over their thighs, reaching down to below their knees, they cannot get a grip on one another, and so it will be some time before one is able to throw the other. They have great difficulty in getting a hold while wrestling, for their arms and their whole body are slippery. Wrestling is a skilled art, and to win the contest one must put the other on his back, which is a matter of great difficulty. If one of them falls on his side or to his knees and the other is still on his feet, that does not mean that he has won, for it is permissible in this kind of wrestling to get a hold on any part of the body, including the legs, and when they get to grips they punch one another and if they manage to get hold of each other's wrists each will try to trip up the other. They will sometimes fight for an hour without securing a throw; but the lookers-on will never be impatient, so pleasant to watch is the bout and so doubtful the issue, fortune seeming to favour now the one, now the other. And if one of them is defeated he will be no worse off than the man who has lost the prize in a fencing match. They sometimes anoint their bodies with oil, and then it makes an even better match, for it is the more difficult to get a hold. They have their special tricks in the matter, neither more nor less than the Bretons in their fashion of wrestling.

40

That the Turks are daring tightrope-walkers

Walking in the air on a rope is not an invention of our own day, for it is mentioned in the writings of the ancients in several places; but there is no nation living that is so good at it as the Turks, for they learn it in their childhood and continue practising it throughout their life. They were anciently called *schoenobates* or *funambuli*. They form a large band of Turks, up to eight or ten in number, who carry their ropes and other baggage with them. One horse is all that they need for the whole troupe, for as they go about the country they do not travel great distances each day; and when they arrive in a village they establish themselves in some spacious place where they unload their baggage and set two tall beams in the ground and run two ropes from one to the other, one of which is much higher than the other.

The upper rope is not used for performing their feats, for they remain on the lower one, on which there are sometimes half a dozen at the same time; and they could be taken for squirrels, so skilled are they at dancing on the rope. The upper rope is only for those who are particularly adept.

They perform their feats in public, for their ropes are set up in the open. But when some of them come down from the rope they go about among the bystanders asking for money, and they are so importunate that it is very difficult to get rid of them.

Many people would find it incredible if I did not specify in detail what they do. If villagers in Europe saw no more than the fourth part of it I have no doubt that most of them would think that it was magic. But they do these things because they were taught to do them from their youth, just like those who do somersaults; for the Turks do not do them. They hang from a long tuft of hair on the top of their head, like a woman's hair. All Turks generally have their head shaved except on the top, where they leave the hair, in order that Mahomet will have something to hold on to when he raises them from the earth on the day of judgment. They are free to decide whether to have the hair short or long. The Turks shave each other's heads, using the same knife with which they cut up their meat; for they sharpen them so well that they cut like a razor. There are also barbers in Turkey, who use razors which differ from country to country; for in Syria and Egypt they are thick and heavy, with a sharp edge and a haft which is not curved, having a kind of head at the end; and since the steel is damascened they have a most excellent cutting edge.

41

Of the dogs of Turkey, and of the Turkish fashion of hunting

The dogs kept by the Turks in Turkey have no particular masters; but dogs in villages are fed without going into the houses, for there are always carpets laid out on the ground in the houses. And for feeding them they have holes in the walls of their houses, where they put what is left over from their pottages and bread and bones, so that the dogs can eat them when they go there. Each dog acts as a guard, and stays near the place where it gets its food, preventing other dogs from going there and driving away the kind of wild wolves which they call *adils* and preventing them from entering the villages.

The greyhounds of Turkey are not so large as ours, but are of the height of those that we call mongrels[472], and have hairy tails and long hanging ears like the greyhounds of Crete; and they keep them always on the leash, as we do with ours. They also have spaniels for retrieving partridges. They also fly hawks and goshawks and sakers and falcons. But when they want to call in their bird they only cry the words *boub boub*, which is the call used to summon them back. Turkish falconers carry their birds on the right hand, and feed them on hardened hens' eggs for lack of fresh meat.

42

The names of plants found on Mount Olympus

Having left Contieum and taken the road over the mountain to Constantinople, we came to a village between the valleys on Mount Olympus, for the mountain is of very great extent. We found great quantities of the plant *tragacantha,* from which the local people gather the gum that we use. On the following day we set out at daybreak and continued over the mountain, and it took us all day to cross it. When we reached the summit we found that there was still much snow, for the great cold at this height, in the middle region of the air, never moderates. This is why it is always extremely cold on the summits of high mountains, which never lose their cover of snow, for it does not melt in summer. It is no great wonder, therefore, if there is sometimes hail in summer when it is very warm lower down.

Here we saw savin junipers, such as we have in our gardens, growing wild. They are so common on this mountain that there is no tree more frequent on the slopes of the hills. Firs grow here to a great height, but produce little resin. There are some *esculus* and *ostria,* which we call beech, and other like trees. The wild pines called *piceae* are very common at some places in the forests, as also is a species of oak different from ours, which I believe that the ancients did not know. It has acorns no bigger than small peas. Here black hellebore produces an abundance of red flowers, and grows in great quantity. This was the first place where I had seen it with red flowers. I also found a kind of plant called ledon which is much larger than the ledon of Greece and of a different species. I also found a number of other trees and plants whose ancient names I do not know, which I will describe at another time.

We continued on our way through forests of wild pines and firs, and spent the night in another village in the mountains. I looked carefully to see if there were any larches, which the Latins call *larices,* but I did not see any anywhere in the mountains, any more than in Asia and Greece. And since they do not grow in Asia and Greece neither the ancient Greek authors nor Theophrastus and

456

Dioscorides speak of them, for any such plant was unknown to them, as to everyone else. I am aware that Dioscorides does mention them, but he has little to say of them, as of a plant unknown to him. And I am surprised that Pliny, in speaking of the thuya, thought that Homer had mentioned it. The mistake arose because when he ought to have put *picea* he said instead *larix*. Here I shall show a portrait of a larix, but will wait to describe it in detail along with other coniferous trees.

Figure: True portrait of the larch or larix

On the following day we descended the whole of the mountain, where I observed only a different species of *picea* with cones scarcely larger than the tip of a man's little finger. I also found the shrub which the people of the Abruzzi in Italy call in their vulgar tongue *spina cerisola*.

Leaving the mountain behind us, we found ourselves in a great plain as level as the sea, a region of very rich soil in which rice is grown; for not only is it watered by numerous streams flowing down on all sides from the mountains but the water is easily channelled and stored by sluices, and released when required.

It is no cause for wonder that the Turks eat a great deal of rice, for they are more skilled at cooking it than we are. Anyone who wants to imitate them should put it in a bouillon and let it boil for a long time without stirring it; for if it is stirred while boiling that spoils everything, as is the custom of the French, who from an ounce of rice make enough to fill a great dish, while in the fashion of the Turks it would require a whole pound.

This rice-growing plain continued for half a day, after which we passed through a gap between two valleys, where we again saw the shrub called *spina cerisola* and the plant called *ephedra*, growing to a great height, which is similar in nature to the *smilax laevis* that grows on Mount Athos; for if it finds itself growing next to a young tree it will grow in company with it, so that if the tree were to grow up to the sky so too would the *ephedra*.

As an example of this we saw planes, scarcely less in height than the tallest firs on Mount Emus, which had led *ephedra* up to their summit. But *smilax laevis* has this advantage over *ephedra* that it can cling on to a tree, while without support *ephedra* droops, and if it is next to a small shrub it will remain small, growing no more than if it were against a wall. I had previously observed this in Sclavonia, between Castel Novo [Herceg-Novi] and Ragouse Veche [Dubrovnik].

43

Of the ancient city of Bursa, which was anciently the seat of the emperors of the Turks

We continued on the road leading to the town of Bursa, anciently called Prusa, which was the seat of the kings of Bithynia[473]. Pliny says that it was built by Hannibal: *Intus in Bithynia Prusa ab Annibale sub Olympo condita*. We saw it from a great distance, situated at the foot of Mount Olympus. We arrived there early and stayed for a long time before leaving. It is one of the most marvellously situated towns in the world, for as it grew it spread out on to the mountain; and it has no walls. It is of greater extent than Lyons, for it is separated into different parts by the foothills of the mountain. It also has valleys which divide it up, making the districts of the town at some distance from one another. When the emperors of the Turks first came into this country they reached Phrygia and, being unable to go any farther, stopped at Bursa and made it their imperial capital. But within the last hundred years they gradually moved into Europe, and after taking Constantinople abandoned Bursa and made Constantinople their capital. And yet at the present day Bursa is as rich and as populous as Constantinople: indeed I would go farther and say that it is richer and more populous.

The great sword of Roland[474] still hangs at the gate of the castle of Bursa. The Turks preserve it as an object as precious as a reliquary, for they believe that Roland was a Turk, at least if what the common people think can be true. Bursa's wealth comes from silk, for there is not a year but a thousand camels coming from Syria and other countries in the Levant and bringing silk to Bursa discharge their loads; and there it is treated, spun, woven and made into various forms of needlework and hangings, in various fashions, for the Turks wear robes of figured velvet in many colours, which are laced with gold and silver and finely fashioned.

44

That the needlework of the Turks is excellently made, and that their robes are well tailored

The Turks, whatever garments they make, whether of stuff, or silk, or camlet, or moncayar[475], sew them with silk thread, and their needlework lasts longer than the cloth. I make bold to say that garments made in Turkey are never sewn but with silk thread, which is mainly spun in Bursa. I will say also that the tailors of Turkey, if their work is compared with garments made in Europe, do their work better and more elegantly than tailors in the countries of the Latins, so much so that tailoring in Europe is but scamped work beside theirs. In brief, the Turks sew so neatly in all their work that the seams cannot be seen, and all their work is so well made that no one could find fault with it.

45

Of the saddlers and shoemakers of Turkey

Turkish shoemakers and saddlers sew leather so neatly that no one could do it better. They do not use pig's bristles, or tar to thicken their thread, but they have wax. They use long; slender needles, and after making a hole with an awl they sew with their needles, which are slightly curved. They commonly also sew all leatherwork with silk. The shoes of the Turks, both great lords and peasants in the villages, are generally shod with iron both in front and behind. The emperor of the Turks himself, as likewise the Bashas, have iron-shod shoes, with no distinction between those of great lords and those of peasants, as also do women, girls and small children When a shoe gets broken it is never repaired, any more than is a horse's saddle, for there are no cobblers in Turkey. All kinds of horse trappings and ornaments are sewn with thread of fine silk, and, as I have already remarked about the shoemakers, a hole must first be made with an awl, for their long, slender needles have no point.

46

Of the shoeing-smiths of Turkey

The shoeing-smiths of Turkey, in whatever part of the country they are, do not have bellows and have no use for coal, for they have no forges. Their shoes are not even half the weight of European shoes, and it takes no more material to make two in Turkey than it takes to make one in Europe. They buy the shoes by the dozen already roughly shaped, as they do the nails. Some are larger, some smaller, but they must then be altered to fit. Squatting on the ground like tailors, the shoeing-smiths shape them on the anvil with blows of a hammer, pierce holes with a punch of good steel and enlarge them with another punch which is square and has an angled head to give a better grip, and, having a sharp point, enlarges the hole in the shoe as much as they desire. They do not cramp their horses' shoes, for they never make their horses circle[476], and also because the nails with which they fix the shoes have a long head the size of a bigarreau cherry; and since they always walk their horses a horse can go for half a year without losing a shoe.

There is a most admirable fashion which I ought to have mentioned when speaking of what gives the Turks an advantage in their wars. When they trim a horse's hoof they do not hollow it out with a paring-knife, as we do, but flatten it by drawing across it an iron implement as wide as a man's hand with a cutting edge turned back towards the haft. When exercising their horses the Turks never make them circle. Accordingly they do not need to cramp the horse-shoe. Also their bridles have only a very small bit. Their curry-combs are toothed like ours, but they have no handle.

47

Of the butchers of Turkey, and of the stones found in the bladder of oxen

I know no butchers more skilled in preparing fresh meat than those of Turkey. All of them, in whatever part of the country they are, are accustomed to look in the gall-bladder when they have gutted an ox to see if there is a stone in it; for frequently there is found in the gall-bladder a stone to which the Arabs have given the name of *haraczi*. The Arab author Avicenna described its virtue in detail. The Jews hold it in greater esteem and honour than the Turks, for the Turks, being healthier than the Jews, have less use for it. The Jews are commonly of an unhealthy colour, and tormented by jaundice, and have this particular nature that they are gloomy and melancholic, not only in Turkey but in Germany, Italy, Bohemia and France; and wherever they are they are slow and pensive. Those living in Turkey know no more excellent remedy for their malady than the stone called *haraczi*.

I have thought it well to touch on this point so that everyone who reads about it may tell the butchers in his country to look in the gall-bladders of oxen to see if there is any such stone. It is not found in all gall-bladders, but in every ten or twelve some will be found to contain one or two.

When they flay a sheep or goat they are quick to bleed it, and they make no use of blood. Then when they take off the skin they set it aside without cutting it so that it can be sewn up and used for carrying some liquor. When the belly is open they cut the little gut close to the paunch below the third stomach, and then choose the part that is joined to the great gut, and put them together at the two ends; then, drawing the little gut out of the belly, leaving no fat, and then hang it from a hook, to do what I am about to describe. They sell the meat by the pound, as they do all other things, and divide it up so skilfully that each piece has some of the bone.

If a Turk has an ox or sheep to sell he will not sell it to a butcher, but will take it himself to the butcher's shop to have it killed by the butchers, whom he will pay for their trouble, and will then sell the meat himself and get the money for selling it. But this does not always happen, for the butchers also buy bestial in villages and markets to sell it by retail in their shops for their own profit.

48

Of bow-strings and lute-strings in Turkey

Late in the evening a man with a basket on his back goes round the butchers' shops and collects the guts that they have kept for him during the day, and takes them to men who make them into all kinds of strings. There are particularly good at making bow-strings; and they are in great demand, for their bows are strung with gut. They also make all kinds of very delicate lute-strings, and E-strings which go as high as ours, but have a less silvery tone, since they are strung with three strings; and they can also be used to string Venetian lutes in default of any others. Such E-strings are found in all colours, red, perse, green, yellow and white, and there is not a haberdasher but sells them in his shop, as well as other kinds of lute-strings that are found everywhere in Turkey. They are as common in Turkey as in Europe, and I can give the reason for this: it is that the Turks have four kinds of gitterns and lutes, and many people play one or the other, which does not happen in France or in Italy, for few people in the villages play the lute or the gittern; but in Turkey many people play them after their fashion.

49

Of lutes and their tuning in Turkey

Anyone who desired to understand something of the music of ancient instruments would learn more from knowing the instruments to be seen in Greece and Turkey than from what is said about them in books. The Turks also play flutes, which are very similar to those of the Germans, with six holes all in a row. But they are more than two cubits long and the mouthpiece is very difficult to use, being different from all the other kinds of flutes that we have in Europe; for they are pierced right through, and are played by taking the large opening at the upper end into the mouth. And so those who play them usually sing into the mouthpiece. I did not find them very tuneful.

I have already mentioned that they also play oboes, tambourins, *fighi*, gitterns, viols or rebecks, and the heptacalamos[477]. They have various kinds of lute, the largest of which have eight strings and are very heavy, with a fairly long head on which there are several keys. The chords that it produces are very different from the chords on our lutes, for the strings on this large lute are not tuned in the same way as on ours.

The second kind of lute is of middle size and is more common than the one just described. It is similar to a gittern, but more tuneful, and much more difficult to play, and it has only seven strings, like our gittern. But the tuning is different, and is well suited to playing branles in the Turkish and Greek fashion. It is more commonly played by seamen, and mainly by those whom the Greeks call *palameriti*, in the Morea, Euboea and the islands in the Aegean Sea, than by those living on the mainland of Natolia. It has no keys like those on a gittern; but after tuning it and putting in keys I played it like a gittern. It also has an E-string to the rear, above the main bass string, which goes up to the octave of the E-string in front. In order that it may go so high they make it short, with the peg low down on the side of the head.

The third kind is smaller than the other two, and has a head fully two cubits long with a number of keys, and with only three strings. To represent it you must think of a spoon with a long, square handle. And since it is not difficult to play and is not expensive, most people play it. It is scraped with a quill like the zither, as is also the large one. The one played by seamen, which has no keys, is played both by scraping and by plucking, like the lute and the gittern. It is made from a single piece of wood which is never split, from the species of savin juniper of which I spoke when I was on Mount Taurus. Half of the case is of wood, but the rest is of the skin of a fish, which has been given various names; for I find that it was called anciently, and by Aristotle, *hyena piscis* and *silurus*. Nowadays the Greeks call it *glagnion*. The bridge of this lute is set on the fish-skin, which holds the strings raised, as on a violin. Some are made of whorled wood, which cost more than 6 ducats; and some seamen do not mind buying them at such a price.

The Turks surpass all other nations in doing fine marquetry work, both in marble and glass as well as in wood. They make small caskets for jewellery which will cost 20 ducats each. In Cairo and also in Constantinople windows are glazed with glass made up of many colours, in the shape of foliage and damascene work. They first make a frame of plaster on a mould and then fit the glass together, a manner of working which came to the Turks from the Arabs.

50

That the Turks are good chess-players, and of the great use that they
make of gum tragacanth

The Turks are good chess-players and take great pleasure in the game. They will sometimes spend a whole day playing without stopping; and so they take their chess-men with them wherever they go, and have only a piece of painted cloth as a board to play on. It is a game in which they are expert, for they spend whole days in idleness, squatting on the ground, without doing anything else.

When I was staying in the town of Bursa I observed that the gum called tragacanth was in such great demand that they use more than 4000 pounds a year to give a shine to their silk. The peasants of Natolia, aware of the profit to be made from it, gather it throughout the countries of Mysia, Phrygia, Gallogreece and Paphlagonia and take it to Bursa to sell, for which they are paid in ready money on the spot. Those who have written that it was brought from Crete to Venice are greatly in error. There is also another drug in common use which was unknown to the ancients. It is a kind of gall that appears on terebinth trees, of which I have spoken in the first book, and is much used in the dyeing of silk, which they make in many colours. They use more than 6000 pounds of it every year. They are hollow inside, about the size of Roman galls, and come from a growth on the male terebinth tree, gathered in spring. If they were not gathered then they would grow half a foot long in the form of a horn.

They speak three languages in Bursa, which are almost common to all the inhabitants. One is Spanish, for the Jews; the other Greek, and the other Turkish, which is the commonest of the three. There are also some Arab, Armenian and Italian families. The signoria of Venice and Chios keeps men here to watch over the traffic in goods.

You can go from Bursa to Constantinople by sea or by land. The journey by land takes five or six days, but by sea it takes only two or three days. From the town of Bursa to the sea of the Propontis is only half a day's journey. From Bursa you go to a village on the shores of the gulf of La Montanée [Mudanya], anciently called the gulf of Nicopolis.

The village is called La Montanée, and is but ill conditioned for ships, for there is no harbour; and so when ships arrive at La Montanée they must be drawn up on land, for fear of the violence of the winds. The inhabitants of La Montanée speak Greek, and are good vignerons. There is a monastery of caloyers. The Grand Signior ordinarily has two fustes stationed here, manned by janissary slaves, which sail without fail every Wednesday, unless they are delayed by a storm: one leaving La Montanée and the coming from Constantinople, carrying those who want to travel between Bursa and Constantinople. The fuste from La Montanée carries a cargo of snow, brought from the nearby mountain, which is part of Mount Olympus. It is brought in horse-drawn carriages, so that the ship can be loaded in two days.

The inhabitants of the shores of the Hellespont and Propontis are almost all fishermen, and they speak Greek. There was a peasant in the village of La Montanée who brought herbs to his house, including the one that the ancient called *caucalis;* he himself called it *cascalitra.* They eat it raw in a salad, along with nipplewort.

Figure: Portrait of the herb called Caucalis

When I got back to Constantinople I found that Monsieur d'Aramont had accompanied the Grand Signior on his campaign in Persia[478], but there was a gentleman from Bourges called Jacques de Cambray[479] acting as vice-ambassador and the king's representative, who treated me with no less courtesy than Monsieur d'Aramont; besides which there were a number of those whom Monsieur d'Aramont had brought with him and who had remained in Constantinople. In addition to the gentlemen whom I have named he had brought a man of good letters called Master Juste Tenelle, whom the late king Francis, the restorer of letters, had sent to recover ancient Greek books[480].

51

*Of the gardens of the Turks and their skill in gardening, and of the
flowers of which they are fond*

There are no people who so much delight in beautiful flowers as
the Turks, and when they find a beautiful wallflower or some other
graceful flower, even though it has no smell they do not prize it the
less. We like to have bunches of different kinds of scented flowers
mixed together, but the Turks care only for sight rather than smell,
and like to have only one flower at a time. Even if they may have
several different kinds of flowers it is their custom to wear only a
single flower in the folds of their turban. Artisans commonly have
several flowers of different colours in a jar of water in front of them,
to keep them fresh in their beauty. And so the Turks think as much
of their gardens as we do, and go to great trouble to get exotic trees,
particularly those that have beautiful flowers, and grudge no money
for the purpose.

They have trees in their gardens that the Greeks call in their vulgar
tongue *kromada* or *cromadia*, which are of the height of an almond-
tree. The Turks call them *cromadia*, from the name of the date-palm,
for their fruits are good to eat. Their leaves are like those of the
andrachne. Beautiful flowers are held in high esteem; as an example
of which we saw a small shrub with leaves like ivy, which remains
green throughout the year and produces a purple flower almost a
cubit long covering the whole branch, which is of the thickness of a
fox's tail. Red lilies are so common that there is no one who has not
some in his garden. These red lilies are different from those that we
have in our country, with a flower resembling that of the white lily;
but the leaves of the Turkish lilies are shaped like those of the cane
called *elegia*, and they have roots like those of couch grass, except
that they are much larger. And so many foreigners who come to
Constantinople in ships from other countries bring with them roots
of plants which have beautiful flowers and sell them in the markets,
and from all the things that they bring they make money.

When I said in another place that the Greeks care only for plants
that are good to eat I did not mean this to apply to the Turks, who

469

have now outdone the Greeks in giving common names to plants; for there is not a plant in Turkey with any claim to beauty to which the Turks have not given a name in their language. And among others they think highly of wild saffron, not only for its smell but because it delights the eye, and also because it has a beautiful cluster of flowers, almost like an artificial flower, and because its leaves seem to be linked with the flower.

The Turks have marvellous devices in many matters, as for example in enabling people to fall asleep quickly. Could anything be more singular than to find a drug which allows someone who cannot rest to fall asleep at once? They go to a druggist (for they have no apothecaries) and ask for *tatoula* seed, for which they pay half an asper. Then they give it to the man who cannot sleep. *Tatoula* is what the Arabs call *nux metel* and the Greeks *solanum somniferum*[481]; which we found growing in the plain of Jericho, near the fountain of Elisha. Jovius, writing of the emperor Selim[482], says that he sometimes ate a seed which makes people happy and removes the memory of things that makes them melancholy and troubled with great matters, and that some hours after eating it a man wants only to rejoice and cannot think of anything that disturbs the mind. He does not know what seed it can be, unless it is *nepenthes*. But I have seen that they use the seed of a herb which is commonly sold in the markets of Turkey called *harmala*, a species of wild rue of which I have spoken in the second book, found in fields and hedges all over Turkey, which does not grow in our countries.

In my quest for plants I visited many gardens; but I saw none more magnificent than the garden of the signoria of Venice in Padua, which I believe was established by Monsignor Daniel Barbarus, patriarch of Aquileia. The next finest, in France, was at Saint-Maur, near Paris. The trees which bear azaroles, and those which bear nectarines, are common in the gardens of Constantinople. As for other kinds of fruit-trees, like almond-trees, apple-trees and other common trees, I have already noted that the Turks are most diligent in cultivating them.

52

The names of animals and plants gathered on the shores of Pontus, and others found in the market in Constantinople, and of the stars that are harmful to bestial in Turkey

There is a time in the year when the Turks do not leave their sheep out at night to graze in the open. The reason is that, as they believe, there are two stars, to which they have given names, which can be seen at night during the months of July and August as they reach their vertical zenith. If the sheep raise their heads and catch the light from them they will die; but if they are under cover at that time of year they will not die.

They declare that they have found by infallible experience that this is so; and to ward off any such danger they put their sheep under cover during the months of July and August. This does not happen in every part of Turkey, but only in some places in the country of Thrace. To prevent it from happening they put their sheep into sheds only during these months, which otherwise they do not do even in winter. Many other nations, who do not have such a practice and suffer great losses by the death of their bestial, and do not know why it happens, have attributed it to some kind of witchcraft; and it seems to me that Virgil was also of this view in his *Eclogues*. I was first told this in Constantinople and have since confirmed it by my own experience; for when I was travelling along the shores of the sea of Pontus with a man looking for vipers we saw in various places flocks of sheep under cover, and I was told by the shepherds that at other times of year they left them in the open. The shepherds did not know the reason for this, but nevertheless said that if they were left in the open they would die.

Having gathered the flowers that I saw as I travelled, I wrote them down at once, as follows. *Cistus* and the *hypocistis* which grows on its root are very common. I also found three kinds of broom, honeysuckle and *aphace*. *Androsemon*, growing wild, is commoner here than anywhere else: I mean the plant that the Italians call *ceciliana*. All kinds of plantain are found here. *Linaria*, *lampsana*, mullein, scented milfoil, *lagochymeni*, pine thistle, common and

471

double mallows, *prassium, marrubium, chrysantemon,* which is good to eat, camomile, dwarf cedars of the two species, dwarf junipers, strawberry-trees, planes, hazel-trees, elder, dwarf elder.

I also found the bones of a dolphin, still joined together, lying on the shore. *Smilax aspera, corruda, trifolium menientes, caucalis,* wild fennel, terebinth, oleander, wild plum-trees, agrimony, *teucrium,* androsaces, horse-radishes, nettles, *aspalathus, agourupes,* arum, two kinds of daisy, a species of comfrey with a round root, which the local people call *sterouli,* lesser burnet, hemp-nettle, calamint, *origanum heracleoticum,* horse-tail, *buphtalmum,* dock, black hellebore, two species of fern, wild poppy, three kinds of hyacinths, two species of spikenard, the third and the first, *satyrions, violes,* heather, giant fennel, then bearing its eggs, which are good to eat, true hyssop, *meu,* yellow-flowered and white-flowered comfrey, hops, *asclepias, cynoglossum,* wild marigold, elms, *chamaedrys, hermodactes,* holy thistle, *sideritis,* sorrel, oak, laurel, apparitory, chicory, wild roses, convolvulus, *stachis, asperula,* hawthorn, styrax, laureola, alkanet, *lycopsis. alaternus, talietrum,* dwarf iris, three species of tree spurge, male tree spurge, *myrsinites* and *helioscopus.* I also found *ornithogalon,* black poplar, aspen, chestnut-trees, alders, sumac, pennyroyal, *sorbus torminalis,* which the French call *alisier,* the tree from which larding-needles are made, *anabasis,* verbena, *peristereon,* two kinds of maple.

The viper-collector whom I had with me, although he was a Turk, nevertheless knew the modern Greek names of snakes, and when we set out to look for vipers and other snakes we found quite a number, including those that the ancients called *driini* and and that are now called *dendrogailla,* which retains something of its ancient name. I have never seen any other that grows so large as this one or that hisses so loudly. I once caught one so large that when I put it in a sack it was so heavy that a peasant could not carry it on his back for more than two leagues without resting. The skin when filled with hay was as thick as the thigh of a heavy man. With the skins of this and other kinds of snake, and of birds and land animals, whole plants, unusual seeds and various sea creatures I had filled a large crate which was loaded on to a Genoese hooker named the *Delphina* belonging to Signior Vivaldi, with one François Brusquet as captain, which was to go to England; but it was captured by corsairs and taken to Algiers, and so I lost the whole lot. There is such a great similarity between snakes while they are alive that it is no great cause for wonder that the portraits drawn of them, in which there is only black and white, are very like another. Nevertheless this is a true depiction of *driinus*[483].

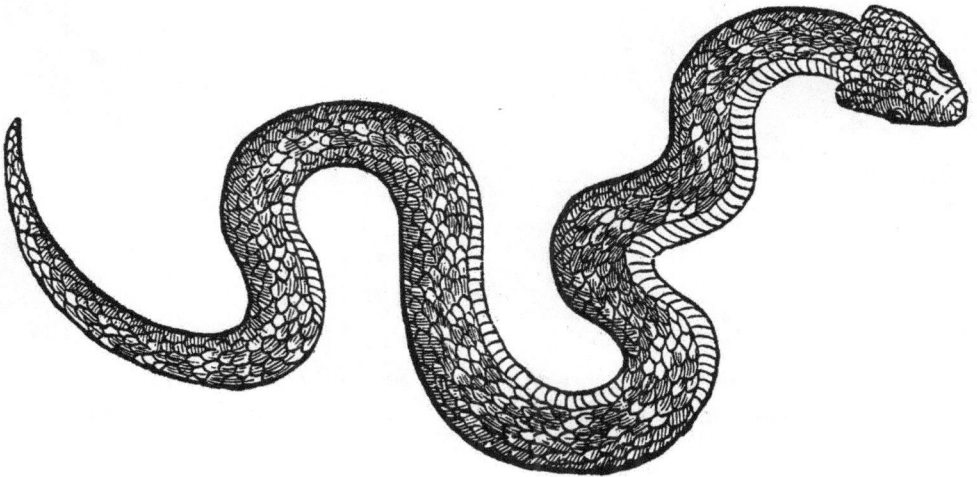

Figure

We also found a snake that had a hard patch of skin like a lump on its forehead, which I believe was the one that the ancients called *aspis*. But that seemed to me too rare, for I had already seen this one in Italy, in the Abruzzi. While the horned viper has two projections like small horns above its eyes, this has only one, and it is of the same colouring as the *amphisboena*. I have already spoken of the horned viper at some length in the second book, and I therefore depict its portrait here, without further discourse, since I shall speak more fully of all snakes in another place.

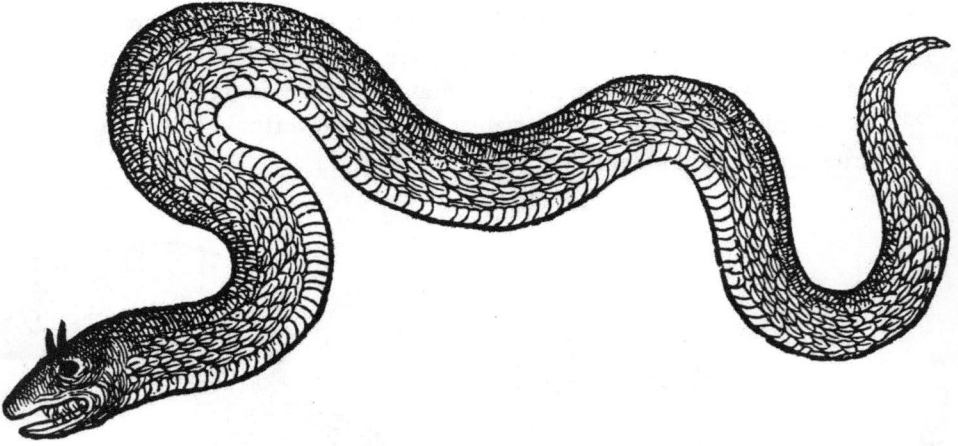

Figure

Salamanders, which we believe to be deaf, *pluvines* and *mirtils* are common everywhere and are frequently to be seen, as are phalangies.

Returning along the shores of the sea, we came to the mouth of the Bosphorus, where the strait of the Propontis begins. Climbing the highest of the nearby hills, we came on a bird-catcher who was catching migrant sparrow-hawks in a manner which I think worth describing. Since it was about the beginning of May, when all birds are busy on their nests, it seemed to me unusual to see so many kites and sparrow-hawks coming from the direction of the right-hand coast of the Great Sea. The bird-catcher was catching them with great industry, never missing one, and taking more than a dozen in an hour. His practice was to hide behind a bush, after laying out a square area in front of him some two paces across and two or three paces from the bush and setting up six posts in the ground round the area, three on each side, an inch thick and the height of a man, with a notch at the top on the inner side. He had a very light net of green thread which was attached to the notches on the posts and hung at the height of a man, and in the centre of the enclosure he had set a stake a cubit high, to which was attached a cord whose other end was held by the man behind the bush. Tied to the stake were a number of small birds feeding on the grain which had been scattered about in the enclosure. When the bird-catcher saw a sparrow-hawk coming from the direction of the Great Sea he caused his birds to flutter about. The sparrow-hawk was a long way away when he saw it and made his birds fly about, for it has such good sight that it could see them from half a league away and, flying at full speed, swooped to steeply down that, thinking to catch the birds, it hit the net and was itself caught, entangled in the meshes. Then the bird-catcher took it, wrapped its wings in a cloth that he had ready, sewn up for the purpose, which also tied down its thighs and tail, and after sewing up its eyelids left it on the ground, for it could not move or struggle. I could not think where so many sparrow-hawks came from; for I stayed there two hours, and during that time he caught more than thirty, so that in a single day a man could catch something like a hundred. The kites and sparrow-hawks came in a stream, one after the other, and could be seen as far away as the eye could reach.

Those who sell herbs in the market in Constantinople, particularly in spring, have many kinds that we do not know or use. Among them is nipplewort, which they call in the vulgar tongue *lapsana;* but when it has formed its head and is beginning to flower they call it *vrouves.* When eaten raw it has the taste of horse-radish, but if it is boiled it becomes bitter. They have cultivated ache so that it becomes sweet, and eat it raw at all their meals, calling it *selino.* Parsley is called *macedonico.* They also sell stems of *smilax aspera,* which they call *smilachia.* They are good in salads, as also are the stems of black bryony, which they call *embegli melena,* a corrupt form of a word meaning black vine. At Ancona they are called *tamarou.*

The Turks hold markets in the towns of Turkey on particular days of the week. In Constantinople the market is held on Monday in one place, on Tuesday in another place, on Thursday in Pera, and so on with the other days. Unless there is some unusual event, they always hold markets on these days. And so when I came back to Constantinople and frequently visited the markets I found many singular things brought from other countries, particularly among the drugs sold by certain theriac-dealers[484], who commission people to get any new things that they can find, so that by displaying them in public they can attract a crowd to whom they sell the products of their art. Some of them show snakes in public, but I will say no more about them here, since I have written about them in detail in the book in which I gave the portraits of snakes. Others sell ointments and various roots and absinth. They often come to Constantinople from Egypt, for I recognised some in Constantinople whom I had previously seen in Cairo, and from whom I got some portraits of fish from the Nile, which I shall publish in another work of mine, the book on fishes[485]. Since they had the animal called an armadillo of which I have already spoken, which comes from Guinea and Newfoundland, of which the ancients make no mention, I have thought it well to give its portrait here.

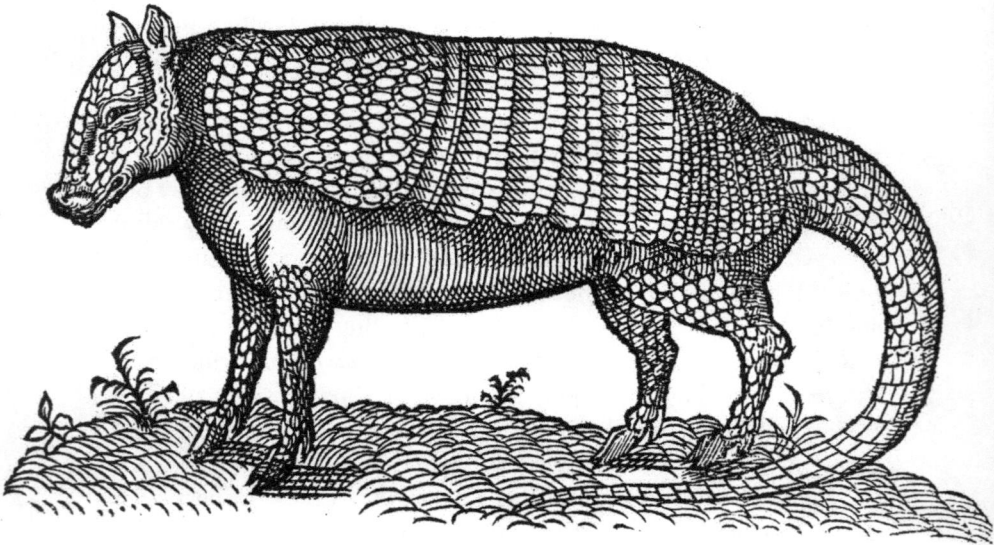

Figure

The reason why this animal is commonly to be seen in cabinets of curiosities is that nature has armed it with a hard skin and large scales in the manner of a corslet, so that its flesh can readily be removed without losing anything of its true appearance. I have already described it as a kind of Brazilian hedgehog; for it curls up in its scales as a hedgehog curls up in its spines. It is no larger than a medium-sized piglet; and indeed it is a species of pig, with similar legs, trotters and muzzle. It has already been seen in France, living on grain and fruit.

The French also know another animal, called a *tartaret* or *tartarin*, which I have thought it right to mention here, lest anyone should be led astray by the similarity of the names to confuse it with the armadillo, which the French call *tatou*. For my part, I take the *tartaret* to be the baboon, which Aristotle calls *simia porcaria*, and which I have already mentioned in speaking of the tumblers of Cairo; for other nations which call it a baboon mean the same animal as the one that the French and other peoples call a magot.

I have given no picture or description of it here, for I intend to describe it in more detail in another work[486], inasmuch as there is still some difficulty about the French name; since there are some who maintain that the magot or baboon is not the same as the *tartaret*.

And now that I am about to conclude my observations I should like to ask the reader not to take it ill if I have sometimes given the portrait of an animal or plant but not made any great mention of it; for if I had described in this book everything that I have named in it I should have lost the opportunity for describing them more particularly elsewhere. Nevertheless, where occasion arose I have spoken in more detail, at greater or lesser length, where it seemed appropriate. But in order that other nations may participate in some fashion in my discourses I propose to publish them on occasion in other languages, not necessarily in the same order and the same words as I have used here. Nevertheless if the reader finds that this work has been of some profit to him, let him render thanks to Monseigneur le Cardinal de Tournon, my most liberal Maecenas and master, who has met the expenses of my travels, and also to our liberal, magnanimous and most wise king, who of his courtesy and kindness has granted me the privilege of being of the number of his scholars, as also has Monseigneur François Olivier, Chancellor of France.

Maps and Other Documents

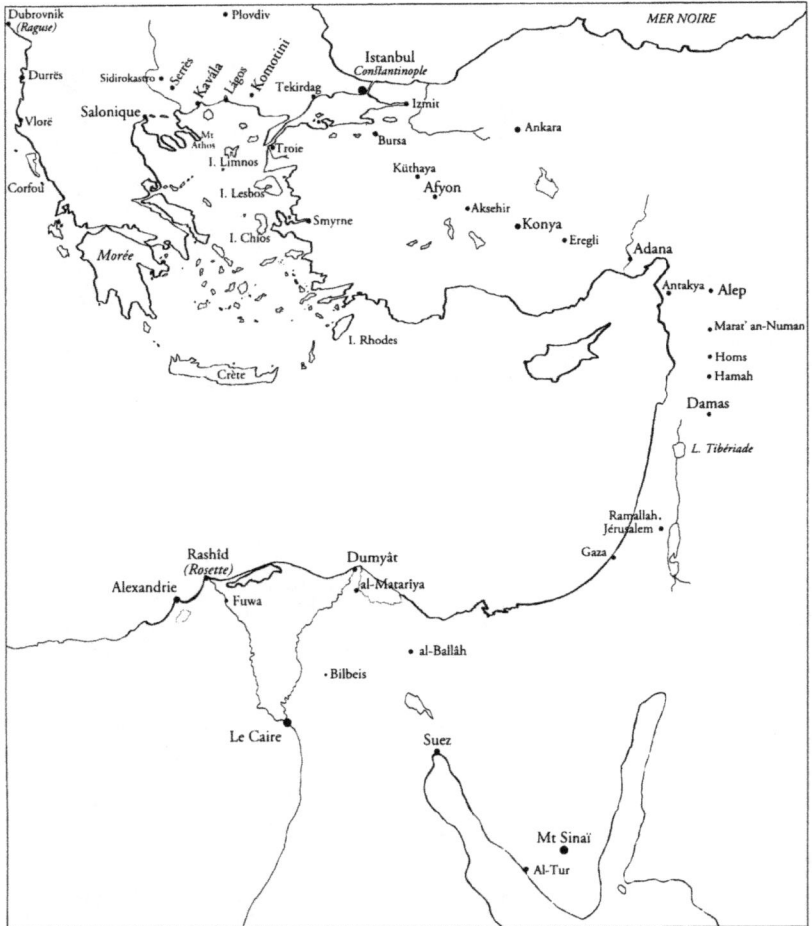

Dubrovnik
(Raguse)

MER NOIRE

• Plovdiv

• Durrës

Sidirokastro • Serrès Kavála Lagos Komotini

Istanbul
Conftantinople

Vlorë

Salonique
Mt Athos
I. Limnos
Troie

Tekirdag

Izmit

• Ankara

• Bursa

Corfou

I. Lesbos

Kütahya
Afyon

Moree

I. Chios

Smyrne

Aksehir
• Konya
• Eregli

Adana

Antakya • Alep

I. Rhodes

• Marar' an-Numan

• Homs
• Hamah

Crète

Damas

L. Tibériade

Ramallah.
Jérusalem •

Gaza

Rashid
(Rosette)

Dumyât

al-Matarîya

Alexandrie

Fuwa

• al-Ballâh

• Bilbeis

Le Caire

Suez

Mt Sinaï

Al-Tur

480

Thevet, Cartographie Universelle, 1575 (detail)

***

Overleaf: Map of the Levant (Du Val, 1677, BnF)

Cracovie · Biecz · Iaslaw · Busk · Shara · Cons Constantinou Kateladic · Kiow

Petite Russie · Premislie · Leopol · Chmiedaw · Winowra Biadacerkiew · PETITE

Bon · Epereis · Crap Zidaczou · Kamionez · Pais · Kudac · TARTARIE · Manaster

Cassouia · Hallcs · Chocim · Bradz · Ochrin · Staf · Slokotak

Fillek · Taskai · Nosma tat · Plopocz · Niesterz · Oczacouvu · Torlnoza

HONGRIE · TRANSILVANIE · MOLDAVIE · Driste Bialogrod · Tandri

Coloza · Gints · Albeule · Hoan · Tartarei · Bouches du Danube · MER NOIRE autr

VALAQVIE · Dobruzes · Daroster · Mangalia · Po

SERVIE · Chiprovac · BVLGARIE · Hazorad Baropoli · Detroit de et autrefois

Pirot · Sophia · Andrinople · Consta nople · Gralari · Famosta

TURQUIE · Philippopoli · ROMANIE · Mer de · Neopoli · Holli

Albanie · MACEDOINE · Thessalie · Epire · ARCHIPEL · autrement

Corfou · MER BLANCHE · Peronatte · Same

Achaie · Teno · Micols · Gyara · Nicones

Poponese · Patras · Corinthe · Moree · Napoli · Paris · Morea · Lero · Milazo

Zante · Malvoisie · Napoli de · Nio · Culoiers · Rhodes

Modon · Milo Santorini · Stampalia · Scarpante

C. Matapan · Candie · Standia

ISLE DE CANDIE · Sfachia

MEDITERRANÉE

C. Razel Jaara · C. Raz augen · C. Razaugen · Bonan dreu · Patraacha

Lebeda · Berebona · Barca · Bouhera

Seches de Barbarie · Molella · PAIS DE BARCA

et Golfe · Catvora

de Sidra · Sarabian · Zanara

I. Sidra · Stagno

45 · 50 · 55

Limen
autrefois
Palus Meotides

Tartares Cornuti

Meot
al Azac
M. Vargada
Vargada
Veroni
Astracan

Balesten
Terras
Copa
Sanach
Balopta
Ria

Temruk
Gisana
Toras
Desert
Bouches
du Volga

Comanie
CIRCASSIE
Rabent
Sanscha

Cudar Mataca
Alba
Abcasses
Serent
Talcan
Salma

Elichia
Avograsie
S.te Sophie
Sanscha
Chiptche
Abuasmedri
Streau

Carbatri
Zitrae
Tehan
Terki
Bazan R.

MER MAIOURE
Sanatopoli
Porto
GEORGIE
Armeni
Gurustan
Casan Kat.
Anders

MER
CASPIENE
aut.
MER DE
KILAN

NT EUXIN
Guriel
Mont Caucas
Kacheti
Baratralu
Karial
Gueorden
Tarku
Derbent

Lanth
Ariva
Imerete
Carduel
Tesla
Scander
Temaki

Guri
Vanthiet
LAZI
Risteurti
Ebbe
Tesla
Exechie
Scamache
Bakuie

Lati
Sunisa
Esmunis
Colior
Ceraunt
Trebisonde
Errezum
Kars
Jenken
Ervaar
Bilagan
Tzauvat

Aloee
Baidizan
Cusalmach
Palk
Bathurt
Mont
Ararat
Fasis R.
Louis R.

Muas
Chemach
Giangeeu
Balu
Roxan
Tygre

PERSE
Tauri

NATOLIE
Amasie
Sivas
Sanastho
Casaria
Serascrubi
Carput
ARMENIE
TURCOMANS

Yuma
Tisama
Gensoul
Hamsaaca
Tal-arejiae
Arsun

Acsare
Acsaror
Arenich
Laza
Melolun
Vardara
Alrass
Matafavequin
Adrzis
Achlat
Van

Iaccem
Nicola
Tinana
Aggar
Saromsada
Malatia
Tal-batris
Manuscut
Arsingan

Apamia
Cogni
Parablais
Aladuli
Mataras
Zusma
Sumiscahar
Betlis

Antioche
Naranda
Venacho
Adoer
Manbeg
Germun
Alleghan
Karkise
Karklise
Asanchut

Perge
Taus Montagne
Turse
Tamasa
Moeser
Karkise
Inclat
Cara-emit
al-Diarbequir

CARAMANIE
Anhachetu
Selechia
Aolman
Curo Ma
Laiassa
Sobcha
Orfan
Resbelta
DIARBECH

Sattalie
Calo
Satalmur
Alexan-
dretha
Nouria
Bir
Tsisire
Sarto
Sahar

Golfe de Sattalie
Vbalde
Alep
Gibrim
Rascea
Bels
Sero
Tapsaque
Nisihin

ISLE
DE CHIPRE
Baffo
Cerines
C.S. Andre
Nicosie
Limitic
Famagouste
Souadie
Antuche
Methula
Chabut
MESOPOTAMIE
Mechabur
Sahar

Tartoee
Saleun
Aman
Achla
Seria
Le Desert
Talba
Mechet

MER
Tripoli
de Sourie
SOURIE
Salamia
Castel
Suberkan

DE
Giblet
Hams
Laudshia
Said el
Tamas
el Palmira
Mechet
Ali
Ana
Eufrat

Sidon
Said
PHENICIE
Barut
Damas
Faras
Soberkan

LEVANT
Tyr
Sur
Clean
d'Acre
Dea
Dahl
Almanaser

Cassaria
Samaria
Napleuse
Terre S.te
Jamm
Sumiscahas

Iaffa
Jerusalem
Mer
Morte
Damas
ARABIE
DESERTE

Rama
Gaza
Savar
Tabuc

Alexandria
Damieta
Mansoure
Geza
Le
Aerrous
Damna
ARABIE
PETREE
Crac al
Heratz

Lac Buchiara
Pisamides
Caire
Suez
Faran
Mont S.te
Caterine

EGIPTE
Kilan
Mont
Orch
Mont Sinai

Grandol
Le Tor

Mer Rouge

DALMATIA

MARE

MACEDO
GRÆ
NIA
Beroea

Apollonia
Thessalonica
Amphi
polis
Philippi
Neapolis
Samotra
cia

TROAS
Assur

Mitilene

Chius

CIA
ACHA
Nicopolis

Athenæ
Cenchræ
Corinthus
IA

Samus

Pathmos

Cous

CRETA
port' Ins.
Phoenice
Lasæa
Salmone

Cyrene
LYBIA
Circa
CYRENEM

484

BITHYNIA

PON TUS

GALA

TIA

CAP

PADO

PHRY

GIA

CIA

Mis...

Thiatira

Sardes

Philadel phia

Hierapolis

Listra

Iconium

Laodicea

Antiochia

LICAONIA

Coloffæ

Pisidia

Derbe

S I A

PI SIDIA

Perge

PAMPHILIA

LYCIA

Atalia

C I L I

Tarfus

CIÆ

Miletus

Mirra

Patara

PAMPHILIÆ ET

CILICIÆ PELAGVS

Rodus

Salamina

Seleucia

CYPRVS

INS.

Antiochia

Paphus

SYRIA

Syro Phœnice

Phœni

cc

Abilena

Cæfareæ Philippi

Damascus

Nazareth

Hierusalem

Alexandria

Sina Mons

Madian

Map: The ancient kingdoms of Asia Minor (two pages)

Turkey (Bellin, 1764)

MER NOIRE

Nord

C. Karempi
Ineboli
Aildun
Istefan
Kitros
Amasra
Durkiani
Kinch
Kiosé
Smub
Kers
C. Jasun
Barin
Hisaroki
Kers
Valusi
Kastemoni
Kafsayanboli
Tshenkeshnebé
Akiurek
Kecre
C. de Terme
Durek
Aladgum
Behre
Ounie
Samsun
Vinrasheher
Moderni
Toric
Kodhjissar
Karky
Liank
Ounie R.
Kerdé
Bainder
Teckes
Karadjé
Osmangik
Terme R.
Tekebu kabad
Aia
Kankesin
Lekib
Tshenike
Sedin R.
Beibasar
Angora
Kiril hermak
Merzifon
Terksal
Yukar
Amoria
Bonsok
Tshurum
Amasie
Sunisa
Insou
Djacenkir
Ceder
Tokat
Kirsheher
Hagibostak
Yous
Jolganeshu
Almous
Tshactelu
Lac
Vale
Monjur
Zilé
Sis
Sivas
ATula
Tshekenagar
Kaisanie
Ruhtsar
Ilqun
Latikié
Ku-hisar
Aksera
Nikde
Keremos ou Kenisou Riviere
Dog Anhisar
Konie
Karabignar
Bour
Bustre
Arca
Kashaelu
Ismil
Artan
Erkah
Islami
Tesamanent
Beisheheri
Kotunserai
Mamut
Bostan
Cocavn
Sudisheheri
Larende
Mes Belger
Bodendo
Guba
Bouzkir
Aladag
Sarikawak
Kars
Sis
Mesrah
Donmanes
Karsadro
Ermenak
Moud
Mesris
Anzarbe
Somisat
Ava
Alame
Castel Ubaldo
Senanbu
Seleski
Sekin
Lamerco
Adana
Melolo
Aias Pala
Aias
Behesni
Antioche
Lebar
Carro
Lingua di Bugass
golfe d'Alexandrette
Alexandrette
Paquas
Antab
Batni
Ainemur ou
Estenmur
C. Bianca
Kelis
Sejun
Reder
Akquia
Berun
S.Simeon
Aadim
MEDITERRANEE
C. Cormaniti
Malandrina
Chili
C. S.André
Bagas
Shagr
Kosten
Elbib
Gebul
EURE
Roum.
Lernssia
Cerbis
Palamisa
Arpaso
Paradisi
Latikié
Gebile
Vinserin
HALEP
ISLE DE CYPRE

30   31   32   33   34   35

***

487

The island of Corfu (Thevet, Cosmographie Universelle, 1575)

The island of Chios (Thevet, Cosmographie Universelle, 1575)

The island of Lemnos (Thevet, Cosmographie Universelle, 1575)

How terra sigillata is mined on the island of Lemnos (Thevet, Cosmographie Universelle, 1575)

491

Mount Athos (Thevet, Cosmographie Universelle, 1575)

Leading lions in Constantinople (Thevet, Cosmographie Universelle, 1575)

Turkish funeral ceremony (Thevet, Cosmographie Universelle, 1575)

Turkish circumcision ceremony (Thevet, Cosmographie Universelle, 1575)

Bibliography

I. OTHER WORKS BY PIERRE BELON
(in chronological order)

L'Histoire naturelle des étranges poissons marins, avec la vraie peinture et description du daulphin, et de plusieurs autres de son espèce, observée par Pierre Belon... – Paris, Impr. de R. Chaudière, 1551.

Petri Bellonii... De Admirabile operum antiquorum et rerum suspiciendarum praestantia liber primus. De medicato funere seu cadavere condito et lugubri defunctorum ejulatione liber secundus. De medicamentis nonnullis servandi cadaveris vim obtinentibus liber tertius. –Paris, Guillaume Cavellat, 1553. Edition shared with G. Corrozet and B. Prévost.

Petri Bellonii... De Aquatilibus libri duo cum iconibus ad vivam ipsorum effigiem quoad ejus fieri potuit expressis. – Paris, Charles Estienne, 1553.

P. Bellonii... De Arboribus coniferis resiniferis, aliis quoque nonnullis sempiterna fronde virentibus... – Paris, Guillaume Cavellat, 1553. Edition shared with G. Corrozet and B. Prévost.

La Nature et diversité des poissons, avec leurs pourtraicts représentez au plus près du naturel, par Pierre Belon... – Paris, Charles Estienne, 1555.

L'Histoire de la nature des oyseaux, avec leurs descriptions et naïfs portraicts retirez du naturel, escrite en sept livres, par Pierre Belon - Paris, Gilles Corrozet, 1555. Edition shared with G. Cavellat. (Facsimile edition by Philippe Glardon, with introduction and notes. – Geneva, Droz, 1997).

Portraits d'oyseaux, animaux, serpens, herbes, arbres, hommes et femmes d'Arabie et d'Egypte, observez par Pierre Belon du Mans. Le tout enrichy de Quatrains, pour plus facile cognoissance des Oyseaux, et autres portraits. Plus y est adjousté la Carte du mant Attos & du mont Sinay, pour l'intelligence de leur religion. – Paris, Guillaume Cavellat, 1557.

Petri Bellonii... De Aquatilium singulis scripta in GESNER, Conrad: *Historiae animalium liber IV, qui est de piscium et aquatilium animantium natura...* – Tiguri, 1558.

Petri Bellonii... Plurimarum singularium et memorabilium rerum in Graecia, Asia, Aegypto, Iudaea, Arabia, aliisque exteris provinciis ab ipso conspectarum observvationes, tribus libris expressae. Carolus Clusius... e gallicis Latinas faciebat. – Antverpiae, ex officina C. Plantini, 1589. Republished in 1605.

Les Remonstrances sur le default du labour et culture des plantes et de la cognoissance d'icelles... par Pierre Bellon... – Paris, Gilles Corrozet, 1558.

Petri Bellonii... de Neglecta stirpium cultura atque earum cognitione libellus... Carolus Clusius... e gallico latinum faciebat. – Antverpiae, ex officina C. Plantini, 1589. Translation of the *Remonstrances...*

La Cronique de Pierre Belon du Mans, médecin, au Roy Charles neufvyesme de ce nom, manuscript preserved in the Bibliothèque de l'Arsenal, ms 4651 (904 H.F.), f. 88r°–141r° and 161r°–250v° (16th century manuscript, copied by François Duchesne).

II. SIXTEENTH CENTURY SOURCES

BUSBECQ, Ogier Ghislain, *Itinera Constantinopolitanum et Amasianum ab... ad Soliman Turcarum Imperatorem,* Amberes, 1581. Translated into French as *Ambassades et voyages en Turquie et Amasie de Mr Busbequius, nouvellement traduites en françois par* S. G. Gaudon. – Paris, P. David, 1646.

CHESNEAU, Jean, *Voyage du Sieur d'Aramont, ambassadeur pour le Roy en Levant, faicts de Paris à Contantinople, l'an 1547, et de Constantinople en Perse, en l'an 1548, escripts par le sieur Jehan Chesneau, secrétaire dudict sieur d'Aramont.* Manuscript published by Charles Schefer in vol. VII of "Voyages et documents pour servir à l'histoire de la géographie". – Paris, E. Leroux, 1887; republished in facsimile, Slatkine, 1970.

DU FRESNE-CANAYE, Philippe, *Voyage du Levant* (1573), published and annotated by M.H. Hauser. – Paris, E. Leroux, 1897.

GILLES, Pierre, *Petri Gylii de Bosphoro Thracio libri III* – 1561.

MAURAND, Jérôme, *Itinéraire d'Antibes à Constantinople* (1544), Italian text published for the first time, with an introduction and translation by Léon Dorez. – Paris, E. Leroux, 1901.

NICOLAY, Nicolas de, *Les Quatre premiers livres des navigations et pérégrinations orientales de Nicolas de Nicolay Dauphinois, seigneur d'Arfeuille, valet de chambre et geographe ordinaire du Roy. Avec les figures au naturel tant d'hommes que de femmes, selon la diversité des nations, et de leur port, maintien, et habitz.* – Lyons, Guillaume Rouille, 1567–1568. The Antwerp edition, 1576 *(Les Navigations, Pérégrinations et Voyages faits en la Turquie)* was reproduced with an introduction and notes by S. Yérasimos and M.-C. Gomez-Guéraud: *Dans l'Empire de Soliman le magnifique* – Paris, Presses du CNRS, 1989.

POSTEL, Guillaume, *De la République des Turcs.* – Poitiers, 1560. THEVET, André, *Cosmographie du Levant,* Lyon, 1554. Critical edition by Frank Lestringant. – Geneva, Droz, 1985.

III. HISTORICAL AND CRITICAL WORKS

ADHÉMAR, Jean and Linzeler, André, *Bibliothèque nationale, département des eftampes, Inventaire du fonds français. Graveurs du XVIᵉ siècle.* – Paris, 1932–1938, 2 vol.

ATKINSON, Geoffroy, *La littérature géographique française de la Renaissance: répertoire bibliographique.* – Paris, A. Picard, 1927.

ATKINSON, Geoffroy, *Supplément au Répertoire bibliographique se rapportant à la littérature géographique française de la Renaissance.* – Paris, 1936.

ATKINSON, Geoffroy, *Les nouveaux horizons de la Renaissance française.* – Paris, E. Droz, 1935.

BERNARD, Yvelise, *L 'Orient du xviᵉ siecle à travers les récits des voyageurs français. Regards portés sur la société musulmane.* – Paris, L'Harmattan, 1989.

BITTAR, Thérèse, *Soliman, l'Empire magnifique.* – Paris, Gallimard, 1994 (Collection "Découvertes Gallimard").

BONNAC, Jean-Louis Dusson, marquis de, *Mémoire historique sur l'ambassade de France à Constantinople.* – Paris, 1884.

BONNAFFÉ, Edmond, *Les arts et les moeurs d'autrefois. Voyages et voyageurs de la Renaissance.* – Paris, 1895. Geneva, Slatkine Reprints, 1970.

BROC, Numa, *La Géographie de la Renaissance (1420–1620).* – Paris, 1980.(Mémoires de la section de géographie du Comité des travaux historiques et scientifiques, n° 9).

BRUN, Robert, *Le livre illustré en France au xviiᵉ siècle.* – Paris, F. Alcan, 1930. New edition, Paris, 1969.

CARRÉ, Jean-Marie, *Voyageurs et écrivains en Egypte.* – Cairo, lnstitut français d'Archéologie orientale, 1932, vol. 1 (1517–1840).

CÉARD, Jean, *La Nature et les prodiges : l'insolite au XVIᵉ siècle en France.* - Geneva, Droz, 1977.

CÉARD, Jean, "Pierre Belon zoologiste", *Actes du colloque Renaissance-Classicisme du Maine.* - Le Mans, 1971; Paris, A.G. Nizet, 1975, pp. 129–140.

CÉARD, Jean et Margolin, Jean-Claude (ed.), *Voyager à la Renaissance,* Paris, 1987. (Actes du XXVIᵉ colloque international d'Etudes humanistes).

CHARRIÈRE, Ernest, *Négociations de la France dans Ie Levant.* – Paris, 1840–1860.

CLOT, André, *Soliman le magnifique.* – Paris, Fayard, 1983.

DAINVILLE, François de, *La Géographie des humanistes.* – Paris, Beauchesne, 1940. New edition Geneva, Slatkine Reprints, 1969.

DELAUNAY, Paul, "L'aventureuse existence de Pierre Belon", *Revue du seizième siècle,* IX, 1922, pp. 251–268, X, 1923, pp. 1–34 and 125–147, XI, 1924, pp. 30–48 and 222–232, XII, 1925, pp. 78–97 and 256–282. Extracts brought together in one vol. under the same title. – Paris, Edouard Champion, 1926.

DELAUNAY, Paul, *Pierre Belon, naturaliste.* – Le Mans, Monnoyer, 2 vol., 1923 and 1926.

DELAUNAY, Paul, *Un adversaire de la Réforme. Les idées religieuses de Pierre Belon du Mans.* – Laval, Goupil, 1922, 23 p. (extract from the Bulletin de la Commission historique et archéologique de la Mayenne, 1922).

DELAUNAY, Paul, *La zoologie au XVIe siècle.* – Paris, Hermann, 1962. New edition 1997 (Collection "Histoire de la pensée").

DELUMEAU, Jean, *La Civilisation de la Renaissance* – Paris, Arthaud, 1967. New edition in the Collection "Les grandes civilisations", Arthaud, 1996.

DEMAIZIÈRE, Colette, "La langue à la recherche de ses origines. La mode des étymologies grecques", *Réforme, Humanisme et Renaissance,* VIII, 1982, pp. 63–78.

DESCHAMPS, Léon, "Pierre Belon naturaliste et explorateur", *Revue de Géographie,* vol. XXI, 1887, pp. 321–333 and 433–440.

Dictionnaire des Sciences naturelles. – Strasbourg and Paris, 60 vol. 1816–1830.

DUBOIS, Claude-Gilbert, *L'imaginaire de la Renaissance.* – Paris, PUF, 1985.

DUGAT, Gustave, *Histoire des orientalistes de l'Europe du XIIe au XIXe siècle.* – Paris, Adrien Maisonneuve, 2 vol., 1868–1870.

FIRMIN-DIDOT, Ambroise, *Essai typographique et bibliographique sur l'histoire de la gravure sur bois.* – Paris, Firmin-Didot, 1863.

HOOKER and JACKSON, *Index kewensis plantarum phaneroganum...* – Oxford, 1895.

IORGA, Nicolas, *Les voyageurs français dans l'Orient européen (du XVe au XVIIIe siècle.* – Paris, 1928.

LAPEYRE, Henri, *Les monarchies européennes du XVIe siècle et les relations internationales .*– Paris, 1967.

LAURENT-VIBERT, R., *Voyages, routiers, pèlerins et corsaires aux échelles du Levant.* Paris, G. Grès, 1923.

LE GOFF, Jacques, *L'imaginaire medieval.* – Paris, Gallimard, 1985.

LESTRINGANT, Frank, *L'atelier du cosmographe ou l'image du monde à la Renaissance.* – Paris, Albin Michel, 1991.

LESTRINGANT, Frank, *André Thevet, cosmographe des derniers Valois.* – Geneva, Droz, 1991 (Travaux d'Humanisme et Renaissance, 251).

LESTRINGANT, Frank, *Arts et légendes d'espaces* : *figures du voyage et rhétoriques du mende*. – Paris, Presses de l'Ecole Normale Supérieure, 1981.

LESTRINGANT, Frank, "Cosmologie et mirabiIia à la Renaissance: l' exernple de G. Postel", *The Journal of Medieval and Renaissance Studies*, vol. 16, n° 2, autumn 1986.

LESTRINGANT, Frank, *Ecrire le monde à la Renaissance*. – Caen, Paradigme, 1993.

LEWIS, Bernard, *Istanbul and the Civilization of the Ottoman Empire*, – Oklahoma, 1983).

MANTRANT, Robert (ed.), *Histoire de l'Empire ottoman*. – Paris, Fayard, 1989. MANTRANT, Robert, *Istanbul au siècle de Soliman le Magnifique*. – Paris, Hachette, 1994 (reedition of *La vie quotidienne de Constantinople au temps de Soliman le Magnifique et de ses successeurs*, Hachette, 1965).

MARGOLIN, Jean-Claude, *L'humanisme en Europe au temps de Ia Renaissance*. –Paris, PUF, 1981.

MARTIN, Henri-Jean, Chartier, Roger (ed.), *Histoire de l'édition française*. – Paris, Promodis, 1983–1986. vol. 1: *Le livre conquérant. Du Moyen Age au milieu du XVIe siècle*.

MERLE, Alexandra, "Les villes ottomanes dans les relations chrétiennes aux XVIe et XVIIe siècles", *Lieux dits, recherches sur l'espace dans les textes ibériques (XVIe–XXe siècles)*. – Presses de I'Université de Saint-Etienne, 1992. }.

MIQUEL, Andre, *L'islam et sa civilisation*. – Paris, Armand Colin, 1977.

Palais et maisons du Caire, collective work (Groupe de recherches et d'études sur Ie Proche-Orient, Univ. de Provence). – Paris, CNRS, 1982–1883, 2 vol.

PARENT, Annie, *Les métiers du livre à Paris au XVIe siècle (1535–1560)*. – Geneva, Droz, 1974.

PAVIOT, Jacques, "L' ambassade de d'Aramon: érudits et voyageurs au Levant, 1547–1583", *Voyager à la Renaissance*, ed. J. Céard and J.-C. Margolin, pp. 381–397.

RENOUARD, Philippe, *Imprimeurs et libraires parisiens du XVIe siècle. Fascicule Cavellat, Marnef et Cavellat*. – Paris, Bibliothèque Nationale, 1986.

RODINSON, Maxime, *La fascination de l'islam*, followed by *Le seigneur bourguignon et l'esclave sarrazin*. – Paris, La Découverte, 1980.

ROUX, Jean-Paul, *Histoire des Turcs. Deux mille ans du Pacifique à la Méditerranée*. – Paris, Fayard, 1984.

SOURDEL, Dominique et Janine, *Dictionnaire historique de l'islam*. – Paris, PUF, 1996.

TODOROV, Tzvetan, *Nous et les autres. La reflection française sur la diversité humaine.* – Paris, Le Seuil, 1989.

URSU, Ion, *La politique orientale de François Iᵉʳ, 1517–1547.* – Paris, Champion, 1908.

VEINSTEIN, Gilles, *Soliman le Magnifique et son temps.* – Paris, La Documentation Française, 1990.

WOLFZETTEL, Friedrich, *Le discours du voyageur. Pour une histoire littéraire du récit de voyage en France, du Moyen-Age au XVIIIᵉ siècle.* – Paris, PUF, 1996 (Collection "Perspectives littéraires").

YÉRASIMOS, Stéphane, *Les voyageurs dans l'Empire ottoman, XIVᵉ–XVIᵉ siècles: bibliographie, itinéraires et inventaire des lieux habités.* – Ankara, Société torque d'Histoire, 1991.

ZINGUER, Ilana, "Narration et témoignage dans les *Observations* de Pierre Belon (1553)", *Nouvelle revue du seizième siècle*, 1987, n° 5, pp. 25–40.

Glossary of weights, measures and coins

asper; a small silver Turkish coin, of which 129 were reckoned equal to the piaster. In the time of Suleiman it weighed about three-quarters of a gram.

carolus: a coin of silver alloy struck in the reign of Charles VIII of France (1470–1498).

cubit: an ancient measure of length, usually about 18–22 inches

drachm: a weight equivalent to rather more than three grams (1/16 of an ounce).

ducat: "a gold coin of varying value, formerly in use in most European countries; that current in Holland, Russia, Austria, and Sweden being equivalent to about 9*s*. 4*d*. Also applied to a silver coin of Italy, value about 3*s*. 6d" (OED).

league: an old measure of length, varying from country but usually about 3 miles.

palm: a measure of length, equivalent either to the breadth of the palm of the hand , i.e. about 3–4 inches, or to the whole length of the hand from the wrist to the finger-tips, i.e. about 7–9 inches.

quintal: equivalent to a hundredweight.

sol, sou: in France of the Ancien Régime, a copper or bronze coin worth 1/20 of a pound.

talent: an ancient Greek measure of weight, varying from place to place and from time to time; usually about 20–27 kilograms (45–60 pounds.

toise: a French measure of length of 6 French feet, roughly equal to 1·949 metres, or 6 2 / 5 English feet.

Notes

[1] There were, however, some exceptions, like the account of a journey by Jean Thenaud in 1512, published in 1530.

[2] "The articles by which the Porte gave special immunities and privileges to French subjects, extended subsequently to those of other nations" (OED).

[3] Stéphane Yérasimos published Nicolas de Nicolay's *Navigations, pérégrinations & voyages faits en la Turquie* under the title *Dans l'Empire de Soliman le Magnifique* (Presses du CNRS, 1989).

[4] The hamlet was called La Soultière. This information comes from Paul Delaunay's *L'aventureuse existence de Pierre Belon du Mans* (Champion, 1926).

[5] According to Philippe Glardon, editor of Belon's *Histoire de la nature des oiseaux* (Droz, 1997), Introduction, p. xvi.

[6] His identification with the painter Pierre Gourdelle is not generally accepted.

[7] The date is uncertain: it may have been 1565.

[8] He was not properly qualified as a physician, gaining the equivalent of a bachelor's degree (but not a doctorate) only with difficulty, after his travels in the Levant.

[9] Op. cit.

[10] Robert Brun *(Le livre français illustré de la Renaissance)* says that these figures of birds, animals and plants are "scrupulously true to life".

[11] He was the author, among other works, of the *Singularités de la France antarctique*, published in 1558.

[12] Book I, chapter 50.

[13] Book I, chapters 73 ff.

[14] Some copies give the publisher as "chez Guillaume Cavellat, à l'enseigne de la Poulle grasse, devant le Collège de Cambray", others as "en la boutique de Gilles Corrozet, pres la chapelle de messieurs les Présidens".

[15] "Sixteenth century books whose illustrator is known with certainty, particularly those in which the engravings are signed, are few in number compared with those – frequently of remarkable quality – which remain anonymous" (Robert Brun, op. cit.).

[16] The first edition of Nicolay's work dates from 1568. Although the engravings (etchings rather than woodcuts as in the *Observations)* were made several years earlier (after Nicolay's own drawings), they are later than Belon's. Stéphane Yérasimos refers to a contract signed

in November 1555 with the engraver Léon Davent, and supposes that the work was done in the course of the year 1556. For the second edition (Antwerp, 1576) a new set of illustrations (woodcuts by a number of different engravers) was used.

[17] *Imprimeurs & libraires parisiens du XVIᵉ siècle. Fascicule Cavellat, Marnef et Cavellat,* Bnf, 1986.

[18] Godfrey Atkinson, *La littérature géographique de la Renaissance: répertoire bibliographique,* Paris, 1927; Jacques Charles Brunet, *Manuel du libraire de l'amateur de livres,* Paris, 1860 (first edition 1809).

[19] See on this point Philippe Renouard, op. cit.

[20] They had already appeared in the *Portraits d'oiseaux* of 1557.

[21] Serge Sauneron, for his part, reproduces in facsimile part of the Paris edition of 1555.

[22] Serge Sauneron's edition reproduces, in addition to the illustrations from the Paris edition of 1555, three from the Antwerp edition of 1589 showing the cassia-tree, the sycamore-fig and the acacia.

[23] This translation of Dioscorides was never published . After Belon's death the manuscript could not be found.

[24] Philosophers of an ancient Hindu sect, who wore no clothes and led the life of contemplative ascetics.

[25] Who gave his name to *eupatorium* (hemp agrimony).

[26] Clymenus was a king of Arcadia; it is also the Latin name of a species of honeysuckle. Belon later describes achillea and *Teucrium scordium*.

[27] Belon is in error: the thyme which grows in France is indeed *Thymus vulgaris;* but he refuses to give that name to the plant of which Dioscorides speaks, which grows in Greece and in Sicily and is properly called *Satureia capitata*.

[28] The grayling.

[29] The two species are indeed different: the former, the Oriental plane *(Platanus)* was of eastern origin. while the latter *(Acer pseudoplatanus* or false plane) is a sycamore maple.

[30] Saltpetre (nitre, potassium nitrate) is found in nature ready formed. Belon's mistake stems from the translators of ancient texts, who rendered the word *nitrum* by nitre, although in fact it means natron (sodium carbonate).

[31] The inhabitants of Arcadia, the mountainous region in the central Peloponnese, were represented as rustic shepherds.

[32] Tyrrhenians: the name given by Greeks to the Etruscans.

[33] The Venetians, after losing the territory they held in the Peloponnese, had been driven out of the Aegean by the Turks. The Turks had

unsuccessfully laid siege to Corfu (which had been held by the Venetians for 150 years), and had then set out to conquer the islands held by great Venetian families. Twenty-five of these islands were taken and devastated by Suleiman's fleet, commanded by Barbarossa, including Patmos, Ios, Naxos and Andros. The Venetians then joined the Holy League (with Genoa, the Pope and the Emperor Charles V), but in 1540 were compelled to sign a treaty under which they abandoned the towns of Nauplia and Monemvasia and all the islands conquered by Barbarossa. At the time when Belon was writing they held only Crete and Cyprus, but Cyprus was lost in 1570.

[34] Modern French *goudron* (tar), from Arabic *qatran*.

[35] Pera is the district in Constantinople which was inhabited by Greeks and was the residence of foreign ambassadors.

[36] "And [does not Plato advise] rather [the free and joyous invitation], drinking in small cups?" *(Saturnalia,* II, 8).

[37] "After the first course, with smaller glasses circulating on all sides, [Praetextatus says:] Men are usually silent while eating but talkative while drinking" *(Saturnalia,* VII, 1.

[38] A semi-nomadic people of Iranian origin.

[39] Albania, Bulgaria, Croatia, Serbia, Wallachia (north of the Danube), Sclavonia and Dalmatia (on the shores of the Adriatic) were among the Balkan possessions of the Ottoman Empire. Circassia (north of the Caucasus) was the country of origin of the Mamelukes.

[40] Later editions correct this to "others by love".

[41] The "mountains of Sphachie", now Lefka Ori, are in the west of the island; Mount Ida, or Psiloreitis, is in the centre; and farther east is the Dikti range, its highest peak being Mount Lasithi, which Belon seems to confuse with the mountains of Sitia, at the east end of the island.

[42] Small galleys.

[43] La Canée is Khania; Candy or Candie is Iraklion; Setie is Sitia; Voulismeni is a small town between Iraklion and Sitia; Chisamo is Kastelli Kisamou, to the west of Khania; Selino is perhaps Ormos Selino, on the south coast of the island; Sphachie is Sfakia.

[44] A member of the Barozzi family of Venice. The archives of the Inquisition refer to a Francesco Barozzi who lived in the second half of the 16th century and was the subject of enquiry in Venice, having previously resided in Candy (Crete).

[45] Fish preserved in brine with added spices, used as a seasoning from Roman times.

[46] Gortyn was capital of Crete in Roman and early Byzantine times.

47 Probably a tributary of the Ieropotamos, the principal river in the region.

48 The cistuses secrete a resinous and aromatic substance known in antiquity under the name of *ladanum* or laudanum.

49 A region in western France (chief town Le Mans). Belon's home village is now spelled La Soultiére. (T)

50 These villages no longer exist, but must have been situated, from what Belon says later, to the north of Mount Ida, between Rethymnon and Iraklion.

51 In his *Histoire naturelle des étranges poissons marins, avec la vraie peinture & description du dauphin, & de plusieurs autres de son espéce* (1551).

52 His *Histoire de la nature des oiseaux, avec leurs descriptions & naïfs portraits retirés du naturel,* published in 1555.

53 Eyebrow in French is *sourcil.* (T)

54 *Effraie* relates to *effrayant* (fearsome). *Capimulgus* is the barn-owl, but Pliny also gives this name to the nightjar, a passerine which hunts insects, flying with its beak open.

55 "It is said that they ferret with thir beak in the entrails [of children…], filled with milk. Their name is *striges;* the cause of their name is that they are accustomed to utter strident cries at night which make men's hair stand on end" *(Fasti,* VI, 137 and 139–140).

56 Belon is referring to his *Histoire des oiseaux,* which was published only in 1555. This is no doubt a means of claiming priority in the subject.

57 Phalangy (pl. phalangies): an anglicised form (now obsolete) of phalangium, a name applied to various kinds of venomous spider. (T)

58 The name of this officer, Jean Choul, was given in later editions. A bailiff was a military or legal officer who dispensed justice in the name of the king.

59 Later editions add: "It is matter for wonder to see the agility of this animal, which is of the nature of the roe deer, for both of them live amid rugged and inaccessible rocks; but the ibex can leap from one rock to another more than six paces away, a thing almost unbelievable to one who has not seen it."

60 The term unicorn is applied both to the animal and to its horn. (T)

61 The *strepsiceros* referred to by the Latin authors, particularly Pliny, is actually a kind of antelope. The animal described here is a sheep *(Ovis aries)* which flourishes in Greece and Crete.

62 The legend of the unicorn stemmed from the existence of two animals, long regarded as fabulous: the rhinoceros, called unicorn, and the narwhal, whose long spirally-twisted horn was sometimes found washed ashore on the coasts of Iceland and Norway.

[63] Ivory from a walrus's tusk or a rhinoceros's tooth.

[64] Indian ass was a name given to the rhinoceros.

[65] Pliny's words are: *Cornigera fere bisulca; solida ungula et bicorne nullum; unicorne asinus Indicus; unicorne et bisulcum oryx* ("Almost all horned animals are cloven-hoofed; none has uncloven hoofs and two horns; the Indian ass has only one horn, the oryx one horn and cloven hoofs."), *Natural History,* book XI, § 255.

[66] The one at Saint-Denis.

[67] The pound was an old measure of length equivalent to 32.4 centimetres. The pound, a unit of mass, ranged between 380 and 550 grams in different parts of France, and was subdivided into ounces. Thus the horn that Belon is speaking of must have been more than 2 metres long and weighed between 5 and 7 kilograms.

[68] These horns were the horns of a narwhal. The treasury of Saint Mark's possessed two, each a metre long. The first, mounted on a silver base and bearing a number of inscriptions, was presented by a jeweller in 1488, and the second was acquired in the early 16th century. They were believed to have medicinal properties, particularly against plague.

[69] A belemnite was a mollusc, a cephalopod, related to the cuttlefish, only the hard interior in the form of a beak could be fossilised.

[70] Francis I of France (1515–1547).

[71] In 1542. Belon went to Luxembourg in the suite of Cardinal de Tournon, after the capture of the town by Charles d'Orléans, in the name of the French king, from the forces of the Empire.

[72] There is some confusion here: Cérigo is Belon's name for Cytherea. (T)

[73] The Calergi were Venetian nobles living in Crete (14th–18th centuries).

[74] Belon quotes Pliny correctly except for his misspelling of the term *scolymos:* "The artichoke flowers late and for a long time... The artichoke, which belongs to the thistle genus, differs from it in that its root can be eaten after being boiled" *(Natural History,* XXI, §§ 95–96).

[75] "A short, heavy, square-headed arrow or bolt, formerly used in shooting with the cross-bow or arbalest" (OED).

[76] "A quarrel or bolt for the cross-bow" (OED)

[77] Saint John the Baptist (Prodromos)? (T)

[78] "Do not you eat monstrous meats, putting in your cups beavers' testicles and the poisonous flesh of vipers and mixing in also products of India and the many herbs of which Crete is so generous?" *(Saturnalia,* VII, 5).

[79] "The wine of Crete is called Pramnian or Protropos (Precursor)" *(Materia medica,* V, 9, quoted by Belon in a Latin translation).

80 Cretan priests who brought up the young Zeus.

81 This was the war dance of the Lacedaemonians.

82 There are many varieties of branles, round dances by a number of dancers holding each other by the hand.

83 The Porte or Sublime Porte: the government of the Ottoman sultan.

84 Like most western visitors, Belon stayed in Pera and had to cross the Golden Horn to Constantinople, where the shops, and particularly the bazaar, were.

85 Simple: "A medicine or medicament composed or concocted of only one constituent, especially of one herb or plant; hence, a plant or herb employed for medicinal purposes" (OED).

86 *Terra sigillata* (a clayey soil hardening when extracted from the earth) is a kaolin which owes its colouring to the ferrous oxide that it contains. It was made into large tablets which were stamped with the Sultan's seal. It was credited with therapeutic qualities, for example against stomach ulcers, but in fact it has only absorbent and adhesive properties.

87 Defluxion: a discharge or flowing of humours and fluid matter. (T)

88 Bole armeniac: a kind of earth from Armenia resembling sealed earth but redder (because it is richer in ferrous oxide) and more astringent.

89 "A Turkish official in command of a district or village" (OED).

90 The Baron de Fumel, sent by Henry II of France to announce the death of Francis I, had arrived in Constantinople in July 1547; Monsieur d'Aramont was already there.

91 The Propontis is the Sea of Marmara, which leads to the Pontus Euxinus (the Black Sea) by way of the Bosphorus.

92 From ancient times the Bosphorus of Thrace (which has preserved its name) was distinguished from the Cimmerian Bosphorus, now called Kerch Strait, which separates the Black Sea from the Sea of Azov. The Hellespont was the strait separating Europe from Asia, now called the Dardanelles.

93 Belon must mean the Mediterranean, which was called the Inner Sea *(Mer Inférieure).*

94 Imbros (now Gökceada) is the first island met with on leaving the Dardanelles.

95 Or perhaps Limni represents the Greek *limen* (harbour) or *limne* (pool, lagoon)? (T)

96 Thasos, Gökceada (Imbros) and Bozcaada (Tenedos) are all close to one another. Skyros is farther south, in the Northern Sporades.

97 The Latin *gracculus* is in fact the jackdaw, a bird of black plumage which bears little resemblance to the jay.

98 The squill *(scille* in French) is a bulbous-rooted plant related to the hyacinth; but Belon may be thinking of the *squine (Smilax china,* China root), an Asian plant with thorny stems.

99 A judge, who might also be a tax-collector.

100 The chapel was evidently dedicated to the Saviour *(Soter* in Greek). Since August 6th is the feast of the Transfiguration of Christ in the Orthodox (as well as the Roman) church, this may have been the reason for the selection of that date. (T)

101 A map by the 16th century geographer Sebastian Munster equates Corsula with Corfu. The "story of the dolphin" presumably refers to the dolphin which saved Arion from drowning; but Arion has associations with the city of Corinth and the island of Sicily, not with Corfu. Corfu was originally colonised by Corinth: could there be a connection there? (T)

102 Pliny describes *cenchris* as a spotted snake. It was probably *Vipera ammodytes,* the nose-horned viper.

103 The island of Thasos lies opposite the town of Kavala. Philip II, king of Macedon from 359 BC, seeking to extend his territory, made a series of conquests on the coast of Thrace and then made war on Athens and Thebes, finally making himself master of the whole of Greece except Sparta.

104 Vatopedi.

105 The cantharides are a genus of coleopterous insects. *Buprestis* designates an insect which is black or dark blue in colour, not yellow. Belon may mean the *mylabres* (buprestids, borers), which are also found on Mount Athos, at a different time of year.

106 *Sphondylion* is the Greek word for spindle or spindle-whorl. The English plant referred to by Belon is presumably hogweed *(Heracleum sphondylium).* (T)

107 Addition in later editions: "We can well call it sea-grasshopper. For what the people of Marseilles call in their corrupt language crayfish could be called grasshopper in pure French".

108 All travellers refer to this unconcern of the Turks, who were not worried about contagion, visited plague victims and wore the clothes of the dead.

109 Chrysites means in Latin "precious stone".

110 Men who had been taken by the Turks in the regular levy *(devshirme,* "collection") of young Christian boys to be trained as janissaries. They were converted to Islam and educated according to their aptitudes, and thus were fitted for useful employment. Most of them became pages or soldiers, but some gained political posts.

111 During his early conquests in Thrace Philip of Macedon occupied the town of Philippi and the gold mines on Mount Pangeo in 358 BC.

112 These were Jews who had settled in Ottoman territory after their expulsion from Spain in 1492 (when the Catholic Monarchs gave them the choice between conversion and expulsion) or in earlier years where they were already under strong pressure to convert.

113 Pyrites and marcasites are natural sulphides of iron.

114 "The action of extracting or elaborating by heat" (OED)

115 Nitric acid.

116 Zinc oxide.

117 Or white arsenic: a name given by the ancients to zinc oxide mixed with arsenious acid (or copper oxide, lead or antimony) which condenses in the form of flakes in blast furnaces.

118 From Latin *lithargyrus*, "silver stone": a natural oxide of lead in crystallised form.

119 A natural sulphide of lead.

120 The Roman consul Lucius Aemilius Paulus, given the cognomen Macedonicus, defeated Perseus, last king of Macedonia, at Pydna in 168 BC. Perseus was taken to Rome, where he died in captivity.

121 Alum was known to the ancients. The industry was a source of profit to Turkey at an early period.

122 Later editions add the information that it was called the Phasis.

123 The Hebrus is now called Meriç in Turkey and Marica in Bulgaria. Pactolus was a river in Lydia which was reputed to carry down gold. The Ticino flows out of Lake Maggiore near a town called Verbania. The Adda is near Lake Como, anciently called Lake Larius.

124 Char.

125 This cannot be the celebrated account by López de Gómara which had just been published in Spanish (in 1552) but was not translated into French until much later. It was probably an earlier book which was the source of the story about the gold of Peru and about Pizarro (who seized Atahualpa's treasury in 1532), and was translated into French in 1534 under the title *Nouvelles certaines des îles du Pérou.*

126 A legendary Christian sovereign whose name first appears in the 12th century. His kingdom was thought to be now in Asia, now in Africa. It was the voyages of the Portuguese navigators that made it possible to identify Prester John as the negus of Ethiopia in the early 16th century.

127 In 1527 there was a war between an Ethiopian king (Lebna Dengel) and a Muslim emir who was occupying the region. Two years later the king, vanquished, had to take refuge in southern Eritrea, in the

mountains of Tigre. In 1535 he sent a member of a Portuguese embassy which had come there in 1529, João Bermudez, to ask for help from Portugal. In 1541 the Portuguese sent four hundred men under the command of Cristóvão da Gama (fourth son of Vasco da Gama), who won a number of battles before being defeated by the Turks, who had established themselves in Africa and now supported the Muslim emir. Almost all the Portuguese were killed (including Cristóvão da Gama); but in 1543 the Ethiopians succeeded in defeating the Muslims.

[128] "The action of heat in preparing any substance" (OED).

[129] "A very smooth, fine-grained, black or dark-coloured variety of quartz or jasper … used for testing the quality of gold and silver alloys by the colour of the streak produced by rubbing them upon it; a piece of such stone used for this purpose" (OED)

[130] A silicate of lime or magnesia.

[131] One of the gulfs round Chalcidice, which projects into the Aegean.

[132] Belon calls it the *Havre neuf,* the new harbour. It had been built between 1517 and 1523, in the reign of Francis I.

[133] Ferns and allied plants (OED).

[134] Known in English as Venus's navelwort. (T)

[135] Theodore Gaza, who had translated Aristotle's *History of Animals* into Latin.

[136] "Nature has given *caprea* antlers, but small ones, [and they do not fall off like those of stags]" *(Natural History,* XI, 124).

[137] "And made them so that they fall off, as for stags". Belon, who identifies Pliny's *caprea* with the roe deer, substitutes "and made them" for "and did not make them".

[138] "Among horned animals the smallest of all those that we have studied is the dorcas, which also belongs to the genus red deer, having horns which fall off each year" (Aristotle, *Parts of Animals,* III, 2, 663b, in the Latin translation by Theodore Gaza).

[139] "And [nature] made them so that they fall off, as for stags". Cf. note 136.

[140] To judge from the drawing, it is a mouflon.

[141] A fabulous animal, half horse and half stag, which is described by the ancient authors.

[142] The river Strymon flows into the gulf of Orfani.

[143] A garbled version of the title *sanjakbey,* an official immediately subordinate to a *beylerbey,* the governor of a province. The sanjakbey governed a district and was in command of the soldiers stationed there, particularly those recruited locally.

[144] Presumably Ibrahim Pasha, Suleiman the Magnificent's grand vizier in

1523 and beylerbey of Roumelia, i.e. the whole of Turkey in Europe with the exception of Albania, Hungary, Bosnia, the Morea (the Peloponnese) and the Greek islands. Thrace was within this territory.

[145] Philippopolis lies to the north of Philippi (of which there are some remains), in Thrace.

[146] Now Vlorë and Durrës in Albania.

[147] "To the muse Naevia in memory".

[148] The name of La Cavalle (now Kavala) reflects the French word for mare, *cavale*. (T)

[149] *Divus* (divine) was the title given after their death to divinised Roman emperors. This was the case with Julius Caesar (called Divus Julius) , and also with Claudius.

[150] See note 147.

[151] A people living in Arcadia, in the Peloponnese.

[152] The name Achaia is applied either to the northern part of the Peloponnese or to the whole of it.

[153] Belon thus identified Bucephala with the present-day town of Kavala (La Cavalle).

[154] Suleiman the Magnificent, seeking to extend his empire westward, had set out to conquer Hungary, and had won the brilliant victory of Mohacs in 1526 over king Louis II of Hungary, who was killed in the battle. He then put the voivode of Transylvania, John Zapolya, on the throne, but this was opposed by Ferdinand, brother of the emperor Charles V, who had married a sister of Louis II. In 1529 Suleiman, at the head of his troops, laid siege to Vienna, but was compelled to withdraw, though still firmly established in Hungary, the whole of which he annexed in 1541 with the capture of Buda. Hungary continued to be the scene of conflict between the Habsburgs and the Grand Signior (though Suleiman himself died during the siege of Szeged in 1566), but remained Turkish until the treaty of Carlowitz in 1699.

[155] Palaiokastro, near Kastelli Kisamou (Belon's Quissamus). (T)

[156] Eastern Thessaly.

[157] See note 143.

[158] Caravanserai.

[159] Esclavine: a pilgrim's cloak.

[160] Mytilene (Lesbos).

[161] A violent purgative made from the juice of wild cucumbers.

[162] This is the river Nestos, to the east of the Strymon, which flows into the sea, as Belon says later, between the islands of Thasos and Samothrace.

[163] *Bistonius* in Latin means "of Thrace".

[164] Soon after his return to France, in 1549, Belon accompanied Cardinal de Tournon to Rome, where a conclave was held which elected Pope Julius III. It was then that he visited Tolfa, where there was a deposit of alum which had been discovered after 1453 by a Venetian who had fled from Constantinople.

[165] "Water impregnated with alkaline salts extracted ... from wood ashes, lye" (OED).

[166] Pliny's *thymus tragoriganum,* which Belon also calls *thymbra.*

[167] Sestos and Abydos lie on either side of the strait of the Dardanelles. The sites of these two ancient towns do not quite coincide with the villages of Kilitbahir (on the west side, near Eceabat) and Çanakkale (on the Asian side).

[168] Mentioned as a coastal town in Thrace.

[169] This term covers chalcedony and other similar silicates (agate, jasper, onyx, flint, etc.).

[170] A type of curd cheese with herbs which was known to the ancient Greeks. (T)

[171] Rodosto is situated on the Sea of Marmara, some hundred kilometres from Constantinople. Belon is wrong in equating it with Perinthus (anciently Heraclea), which is a different town (now called Marmaraereğlisi).

[172] Later editions add: "although there are people who think that Perinthus was the town now called Heraclea". This was in fact right: see note 170 and page *431.*

[173] There are several towns named after Hercules, including Heraclea in Thrace (now called Marmaraereğlisi), of which Belon is speaking here, Heraclea in Lycaonia (see page *428)* and Heraclea on the Black Sea in Paphlagonia.

[174] Presumably Rye, which, like Silivri, is situated on a hill, and could have been visited by Belon when he was in England in the 1540s. (T)

[175] Names given in antiquity to the provinces of Turkey in Asia. Details in the Index, pages *565–574.*

[176] Suleiman the Magnificent had gone to war with the shah of Iran, his neighbour. The hostility between the Ottoman sovereigns, who were Sunnites, and the Shiites who reigned in Persia was of long standing, and Sultan Selim I had had already made an unsuccessful attempt to vanquish the Safavids of Persia. At the end of his expedition, in 1534, Suleiman took Baghdad, the city of the Caliphs, but without totally overthrowing the shah. Some years later war flared up again, and in the spring of 1548 Suleiman set out once again at the head of

his army and won further victories. Other campaigns followed until the temporary peace of Amasya in 1555.

[177] A settlement on the opposite side of the Golden Horn from Constantinople, occupied by Greeks and westerners.

[178] Gabriel de Leuls, Seigneur d'Aramon (or d'Aramont), spent many years in Constantinople. He first went there in 1542 as ambassador *ad interim*. Returning to France in 1545, he went back to Constantinople in the following year with the title of ambassador. It was his first mission, in the course of which he accompanied Suleiman to Persia. During his second mission, in 1551–1553, he also had to travel, following the Turkish galleys on a campaign in Apulia. He died soon afterwards.

[179] The pinna *(Pinna marina)* was a shellfish, not a fish.

[180] These are the Princes' Islands.

[181] The largest of these islands in the Sea of Marmara is still called Marmara Adası. Of the others the most important are Türkeli Adası and Paşalimanı Adası.

[182] Belon is here thinking of the French. He adds in later editions: "We mean those who from stubbornness eat meat secretly on Fridays, and scarce even have fish on Sunday".

[183] A *carrelet*, a square net suspended from two crossed half-hoops attached to the end of a pole.

[184] Barbarossa died in Constantinople in 1546.

[185] The French term *chien de mer*, generally translated as dogfish, was applied to various members of the shark family. Among them was the *roussette* (catshark), also called *chat de mer*.

[186] The Latin word *taeda* means a pine-tree.

[187] "A sauce prepared from fermented fish, much used by the ancient Romans" (OED).

[188] Belon transcribes the quotation from Pliny with fair accuracy, but it requires some correction to restore the logic of the passage: *Aliud vero est, castimoniarum superstitioni etiam sacrisque Iudaeis dicatum, quod fit e piscibus squama [non] quarentibus;* that is (apropos of garum): "There is another kind, reserved for the superstitious practices of continence and for the religious ceremonies of the Jews, which is made from fish *not* lacking scales" *(Natural History,* book XXI, § 95). The book of Leviticus holds that aquatic animals without fins or scales are impure.

[189] Constantine I, the Great, son of St Helena, made Constantinople the new capital of the Empire in AD 330. He granted Christians a tolerance which amounted to the recognition of Christianity as the

state religion and built the first great Christian monuments, including St Sophia in Constantinople and the Holy Sepulchre in Jerusalem.

[190] The Hippodrome contained an obelisk and a column consisting of three intertwined brass snakes. The column was an offering by Greeks to the oracle of Delphi which Constantine had caused to be transported to Constantinople.

[191] A traditional comparison. In fact seven eminences can be distinguished in the city, but only five of them (bearing notable buildings) really deserve the name of hills.

[192] The walls were built by Theodosius II in 414 and 447 and were several times restored in later periods.

[193] Again a traditional comparison, though here it is more openly in favour of Saint Sophia than usual.

[194] The Byzantine church of St John the Evangelist, near St Sophia.

[195] The *bubalus* of antiquity was a large African antelope.

[196] Belon is confusing two medicinal substances: red behen *(behen akmar* or *hamer)*, which is perhaps the root of *Statice limonium*, and white behen (or *behen abiad*), the root of *Centaurea behen*.

[197] "A medicinal preparation of the substance of mummies; hence, an unctuous liquid or gum used medicinally" (OED).

[198] Belon uses the word *chaoux,* a version of the Turkish word *çavuş,* the uniformed attendant of an ambassador or consul.

[199] The Propontis (Sea of Marmora) is closed on the east by the Bosphorus (formerly known as the Bosphorus of Thrace) and on the west by the Dardanelles, formerly called the Hellespont. Belon must be thinking of the Black Sea (Pontus Euxinus), which lies between the Bosphorus of Thrace and the Cimmerian Bosphorus (Kerch Strait).

[200] The Gulf of Izmit (Nicomedia) is situated before the Gulf of Gemlik (on which is the town of Mudanya), coming from Constantinople.

[201] See notes 170 and 171.

[202] Ragusa (present-day Dubrovnik), a merchant republic, was under the suzerainty of Venice (from 1205 to 1358) and then of Hungary, but reached a rapprochement with the Ottomans in the 14th century and became their vassal in 1458. On payment of a tribute they enjoyed considerable commercial advantages. Other states were already trading with the Byzantines (notably the Genoese, who at this period were called Genevese, and the Venetians), and these relations developed after the capture of Constantinople by Mohamed II. Mohamed confirmed the privileges of the Genoese and Venetians who were already installed in Galata, and they preserved their primacy even when other "Frankish" traders obtained

permission to establish themselves in the capital

203 Fuste: a small boat, long, with low freeboard. Mahone: a large Turkish galley.

204 The Turks had developed their navy in the 16th century, and the Kasim Pasha arsenal (from the name of the vizier who developed a whole township devoted to the construction of ships round an arsenal founded by Mohammed II) was one of the largest in Europe. Some 30,000 slaves worked there in the time of Suleiman

205 The town of Scamandria was near Troy.

206 The site of Sestos, facing the town of Kilitbahir, is not very far from the old village of Maito or Madhytos, now Eceabat.

207 Pitch is an impure resin obtained by the distillation of resinous wood. *Cedria* or *catran* is a vegetable tar, oily and brown or black in colour, obtained in the same way.

208 Mineral pitch, which we call asphalt, a natural mixture, blackish in colour, of limestone, silica and bitumen.

209 This is the island of Marmara, in the sea of the same name, below which are a number of smaller islands.

210 Sea foam; the colloquial name for magnesite.

211 Black coral.

212 The two fortresses in question, of modern construction, were built near the ancient sites of Sestos and Abydos. They are the fortresses of Kilitbahir (in Europe) and Çanakkale (in Asia), built in 1463, ten years after the capture of Constantinople.

213 A cold wind from the north-east.

214 Hecuba was the wife of Priam. Protesilas was the first Greek to be killed on the shores of Troy.

215 A promontory about the latitude of Troy, at the exit from the Dardanelles, now known as Kum Burun.

216 Between the coast and Bursa there are a Mount Ida (Kaş Dağı] and a Mount Olympus (Ulu Dağ).

217 The cape opposite Mytilene (Lesbos) is Cape Babra (in Turkish Baba Burun).

218 This promontory, situated at the beginning of the Gulf of Edremit (north of the island of Mytilene).still bears the name of Cape Assos.

219 The river Xanthus, also called Scamander in Latin, is now called Menderes. The Simois was formerly joined by the Scamander, but the accumulation of alluvium at the confluence has separated the two rivers.

220 There are remains of the baths a little way south of the Gulf of Çandarlı. Pliny mentions a number of places, including *Larisa Troade* (Larissa in the Troad) in book XXXI of the *Natural History* (§ 61).

[221] The promontory of Sigaeum, now called Kum Burun, where there are still the ruins of a castle.

[222] *Maza* was a kind of porridge eaten by soldiers.

[223] A small island to the west of Chios.

[224] This port and promontory on the island of Chios, which was famous in antiquity for its wines, is now called Cavo Melanios.

[225] The city of Ephesus and the river Meander (Menderes) are not in Thessaly but on the west coast of Turkey, opposite the island of Samos. The town of Magnesia is near it. The district of Magnesia in eastern Thessaly (in Greece) has neither a river Meander nor a town called Ephesus.

[226] Chios, the last possession of the republic of Genoa in the Archipelago, paid tribute to the Turks from the 15th century onwards It was taken in 1566 by Grand Admiral Piyale Pasha.

[227] In the second book of his *Methodus medendi,* which is dedicated to Glaucon.

[228] Mastic, a resin produced by the lentisk or mastic tree, was used in the making of raki, a kind of anisette much favoured by the Turks, refreshing and intoxicating.

[229] The reputation of the people of Chios for courtesy is referred to by all travellers, who also agree that the women of Chios are notable for their beauty and not at all coy.

[230] In fact Ios lies to the south of Naxos.

[231] A reference to the invasion of Greece by Xerxes I, king of Persia from 486 to 465 BC.

[232] A small vessel so called because it originally resembled a lute. By the 15th century it had increased in size and become long and slender.

[233] Paxi, a small island to the south of Corfu.

[234] To the south of the Fourni there are a number of small islets which now have no names.

[235] The island of Leros lies off a promontory on which is ancient Halicarnassus.

[236] There are some remains of ancient Halicarnassus beside the town of Bodrum.

[237] Suleiman had conquered the island of Rhodes in 1522, obliging the knights of St John of Jerusalem to withdraw to Malta.

[238] *Eryx jaculus,* a non-venomous pythonid.

[239] *Storax* or *styrax,* an odoriferous resin or the tree which produces it, the styrax tree or snowdrop bush.

[240] Properly Negroponte is the name of Euboea. The Morea is the Peloponnese.

[241] For Belon the two terms are frequently synonymous, though "Moors" generally means either the Arabs of the towns (the name Arabs being reserved for the nomads), or the general body of Muslims, or Muslim populations under Turkish rule. "Egyptians" may mean the inhabitants of Egypt, Christian and Muslim, under Turkish rule, or Egyptian Muslims, or only the original inhabitans of the country. Another marginal sense is gipsies.

[242] Peter I of Lusignan, king of Cyprus from 1359, briefly occupied Alexandria in 1365 (in the reign of Charles V of France), when Egypt was ruled by the Mamelukes, who had made it a centre of Islam. Sultan Selim I conquered Egypt and Syria, which were still governed by Mameluke sultans (often called by westerners soldans), in 1517.

[243] Agrippa, an ally of Augustus, was the builder of the Pantheon.

[244] Granite.

[245] Caesar, after routing Pompey at Pharsala in 48 BC, pursued him to Egypt, where he was assassinated in the same year. The column, almost 30 metres high, was erected, according to other sources, in honour of Pompey.

[246] Belon is probably thinking of the anonymous compilation entitled "Library of Apollodorus".

[247] Cleopatra's needles.

[248] The Flaminian obelisk, erected in the Circus Maximus by Augustus in AD 10, then moved to the Piazza del Popolo, where it was set up in 1587.

[249] One of the mounds of ancient debris is still called the "hill of broken pots".

[250] Correction in later editions: "of stone and tile [i.e. brick]".

[251] The name *ichneumon vespa* comes from Pliny and Aristotle and designates a sphex (digger-wasp), a predator which paralyses its prey by stinging it and deposits it in its nest in the sand as food for its larvae.

[252] The Wadi el Natrun, the Western Desert, which Belon confuses with the desert on the shores of the Red Sea where Saint Anthony lived.

[253] Eagle-stone: aetites, a variety of hydrated iron oxide, which eagles were said to carry off to their eyrie to facilitate the laying of their eggs. Belon confuses this stone with *cittites* (Pliny's *cissitis),* a white stone with an ivy-like surface pattern.

[254] An island near Alexandria, on which was the celebrated lighthouse.

[255] The Evangelist Saint Mark is sad to have established the church in Alexandria. Tradition has it that he was put to death by the idolators at Serapis in AD 68.

²⁵⁶ Master Benoît Badiolus, from Avignon, was consul for both Florence and France. He showed Belon idols, vases, coins and papyri found inside mummies.

²⁵⁸ These galls, which contain a dry, brownish substance, are used in preparing decoctions and infusions (in the treatment of haemorrhages among other things), in toothpastes for firming up gums and in poultices. The form *chermasel* is a transcription of the Persian name of the substance.

²⁵⁹ The Latin name of the dasheen, *colocasia,* also designates the lotus, a name given to various kinds of water-lily on the Nile.

²⁶⁰ The leaves of water-lilies.

²⁶¹ This is *Chenalopodex aegyptiaca,* the Egyptian goose.

²⁶² A slip by Belon for "on the right".

²⁶³ *Accipiter* designates any bird of prey. The Egyptian saker is a vulture.

²⁶⁴ "Most conspicuous sailing on the river, coming from any direction" *(Natural History,* XXXVI, 76).

²⁶⁵ The name *crex* is sometimes applied to the Egyptian barge-bird, but it also has other meanings (in particular the moorhen and the rail).

²⁶⁶ The ruins of Canopus lie between Alexandria and Rosetta. The ruins of Pelusium lie well to the east of Damietta, beyond Port Said.

²⁶⁷ Scaurus is a name common in the Roman gentes Aemilia and Aurelia. The reference here may be to M. Aemilius Scaurus, who was accused of misappropriation of public funds and defended by Cicero.

²⁶⁸ The hippopotamus was little known in Belon's time. The descriptions by ancient authors had created confusion. For Aristotle it was a monster with the feet of an ox, a horse's mane and the tail of a boar, while Herodotus said that it was the size of a donkey and had the tail of a horse.

²⁶⁹ Properly germe, a type of boat on the Nile.

²⁷⁰ "Pine wood is the best fuel for smelting copper and iron, but Egyptian papyrus can also be used; for gold, a fire of straw" *(Natural History,* XXXIII, 94).

²⁷¹ The square-bracketed paragraphs and the illustrations are not in the 1553 edition.

²⁷² This passage and its illustration are not in the 1553 edition.

²⁷³ The Mamelukes who ruled Egypt until 1517 were originally Bahrids (from 1250 to 1381; named after the region from which they came on the river Bahr, which became the White Nile} and thereafter Circassians.

²⁷⁴ An ancient name for Cairo, as Belon explains below. The capital of the Fatimid dynasty, it lay close to the modern town.

275 The Turkish word is *bedesten,* the main part of the bazaar.

276 The crypt of the church of Abu Sarga or St Sergius.

277 The aqueduct built by Saladin to the south of Cairo.

278 Probably the *kemençe,* a kind of viol.

279 The Lendit fair was held in the 16th century at Saint-Denis, just north of Paris.

280 The balm-tree or balsam-tree is a shrub which produces myrrh, an aromatic resin.

281 "The balm fruit which comes from the fortress of Petra is adulterated with a seed similar to that of Saint John's herb" *(Materia medica,* I, 18, quoted by Belon in a Latin translation.

282 "The wood called balm-wood is appreciated fresh, in delicate shoots, gold-coloured, odoriferous, with the scent of balm" *(Materia medica,* I, 18), in a Latin translation.

283 "In sandy places near the river there grows underground what is called *malinathallë"* (Theophrastus, 1989, II, book IV, ch. 8, § 12). In fact this word is thought to mean the yellow nutsedge *(Cyperus esculentus),* an edible tuber with a nutty taste which was much consumed in Egypt.

284 Properly, a territorial subdivision of a Turkish province; also used to mean the governor of a sanjak. Belon may be using the term loosely to mean a Turkish official of some kind. (T)

285 Belon published in 1553 a work in Latin, *De admirabili operum antiquorum et rerum suspicindarum praestantia liber, quo de Aegyptiis Pyramidibus, de Obeliscis, de Labyrinthis sepulchralibus, et de antiquorum sepulturis agitur,* which contained lengthy descriptions of the pyramids.

286 Pliny says: *Vestigia aedificationum nulla existant, harena late pura circa, lentis similitudine, qualis in maiore parte Africae* ("There remain no traces of buildings. The sand, extending widely around, is unmixed, with grains the size of a lentil, as in most of Africa" *(Natural History,* XXXVI, § 81).

287 Point: a point on the scale used by shoemakers to measure the size of a shoe.

288 In fact, crocodile excrement, which the ancients used as a medicament.

289 Belon seems to be thinking of the pyramid of Caius Cestius, near the Porta S. Paolo in Rome, which is 37 metres high and 30 metres wide at the base.

290 Francis I of France (1515–1547).

291 Plato's actual words are: *Ante est sphinx vel magis miranda de qua*

silvere, numen accolentium. Harmain regem putant in ea conditum et volunt invectam videri. Est autem saxo naturali elaborata; rubrica facies monstri colitur. Capitis per frontem ambitum centum duos pedes colligit, longitudo pedum CXLIII est, altitudo a ventre ad summum aspidem in capite LXII ("Before treating of them [the pyramids] I must first speak of the sphinx, of which nothing has been said, and which is the divinity of the local people. It is thought that the body of king Harmais was enclosed in it, and it is said that he was brought here. It is carved in the native stone, and in honour of the monster they paint its head red. The circumference of the head at the forehead is two hundred feet, the height from the belly to the top of the snake on the head sixty-one and a half feet", *Natural History*, XXXVI, § 81).

292 Chimera: "A fabled fire-breathing monster of Greek mythology, with a lion's head, a goat's body, and a serpent's tail (or according to others with the heads of a lion, a goat, and a serpent)" (OED).

293 From the end of July to the end of September.

294 Pliny's actual words are *Harmain regem putant in ea conditum* (see above). The name Harmais may be a deformation of Harmachis, the Greek name of the sun-god (Horemakhet, "Horus in the horizon"), with whom the dead king was identified

295 Bitumen, which was used in embalming bodies. The term *mummy* was applied both to the embalming fluid and the embalmed body. Great properties were attributed to this "mummy".: it was believed to fluidify coagulated blood, and was therefore administered to patients suffering from the effects of a fall. All great personages took it with them when travelling. Originally it was taken from embalmed bodies, but later matter taken from ordinary corpses dried in the sun or in an oven, with no trace of any aromatic substance, was imported. Belon aroused opposition by protesting against this repellent practice.

296 Catfish..

297 A soldier's pike in the 16th century was about 7 metres long.

298 The giraffe is mentioned by Pliny, Strabo and Solinus and appeared in Roman circus games, but was little known in the 16th century.

299 Asamia (Belon's *Asamie)*, was the Turkish name for Mesopotamia and Assyria. See chapter 96 below.

300 The Latin name *bubalus* is applied to both the buffalo and the bubal, a large African antelope. The animal represented here, however, looks more like a zebu.

301 The quotation is correct but for one word: Belon writes *bubalos bisontes* instead of *jubatos bisontes*. Pliny's phrase (in his account

of Germany and its animals) means "It has, however, remarkable species of wild oxen, bisons with manes, of a strength and speed without equal, the urus (aurochs), which the ignorant common people call bubals, although the bubal is a product of Africa with a certain resemblance to a calf or a deer" *(Natural History,* VIII, § 38). Pliny, followed by Solinus, who picks up this passage, take no account of the double meaning of the word *bubalus.*

[302] Pliny's actual words are: *In India et boves solidis ungulis, unicornes, et feram nomine axin inulei pelle pluribus candidioribusque maculis, sacrorum Liberi patris* ("In India there are still oxen with uncloven hoofs and a single horn, and an animal called *axis,* with the coat of a fawn, but with more numerous and whiter spots, which is offered as a sacrifice to the god Liber" *(NaturalHistory,* VIII, § 76).

[303] Evidently *Cercopithecus callitrichus,* a kind of green monkey found in Mauritania.

[304] Black henbane is a poison, whose Arabic name is "rat's poison". According to Sauneron the species which grows in Egypt is *Hyosciamus muticus* and in Sinai *Hyosciamus boveanus.*

[305] Belon adds in later editions: "Those who say that when travelling through desert country the Arabs sing to their camels to give them better heart for travelling are right; for the cameleers keep pace with their camels, following them on foot and pausing in their singing in time with the camels' paces".

[306] Agathocles' *palinurus* is the African form, while Theophrastus describes *Palinurus spina-christi,* Christ's thorn.

[307] "It bears its young in membranes which are torn open on the third day. It sometimes happens that those which are in its belly perforate it, having eaten away the membranes. It bears one young one each day, and altogether there are more than twenty of them" (Aristotle, *History of Animals,* V, 34, 558a, quoted by Belon in Theodore Gaza's Latin translation).

[308] It is *Acacia arabica* or *nilotica.*

[309] The Italian cassia-tree.

[310] *Colutea haleppica.*

[311] Exodus XV, 22–27. (T)

[312] Still known today as the "springs of Moses", they lie close to Suez, at the tip of the Red Sea. The Bitter Lake is farther north.

[313] *Dejectamenta marina,* the term applied to fish and other marine creatures that were not edible.

[314] This channel was begun by king Necho in the 8th century BC and continued by Ptolemy I (360–283 BC) and his successors, but it never extended over the whole width of the isthmus.

³¹⁵ Belon adds in later editions: "For they hew their houses out of the ground, like those to be seen in Touraine and Lodunois and in several other places along our rivers in France. Here a janissary killed a crow with his arquebus and presented it to Monsieur de Fumel".

³¹⁶ According to Sauneron, these would not be *Balanites aegyptiaca* Wall., a thorny shrub whose fruit is the myrobalan of Egypt, but *Moringa aptera*.

³¹⁷ The monastery of the "Forty Fathers" (also called Quarentapadri), named after forty martyrs killed by the Beduin.

³¹⁸ The monasteries of St Anthony and St Paul, on the other side of the Gulf of Suez. The monastery of St Macarius is in the Libyan Desert.

³¹⁹ See note 48.

³²⁰ Belon makes it clear in a later edition that this was the dignitary who had accompanied Monsieur de Fumel from Cairo. The term *schecarab* is his transcription of *cheikh arabe* ("Arab sheikh").

³²¹ Properly *chavein*, or "dragon's blood", a resinous exudation, carmine red in colour, which covers the fruit of the plant called *calamus draco;* but this name is also given to the fragments of a polyp (coral), *tubipara musica*, a tubipore commonly known as organ-pipe coral, for it consists of juxtaposed tubes resembling organ-pipes. Corals at this period were considered to be either mineral or vegetable.

³²² Gold marcasite, a natural sulphide of iron, crystalline, occurs in the form of balls of radiate structure. Androdamas, which was reputed to quell anger, is perhaps haematite, a natural oxide of iron which can be ground into a red powder.

³²³ A spice consisting of the dried outer covering of the nutmeg.

³²⁴ Round-bodied cargo vessels, originally built in Holland.

³²⁵ Later editions add: "They are as common along the shores [of the Red Sea] as are ours in the Ocean; and the caloyers of this country are fond of eating them".

³²⁶ Here, the Pole Star.

³²⁷ A tributary of the Rhône in south-eastern France. (T)

³²⁸ Arsinoe was the name of several princesses of the Ptolemaic dynasty. Lysimachus married Arsinoe, daughter of Ptolemy I. Her brother Ptolemy II Philadelphus ("who loves his sister") first married their daughter, also called Arsinoe, but then repudiated her to marry his sister, now widowed. The brother and sister were deified as *theoi adelphoi* ("divine brother and sister").

³²⁹ No doubt Zebid in Yemen, captured by the Turks in June 1516. Yemen was conquered in 1547 (i.e. at the time of Belon's travels) by Ozdemir Pasha, and remained in Turkish hands until 1636.

³³⁰ According to Paul Delaunay, this is a mutilated specimen of one of the iguanians of the East Indies and the Indian Archipelago, quadrupeds with "wings" which act as parachutes.

³³¹ Murex is a gasteropod with a thick spiny shell which yields a purple dye. *Murrha* is the name of a mineral substance formerly used in the making of precious vases.

³³² The *maidin* (from the Arabic *mu'ayyidi*) corresponded to the Turkish *para*, which varied in value between 3 and 4 aspers. There were 120 aspers to a piastre.

³³³ Yellow amber is indeed a fossilised resin, hard and transparent, which has the property of being electrified by rubbing (hence the comparison with lodestone). Grey amber, however, is a substance which comes from the excrement of sperm whales and floats on the surface of the sea.

³³⁴ *Batega*, from Arabic *al-battikha*, is the watermelon.

³³⁵ Cataro (al-Kattara) lies between Bilbez (Bilbeis) and Salatia al-Salhiya), two villages mentioned below. Belon has inverted the order of two days' journeys.

³³⁶ The following edition adds: "But the turrets of the Arabs' mosques differ from those of the Turks in that they have three storeys but those of the Turks have only one".

³³⁷ Spanish or Portuguese Jews who had been baptised but still practised their faith in secret.

³³⁸ Belon adds in a later edition: "Great lords in Turkey travel in litters as in Europe; but where we have mules they have camels".

³³⁹ The text has "Egypt", but this must be a typographical error. (T)

³⁴⁰ *Phinis* is thought to be the young of the white-tailed eagle.

³⁴¹ Perhaps a species of shrike.

³⁴² See note 280.

³⁴³ The Franciscans had established themselves in Palestine in the 13th century and had undergone many vicissitudes in their struggle for the right to guard the Holy Sepulchre and other sanctuaries. The conquest of the Holy Land by the Ottomans was favourable to them, for their rôle was the subject of a number of treaties between the Ottomans and the Christian princes. Thus the security of the Franciscans' position was covered in the negotiations conducted on the order of Francis I of France.

³⁴⁴ *Viscum cruciatum*, a parasite of the olive-tree.

³⁴⁵ Saint Stephen, deacon of the first Christian community in Jerusalem, who was stoned to death by the Jews, is regarded as the first Christian martyr.

346 Saint Helen, born in Bithynia about 255, made the pilgrimage to Palestine and built the basilicas on the Mount of Olives and in Bethlehem. She was later credited with the discovery of the relics of the True Cross.

347 Vespasian, Roman Emperor from 69 to 79, took Jerusalem, along with his son Titus, in 70.

348 A pool near the Temple of Jerusalem in which animals destined for sacrifice were purified. The word probatic comes from the Greek probatikos, "relating to cattle".

349 Pisa, then an independent republic, played a major part in the crusades of 1099 (after which the city became capital of the Latin kingdom of Jerusalem) and 1189, and remained prosperous until 1284, when its fleet was destroyed by the Genoese.

350 The Syrian church, of which the Jacobites are members, was in fact founded by Jacob Baradaeus.

351 After the leather belt worn by Coptic monks? (T)

352 Abyssinians: inhabitants of Abyssinia, a province of the Ottoman Empire roughly corresponding to present-day Ethiopia.

353 The 1555 edition adds that they are circumcised.

354 Disciples of Nestorius, patriarch of Constantinople in the 5th century, a heresiarch who asserted that the two natures of Christ (divine and human) possessed their own individuality. The Nestorians were condemned by the Council of Ephesus in 431.

355 Christians of Syria and Lebanon.

356 Perhaps the catechu-tree *(Acacia catechu)*.

357 The reference must be to Aetius, a physician of the 6th century born in Mesopotamia, a Christian, who practised his art at the court in Constantinople and wrote a vast compilation summarising the medical knowledge of the time (based on Hippocrates, Galen and Dioscorides).

358 Saint John the Baptist.

359 Saint Elizabeth was the barren wife of Zachariah, who miraculously became mother of the Baptist. Saint Anne was the mother of the Virgin.

360 This mobility was at the origin of the cupidity of Turkish officials, who sought to make as much money as possible from a wealthy territory before being posted elsewhere.

361 Taman, on the strait of Kerch, between the Black Sea and the Sea of Azov.

362 See note 274.

363 Philo's collyrium (a remedy devised by the Greek doctor Philo).

364 A common remedy composed of several simples and purgatives, named after the Arab doctor Hamech.

365 Islands off Marseilles.

366 Used in the treatment of asthma.

367 *Ervum:* vetch. *Ervilia* (diminutive of *ervum):* vetchling, a leguminous plant, some species of which are grown as fodder.

368 Trehala, a sugar-like substance obtained from the pupal case of a beetle of the genus *Larinus*.

369 This was Canberdi al-Ghazzali, who had been in the service of the Mamelukes before the conquest, and had betrayed them in favour of the Ottomans. By way of reward he had been appointed governor of Syria, but soon seized Damascus, Beirut and Tripoli. He then laid siege to Aleppo, but was obliged to retreat and barricade himself in the citadel of Damascus against the advance of Turkish troops led by Ferhad Pasha. Ferhad, with 40,000 men, had no difficulty in taking the place, and the traitor was put to death.

370 A gummy substance exuded by *Atractylis gummifera* (the gummy carline or pine thistle).

371 Cassia.

372 The bracketed passage and the illustration are not in the 1553 edition.

373 An error by Belon.

374 Belon shows a remarkable openness of mind in face of the absence of any stable social hierarchy which characterises Ottoman society, unlike most western travellers, who are concerned only to express their indignation about it. His interpretation of the simple nature of their houses is pertinent. Other authors say that the Turks do not build sumptuous dwellings out of humility and piety. On the contrary, their detractors attribute this lacuna to a lack of social graces and "civilisation".

375 A province in southern Turkey in Asia (Mount Taurus region).

376 Julius Caesar.

377 A mixture of water and vinegar used in Greek antiquity.

378 Belon must be referring to *boza*, a drink similar to beer made from barley or millet, inexpensive and very common in Turkey.

379 Belon is confused: Hamah, which has preserved its ancient name, is in Syria, while Tarsus is in Cilicia, in southern Turkey.

380 A common misapprehension.

381 Belon means Hama.

382 Trochisk: "A medicated tablet or disk; a (round or ovate) pastille or lozenge" (OED).

³⁸³ *Galbanum* is a gum-resin of vegetable origin common in Syria; styrax is an aromatic gum from the tree of the same name; *serapinum* is related to asafoetida and very similar in appearance.

³⁸⁴ The oil of bitter almonds.

³⁸⁵ The range lying between Syria and Cilicia.

³⁸⁶ The hill of Fourviéres.

³⁸⁷ North-west of Lyons in south-eastern France. (T)

³⁸⁸ This is the Gulf of Iskenderun (formerly Alexandretta), on the shores of which was the town of Issus or Issos, famed as the scene of Alexander's victory over Darius III, king of Persia, in 334 BC).

³⁸⁹ A jackal.

³⁹⁰ "Green cheese".

³⁹¹ A conical bag of cotton, linen, or flannel, used as a filter or strainer (OED). The term used by Belon, *chausse d'hippocras,* also occurs in Rabelais, and is rendered by Urquhart and Le Motteux as "a felt to distil Hjppocras" (T)

³⁹² A fabric originally made from camel-hair, later from goats' wool, frequently mingled with silk.

³⁹³ Wools from the city of Miletus in Ionia, which was famed in antiquity for its wool.

³⁹⁴ "The goats are shorn, because of the length of their hair, in much of Phrygia, from which are made fabrics called *cilicia.* It is said that since this shearing was first practised in Cilicia the name *cilicas* was introduced" (Varro, *Agriculture,* II, 11, 12). Belon wrongly attributes the quotation to Pliny.

³⁹⁵ Apparently a mistake for Ismil, from which Belon reports his depsrture in the next chapter.

³⁹⁶ See note 63.

³⁹⁷ Ankara, the present capital of Turkey, called Angora by the ancient Greeks, was called Engürü by the Turks. Belon, however, is confused, for Ankara is much farther from Konya (Iconium) than he says.

³⁹⁸ The passage in brackets was added in later editions.

³⁹⁹ Ancient Paphlagonia lay to the north of Ankara. Belon stayed farther south, at Afyon Karahisar.

⁴⁰⁰ The chronology of Mahomet's life is difficult to establish. Only the date of the Hegira (his flight from Mecca to Yathrib, later called Medina) is known with certainty: AD 622. Tradition has it that the Prophet was then forty years old. He died in 633. The dates given by Belon are thus wrong.

⁴⁰¹ According to the Sira, Mahomet lost his parents early and was brought up by his grandfather, Abd el-Mottalib (whose name is

confused here with that of his father, Abdallah) and an uncle called Abu Talib.

402 It is known that Mohammed entered the service of a wealthy widow, Khadija, whom he soon afterwards married. He then became a merchant and caravaneer.

403 According to tradition the angel appeared to Mohammed during the month of Ramadan and said the one word, "Recite". Then Mohammed knew that he had been chosen to "recite" the word of Allah to men, and these revelations constitute the Koran (Quran, or "Recitation").

404 Omar and Abu Bakr, two intimate friends of Mohammed who were among the first to follow him.

405 Yathrib, north of Mecca, where Mohammed and his followers found refuge in the Hegira, and which was later renamed Medina (Madinat al-Nabi, the city of the Prophet).

406 After increasing his influence in Mecca (and driving out the Jewish tribes) Mohammed returned to Mecca and conquered it in 630 without a fight.

407 On Mohammed's death (leaving no male heir) Abu Bakr became the first Caliph. He appointed as his successor (in 634) Omar, who was assassinated ten years later. The next Caliph was a son-in-law of the Prophet called Othman, of the family of Muawiya. This was the origin of the Umayyad Caliphs, who remained in power until 750. The Koran was not compiled during Mohammed's life. It was Omar who, after his death, had all the transcriptions of the revelation brought together; but various versions were in circulation. Caliph Othman later appointed a commission which established an official text of the Koran.

408 Turks: Belon means Muslims.

409 Sunna: "The body of traditional sayings and customs attributed to Muhammad and supplementing the Koran" (OED).

410 The Caliph.

411 The Ottomans were Sunnites, and the rulers of Iran were Shiites.

412 The Sultan of Cairo.

413 An error, since Mohammed died only ten years after the Hegira.

414 Monkar and Nakir: the two angels who, in Islamic tradition, interrogate the dead as to their religion. (T)

415 Apart from the profession of faith, a Muslim's obligations are prayer (Belon's Zala, Turkish çalat), five times a day according to the Sunna, the Ramadan fast, and the legal alms (a kind of tithe, under which every Muslim with a certain level of income must pay a tenth of

it and a twentieth of his profits or harvest), added to which are voluntary alms. His final obligation is to make the pilgrimage to Mecca once in his life.

[416] The feast of the sacrifice (in Turkish *kurban bayramı*), which lasts four days, in the course of which every head of a family ritually cuts a sheep's throat.

[417] As long as Khadija, the rich widow whom he had married, was alive Mahomet had no other wife. After her death (which was before the Hegira) he had nine other wives.

[418] Shortly before the Hegira Mahomet had his "night journey". The angel Gabriel awoke him and took him to a winged animal called Buraq. Mounted on Buraq, the Prophet was transported to Jerusalem, where he prayed along with Abraham, Moses, Jesus and other prophets. Then, after passing through seven heavens, he came into the divine presence.

[419] A fabulous stone in Pliny and other authors. The name was later applied to garnets and dark red rubies.

[420] Paradise is described in the Koran as a peaceful place in which there are gardens and streams of sweet water and wine or honey, where good Muslims will be able to eat and drink in the company of houris.

[421] More precisely, hell has seven parts or levels, the highest of which is the purgatory of erring Muslims, while the others are reserved for different categories of infidels.

[422] A transcription of the profession of faith in a verse of the Koran: "There is no God but God, and Mohammed is his prophet".

[423] Judge.

[424] "The architect Democrates began to use lodestone in constructing the vaults of the temple of Arsinoe in Alexandria, so that a statue of her seemed to be suspended in the air in the temple" *(Natural History,* XXIV, § 148).

[425] "A dish made by boiling bread in water to a pulp, and flavouring it according to taste with sugar, currants, tmegs or other ingredients" (OED).

[426] French *billard,* originally a stick with a curved end used in the game of bowls. (T)

[427] The kingdom of Armenia was a dependency of the Byzantine Empire when the Seljuk Turks seized it in the 11th century.

[428] Here, as frequently, Turk means a Muslim.

[429] Asamia: Mesopotamia and Assyria (see chapter 96, Book II). Adiabene: an ancient kingdom in northern Assyria, now in Iran.

[430] These schools were fairly rudimentary, and the essential element in

the education they gave was learning by heart verses from the Koran (which the children did not understand, since they were in Arabic). The sons of well-off families were taught at home by tutors.

431 The first work printed in Turkish appeared only in 1729.

432 The Parthians were a people of Iranian origin who moved into Syria and Palestine and concluded a treaty with Rome in 20 BC. The Medes were the inhabitants of Media, in western Asia.

433 Except those who claim to be of the family of Mohammed, who wear green turbans. See page 294.

434 The Latin name of a physician and philosopher born at Razy, near Teheran (865–925).

435 Belon continues in later editions: "It could scarcely believed in our countries that embroidery on linen is so highly prized and priced so dear in Turkey, and that such a great quantity of it should be made. The reason is that since women ordinarily live such an enclosed life and have no housework to do they must find something to employ themselves with. And so, being accustomed to doing needlework, they spend their time embroidering linen."

436 Half-drachm: about a gram and a half.

437 Belon is wrong: women *are* permitted to take part in the prayers in mosques. They must be veiled, and are confined to the sides of the mosque, separated from the men, who are in the centre, by low barriers, or, if the mosque has galleries, in the galleries on the upper storey.

438 Later editions add: "Their shoes are always open in front, so that the fore part of the foot is bare, and they commonly wear rings or bracelets round their legs, above the ankle, which is a very graceful ornament. You will find few women in Cairo without damascene patterns on their arms and thighs, for when they go to the baths they have their skin patterned as in the portrait, and the black colour enters into the skin and stays there, leaving well marked circles on the arms and other parts of the body; but this fashion is not yet common among women in Asia. And since Mahomet's law prohibits them from appearing in public with their face uncovered, they always have a veil hanging from their forehead over their eyes, and also have their throat and hands hidden. They wear high boots with iron-shod heels, as can be seen from the drawing." The term "damascene" means "having the watered pattern of dark lines characteristic of Damascus blades" (OED).

439 "A supposed flow of 'humours' to a particular part of the body, in certain diseases" (OED).

[440] Cauterisation.

[441] There are several orders of dervishes, who live either in a community (having taken vows and following a rule which is sometimes extremely austere) or in the world. In Constantinople the most important are the *bektashis* and the *mevlevis*, better known as the whirling dervishes from the dances which bring them into a state of ecstasy.

[442] A state of ecstasy (literally, the state of being out of oneself).

[443] A small coin; in English usage a halfpenny. (T)

[444] "Alas, prodigies of gluttony; ... some drink snow, others ice, transforming the toils of the mountain into pleasures of the belly. The cold then protects against burning heats, and one wonders how to preserve snow during the months when there is none. Others first boil their water so that then they may give it a winter temperature" *(Natural History,* XIX,§ 54–55).

[445] "It was an invention of the emperor Nero to boil water and then chill it in a glass vessel plunged into snow. Thus the pleasure of the coldness of the water is produced without the inconveniences of snow" (XXXI, § 40).

[446] *Apus* is the swift.

[447] A headdress consisting of a pad on the head with a ribbon of cloth hanging down behind.

[448] The French word *rave,* taken into English but long obsolete, can mean either a turnip or a radish. (T)

[449] Circumcision is usually performed during a boy's seventh or eighth year.

[450] It is not a priest, but a "barber-circumciser" *(sunnetji),* who performs the operation, which is not accompanied by any religious ceremony and is not prescribed in the Koran.

[451] The Shah of Persia.

[452] An error.

[453] The *harac* or *cizye* was a tax paid by non-Muslim subjects of the Sultan. It applied to adult men except the aged and infirm.

[454] A beylerbey, the governor of a province.

[455] In fact this is an extract from book III of Martial's *Epigrams:* "Scarcely had I taken off my shoes than I was brought an enormous volume. along with lettuces and fish sauce".

[456] Varro says: *Gallinae Africanae sunt grandes, variae, gibberae, quas meleagridas appellant Graeci. Haec novissimae in triclinium cenantium introierunt e culina propter fastidium hominum:* "African hens are large, many-coloured, humped; it is these that the Greeks call

meleagrides. They are the latest things to be brought from the kitchen into the dining-room to cater for the spoiled taste of the diners" *(Res rusticae,* chapter 9).

[457] The quotation is not entirely correct. Suetonius says: *Convitatum assidue per provincias duobus tricliniis, uno quo sagati palliativi, altero quo togati cum illustrioribus provinciarum discumberent* ("In the provinces he continually gave feasts, with two separate tables, one for his officers and the Greeks, and the other for the notabilities of the province" *(Life of the twelve Caesars,* book I, "Divus Julius", chapter 48).

[458] Suetonius says, speaking of Augustus: *M. Antonius super festinatas Liviae nuptias obiecit et feminam consularem e triclinio viri in cubiculu, abductam, rursus in convivium rubentibus auriculis incomptiore capillo reductam* ("Marcus Antonius reproached him not only for his hasty marriage with Livia but also with having caused to leave the table, under the eyes of her husband, a woman of consular rank and taken her to his bedroom, and then brought her back, with red ears and her hair in disorder" (book II, "Divus Augustus", chapter 69).

[459] "He admitted to all his dinners not only his children but also young men and girls of noble families, who, following the usage of earlier times, took their meal sitting at the foot of the couches. They hardly ever left the dining-room without being stuffed with food and gorged with wine" (book V, "Divus Claudius").

[460] A legendary queen of Assyria who was supposed to be of divine origin, the absolute mistress of an immense empire.

[461] This was an Egyptian eunuch of the second half of the 1st century BC, governor of Princess Arsinoe. When Caesar came to Egypt in 48 BC he left Alexandria with the princess and then took command of the army and won several victories over the Romans.

[462] The reference is to pastry-cooks selling their wares (probably carried in baskets) in the street.

[463] The call to prayer is here considerably reduced. It consists in fact of various invocations repeated several times. There are, as Belon says, five calls, at dawn, at midday, about three o'clock in the afternoon, in the evening and finally some hours after sunset.

[464] Goitre. Belon's explanation of the cause of this disease is wrong: it is the result of a lack of iodine.

[465] The gulfs of İzmit (Nicomedia) and Gemlik; the town of Gemlik is near Mudanya.

[466] The river is now called Sakarya Nehri and the lake Sapanca Gölü.

[467] This episode, somewhat altered by Belon, dates from the last years of the reign of Beyazit II, a time of instability in the Ottoman empire,

coinciding with the coming to power in Persia of an ambitious sovereign, the young Safavid Shah Ismail. He was the moving force behind a rebellion led by one Shah Kuli ("servant of the shah") which broke out in 1511 in Anatolia. The rebels seized Antalya and then marched on Kütayha, routing the troops of the beylerbey Karagöz Pasha (here called Corague), who was beheaded. The grand vizier Hadim Ali Pasha led troops against the rebels, and was killed in the battle, as was Shah Kuli.

468 An old word for depilatory.

469 "A bright yellow mineral substance, the trisulphide of arsenic" (OED), which is used in paint and in the preparation of depilatories (from Latin *auripigmentum,* which means "gold paint").

470 "It lengthens the face, smoothes out the wrinkles and makes it resplendent, heightens the colour of the face and the whole body and cleans the skin in the baths like soda" *(Materia medica,* V, 173, quoted by Belon in a Latin translation).

471 "We get rid of our daily indigestion in the warmth of the Spartan baths" *(Agriculture,* preface, § 16).

472 Public baths had a bad reputation in France.

473 The word used by Belon *(métifs)* was applied to mongrels in general but to a cross between mastiff and greyhound in particular.

474 Bursa, capital of Bithynia, was taken by the Turks in 1326 and became their capital.

475 Roland, one of Charlemagne's paladins, became the hero of the *Chanson de Roland* and other *chansons de geste* and was credited, like Charlemagne himself, with expeditions all over the world, including the East and Constantinople.

476 A kind of serge.

477 A cavalry manoeuvre: "to sweep round on a moving flank over a more or less wide circle" (OED).

478 The rebeck was similar to the viol, but had only three strings. The heptacalamus was evidently a seven-holed flute.

479 Gabriel d'Aramont, sent by Henry II of France to ask Suleiman the Magnificent to attack the Emperor Charles V in Hungary and to prepare for an expedition to North Africa, arrived when a campaign in Persia had been decided on, and accompanied Suleiman in the spring of 1548, a journey recorded in an account by Jean Chesneau.

480 Jacques de Cambray, canon of Saint-Étienne in Bourges, had accompanied Jean de Montluc to Constantinople in 1545. Later he was appointed acting ambassador on several occasions, particularly during Monsieur d'Aramont's absence (in 1548–1550).

[481] Juste Tenelle had come to Constantinople to look for manuscripts to enrich the royal library, but his journey was not particularly fruitful.

[482] Nightshade.

[483] Jovius: the Italian writer Paolo Giovio, whose treatise on the Turks, published in Italy in 1529, was translated into several languages and was one of the main sources of the abundant literature on the Ottoman empire. The sultan in question was Selim I (1512–1520), Suleiman's immediate predecessor.

[484] This is the name, borrowed from the ancients, of a tree-living snake, perhaps *Vipera ammodytes*. Belon no doubt exaggerates the size of the specimen he mentions, for his description would fit a python better than a viperid.

[485] Theriac: "an antidote to poison, esp. to the bite of a venomous serpent" (OED).

[486] *L'histoire naturelle des étranges poissons marins…*

[487] In *Portraits d'oyseaux, animaux…*, 1557.

Index

Botanical index

(* indicates illustration)

A

Abies, see fir

absinth (Fr. *absinthe, aluyne, mort-aux-vers*), *Absinthum marinum, Absinthum seriphium* 293, 298, 342, 351, 380, 381, 382

absinth, pontic *Artemisia pontica* 298

acacia 58, 99, 121, 174, 192, 242, 248, 249, 280, 283*, 288, 299, 303, 309, 321

Acacia altera 99, 330

ache (Fr. ache), Apium, a name given to several plants, smallage, wild celery etc. 105

Achillea 8n: see also eupatorium, Mesue's

Achinopoda, broom 51, 67

Acillaca (Fr. alisier): see Whitebeam and Service-tree, wild

Adam's apple (a variety of lime or bergamot) 26, 99

Ageraton: see Mesue's *eupatorium*

agnus castus, chaste tree, chasteberry 51, 330, 367

Agourupes, agurupes 67, 474

agrimony 293, 474

Agrimony, hemp (Fr. *eupatoire des Arabes, eupatoire chanvrine*) see absinth

Agriomelea, serviceberry 49

Alaeprini, alaeprinos, eleprinos (Gr.): *Rhamnus alaternus*, evergreen buckthorn, mock privet: see also *Rhamnus* 95

Alaternus, Alinternus: *Rhamnus alaternus* L.: see *Alaeprini*

alder 50, 474

Alevo, Aleppo pine 97, 379

Alga latifolia 187

Alga tertia 317

alhansegi, corona spinea 334

alkanet 66, 474

almond, almond-tree 26, 67, 120, 207, 291, 349, 374, 380, 471, 472

ambrosia 280, 298, 316, 317, 380, 382, 383

ammi 58, 68, 174

amomum (Fr amome): see Cardamom

anabasis, Ephedra anabasis, Atriplex halimus L. 99, 484

anagyros, stinkwood 49

anapala (Gr) 101

anchusa, Hermuzakia aggregata, bugloss 317

andrachne, *Arbutus andrachne*

537

chameleon 367

chameleon, black (*Carthamus* Tourn., *Cardopatium corymborum* L.) 53, 66, 68-9, 77, 79, 189

chameleon, white (*Carlina acaulis* L.; but probably also *Carlina gummifera* L.) 53, 69, 77-8, 79, 343

chermasel, tamarisk gall 229

cherry 120, 360, 464

cherry-plum(-tree) (Fr *mirabellier*, *myrobolan citrin*) 328, 330

cherry-tree 120

chestnut 103, 120, 133, 316, 340, 474

chestnut, water (see also *Tribulus*) 52, 123

chickpea 331

chicory 50, 66, 100, 474

chrysanthemum 66

cistus 28, 124, 322

citron (Fr *poncire*, *citre*) 26, 405, 406

clematis or snakewort (Fr *aristoloche*) 49

clover, *Trifolium* L. 48, 309

coccus, gall of kermes oak, "scarlet-grain" 49, 99, 340

codomalo (Fr *malaucier* according to Belon, Fr *amélanchier* according to other authors), serviceberry 49

colocynth, bitter-apple 174

comfrey (Fr *consoude*) 474

comfrey, great (Fr *grande consoude*) 474

convolvulus, bindweed 474

coris 49

corn-cockle (Fr *nielle*) 66

corruda, wild asparagus 53, 145, 474

costus (root), a name applied by the ancient authors to various plants, including *Costus arabicus* L. 53, 58, 249, 335

costus indicus 53

cotyledon 16, 66, 125, 126*, 322

cotyledon alterum (in the ancient authors = houseleek) 16

cotyledon umbilicus: see Umbilicus

crabonella (It), leadwort 67

creeping spurge 132, 474

cress *Lepidum sativum* L. 105, 330

cress, water 290

cucumber xxxiii, 69, 78, 105, 150, 193, 299, 313

cucumber, wild 67

cumin, wild (Fr *nigelle franche*) 215, 373

currant-bush (Fr *groseillier*) 144, 232

cyclamen 322

cydonia, quince 24

Cynoglossum L., hound's tongue 474

cypress 48, 99, 143

cytisus 136, 144, 150, 157

D

daisy (Fr *pâquerette*) 474   daphne (Fr *thymélée*, *Thymaelae* Tourn.) 51

dasheen (Fr *colocase*, *Colocasia esculenta* Schott: a cultivated variety of taro 215, 232, 523

date 17, 249, 284, 302, 313, 320, 330, 361, 471

date-palm 471

Daucus L., carrot 67

dictamnum, *Origanum dictamnus*

L., dittany of Crete 41

dock (Fr *parelle*, *Rumex patientia* or *R. hydrolapathum*) 67, 474

dogwood (Fr *cornailler*, *cornouiller*, *sanguin*) 137, 427

dolceguini (It: *dolzolini*), *Cyperus esculentus* L., yellow nutsedge 22

dolicos (Gr), *Dolicus* L., climbing bean 215

draba, whitlow-grass 66

Dracunculus vulgaris Schott, arum arrowroot 51

E

elder (Fr *sureau*,) 19, 47, 71, 474

elder, dwarf (Fr *hièble*) 47

elegia, reed 104, 330, 471

eleprinos, *eleprin*: see *aelaeprini* (buckthorn; Fr *nerprun*) 335, 363

elm 10, 15, 35, 47

enula campana, the ancient pharmaceutical name of *Inula helenium*, elecampane 436

Ephedra L. (Fr *uvette*) 49, 99, 100, 461

epithymum (*Cuscuta epithymum* Murr.), dodder of thyme 52

ervilia, vetchling 342

ervum, vetch 530

Eryngium L. (Fr *panicaut*), blue thistle 54

esculus, *Quercus aegilops* L., *oak esculus* 75, 76, 99, 121, 137, 145, 192, 208, 248, 335, 340, 363, 367, 458

eupatorium, Mesue's (*Achillea ageratum*), yarrow 349, 351

euphorbias: see spurge

F

fennel 50, 101, 357, 474

fennel, giant (Fr *férule*) 50, 101, 357, 474

fennel, wild 474

fenugreek 68

fern 474

ferula 49, 81, 319

fig 26, 67, 78, 96, 207, 288, 289, 320, 324, 325, 330, 332, 335, 336, 351, 354, 356, 366, 508

fir (Fr *sapin*) 97, 350, 376, 378, 379*

fleabane (Fr *conise*) 293

G

Galeopsis, hemp-nettle 474

galingale (Fr *souchet long*, *Cyperus longus*) 66, 220

Galium see *aparine*, *asperula*

garlic 76, 78, 105, 106, 154, 200, 291, 339, 381, 416, 426, 435, 436, 445

germander 66

germander, water: see scordion

gladiolus 51

glans unguentaria (?) 99

glycirizon 50

gnaphalion (Fr *diotis blanc*, *Otanthus maritimus* L.), cottonweed 51

goat's beard, (Fr *barbe de bouc*, *Tragopogon pratensis* L.) 66

gourd 150, 164, 167-8, 280, 299

grapes 289, 313, 339, 345, 347, 349, 373, 430

H

halimus: probably privet 51, 99, 144, 237, 319

harmala: *Peganum harmala* L.,
Syrian rue   220, 228, 472
hastula regia (?) 319
hawthorn (Fr *aubépine*) 53, 474
hazel-tree (Fr. *coudrier*) 132, 158,
474
hazelnut (Fr *noisette, armeline*)
132, 153, 174, 343, 431
heather 66, 99, 123, 124, 474
hebulben, Staphylea pinnata L.,
bladder-nut 174
heliochryson: *Helichrysum* Miller,
everlasting daisy 48
Heliotropium magnum, heliotrope
52, 299
hellebore, black, *Helleborus niger* L.
49, 95, 458, 474
hellebore, white, *Veratrum album*
L. 49
hemp 65, 91, 427, 474, 508
henbane, black, *Hyoscyamus niger*
279, 313
henbane, Egyptian, *Hyoscyamus
muticus* 329, 349, 526
henna-tree (alcanna), *Lawsonia
inermis* L. 99, 260, 312
heracleoticum (*Origanum
heracleoticum*) 50, 322, 332, 474
hermodacte, root of *Iris tuberculosis*
474
hernia, rupturewort 66
hippoglosson (*globularia alypum*),
wild senna (?) 95
hipposelinon: horse-parsley 67
holly 49
honeysuckle 44, 50, 473, 508
hops 474
horse-tail (Fr *queue-de-cheval*)
474
horseradish (Fr *raifort, cranson
rustique, armorache*) 474, 477
houseleek (Fr *joubarbe*) 15, 16, 52

hyacinth 513
hypocistis (*Cytinus* L.) 473
hyssop 14, 52, 154, 175, 322, 474

I

ilex, ilices: see oak, holm 67, 99,
335, 367
iris, dwarf (Fr *petit iris*) 72, 474
ivy, white 51, 99, 363, 471, 522

J

jasmine (Fr *jasmin, josuim*) 225,
260
jujube-tree 380
juniper 375, 383, 467
juniper (Fr *genévrier*) 99, 368,
375, 383
juniper, savin (Fr *savinier*) 99,
368, 375, 383, 458, 467

K

kali: see *anthillis* 227, 228, 248
kellerkraut 369
kromada, cromadia (?) 471

L

lagochymeni (*Lagoecia cuminoides*
L., Fr *gite-de-lièvre*), hare's form
68, 473
larix, larch 97, 99, 379, 459, 460*
laurel 99, 474
leadwort (Fr *dentelaire*): see
crabonella, mauronia
ledon (Fr *lédon, lède, Cistus
ladanifer* L.), crimson spot rock-
rose 27, 322, 383, 384, 458
leek 105, 291, 362
lemon(-tree) (Fr *citron, limon*) 26,

405, 406
lentil 524
lentisk (Fr *lentisque*, *Pistacia
lentiscus* L.) 33, 197, 257, 521
leontopetalon (*leontice leontopetalum*
L.) 48, 353
letron: see sow-thistle 50
lettuce 50, 291, 362
lettuce, wild 67
libanotis 49, 316, 335
libanotis, *libanotides*, applied by
the ancient authors to a number
of plants, including rosemary,
seseli and plants of the genus
atamantha
licion, *licium*, catechu-tree (*Acacia
catechu* Willd.) 99, 330
ligusticum, lovage (Fr *livèche*) 317
lily, red 471, 523
lime (tree) (Fr *tilleul*, *tillet*) 45,
103, 146, 227, 264, 266, 384,
448, 449, 515
linaria 473
lonchitis altera (*Serapias* sp. L.,
(fern) 125
lotus (water-lily) 50, 158, 367,
523
lotus-tree (Fr *arbre de lotus*,
micocoulier) 50
lycopsis (in Dioscorides): viperine,
Echium L. 474
lysimachia purpurea, loosestrife
157

M

malaucier (serviceberry) 49, 132
mallow 474
mandragora 48
maple 14, 16, 150, 427, 474, 508
maple, mountain: see
Asphendannos

marigold (Fr *souci*) 474
marjoram (Fr *marjolaine*) 48, 66
marjoram, wild (Fr marjolaine
sauvage) 48, 66
marrubium, horehound 474
marsh mallow 136
mauronia: *Plumbago* sp. L.,
leadwort 67
melilot 48
melon 192
menstatrum, wild mint 53
meu, *meum*: a name given to
three umbelliferae of different
genera; probably here *Meum
athamanticum* Jacq., spingle 474
milfoil (Fr *mille-feuilles*) 473
mint 342
millegrana: see *hernia* 66
mistletoe 72, 134, 135, 336
moly (wild garlic) 20
mother-of-thyme, wild thyme (Fr
serpolet) 12
mouronne (?) 69
mulberry-tree, white (Fr *mûrier
blanc*) 16, 369
mullein (Fr *molène*) 473
mustard 436, 440
myrrh-tree 321
myrsinites: see spurge, creeping
myrtle 33, 192, 369

N

napeca, *nabca* (Ar), jujube-tree 99,
193, 242, 318, 320, 339,
napellus: *Aconitum napellus* L. 174,
226
nepenthes 472
nettle, Roman (Fr *ortie romaine*,
Urtica pilulifera L.) 50, 67, 68,
474
nightshade, *Solanum somniferum*

sainfoin (Fr *foin de Bourgogne*, *atrivola*, *atrivolo*) 67

salsola: see *anthillis*, *soldanella*

sanguin: see dogwood 138

sarcophago: see *mauronia* 67

satyrion, a species of orchid 474

savin 368, 375, 383, 458, 467

savory 12, 13, 52, 99, 148, 257

savory, wild (*thymbra*, *tribi*) 13, 52, 257, 322, 332

scabious 67

scammony, *Convolvulus scammonia* L. 52, 361

scarlet-grain: see *Coccus* viii, 47, 49, 99, 335, 358, 366

scordion, *Teucrium scordium* L., water germander 144

scorpiodes (*Scorpiurus* L.) 66

scorpiuros, ancient name of the heliotrope: see Heliotropium

sebesten(-tree) (*Cordia myxa*) 99, 207, 259

securidaca: *Securigera coronilla* 51

Sempervivum L., houseleek 15

senna, false (Fr. *bagenaudier*, *Colutea haleppica* L.) 99, 280, 284

serre: see cerrus

serrus: *Quercus serris* (holm oak, q.v.)

service-tree, wild (*Sorbus tormentalis*, Fr *alisier des bois*) 13

serviceberry (Fr a*mélanchier*): see *malaucier*

sesame 52, 78, 153, 192, 335, 358, 359, 440

seseli 49

sideritis, ironwort 211, 474

skirret (Fr. **chervis**) 66

smilax 49, 100, 101, 322, 369, 461, 477

smilax aspera, rough bindweed 49, 100, 322, 369, 474, 477

smilax china, China root 68n

smilax laevis: *Smilax excelsa* L. 96, 100, 461

smilax, *sarsaparilla* 49, 100

smyrnium (Fr *maceron*), horse-parsley 317, 318, 353

snakeroot (Fr *serpentaire*) 66

snakewort: see Clematis

snowberry: see Styrax

solanum somniferum: probably the climbing nightshade 472

soldanella, *salsola*, saltwort In the ancient authors, a species of bindweed growing in coastal regions, *Calystegia soldanella* R. Br. 51, 67, 132, 227,

sorbus, the service-tree 474

sorghum 357

sorrel 67, 474

southernwood (Fr *aurone*) 174

sow-thistle (Fr *laiteron*, *letron*), *Sonchus* 50

sphondilion (*Spondylium*, ancient Latin name of cow-parsley, *Heracleum* sp. L. 103

spikenard, ploughman's (Fr *conise*, *conize*), *inula conyza*; but the term was also applied in the ancient literature to other plants in the genera *Ageratum*, *Gnapalium*, etc. 100, 290, 474

spina cerisola 461

spruce (Fr *picéa* , *pigne* 367

spurge 66

spurge laurel (Fr *lauréole*, *Daphne laureola*) 474

spurge, broad-leaved, *tithymalus platyphyllos*, *Euphorbia platyphyllus* L. 271

spurge, creeping, *tithymalus myrsinites*, *Euphorbia myrsinites*

546

and woody thyme332, 335, 517
tree of life, *Thuja orientalis*,
  Chinese arbor-vitae 375, 379
tree spurge: see spurge, tree
tribulus (*Trapa* L., Fr *macle, macre,
  châtaignier d'eau*), water chestnut
  52, 67, 133
trifolium menientes: *Menyanthes
  trifoliata* L., bog bean 474

U

*umbilicue seu cotyledon, umbilicus
  veneris*, Venus's navelwort

V

valagnida: *quercus macrolepsis* or
  aegilops 99
venus's navelwort
verbena 474
viburnum 50
vine 14, 100, 257, 477
viole (?) 474
Viscum cruciatum Sieber, red-
  berried mistletoe 324, 336

W

wallflower (Fr *giroflée*)n 471
walnut-tree 120
water chestnut (Fr *macle, macre,
  chataîgnier d'eau*) 52
water-melon (Fr *pastèque*)
wheat 73, 74, 106, 195, 358, 418,
  430
whitebeam (*Sorbus aria*, Fr *alisier
  blanc*): see aria
willow 71, 103, 144, 384
wool-bearing tree (*Calotropis
  procera* according to Sauneron),
  giant milkweed

wormwood (Fr *armoise, barbotine*)
  174, 175, 266, 293, 349: see
  absinth
wormwood, Roman (Fr *absinthe
  pontique, aluyne pontique,
  Artemisia pontica* L.) : see
  absinth
wormwood, sea, *Artemisia marina*
  L. see absinth

Y

yarrow, woundwort (Fr *mille-
  feuilles, Achillea millefolium*) see
  Achillea
yew 99, 383, 425, 426

Z

zygis, wild thyme 332, 335

Geographical index

549

Cicèrigo, island: see Antikithira 46
Cidnus, river, now called Tarsus, at the town of that name 356
Cilicia, region in south-eastern Asia Minor, between the central Taurus mountains to the west and Nur Dağları (Mount Amanus) to the east xv, 14, 80, 353, 356, 357, 363, 369, 370, 373, 382, 385, 418, 446, 530, 531
Cimmerian 512, 519
Cingualinus, Crete
Cio, island: see Kea 202
Circassia (*Cercassie*), ancient name of the piedmont area north of the Caucasus 90, 509
Civitavecchia (*Civita Veche*), Italy 146
Co or *Stancou*, island: see Kos
Cochino, *Cochyno*: see Ifestia 64, 72, 75, 79
Cogne: see Konya xvi, 381, 383, 384, 415, 416
Comasco, Comacchio, Italy 166
Commagene, an ancient province of the Seleucid kingdom of Syria, extending from the foot of the Taurus to the Euphrates, later split between the provinces of Cilicia and Syria 359
Commercine: see Komotini 145, 147, 148
Como xii, 514
Como, Lake (*Larius*) xii, 514
Constantinople, now Istanbul viii, x, xi, xii, xviii, xix, i, ii, iv, v, vi, vii, viii, ix, x, xii, xiii, xiv, xvii, xxiv, xxvii, xxviii, xxxii, xxxiii, xxxiv, 9, 20, 26, 33, 57, 58, 60, 61, 62, 74, 83, 84, 92, 113, 124, 135, 141, 143, 145, 146, 147, 148, 151, 153, 156, 157, 158, 159, 160, 161, 162, 164, 165, 168, 169, 170, 171, 172, 173, 174, 175, 179, 180, 181, 182, 189, 190, 195, 202, 211, 213, 214, 230, 240, 256, 260, 261, 277, 305, 312, 334, 340, 344, 348, 350, 365, 372, 383, 412, 413, 415, 416, 427, 430, 431, 432, 436, 445, 446, 450, 453, 458, 462, 468, 469, 470, 471, 472, 473, 477, 478, 483, 495*, 500, 501, 503, 509, 512, 517, 518, 519, 520, 529, 535, 537, 538
Corfu vi, xiii, xxviii, 15, 21, 23, 64, 69, 95, 132, 202, 357, 363, 490*, 509, 513, 521
Corsula, island 513
Cos, island: see Kos xii, xxviii, 21, 193, 205, 206
Cothleomuz 89
Covios, lake (or village): see Volvi 124, 125, 132
Crete xiii, xxv, 15, 18, 19, 21, 23-56, 66, 67, 69, 77, 95, 99, 101, 139, 144, 148, 150, 157, 205, 209, 222, 232, 264, 293, 322, 343, 368, 372, 374, 414, 457, 468
Çurlidere (*Chiaurlic*), river flowing into Sea of Marmara north of Tekirdağ
Cute: see Kütahya 446, 447
Cyclades, islands 62, 195, 206, 309
Cypsella: see Sapes x, 145, 146
Cytherea: see Kithira xiii, 24, 30, 148, 511
Cytie see Sitia 25

D

Meander, river: see Menderes 196, 521

Mecca xiv, xv, xxxii, 258, 259, 278, 279, 301, 344, 389, 390, 392, 403, 430, 433, 531, 532, 533

Medina (*Almedine*) xxxii, 278, 531, 532

Mediterranean Sea i, iii, vi, viii, ix, x, xiii, 28, 54, 62, 63, 65, 119, 162, 164, 189, 190, 199, 206, 212, 214, 228, 296, 300, 302, 315, 317, 360, 369, 373, 382, 512

Megalivigla, peninsula, Chalcidice, Macedonia 88

Melane, river, Turkey 150

Menderes or Küçükmenderes, Meander (Scamander, Xanthus), river at Troy 520, 521

Mesara (*Messarie*), Crete 46

Mesopotamia 255, 353, 360, 396, 414, 525, 529, 533

Messina, Italy 106

Metaria, near Gortyn, Crete 27

Metelin, island: see Lesbos (Mytilene) xii, xxviii, 141, 147, 191, 195, 196, 205

Metelin, town: see Mytilini

Milan, Italy iii, vii

Milos, island in Cyclades

Mingrelia, province of Georgia 83, 90, 372, 428

Miniet al-Said (*Elminie*), delta of the Nile, Rosetta branch 232

Mirina (*Myrina*), island of Lemnos

Monte Negro or *Mont Noir*: see Amanus 368

Morea: see Peloponnese i, 212, 334, 467, 516, 521

Mudanya (*La Montanée*), on Sea of Marmara (port of Bursa),

Turkey 164, 180, 469, 519, 536

Muscovy 90, 92

Mutubis (*Nantubes*), delta of the Nile, on the Rosetta branch, half-way between Dibi and Birimbal 232

Mysia, ancient region in north-western Asia Minor (now Balikhesir region) 430, 468

Mytilene, island: see Lesbos 147, 191, 195, 205, 516, 520

Mytilini (*Metelin*), town on the island of Lesbos q.v.

N

Nablus (*Napolosa*), Palestine 335

Nantubes: see Mutubis 232

Naples, Italy iii, v, vii, ix, 106

Napolosa 335, 336

Narni, Italy 364

Natolia: see Anatolia 157, 418, 419, 431, 446, 467, 468

Naxos (*Naxia, Naxie*), island in Cyclades, Greece vi, xxviii, 21, 199, 322, 509, 521

Nazareth, Palestine xv, 336

Negroponte, Nègrepont: see Euboea 521

Nestos (*Nesus*), river, Macedonia 516

Nesus 143, 144, 149

Newfoundland xxi, 11, 478

Nicarie, island: see Ikaria

Nicomedia: see İzmit xi, xiv, xxxiv, 67, 160, 161, 180, 365, 446, 483, 519, 536

Nile, river xii, xiii, xxxvi, 212, 213, 215, 221, 227, 228, 229, 230, 231, 232, 233, 234, 235, 236, 237, 238, 239, 240, 241, 242, 243, 249, 250, 251, 252, 255,

260, 261, 262, 263, 265, 267,
268, 269, 271, 279, 280, 284,
286, 305, 306, 307, 312, 313,
314, 316, 478, 483, 523
Nîmes, France 137

O

Ochomenus, lake near Athens,
Greece 136
Oeta, Mount, now Katavothra,
Greece 293
Oise, river, France 28, 235
Olives, Mount of (*Olivet*) 325,
326, 529
Olympus, Mount (Ulu Dağ),
Turkey xviii, 100, 190, 293, 432,
446, 458, 462, 469, 520
Olympus, Mount, Greece 45, 293
Oreb, Mount, Sinai xiv, 291, 292,
293, 297
Orléans, France xiii, 361
Orous, river: see Asi Nehri 355,
365, 367
Ostia, Italy xi
Ostium Canopicum: see Rashid xii,
230, 239
Ostium Pelusiacum: see Dumyat
262

P

Pactolus, river in ancient Lydia,
Turkey 115, 514
Padua, Italy xii, xiii, 69, 380, 472
Paladru, Lac de, France 115
Palaiokastro (*Paleo Helenico
Castro*), Crete 25, 516
Palestine xv, xiv, 318, 528, 529, 534
Palmira, Egypt 315
Pamphylia, ancient region on
north coast of Asia Minor,

between Cilicia and Lycia 369,
385, 414, 446
Pangeo (*Pangeus*), Mount,
Macedonia 134, 514
Panormus, Crete 24
Paros, island in Cyclades vi, 77,
322
Patmos, island in Sporades xii, vi,
xxviii, 21, 204, 509
Pavia, Italy iii, iv, 227
Paxi (*Paxo*), island, Greece 521
Pelinaion (*Pellenium*), Mount,
island of Chios 196
Peloponnese 138, 334, 508, 516,
521
Peneus, river: see Pinios 203
Pera (*Pere*), suburb of
Constantinople xi, 57, 159, 164,
168, 172, 261, 452, 453, 477,
509, 512
Perinthus or Heraclea: see
Marmaraereğlisi xi, 154, 156,
181, 381, 517
Persia vi, viii, x, xiv, 360, 390, 412,
418, 442, 447, 517, 518, 521,
531, 535, 537
Peru x, 113, 114, 115, 116, 117,
514
Pesaro, Italy 334
Peschiac, Peschar, Pischar, lake: see
Covios 124, 132
Peschiera, Italy 115
Pest, Hungary 138
Pharan (Pharagou), on the road to
Sinai 289, 290
Pharmaco, island: see Farmakonisi
204
Philippi, ruins of, now Filippoi,
Macedonia x, 134, 135, 136,
137, 138, 139, 148, 194, 350,
366, 483, 514, 516
Philippopolis: see Plovdiv x, 135,

139, 516
Philotheou, monastery, Mount
    Athos 88, 89
Phoenicia 96, 340, 350
Phrygia, ancient region in Asia
    Minor, between Lydia and
    Cappadocia xii, 14, 67, 80, 121,
    157, 180, 186, 195, 214, 446,
    449, 462, 468, 531
Piavits, near Sidirokastro,
    Macedonia 122, 123
Picardy, France 20, 34, 158, 329
Pierius, Mount 368
Pinios (Peneus), river, Thessaly,
    Greece 203
Piombino, Italy 212
Pischar, village on Lake Volvi,
    Macedonia 125
Pisidia, ancient region in Turkey,
    between Phrygia and Pamphylia
    414
Plovdiv (Philippopolis), Bulgaria
Po, river, Italy xiii, vii, 115, 152,
    166, 193, 234, 235
Pontoise, France 149
Pontus xix, 7, 28, 62, 63, 83, 87,
    114, 145, 157, 162, 165, 166,
    171, 413, 414, 446, 473, 512,
    519
Pontus Euxinus: see Black Sea
Pontus, ancient kingdom in Asia
    Minor, in north-eastern Turkey,
    on the Black Sea
Portugal 117, 118, 413, 515
Propontis: see Marmara, Sea of xi,
    xxxiv, 28, 62, 87, 125, 145, 148,
    156, 157, 161, 162, 164, 165,
    166, 168, 180, 181, 187, 188,
    189, 381, 446, 469, 476, 512,
    519
Provence, France 13, 197, 227, 503
Prulacas, peninsula, Chalcidice,

Macedonia 88
Psara, island, Greece 196
Pserinos (*Psermo*), Sporades,
    Greece 204, 205
Psiloreitis: see Ida, Mount 509
Pyramus, river: see Ceyran Nehri
    371

R

Ragouse Veche: see Dubrovnik 461
Ragusa: see Dubrovnik viii, xiii,
    134, 159, 186, 198, 207, 432,
    483, 519
Rama xv, 320, 321, 333
Ramallah (*Rama*), Palestine 320
Rapanidi, island of Lemnos 70,
    75, 79
Rashid (*Raschit, Rosette*; Rosetta),
    delta of the Nile 229
Ravenna, Italy 50
Red Sea xiv, 83, 282, 285, 286,
    293, 297, 299, 300, 301, 302,
    303, 304, 305, 329, 394, 522,
    526, 527
Rentina (*Redina*), on Lake Volvi,
    Macedonia 125
Rethymnon (*Rethymo*), Crete 24,
    510
Rhine, river 115
Rhodes, island xii, i, xxviii, xxx, 21,
    25, 204, 206, 207, 208, 209, 210,
    212, 214, 269, 373, 411, 521
Rhodes, town
Rhodopes, mountains (Bulgaria,
    Macedonia, Thrace): see *Despota*
    and *Emus*
Rhône, river, France 232, 527
Rodosto: see Tekirdağ xi, 156, 381,
    517
Rome, Italy ix, x, xii, xiv, xxxv, 22,
    50, 73, 82, 87, 90, 127, 128, 135,

Vistonida or Bistonida (*Bistonius, Bouron*), lake, Macedonia

Vlorë (*Valonne*), Albania 516

Volvi (*Covios*), lake and village, Macedonia

Voulismeni, ancient Panormus, between Iraklion and Sitia, Crete 24, 52, 509

W

Wadi el-Natrun (*Saint-Macario*), desert 225

Wallachia, region in Romania, between the southern Carpathians and the Danube i, 90, 92, 106, 261, 312, 509

X

Xanthus, river: see Menderes 520

Xenophontos (*Xenopho*), monastery, Mount Athos 89

Y

Yuero 88, 106

Z

Zakynthos (*Zante, Zacinthe, Alzante*), island, Greece xiii, xxviii, 21

Zebid (*Zibit*), Yemen 527

Zia, island: see Kea 202, 322

Zographou (*Sguraf*), monastery, Mount Athos 88

Zonari, Cape (*Cavo del Bo*), Rhodes 210

Index of people
Names in italics are Belon's spelling of the name

A

Abd al-Mottalib (*Abdola Motalip*). Mahomet's grandfather 390n

Abd-Allah, Mahomet's father 390

Abdola Motalip 390

Abraham 332, 390, 394, 398, 401

Abu-Bakr (*Ubecar*), disciple of Mahomet 390

Abu-Talib, Mahomet's uncle 390n

Achilles, Greek hero of the Trojan War 8, 195

Actuarius, Greek physician 167

Adam 26, 99, 332, 333, 393, 397, 400, 402

Aeacus: an error for Aetius 330

Aelian, Italian author who wrote in Greek 42, 130, 382

Aemilius Paulus, Lucius, Roman consul 112, 514, 523

Aesculapius, in classical mythology the god of medicine 7

Aetius, a physician who practised at the emperor's court in Constantinople (6th c.). 529

Agathocles of Chios, Greek naturalist 280, 526

Agrippa, Marcus Vipsanius, Roman general (1st c. BC) 522

Aimars, Antoine Escalin, also know as Captain Polin, French ambassador in Turkey vii

Albertus Magnus, German theologian and philosopher (13th c.) 211, 319

Alexander the Great, king of

Pliny, Greek naturalist and writer (1st c. AD) xix, xx, 33, 34, 43, 51, 63, 66, 72, 77, 95, 101, 103, 115, 125, 128, 129, 133, 134, 138, 148, 149, 167, 169, 194, 214, 225, 231, 232, 237, 238, 242, 257, 263, 264, 267, 268, 269, 270, 271, 275, 276, 278, 281, 284, 286, 288, 319, 330, 332, 349, 368, 382, 408, 431, 441, 446, 459, 462

Polin, captain: see Aimars vii, viii

Pompey, Roman general (1st c. BC) 7, 213, 219, 240, 296, 350, 522

Postel, Guillaume, French traveller (16th c.) ii, vi, viii, xix, 500, 503

Prester John, legendary Christian ruler variously located in Asia or Africa, later in Ethiopia 117, 118, 323, 328, 438, 514

Prez, René des, French apothecary (16th c.) xi

Protesilas, mythological hero 520

Ptolemy I, founder of the Greek monarchy of Egypt (3rd c. BC) 526, 527

Ptolemy, Greek geographer (2nd c. AD) xix

Ptolemy Lagus 305

Ptolemy Philadelphus 305

R

Rhazes (Rasis), Persian physician (9th–10th c.) 415

Richelieu, Cardinal, French statesman (17th c.) x

Rinçon, Antoine, French emissary (16th c.) iv, v, vii

Roland, one of Charlemagne's paladins 462, 537

Romulus, legendary founder of Rome 221

Rondelet, Guillaume, French physician and naturalist (16th c.) xx

S

Sarah, wife of Abrahamn 390

Sauneron, Serge, editor of Belon's travels in Egypt xxxvii, xxxviii, xxxix, xl, 508, 526, 527

Savary, François, French ambassador to Constantinople (16th c.) x

Scaurus, Aemilius, Roman consul in 115 BC 523

Selim I, Ottoman sultan (16th c.) i, 517, 522, 538

Semiramis, legendary queen of Assyria 441

Serapion, Arab physician 313, 354, 415

Shah Kuli, rebel against Ottoman rule (15th c.) 537

Sinan Pasha, Turkish admiral (16th c.) ix

Socrates, Greek philosopher (5th c. BC) 429

Solinus, Latin geographer viii, 27, 45, 112, 127, 275, 281, 525, 526

Spandugino, Italian traveller (16th c.) ii

St Anne 326, 333

St Augustine xx

St Catherine 296, 297

St Elizabeth 333

St Helen 326, 331

St James the Greater 327

St John i, ii, xx, 53, 78, 204, 331, 333, 355, 519, 521

St Mark 226

Thematic Index

scarlet-grain (dye) 49-50
sesame (oil) 440
storax (styrax) 208-9
tamarisk galls 229, 233
terebinth galls 153, 468
terebinth seeds 253
white chameleon (gum) 53
wild rue 472
wool-bearing trees 288
yellow amber 310

WOMEN
alms of Turkish women 143-4
beauty of the women of Chios 197
circumcision of women in Persia
   438
condition and way of life of
   Turkish women 423-4, 453
depilation of Turkish women 448
dress of Cretan women 56
dress of Turkish women 420-1
fables concerning the women of
   Lemnos 73
Greek criteria of beauty 453
Greek women of Pera
   (Constantinople) 453
Greek and Turkish women do not
   appear in public 22, 23, 362,
   417, 420
gypsy women 261
polygamy and repudiation of
   wives among the Turks 407
use of henna as a dye 312
the Turks buy their wives 443
Turkish women are much
   concerned for their beauty 355,
   449-50, 452
women of Cairo 243-7*, 255-6
women chewing pine thistle gum
   343
women slaves of the Turks and the
   Jews 403-4, 425

Zoological Index

A

alcyonium 188
amphisboena (snake) 77, 475
angelfish (Fr *ange; Squatinus
   angelus*) 167
antelope 510, 519, 525
apus (swift) 517
armadillo 20, 478*, 479
asp 224
ass 43, 66 79, 247, 325 361, 399,
   511
ass, Indian (rhinoceros) 43, 361
atherinae, atherines (sand smelts)
   75

B

baboon 479
badger 218
barbel 19, 133
barge-bird (*Crex*) 523
barn-owl (Fr *fresaie, effraie*) 35, 510
bass 167, 215, 300, 467
beaver 233
bee (Fr *abeille, avette, mouche à
   miel*) 224
bee-eater (*merops, apiaster*) 32*
belemnite 511
blackbird 34, 347
blackbird, white-collared (ring
   ousel) 34
blackbird, blue (*petro cossipho,
   Petrus-cossuphos*) 34
blackfish (Fr *lampugne;
   Centrolophus niger*) 163
bleak (Fr *able, ablette*) 145
boar, wild 384, 523
bonito (Fr *pélamide; Sarda sarda*)
   163

bream 163, 215, 297, 300, 385
bubalus (large antelope) 274, 275, 519, 525, 526
buffalo 274, 275, 388, 525
bullfinch (Fr *pivoine*) 37
bunting (Fr *bruant*) 37, 303
burbot (Fr *lotte, barbote*) 125
bustard, little (Fr *canepétière*) 33, 36, 347

C

camel 272, 279, 313, 344, 353, 531
canary 37
cancer cursor (crab) 317
cantharid 100
caprimulgus (barn-owl, night-jar) 35
carp 19, 115, 169, 339, 385
caterpillar
catfish (*glanis*) 20
catshark (Fr *roussette*) 503
cenchris, cenchriti, nose-horned viper (*Vipera ammodytes*) 77*, 513
cephalopola, mullet 125
cephalos (fish) 133
cercopitheci (monkeys) 223
chaffinch 37
chameleon 53, 66, 68, 69, 77, 78, 156, 189, 229, 287*, 367
chamois 43, 128, 129*, 130, 277
char (Fr *omble chevalier, emblon*) 115, 499
chella, chelli, eel 20, 125, 133
cheriscaria (fish) 133
cheronia (fish) 125
cholios (Turkish *kolyoz*), mackerel 163
chub (Fr *chevesne, dard, vandoise*) 145, 339
cicada 32
civet 218-9*

claria, common burbot 124, 125
conger 165
coral 249 300, 520, 527
crab (Fr *cancre*) 105, 106, 316
crane, Balearic 361
crave (chough?) 44
crayfish (Fr *écrevisse, langouste*) 16, 104, 106, 107*, 513
crex (according to Aristotle, a long-legged bird) 238, 523
crocodile xxii, xxxvi, 224, 240, 241*, 265, 524
crow 95, 236, 527
cuckoo 32, 35
cuttlefish (Fr *seiche, casseron*) 105, 167, 511
cynocephali (baboons) 278

D

deer 40, 43, 127, 128, 129, 130, 131, 276
deer, fallow 43, 127, 130, 131, 276, 277
deer, red 43, 127, 276, 277
deer, roe 43, 127, 128, 129, 131, 277, 286
dental 163, 167
diver 36, 37
dog 222, 224, 370, 371, 457
dogfish 166, 167, 215, 316, 518
dolphin 74, 168, 472, 513
donzelle (fish) 75
dorado, *dorade*, gilthead 163, 300
driinus, nose-horned viper (?) 475*
duck 36, 366
duck, tufted (Fr *morillon*)

E

eagle 38, 225, 226, 236, 319, 506 528

eagle, white-tailed (Fr *orfraie*) 35,
 319
eel 20
elephant 171, 174, 441
ermine (stoat) 171
esculus (iaculus, acontius) 208*
exocetus (fish) 166

F

falcon 38
fieldfare (Fr *litorne*) 34
fieldmouse 150, 318
finch 92
finch, royal (Fr *pinson royal*),
 hawfinch 92
flascopsari 240
fly 31, 32, 172, 233, 306, 308, 457,
 477
fox 469
francolin 33, 161
frog 223, 236

G

gazelle xiii, 274, 276, 277
gecko (Fr *tarente*) 265
gilthead (Fr *dorade*): see dorado
giraffe 272-4*, 277, 525
girole (*girelle, jule*), rainbow wrasse
 (?) 163
glanis, glanos: see Silurid 20, 125,
 133, 218
glini (fish) 75
goat 34, 40, 66, 73, 122, 130, 195,
 277, 374, 381, 426, 465, 525
goby 75
goldcrest (Fr *roitelet*) 34
goldfinch 16, 37
goose 104, 168, 193, 207, 257,
 372, 523
goose, Nile (Fr bièvre) (*Chenalopex*

aegyptiaca) 233
goshawk 38
gracculus, jackdaw (?) 66
grayling (Fr *ombre, themelo*) 508
grebe, little (Fr *castagneux*) 37
greenfinch (Fr *verdier, serrant*) 37
greyhound 537
grinadies, grenadier fish (?) 133
grivadi, carp 125
guillemot 36
gurnard (Fr *gournal, grondin gris*)
 215
gyrfalcon 38

H

hake 19
hare 68, 224, 277, 374
hawfinch (Fr *gros-bec, pinson royal*)
 92, 320
hedgehog 20, 479
hen 34, 36, 38, 144, 223, 288
hiena: see Silurid 133
hippelaphus (half horse, half stag)
 130, 132
hippopotamus 239, 240, 383, 523
horse 64, 74, 130, 137, 138, 240,
 243, 247, 249, 272, 274, 345,
 367, 368, 426, 434, 435, 441,
 456, 463, 464, 469, 474, 477,
 515, 523
hyena 465

I

ibex (Fr *bouquetin*) 40, 41*, 127,
 130, 132, 338, 374, 513
ibis 238, 239
ichneumon (mongoose) xii, 20,
 218, 222-4*, 522
ichneumon vespa (sphex, digger-
 wasp) 224, 522

www.ingramcontent.com/pod-product-compliance
Lightning Source LLC
Chambersburg PA
CBHW030632270326
41929CB00007B/40